MIND AND LABOR
ON THE FARM
IN BLACK-EARTH RUSSIA,
1861–1914

MIND AND LABOR
ON THE FARM
IN BLACK-EARTH RUSSIA,
1861–1914

DAVID KERANS

CEU PRESS

Central European University Press

Published by
Central European University Press

Nádor utca 15
H-1051 Budapest
Hungary

400 West 59th Street
New York, NY 10019
USA

An imprint of the
Central European Share Company

Distributed in the United Kingdom and Western Europe by
Plymbridge Distributors Ltd., Estover Road, Plymouth PL6 7PZ,
United Kingdom

ISBN 963 9116 94 7 Cloth

Library of Congress Cataloging in Publication Data
A CIP catalog record for this book is available upon request

Printed in Hungary by
Akadémiai Nyomda Kft., Martonvásár

Table of Contents

PART ONE

FARMING THROUGH THE PEASANT'S EYES.
THE EVOLUTION OF LABOR, 1861–1914

PART TWO

TOWARDS A HISTORY AND UNDERSTANDING
OF AGRONOMIC APTITUDE

PART THREE

THE THREE-FIELD SYSTEM AND BEYOND

PART FOUR

GOVERNMENT'S SOLUTION TO THE AGRARIAN PROBLEM: THE STOLYPIN REFORM IN TAMBOV

PART FIVE

ALTERNATIVES FOR REFORM, PROSPECTS FOR DEVELOPMENT

List of Figures

List of Tables

List of Maps

Map 1.1. The Provinces of European Russia
(*Source:* Yaney, *The Urge to Mobilize,* frontispiece)

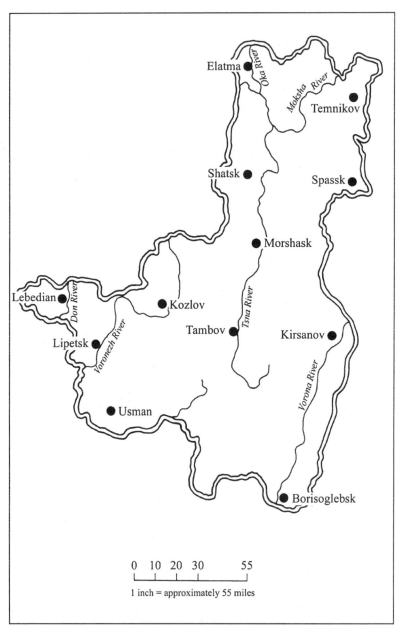

Map 1.2. Tambov Province and Its *Uezd* Towns
(*Source:* Hoch, *Serfdom and Social Control*, p. 6)

Sokha tillage. The dust and the sweat are evident

A good farmer—he is checking the condition of the ears of his grain

A good farmer—he is cleaning the teeth of an iron "zig-zag" harrow before continuing work

Sickling. Judging from the standing posture of the sheaves in the background, this is in a province somewhere north of Tambov

Children bringing water out to the fields

Binding the sheaves, right behind the sicklers

Loading up the sheaves

Flail threshing I

Flail threshing II

Spade winnowing

A simple reaping machine
in action

A sorting machine

A large threshing machine
on a landlord's estate

An agronomist describing
the virtues of a multi-field
system to a village assembly, in the late 1920s

INTRODUCTION
The Agrarian Problem as a History of Work

"The whip of authority, the pull of tradition, or the lure of gain." In the words of a great historian of economic thought, these are the three alternative principles that can organize the economic life of a society.[1] The three principles correspond to great historical stages, the last among them—the lure of gain—underpinning the market society which first arose in a mature form in Western Europe less than three centuries ago. The transition from one stage to another is bound to be unsettling in any society, no matter how gradually it may transpire. In Imperial Russia the transition was so traumatic as to lead towards cataclysmic revolutionary upheaval.

Over just three generations, from the middle of the nineteenth century to the beginning of the twentieth, the will of Russian monarchs and the pressures of international market mechanisms fated Russian society to experience all three patterns of economic organization. Just thirty years after Emperor Alexander II laid the age of serfdom to rest in the 1860s, Russia was undergoing one of the greatest industrial booms in history. The first decade and a half of the twentieth century witnessed the birth of commercial and legal frameworks that lie at the foundation of any market society. On the eve of the First World War Russia remained an overwhelmingly peasant nation, but the society as a whole was beginning to shed its agrarian character.

The telescoping of economic epochs into such a short span of time jolted the fortunes, allegiances, and composition of all social groups in Russia. Fundamental problems facing the Russian State in the late nineteenth century—such as the priority of industrialization with its attendant social perils, the scope of political freedoms within the country, and the unstable alignment of the population into estates—acquired tremendous intensity. No less formidable was a fourth problem, the agrarian problem, by which contemporaries understood the task of improving the lot of the huge peasant population while simultaneously

stimulating economic growth through increasing the marketable surpluses of the agricultural sector.

The present study analyzes the evolution of peasant agriculture, the
heart of the agrarian problem in late Imperial Russia. Considering the
voluminous literature that has accumulated on the peasant economy
over the last hundred years, such a design might appear to be superfluous at first glance. Yet there is an enormous gap in this literature,
conditioned by a lopsided emphasis on agrarian relations as opposed to
the history of agriculture itself. Five themes have dominated all discussions: the history of differentiation (or class formation) within the
peasantry, the fate of the peasant commune,* the peasantry's standard
of living, the struggle of the peasantry versus the gentry up to 1917, and
the productivity of the peasant agricultural sector. Only portions of the
work of a handful of scholars have ventured into *agricultural*, as opposed
to agrarian, history, by attempting to explain the means, the obstacles,
and the processes of agricultural change from the agriculturists' point
of view.[2] We have no agricultural history of the Russian peasantry in
the proper sense. Consequently, we have no material history of peasant
agriculture. Nor, speaking more broadly—and this applies to Europe as
well as to Russia—do we have a history of peasant work.[3] The present
study is primarily devoted to providing such a history, and to re-framing
our conclusions on the agrarian problem in its light.

An analysis of agricultural work must encompass two separate elements of the labor process. The first and more visible element is the
technology of work, which includes both the organization of production and the domain of material history in the strictest sense—namely
the tools and equipment with which work is carried out. The second,
more elusive element is the laborer's comprehension of the employed
technology. In factory labor the degree to which workers understand
technology is largely irrelevant. Individual workers perform a limited
number of duties along lines that the technology has clearly defined.
Variables are few, management reserves control over all important
decisions. For the manager—or for the family farmer—on the other
hand, the comprehension of technology is vital. By its very nature,
agricultural labor is much more variegated than industrial. There are
more processes to master, more variables to which to react. And as the
present study will illustrate, the lower the level of the farming technology, the greater the number and the intensity of these variables. The

---

*Normally organized on the basis of a single village, the peasant commune was the
peasantry's organ of self-administration.

fate of agricultural endeavor depends on the keenness and insight with which farmers select technological alternatives to fit the environment.

Therefore, a history of the comprehension as well as the technology of work—of the mental as well as the physical dimensions of labor—must form the foundation of a history of peasant agriculture. Such a perspective yields a host of important insights on the agrarian problem in Imperial Russia. First, it uncovers the features that distinguished peasant farmers from gentry estate-holders or other private agriculturists. Exactly how did they work, and why? How well did they perform their work, and how did they appraise it? Who taught them how to work, and how did they subsequently teach themselves? To what extent could they improve their work without help from agricultural science, and how did they react to this science when confronting it? These vital questions remain not just unresolved, but unposed. Further, an agricultural history helps to explain the direction and pace of the rural economy in the last half century of the Tsarist regime. Without a technological perspective we cannot fully identify the circumstances that aggravated the pressures on the agrarian sector, nor can we see how the peasantry responded to these pressures. Only a technological perspective will allow us to evaluate the viability of the government's great campaign to solve the agrarian problem, the Stolypin reform, or to gauge the potential of the peasant economy to evolve—perhaps even to preside over an agricultural revolution—had there been no war in 1914.

Existing scholarship on the agrarian problem has not entirely ignored the question of the mentality of the peasant farmer. Ever since the German traveler August Von Haxthausen's analysis of the peasant commune appeared in the 1840s, the dominant wing of pre- and post-revolutionary Russian agrarian thought has maintained that the peculiar institutional features of the commune did much to shape the mentality of the farming population.[4] In this context, scholars have proposed that three separate features of the commune served to limit the potential of peasant agriculture.

1) *The open fields.* For reasons to be explained in detail in the main text, the commune parcelized its arable land into strips, such that each household possessed its lands in a number of locations, not in a unified plot. Since the village's herds of livestock grazed on the crop stubble left on these interspersed holdings after harvest time, the commune necessarily homogenized all households' sowings and labor operations. The roving herds would devour any crops growing outside of the

established pattern, so individual farmers had no option to vary from this pattern. It is assumed, therefore, that farmers could neither experiment with innovations nor rearrange their sowings so as to take advantage of market opportunities.

2) *Land redistribution.* Across most of European Russia the commune periodically redistributed arable land among member households in accordance with fluctuations in family size. The fact that the land belonged to the collective, and not to the individual household, is said to have dulled peasants' attentiveness to soil care. Redistribution acted as a disincentive to manuring, drainage, and weeding. The household simply sought to extract as much from their strips of land as they could before they lost these strips upon the next redistribution.

3) *Welfare.* The commune is thought to have acted as a safety net for the failing farm. In times of need neighbors would supposedly help each other out, and the commune would provide assistance, covering helpless families' tax payments and loaning them grain. In so far as this was true, it could be argued that the commune preserved impoverished farms at the expense of the sturdy, and stunted the development of an independent and self-reliant spirit among peasants.

This set of arguments has always dominated scholars' perceptions of agriculture in the commune, especially so since 1906, when the Tsarist government launched its propaganda campaign against the commune in connection with the Stolypin reform. Hence the popularity to this day of the image of the peasant farmer as an indolent, mentally conservative, and backward creature, given to passive egalitarianism at the expense of initiative and entrepreneurialism. It is imperative for us to note, however, that this characterization of the peasant is based more on inference and supposition than on detailed study of peasant agriculture. Indeed, already before the turn of the twentieth century researchers were challenging this generalized picture of agriculture in the commune. Defenders of the peasantry and its institutions, including the commune, showed that communes did sometimes manage to adopt multi-field systems and to encourage manuring and proper care for the soil. In some areas of the country peasant farmers were acquiring improved tools and raising higher quality animals.[5] Moreover, the official data establishing nationwide increases in grain yields throughout the half-century preceding the First World War testify that technological advances were widespread.[6] Meanwhile, contemporary observers with an anti-populist ideological bent produced evidence that both attacked the notion of the commune as a safety net for failing farms and demonstrated plenty of "capitalist" entrepreneurial behavior in the peasant economy.[7]

Unfortunately, research on agricultural life in the commune did not develop very far beyond the stage reached at the turn of the century. Up to the revolution and throughout the 1920s the questions of the mentality of the peasant farmer and the vitality of the commune remained politically charged issues in Russia. But the debates were far more polemical than analytical in substance. Our understanding of these issues has advanced very little since then, because nothing even approaching a comprehensive picture of peasant agriculture has ever emerged.[8] Therefore, the primary object of the book is to provide this picture. In the process, we will see that the role of the commune in shaping peasant mentality and labor has been greatly exaggerated.

For purposes of the present study I have focused primarily on Tambov province in the Central Agricultural Region of European Russia. Tambov is an attractive choice for several reasons. In the first place, the circumstances surrounding agricultural labor in the province conformed to the picture in the standard literature on the agrarian problem: the peasants held their land almost exclusively in communal tenure, the plowland was divided up into strips and periodically redistributed; the supposedly backward three-field system of farming* was ubiquitous on peasant lands; the peasant population grew at a fast rate after the emancipation of 1861, creating pressure on the land; gentry landowners retained large estates in the countryside until 1917, such that traditional frictions and animosities remained in place. The typicality of these circumstances allows me to extend the significance of my findings beyond the scope of a local study.

In the second place, other features of Tambov's demographic and economic profile over the period 1861–1914 permit an agrarian historian to draw clearer conclusions than would be possible with other provinces. In contrast to the complex ethnic composition of many other provinces, Tambov's population was overwhelmingly of Great Russian stock. The economy was similarly homogeneous, with very little industrial and commercial activity to challenge the preeminence of the agricultural sector. Finally, while the shadow of the land problem was lengthening over Russia throughout the half century following the emancipation, it covered Tambov more quickly and more thoroughly than most other areas of Russia. In consequence, tendencies that remained latent in other areas developed to their maturity here. The

*See glossary on pp. 483–484.

most important of these tendencies was peasant farmers' search for ways of increasing their production of food per unit of land. As we shall see, this quest was central to the agricultural evolution of the province throughout our period. Tambov peasants' performance in this pursuit will go far towards revealing the proclivities and capacities of the Russian peasant as a farmer.

The book begins with a presentation of the economic setting in Tambov for the entire period 1861–1914. While the health of the agricultural sector has been and will remain a contentious issue in the study of late Imperial Russia, the evidence for the peasantry of Tambov points clearly to stagnation and decline. Across the whole province peasant farmers were under mounting pressure to improve their per-formance in the fields.

The main body of Part I reviews peasants' performance with respect to grain farming, which towered over all other branches of agriculture throughout black-earth Russia. It traces the evolution of labor prac-tices, and provides physical, mental, and psychological portraits of peasants' work. The first goal here is to demystify peasant agriculture, by uncovering the environmental and demographic circumstances that shaped the agricultural system and conditioned its development over space and time. As we will see, there was no gray uniformity of labor practices among villages, on the one hand, nor endless local variety on the other hand. The geography of soil, water sources, vegetation, climate, and population density determined the outlines of agricultural work.

A parallel goal is to demystify the peasant farmer himself. In present-ing how farm work was actually done we will pull him out from under the generalizations and generalities concerning the peasant commune and establish his identity. We will see the decisions in front of each family, and how they thought these decisions through, however unre-flectively. *In the process we will show that the farmer controlled his own fate, and that with the exception of a few key moments the commune played no role in the family's agricultural year.* This control gave the farmer equal freedom to succeed or to fail. In dissecting peasants' labor we will identify the decisions or circumstances that separated success from failure, and the personal qualities that made the difference.

At the same time, analysis of the paradigms of agronomic folk wis-dom reveals the limited competence of the great mass of the popula-tion to orient themselves within the confines of their own craft. In spite of occasional famines, over the last half of the nineteenth century the peasantry managed to intensify tillage and other operations enough to support population growth to a (by European standards) modest level. All of this transpired under the guidance of their traditional paradigms. But by the early twentieth century folk wisdom was proving to be utterly bankrupt for further intensification.

Part II seeks to discern why folk wisdom arrived at dead ends. Two tasks are involved here. The first is to uncover the principles through which peasant farmers understood their technologies and to trace the manner in which they adjusted these principles. The second is to situate peasant technological thinking in the religious, social, and psychological worlds of the village. Along the way we will see just how much distance separated peasant farmers from agronomists in their approach towards the theoretical and practical problems of agriculture. The challenge is to reveal concretely how certain aspects of peasant society served to routinize attitudes towards work, and thus to limit peasants' success in coping with the rapidly changing economic environment of the post-emancipation period. At the same time, it will be possible to locate the emergence of new forces in the village that promised to condition more flexible approaches to work and technology.

Part III analyzes the prospects for an agricultural revolution akin to those experienced in Western Europe in the nineteenth century. The task here is to investigate the possibilities for a reorganization of labor into systems of farming that would yield more production per unit of land. We begin with a detailed treatment of the functioning of the three-field system in Tambov and its evolution over time. We also examine farmers' performance in organizing their family farms amidst the evolving economic climate of the pre-Revolutionary period. As with our evaluations of individual farming operations in Part I, we will identify serious flaws in farmers' performance.

The rest of Part III addresses the problem of transitions from the three-field system of farming into more productive systems. Here the task is to explain why intensive systems were so slow to appear in peasant Russia, and what the prospects were for their development as of 1914. Key questions concern the extent to which economic conditions permitted profitable implementation of these systems, and whether or not farmers understood or desired to employ them. Could agriculture evolve past the three-field system without substantial help from the industrial sector? Did the intensification of agriculture depend as much on the presence of transport networks and enterprises that processed agricultural products as it did on the peasantry?

Parts IV and V of the book compare the two very different campaigns designed to solve the agrarian problem after the political upheavals and peasant rebellions of 1905–06. Both campaigns sought to stimulate farmers to reorganize their farms along lines leading towards more intensive systems. Part IV analyzes the Stolypin reform, the great campaign on which the government placed so much hope. The idea behind the reform was to rescue the family farm from the supposed restrictions of open-field, communal agriculture by forming individual homesteads on consolidated plots of land. While the Stolypin reform was a clumsy approach to the agrarian problem in central Russia, it was not without real prospects for promoting agrotechnical progress among an important layer of the peasantry. After examining the theory behind the reform, we proceed to chart its progress and its consequences in Tambov.

While the government exerted almost all of its energies in the countryside towards breaking up the commune in favor of consolidated farms, zemstvo* agronomists all over Russia embarked on a vast crusade of their own. This was the agronomic aid effort, a momentous but entirely unstudied movement that aimed primarily at providing the benefits of agronomic science to the peasantry.[9] To many observers at the time, and not only to those within the ranks of the agronomic community, this movement promised to play at least as great a role in deciding the development of Russian society as would the other cultural campaigns—most importantly those concerning education and medicine—then underway in the countryside. Part V covers the zemstvos' agronomic aid effort in Tambov as it took shape in the final years before the First World War. Here we trace the course of the confrontation of the farming population with agronomic science, and offer a prognosis of the peasantry's capacity to assimilate the achievements of science into their agricultural practice had the outbreak of war not severed the peasant–agronomist relationship in 1914.

In addition to covering the progress of professionally guided agricultural innovations in these years, Part V also treats the evolution of the methods of the agronomic aid effort. The agronomists initially shared a naive faith in the power of their teachings to transform peasant agriculture. In keeping with this faith, they went to the countryside with an overtly paternalistic approach: *they* knew the farmers' problems, and *they* would prescribe the solutions. However, after encountering cultural barriers of various kinds standing between themselves and their audiences, they began to sense how difficult it would be to

---

*Zemstvos were semi-autonomous provincial- and district-level organizations that fulfilled a wide range of administrative functions in the countryside.

influence peasant farmers directly. These cultural barriers, combined with rising suspicions among the agronomic community as to the immediate applicability in peasant conditions of some of their standard prescriptions for agricultural improvements, prompted a recasting of the agronomic aid movement. The agronomists willingly ceded some initiative to the farmers. The movement came to depend ever less on the individual agronomist and ever more on popular initiative, as expressed in the agricultural press and the agricultural cooperative movement.

The flexibility of the agronomic aid campaign augured well for the economic future of rural Russia. Given enough time, the technological and cultural evolution of the countryside could have acquired real momentum. Already by 1913–14 it seemed to many agricultural officials in St. Petersburg and the provinces that the tremendous burden of backwardness vis-à-vis Western Europe that had so preoccupied Russia's rulers ever since Peter the Great could be lightened, even thrown off, in the matter of a generation or two. But how much time did the agronomists—and the Empire—have to propel this evolution? The outbreak of the First World War in the summer of 1914 would force Russia to meet the challenges of modernization on the field of battle. Alas, 1914 was only so far removed from 1917....

A Note on Sources

I very much wanted to go out on the street and to walk around the village. But in doing so I would disturb the peasants' conversations: they would cease talking, because for them I was a complete outsider.

—F. M. Reshetnikov, 1868[10]

Formerly I had doubts about the data we collected from peasants, but no longer.... The population is brighter and more developed than it was ten years ago. Everyone who participated in the previous survey as well as the current one agrees on this. The old peasant men still hesitate, strain to remember, and get confused. But the overwhelming majority of the young men running their own farms answer questions clearly and knowingly, without straying off into unnecessary details.

—M. V. Rklitskii, 1914[11]

The data available on peasant agriculture give the historian of Russia great advantages over scholars of other countries. The sheer quantity of the Russian data dwarfs that for any other nation before the twentieth century. What is more, the sources are varied in nature, offering a great many perspectives. The sheer number of categories of sources available to the historian is startling: statistical surveys (surveys and land appraisal studies from the *zemstvos* and state statistical services); compilations of reports from agricultural correspondents (most of them peasants); *belles lettres* (many of the authors being peasants themselves); budget studies; reports of local agronomists; agronomic conferences; proceedings and reports of special commissions addressing agrarian problems; records of *zemstvo* assemblies and their sub-committees (as much as half a million pages published annually in this category alone); ethnographic studies; peasant memoirs; journals of agricultural societies; peasant letters to agricultural journals; folkloric collections; newspapers; paintings; photographs. All these categories of sources pertain to both the Soviet period and the Tsarist; almost all are available in great quantities. I have supplemented these categories of sources with two more: interviews with surviving peasants and personal field work with traditional technologies.

The statistical data are not only abundant, but of high quality. Data on peasant livestock in Tambov are the best in all of Russia.[12] Grain production statistics improved markedly in the early 1880s. In 1881 the Ministry of State Domains' Department of Agriculture and Rural Industry established a network of correspondents to report on yields in their localities, and in 1883 the Ministry of Internal Affairs' Central Statistical Committee began collecting data from all *volost'* administrations. Western and Soviet specialists agree on the reasonably high quality of the Central Statistical Committee's data.[13] From 1896 the Tambov *zemstvo* joined many other *zemstvos* in establishing a dense network of its own to report on grain production and other branches of the rural economy. These data are still better than the Central Statistical Committee's.[14] Independent *zemstvo* investigations such as the mammoth, turn-of-the-century tax appraisal study and the budget study of 1914 offer even more information.[15]

As important as they are, statistics cannot solve many of the problems the present study will pose. Fortunately, the qualitative data are broad, deep, and plentiful. Peasant voices are well represented in the sources.[16] Moreover, most of the non-peasant sources speak from a position of familiarity with the peasant world. Russia was an overwhelmingly agrarian country. The layers of Russian educated society that took an interest in the peasantry tended to have some degree of acquaintance with the village before they published their opinions or findings on it. Their non-peasant upbringing did not necessarily make them ignorant outsiders incapable of understanding their own people. "It seems to me," remarked the writer Ivan Bunin, "that the Russian gentry share the same life and soul as the peasant.... In no other country do the gentry and the peasants live in such proximity, in such close contact, as with us. I think the soul of each is identically Russian."[17] Further, a large portion of those who wrote on rural affairs harbored populist sentiments, and looked on peasant life and traditions with sympathy. The source base as a whole, therefore, does not suffer irremediably from "urban bias" or "anti-peasant bias."[18]

Sources of peasant origin are available to correct misleading characterizations, as are the voices of conscientious non-peasants. Still more significant is the variety of methods authors used to collect and analyze their data. Studies were composed in any number of unlike ways, and towards unlike ends. Analysts applied a bewildering variety of sociological categories to subdivide the peasants they studied. The incomparable weight and diversity of the information available on the Russian peasantry thus serves to protect the historian from following false leads.

Where this enormous arsenal of sources is not enough, geographical and political circumstances effectively multiply the historians' weaponry for most topics in agrarian history. Although a dense trail of data on questions of economic geography goes back no further than 1880, the relative homogeneity of Russia's topography allows the historian to substitute space travel for time travel. For example, many farming practices bore a close connection to population density, which tapered off to the south and east of European Russia. Thus the historian of Tambov in the late Imperial period can look to the contemporaneous south and east for clues as to Tambov's own farming practices in earlier times. This circumstance will come in very handy in the present study.

Meanwhile, the revolution of 1917 brought agrarian historians invaluable reinforcement of the sources. Naturally the revolution exposed previously classified materials of many kinds. More importantly for agrarian studies, the revolution generated a new wave of research on rural Russia. Politicians, agronomists, and agrarian specialists tried their hands at repeating much of the research and analysis of Tsarist times. Much of this work was inspired by, or beholden to, an ideological framework quite distinct from that prevailing before 1917. In bringing fresh perspectives to Russian agrarian problems, scholars in the early Soviet period provided innumerable corroborations and correctives to late Imperial work.

It is possible, therefore, to reconstruct the peasant world of late Imperial Russia with some confidence.

Notes

[1] Heilbroner, *The Worldly Philosophers*, p. 18.

[2] Here I have in mind the works of P. N. Pershin, A. M. Anfimov, V. P. Danilov, Lazar Volin, Judith Pallot, Esther Kingston-Mann, and Leonard Friesen, to give the most prominent examples.

[3] A recent overview of European agricultural history announced "a crying need for studies of work practices" (Overton and Campbell, "Productivity Change in European Agricultural Development," p. 37). They and I might be unaware of some work in this vein.

[4] Von Haxthausen, *Studies on the Interior of Russia*.

[5] The most thorough work in this vein is Vorontsov, *Progressivnye techeniia*.

[6] According to the Soviet Commissariat of Agriculture's treatment of these figures, average peasant yields by decades from the 1860s to the 1900s (in centners/hectare), were 4.4–4.7–5.1–5.9–6.3 (Danilov, *Rural Russia*, p. 275).

[7] Lenin's 1898 work *The Development of Capitalism in Russia* is merely the most famous of the publications devoted to this perspective.

[8] Historian Michael Confino did provide a thorough examination of many of the relevant topics, but he focused primarily on landlords, and exclusively on the late eighteenth and early nineteenth century. See his *Domaines et Seigneurs en Russie vers la fin du XVIII siècle*; and especially *Systèmes Agraires et Progrès Agricole: l'assolement triennale en Russie aux XVIII–XIX siècles*. Recent works pointing up the flexibility of the post-emancipation commune to accommodate new crops and techniques within the framework of open-field farming are Pallot, "Agrarian Modernization on Peasant Farms in the Era of Capitalism;" and Kingston-Mann, "Peasant Communes and Economic Innovation." Robert Bideleux is also noteworthy for having intuited the significance of subtle alterations in peasant farming technology in the late Imperial period ("Agricultural Advance under the Russian Village Commune System"). None of these articles confronts the topic deeply or broadly. None of them attempts a critique of peasant agricultural performance.

[9] Be it noted here that in 1996 a Tambov-based historian named Sergei Esikov published an article echoing (in condensed and sometimes distorted form) some of the themes and conclusions of my work, especially of Part V (Esikov, "Trekhpol'naia sistema i zemskaia agronomicheskaia pomoshch'"). Much of Esikov's article is in fact translated—often word-for-word, and with no mention of me—from my 1994 dissertation and a conference paper I gave in Moscow in 1993. I gave him a copy of my dissertation in May 1995, and am pleased to see he made such honorable use of it.

[10] Reshetnikov, p. 95. In the middle of the nineteenth century, if not later, urban lower classes could be just as suspicious of officials or other outsiders as were peasants.

They too might cease talking when such a person appeared. See, e.g., Aksakov, *Pis'ma iz provintsii*, p. 338 (pertaining to the town of Liubim, in Iaroslavl province, 1850).

[11] Rklitskii, p. 22.

[12] The *zemstvo* livestock study of 1912 (many entries in the bibliography) eclipses any similar study. It extended far beyond the recording of animals' numbers to provide detailed information on breeds, age structure, care, living conditions, health, and other topics. The *zemstvo* enhanced the precision of the study by hiring qualified data-takers, and running two series of inspections of their work (*Materialy po podvornomu obsledovaniiu zhivotnovodstva Tambovskoi gubernii v 1912 godu. Kozlovskii uezd*, pp. 4, 8; Pridorogin, "Zakliuchenie professora," pp. 812–813). As we shall see in the main text, the *zemstvo* did other studies of livestock, in the 1880s and late 1890s. National surveys of horses (the *Voenno-konskaia perepis'* volumes) provide some confirmation of the *zemstvo* studies.

[13] Wheatcroft, "The Reliabilty of Russian Pre-War Grain Output Statistics," pp. 170–171, discussing early Soviet analyses as well.

[14] The Tambov network was a bit less reliable than most others, since they did not pay their correspondents (*ZhTGZS ocherednoi sessii 1910 goda*, pp. 94, 622). Nevertheless, the data are very good, especially for the peasant economy. They had about 1,000 reports every year, only 5–6% being from landlords. See Anonymous, "Po voprosu ob uluchshenii dela organizatsii tekushchei statistiki," pp. 657–660.

[15] The tax appraisal study was published as the *k otsenke* volumes (on the independence of these data from all others, *k otsenke*, Usman, pp. 36–37). Chelintsev's *Opyt izucheniia organizatsii* provides extended analysis of the budget study. The *zemstvo* data are ordinarily rated more highly than the Central Statistical Committee's (see, e.g., Eropkin, "Ob upadke zemledeliia," no. 5, p. 196, no. 6, p. 2). On the other hand, a researcher in charge of the tax appraisal study in Morshansk *uezd* was hesitant to pass judgment after comparing the various sources with the findings there (*k otsenke*, Morshansk, p. 41). By the early twentieth century demand for speedy information on grain production prompted other private and public organizations to provide estimates of yields (see B. M.'s overviews, "O khlebnoi statistike," pp. 5–6; and "Ob uchete urozhaia khlebov," pp. 5–6). I have not used any of those sources.

[16] No less an authority than the current editor of the journal *Agricultural History*, historian Douglas Hurt, endorses the view that the sources by their nature stem exclusively from the intelligentsia. This is a gross mistake. Professional correspondence, November 4th, 1999.

[17] "U akademika I. A. Bunina (beseda),"*Moskovskaia vest'*, September 12th, 1911 (as cited in Dmitrieva, "Problema natsional'nogo kharaktera," p. 70. Of course there were educated Russians who felt very alien in the village world. The famous writer Alexander Kuprin, for instance, described the inability of some visiting Petersburgers even to understand peasant speech in Riazan province (Kuprin, "The Song and the Dance"). But people so completely removed from the peasant world took very little part in analyzing or depicting it.

[18] The aforementioned Hurt is willing to dismiss non-peasants' criticisms of peasants on just these grounds (Professional correspondence, November 4th, 1999). He is by no means alone, as we shall see in the main text of this book. Yet the trend towards sympathetic portrayals of the common people was sufficiently strong among publishers in early twentieth century Russia as to be labeled a "dictatorship of the left" by some (Sigov, "Narodnyi kharakter i sud'ba Rossii," p. 102). Plenty of censorious commentary did appear in print, to be sure.

PART ONE

FARMING THROUGH THE PEASANT'S EYES. THE EVOLUTION OF LABOR, 1861–1914

Methods of Cultivation

Sokha Tillage

Imagine a hot day in June, the year 1900. We are in Tambov Province, Kozlov *uezd*, Petrovsk *volost'*. Together with his horse, a young man, Osip Lokhin, has walked out to a field that has lain fallow all spring. The whole field is 80 *sazhens**** long, very wide, and speckled with weeds of all kinds. The strip belonging to Osip is only four *sazhens* wide.[1] He now harnesses the *sokha* to his horse [Figure 1.1].

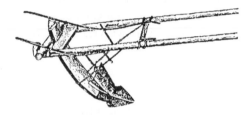

Figure 1.1. The Sokha *(Source:* Kushner, *Russkie,* p. 40)

The two metal blades attached to the tool's wooden body dig into the soil and lift out a trough of earth. The *sokha* cannot cut a clean layer of soil and turn it over like a plow. The shovel-like attachment resting on the body above the blades channels the lifted soil off to one side of the tool. The tiller repositions this iron attachment, known as the *politsa* in Russian, when he turns around after completing each furrow. This allows him to begin the next furrow right alongside the previous one as he tills in the opposite direction, channeling soil from the second furrow over towards the first furrow. Were he to try this without repositioning the *politsa*, then the raised soil would interfere with tillage of the third furrow.

After having had a look at the condition of the soil, Lokhin may decide to adjust the *sokha* for depth of tillage. To do so he re-attaches

****1 *sazhen* = 7 feet.

the sidebars to the horse's girth, and tightens or slackens the ropes that support the main body of the tool.

Now horse, man and tool are ready. Once the team has taken position at one corner of the strip, Lokhin commences tillage with the command *pah-shoal!*[*], or *davai*, or simply a kissing sound. He watches the right rear hoof, aiming the *sokha* at it. The first furrow runs lengthwise along either the right or the left edge of the strip. Reaching the end of the strip, he and the horse reverse direction and begin the second furrow alongside the first. The four-*sazhen*-wide strip will demand about 32 furrows in all.

The *sokha* was the defining feature of Russian peasant agriculture. This tool, more than any other, supported the Russian population from the Middle Ages to the 1930s. It was the team of man, horse, and *sokha*, moreover, which established the peasant within his society. In village parlance a "genuine" or "full-fledged" peasant had his own horse, his own land, a cow, and of course a *sokha*, together with some supplementary equipment.[2] Before drawing back to examine the economic setting in which Osip and his horse are working, let us remain on the scene to observe the characteristics of work with the *sokha*, from the problem of directional control to the technique of turning around at the end of each furrow.

The Tillage Line

The Tiller. On every furrow except for the first, the *sokha* will constantly threaten to skid into the previous furrow. This is because the blades run alongside the previous furrow, where the freshly tilled earth offers less resistance than the earth in the tillage line. The iron parts of the *sokha* compound the difficulty of keeping the tool steady in the furrow. Earth sticks easily to the *politsa*, and the iron blades of the *sokha* dull faster than the steel share of good plows. Each of these drawbacks creates more resistance to the tool, such that the *sokha* might veer off line, or the horse might lurch off course under the extra strain.[3] The tiller can cut the furrows at a safe distance from one another, so as to eliminate the possibility of skidding into the previous furrow. But this somewhat defeats the purpose of tillage, by leaving broad ribbons of untilled land in between the furrows. Decent tillers tried to fit at least eight furrows per *sazhen* of land, measured by width. Careless ones dropped down to as few as five.[4]

[*]If the horse is female, either "pah-shla" or "pah-shoal" is used.

When the *sokha* starts to skid off line the tiller must react instantly to avoid spoiling the ongoing furrow. The handle furthest from the previous furrow must be driven down, while the other handle rises. This will re-aim the tillage line away from the previous furrow. Imagine the view of the *sokha* handles from the point of view of the tiller's waist. The left handle stands at 9 o'clock, the right handle at 3 o'clock. Now picture the *sokha* slipping off towards a previously cut furrow on the right. Recovery back to the tillage line requires moving the left handle down to 8 o'clock, or even to 7:30, while the right handle rises to 2 o'clock, or 1:30. The natural reaction—at least for me, when I was new to the *sokha*—is the opposite. I instinctively wanted to move the blades further away from the previous furrow. Thus I wanted to pull up on the left handle and push down on the right. This is no solution at all. Note that regulating the tillage line is not like using the handlebars of a bicycle. If we imagine the view of the *sokha*'s handles from directly above, with the left handle again at 9 o'clock, and the right handle at 3 o'clock, then, unlike steering a bicycle, in redirecting tillage to the left, the handles' positions will barely change. The left handle might move a bit towards 8 o'clock, and the right handle towards 2 o'clock. A bicycle's handlebars, naturally, would move much more strongly towards 8 o'clock and 2 o'clock. In the process of realigning the *sokha* the tiller's feet must often skip over to the side away from which he wishes to till. Thus in our example of a recovery back to the left, he would scamper over to the right. In loose earth this is not the simplest of tricks. The more experienced the tiller, the smoother, less strenuous, and less perceptible are his recoveries.

Holding the tillage line is the trickiest aspect of tillage, with a *sokha* or a plow. This difficulty accounts for the fact that a small minority of otherwise capable peasants would hire more skilled neighbors to till for them.[5] More importantly, it also helps to explain the tendency to till eight or fewer furrows per *sazhen*. Cutting fewer furrows was less work, of course. But it also lowered the frequency of the tool skidding off the tillage line. This convenience came at a substantial price, however, as we shall now see.

To a casual observer the *sokha* appears to cut furrows wider than the tool's blades. Unless the soil is sandy or dusty, a bit of earth up at the surface adheres to the soil that the blades are raising. *Sokha* furrows are therefore trough-like, such that the furrow is wider at the surface than it is where the blades passed. At the edges the furrows are barely tilled at all. Where the gap between furrows is reasonably small, this deficiency is not easy to see, because the *politsa* immediately hides the land that goes unworked or barely worked by throwing fresh earth from the trough off to that side. All too often, however, the gap between furrows was so wide as to remain visible, as chronic complaints about *ogrekhi* (surface missed by the *sokha*) attest.[6]

By tilling the norm of eight furrows per *sazhen*, farmers were leaving 10–15% of the surface of the land more or less unworked. Those who dropped down to six or even five furrows were missing about a third of the land.[7] The *sokha*'s instability along the tillage line was largely responsible for such sparse tillage norms, and was therefore a serious weakness of the tool—a weakness that has never been fully analyzed in the agronomic or historical literature.[8]

The Horse. With the exception of temperamental stallions, well-trained horses will walk a straight furrow every time. Green horses or agitated stallions are less reliable. They will charge ahead too fast, walk a crooked furrow, turn too widely. If the horse does stray off-line, the tiller is helpless to save the furrow. The value to the farmer of a well-trained, calm, experienced workhorse cannot be overestimated. If there is one overriding message to be drawn from this first discussion of tillage, it is the importance of communication between the horse and the tiller. A good tiller and a good horse can work many hours in a day without tiring, and almost without reins. It is interesting to note that according to the results of a plowing competition in Tambov in 1871 the connection between the horse and tiller is less delicate than the connection between the plower and his plow. When plowers at such competitions worked without their own plow, the level of their work dropped off further than when they worked with new horses.[9]

Distractions

The Tiller. The tiller must be attentive all the time, because irregularities in the soil can pull tillage off-line at any moment. In trying to keep control of the handles an inexperienced tiller will quickly develop painful blisters. Dusty air, the horse's tail, and especially flying insects can disturb his concentration or his view. Swarms of midges and mosquitoes can make work almost impossible in some places, especially in the spring. Horses defecate and flatulate on the move. The furthest-flying liquid from a strong spray of diarrhea will just reach the tillers arms and shirt (I have never experienced worse, anyway). When tilling a large area in a single day the mental strain is considerable, even for an experienced tiller. Halts to reset loose harnessing or support ropes on the tool offer occasional respites.

The Horse. Hunger, thirst, and fatigue are the main challenges to the horse's concentration, as we shall see below. In some cases horseflies can make work in the daytime an ordeal for horses. If the animal has exposed, broken skin, the torment from horseflies can be unbearable. Another complication can arise on strips closest to the village. If the horse sees his home in front of him then he might accelerate through the furrow. If then he must turn around and continue work, he will walk a very weak and slow furrow in the direction away from home. Exhausted or recalcitrant horses might sometimes stop working, even in mid-furrow. Shouts, whips, and fists might or might not get them moving again.

Obstacles

The *sokha* is light enough to lift up so as to avoid obstacles such as roots or rocks. Of course this advantage over plows is most significant on lands newly converted from forest or scrub, but even in areas like Tambov it is helpful, since some patches of soil become nearly untillable with a *sokha*. They might harden from loss of moisture, or might contain rugged clumps of crop stubble.

Soil Relief

When coming into a rise the *sokha* does not seem to dig in deeper. The problem is on the downslope, where tillage will be too thin, unless the tiller hustles to bring up the handles a little bit at just the right moment so as to let the blades dig in.

Corrections

Mistakes happen in tillage; some spots of land will be missed. One option is to leave these spots behind. Otherwise, *nazad!*: the horse's most hated command. He or she must retreat, step by step, over uncertain footing that he or she cannot see. Meanwhile, the tiller must hold up the *sokha,* yank on the reins to convince his friend of the necessity to move backwards, and perform the same careful retreat himself. The best tillers hardly ever have to retreat; the worst tillers hardly ever bother to retreat.

Turning Around

The Tiller. Changing direction at the end of each furrow is in many ways more arduous than cutting the furrow itself. *Tprruu!* was the common command to halt the horse. *Stoiat'!* could also be heard (this is the more military sounding command; "stoi!" is softer). Turning around demands at least 3 meters, it seems to me. The horse must really listen and respond quickly and accurately. Otherwise, turning around is arduous. The *sokha* is lighter than the plow, but at 30–40 pounds its weight is not negligible, especially if good-sized clumps of earth have stuck on top of the blades, as they almost always do. If the tiller has sufficient energy he might try to shake this earth free. The horse will respond to reins and the pressure of the sidebars on his flanks. The faster he responds the easier on the tiller. If the tiller is using the reins actively, then he must support the weight of the *sokha* with only one arm. Once the turn is completed a good horse will come to a halt, or near halt, at the starting point for the next furrow. This gives the tiller a moment to align the *sokha* accurately and to prepare to set the blades into the soil right at the border of the strip. A less experienced or off-form horse needs reminding: *Stoiat'!*

The Horse. After the first few furrows, a good horse quickly orients to the length of the strip, and the teamwork between man and horse improves. The horse works at an even pace, and thus instinctively knows when the furrow is coming to an end. The shorter the furrow, the more precise is this sense. Naturally he can see the end of the strip, and if any of his hooves are trodding through the furrow alongside the current one then he will notice the firmer ground at the end of the strip. His sight and memory tell him which direction to turn at this point, right or left. Of course he is supposed to pull for a couple more steps, so as to allow the tiller to guide the *sokha* all the way to the end of the strip. But the horse will not always do this. As the work session lengthens, his concentration will lapse. He might turn too early: "Enough already. This furrow is done. Let's get on with the next one." Alternatively, a strong horse might keep pulling out of inertia. The tiller then has to yell for a halt, and yank back on the reins. If the horse is hungry he will halt and reach down to feed on any greenery that might be available on the borders of the strip. If the current job is planting and covering potatoes or beets, then he might even stop in mid-furrow and help himself to a bite or two.

Why Till?

Tillage might be considered the defining feature of farming. Social groups that rely on fishing, hunting and gathering, or pastoral live-stocking can make do without tillage. Without any great expenditure of effort, such peoples can harvest and make use of fruits, vegetables, and even grains that grow on their own. But once the population density grows past a certain point then men must begin working the land. Some farming can be done without significant tillage operations, but only at a very primitive and under-productive level. When properly executed, tillage greatly improves crop yields by performing the following functions:

1) It crumbles up the surface layer of soil, which in turn:
   a) allows the easier passage of air into the soil,
   b) allows water easier entry into the soil,
   c) slows water evaporation from the soil.
2) It reduces weeds, which take moisture and nutrients from the soil to support their own growth.
3) It covers seeds, protecting them from birds and allowing them to begin their growth underneath a favorable layer of soil.
4) It covers manure or other fertilizers with soil, facilitating their absorption into the soil.

The first point above surely deserves some elaboration. As any Tambov peasant could tell you, soil that is left untilled will slowly settle, becoming ever more firm and dense. He could tell you that such soil dries out and forms a tough, infertile crust (*korka*). By directing your attention to a dirt road, he could also show you how pressure on the soil from above will exaggerate this process.

What the peasant would almost certainly not be able to tell us is why tillage so effectively maintains soil fertility. The first and most obvious point concerns the retention of soil moisture. Of course plants need water to grow, but the quantity of water that they demand can be quite enormous. Thus, to obtain a yield of 150 *puds* of grain and 300 *puds* of straw, a *desiatina* of land in the central black-earth region requires approximately 180,000 *vedros* of water.[10] In other terms, anywhere from 300 to 500 *puds* of water are needed for every *pud* of dry matter (grain, chaff, straw and roots).[11] Tambov did not suffer from an overabundance of rain. Average precipitation ranged from about 400 mm per year in the south of the province to 550 mm in the north. In rainy years some areas would get over 800 mm, but in the occasional dry year the rainfall would dip below one half of average levels.[12] Thus the threat here was drought, not an excess of water. And so the primary function of tillage in Tambov was the retention of soil moisture. As gravity, rainfall, and other pressures compact the soil, the canals through which air and water pass, are narrowed [Figure 1.2]. When these canals are relatively

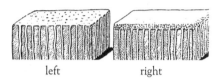

left   right

Figure 1.2. The Capillary Structure of Soil. *Left:* Unworked soil. *Right:* Soil worked shallowly, with a harrow (*Source: KSE*, vol. 4, Prilozhenie)

wide, the soil will easily absorb precipitation. But the canals will narrow if the soil settles. Then water will run off downslope or lie on the surface in puddles, blocking the passage of air through the soil. Furthermore, narrow channels allow water deep in the soil to climb up to the surface and evaporate in tremendous quantities. By keeping the upper layer of soil loose and crumbly the tiller can prevent the narrowing of the canals, and retain the necessary moisture in the soil, even in the case of significant drought.

The retention of soil moisture for plant usage is not the only benefit of loose and crumbly soil. All fertile soils contain the elements without which plants cannot flourish, namely nitrogen, phosphorus, and potassium. But these elements are inaccessible to plants in their raw form. Plants cannot absorb nitrogen, for instance. They depend on microbes in the soil to transform nitrogen into saltpeter, which they can absorb. But these microbes are living organisms, which cannot survive without air, heat, and water. By maintaining a friable layer of soil on the surface the tiller maintains life in the soil. The all-important microbes flourish, and the soil's fertility rises dramatically.

Of course the task of tillage is extremely subtle. The tiller must decide when, how deeply, and with what implements to till. He must know how to arrange his furrows, and he must know how much time he has to complete the job, for other operations also demand his attention. Poorly executed tillage will cost him dearly. Undertilled areas will dry up and die, while over-tillage will reduce the upper layer of soil to dust, narrowing the channels for air and water, and the next good dose of rain will turn this dust into packed mud.

When to Till

The crucial factor here is the moisture level of the soil. It must fall within a small range. Soil that is too moist is very arduous to till, and if the raised soil is really wet then it will bind into clumps. Ensuing winds will harden these clumps into bricks that will be impervious even to a good rain, and the field will be useless until the next spring thaw sinks in and allows another try.[13] This danger is present every spring, when the tiller is in a hurry to work the soil so as to help it retain as much of the moisture of the spring thaw as possible. He must wait approximately until the horse's hooves do not leave a full imprint in the soil. If he waits any longer before tilling, then the soil will start to harden and dry out. Tardy tillage can yield more of a dusty than friable soil, leading to erosion and increased density. One exception to these rules may be mentioned here: lighter soils, which in Tambov are situated mostly in the four northern *uezds*, can be tilled when wet with less trepidation, for they will not tend to clump up as badly as heavier soils.

How Deeply to Till

By comparing crop yields on tilled versus untilled soils peasants could easily identify the connection between tillage and soil fertility. But, in some cases thanks to the influence of landlords and estate managers, many of them came to assume that tillage increased the fertility *of the layer of soil tilled.* And so they were inclined to believe as a general rule that deeper tillage was better.* They might also have felt that deeper tillage facilitated the penetration of crops' roots into the soil. But roots will quickly grow down and seek nourishment below the tilled layer of

---

*For discussion of the stages of peasant thought on the depth of tillage, see the opening section of Part II.

soil, no matter what its depth.[14] Before the turn of the century prejudice in favor of deep tillage reigned all over Europe, not just in Russia. Russian landlords were buying heavy plows to till grain at 18–26 cm, beets at 35 cm.[15] But agronomic science determined that the depth of tillage was much less important than the timing, especially in drier climates.[16] After the discussion above concerning the timing of tillage this should come as no surprise. And so there is rarely any need to till deeper than about 13 cm.[17] Data from experimental stations in Samara and Simbirsk indicated that, with some exceptions, deeper tillage was simply a waste of time and effort. Crop yields would increase by only a few percent.[18] We might add here that some crops do need slightly deeper tillage than others; and most soils will benefit from an occasional deeper tillage if continual working at a shallow depth is pulverizing their structure. Of the crops prevalent in Tambov, rye prefers loose soil to a depth of about 4 *vershki*, oats a bit deeper, potatoes and beets a bit deeper still.[19]

No matter what peasants' perceptions may have been concerning tillage depth, before the appearance of plows it was difficult for them to get any deeper than about 12 cm (2.7 *vershki*) with the *sokha*. How deeply did they actually till, when raising fallow for example? Information on this issue is not plentiful. A study of agricultural technology in 1914 in Voronezh *uezd* (on the southern border of Tambov province) found a rather wide range of depths—anywhere from 2.2–2.7 *vershki*.[20] Boris Bruk, the director of the Voronezh experimental station in the 1920s, writes that the range was anywhere from 2–3 *vershki*, but he was including work with plows.[21] An official inquiry across Kozlov *uezd* in 1920 yielded responses on this question for only two *volosts*. In both cases the depth was 2.5 *vershki*.[22] Peasants from the period attest that they did not think in terms of any such measurement when tilling. They simply looked down at the furrow, and adjusted the *sokha* as described earlier, should they wish to change the depth significantly. They recall tilling at about 10 cm.[23] Lazy farmers, or those with weak or failing horses, might till even more shallowly.[24]

These then, are the sensory features of *sokha* tillage, unchanging for hundreds of years. The talents, skills, and strengths of man and horse always determined the quality of this work. But the relative success of the family in keeping itself and its livestock fed depended in large part on the economic context surrounding the work. As we shall now see, the stresses accumulating on the peasant economy in the nineteenth and early twentieth centuries were placing unprecedented demands on partners like Osip and his horse. The manner in which they met—or failed to meet—the challenges of the times forms the heart of our story, and the core of Russian agrarian history for the entire period from emancipation to collectivization.

An Agrarian System under Stress

As soon as we left the lilac alley Turgenev's Russia opened up before us, with its green rises, blue groves and copses, softly waving, silvery-green grain fields, white churches, villages and manor homes. The hint of smoke we spied from afar was a warm steam rising from the land. The sun had not come out from behind the clouds, but its warmth was already with us. The moist ground rustled under the carriage's wheels and the horses' hooves. A warm breeze came head on, carrying the soothing scent of the rye fields. The trilling sound of skylarks fell all around.

—F. Kriukov, 1914[25]

Given all the advantages accruing to Russia, given all its material resources and moral wealth, why does nothing come of it but mutual face beating?

—A character of G. I. Uspenskii, 1882[26]

Nature blessed the central Russian grain belt with beautiful scenery and tremendous soils. Nineteenth-century travelers would reach the black-earth zone about 120 miles (or 3–6 days) southeast of Moscow, near the border between Riazan province and Shatsk *uezd* in north central Tambov province. Here they would leave behind certain features of the scenery of non-black-earth Russia. Thick forests gave way to open spaces; the dark green coniferous woods they were accustomed to seeing in the background of northern landscapes were nowhere to be found. If they arrived in spring or autumn the entire countryside would seem to be covered in the bright emerald hue of grain sprouts. In summer the land was transformed into a golden sea of gently waving, ripening grain surrounding islands of birch, oak, asp, and other leafy trees. If the travelers had never before visited the region, the soil below the flora would likely catch their attention. Wherever the ground was laid bare by recent tillage, its dark brown hue, sometimes truly verging on the black, betrayed the fertility of the land.[27]

Moving a substantial distance along any road in a southern or easterly direction, an observant traveler would note that the gently rolling terrain began to flatten out, and that the rivers and water sources became sparser. If he took the initiative to inquire of the locals along the way, he would learn that the rains fell less consistently towards the south and east, and that the winds blew a bit stronger. Already by the time he reached the southern third of Tambov, the surroundings would begin to resemble the bare, flat steppelands of southern Russia. Here the monotony of the landscape was joined to the unpredictability of precipitation. The quality of the soil remained superlative, but the threat of drought could never be far from the farmer's mind.

Given the natural conditions of the central black-earth region, it would come as no surprise to our travelers to learn that agriculture and its complimentary crafts dominated economic life in Tambov, to the point of exclusivity. Among a population of 2,684,030 in 1897, 92% lived in villages, 84% relying primarily on agriculture to make a living. 94% of the province's inhabitants were peasants, and, apart from an enclave of 90,000 Mordvinians (a Finnic people) residing mainly in Spassk *uezd*, 99% were Russians. 99% were registered as Orthodox Christians.[28]

What might puzzle the travelers, on the other hand, was the apparent material want of the peasantry in Tambov. The superabundance of flies and cockroaches inside peasant huts would shock them most of all.[29] If they were visiting around the turn of the century, they would surely be prepared to encounter poverty. By this time the condition of the peasantry throughout the central black-earth region had become shameful and alarming to the Tsarist government. The area was a symbol of a widely perceived agrarian crisis. Voices both inside and outside the circles of power warned that this crisis could shatter the stability of Russian society. Freshly arriving travelers might understandably ask just how serious the crisis was, and how it might have arisen in such a blessed land. To answer these questions, let us now survey the primary features of the peasant economy in Tambov province in the late nineteenth century.

In the decades following emancipation, the most glaring and alarming development in rural Russia was the population explosion among the peasantry. Both in Tambov and in European Russia as a whole the rural population doubled between 1861 and 1914 [Tables 1.1–1.3].

The population of the average village in Tambov also doubled, reaching almost 1,000 by 1914—more than that in the southeast, where the scarcity of the water sources conditioned the formation of oversized villages positioned near rivers and streams.[30]

Table 1.1. Pressure on the Land (rural population growth, 1858–1914)

	1858	1882	1897	1914
European Russia	53,748,684	68,616,418	81,378,100	109,179,700
Tambov	1,770,991	2,323,018	2,457,766	3,225,600

Sources: For 1858, Statisticheskie tablitsy Rossiiskoi imperii. Vyp. 2. Nalichnoe nase-leniia imperii za 1858 god. pp. 182–183, 199–200, 242–243. For 1882, Sbornik svedenii po Evropeiskoi Rossii za 1882 god, p. 50. For 1897, Pervaia vseobshchaia perepis', p. 1; and A. G. Rashin, Naselenie Rossii za 100 let, pp. 44–45, 87. For 1914, Rashin, op. cit., pp. 44–45, 87, 101.

Table 1.2. Rural Population Density, 1858–1914 (inhabitants per square *versta*)

	1858	1882	1897	1914
European Russia	12.9	16.2	19.1	25.7
Tambov	30.5	39.7	42.0	55.1

Sources: as for Table 1.1.

Table 1.3. Tambov: Allotment Land per Capita, 1858–1914

1858	1882	1897	1914
1.74 *des.*	1.26 *des.*	1.19 *des.*	0.91 *des.*

Sources: For 1858, *Statisticheskii tablitsy Rossiiskoi imperii,* pp. 182–183, 199–200, 242–243. For 1882, *Sbornik svedenii po Evropeiskoi Rossii za 1882 god,* p. 50. For 1897, *Pervaia vseobshchaia perepis',* p. 1; and Rashin, *Naselenie Rossii,* pp. 44–45, 87. For 1914, Rashin, *op. cit.,* pp. 44–45, 87, 101.

The surging population struggled to feed itself. Grasslands and forests were cut down, plowed up, and sown with grains. Whereas forest and shrub had covered 60% of the land in the northern third of the province in 1800, by 1914 their share fell to about 40%. In the rest of the province the amount of land categorized as meadows dropped over the same period from 27% to 5%. Already by the early 1880s over four-fifths of the land allotted to the peasantry after 1861 was under the plow.[31]

Unable to extend sowings any further on their own territory, and needing still more cropland, peasants eyed nearby private and govern-ment holdings. The terms of the emancipation had left 50.2% of the province's land in the hands either of gentry landowners (37.6%), the government, the Imperial family, or the church.[32] The other half of the land, coming to approximately 3,000,000 *desiatinas,* had been reserved as "allotments" to peasant communes to be doled out and periodically reapportioned among villagers as the communes saw fit. Often extending themselves to the limit of their means, by 1901 peasants were renting about 850,000 *desiatinas*, at a roughly estimated cost of 11 million rubles* annually.[33] Moreover, by 1912 they had bought 622,000 more *desiatinas* of privately owned land.[34] Nevertheless, peasant land per capita (allotment, purchased, and rented land) dropped to 1.74 *desiatinas* in the early 1880s, and to 1.35 in 1912 (see Map 1.3).[35]

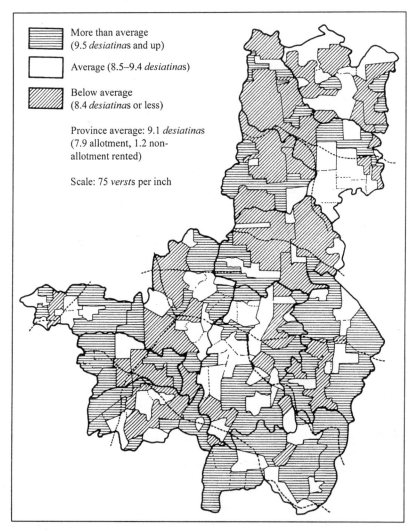

More than average
(9.5 *desiatinas* and up)

Average (8.5–9.4 *desiatinas*)

Below average
(8.4 *desiatinas* or less)

Province average: 9.1 *desiatinas*
(7.9 allotment, 1.2 non-
allotment rented)

Scale: 75 *versts* per inch

Map 1.3. Average Amount of *Desiatinas* of Land per Peasant Household, by *Volosts*, 1912 (*Source:* Chelintsev, *Opyt izucheniia organizatsii krest'ianskogo khoziaistva*, p. 29).

*One ruble was equal to 51 cents in 1913 (according to a note of S. Strumilin, in Vainshtein, *Narodnoe bogatstvo*, p. 6).

Under the pressure of land shortages, peasants sought supplementary income in growing numbers. Unfortunately for them, the economy of Tambov remained overwhelmingly agricultural. After textiles, all of the primary industries in the province were closely tied to agriculture: grain milling, distilling, beet-sugar extraction, and tobacco processing. Gross output from all industries in Tambov in 1913 was a paltry 44 million rubles.[36] And so industry never supported significant quantities of laborers—factory employment stagnated between 12,500 and 14,000 from the 1860s to 1902.[37] A small industrial boom in the next decade brought the figure no higher than 23,000.[38] Shut out of factory work, peasants tried to find odd jobs. They might gain temporary employment in transporting goods, for instance, or they might practice carpentry, masonry, leatherwork, or a multitude of other trades. All told, the 1897 population census registered 18.6% of all peasant families as receiving income from some non-agricultural work in their locality.[39]

Agricultural labor was another, obvious avenue for off-farm employment. But there was not enough of this work to go around.[40] Landlords held ever less of the province's land over time, and frequently they opted to lease out their land rather than accept the risks of conducting their own farming operations.[41] While wages for farm labor were unenviable throughout Russia, local circumstances guaranteed that they were exceptionally low in Tambov.[42]

If local employment opportunities did not suffice, families could always try to send a member or two away for seasonal, migrant labor—*otkhod*. They might look for jobs in the factories around Moscow, or head south to work on the big grain farms there. *Otkhod* naturally became more attractive, and more necessary, as the local economy faltered. Decade-by-decade statistics of passport issues demonstrate the scope of the trend (passports are a rough indicator of *otkhod*, since by law peasants could not travel more than thirty *versts* from their home village without a passport obtained from local officials) [Table 1.4]:[43]

Table 1.4. Passports Issued to Tambov Peasants, 1861–1910

	1861–1870	1871–1880	1881–1890	1891–1900	1902	1906–1910
# issued, per year	34,900	88,900	115,300	167,300	235,900	251,300
% of population	1.9	4.2	4.7	5.9	8.8	8.2

Source: Burds, "The Social Control of Peasant Labor," pp. 56–59.

As closely as the statisticians could figure, by the year 1900 about 39% of all working-age peasants were gathering income from *promysly*, *otkhod*, or local agricultural labor. But still there were not enough of these jobs to support all those in need. Contemporaries even complained of the shrinking of opportunities for such earnings. They sensed that the appearance of manufactured goods and railroads was depriving peasants of much needed income from craftwork and cargo hauling.[44] The final alternative for peasants was to abandon their homes in favor of migration to Siberia or the North Caucasus. Perhaps as many as 200,000 peasants left Tambov between 1885 and 1915. Nevertheless, the migrations did little to ease the pressure of population growth. For every ten new mouths to feed in these decades, perhaps one found refuge outside of the province.[45] For many the refuge was all too brief—up to 20% of the migrants died en route or shortly after reaching their destinations.[46]

Population pressure was not the only trend fueling the crisis in the countryside. The worldwide agricultural depression of the late nineteenth century and the Tsarist government's financial policies also played their roles. Virtually all peasant families had to sell some of their grain in order to pay taxes, so they benefited from relatively high grain prices. Prices dipped sharply in the late 1880s, when the depression hit, and did not recover before the turn of the century [Table 1.5].

Table 1.5. Average Grain Prices in Tambov Province, 1862–1900
(all prices in kopecks per *pud*)

	1862–70	1871–75[*]	1876–80	1881–85	1886–90	1893–95	1896–1900
RYE	40	54	56	72	55	44	48
OATS	41	53	51	55	41	42	50

[*]Excluding the years 1873 and 1874, for which data are not available.
Note: I have also excluded the two exceptional years following the massive crop failure of 1891 (which drove prices up very high for two years).
Source: Mironov, *Khlebnye tseny v Rossii*, prilozhenie, tables 11 and 14.

Thanks to Russia's size and inadequate transport networks, grain prices in surplus areas like Tambov were languishing at about 15% below national averages in the last twenty years of the nineteenth century.[47] Transport problems within the province, moreover, meant that prices in the villages were anywhere from 3–15% lower than in the *uezd* towns. This impelled many farmers to make long, costly trips to market. In the southern two-thirds of the province the average distance from farm to marketing point was about twenty *versts*—over poor roads—in all of the *uezds*, reaching twenty-five in some.[48] Grain merchants' collusion against small peasant sellers was widespread, depressing farmers' profits still more.[49]

While the economic conjuncture was turning against agriculture, the government decided to extract still more resources from the countryside in order to finance industrial development. Although direct taxes on the peasant population and their lands rose only modestly in real terms from emancipation to the turn of the century, indirect taxation on goods such as sugar, alcohol, salt, and kerosine multiplied. By 1900 the peasantry was paying more indirectly than directly—c. 5,500,000 rubles, or about 13 rubles per family (at local rye prices, enough to provide an average family with as much as three months' worth of grain).[50] Finally, it was clear to contemporaries that government programs were ignoring the agricultural heartland in particular. Central government expenditures in the region equaled at best 50% of the money extracted there.[51] A geographical breakdown of government expenditures per capita reveals startling contrasts [Table 1.6]:[52]

Table 1.6. Central Government Expenditures, by Region (per Capita, c. 1900)

St. Petersburg province	48.20 rubles
Moscow province	13.60 rubles
Central agricultural region	78 kopecks

Note: These are the cumulative expenses of five ministries—Agriculture and State Domains, Internal Affairs, Education, Communications, and Justice.
Source: Stakhovich, "Ob obshchei finansovoi politiki," p. 347.

As we shall subsequently detail, peasants all across the province responded to the demands of the time by working harder so as to raise crop yields. They worked the land more intensively, and expended effort on manuring. They reduced their sowings of oats (which required little labor to grow and could bring in much needed cash) in favor of "poor man's crops" like millet and potatoes—which raised the labor requirements per *desiatina* about twice as fast as they boosted returns.[53] Labor intensification brought some results. Rye yields rose by about 50% over the course of the half-century following 1861. Peasant per capita production of rye and other consumption crops grew slowly but surely throughout the period.[54]

Increasing *production* per capita did not, however, guarantee increasing *consumption* per capita. Peasant standards of living depended in part on the economic conjuncture. Were rising payments for land and taxes forcing farmers to sell ever more of their foodstuffs and animals? Assessment of shifts in the standard of living can be divided into two related tasks. The first is to establish the biological standard of living—the health of the population, in other words. The second is to assess their standard of living in the stricter sense—their wealth, in short.

The data in the Appendix "Nutrition and Mortality" starkly illustrate the severity of the economic crisis in Tambov, and imply a decline in the biological standard of living in the late nineteenth century. Despite increasing production of foodstuffs per capita, peasants had less food on the table in the late 1890s and 1910s than they had had in the early 1880s. Quite in contrast to the national trend, nutrition levels in Tambov troughed in the 1890s, coinciding with increased mortality.[55] Further, data on the condition of army recruits suggest a declining level of popular health stretching back to the 1860s—a period for which we cannot establish the amount of food available to the desired degree of accuracy.[56] Thus the decline of the peasant economy might have been a long-term trend in Tambov.

Data available for analysis of the peasantry's wealth cannot pretend to as much precision as the data on nutrition and mortality. Yet here too the sources portray an increasingly impoverished population. The declining availability of rye, meat, dairy products, and vegetables in the 1890s surely represented an unwelcome deterioration of peasant diets. The intensive work required to grow potatoes and millet, and to raise crop yields generally, was a very serious concession to the times. So too were the migrations to Siberia, and the reduced numbers of horses per farm. Horses were fundamental capital in the peasant economy, and performed important functions beyond fieldwork. Farmers would not part with them easily.[57] They held 30 horses for every 100 capita in the early 1880s, but only 24.1 in 1897 and 19.5 in 1912.[58]

Contact with urban Russia did bring the peasantry important compensations in the decades after emancipation. Fabrics, manufactured clothing, household conveniences, and amusements of new kinds became available to villagers, at least in principle. Samovars, liqueurs, cosmetics, hand tools, boots, decorations, and a great variety of other goods—including the printed word—now competed for peasants' scarce cash. One historian has labeled the peasants' manifest appetite for urban products a "culture of acquisition," implying a reformation of material values.[59] In other words, partaking of the ever-increasing repertoire of refinements and diversions on the market might have meant more to peasants than maintaining a full complement of live-stock. Peasants might also have invested more resources into their houses and other structures. Some data points in that direction, any-way.[60]

The absence of good data on peasant consumption of commercial goods precludes firm conclusions regarding the wealth of the popula-tion in Tambov. But the character and intensity of the material burdens on the peasantry's shoulders in the last decades before the war squares well with the hypothesis of distress. Further, the material difficulties appear to have burdened all strata of the peasant population, not just the poorer families. The breakdown of horse holdings over our time period points strongly to the conclusion of immiserization of the peasantry, not stratification [Table 1.7].

Table 1.7. Horseholding per Peasant Farm, 1888–1912

% of farms with:	1888	1899	1905	1912
0 horses	22.2	29.4	28.0	33.7–36*
1–2 horses	44.3	48.5	47.7	49.4
3 horses	14.0	10.9	11.8	9.0
4 horses	8.6	5.5	6.1	4.2
5 or more horses	10.9	5.9	6.4	3.6

*The data from the 1912 military horse census employed in this table varies from the Tambov *zemstvo*'s animal holding census findings for the same year. The percentage of horseless farms is 36% in the latter. The military census was not contemporaneous with the *zemstvo* study. The discrepancy is significant, but unresolvable.
It should be noted that although the 1911 harvest was well below normal, the quantities of livestock holdings appear to have been little affected. The animals ate very poorly in the winter of 1911–12, but peasants did not sell or consume inordinate numbers of them. A summary of opinions on this matter from the agricultural correspondents of the Tambov *zemstvo* appears in SKhVIuV, 1912, no. 10, p. 16.
Sources: *Voenno-konskaia perepis' 1888 goda*, pp. 8, 80–81; *Voenno-konskaia perepis' 1899–1901 goda*, p. 62; *Voenno-konskaia perepis' 1905 goda*, pp. 5, 36–37; *Voenno-kon-skaia perepis' 1912 goda*, pp. 14, 134–135.

Rising grain prices [see Table 1.8] and reduced taxation offered some relief after 1900.[61] Even though the amounts of nutrition available did not recover to the levels of the 1880s, the sharp decline in the mortality rate by the eve of the First World War does suggest improved popular health. A combination of causes might have been at work, including advances in hygiene, the slight increase in nutrition, a favorable disease climate, and government-organized, railroad-borne food relief cam-paigns following harvest failures.[62]

Table 1.8. Price Indexes, 1890s–1913

Years	All goods, averaged	Grain products	Animal products	Textiles	Groceries
1890–99	100	100	100	100	100
1901	112.6	106.8	115.3	109.1	114.9
1905	111.1	117.0	127.8	110.0	115.2
1910	127.8	117.8	154.6	116.7	128.9
1913	139.8	128.9	168.7	168.8	137.5

Source: KSE, vol. 2, pp. 215–216.

While the degree to which the peasant economy recovered in the first decade and a half of the twentieth century must remain unclear, the import of the rural crisis for peasant farmers is unmistakable. Farmers were exerting tremendous efforts to improve yields. As hard as they tried, failure loomed ever larger as time went by. By 1912, 15% of the farms had no livestock at all, another 4% had neither an adult horse nor an adult cow, and another 22.5% did not have both animals. 25.5% more had only one horse and one cow.[63] No reserves were left on two farms out of three. Most peasant farmers were losing the battle to refine and advance their mastery of the natural environment at the pace dictated by the times. Did they stand to lose the war, and to face the choice of either starving or giving up farming?

The rest of Part I seeks to analyze peasant tactics in the struggle to raise yields. Only on this foundation will it be possible to assess the capacities of peasant agriculture and its prospects on the eve of the World War.

Green Fallow and Other Shortcomings

When one considers all the patient observation, practical intui-
tion, and willing co-operation, unsupported by any proper
scientific knowledge, which from the dawn of our rural history
must have gone into the cultivation of the soil, one is filled with
feelings of admiration akin to those which inspired Videl de la
Blanche, after a visit to the Museum of Ethnography, to one of
his finest flights of prose. But our sense of gratitude to those
remote forefathers of ours who discovered grain, invented plowing and joined arable, woodland and pasture into in a fruitful
union, should not blind us to the imperfections of their labors,
to the poverty of their fields, and to the narrowness of the
margin which separated them from famine, their ever-present
companion.

                         —Marc Bloch, 1930[64]

Agronomist's Criticism of Peasant Tillage

Having noted the inability of the *sokha* to till deeper than 10–11 cm, we may now point out that the constant tillage of a thin upper layer does damage to the soil structure. First clumps of soil begin to turn into dust during grazing or fieldwork, then deep freezes in the fall break up remaining clumps still further. Soil ought to be tilled more deeply once per year, to 5–6 *vershki*. This brings crumbly soil up to the top, and sends dust down below to reform.[65]

Peasants sometimes tried too hard to improve the condition of their soil. Good black-earth soil is not overly dense and heavy. It is loose and crumbly, with plenty of air in it. Observers recorded how peasants sought to fluff up their soil, to which end they might work the soil too much.[66] Over-tillage leads only to dust, not to improved soil structure.

We have reason to believe that some, even many, peasants did not really know exactly when to till. According to Vasil'ev, the ranking agronomist in the south of Tambov, writing in 1912, *no one* knew when to till—neither peasants nor landlords. While in the morning conditions may be too wet for tillage, by noon or evening it may already be too late. "Our peasants and landlords pay almost no attention to this whatsoever, since they just do not understand how important it is."[67] One suspects this criticism is slightly exaggerated. The best farmers would not have been guilty. They had their own ways of telling when to begin tillage. Some would put their hands deep into the soil so as to estimate the degree of warmth below the surface. Others would rely on their nose, since moisture influences the smell of the soil.[68] Some farmers were finer judges than others, of course.

Green Fallow. Far and away the worst problem with the peasants' timing of tillage was the entrenched practice of green fallow. All agronomists of the day agreed that green fallow was a plague on Russian farming. It was enemy number one. Getting rid of it in his district was the primary goal of every local agronomist in the province. What is green fallow?

Green fallow is fallow land used as temporary pasture for farm animals. Since the animals graze on the various weeds and grasses growing there, such fallow land cannot be tilled. Tillage immediately reduces or even eliminates the fodder available on arable land. In Tambov the communes sent their herds out to the fallow fields in April or early May, once sprouts had appeared there, and after the herds had "grazed out" any other suitable pasture sources. The herds—including sheep and often pigs as well as cattle[69]—stayed on the fallow fields for

6–8 weeks, well into June, in unusual cases even into early July. Only when the *skhod* elected to take the herds off the fallow land was anyone permitted to till it. The fallow grazing period was shorter in springs with a lot of rain—more grass would grow elsewhere, herds could eat better there, and so the commune would move them off the fallow land earlier.[70] In especially dry years, which were more frequent in the steppe lands of southern Tambov, virtually all of the vegetation on the fallow lands would die out during the second half of May. Most peasants would then try to till this land quickly, before it became so hard as to render tillage prohibitively difficult.[71]

What were the benefits of this system? In 1912 a local agronomist in Tambov *uezd*, V. Gudvilovich, calculated that each *desiatina* of fallow land in the *uezd* was then supporting 0.33 cows an 6–8-week grazing period.[72] Translating these numbers into cattle equivalents, we get 2/3 of a head of cattle per *desiatina*. Meanwhile estimates of the average amounts of fodder available on green fallow for the entire grazing period range from 15 to 25 *puds* per *desiatina*.[73] And so green fallow was providing the peasants' cows with the equivalent of about 15 *puds* of hay per month. This is a starvation ration even on average quality hay, but the fodder on green fallow was inevitably of inferior quality.[74]

In return for this miserable fodder ration for their animals the peasant farmers faced the following consequences. First, the pasturing of the herds on the arable tapped the soil down, with the inevitable effects on the health of the soil. If sheep were sent out on the fallow as well as cows, then their small hooves served to generate extra doses of dust. And the grazing process itself did not always go according to plan. It was not unheard of for animals to get out of control and charge onto the standing crops nearby, causing great damage.[75] Second, lack of tillage allowed weeds and pests to flourish. The animals would not eat most of the worst weeds unless as a last resort, and so these weeds thrived most of all.[76] Studies found prodigious quantities of weed seeds on peasant land.

Next, green fallow was devastating to soil moisture. We know that poorly worked soil absorbs only 20–25% of the moisture that well-worked soil does.[77] Moreover, dry winds, dry air, and the heat of the soil force the evaporation of almost 90% of all precipitation during the warmer months, even on the best-kept soils.[78] With each month that tillage is postponed the moisture in the soil at the time of sowing sharply declines.[79] In an average year, green fallow would tend to have around 10% water by weight at a depth of 20 cm, while early fallow would have about 20%.[80] Green fallow would have 2% oxygen, well worked land about 12%.[81] The microbes could not thrive in green fallow soil, and so the quantities of potassium nitrate, for example, would be two to three times less than in well-worked soil.[82] Furthermore, we must emphasize that these drastic differences reflect *average* conditions. In dry years green fallow is simply catastrophic. Water content by weight at a depth of 30 cm declines to 1% in drier years, as compared to 8% for early fallow soil.[83]

By waiting so long to till peasants ran the risk that in a dry year the soil would become so hard as to forbid tillage with the *sokha*. The wooden body of the *sokha* could simply bust trying to pass through such ground.[84] Even if the *sokha* could handle the soil, tillage in such conditions is very difficult work, and it only furthers soil decay. Hooves and equipment bang on the dry earth and generate dust. Soil breaks up into tough chunks—"the size of a hat" peasants sometimes said—which harrows cannot handle.[85]

The Tambov agronomist Gudvilovich estimated the cost of green fallow to the rye yield to be 35 *puds* of grain per *desiatina*.[86] In a good year (with a long, cool spring, which gave weak rye time to develop before the dry heat of the summer) green fallow might cost something like 15% of the yield. In a bad year it could cause terrible crop failure. Green fallow even affected sowing and manuring. Peasants were quite rightly reticent to throw seeds onto such soil, and would often wait for rains before sowing.[87] But since this delay could stretch out to an entire month, it carried its own risks, as we shall see later, in our criticism of the traditional sowing techniques. Meanwhile, the interval between the raising of fallow (at which time manure, where used, was tilled into the soil) and sowing was too short for manure to be absorbed evenly into the soil.[88]

The Russian agronomic community's unanimous recognizance of the seriousness of the green fallow problem led to a wave of tests at experimental stations throughout the country in the first two decades of the twentieth century. These tests established that black fallow (fallow tilled in the fall following the harvest of spring crops there) had no significant advantages over fallow raised in April.[89] On the other hand, the difference between green fallow and early fallow—raised in April or May—was tremendous. An eight-year study in Tambov produced the following average figures, in *puds* per *desiatina* [Table 1.9].

We have already seen why green fallow had gained currency among Russian peasants. They simply needed some place to graze their animals before other sources of fodder, hay and crop stubble, were available. Sources occasionally record peasants maintaining that the herds helped

Table 1.9. Timing of Tillage and Consequent Yields

Timing of first tillage	Grain yield
Early fallow	136
June fallow	106
June fallow, with herd grazing[*]	71

[*]This is the average rye yield on peasant lands in the area of the experimental station during the test period. I note here my suspicion that herd grazing alone could not account for all of the large disparity between peasant and experimental station yields on late fallow.
Source: KSE, vol. 4, p. 296.

the fallow soil by killing off the weeds growing there.[90] The cost of this weeding to soil fertility escaped their attention.

There is no sound agronomic rationale for green fallow. Or is there?! Against the flood of criticism of green fallow I have come across only one rebuttal. In 1913 a soil scientist from Poltava published an article outlining the results of experiments designed to assess the affects on soil of various tillage techniques.[91] Over a period of fourteen years they compared green fallow to black, and shallow tillage to deep, within the context of a three-field system. The results were quite startling. They found that both humus and nitrogen in the soil declined faster with black fallow than with green, given no manuring. Tillage at a depth of six *vershki*, depleted nitrogen faster than tillage at a depth of three *vershki*, on both black and green fallow. Phosphoric acid also survived better with green fallow and with shallower tillage. Green fallow even had a superior soil structure—thanks to the depletion of humus, black fallows created more dust than green. Yields on black fallow were indeed higher, but only for about 9–10 years, after which green fallow gave higher yields. In fact, the damage done to the soil by black fallow was such that yields on these lands were lower than on the green fallow lands ten years after the experiments had been halted and all lands worked identically.

To my knowledge no agronomist ever responded to these findings. What are we to make of them? We must point out that black-earth soils were not included in the experiments. All of the work was done on *lesnoi suglinok*, whereas all of our analysis has been focused on black-earth soils. Since black-earth studies never hinted at findings akin to those from Poltava, we need not question the agronomists' disdain for green fallow in the black-earth zone. But the Poltava study does remind us that the genesis of Russian peasant agriculture was in soil zones similar to that tested in Poltava. As the three-field system matured in the areas north of the black-earth zone, primitive peasant technology, including green fallow, really might have been appropriate.[92] In this context we should note that rye and oats, the staple crops of the Russian peasant, do not actually need soil to be as well worked as other crops. Green fallow was more tenable with rye than with any other grain crop.[93] It was only after this technology had congealed that peasants began to settle the southern half of European Russia, including Tambov. They took their tillage traditions with them, and perpetuated them all the way down to the twentieth century. But what was apparently permissible on one set of soils was highly dubious on another.[94]

Harrowing

... the hard clods of earth bounced around under the harrow's iron teeth without breaking up, especially in those places where the cattle had spent a lot of time walking around, beating down the ground to the consistency of roads. The harrow popped into the air over these, raising dust to the height of Van'ka himself. The dust wafted under his nose, and got into his eyes. In vain he twisted around, holding his nose—this only forced him to breathe the dust in through his mouth while he walked behind the horse. The dust penetrated his shirt and stuck to his body, covered as it was in sweat on account of the work and the hot sun. The shirt clung to his dirty torso and made him itchy.
—Aleksei Demidov, *Zhizn' Ivana*, 1923[95]

Performance of Harrowing. Let us now return to Kozlov *uezd* in the summer of 1900. Having raised the fallow strip to which we are paying attention, Osip Lokhin now brings out his harrow. If he is attending to other work he might send his son Fedor, but not his wife or daughter—harrowing, like plowing, was traditionally a male preserve.[96] The harrow has twenty-five long wooden teeth (up to a foot long or more, commonly) attached to a light, square wooden frame.[97] The harrow was usually drawn corner first, since drawing it side first would leave significant surface area unruffled [Figure 1.3].[98]

Before starting out, Osip will have a look at the soil, and feel it under his feet. If it is dry and bumpy he will want to weigh down the harrow with a sack of rocks or a wheel, so as to help the teeth dig in. He or his son Fedor might even stand on the harrow, holding the reins in his hands. A different strategy was required if the clods on the surface were especially large and numerous, as could happen in dry years. Then Osip

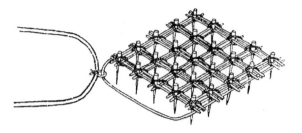

Figure 1.3. A Standard Wooden Harrow (*Source:* Kushner, *Russkie*, p. 46)

would bring an axe, and strain to break up the clods with the butt end. In this case harrowing became almost as arduous as chopping wood.[99] The footing on rough soil could be harsh enough to drive an inexperienced man off in just a half day of harrowing, even if he were wearing decent boots.[100]

Now, beginning at whichever side of the strip is more comfortable, he leads his horse by the bridle down the furrow line at a walking pace (the passage at the outset of this section illustrates the drawbacks of walking behind the harrow).[101] Reaching the end of the strip, they simply turn around and head back, always harrowing along the furrow lines. Harrowing was not done cross-furrow, even on relatively wide strips, because of the time that would be wasted in turning around.[102] If the work is going easily it becomes boring and then Osip must exercise some patience to avoid the temptation to increase the pace of his walk. For the faster the harrow moves along the furrows the less deeply it works the soil.[103] After a full harrowing the soil will be looser, more level, and more uniform than before. But some of the weeds will be left on the land, and Osip will usually wish to make another full pass, so as to clear them off and simultaneously to reduce remaining clods of soil.

Harrowing—Other Considerations. As the above account of the work process indicates, the chief motivations to harrow are to break up clumps in the soil, level off tilled furrows, and rip out weed roots. Harrows are also employed to help cover seeds or fertilizers, which have been distributed on the soil (or, in advanced fallow care, to break up the top layer after a hard rain). Good harrowing is just as important as good tillage. Land left in furrows will dry out much more quickly, and unevenly. Subsequent rains will leave puddles, greatly exacerbating the unevenness of moisture levels in the soil. Overly harrowed land, on the other hand, will turn into dust, with all the consequences described above [see "*Sokha* Tillage"]. Since the work is simple and the tool so cheap to construct, even the poorest peasants harrowed on their own, provided that they had a horse. Before the acquisition of a plow, which can leave layers of soil too thick for simple harrows to handle, the only real hindrance to harrowing was the time involved. But only in extraordinary cases would families with large amounts of land have to rush through the work, doing one pass instead of two, or simply going over their strips too quickly. Two passes would appear to be the norm, three if the soil were very dense at the moment.[104]

Agronomist's Criticism

Evidence concerning the quality of peasants' harrowing is sparse. Nevertheless, several important shortcomings can be uncovered here. Firstly, the agronomist S. Kliuev noted that ideally one should clean the harrow off after each pass through the field, so as to prevent uprooted weeds from taking root once more in the prepared soil.[105] Survivors recall that peasants were not bothering to do this.[106] The fact that peasants tended to lead their horses by the bridle when harrowing inevitably limited their awareness of weed build-up around the harrow's teeth.[107] Secondly, Kliuev and other observers accused peasants of not paying proper attention to the condition of their harrows. Some of the teeth would be out of line, bent, or too short to be in full contact with the soil.[108] A look at harrows of the period in museums and photographs lends credence to the charge. As in virtually every aspect of farming, the state of the harrow depended on the quality of the farmer. Thirdly, dragging harrows "corner first" draws some of the tines through tracks the forward teeth have just cut. Harrows ought to have been attached obliquely, so that all of the teeth could contribute.[109]

More seriously, the chief agronomist of the Borisoglebsk *uezd zemstvo*, N. M. Vasil'ev, insisted that peasants' harrows were poor, and that the farmers themselves simply did not understand how to harrow—they might work too hard:

> Observing peasant work on the fields lying fallow, ... you can see how they carefully apply their light, wooden, iron-toothed harrows to breaking up the large, dry, rock-hard clods that remain after tillage [of green fallow] with the *sokha*. The harrow bounces over the clods, scratching and splintering them while raising a column of dust over the strip.
> Having turned the land into powder, the peasant is satisfied, as though that is the way it should be. According to the long-established experience of the grandfathers and great-grandfathers, the more fluffy is the land the better it is for the crop.[110]

> Anyone taking 8–10, or especially 20–30, passes with a harrow, has effectively ruined his land for two or three years.... 1–3 passes with a heavy harrow will suffice. Wooden and light iron harrows only damage the soil. They only bounce around on the surface and create dust. Get rid of them.[111]

These farmers were trying to break up hardened clods of earth, no matter how long it took.[112] This is indicative of one or both of two trends in peasant conceptions of tillage. The first is the prejudice towards fluffing up the soil, discussed earlier [see "Green Fallow and Other Shortcomings"]. The second is the conviction that more tillage is better tillage [to be discussed in the section "The Evolution of Tillage Regimes"].

Under different circumstances, ignorance concerning the dynamics of soil moisture conditioned the under-application of harrows. Thus, agronomists frequently harped on the need for peasants to use harrows after strong summer rains.[113] Rains beat down the soil, compressing dust into the wide vertical canals which are so important in minimizing water evaporation. Harrowing is very useful after rains, so as to break up the soil surface and prevent a hard crust from forming. Did peasants regularly do this? Probably only the very best farmers in certain villages did so. Why else would agronomists be instructing them thusly? Interviewed peasants admit that this practice was unknown to them.[114]

Generally speaking, peasants ought also to have harrowed their rye sprouts after the spring thaws. Springtime harrowing of rye provides insurance against a dry spring and summer by loosening up the soil and uprooting the weakest sprouts, which leaves more space and nutrients for the viable sprouts.[115] But few, if any, peasants appreciated the merits of this technique, as one landlord/agronomist found out for himself:

> Quite often I have advised peasants ... to run harrows over their rye, but my advice has always seemed strange to them. They simply cannot square the advantages I promise them with the uprooting of the sprouts that they see before their eyes.[116]

Above and beyond difficulties in the performance of harrowing in the field, huge numbers of peasants in Tambov seem to have been in the dark about the proper time to harrow. They simply did not understand how quickly soil could lose moisture. In a hot wind soil must be harrowed as soon as possible—even a delay of one or two hours is a serious error. By taking lunch breaks or waiting overnight peasants were violating fundamental principles of soil care.[117] Just how many peasants tended to wait just how long after tillage to harrow is not known. In interviews survivors claim to have harrowed right away, but one gets the impression that delays were commonplace, even chronic.[118] Of course for farms with two horses tillage and harrowing could be almost simultaneous.

The most striking violation of harrowing principles was the practice of waiting *from one to four weeks* to harrow after the raising of fallow! According to the budget studies of 1914 half of the farms in the central *uezds* and three-fourths in the south were doing this.[119] Another 10% in the south made no effort to harrow at all![120] General descriptions of agricultural practice in the *zemstvo* studies from the early 1880s mention delayed harrowing of fallow as standard procedure throughout most of the province at that time.[121] By at least one indication, farmers were also delaying harrowing on land planted with potatoes (in the spring-sown section of their fields, not on fallow).[122]

It is not easy to make sense of delayed harrowing. At first glance, it might be thought that peasants were simply waiting for a rain to soften up the hard green fallow soil before attempting to harrow it. But the sources insist that they observed a customary delay of at least a week, regardless of rainfall. Why? When pressed for an explanation, peasants told agronomists that the delay allowed the soil to warm up and to soften. This reasoning holds no water, it only betrays peasants' ignorance concerning fundamental principles of soil care. The same peasants added, however, their conviction that a particularly insidious weed, couch grass (*pyrei* in Russian, also known as "twitch" or "quitch grass" in English), died off in the long interim between tillage and harrowing.[123] A couple of early sources confirm that fear of couch grass was indeed the origin of delayed harrowing.[124] If rains come after tillage, couch grass can multiply very quickly (root fragments remaining in the soil will redirect themselves to grow vertically up to the surface and horizontally just beneath the surface). If, however, these root fragments are exposed to hot, dry air, they will die.[125]

While the threat of couch grass explains why peasant farmers originally decided to delay harrowing, it does not justify this decision. By waiting so long before harrowing peasants were killing off not only the weeds, but almost all life in the soil![126] If they wanted to rid themselves of couch grass, they ought to have delayed harrowing for a shorter time, then harrowed periodically, and occasionally sent sheep out to graze some more on the most infected fields. Instead of looking for this kind of solution, however, farmers across large areas of the province settled for long delays before harrowing.

Furthermore, many agronomic reports either specify or imply that the peasants observed long delays by rote, not understanding or caring to adjust their work in accordance with the weather or the extent of the couch-grass problem. V. Gudvilovich, a local agronomist in Tambov *uezd,* noted that *all* peasants in his sector were convinced that one should not harrow in the fallow field soon after tillage. But none of them could offer any rationale for this practice:

> If you ask peasants why delayed harrowing is necessary, you will get only one answer—"That's the way our elders taught us."[127]

As we shall see many times throughout Part I, this kind of passive, indifferent attitude to learning and to work acted as a tremendous weight on the peasant agricultural system. In the case of delayed harrowing, peasants were throwing away an average of perhaps 15% of their rye yield per year.[128]

The Evolution of Tillage Regimes

From our opening discussion of tillage we are quite familiar with the complexity of any individual tillage operation. Now it is time to become acquainted with the additional challenges, which various combinations of tillage operations posed the peasant farmer. These combinations provided farmers with a wide range of options to boost productivity within the framework of the three-field system. As long as more advanced systems of farming failed to appear, and insofar as pressure on the land intensified in the decades after emancipation, peasants' ability to make proper use of these tillage options would play a large role in determining the viability of their economy.

The Fallow Field

Having raised and harrowed the fallow field sometime in June, the natural continuation in the traditional agriculture was to leave this field alone until the commencement of the rye sowing, in early August. So long as rye yields sufficed to meet consumption needs, there was no need to do any more work. Indeed, so long as weeds were not choking the fields some farms—as much as half of a village—would even forego harrowing after raising fallow![129] Moreover, since the *sokha* left some weeds alive, under this labor-minimal tillage regime the commune retained the option to use the fallow field as grazing land well into July.[130] A. A. Kotov found this tillage regime to be dominant in Voronezh *uezd* (just south of the Tambov border) right up to 1914, and it was certainly prevalent in the black-earth areas of Tambov for a long time after the emancipation of 1861.[131] Indeed, land appraisal studies noted the popularity of this regime across most of the southern *uezds* at the turn of the century.[132]

Once economic circumstances began pressuring peasants to produce more per unit of land, more intensive tillage regimes appeared. The cornerstone of intensified tillage was *dvoenie*, or *dvoika*—a second tillage of the fallow field, anywhere from ten days to five weeks after the raising of fallow.[133] It should be clear from our earlier discussion of the fundamental functions of tillage that, in principle, *dvoenie* represented improved care for the soil. Even when raised very late, at the end of June, fallow would not be sown for a minimum of five weeks, during which time the soil would certainly benefit from some form of tillage. By way of confirmation, Kotov's inquiries found that *dvoenie* raised peasants rye yields from 78 to 82.1 *puds* of grain per *desiatina* in one year, as well as giving nine extra *puds* of straw.[134] The figure of 78 *puds* per *desiatina* is of course quite high for Voronezh peasants. This year must have been quite good in this area. *Dvoenie* would improve yields significantly more in drier years.[135]

The execution of *dvoenie* did not present many individual problems. According to one source, peasants tilled *dvoenie* at a very shallow depth, only about 1.5 *vershki*.[136] Several other sources maintain that they usually tried to do *dvoenie* 1/2–1 *vershok* deeper than the raising of fallow.[137] This would not necessarily represent any additional strain on the horse, the tiller, or the *sokha*, since the soil would not be as tough as it had been upon first tillage. The timing of *dvoenie* was of course a difficult judgment. Naturally the farmer wanted to wait for a rainfall, so as to ensure that he could till at the desired depth. But if he waited for a long time, and no rain came, then soil moisture would decline precipitously. Additionally, by waiting for a rain he would be running the risk that after *dvoenie* the soil would not properly settle before the rye was sown. Were the soil to continue to settle after sowing, then many of the seeds would lie too close to the surface, and grow poorly, if at all.[138]

How exactly did *dvoenie* gain license among Tambov peasants?* We have no direct evidence on its origins, but there must have been several ways in which peasants became acquainted with it. *Dvoenie* was a standard procedure on the great majority of landlords' estates by 1900, and peasants working on such estates would have seen *dvoenie* there.[139] The practice might also have filtered down from neighboring provinces to the north. Surely in many villages some farmers tried it out when a superabundance of weeds threatened to choke the impending rye sowings, thanks either to manuring or to rains following the raising of fallow.[140] If *dvoenie* seemed to work, then they might decide to do it in subsequent years even if the weeds were not so thick. More interestingly, we might speculate that *dvoenie* first appeared in some villages thanks to the incompetence of some tillers. If a farmer raised fallow very poorly, leaving many untilled spots or weeds, he would be unable to run his harrow over the soil, and so would be forced to till again.[141] Should a good grain yield subsequently accompany such an accidental *dvoenie*, the more able farmers might begin experimenting.[142]

Whatever the origins of *dvoenie*, two remarks are warranted. First, it neither issued from nor produced an advanced understanding of soil structure among more than the slimmest layer of peasant farmers.[143] This is a theme to which we shall return later in this section, and in Part II. At the same time, and secondly, it seems that all peasants who had seen *dvoenie* readily conceded that it raised yields.[144]

Sufficient data do exist to trace the spread of *dvoenie* in Tambov during the last two decades before the First World War. The land-appraisal studies of the turn of the century found *dvoenie* to have made the least headway in the steppe *uezds*, just as we would expect, given the sparser population there. *Dvoenie* was said to be uncommon in Borisoglebsk, and in Lebedian only one-third of the communes were generally doing *dvoenie*, even fewer in the best black soil areas of the

---

*Note in this context that if the commune elected to leave the herds on the fallow to the end of June and beyond, it was effectively precluding the option of *dvoenie* for all *dvors*. The author of the Kozlov volume of *k otsenke* speculated that this might have been an obstacle to the introduction of *dvoenie* (*k otsenke*, Kozlov p.37). If this was so, then the shift to *dvoenie* would have been possible only after a communal decision to raise fallow earlier than normal, with the specific intention of allowing *dvoenie*. This would be an impressive example of communal cooperation. But this seems a very unlikely scenario. Few communes would have reason to leave their herds on the fallow into July—already by late June there was little left on the fallow for the animals to graze. Thus I assume that the spread of *dvoenie* did not depend on cooperation from the *skhod* (communal assembly of heads-of-households). But there might have been cases of this. We cannot be sure.

uezd.[145] In Lipetsk and Kozlov, just to the north, already more than half of the peasants tended to do it.[146] And in Kirsanov *dvoenie* was standard in 76% of the communes studied.[147] The 1914 budget study registered a tremendous increase in *dvoenie*—92.5% of the farms in the central *uezds* and 81% in the southern *uezds* were now performing this tillage.[148]

The extremely rapid rate of adoption of *dvoenie* is very thought provoking. *Dvoenie* was a fundamental change in the peasantry's tillage regime. Its timing often fell within one of the most critical periods of the labor calendar for men (but not for horses)—the reaping of rye. It thus represented a significant increase in labor intensity during a time of the year when hands could be put to good use elsewhere on the farm. Moreover, *dvoenie*'s contribution to land productivity was rather modest—it could not provide any revolutionary increase in grain or straw yields. And yet within the space of twenty to forty years virtually all of Tambov inserted *dvoenie* into their traditional tillage regime. Certainly the aggravation of the land question in these years was one of the primary stimuli here. Data from Kozlov in 1898–99 show that 90% of the communes in 9 congested southern *volosts* were doing *dvoenie*, while 62% of communes in other areas still avoided a second tillage of the fallow field.[149] For whatever reasons, more and more peasants were agreeing to work harder so as to produce more per *desiatina,* and their social organization (the peasant commune) was flexible enough to accommodate this intensification.

The Spring Field

Tillage regimes in preparation for spring crops evolved in much the same way as tillage regimes on the fallow fields: peasants began to do more work in order to ensure higher and more reliable yields. On the spring field, however, the traditional regime as of the mid-nineteenth century involved no preparatory tillage whatsoever for the crops sown earliest in the spring. Thus there was still more room for labor intensification here than on the fallow field.

Oats. What exactly was the traditional tillage regime for spring crops? To begin with, let us concentrate on the most important of these crops, oats. As the earliest sown spring crop, oats always forces the farmer to work quickly once the snow has thawed. But of course if he attempts to till prematurely he can ruin the soil. The simplest and most obvious solution is to avoid this problem altogether, by not tilling at all. Oats can be sown straight on to the remnants of the rye stubble, and then tilled in and harrowed right away.[150] This method hardly generates high yields, as peasants themselves realized.[151] But so long as the yields satisfy the farmer, why should he work harder? Since this regime remained current in over 90% of Voronezh *uezd* communes up to 1914 and beyond, we can be certain that it was dominant in Tambov up to the last decades of the nineteenth century.[152] We know for instance that at the turn of the twentieth century most communes in Lebedian and Kirsanov were still sowing oats straight onto rye stubble.[153]

Just as with rye, once peasants felt the need to boost oats yields they responded with preparatory tillage. The 1895–97 land appraisal study in Kozlov noted the prevalence of pre-sowing tillage, especially in the more congested southern *volosts*, where land tended to be tilled twice before sowing.[154] And by 1914 only 28.6% of the farms in the southern *uezds* and 25% in the central *uezds* were not tilling land before sowing oats.[155]

As significant as preparatory tillage for oats might have been in peasants' quest to intensify production, the hazards and hastiness of tillage in early April remained problematic. The optimal solution was to till the rye stubble in the preceding fall, a technique known in Russian as *ziablevaia vspashka*, or simply *ziab*. By breaking up the upper layer of soil and tilling in the rye stubble, *ziab* makes all of the positive contributions of other categories of tillage discussed earlier. The Tambov experimental station found that it improved yields by an average of 7–15%, and was several times more effective than that in dry years, as we would expect.[156]

Perhaps most importantly for many peasants, *ziab* offered relief from much of the April labor crisis. For horses badly weakened by malnutrition or illness over the long winter, tillage in April was the most arduous and unpleasant task of the entire year. Horseless farms, meanwhile, were paying dearly to get their land tilled on time in April. In contrast, the horse and the farmer could do *ziab* at their mutual convenience, sometime in September or October for instance. And since the snows were already imminent at this time, there was no need even to harrow after *ziab*. The harrowing could easily be left until after the spring thaw.[157] Further, by preparing the land earlier, *ziab* permitted farmers to begin sowing earlier in the spring, which was often an important advantage.[158]

Ziab worked well in peasant practice—communes in Kotov's 1914 study were reporting *ziab*-tilled oats' yields of 80 *puds* per *desiatina*, some 10–20% over other tillage regimes.[159] *Ziab* can in certain cases pose a problem for the communal herds, however. Should the rye stubble be indispensable for supporting livestock, then at least a portion of the stubble will be off-limits to *ziab* tillage.[160]

Given the convenience and effectiveness of *ziab*, we would expect to find it spreading rapidly in Tambov from around 1880 on. Indeed, data from Voronezh in 1914 correspond closely to earlier data from Lebedian *uezd*, in 1895–98. In both locations anywhere from 1–30% of the farms in some communes were doing *ziab*, and these only on the earliest sown of their oats strips.[161] Meanwhile, in Kozlov *uezd* in 1895–97 *ziab* was already becoming common.[162] The most convincing evidence of the popularization of *ziab* comes from the 1914–15 budget study, which found 75% of the farms practicing *ziab* in the central *uezds*, and 50% in the southern *uezds*.[163]

Millet. The evolution of tillage regimes for millet is more difficult to trace. The sources simply are not as clear on the tempo or mechanics of intensification. Two trends stand out however. Firstly, while sowing straight onto untilled stubble was very rare in Kotov's study of Voronezh, it was already unheard of in Chelintsev's budget study.[164] The practice of sowing millet on rye stubble had probably never been widespread, and so in looking for the evolution of tillage regimes for millet we must focus on pre-sowing techniques. Here the data for our period clearly indicate increasing interest in *ziab*, much as for oats. By 1914 30% of farms studied in the southern *uezds* of Tambov and 50% in the central *uezds* were performing *ziab* tillage for millet, whereas only 1–30% of the households in a moderate number of communes in Voronezh had by then adopted the technique.[165] This acceptance of *ziab* proceeded in spite of the fact that the new technique was significantly less powerful in raising millet yields than it was for oats (communes in Voronezh reported an increase of some 7%, exactly as the Tambov experimental station established for millet.)[166] Furthermore, the convenience of *ziab* in overcoming the spring labor crisis could not have been as important to its adoption for millet as it was on oats strips. In addition to the spread of *ziab*, the sources agree that the more congested the region, the more tillage peasants were performing (two pre-sowing tillages in place of the traditional one, e.g.).[167]

Conclusions

In sum, we see that peasants in Tambov were intensifying their tillage regimes at an extremely rapid rate. The new techniques very quickly conquered the more congested areas of the province, indicating a clear connection between population density and the intensification of tillage regimes. However, the speed at which the new methods were accepted, and their extension into the less crowded regions proves how long overdue they had been for much of the peasantry in Tambov. Rising population density certainly created a favorable climate for tillage intensification. But more had to happen before these innovations could take hold: someone had to import or invent the technology. As far as *dvoenie* and *ziab* are concerned, local landlords must have performed this important function, perhaps together with some observant peasants who traveled to other areas of Russia and reported what they had seen.[168] For reasons which we shall discuss later, it took a fair amount of time for the peasants to imitate the new tillage regimes on the landlords' estates. But once underway, the process was inexorable.

Agronomist's Criticism

The tremendous speed at which the intensification of tillage took place should warn us to look for imperfections and distortions in the execution of the new regimes. Upon closer inspection we find a limited amount of evidence of this. At times peasants did *dvoenie* too late, perhaps failing to leave enough time for the soil to settle before the rye sowing. Chelintsev found 12–13% of the farms tilling in the latter part of July.[169] On other occasions (17% in the southern *uezds*) they waited too long after *dvoenie* to harrow, much as with harrowing after the first tillage of fallow.[170] However we should note here that with *dvoenie* this delay might in many cases have been justified by the constraints of the labor calendar. In the southern half of the province, where the crops ripen a bit earlier than in the northern half, the reaping of rye could certainly overlap with *dvoenie* tillage.[171] More damagingly, there were some places where peasants dispensed altogether with harrowing after *dvoenie*.[172] Alternatively, having adopted *dvoenie* they simply abandoned harrowing after the raising of fallow.[173]

With respect to *ziab* tillage, it is much more difficult to assess the quality of peasant work. Firstly, we know that peasants rarely if ever tilled at the optimal moment. Experimental stations verified that the earlier *ziab* was done the more effective it was, but Chelintsev found no instances of *ziab* before late September.[174] All the same, tardy *ziab* was not nearly as harmful to ensuing yields as tardy raising of fallow, so the delay was not critical. Moreover, the herds grazed on the rye stubble before *ziab*, in August–September. Communes were always very reticent to allow any alteration of the grazing cycle, and so they would resist early *ziab*. More importantly, since the labor calendar was so full up to mid-September, virtually no one wanted to do *ziab* any earlier. And so they did *ziab* later.[175]

When *ziab* was done, it was not always properly organized. To begin with, some peasants pioneering the use of *ziab* failed to capitalize on the opportunity it provided for earlier sowing. They stuck to their traditional sowing schedule, to their own detriment.[176] Further, Vakar found peasants always tilling *ziab* before millet, a late-sown crop, but sometimes doing without *ziab* for oats.[177] This is not good farming. Experiments in Kharkov established a 35–40% increase in yields of early-sown spring crops with *ziab*, but only a 14–20% increase for late-sown spring crops.[178] However, the communes, which Vakar studied must have been exceptional in this regard, judging from other sources.[179]

Intensification, or Over-Intensification?

Before concluding this analysis of the execution of tillage and its intensification, it will not be amiss to investigate whether or not peasants actually *over*-intensified their tillage regimes. Let us examine this both from an economic and from an agronomic point of view. From an economic point of view it is clear that some of the new techniques represented a major investment of horse and human labor for a minimal return in the form of crop yields. Swarms of calculations in the land appraisal studies and elsewhere show that the costs of this labor often exceeded the value of the extra crops produced. The same sort of calculations is superabundant in studies of peasant land renting during this period (these studies disseminated the term "hunger renting"). And yet it does not follow from such calculations that the peasants were over-intensifying their tillage regimes. For, in the absence of other opportunities for employment, the application of labor was profitable to the farm no matter how minimal was the return.

From an agronomic point of view, on the other hand, there might have been cases in which some of the new tillage techniques ought to have been avoided. *Dvoenie*, for example, is dangerous in a dry year. In dry weather the sound tactic is to wipe out weeds and work only a thin layer of soil with a cultivator.[180] It is important to know if peasants refrained from *dvoenie* in dry years. Naturally evidence on this question is very rare, but there are sources indicating that Tambov farmers went ahead with *dvoenie* regardless of the weather.[181] Once *dvoenie* had established itself within the commune's tillage regime, most farmers would follow this regime by rote. Meanwhile, there is evidence that most peasants tilled *dvoenie* too deeply. Studies at the Shatilov experimental station in Orel province determined that shallow *dvoenie* (at about 1.5 *vershki*) gave better results than the most widely established peasant method, when *dvoenie* was deeper than the first tillage.[182] Nevertheless, on the whole we cannot conclude that peasants were going too far in the intensification of their tillage regimes. They understood enough not to pulverize the soil into dust in a desperate quest for higher yields.

The Plow and the *Sokha*

As Figure 1.4 shows, these tools contact the soil in dramatically different ways. While the *sokha*'s blades scratch through the soil surface and lift up enough earth to form a furrow, the plow's coulter and share slice off a clean, even section of land. Moreover, as the plow moves forward along the furrow, its moldboard rolls this layer of earth over, and lets it fall off, upside down, just to the right of the furrow (much more rarely, the plow is constructed inversely, to send the layer of land off to the left). And so the arrival of the plow presented peasants with the opportunity to fundamentally revise the manner in which they furrowed the soil. In order to appreciate peasant reactions to plows, we must first explore the significance of the differences between the *sokha* and the plow.

Sokha   Plow

Figure 1.4. The Blades of the *Sokha* and a Plow (*Source:* Kushner, *Russkie,* pp. 40, 282)

The *sokha* has quite a few advantages over the plow. Being light, it is easy to lift up or maneuver around obstacles, and it is not strenuous to cart around from strip to strip during the workday. It can turn tightly when changing directions at the end of each furrow, which is important when little or no space is available at the end of the strip. Wheeled plows need as much as five yards to make a comfortable turn. The *sokha* is less expensive than the plow, both to purchase and to repair.[183] Local blacksmiths could always repair a *sokha*, but such was not always the case with plows.[184] Likewise, *sokhas* were simpler to assemble. In every village peasants could find some experts at attaching blades and other spare parts to a *sokha*, whereas plows could be more complex.[185]

The *sokha*'s adjustable *politsa* allows the tiller to direct all lifted soil towards one side of the strip. Conversely, when a plowman turns around at the end of a furrow, he must walk to the other side of the strip [see Figures 1.5 and 1.6]. Thus tillage with the plow costs more time and doubles the number of dead furrows per strip. If a farmer has thin strips then this becomes a very significant consideration. Finally, the *sokha* is a universal tillage tool. It can fulfill all kinds of secondary functions, such as covering seeds, planting potatoes, or inter-tillage (tillage in between furrows on ribbon-sown crops—see discussion of seed drills). And it performs all of these functions with just a single horse, whereas many plows in the period under discussion were difficult or even impossible to use without harnessing two horses.

But in many respects the *sokha* cannot compete with the plow. The *sokha* cannot turn the soil over so as to kill weeds or properly till in manure.[186] Of course by not killing all of the weeds the *sokha* allows

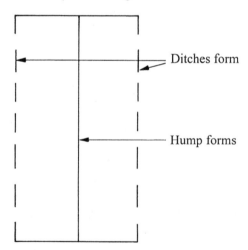

Figure 1.5. A Style of Plowing: "Gathering." The most common method, "gathering" (*v sval*)—the plowman begins just left of center. The plow throws the raised layer of earth to the center. The second furrow is thrown onto the centerline as well, forming a hump. This method leaves the hump in the center, and ditches on the edges. The hump could reach fifteen inches in height (Preobrazhenskii, *Opisanie Tverskoi gubernii*, p. 239), but harrows could bring it down lower.

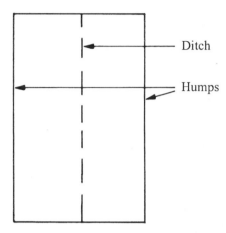

Figure 1.6. A Style of Plowing: "Casting." The less common method, "casting" (*v razval*). This is the reverse of "gathering." The plowman begins on the right edge. Humps are left at the sides, a ditch in the middle. Combining "gathering" and "casting" alternately, farmers could keep the land more level. Cases of this can be found in the sources (e.g., Rusov, *Opisanie Chernigovskoi gubernii*, p. 338; Dmitriev, *Opyt prakticheskikh zamechanii*, p. 12), but appear to be rare. An American agronomist reported peasants in Bessarabia not bothering to alternate their style of plowing for generations (Guy Michael, "My Russian Experience," p. 10).

herds to stay out on the fallow after tillage. A plow cannot do this, but the same effect can be achieved with cultivators. As a wooden tool the *sokha* will swell up in wet weather, and become brittle in dry weather. Unlike the plow, it can break. While women and adolescents can use a plow, the *sokha* requires a bit more strength, attention, and agility from the tiller.[187]

Every furrow is more troublesome with the *sokha*. We have already seen how in difficult soil the *sokha* can—and will—stray from the tillage line at any moment. Likewise, the tiller is hard-pressed to keep tillage at an even depth with the *sokha*. The plow is much easier to guide; wheeled plows are particularly stable along the tillage line.

Naturally then, stubble and tough soil pose fewer problems to plows than to *sokhas*. Especially in dry years *sokha*-tilled fields were littered with thin chunks of untouched land, where the tool had strayed well away from the tillage line.[188] Tillage of newly cleared land is a nightmare with the *sokha*. Roots and stubble of scythed growth quickly clog up the cutting area. The furrow becomes ever shallower, until soon the blades are uselessly skimming along the surface. The plow's stability also allows it to cope easily with cross-tillage (perpendicular to previous furrows), which is an excellent measure for leveling off the surface.

I found cross-tillage to be very uncomfortable with the *sokha*, because the soil offers such uneven resistance.

Plows have a much wider range of adjustment than do *sokhas*. While the *sokha* could hardly get deeper than 11 cm, plows could go 30 cm and more deep.[189] And plow furrows reach an even depth. As we saw earlier, *sokha* furrows are trough-like, such that the edges of each furrow are much shallower than the center. Plows could adjust the width of their furrow as well, up to 50 cm wide in extreme cases. As we saw earlier, tillage with the *sokha* left 1/10–1/3 of the surface virtually untilled. Farmers new to the plow had to learn how properly to select furrow width, in correspondence to soil moisture.[190] If the width is set incorrectly, the layer of lifted soil will come off the moldboard sloppily, and harrows will not easily correct the flaw.

Finally, by improving care for the soil plows allow farmers to conserve on the amount of seeds sown per unit of land. This assumes of course that the farmer understands the connection between soil care and sowing norms—a big "if" among peasants, as we shall see in our discussion of sowing. Peasants in Moscow province did eventually make this connection, and economized on seed grain.[191] In sum, for most farms the plow was a very wise investment. Any family holding more than two or three *desiatinas* of arable land and a pair of horses (or one very fit horse) would stand to benefit from the acquisition of a plow.

Use of the plow demanded certain adjustments from the peasant accustomed only to the *sokha*. Consider the issue of draft power. Not all plows are alike. As noted above, many models require 2 horses, or work sub-optimally with only one.[192] Powerful draft horses of various European breeds can accomplish virtually any tillage task singly, but Tambov peasants did not acquire such horses in any numbers before about 1910. Furthermore, if conditions are damp and wet, soil sticks to the larger cutting surface of the plow much more than to the *sokha*, and draft power requirements spiral upward.[193] For many peasant horses a plow was simply too difficult to pull at any depth below that of standard *sokha* tillage, no matter what the conditions. Finally, horses had to be trained to work together properly before being paired. Not all horses take to this as easily as others, and sometimes two horses have difficulty harmonizing their gaits with each other.[194]

If deep tillage was an option, the farmer had to be careful not to till too deeply right away. Plowing more than about 1 1/2 *vershki* deeper than the soil has previously been tilled brings up "dead" soil, which has not been in contact with air for a long time. Its composition will not be friendly to crops, and it can destroy soil fertility.[195] Once plowing was done, peasant harrows, even those with metal teeth, could not necessarily handle the thick layers of overturned earth. Depending on conditions, these harrows might simply skip over the surface and create dust. There was a way around this without buying all-iron harrows or cultivators. One could plow, level the overturned layers a bit with a harrow, then till with a *sokha*, and then harrow again with good effect. This technique was spotted in Moscow province in the 1880s.[196] Still, it demanded quite a lot of labor time. It was no real solution to the weakness of peasants' harrows.

Peasant Reception of the Plow

Our best sources in tracing the Russian peasantry's attitudes towards plows do not come from Tambov or any other central black-earth province. From Moscow province, however, where *zemstvo* agronomic services began much earlier, come several fine sources on this topic. Since scattered and less complete sources from Tambov correspond to those from Moscow, we will now borrow heavily from the latter. To begin with, it seems that peasants greeted the arrival of plows coldly. Most farmers saw plows for the first time on landlords' estates or in the hands of wealthier villagers plowing non-communal lands. But they did not generally take much interest in their neighbors' results with the new tools. These neighbors had strong, well-fed horses, and their land was simply in better condition. When a plow then appeared in the village and the question of plow usage on communal arable land arose in earnest, they would defensively reject the plow. "Many peasants not only insisted on keeping the *sokha*, but even refused to witness their neighbors working with a plow."[197] They would, for example, declare the plow to be unnecessary, since they had lived so long without it.[198] "I will not till with a plow. Our fathers and grandfathers kept themselves fed with the *sokha,* and it would be sinful for me in my older years to part with the *sokha.*"[199]

Such emotional objections rarely sufficed for long. Someone would want to try out the new tool. The great majority of peasants would continue to resist, however, contesting that the conditions of communal agriculture were inconducive to the usage of plows—the plow demands more draft power, it leaves twice as many dead furrows, it costs more cash, etc. These objections were reasonable. But, as a Moscow agronomist named Bazhenov put it, they stemmed in large part from the peasants' unfamiliarity with the tool, its parts, and its capacities.[200]

If some members of the community could see the usefulness of the plow despite such criticisms, then they would begin to work with a plow....

> Came the time to raise fallow. We'd long since put out manure, but it had fully dried up—there wasn't a drop of rain. That summer was dry, the land baked into brick. We waited for some rain, but God sent us none. Like it or not, you had to go out and till. So out we went, the whole village with *sokhas* but for my Vasilii, with a plow. He went off to one strip while my younger son and I set up on another. Well, we got nowhere. You couldn't take ten steps before stopping—either the support ropes slackened, or the blades got stuck or lifted out of the ground. There was nothing to be done, the job was impossible. But then I looked over towards Vasilii, and there he was working away without a hitch. At first he had his wife with him, leading the horse, getting the horse used to it [to the plow—DK]. Well, after a dozen furrows the horse was fine, and he sent his wife home. She came by us on the way.
>
> "Why are you torturing yourself grandpa? Give up the *sokha* and pick up a plow."
>
> "Is it really easier?"
>
> "Go see for yourself."
>
> So I walked over to look, and I could hardly believe my eyes: the horse was walking at an even pace, flicking his tail at flies and gadflies; the plow was going beautifully, taking a wide, clean furrow, turning over a layer of soil and covering the manure better than a *sokha* could do with moist earth. Vasilii was holding it with only one hand, in the other the reins and whip.
>
> I took hold of the plow and cut a few furrows. I was almost in shock: it didn't take any muscle at all; it was like I was taking a walk....
>
> Well, Vasilii went off to the city, and people all came to me. Everyone tried out the plow and was surprised, they all loved it. In that very summer half of the village got plows, and by the next year almost everyone had replaced the *sokha*. Let God be my witness, it's true what I'm telling you.[201]

This account clearly illustrates the primary attractions of the plow to a peasant farmer. He might not understand or even suspect the influence of the plow on soil structure, but he could not help but be impressed by the grace of the new tool in action. This by itself was enough to win him over, and once the plow justified itself by killing weeds and netting higher grain yields, its popularity was ensured. Farmers held on to their *sokha*, but they used it ever less for primary tillage tasks such as raising fallow or clearing stubble.

Distribution of Plows, 1900–1914. As its advantages over the *sokha* became clear, plows spread quickly across Tambov. Statistics on this trend are limited, however. Sketchy data from the turn-of-the-century land appraisal studies show that the plow was still very rare at this time, even in the steppe *uezds*, where conditions were most amenable to its adoption. "Some" farms were plowing in 10 of 120 communes in Lebedian, in Lipetsk the same was true in just 10 of 135.[202] Plows were very rare among peasants in Usman and Kirsanov *uezds*.[203] Already by 1910 the plow had gained a lot of ground in the black-earth *uezds*, and the pace at which the tool spread must have been accelerating in the last years before the First World War. Given the economic disruptions that followed Russia's entry into the war in 1914, the data in the "1917" column of the following table probably differ little from tool holdings in 1914 or 1915. As we would expect, plows were most common among families with larger amounts of land and horses [Table 1.10].[204]

Table 1.10. Metal Plows per 100 Peasant Households, 1910 and 1917[*]

	1910	1917
Northern *uezds*	1.2	7.3
Central *uezds*	10.0	15.3
Southern *uezds*	13.1	17.2
Provincial Total	8.9	14.3

[*]Since some farms had two or more plows, the percentage of farms with plows would be a bit lower than these figures. Moreover, the 1910 column is more accurate than the 1917 column, because the numbers of households for both columns are taken from a 1912 *zemstvo* study.
Sources: *Sel'sko-khoziaistvennye mashiny i orudiia*, pp. 68–69; *Podvornoe obsledovanie zhivotnovodstva*, Prilozhenie 1; *Trudy Tsentral'nogo Statisticheskogo Upravleniia. Tom 5, vyp.2*, pp. 114–121.

Use of the Plow

Restricting the Plow.

In order to persuade peasants to improve tillage, the local agronomist must do more than simply encourage them to acquire better tools. Sometimes he must prove to them the superiority of these tools, even in cases where this superiority would seem to be indisputable.

Take, for example, the opinion of a slew of peasants in Sosnovka and other villages. They are convinced that plows

work well only with spring-sown crops, and that rye does better
after *sokha* tillage. Indeed, a mass of plow-holding peasants till
their fallow fields with *sokhas*.[205]
        —Local Agronomist V. Gudvilovich, Tambov *uezd*, 1911

Folk agronomic wisdom could not give farmers any direct guidance
on the use of plows, and until 1910 the *zemstvos* did not begin to
establish the agronomic aid networks that would in later years be
available for consultation. Thus the first farmers to acquire plows had
to teach themselves about the characteristics and capabilities of the
tool. Assembly of the tool was the first hurdle—it took years before
most peasants were attaching the coulter, the wheels, and other parts
properly.[206] Eventually farmers must have got past these growing pains.
But more complex challenges looed. Some exceptionally insightful
sources—such as the passage quoted above—reveal that peasants'
inadequate understanding of agronomy served either to exclude the
plow or sharply restrict its application in many areas.

    To begin with, it is probable that farmers in many locales transferred
their frustration with couch grass (*pyrei*, as discussed above, with
respect to harrowing) onto the plow. They could see how tillage
severing the roots of couch grass did not kill this grass. On the contrary,
the grass simply re-sprouted from the root fragments, and occupied
even more territory than before tillage. Plows' shares cut under the
entire surface of the soil and turned it over, protecting most of the root
fragments. In comparison, the *sokha*'s blades undercut about 2/3–5/6
of the surface, and brought most of the root fragments up to the surface
where they would dry out and expire. It must be admitted that on lands
presently suffering from couch grass, plowing might be counter-productive.[207] And so peasants familiar with couch grass were understandably
opposed to plowing during the spring and especially late spring and
summer—when the couch grass could recover very quickly.[208] The
problem, however, is that this circumstance must have reinforced many
peasants' categorical allegiance to the *sokha* and antipathy to the plow.
Over time, the proscription of the plow specifically on lands infested
with couch grass could easily fade in people's minds, and become a
proscription of plowing altogether, or at least in the late spring and
summer.

    Surely most peasants who had continuous problems with couch grass
remained aware of the particular dangers of plowing on lands so
infected. But, misled by their ignorance of soil structure, such farmers
often conjured up other reasons to restrict the application of plows.

The following passage, taken from Vakar's discussions with peasant farmers in the 1920s, records how peasants might fear to turn the soil over in the heat of the summer:

> ... virtually unanimously, all assert that fallow must be raised with the *sokha*, since plows give lower yields of winter crops [i.e., rye—D.K.]. Peasants explain that the plow's turning the soil over and exposing moist earth dries up the soil. Additionally, plowing exacerbates the couch-grass problem, while after tillage with the *sokha* the land 'holds its juices better', and couch grass 'fears' the *sokha*, and dies off from it.[209]

On dry, hard soil in June and July, this wariness of plowing was not illegitimate. It is often better to till such land very lightly, avoiding the risk of raising large brick-like clods that no harrow can reduce. But of course peasants were very mistaken in deciding categorically that they should not turn the earth over with a plow in the summer months. On those occasions when rain or cool weather left their fallow land in decent shape, they should have used their plows. All too often, alas, they did not:

> Conversations with peasants confirm ... that all plow-holders ordinarily plow their fallow land only when the soil is so dried out, and beaten down by grazing animals, that they cannot possibly drive their *sokha* into the earth....
>
> This year the fallow was barren of grazeable fodder very early, so they began tilling it relatively early ... But, since the land had not yet dried out, for the most part they worked with *sokhas*.[210]

In practice, therefore, many farmers, *even plow-holders*, blindly rejected the efficacy of plow tillage on any land in the summer. According to the 1914 budget studies about one plow-holder in three was reserving the plow exclusively for spring crops.[211] At the same time, we must suspect that quite a few farmers were actually *over-using* their plow. Whereas agronomists endorsed the *sokha* for *dvoenie* under typical weather conditions in the black-earth zone, surviving peasants admit that they indiscriminately applied their plows for *dvoenie*.[212] Because of their very limited understanding of the structure of soil, therefore, many farmers found it difficult to apply plows properly.

Depth of Plowing. With one of the primary advantages of the plow being its capacity to till deeper than the *sokha*, peasants and landlords alike were naturally anxious to experiment with turning the soil over at depths of 20–30 centimeters, or even deeper. However, work at such depths requires prodigious draft power. One survivor recalls seeing 6 or even 8 oxen pulling a plow at a depth of 40 cm on the estate of Count Vorontsov-Dashkov in Shatsk *uezd*.[213] Peasants (and most landlords) were forced to work on a much more modest scale. Unfortunately we have no evidence on depth norms from this time, apart from a survey of landlords conducted during the land-appraisal study of Lebedian *uezd* over the years 1895–1898. This survey found landlords instructing hired peasant plowmen to raise fallow at depths ranging from 3–4 *vershki* (5.25–7 inches). The average was about 3.5 *vershki*.[214] No one was tilling any deeper. This range of depths was entirely appropriate (we have already noted how dubious deeper plowing is—see the section "*Sokha* Tillage"). The Lebedian survey also recorded width of plowing. The range always fell between 7–8 furrows per *sazhen* (10.5–12 inches per furrow), which was acceptable—the recommended width : depth ratios on black-earth soil ranging from 7:5 to 9:5.[215]

Types of Plow

> It cannot be disputed that to see Sack one-shared plows on peasant fields is the dream of every agronomist.
> —agronomist P. E. Popov of Usman *uezd*, 1914

Characteristics. One plow is not the same as the next. Throughout the nineteenth century designers tinkered with many aspects of the tool—the shape of the moldboard, the angle of the shafts, the rolling coulter, the steel for the share, etc. By the beginning of the twentieth century manufacturers had a huge selection of plows in production. For most farmers the quality of the share and the moldboard separated one plow from another. Of course the best shares were steel, not iron; but steel comes in many grades, and some firms produced better material than others. The shape of the moldboard in particular defined the soil types appropriate to each model. Speaking generally, clay soils need "spiral" moldboards, while sandy soils need "cylindrical" moldboards, which are nearly straight, or slightly curved. For black-earth soils moldboards shaped between these two extremes are best [Figure 1.7].[216]

The Best Plow? It will come as no surprise to learn that the best plows in Russia came from Germany and Austria. Before the turn of the century models from the Liphardt and Ekkert firms competed for the top positions in the market.[217] Their models would maintain popularity up to 1914 and beyond, but by the time plows began to make significant headway in Tambov the world's best plow was already available. This was the Sack plow from Germany [Figure 1.8].

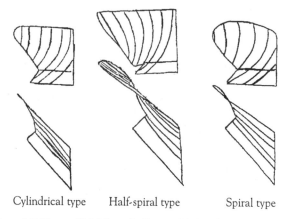

Cylindrical type   Half-spiral type   Spiral type

Figure 1.7. Types of Moldboards (*Source: KSE*, vol. 4. Prilozhenie)

Figure 1.8. A Sack Plow (*Source:* Vasil'ev, N.M.,*Kak obrabatyvat' parami*, p. 1)

Agronomists and farmers were virtually unanimous in their adulation for Sack plows.[218] Thanks to its simple and elegant construction it was easy to adjust and free from malfunctions or breakdowns. It could accept various moldboards, should conditions dictate a change. But what set it apart more than its design was the excellence of the steel. Sack's mastery of steel production processes was unparalleled. Competitors tried for decades, but no one in our period (up to 1930) was quite able to match the quality of Sack's steel. Plowmen recognized this immediately, on the very first furrow:

> I could feel it from the very first furrow. I set it up and it just moved, just right. I hardly had to guide it at all, it was so stable. When it came out of a furrow it shone like the sun. It was so clean that it looked like a mirror.[219]

The plow worked ideally with two horses, but its extraordinary steel increased efficiency such that one good horse could do first-class work. Such was the case with other plows as well—other firms did produce superb equipment—but the Sack plows were on a level of their own. Sack plows were not inordinately expensive, running about 25–30 rubles before the World War.[220] Poorer and wealthier peasants alike could and did find ways to afford one.[221] As further testimony to the excellence of this tool, let it be noted that Sack plows from the 1920s can still be found in private use in Russia [Figure 1.9].[222]

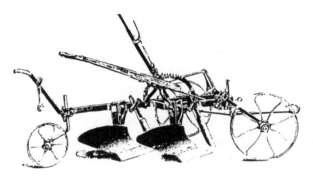

Figure 1.9. A Two-Shared Plow (*Source: KSE,* vol. 4, Prilozhenie)

Two-Shared Plows. Up to now our discussions of the plow have focused on the standard one-shared tool. The two-shared plow was a very popular alternative with independent characteristics. The major advantage of the two-shared plow was its speed. The two shares could work much more territory in any given amount of time than could a *sokha* or one-shared plow. One man and two horses with a two-shared plow can do the work of two men and two horses with *sokhas.*[223] Additionally, the two-shared plows were the easiest for adolescents to use.[224] On the other hand, two-shared plows were awkward to turn at the end of furrows, could not till deeply, were not as sturdy, could not adjust the width of the furrow they were cutting, demanded two or more horses, and were more expensive than one-shared plows.[225]

The many disadvantages of two-shared plows restricted their popularity among peasant farmers. Naturally their speed made them ideal for lighter work, like shallow *dvoenie,* or tilling in seeds, for example. Peasants appreciated the two-shared plow's universality.[226] But the *sokha* could still fulfill these functions, albeit without turning over the soil or tilling at such an even depth as the two-shared plow. Peasants who chose a two-shared over a one-shared plow were depriving themselves of the latter's unique capabilities. Two-shares made sense only for landlords or families with relatively large amounts of arable land, who had trouble tilling all of their territory at the appropriate moment. Since very few households could afford to purchase both types, the cheaper one-shared plows predominated in most villages where plows gained a foothold. Nevertheless, two-shared plows acquired remarkable popularity. Why?

However clear the advantages of the one-shared plow might have been to agronomists and experienced farmers, it is easy to see why peasants were initially more attracted to two-shared varieties. We have already discussed how suspiciously peasants received the arrival of plows. In such circumstances two-shared plows enjoyed a significant advantage over one-shared: their strong point—speed of work—was readily apparent. Peddlers, traders, and storekeepers were well attuned to peasants' points of view on tools, and recognized that the two-shared plow would be easier to sell. Some of them only sold two-shared plows, and so the peasant's choice was made for him.[227] Alternatively, some poorer families would choose a two-shared plow if they wanted to spend the least amount of time possible on their own farm during critical periods of the agricultural labor calendar, so as to gain employment on the landlord's fields. Finally, the example of landlords and larger peasant farms using two-shared plows sometimes lent these tools a certain amount of prestige. In such cases co-villagers would overestimate the value of the two-shared plow. In short, agronomists agreed that the two-shared plow did not deserve much of its popularity among peasant farmers.[228] The one-shared plow was simply better for the great majority of farms.

Plow Selection in Practice. Whatever farmers might have had in mind when looking for a plow, they were dependent on the inventory of local suppliers.[229] Before the agronomic aid networks developed after 1910, villages acquired haphazard collections of plows, some of which were not best for prevailing local soils.[230] After 1910 or so, if farmers were fortunate enough to live close to a *zemstvo* equipment-lending point (see discussion of agronomic aid networks in Part V), then they could try out various models before placing an order. But even if they found something that they liked, the *zemstvo* warehouses were not always well-stocked. Popular models would sell out quickly, and so many farmers had to make do with second-rate equipment. This problem would persist throughout the 1920s as well.

Growing Grain

Having acquainted ourselves with peasants' relationship to the soil, it is now time to observe their handling of grain. The operations that concern us here will be easier to explain than tillage. None of the nuances of sowing, reaping, and threshing grain involve features as hidden to the naked eye as the capillary structure of the soil or the action of microbes on elements in the soil. Consequently, we might expect to find more accurate work on the peasant farm in regard to these operations. What we find, however, may surprise us.

Sowing

From the technological point of view, broadcast sowing—that is, sowing by hand—is one of the simplest agricultural operations. But not every peasant could do a first-rate job. Patience and physical coordination determine the quality of sowing work. The sower fills up a special tub (*lukoshko*) with seeds, and throws them in handfuls across the surface of his land. Since the tub hangs in front of him from a string around his neck, he can alternatively throw the seeds against the front of the tub such that they bounce off and land in a wide arc in front of him.[231] Grain seeds fly a maximum of about three steps away from the sower. Of course he must try to spread the seeds evenly over the land, a task which is not so easy to do, especially on a windy or rainy day (seeds stick to the hands when wet). Smaller seeds, such as grasses, are naturally more difficult to sow properly than bigger seeds, such as rye.[232] The sower's accuracy declines if he walks at an uneven pace, or tries to save time by increasing the arc of his cast, or throws out seeds with his left hand as well as his right (the Russian tradition was to use the right hand only, unlike in Europe, where two-handed work could be seen.)[233] In these cases the grain would grow unevenly, exposing the lazy work of the sower for all to see.[234]

The sower always has to take care not to waste seeds by throwing them beyond the border of his piece of land. If he is sowing a crop different from that sown on a neighboring strip, then he ought to take extra care not to spray any of his seeds onto that strip. At least three methods existed to avoid wasting seeds. One way was to walk slowly down the border of the strip, bending over slightly and distributing seeds along the edge.[235] Another method, known as *leshenie*, was for a helper to position some straw (or cut a shallow furrow) two or three steps to either side of the sower each time he went up and down the strip. The straw or furrow would help the sower regulate the distance the seeds were flying and avoid throwing seeds beyond the family's strip.[236] The final, and likely most common, method was for the sower to throw very few seeds towards the edges of his strip.[237] But this was no solution at all. The seeds in the middle were sown too densely, those on the edges too sparsely. In consequence crop growth suffered, and the grain ripened unevenly. The importance of the uneven distribution of seeds will become clearer after subsequent discussions of the density of sowing and the timing of reaping.

The process of sowing is technically uncomplicated and physically undemanding, apart from the weight of the seed bucket hanging from the sower's neck. Still, the farmer must make a number of difficult decisions before he actually sows the land. He must choose when to sow, how many seeds to use, and which seeds to sow on each strip. Let us now review what these choices involve, and see how farmers made them.

When to Sow

> The frogs are croaking—time to sow.
> When the swallows fly in, sow the millet.
> Sow when the land is ready, when it gives off a sowingtime odor.[238]

These sayings are among the finest examples of Russian agricultural folk wisdom. At first glance they appear to be raw superstitions, but in fact they are all based on shrewd observations of nature. The singing of certain birds, the croaking of frogs, or the appearance of certain leaves or flowers all testify to shifts in the temperature of the air or the soil. These shifts in temperature are cues to the farmer, confirmations that the climatic conditions are ripe for the sowing of various crops.

Similarly, the smell of the earth reflects a combination of the temperature of the soil and the level of soil moisture. A good farmer's nose really is a useful asset.[239]

In evaluating the body of folk wisdom governing the timing of sowing, we must mention that this wisdom was not limited to observations connected to air and soil temperature. For the most part, other types of sayings were nothing more than primitive superstitions. They advised sowing to be timed based on the weight of the first and last eggs of a chicken, or on the weather on a certain winter holiday, for example. Other sayings declare that "in order for wheat to grow well, it should be sown on Wednesday and Friday," or "before the commencement of winter sowing, hay must not be used either as fodder or as ground cover for livestock."[240] We cannot know how many peasants really believed in these sayings. The influence of such superstitions was probably weakening in our period. But the fact of their survival in village lore into the twentieth century suggests a lingering, insidious presence.

The proper timing of sowing is critical to crop yields for all farmers. But for the Tambov peasant timing decisions were even more important, for, as we have already seen, shoddily kept soil does not retain moisture for very long. In springtime, when the snows have thawed and their water is running off, the best conditions for sowing on such land can pass in as little time as one or two days. Crops sown too early in the spring can be wiped out by sudden frosts, or will fail to grow in the cold soil, while tardily sown grain will develop poorly in earth that has dried out or been occupied by weeds. The sowing of millet is especially tricky to judge in this respect. With farmers straining to divine the weather in advance, village elders acquired maximal influence at this time. The timing of winter rye sowings is less tricky, of course, since soil moisture conditions are much more stable in the summer than in the spring. All the same, late sowing of winter grain could reduce yields by 50% or more on peasant lands.[241] The crop needs at least six weeks to develop a strong root structure before the first frosts arrive in the fall. In poorly prepared soil this takes more time, and so peasants needed to sow early (no later than mid- to late August, in Tambov).[242]

Agronomist's Criticism (of the timing and technique of sowing). Despite all the value of folk wisdom with respect to the timing of sowing, agronomists found flaws in peasant practice. In obeying traditional counsel to sow oats early ("sow oats in mud, and reap a good harvest"),[243] farmers tended to sow oats at the first opportunity.[244] But at least one important agronomist and one estate manager insisted that they ought not to have done so, except for years in which spring came late. Early sowing left the oats in cool soil, such that weeds got a head start on the oats sprouts, and farmers had to till the field several days after sowing to cut down the weeds (*lomka* tillage, as discussed earlier).[245] In addition, religious custom often got in the way of sound agronomic practice. Peasants would not work on holidays, no matter how urgently conditions might call them to the fields. The best days for oats sowing often coincided with the Easter holiday, but no one would sow on these days, regardless of the hazards delay entailed.[246] As we shall see in Part II, adherence to the observance of religious holidays was slowly weakening, and would recede still further after the Bolshevik revolution. Yet, as late as the great drought year of 1924 most peasants waited until after Easter to sow.[247] This was a very expensive and dangerous custom in dry years.

In places, the communal grazing of livestock exercised further constraints on the accuracy of peasant sowing. Villages might try to sow the fields adjacent to the village first, and gradually work their way outwards. The idea was to reap the fields in the same order, thereby allowing the herd to spread out slowly, without trampling any standing crops. Of course, in ordering their sowings in this way they could not adjust the timing very closely to soil conditions.[248]

With rye, tardy sowing was a chronic problem. Decent farmers would be sure to sow their best strips on time, but many of them had to wait before getting around to the rest of their land.[249] Other tasks demanded their attention simultaneously. Everyone had to be concerned with the harvest of spring crops, and most would have to thresh at least some of the just collected rye, either for seed grain or for paying off debts. For some peasants, work for landlords or co-villagers who offered them a needed wage impinged on their sowing. It is almost certain that this complex of competing concerns, and not any significant variation of opinion as to when would be the optimal time to sow, accounts for the great length of time over which farmers could be found sowing rye on one and the same section of land.[250] Fedor Lokhin describes how in his village farmers spoke of "early," "middle," and "late" periods for rye sowing.[251]

Finally, we may note here an important shortcoming of peasant sowing practice, as reported by a peasant of Elets *uezd*, which bordered Tambov to the west. According to him, peasants chronically failed to pay appropriate attention to the distribution of seeds (of oats, at least) when throwing them on the ground. They mistakenly felt that the action of the *sokha* and the harrow after sowing would suffice to spread the seeds out. In actual fact, however, they ended up with alternating stripes of over and underseeded land.[252] Just how widespread was this behavior we cannot say, but a source from southeastern Russia reports the same tendency.[253] At any rate, such carelessness comes as no surprise. Sloppy sowing could cut yields in half, according to one estimate.[254]

How Densely to Sow

In selecting the quantity of seeds to sow per unit area, the farmer must keep in mind several variables. The first is his own talent. More experienced and coordinated sowers take less seed than their neighbors.[255] Much depends on the condition of the land. Poorly prepared soil—or soil left drying out for too long after the spring thaw—will give seeds less nourishment, and so will demand denser sowing.[256] The quality of the grain also matters: smaller, weaker seeds are less likely to sprout and mature than are better seeds. The weaker the seeds, the denser should be the sowing. The timing of sowing also plays a role in the selection of sowing density. If sowing is slightly tardy, then an additional 1–2 *puds* per *desiatina* may be sown in compensation, and yields will not suffer from the delay. On the other hand, should sowing be delayed by a month or more, extra seeds will only be wasted.[257]

Did villages have norms to guide farmers on the quantity of seeds typically needed per unit of land? This question is pertinent in evaluating the degree to which family farms were exercising judgment independently of local traditions. Because of the many variables influencing selection of sowing density, it is probable that many villages never established sowing norms, and that many farmers did not even conceive of sowing densities in terms of a certain quantity of *puds* per *desiatina*. All surviving farmers with whom I personally spoke declared that they intuitively "eyeballed" the amount of seeds needed for each strip of land. They learned to sow by watching their fathers and grandfathers at work. No one ever formularized for them the amount of seeds of each crop to be sown per *desiatina*.[258]

Sowing Densities in Practice. Unfortunately (astonishingly?), farmers did not necessarily understand that poorer land requires denser sowing: "Farmers frequently err with respect to the density of sowing. They feel that one should sow more on fertile land, and less on exhausted land. In fact the opposite is true."[259] Although this misconception was not all that common, it could be found all over Russia, especially among peasants.[260] Moreover, owing to poor tillage, tardy sowing, weak seeds, and impure sowing material, Russian fields were very thickly sown on average. Compiled from data gathered all over European Russia at the end of the nineteenth century, this chart is powerful testimony to technological backwardness [Table 1.11]:

Table 1.11. Sowing Densities in Theory and Practice

	Area required for full development of each plant, in square inches	Theoretical ideal sowing norm, in *puds* per *desiatina*	Average amount of seeds sown on peasant lands, in *puds* per *desiatina*
Rye	8	2.2	9.0
Oats	9	1.43	12.0

Source: A. S., "Sev i seialki," p. 324.

In Moscow province, Zubrilin located peasants sowing up to 16 *puds* of rye, and 24 *puds* of oats per *desiatina!*[261] Statistics for the period 1896–1900 painted a similar picture for our province, as we would expect (all figures in *puds* per *desiatina*) [Table 1.12]:

Table 1.12. Sowing Densities in Tambov

Uezds/Crops	Rye	Oats
Borisoglebsk	9.3	11.3
Usman	8.9	11.1
Shatsk	8.7	10.3
Elatma	9.6	10.7

Source: Proekt obshchikh osnovanii, p. 19, citing Central Statistical Committee (Ministry of Internal Affairs) figures.

Apart from the high density of sowings, the information from Tambov implies that peasants had conflicting opinions on sowing norms. The norms in the chart above do not vary in accordance with the characteristics of the soil or climate. The meticulous *zemstvo* land appraisers noted wide variations within the individual *uezds* as well, but could not come up with any logical explanation for this. They had to settle on blanket figures of 9 *puds* of rye and 11 of oats as the standard norms for the whole province.[262] Thus, in the absence of agronomic advice, a certain amount of guessing was going on in the countryside. Those who sowed too sparsely reaped sub-optimal harvests, while those who sowed too thickly lost in other ways. If sown too densely, grain crops produce fewer grains per plant, and have thinner stems, which makes lodging (falling over) more likely.[263]

Selection of Seed Grain

In practice, the preparation of seed grain begins with reaping. The timing of reaping, and the techniques of drying, threshing, winnowing, and storing grain all affect the quality of the grain from which the farmer will select his seed. Because we will be analyzing these operations later, for the moment we will concentrate on the final step, the selection of seed proper.

The peasant farmer had two simple decisions to make in selecting seed grain: what size grains he would sow, and what year's grain he would sow. The size of grains is usually a direct reflection of their strength. Larger, heavier seeds give much better yields than smaller seeds, by as much as 100% or more.[264] Bigger seeds sprout more quickly, choking out weeds, and stand up better to pests and bad weather.[265]

It has always been taken for granted that peasants were fully aware of the advantages of larger seeds. Accounts of traditional spade winnowing (which we will discuss later) insist that the technique was designed to segregate larger grains for sowing material.[266] And it seems that another technique, the beating of sheaves across rails, was so designed. Ermolov's collection of agronomic folklore includes sayings counseling the sowing of the largest seeds, and all survivors declare that they did so.[267]

Yet, astonishing as it may seem, a number of reports from local agronomists give us reason to believe that huge numbers of peasants failed to comprehend the superiority of larger seeds over smaller. Writing from Lipetsk *uezd* in 1911, one agronomist comments that "… in its broad mass the population attaches little significance to sowing material, in many cases they even sow the worst grain."[268] An agronomist in Shatsk *uezd* in 1915 commented that "… peasants always sow bad grain."[269] Similarly, Morshansk agronomist F. Ia. Levin's report for 1911 asserts that the peasant "… attaches only secondary significance to physiologically healthy [seed] grain". He noticed willingness on peasants' part to remove weed seeds from seed grain, but never any interest in segregating the better seeds from the worse.[270] A. Ia. Gorokhov's annual report from a sector of Borisoglebsk *uezd* in 1912 confirms and elaborates these observations:

> Seed grain leaves much to be desired. Only when grain is earmarked for sale is it sent through a sieve, and even in that case not always. They use the wind [spade winnowing—D.K.] or a winnowing machine to prepare seed grain. When selecting

seeds by spade winnowing, they do not even try to collect the grain at "the head" [In spade winnowing, the heaviest grains fall at the winnower's feet. Lighter seeds drift off in a line thanks to the wind. The heavier seeds are "the head", the lightest are "the tail".—D.K.], but, in most cases, they select grain from "the tail", and all other grains that have in some or another way lost market value. Stray grain from the threshing floor, including stained leftovers [spotted or stained grains are damaged, and unfit to sow—D.K.]—any such grain is thrown together for sowing. For the most part, therefore, seed grains are mechanically damaged, about 50% non-germinating, and quick to dislodge from the ears [The shock to the stalk from reaping tools, or simply wind, causes individual grains to fall out of the ears, leading to substantial losses. See discussion of reaping.—D.K.].
... peasants do not yet clearly conceive the importance of good seed grain ...[271]

None of the Tambov agronomists related any rationale underlying peasants' indifference to larger seeds. An agronomist in Samara province did supply an explanation gathered from peasants there. Their aim was to economize on the value of grain expended on seed. They did not perceive any advantages pertaining to large seeds. So, since a seed was a seed, they might as well eat or sell all the larger ones.[272] Larger seeds did fetch a higher price.[273]

Taken by themselves, these agronomists' accounts do not allow us to conclude that the mass of the province's farmers were incompetent with respect to seed grain. But supplemental information regarding the replacement of seed grain serves to reinforce our suspicions to this effect. We know, for example, that poor growing conditions or premature reaping can reduce grain's quality over the course of several years. Such grain ought to be replaced with new sowing material. The following account, from Kozlov *uezd* in the late 1880s, paints a sufficiently clear and poignant picture of popular attitudes towards grain replacement.

God only knows what kind of seeds we put in the Mother earth.... Almost no one takes care to replace his seeds, and if someone does make an attempt, then they do so solely on the basis of rumors to the effect that "look, they say that neighbor so-and-so's seeds are very good, we should try some of them". And then it turns out that the new seeds are worse than the old.[274]

Russian folklore did address the need to replace seed grain periodically. Thus Ermolov's collection of folk agricultural wisdom contains
a saying advising the replacement of seed grain once every few years.[275]
But, as with advice concerning the sowing of the largest seeds, this
wisdom was not always getting through to the farmers in the field.[276]
One survey comparing peasants' rye and oats to the grain of landlords
revealed the latter's grains to weigh an average of about 15% more
(per individual grain).[277] Another registered an average difference of
65%.[278] Russian experimental stations were achieving results of as much
as 100% above peasants'.[279]

Finally, if large numbers of peasants ever did come to understand the
significance of good seed grain, we must ask why the records of the
zemstvo agronomic aid organizations always show their local agronomists spending precious time explaining sowing fundamentals in their
traveling agronomic lectures? We do not know exactly what went on
in these lectures, since not a single one—from Tambov, at any rate—
has survived. But we do know that, after tillage, sowing was often the
primary topic of these lectures.[280] And we can infer that if the agronomists had felt more confident concerning peasants' handling of seed
grain then they would not have focused so much of their attention on
this issue. Our evidence is quantitatively limited, but it seems clear that
*a substantial portion, perhaps even a majority, of peasants were failing to
select the strongest grains for sowing.*[281] This assertion will be more
convincing later, once we examine how shoddily peasants cleaned their
grain.

Peasants also experienced difficulties in deciding from which year's
harvest to select seed grain. The problem here was to avoid grain with
a low germinating percentage. Grain loses germinating power for
various reasons: if reaping is premature, if the sheaves are rained on in
the field (or are stored in moist air), or if the grain is exposed to high
temperatures (60 °C in dry air, 42–50 °C in moist air, which can happen
in artificial grain drying). Aging always influences grain fertility. Even
under excellent storage conditions most grains cannot be sown after 4–6 years. The younger the grain, the higher the germinating percentage.[282]

By all indications, peasants appreciated the fact that seed grain
deteriorated over time. Thus families who still had some of last year's
grain when sowing time came, and so had a choice of which year's grain
to choose, preferred to sow the youngest grain, from the harvest just
completed. All survivors maintain that this was the case in their
families.[283] Indeed, a general assessment of Russian farmers on this issue

described their preference for new seeds as "strongly entrenched," "almost everywhere in Russia," among virtually "every farmer."[284]

But in the all-important case of rye it is possible that farmers'—not only peasants'—loyalty to new seeds was often counter-productive. For the rye sowings overlapped with the reaping period for oats (sometimes even with the reaping of rye itself). In order to prepare new rye seeds for immediate sowing families had to take hands away from the ongoing reaping so as to collect, dry, and thresh new sheaves of rye. The rush to prepare seed grain could be very costly. Quoting again from the report cited just above:

> Often they lay out the sheaves and thresh them on an impro-
> vised threshing ground right in the field, where substantial
> quantities of grain are lost [after the inevitable scattering during
> flail threshing it is difficult to sweep seeds up on such an
> improvised threshing ground—a fact that will become clearer
> after treatment of threshing technologies—D.K.].... I have
> observed how, out of fear of delayed sowing, peasants sow
> uncleaned, unwinnowed grain."[285]

Moreover, as we shall see in the discussion of reaping, delays during the harvest deprived farmers of a substantial amount of their standing crops. Farmers should have been more willing to sow year-old rye. But "the inaccurate, unfounded prejudice that old seeds give poor yields" was too strong.[286]

Covering the Seeds

Once the seeds were on the soil, the next step was to cover them by lightly tilling with a *sokha*. Plows are not necessary for this job, since seeds need not be deeply covered (1.5–2 inches is about the maximum for spring grains, 2–3 inches maximum for winter grains).[287] With spring crops, the land should then be leveled off with a harrow, to help the soil warm up evenly. Since fall crops are sown in the summer, and since they have so much more time to grow, this harrowing was tra-ditionally omitted for them. As scythes gradually replaced sickles for the reaping of rye, however, peasants began to harrow the rye seeds after covering them with a *sokha* (scythes are easier to use on level soil).[288]

Sowing operations are complete at this point for most crops. But for millet, and sometimes for oats as well, peasants would return to the field 4–12 days later, for another light tillage with a *sokha* or harrow (or even both) over the sprouts. The ideas behind this technique, known as *lomka*, were to kill off weeds (which always afflict millet), and to compensate for inadequate pre-sowing tillage.[289] The surface would be crumbled up a bit, while the sprouts' roots would remain unharmed. Statistics from Voronezh in 1914 show that yields after *lomka* were no better than yields on lands where *lomka* was not done.[290] However, it does not follow from this that peasants were mistaken in performing *lomka*. *Lomka* was a necessary measure of last resort for those fields most badly choked with weeds. Its practice is testimony to the inadequacy of tillage before sowing. In 1914 approximately 25% of the farms in the central and southern *uezds* were doing *lomka* for millet, about 15% for oats.[291]

Agronomist's Criticism (of Seed Covering). Agronomists very rarely criticized peasant techniques for covering seeds. But this was at least in part because of a lack of information on the subject. The rare existing data reveal several imperfections. First, it appears that peasants sometimes tilled more deeply than necessary when covering rye seeds with their *sokhas* (plows were not employed for the covering of seeds).[292] They were trying to lodge the seeds in a deeper, moister layer of soil. But they could have spared themselves some of the effort involved. Seeds can, and did, die when lodged too deeply.[293] Likewise, one source accuses peasants of taking too many passes—up to 10 or 15!—when using their harrows to cover seeds left exposed after the passage of the *sokha*.[294] It was true that the standard two passes always left many seeds exposed. But of course it was better to sacrifice some of the seeds than to over-harrow the land. Conversely, a minority of farmers was too lazy when covering seeds. According to the budget study of 1914 about 20% of the farms in the central and southern *uezds* were not bothering to use the *sokha* to cover millet sowings. They tried to get by with a harrow only. For oats the figure was 13–14%.[295]

Technological Advance in Sowing: The Seed Drill

Up to this point all of our analysis has concerned sowing by hand. The arrival of seed drills in Tambov at the turn of the twentieth century offered peasants a tremendous opportunity to improve their sowing technology. But, as we shall see, a complex of circumstances combined to retard the adoption of this tool.

Advantages of Seed Drills. The seed drills of our period ranged from 7–13 rows. As the tool moves forward its teeth cut thin furrows in the surface of the soil. Meanwhile, at a pace regulated by gears, seeds drop down behind the teeth and fall into the furrows. The first advantage of the seed drill is that it sets seeds at a predetermined depth, so as to maximize their growth potential. Seeds sown by hand and covered with a harrow or other tillage implement inevitably come to rest at various depths, such that many seeds lie outside the optimal layer of soil [Figure 1.10]. Furthermore, the seed drill places seeds apart from each

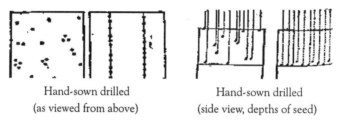

Hand-sown   drilled   Hand-sown   drilled
(as viewed from above)   (side view, depths of seed)

Figure 1.10. Broadcast vs. Drill Sowing (*Source: KSE*, vol. 4. Prilozhenie)

other at an appropriate distance, so that they will not compete with each other for light or root space. Drilled crops thus take root faster and stronger, and sprout up evenly, which gives them a large edge against weeds. The evenness of their growth results in more uniformity among the plants at harvest time, meaning that fewer ears will be reaped prematurely. These considerations allow the farmer to reduce the grain expended on sowing by 25–33%, or even more.[296] Finally, by arranging the sprouts in straight rows, and leaving some rows set widely apart (a tactic known in Russian as *lentochnyi posev*—"ribbon sowing") the seed drill permits the farmer to run small tillage implements between the rows at his convenience, killing weeds and breaking up the soil for the retention of moisture at the same time (this tactic is known in Russian as *mezhduriadnaia obrabotka*, which in the present work will be translated "inter-tillage"). Drilled crops remain stronger than hand-sown crops through maturation, which makes them less likely to lodge.

The seed drill cannot be used in all conditions. The tool is wide, especially the 11- and 13-row models, which makes it awkward on very thin strips of land. If weeds are present in sufficient quantity, they will clog up the drill's teeth, either precluding penetration to the desired depth or disturbing the descent of the seeds. Wet soil in the early spring can also be off-limits to the tool. The horse's hooves will sink into the ground and spoil the path of the teeth. In all cases the ground should be as level as possible for the seed drill, and not very sloped. Clumpy soil will impede it as well. Additionally, the farmer must have access to a horse (or two horses, for the largest models of the period) to pull the tool.

The preparatory tillage required for seed drilling made it difficult for agronomists of our period to gauge the effect of this tool alone on grain yields. Yields of drilled crops rose above hand-sown crops owing in part to the improved tillage. Moreover, the quality of post-sowing tillage could be crucial to the performance of some drilled crops, as we shall see below. As a very rough estimate, we can credit seed drills with the power to raise peasant yields by 30%.[297]

Promotion and Reception of the Seed Drill. The effectiveness and simplicity of the seed drill made it a natural favorite with the *zemstvos'* agronomic aid organizations. Whenever the Agricultural Commissions of the *uezd zemstvos* gave local agronomists explicit guidelines for their work, they always attached high importance to acquainting peasants with seed drills.[298] Every local agronomist's report in the Tsarist period mentions propaganda in favor of the tool, and most also list those peasants trying out drills under the agronomist's supervision.

Since very few peasants had seen seed drills at work before the arrival of the local agronomists, they generally greeted the tool coldly.[299] To many, the notion of reducing sowing densities by 25% or more violated long-established balances, and seemed to portend corresponding reductions of yields. Thus, agronomist A. I. Moller instructed peasants in his sector to sow 7.5–8 *puds* of rye per *desiatina*, but when he left them alone to sow, and then doubled back to check on them, he frequently caught them having dumped 10–20% more rye into the machine in his absence.[300] Farmers expressed similar trepidation at leaving the land in between the sown rows empty of seeds. To them this was just so much territory lost to their crops, and surrendered to weeds. The agronomists always explained that the rows in fact allowed for elimination of weeds with subsequent inter-tillage, but this argument was not persuasive to peasants. "Many [peasants] come right out and declare that nothing will come of such sowings."[301]

Naturally some peasants could always be found to try out seed drills, especially in hard years when seed grain was in short supply. In such years many people were willing to compromise their trusted notions of proper sowing densities. But to them the main attraction of the drill was simply its economization of seeds, not the features of its work, which allowed for this economy and increased yields. They had not achieved any understanding of the principles behind the tool.[302]

Inadequate comprehension of the seed drill led to many distortions in peasant practice, which slowed adoption of the tool. We have already seen how peasants often put too many seeds into the drills. Their crops' sprouts interfered with one another, thereby minimizing yield increases.[303] Farmers frequently failed to prepare their land properly for seed drills, and as a result the seeds did not fall into a moist layer of soil. Sowing poor seeds on poorly worked soil was no recipe for good results. Peasants cursed the seed drills, but the tools were not to blame.[304] Lastly, farmers' ignorance of fundamental principles of soil science prevented them from understanding how to care for ribbon-drilled crops. Agronomists commonly noted peasants' incomprehension of the need to perform inter-tillage on ribbon-drilled crops:

> ... peasants tend to see the advantage of ribbon sowings as the manner of sowing itself, and not the possibility of subsequent inter-tillage, for which purpose such sowings are done."[305]
>
> "When ribbon sowings are promoted peasants agree to all the advantages plants derive from such sowing. But when the time comes to perform inter-tillage ... it seems strange to them that such tillage is truly necessary. And so ribbon sowings are left unworked most of the time.[306]

Despite these common flaws in the application of seed drills, peasant pioneers soon began to achieve good results with drilled crops. As with most other innovations, the tool gained authority among peasants most quickly during dry or otherwise poor years, which exposed the disadvantages of sowing by hand. Neighbors slowly began to imitate the pioneers, and the tool's popularity rose all across the province in the years before the First World War. In areas where plows had made headway before the appearance of the local agronomists, farmers acquired more seed drills in the pre-war period than any other advanced equipment [Table 1.13].[307] Good seed drills were expensive for

Table 1.13. Seed Drills in Tambov

Seed drills on peasant farms in Tambov	1910	1,132
	1917	5,978

Sources: Sel'sko-khoziaistvennye mashiny i orudiia, pp. 68–69; Trudy Tsentral'nogo Statisticheskogo Upravleniia. Tom 5, vyp.2, pp. 116–17, 120–21.

peasant farmers, with quality American and German models ranging from 60–120 rubles, depending upon their size.[308] But, to agronomists' chagrin, peasants often settled for inferior makes, which cost a bit less.[309]

Reaping

The clouds chase the carriage through the fields. Wherever you cast your eye, all the way to the distant trees, you see the tall rye waving, looking just like the fur of some unknown, angry gray beast, its bristles sparkling in the wind, which rustles through its pelt.

—Garin-Mikhailovskii, 1897[310]

Once spring tillage and sowing are completed, the hay has been made, and fallow has been raised, the farmer must prepare for reaping. The harvest is the family's reward for the hard work that has preceded it. Unless the crops have failed miserably, this period is filled with satisfaction and celebrations. At the same time, reaping is the most grueling work of all. Neither the sickle nor the scythe is heavy to hold or swing at first. After a spell of work under the hot sun, however, fatigue, numbness, and pain invade the body, commencing in the arms if using the scythe, or the back if using the sickle. The more land per worker that the family has, and the greater the yield per *desiatina,* the better is the mood in the fields. But more grain requires more labor. Day after day the reaping continues, always under the pressure to go faster, so as to finish the job before grain overripens or rain spoils the crops. The grain stands tall—rye rose six feet or higher in good years—and looks even heavier and more difficult to handle as exhaustion sets in. Dust gets into the peasants' eyes, causing painful and long-lasting irritations for many. Constant contact with dry ears of grain and straw rubs the sicklers' hands raw, sometimes opening up deep, painful cracks in the skin. The only treatment for these wounds is to take the thickened tar accumulating around cart axles, heat it in ashes, and spread it on the injury. The peasants stay the night when reaping the fields most distant from home, leaving them exposed to all sorts of weather. Some of them inevitably fall ill under the strain, leaving the rest with still more to do. Not without reason did the peasants call the reaping period *strada,* "the suffering."[311]

Fundamentals of Reaping

> Peasants were starting for their fields—some in springless carts
> lurching through the mud, some on foot; barefooted most of
> them, with the inevitable white lunch-sacks and the visible
> lumps of black bread on their backs; some with scythes, some
> with hoes, some with sickles or spades. They walked singly and
> in groups, the young people by themselves, chatting, laughing,
> teasing one another, some of them singing. They walked fast,
> for it was a glorious day, cool, sunny, bracing—one of those days
> that bring joy and hope and zest to the farmer—and they were
> in a hurry to get to their fields.
>
> —Maurice Hindus, 1926[312]

When to Reap. As with tillage and sowing, reaping must be properly
timed. Unfortunately, it is not easy to judge the best moment to reap
grain crops. To begin with, one must gauge the ripeness of the field as
a whole. On land sown by hand the strength of the individual plants
varies widely. Plants with more space, more light, and more nourishment from the soil will grow larger and ripen sooner than other plants,
and will give the best quality grains. The trick is to start work when the
greatest number of plants is reaching the proper stage of ripeness.

Judging the proper stage of ripeness for any individual grain plant is
a task all its own. Take rye as an example. As the plant ripens, the grains
within the ear develop unevenly. The grains higher up and in the middle of the ear are the first to mature, followed by those, lower down.
Grains just reaching full size are said to be at the "milk-like" stage of
ripeness. They are greenish-yellow and quite soft, emitting a whitish
liquid if broken by a knife or fingernail. At the next stage, "yellow
ripeness", the grain has almost completed its maturation. The grain is
malleable like wax, while the material inside is mealy and soft, but
hardening. Soon the crop reaches "full ripeness", when the straw is
completely dry, and the grain is difficult to break with a fingernail, but
is still elastic. If the crop remains standing any longer, it reaches the
stage of "dead" ripeness, when the grains get very hard, and the straw
becomes a dirty yellow, or even darker.

How was the peasant to determine the ideal moment for reaping? If
he waits for the "full ripeness" stage, he increases the risk of a sudden
storm knocking the crop down, and of the grain becoming overripe.
Hot summer air sucks the moisture out of the grains, leaving them ever
more prone to dislodgment—in cutting through the straw, reaping tools
send a shock wave up to the ear, shaking the drier grains loose. Even

at "full ripeness" a lot of grain is lost in this manner, but once the crop reaches the "dead" ripeness stage, losses to dislodgment are prohibitive. If a stiff, hot wind is blowing, more than half of the crop can disappear by the time scything is done.[313] "The space of one day decides the year's food supply", went a profound peasant saying.[314]

Because of the severity of the penalties for tardy reaping, the natural, and correct, response is to try to begin work as early as possible. Agronomic studies of the late nineteenth century established that grain cut down at the "yellow ripeness" stage is not significantly inferior to grain reaped at the "full ripeness" stage, once the grain has been dried. Whether the grain stays on the root after "yellow ripeness" or not is of little consequence. Grain reaped a bit early is more difficult to thresh, but this is a small price to pay for the minimization of losses to dislodgment.[315] The following chart, taken from a study of wheat, is a powerful illustration of the consequences to the grain of reaping at various stages of ripeness [Table 1.14]:

Table 1.14. Changes in Grain during Ripening

Stage of ripeness	Day of reaping	Water as a % of the total weight of the grain		Volume of 100 grains, in cubic cm		Dry weight of 100 grains, in grams
		Fresh grain[*]	Set grain[**]	Fresh grain[*]	Set grain[**]	Set grain[**]
Milk-like	July 21st	*51.47*	**11.82**	5.31	2.41	2.97
Milk-like	July 25th	*47.69*	**11.67**	5.17	3.00	3.71
Yellow	Aug. 1st	*25.73*	**11.61**	4.28	3.43	4.22
Full	Aug. 4th	*12.97*	**11.57**	3.52	3.43	4.19

[*]This grain was measured just after reaping.
[**]This grain was allowed to ventilate and dry out for several days in the field, in sheaves.
Source: Sovetov, "Zhatva," p. 728. Although this study was performed in Germany, its conclusions apply perfectly well to Russia.

The figures in italics here demonstrate the speed at which moisture leaves the grains as they approach full ripeness. Meanwhile, the bold figures testify to the hazards of premature reaping—grains reaped too early will be both smaller and lighter than grains left on the root to continue ripening.

We have limited information on the stage of grain ripeness at which Tambov peasants preferred to commence reaping. We would like to assume that most farmers had the sense to begin once grain reached "yellow ripeness." *Zemstvo* investigations in Borisoglebsk and Kirsanov *uezds* in the late 1870s and 1880s specify landowners commencing reaping at precisely this moment.[316] It appears, moreover, that farmers preferred the flour obtained from early-reaped rye and wheat. Such flour was lighter in color, and so was reserved for special occasions or sold for a higher price.[317]

Nevertheless, authoritative sources cast serious doubt on the competence of farmers regarding the all-important matter of the timing of reaping. L. A. Pel'tsikh, the director of the Tambov Agricultural Experimental Station throughout the 1920s, remarked that peasants were chronically late in the reaping of rye.[318] A. V. Sovetov, one of the greatest Russian agronomists (and a man well traveled over European Russia), spoke more broadly:

> It happens often that, partly out of inability to cope with other tasks preceding reaping, and in part *thanks to an incomplete understanding of the dangers of tardy reaping, peasants are late in reaping their fields.* Larger farmers are likewise often guilty of improperly determining the appropriate time at which to begin reaping.[319]

A peasant from a district on Tambov's western border made a similar accusation, as did agronomists in other provinces.[320] "Very often," noted an agronomist working just across Tambov's southeastern border, A. Iudin of Balashov *uezd,*

> ... farmers reap grain when it has reached 'dead' ripeness.... When it comes time to reap, farmers often direct their attention to the straw: if the straw is green, then they think that the grain must be green as well. But this conclusion is incorrect. Grain can be ripe even when the straw looks greenish.[321]

The following passage is the most explicit, and most damning criticism of Russian farmers concerning the timing of reaping:

> Unfortunately, we [estate owners and peasants alike—D.K.] decide to begin reaping only when the entire field has fully ripened. By the time work begins, the ears and the straw have dried to a crisp. Naturally no one pays any attention to the lay of the land in this context; raised spots, level areas, and hollows are reaped in no particular order.[322]

According to the Balashov *uezd* agronomist Iudin, cited above, the preference in favor of late reaping stemmed from farmers' "... fear of netting a smaller yield and poor, frail grain if they reap when the grain is at wax-like ripeness." As he quite rightly pointed out, this preference was absolutely wrong. Sources record peasants offering only one other justification for late reaping: the concern that the moisture remaining in incompletely ripe grain would ruin it when it stood in stacks. This concern too was unfounded.[323]

The dislodgment of tardily reaped grain continued after the reaping operation proper. Every time dried out sheaves were handled, be it for placement in the field, carting home, or positioning on the threshing floor, more grains streamed out of the ears.[324]

Thus problems with the timing of reaping often stemmed from agronomic ignorance. The Russians were certainly not alone in this matter. It seems that nowhere in Europe (apart from the most northern latitudes, where the brevity of the growing season forbade tardy reaping) had farmers appreciated the virtues of earlier reaping of wheat and rye, until the early 1840s. It was then that the Scottish farmer Hannam conducted pathbreaking experiments on the issue.[325] Word appears to have got around more quickly in Western Europe than in Russia.[326]

Obstacles to timely reaping that are more visible to the historical eye than agronomic ignorance included physical and economic constraints. Without horse-drawn reaping machines, no one could cut down all of his crops at the ideal time, especially so in the odd year when oats matured ahead of schedule, at the same time as rye. Some losses to dislodgment were inevitable. According to the only scientific study of its kind which I have ever found, 14.1% of the rye grains present in the ears at the outset of reaping were lost during sickling, binding, stacking, sun drying, and carting the grain home.[327] And this study concerned grain not yet at "yellow" ripeness. All serious observers estimated that on longer-standing crops the losses increased dramatically, reaching 50% or more.[328] It is possible, moreover, that the ripening process of rye sown after green fallow was faster than for rye sown on better prepared soil. If so, then green fallow was partly responsible for losses from shattering.[329]

In sum, reaping inaccuracies were tremendously wasteful. Perhaps more importantly, the village did not absorb these losses uniformly. The frenzy of the period inevitably resulted in uneven work as between well-off and poor households. The better off would buy the poor's labor with cash or food at the critical moments. The poor's grain would have to wait. Alternatively, some poor families would harvest too early out of need or hunger.

The Binding and Drying of Grain

Once the grain has been cut down, the technical complexities of the harvest period are virtually over. Nevertheless a great deal of labor remains to be done before threshing can begin. The grain must be bound, set to dry, and carried home to the threshing floor before the harvest can be realized. None of these tasks require any equipment at all, apart from a rake and a cart. The farmer is no longer burdened with choosing between various tools or methods of using these tools. Yet, once the grain is set to dry in the fields, the psychological tension rises. If rain threatens at this point, a final decision must be made: to leave the grain exposed or to bring it under cover? A mistake at this point can cost the family dearly. As we shall see, analysis of this part of the work year will help to illuminate the psychological atmosphere that accompanied peasant farming and the qualities which set successful farmers apart from their neighbors.

Binding. As the scyther moved along a strip of grain, a woman or an adolescent would generally accompany him, walking behind, raking the reaped plants together, and binding them into sheaves with lengths of straw or sturdy grass. The straw might be prepared ahead of time, or a young child might be there to get them ready as the work proceeded. If the strip is full of weeds, the binding would be put off for a day or so, to ensure that the grasses would dry out and not rot the grain in the sheaves.[330] Binding helped to even the rate at which the ears dried, and simplified threshing by concentrating all of the ears in one place, at the end of the sheaf.

The diameter of sheaves varied from 6–9 inches in the northern *uezds*, versus 8–12 inches in the open, drier terrain of the center and south of Tambov.[331] Grain tied into smaller sheaves dries better than in larger, and is also easier to thresh, but when the binder was in a rush larger sheaves saved time. In an average rye field the scyther would make up to ten swipes with the scythe to cut down enough grain for a large sheaf.

Drying. Once the crop was bound, it had to be arranged for drying in the field. Sheaves could not be put into big stacks right away, for there were always weeds lodged inside the sheaves. If the sheaves were not given ventilation and properly dried, then these weeds would not dry out, and could spoil a whole stack of grain.[332] In all provinces of the central black-earth region and further south, peasants exclusively laid out their sheaves horizontally, in *krestsy* ("crosses"). They placed four sheaves together on the ground in the form of a cross, with all of the ears converging in the center of the cross. If the ground was wet or rain expected, they might bend back the ears of the two bottom-most sheaves so as to keep the ears off the ground. The next step was to lay four more sheaves directly above the first four, in the same positions, thus forming a second layer of the cross. Four more sheaves comprised the third and final level. Then an unbound, thirteenth sheaf was fanned over the ears on the top of the "cross" as protection against light rains.[333] On the same evening as reaping, ordinarily, peasants would arrange the crosses into *kopny*—stacks composed of four crosses, which provided better protection against rain.[334] Families would then cart the grain home as soon as the work schedule permitted, but never sooner than a week after it was reaped.[335]

Placing grain in *krestsy* was much quicker than arranging the sheaves to lean into each other in a vertical posture, as peasants tended to handle crops in the northern, colder half of Russia.[336] The significant disadvantage of horizontal drying became apparent when heavy rains came. The single sheaf over the top of the cross could not keep water off the other sheaves for very long. The moisture and summer heat would then prompt the grains to begin growing inside of the ears, and much of the crop would be ruined.[337] In rainy summers local agronomists' estimates of the grain lost in their sectors in this manner reached as high as 18%.[338] This is a huge loss.

Thus, much as with haymaking, storms arriving after reaping time were a terrible threat to farmers of this period:

> At this time of year thunder often sounds, almost always accompanied by hail. The thunderhead strikes fear in the farmer: all of his labors, all of his hopes can be shattered in the space of half an hour. Each and every one prays from the depth of his soul. I dare say that the city-dweller never prays like this.[339]

The whole countryside strained its senses for clues to the coming weather. Nearly every day in the summer they could hear thunder or see lightning in the distance.[340] A big storm on the approach would summon a frenzied burst of energy as everyone tried to bring as much as they could under shelter. It was just at this time that all were exhausted from the reaping and binding work (of course if the storm came just after the winter crop had been sheaved, then the reaping of spring crops was still going on). Even a moment's delay at a time like this could be critical, especially to families with most of their land located more than two or three miles from home. A heavy, prolonged rain could easily turn the roads into quagmires, and slow transport to a crawl.

When a storm did arrive, the stamina and strength of men, women, and horses played a decisive role in the success of families relative to one another. Households that were physically weaker, either because they had fewer men, or because these men were not fit, faced a tremendous disadvantage. The same was true for households without horses or carts. No data exist for Tambov, but in other provinces 10% or more of the farms did not have their own carts.[341] And not all carts were alike, of course. The more prosperous families had special over-sized carts specifically for transporting grain. A good horse could haul up to 80 sheaves at once on such a cart, as opposed to the typical 50–60.[342] This saved a lot of time, which was a meaningful advantage, even in clear weather.[343]

Quite independently of the pressures imposed by inclement weather, peasants disappointed observers with their carelessness in carting home and stacking grain. Various sources and photographs confirm that few peasants made an effort to seal their wagons' rickety lattice cargo beds with canvas or any other fabric while transporting sheaves. One observer estimated that peasants were losing 40–60 pounds of rye per full day of carting.[344] Meanwhile, it seems that farmers rarely took adequate measures to protect their grain at home from mice and other vermin. They did not generally build special platforms to keep mice out of the stacks. They settled instead for a thick layer of straw, sometimes atop a layer of twigs, perhaps together with a few sacred trinkets intended to ward off the mice.[345] We shall have occasion to consider the consequences of this negligence in our discussion of threshing.

The Disappearance of Artificial Drying of Grain. Judging from the seriousness of the danger posed by poor weather in August, we might expect artificial grain drying techniques to have been very widespread in Tambov. Unfortunately, statistics on this are lacking, but we do have limited evidence of the evolution of such techniques, thanks to two turn-of-the-century *zemstvo* inspections of rural buildings. Before analyzing this evidence, we must first examine existing technology for artificially drying grain.

The Ovin.[346] The *ovin* is a simple structure in which sheaves of grain can be slowly dried by means of heat from fire in a subterranean chamber. A small pit would typically be filled with straw, twigs, and bark, then set alight. Anywhere from 200–400 sheaves could usually fit in the upper chamber, where the heat of the fire would slowly dry the grain. The labor involved in the process was not prohibitive.

Properly loading the sheaves was demanding, and an elderly member of the family would have to keep watch on the height of the fire overnight. In a typical year a family with six *desiatinas* of sown area and a medium-sized *ovin* could dry all of its grain in nine nights or so.[347] Thus the *ovin* appears to have been perfectly well suited to protecting peasants in years with August storms. At least some of the grain, if not all of it, could be dried before it began to fester.[348] Further, artificially dried grain was much quicker to thresh than air-dried grain.[349]

On the other hand, *ovin* drying had many drawbacks.[350] Fire was a real threat if the process was carelessly overseen. Further, the smoke of the fire contained the moisture evaporating from the fuel source. The action of this moisture on the grain significantly slowed down the drying, and hence a great deal of straw and twigs were required to do the job. In a province like Tambov, where rising population density was occasioning deforestation, wood of any kind was too valuable to be wasted in *ovins*. And the scarcity of wood made straw valuable as a substitute heat source for the winter. Moreover, the flour from smoke-dried grain retained an unpleasant flavor, as did the straw. Cows not accustomed to this flavor will not eat such straw unless they have nothing left to eat whatsoever, and if they do the quality of their milk declines. Straw had been superabundant in the central black-earth region as recently as the middle of the nineteenth century. But by the twentieth century this was no longer the case. Could farmers really afford to let smoke spoil what straw they had? Moreover, to the people of the central black-earth provinces deforestation appeared to have altered natural balances, causing a gradual drying out of the climate.[351] Meteorologists found no long-term disruptions of precipitation patterns, but farmers were free to form their own opinions.[352] Once they believed or sensed that summer rains were less likely, the *ovin* became less necessary. Additionally, as we shall see later, the appearance of threshing machines made artificial drying still more superfluous for the growing number of farmers with access to them.

In sum, then, it will come as no surprise to learn that peasants were abandoning *ovins en masse* by the start of the twentieth century. *Zemstvo* inspections conducted in Morshansk and Borisoglebsk *uezds* from 1900–1902 found many *ovins* out of use and falling into complete disrepair, among both peasants and landlords. A follow-up inspection in Morshansk in 1909 located even fewer.[353] Only in the northernmost *uezd*, Temnikov, were *ovins* still in general use.[354]

The Threshing, Winnowing, and Sorting of Grain

Threshing

While the harvest period proper ended when the last crops were hauled home from the fields, the constant grind of work did not let up for a moment. Even while the spring crops were still drying in *krestsy*, the threshing of the winter grain was underway. The sheaves were stored under cover, either inside or nearby the threshing floor. Families in debt or going hungry would rush to begin threshing as quickly as possible, as would those trying to make some quick sales before grain prices dropped once everyone else began threshing. Unless the family had access to a mechanical threshing machine, the work went slowly, dragging out over many months thanks to interruptions from other, more pressing tasks. As we shall see, threshing was hard work. But, as with reaping, the more the work, the more the reward.[355]

Flail Threshing. The flail is an ancient instrument, consisting of two lengths of wood usually joined together by a leather strap. The longer piece serves as the handle, the shorter piece (often termed the "swingel" in English) swings through the air and strikes the ears of grain (or hits the sheaves just below the ears, ideally), thereby dislodging the grains from the ears. The weight of the swingel varies in accordance with the crop being threshed—for most crops a heavy piece of oak is to be preferred, while for a crop with more delicate grains, like millet or lentils, a lighter wood like pine works better. Naturally the threshing area must be hard and flat for flailing. Even under optimal conditions, however, earthen threshing floors deposit a mass of dust, pebbles, and chips of earth into the threshed grain. And rainy weather would some-times hold up work for weeks at a time in the fall. So families were quick to set down a layer of ice as soon as frosts came, after which the work proceeded with facility [Figure 1.11].[356] Threshing ordinarily began

Figure 1.11. A Flail (*Source:* Kushner, *Russkie*, p. 87)

before sunrise, and continued until mid-afternoon. To begin work a long row of sheaves was aligned on the ground, with the ears all at the same end. Then a second row was laid down against the first row, with the ears meeting the ears of the first row. Thus was established a wide target zone for the flails. If mice had infested the stacks before threshing, the task of laying out the sheaves took on another dimension:

> I myself have witnessed the extermination of up to 1,500 mice from one set of grain stacks. Besides which, many other mice managed to run away, and bystanding dogs rushed in to eat plenty more.[357]

Flail threshing is tiring, dreary labor—"threshing was real, downright slavery," recalls one farm worker[358]—so families tended to work in groups. In order to establish a steady rhythm to the work, flailers would often time their blows in synchrony with each other: rat-tat-tat-tat, rat-tat-tat-tat, rat-tat-tat-tat, and so on. Songs might even be sung.[359] Usually the ears were beaten for a while, then the sheaves were turned over and unbound for further flailing. Children would help out by turning over the clumps of grain every so often, so as better to expose all of the ears.[360]

The job always took a long time, especially when the crop had been reaped early or had not fully dried out after reaping. At a typical work-rate of 30–40 blows per minute per worker, four flailers could thresh about 60 sheaves per day.[361] The arduousness of flail threshing becomes more apparent when compared to the 8–10 times as much grain, which the best threshing machines of the day could handle *in a single hour*.[362]

The slowness of the flail not only demanded more labor from the family, but also cost them a large amount of grain. Only rarely would all sheaves be thoroughly dry after lying in the fields in *krestsy*. Some moisture would remain, and the inevitable delays in threshing meant that some of the grain would fester. How much grain would be lost depended only on the weather and the speed at which the threshing could be completed. Additionally, flail threshing cannot separate all grains from the ears. Up to 5–7, or even 10% of the grains will not be dislodged at all.[363] With fodder crops this is no loss at all—the straw, chaff, and grain will all end up in the feed anyway. But with crops earmarked for sale or consumption 5% or more can be quite a sacrifice. And much more grain than this is lost in practice: "... just take a close look for yourself at a few blows of a flail, and see how the grains fly off like rain with each blow."[364] A scrupulous study measured the loss from this spraying to be about 4% of the grain that reached the threshing floor in the first place.[365] Of course if a family worked harder, longer, and more carefully, it could marginally reduce losses in flailing. Nevertheless, it is easy to understand why peasants were so willing to discard the flail in favor of threshing machines.

Other Threshing Systems

All sources agree that the flail was by far the most common method of threshing in the central black-earth region before the adoption of threshing machines. Yet, among the several alternative techniques we must mention rail beating and animal trampling.[366] The former method, which entailed simply beating the ears against a framework of horizontal rails, was usually employed on rye as a means of selecting seed grain in the rushed period between the reaping of rye in mid- to late July and its sowing in early to mid-August.[367] The heavier seeds would shake loose first, and be set aside for sowing. This might appear to be a logical means of selecting seed grain—certainly it demands much less effort than spade winnowing, which we shall examine shortly. In reality, however, the grains, which come loose from rail beating, are not only the larger, stronger grains, but also those whose shape allows them to slip out of the ear upon the slightest shock. Once sown, these grains pass on this shape as a hereditary trait, and, if the farmer is not careful enough to select his seeds in another manner, within a few years' time he will find himself with a whole field of *rozh-plivun'ia*—"quicksand rye", which dislodges in great quantities during reaping.[368] Rail beating was not the most common method of selecting seed grain. It was probably rare in the central black-earth region.[369]

Animal trampling is another ancient threshing procedure, but it was little practiced in Tambov, except on millet, because it ruins the straw and forfeits some of the grain. The work goes much faster than flailing, but animals' hooves rip up and soil the straw, and also crush a fair amount of the grains. They can also foul the grain with excrement.[370] And of course the animals will try to help themselves to some of the grain ears while they work.[371]

Threshing Machines.

> The threshing drum hums and drones as it slowly works up speed. Horses walk, swaying, round and round tugging lazily at their traces and thrusting their legs into a manure-strewn path.

The driver sits on a little stool fitted on to the driving bar, and as he revolves he shouts monotonously at the horses, his whip falling on the brown gelding alone, the laziest of the lot, sleeping as it walks, since its eyes are blindfolded anyway....

"Godspeed!" he says and the first trial cluster of rye flies through the buzzing, squeaking drum and is tossed up in an untidy arc. The droning of the drum grows more and more insistent, work goes on apace, and soon all the sounds merge in the one pleasant hum of threshing. The master stands at the barn door and watches the red and yellow kerchiefs, the hands, the forks and the straw flickering in the darkness within, all of it moving rhythmically and busily to the roaring of the drum, the monotonous shouts of the driver and the cracking of his whip. Clouds of chaff come flying to the door, and the master stands there getting covered with this gray dust.

—Ivan Bunin, 1900[372]

By the beginning of the twentieth century, farmers with a couple hundred rubles of capital and a desire to market large quantities of grain had a huge variety of horse- and engine-powered threshing machines from which to choose. As far as the great mass of peasant farmers in Tambov was concerned, threshing machines—even primitive hand-powered machines—were an over-priced and unnecessary luxury. The simplest horse-driven, Russian-made models cost nearly a hundred rubles at this time, and required 4–6 horses to operate.[373] But the machines were very useful. They could thresh 20–25 *kopen** of grain per day, which was around half the quantity an average family would harvest in a typical year.[374] And, since threshing machines could handle freshly reaped, undried grain, they represented an answer to the threat of rain on standing sheaves and stacks.[375] Nevertheless, only the strongest families could round up the capital to make such an investment.[376] Thus the numbers of threshing machines in the province remained small all the way up to the First World War and beyond. The 1910 census registered about 13,500 threshing machines among peasants (99% of which were horse-powered), while in 1917 there were still only about 16,000 in peasant hands.[377]

The small numbers of threshing machines do not, however, indicate the influence of this equipment on the farming sector. Their tremen-

*Four *krestsy*, each with 13 sheaves, made up a *kopna*. Let it be noted here that in peasant parlance a *kopna* of spring-sown grain could occasionally mean five *krestsy*, or 65 sheaves (SSS, Spassk, p. 29). This must have been rare usage, however. Sources from Tambov are more consistent than those from other provinces on the norm of 52 sheaves per *kopna*.

dous work rate allowed owners to finish their own work quickly, and then hire out the machinery to other families for a fee. Ordinarily the owning party supplied a couple of horses and a couple of workers to help out.[378] By the early 1900s *zemstvo* researchers estimated that more than half of the peasants were already using machine threshers.[379] The machines did have drawbacks. They would smash a minimum of 2–4% of the grains, or even 20–26% when improperly adjusted or operated.[380] In addition, they caused serious or fatal injuries to anyone caught in the machinery.[381]

Winnowing

Like so many other agricultural operations, the task and tools of winnowing are relatively simple. Shovels, sieves, or winnowing machines help to separate the threshed grain from chaff, weed seeds, and any other foreign matter with which it is mixed. But, again as with other operations, top quality winnowing work was not a common achievement in the villages.

Spade Winnowing. The spade is probably the oldest of all winnowing tools. The winnower simply tosses amounts of threshed mixtures into the air, letting the wind carry the chaff away from the seeds. The ordinary technique was to throw the mixture into a crosswind, or just slightly against it. The chaff would return to earth a bit downwind; the seeds would spread out in a stripe in the direction they were thrown, with the lightest grains landing near the worker's feet. This permits segregation of grain into rough categories, according to their weight.[382] Spade winnowing is possible in the absence of wind, if the winnower gently tosses the mixture forwards across the threshing floor. But this method is much more time-consuming, demanding three or four runs through the mixture to segregate the grain properly.[383] Spade winnowing is not without cost—as much as 10% of the winnowed grain can be lost in the process.[384]

Sieves. Statistics are lacking, but sieves probably winnowed better than spades. They allowed chaff and the smallest seeds through, thereby collecting the largest seeds. Ideally, the winnower then picked off the largest weed seeds by hand. Some sieves had two screens, with different gauges of openings, so as to sift seeds by two sizes.[385] Since sieves would work less quickly than spades, it is clear that peasants often used them on grain that they had already spade winnowed. Such two-fold winnowing appears to have been a typical method of preparing grain for sale at market places.[386] Despite their simplicity and effectiveness, sieves do not appear to have been common among peasants in Tambov or elsewhere in the central black-earth region.[387]

Winnowing Machines. Most of the winnowing machines available to peasants in the late nineteenth century were simple, hand-powered models manufactured in neighboring Riazan and Saratov provinces. While prices varied widely, a winnowing unit of adequate quality would usually cost about 30 rubles.[388] Typical versions of these tools worked best with three workers in attendance—one pouring in the threshed mixture, a second turning the crank, and a third to direct all of the chaff and seeds as they came out.[389] Under the best conditions, these machines could winnow 100–150 *puds* from the threshing floor in only one hour. But peasants did not really need such a work rate, so they purchased slower, flimsier winnowing machines "of imperfect construction, made with poor screens."[390]

We have no way of knowing exactly how many farms machine winnowed their grain. From tool census data we can infer that in good years about 50% might have been doing so in the last years before the World War, at least on some of their harvests [Table 1.15].

Table 1.15. Winnowing and Sorting Machines in Tambov

Tools on peasant farms	1910	1917
Winnowing machines	20,403	25,856
Sorting machines	no data	712 (figure for 1920)

Sources: Sel'sko-khoziaistvennye mashiny i orudiia, pp. 68–69; Trudy Tsentral'nogo Statisticheskogo Upravleniia. Tom 5, vyp.2, pp. 116–17, 120–21; RGAE, f. 478, op. 2, d. 2012, p. 135.

Sorting Machines. Sorting machines represented the height of winnowing, cleaning, and sorting technology all in one piece of equipment. At high speed and with little effort, these machines could segregate chaff, weed seeds, and different sizes of grain seeds to near perfection. Thus they could prevent crop losses from *chrezzernitsa*—a condition in which a few grains in the center of the ear over-developed, killing up to 90% of the other grains. Most farmers traced the absence of grains in the ears to dislodgment from wind, rain, or cold.[391] In fact, however, *chrezzernitsa* stemmed from the sowing of the oversized grains, which passed on the condition to the next crop by heredity.[392] Sorting machines could clean sowing material of these grains.[393]

Unfortunately, with the best models costing up to 200 or more rubles each, sorting machines were far too expensive for farmers to purchase individually.[394] But once agronomists—or, much more rarely, land-lords—convinced peasants of their usefulness, then various coopera-tive organizations in the countryside began to acquire them for collec-tive use. The chart above shows that sorters were becoming a bit less rare in this period. As we shall see later, almost every local agronomist directed peasants' attention to the virtues of sorters.

An Important Crossroads of Technology:
The Spade, the Winnowing Machine, and the Sorter

To the agronomic community of our period the characteristics which set these three winnowing technologies apart from each other con-cerned the preparation of seed grain. For masses of peasants, quite likely a majority, healthy seed grain was a foreign concept, as we have already seen. To their minds these technologies represented nothing more than opportunities to save labor. Regardless of this ignorance on the part of the farmers themselves, it is incumbent on us to analyze the features of the competing winnowing technologies with respect to seed grain, so as to ascertain as best we can exactly what peasants were sowing on their fields.

According to generally accepted standards for good seed grain—rye in this case—in our period, the weight of foreign matter (broken seeds, extraneous seeds, and clods of earth) should not exceed 1% of the sown seeds' weight.[395] Unfortunately, peasants' seed grain almost never ap-proached this standard. Studies in various provinces found 80% clean-liness to be the norm. No province was found with an average purity of seed grain of 90% or more.[396] Measurements in various sectors of Tambov produced similar figures: an average of 20% purity in 1912, occasionally descending to 70%.[397] The actual numbers of weed seeds present in seed grain were spectacular. A study of peasant seed grain in Kazan province on the Volga (to the east of Tambov) found approxi-mately 36,000 weed seeds in every *pud* of sown rye, 56,000 per *pud* of oats, and 80,000 per *pud* of millet.[398] And so the weeds fared about as well as the crops. One specialist in Leningrad province in the 1920s estimated that weeds cost peasants approximately 50% of their harvest every year.[399]

The seriousness of the weed problem invited solution from advanced winnowing technologies. Interestingly enough however, only the sort-ing machines offered significant progress in this respect. Winnowing machines worked fast, but they could not separate larger weed seeds

from grain, and thus were little better than good spade winnowing.[400]
At the same time, much depended on the eyesight, coordination, and
talent of the person using the spade. The shaded portions of the
following chart, from a study in Tver province, testify first to the
insufficiency of winnowing machines (*figures in italics*), and second to
the very unequal ability of peasants to winnow with spades (bold
figures) [Table 1.16]:

Table 1.16. Grain Cleaning Technologies Compared, #1

Tool	Weight of foreign matter, in %	Range of results
Spade	*5.65*	**0.58–19.55**
Winnowing machine	6.18	3.19–11.93
Sorting machine	4.01	2.63– 5.81

Source: M. Arnol'd, "Posevnye semena krest'ianskikh khoziaistv Bezhetskogo uezda,"
p. 192.

The weak performance of the sorting machines in the Tver study
should not be taken too seriously. The survey measured only three
samples of sorted grain. Data from tests at the Moscow Seed Control
Station in 1913 reflect better on the sorters [Table 1.17].

Table 1.17. Grain Cleaning Technologies Compared, #2

Tool	# of weeds found in 2.35 lbs. of rye
Spade	9,588
Winnowing machine	4,285
Sorting machine	155

Source: Bauer, *Ukhod za parom*, pp. 53–54.

In combination with sorting machines' protection against *chrezzernitsa*, such a result against weed seeds makes it easy to understand how
agronomists could promise farmers that merely by employing a sorting
machine they could raise yields by a minimum of 15 *puds* per *desiatina*.[401]

***

The account of peasant labor we have offered in Part I is not meant
to be complete. Elements of agriculture, such as haymaking and
beekeeping, have been omitted, since they were much less important
across most of the black-earth zone than the basic operations of grain
farming. Nor have we treated many aspects of peasant labor, such as

the construction and repair of dwellings, outbuildings, fences, carts, and tools, likewise the milling of grain and the baking of bread. All of these themes helped to define peasant life and labor, but their presentation would not affect our analysis of the agrarian problem.

By focusing on the fundamentals of grain farming, Part I has demonstrated the diversity of agricultural labor. It has exposed this diversity along geographic, sociological, and chronological lines. On the basis of this analysis, we can now proceed to look for diversity in another dimension—in peasant farmers' understanding of technology and attitudes to agricultural work.

Notes

[1] 80 *sazhens* was the standard length of a field. Examples of 60 or 100 *sazhen*-long fields were not rare, however. E. g., *Materialy po podvornomu obsledovaniiu zhivotnovodstva Tambovskoi gubernii v 1912 godu. Kozlovskii uezd*, p. 7.

[2] SSS Borisoglebsk, otdel II, p. 20; Fenomenov, *Sovremennaia derevnia*, vol. 1, pp. 158–59.

[3] See, e.g., S. D., "Po povodu konkursa odnokonnykh plugov," p. 449. This source reports that steel *politsy* could be found, but only for a high price. The *politsa* might also be wooden (e.g., F. Nikonov, "Byt i nravy poselian-velikorussov Pavlovskogo uezda," p. 73).

[4] The norm of eight *sazhens* per *desiatina* with standard models of the *sokha* is widely attested. A couple of reprinted tillage contracts from Tambov stipulate eight and nine furrows per *sazhen* (SSS, Borisoglebsk, Otdel I, p.65; *ibid.*, Kozlov, p. 123. An early nineteenth century Tambov landowner reported a range of 7.5–9 (N. Bunin, "Vedemost' o zemledel'cheskikh rabotakh," p. 388). See also Preobrazhenskii, *Opisanie Tverskoi gubernii*, p. 239; F. Posashev, "Razvedenie probshteiskoi i shampanskoi rzhi," p. 704; and V. Goriachkin, "Sokha," p. 204. The second source mentions work at five furrows per *sazhen*. According to a specialist in Saratov province, on Tambov's southeastern border, eight furrows was the maximum there (S. Kharizomenov, "Lentochnaia obrabotka," p. 8). The best known history of the *sokha* states six or seven to be the norm (Zelenin, *Russkaia sokha*, p. 51).

[5] S.V. Kuznetsov notes such hirings, but does not pin down any particular explanation for them (*Traditsii russkogo zemledel'tsa*, p.63). The most descriptive account of the traumas boys experienced when first attempting to master the *sokha* is Demidov, *Zhizn' Ivana*, pp. 173–175. Other peasants did not experience as much anxiety or difficulty as Demidov (Interviews; Ivan Vol'nov, *Povest'*).

[6] A few examples: F. Posashev, "Sel'skoe khoziaistvo v Eletskom i Dankovskom uezdakh," pp. 5–6; P. Kharchenko, "Obrabotka para—kak ona obychno vedetsia i kak ona dolzhna by vestis'," p. 904; S. D., "Po povodu konkursa odnokonnykh plugov," p. 449.

[7] Of course the amount of land missed depended on the width of the *sokha*'s furrows. The typical width appears to have been only 18–22 cm (Rusov, *Opisanie Chernigovskoi gubernii*, p. 356; Milov, *Velikorusskii pakhar'*, p. 194; and my personal experience in Tambov). Supplementary evidence corroborates this estimate. Thus Kharizomenov noted gaps of 8 to 17 inches between the centers of furrows (*op. cit., loc. cit.*; see also Dmitriev, *Opyt prakticheskikh zamechanii*, chast' 1, p. 30). Provincial committees formed in the late 1850s to discuss the impending emancipation of the serfs left valuable evidence confirming the 18–22 cm width. The landlords specified ten or even twelve furrows per *sazhen* as proper tillage norms,

and sometimes explained that they meant for the entire surface to be worked. Ten or twelve furrows per *sazhen* would indeed be full tillage, given furrows of 18–22 cm in width. The Tambov committee asked for twelve furrows in black-earth soil, and fifteen in the northern part of the province (where *sokhas* must have been narrower). The emancipation committees' statements are collated in A. Skrebitskii, comp., *Krest'ianskoe delo v tsarstvovanii Imperatora Aleksandra II. Materialy dlia istorii osvobozhdeniia krest'ian. Tom III. Gubernskie komitety, ikh deputaty, i redaktsionnye komissii v krest'ianskom dele.*, Bonn 1865–66, pp. 361–362. The full text of the Tambov committee's deliberations appears in Tambovskii gubernskii komitet..., *Proekt polozheniia ob uluchshenii byta pomeshchich'ikh krest'ian*, Prilozhenie 3. The tillage contract from Borisoglebsk *uezd* cited above stipulates "at least eight furrows" with the *sokha*. The source goes on to explain that twelve furrows would be best, but hired peasants cannot be trusted to do even eight in the absence of an overseer. *SSS*, Borisoglebsk, otdel I, pp. 65–66. Sources from Simbirsk, Voronezh, and Kursk describe landowners making similar concessions. They wanted laborers to cut at least nine furrows, but often struggled to get them to do just seven. Rodionov, "Vol'nonaemnyi trud v sele Varko-Veshnaima," p. 176; Beketov, *Voronezhskaia guberniia v sel'skokhoziaistvennom otnoshenii*, p. 61; Chuikov, *Kurskaia guberniia v sel'skokhoziaistvennom otnoshenii*, pp. 75–76.

The historian L. V. Milov portrays tillage practice with the *sokha* very differently, without gaps between furrows (*op. cit.*, pp. 90, 194–195). One of his sources does explicitly support this portrayal (*TVEO*, 1768, ch. VIII, p. 193). This source presumably reflects landlords' instructions to their serfs. The weight of the evidence points to peasants leaving a significant portion of their own land unworked with the *sokha*. One Russian historian, D. V. Naidich, reports the maximum width of *sokha* furrows to be 27 cm ("Pakhotnye i razrykhliaiushchie orudiia," p. 39). He does so without citations, however, leading me to believe that he simply assumed peasants cutting the norm of eight furrows were not leaving any of the surface unworked (27 cm is almost exactly one-eighth of a *sazhen*). On the other hand, at least two source (from Tambov, moreover) describe local *sokhas* being inordinately wide (N. Bunin states they could be up to 36 cm wide, "Vedemost' o zemledel'cheskikh rabotakh," p. 433; Gruzinov gives no figure, "Byt krest'ian Tambovskoi gubernii," p. 6).

The only black-earth zone source I have seen describing *sokha* furrows as narrower than 18–22 cm is *Sbornik statisticheskikh svedenii po Samarskoi gubernii*, p. 90. This source reports furrow widths of 14–18 cm.

In light of discussion to follow in a later section, it should be noted that *dvoenie*—a second tillage of the fallow field—did not necessarily hit the ribbons of land left shallowly tilled or untilled the first time around. The *sokha* tends to return to the pre-existing furrows, where resistance is less. The very limited information available on the placing of *dvoenie* furrows confirms this (see Milov, *Velikorusskii pakhar'*, pp. 79–81).

[8] Of course plows can veer off line as well. They require considerably less skill to keep straight, however.

[9] Cherniaev, "Sostiazanie pakharei," pp. 373–6.

[10] *KSE*, vol. 4, p. 276. About 25% more water is necessary in the drier air of the southeast.

[11] Gorev, *Agronom priekhal*, p.36.

[12] Data available for the two periods 1849–99 and 1912–27 concur on these figures (respectively, Sakharov, *Sel'sko-khoziaistvennye raiony Tambovskoi gubernii*, pp. 7–9;

and Kravchenko, "Piatnadtsat' let izucheniia klimata Tambovskoi gubernii," pp. 16–18). The same sources provide monthly distributions of precipitation. Rainfall was a bit heavier from June to August than in other months.

[13] Selivanov "God Russkogo zemledel'tsa," p. 35; Kliuev, *Chto nado znat' o pochve*, p. 58.

[14] *KSE*, vol. 4, pp. 269–74.

[15] *Ibid.*

[16] See *ibid.*, vol. 4, p. vii, e.g.

[17] *Ibid.*, vol. 4, pp. 269–74.

[18] *Ibid.* Obviously this discussion is simplified. A fuller treatment of depth of tillage would require a lot of space. I have restricted myself to some fundamental considerations.

[19] Sobichevskii, "Vspashka," p.410.

[20] Kotov, *Opyt issledovaniia*, p. 38.

[21] Bruk, *Kak naladit'*, p. 9.

[22] GATO, f. R-956, op. 1, d. 124, p. 11.

[23] Interviews.

[24] *Sokha* tillage was shallower in some areas of Russia. One observer found 1.5 or even 1 *vershok* to be a common depth in those areas of Chernigov province where the *sokha* predominated over other tillage tools (Rusov, *Opisanie Chernigovskoi gubernii*, p.356). 1.5–2 *vershka* appears to have been the standard in mid-nineteenth-century Tver province (Preobrazhenskii, *Opisanie Tverskoi gubernii*, p. 238). Naturally, lazy, shallow work was a chronic problem with hired or serf labor. See, e.g., Selivanov, *God Russkogo zemledel'tsa*, p. 37.

[25] F. Kriukov, "Mel'kom (Vpechatleniia proezzhego)," *RB*, 1914, no. 8, p. 199.

[26] The character Protasov, in G. I. Uspenskii, *Iz razgovorov s priiateliami*, in *Polnoe sobranie sochinenii*, vol. 8, p. 126.

[27] The humous content in the soil rose above 10% in the south of Tambov. It was only about one-fourth of that in the northern quarter of the province (Sakharov, *Sel'sko-khoziaistvennye raiony Tambovskoi gubernii*, p. 8).

[28] All data from *Pervaia vseobshchaia perepis'*, pp. x–xvii, 1–3.

[29] This is said to have struck all first-time visitors to the central black-earth region (V. P. Semenov-Tian-Shanskii, *Rossiia. vol. 2*, p. 110). The most ghoulish account of all is Belokonskii, *Derevenskie vpechatleniia*, pp. 33–34.

[30] Some of the large villages in Tambov and elsewhere in the central black-earth region were as much the product of state policy as geography. They were legacies of the pre-Petrine era, when the Tsars had partially subsidized the formation of semi-militarized peasant outposts. along the state's southern frontier as protection against steppeland marauders. See, e.g., Anonymous, "Doklad (No. 17-i)," pp. 414–415.

[31] All figures from *Sbornik ocherkov*, pp. 16–20.

[32] *Krest'ianskoe dvizhenie 1905–07 gg.*, p. 6.

[33] The precise cost of land rental is unknown. Instead of paying cash peasants often sharecropped, or performed labor services elsewhere on a landowner's estate in return for land rental. Where they paid money for rental, the average price in 1901 (the only year for which the statistics are reasonably thorough) was 13.33 rubles per *desiatina* (*Krest'ianskoe dvizhenie 1905–07 gg.*, p. 6). I have used this figure to estimate the cost of renting 850,000 *desiatinas* (the latter figure coming from *Kom tsentra*, vol. 1, p. 148).

[34] Oganovskii, *Sel'skoe khoziaistvo Rossii*, p. 55; *Podvornoe obsledovanie zhivotnovodstva*, prilozhenie 1. Land prices in Tambov rose in our period—the average price of a

desiatina of land was 95 rubles for the years 1896–1900, up from 48 rubles in 1868–1877 (*Statisticheskie svedeniia po zemel'nomu voprosu v Evropeiskoi Rossii*, p. 69)—so one might be tempted to conclude that farm incomes were rising. Economist Paul Gregory offers this perspective in questioning the thesis of agrarian crisis in late Imperial Russia (*Before Command*, pp. 52–53). It is an uncharacteristic slip. Rising land prices might indicate rising income *per unit of land*, but not *per farm*, unless farm sizes remain static over time. Even then, increasing prices of land can reflect increasing demand for that land, where circumstances persuade farmers to work for decreasing marginal utility. None of this is meant to reject Gregory's broader arguments, but rather to doubt their applicability to the central black-earth region in late Imperial Russia.

[35] Computed from Oganovskii, *Sel'skoe khoziaistvo Rossii*, p. 55; *Podvornoe obsledovanie zhivotnovodstva*, prilozhenie 1 (for allotment land and purchase of non-allotment lands); *Sbornik ocherkov*, pp. 42, 53 (figures for land rental in 1880/84); Part II of Kerans, "Agricultural Evolution" (section estimating non-allotment land rental as of 1912). Having purchased more land, peasants were renting less non-allotment land in 1912 (c. 500,000 *desiatinas*) than in 1901.

[36] Oganovskii, "Tambovskaia guberniia," p. 767.

[37] *Kom tsentra*, vol. 1, pp. 216–217; Pogozhev, *Uchet chislennosti*, Prilozhenie, table 1, pp. 2–11 (as cited in Ryndziunskii, "Gorodskie i vnegorodskie tsentry, p. 115).

[38] Chermenskii, *Ot krepostnogo prava*, p. 56. The same history provides the best figures on pre-war industrial growth (pp. 55–56).

[39] RGAE, f. 478, op. 5, d. 3719, p. 19.

[40] Official statistics (such as those presented in *Kom tsentra*, vol. 1) are not very useful in determining the number of peasants involved in labor on others' farms. Untold quantities of deals went unregistered, many of them, moreover, not even involving exchanges of money.

[41] See, e.g., some interesting discussions in *SSS*, Borisoglebsk, otdel I, pp. 50–77.

[42] According to official statistics for the year 1901, average wages for all necessary work on one *desiatina* of grain were 12.2 rubles in Tambov, versus an average of 15 rubles for all of European Russia (*Kom tsentra*, vol. 1, pp. 230–231).

[43] As widespread as *otkhod* was, at the turn of the century about half of the villages in the province were taking no part in it whatsoever [according to the author of *Krest'ianskoe dvizhenie 1905–07 gg.*, citing *Kratkii ocherk ob otkhozhikh promyslakh*, p. 3].

[44] One prominent example is Kononov, "Zapiska M. A. Kononova," p. 251.

[45] All estimates derived from *Kom tsentra*, vol. 1, pp. 18–19, 24; Oganovskii, *Sel'skoe khoziaistvo Rossii*, pp. 32–33; and Chermenskii, *Ot krepostnogo prava*, p. 60—citing a work by I. V. Chernyshev entitled *Agrarnyi vopros v Rossii*, pp. 142–143). By no means were all of the migrators poor. Indeed, the very poorest peasants had trouble raising enough money to finance their own migration. The most influential study of migration from the central agricultural region identified a wide range of peasants among those heading for Siberia, including very well off families (V. Grigor'ev, *Pereselenie krest'ian Riazanskoi gubernii*, Moscow 1885, as analyzed in Chuprov, *Rechi i Stati*, vol. 1, pp. 362–363). Following Grigor'ev, assessments of the social composition of migrators have varied. Only the most recent work has clarified that the poorest peasants predominated in the migration movement (N. A. Iakimenko, "O sotsial'nom sostave krest'ian-pereselentsev"). Migration statistics do register economic distress, in other words. And we must keep in mind that most of the families

leaving their homeland, even the more prosperous households, were choosing to do so because of dissatisfaction with their living standards.

[46] Iakimenko, *op. cit.*, p. 178.

[47] Computed from average autumn rye and oats prices, central agricultural region versus European Russia (*Svod statisticheskikh svedenii po sel'skomu khoziaistvu Rossii, vyp.III*, pp. 3,10). Regional disparities in grain prices would level out a bit in the last years before the First World War, as the railroad network improved. See Part II of Kerans, "Agricultural Evolution," for a brief treatment of the evidence.

[48] *k otsenke*, Lipetsk, p. 59; Kozlov, p. 46; Lebedian, p. 92; Usman, p. 47; Borisoglebsk, pp. 58–59; Kirsanov, p. 82; Tambov, p. 57; Morshansk, p. 66. Some villages stood over 50 *versts* from their marketing point (Romanov, *Gruntovye dorogi*, p. 64). Meanwhile, the low quality of Russian roads and access paths to bridges and stations was a common lament. The difficulties precluded loading carts fully (e.g., Engel'gardt, *Ocherk krest'ianskogo khoziaistva*, p. 63).

[49] Observations on this score are plentiful in the literature. Useful examples are Sokolovskii, "V odnom iz zakholust'ev," pp. 108–110; and Serezhnikov, "Sel'sko-khoziaistvennyi krizis," p. 6. Another, from Tambov, is Sazonov, *Voprosy khlebnoi promyshlennosti*, p. 260. The standard margin by which merchants underweighed peasant grain with rigged scales was said to be 1/16 in Voronezh *uezd* (on Tambov's southern border), sometimes rising to 1/8 (Astyrev, "Krest'ianskoe khoziaistvo v Voronezhskom uezde," p. 174). Peasants had to pay burdensome fees for space, weights, etc. if they wanted to stand at a marketplace and sell straight to consumers (*TMK. T. 41*, p. 171; Reshetnikov, "Tetushka Oparina," p. 101).

[50] The direct tax burden was actually dropping from the mid-1880s on, when it fell below five million rubles per year (*Sushchestvuiushchii poriadok vzimaniia*, p. 66). Indirect taxes quickly became a huge source of revenue in Tambov. In 1899 the province as a whole contributed 8,703,071 rubles to the state alcohol monopoly, and another 2,392,086 rubles in other indirect taxes (Romanov, "Tambovskaia guberniia", p. 565). As a rough guess, I estimate peasants to have been paying one half of this total. Nationally, the government was collecting four times as much from indirect taxes as from direct taxes in 1903, three times as much in 1913 (Pasvoldsky and Moulton, *Russian Debts and Russian Reconstruction*, p. 53).

Tambov's per capita consumption of *bezvodnogo spirta* (undiluted alcohol), in *vedros*, was 0.23–0.25–0.20 for the 1870s, 1880s, and 1890s, respectively (*Kom tsentra*, vol. 1, p. 42). The drop in the 1890s was noticeable all over the nation. Tambov alcohol consumption figures were below the national average, which was in turn below that of most countries in Europe at the time (for comparative data, see Bideleux, *Communism and Development*, p. 12).

Additionally, we can note here that Russia had no progressive income tax. Of all the countries in Europe, only France, Turkey, and Russia did not have such a tax at the turn of the century (Stakhovich, "Ob obshchei finansovoi politiki," p. 354). The lower classes were pulling more than their weight in the state budget.

[51] Stakhovich, "Ob obshchei finansovoi politiki," p. 347

[52] Taxes extracted from the three areas at this time, in millions of rubles per year: St. Petersburg 342.9, Moscow 112.7, central agricultural region 106.4. Eropkin, "Ob upadke zemledeliia," p. 197.

[53] Analysis of the spread of labor intensive crops appears in Part III.

[54] Statistics concerning land rental are too sparse to allow for precise calculations, but according to my estimates peasant production of rye per capita was 14.1 *puds* in the 1860s, 17.1 in the 1880s, and 18.5 in the 1890s. Were supplementary

consumption crops like millet and potatoes to be included in these calculations, the surplus of production beyond subsistence needs would be still higher. For the derivation of the data, and discussion, see Kerans, "Agricultural Evolution," Part II.

[55] Nationally, peasant food consumption rose by 3.5% per annum from 1885–89 to 1897–1901 (Bideleux, *Communism and Development*, p. 16).

[56] The most common reason for rejection of recruits was short stature. The stature of recruits at the age of induction reflected levels of nutrition and other health conditions in early childhood, up to about age seven (Hoch, "Tall Tales," p.3). Thus the rising percentage of rejected recruits from the period 1874–1883 to the period 1894–1901 implies—but does not prove, certainly—a decline in the biological standard of living between a period in the 1860s to a period in the 1880s. This evidence is not especially strong, however, since it is so incomplete. Data on the height of the recruits who *were* accepted into the army might show the young men of the province to have been getting taller.

[57] Peasants needed horses for hauling, breeding, recreation, and trips to market or administrative centers. They were naturally a primary source of status in the community. Apart from the short comments at the outset of Part I here, see David Kerans "The Workhorse in Late Imperial Russia. An Exploration." Forthcoming.

[58] Computed from *Materialy po podvornomu obsledovaniiu zhivotnovodstva*, vol. 2, prilozhenie.

[59] Burds, *Peasant Dreams and Market Politics*, ch. 6. While Burds connects the rise of the culture of acquisition to the emancipation, the phenomenon must stretch back further, at least among non-serfs (one example is Arkhangel'skii, "Znachenie plugopolol'nykh rastenii," p. 2).

[60] In 1912 12% of village structures in the province had iron roofing, as compared to just 5% in 1877. The average value to which rural structures were insured rose from 40 rubles per family to about 100 in the same years. Zhikharev, "Ocherk razvitiia strakhovaniia," pp. 228–229.

[61] Prices for rye were 60 kopecks per *pud* in the first half of the 1900s, 85 in the second half, and 80 for the years 1911–1914. Corresponding prices for oats were 54, 66, and 71 (Mironov, *Khlebnye tseny v Rossii*, prilozhenie, tables 11 and 14). Despite rising grain prices, the economic conjuncture was not unequivocally favorable towards peasant agriculture. National price indexes demonstrate that grain prices did not improve relative to other commodities [Table 1.8].

[62] Although the zemstvos' medical services in the countryside were much maligned at the time, a recent assessment declares them to have been "remarkable" (Hutchinson, *Politics and Public Health*, pp. 65–66, 72). The zemstvo rural medical network in Tambov grew from 29 points in 1890 to 67 in 1900, and 114 in 1912 (Sadovnikov, "Kratkii ocherk razvitiia," p. 222). Hygiene and disease control must have improved a bit in consequence.

Concerning famine relief, the government delivered 27.6 million rubles worth of grain to Tambov after ten separate harvest failures between 1867–1908. Six of these fell in the period 1901–1908, another three in the 1890s (Kahan, *Russian Economic History*, pp. 111–114). Wider data make clearer the magnitude of famine relief during the difficult period around the turn of the century. The government spent 203 million rubles on famine relief in nine central black-earth and Volga provinces in the years 1893–1902, as against tax revenues of just 407 million (Miliukov [quoting Ministry of Finance official Shvanebakh], *Russia and its Crisis*, p. 444).

[63] *Podvornoe obsledovanie zhivotnovodstva*, prilozhenie 1. Cowlessness was holding steady at 25–26% (*Materialy po podvornomu obsledovaniiu zhivotnovodstva*, pri-

lozhenie, pp. 15–16; *Podvornoe obsledovanie zhivotnovodstva*, Tambov 1914, prilozhenie 1).

[64] Bloch, *French Rural History*, p. 26.

[65] Vasil'ev, *Kak obrabatyvat' parami*, p. 8.

[66] Vakar, *Rezul'taty obsledovaniia tekhniki*, p. 6; Vasil'ev, *Kak obrabatyvat' parami*, pp. 7, 9–10; V. V. Selivanov (writing from neighboring Riazhan province, in the mid-nineteenth century), *God russkogo zemledel'tsa*, p. 39; Rusov, *Opisanie Chernigovskoi gubernii*, p. 360.

[67] Vasil'ev, *Kak obrabatyvat' parami*, p. 8. An earlier criticism along the same lines is Posashev, "Sel'skoe khoziaistvo v Eletskom i Dankovskom uezdakh," pp. 5–6.

[68] See the sayings in Ermolov, *Narodnye primety na urozhai*, p. 127.

[69] A survey of grazing practices found pigs being pastured on crop lands in about half of the villages (*Materialy po raionnomu kachestvennomu obsledovaniiu zhivotnovodstva*, vol. 2, p. 220).

[70] *Ibid.*, p.7, e.g.

[71] Chelintsev, *Opyt izucheniia organizatsii*, p. 369; *Otchety uchastkovykh agronomov za 1914 god*, p.107.

[72] Gudvilovich, "Stoimost' vypasa skota," pp. 324–6.

[73] RGAE, f. 478, op. 5, d. 3719, pp. 124, 138; Trifonov, *Zaniatoi par*, p. 6. Only twice have I come across higher estimates. One estimated 30–50 *puds* per *desiatina* in hay equivalent (KSE, vol. 6, p. 386), another 28–80 *puds* of plants, including all inedible material (Troitskii, "Iz nabliudenii nad kul'turoi ozimykh khlebov," p. 6).

[74] Vasil'ev, *Kak obrabatyvat' parami*, p. 6.

[75] *Kratkii sel'sko-khoziaistvennyi obzor Tambovskoi gubernii za 1912 g.*, p. 4 is one among many sources noting cases of this.

[76] Vasil'ev, *Kak obrabatyvat' parami*, p. 6.

[77] KSE, vol. 4, p. 302.

[78] *Ibid.*, p. 274.

[79] *Ibid.*, pp. 279–80.

[80] *Ibid.*, p. 303. The actual data, from a study in Simbirsk, were 12% and 19%, respectively. But since the experiment did not include animal grazing these data are imprecise for our purposes here.

[81] *Ibid.*, p. 308.

[82] *Ibid.*, pp. 284, 306.

[83] *Ibid.*, pp. 279–80.

[84] See, e.g., *Uchety uchastkovykh agronomov za 1911 god*, p. 10; Zubrilin, *Chem obrabatyvat' zemliu*, p. 13; and Elenev, "1868 god," p. 253.

[85] Vasil'ev, *Kak obrabatyvat' parami*, p. 6; V. Sobichevskii, "Vspashka", pp.409–414; et al. "The size of a hat" expression appears in Dmitriev, *Opyt prakticheskikh zamechanii*, chast' 1, p. 37.

[86] Gudvilovich, "Stoimost' vypasa skota," pp.324–6. To this estimate we should add 50–60 *puds* of straw, plus a modest increase in the yield of the crop which follows rye in the next spring.

[87] Vasil'ev, *Kak obrabatyvat' parami*, p. 5; KSE, vol. 4, p. 294.

[88] Bauer, *Ukhod za parom*, p.9.

[89] KSE, vol. 4, p. 298.

[90] E.g., Milov, *Velikorusskii pakhar'*, p. 62 (citing a late-eighteenth-century source from Tambov); SSS, Borisoglebsk, Otdel 1, p. 54, Otdel 2, pp. 18, 40, Prilozhenie 1, p. 18; Vorob'ev, "Sel'sko-khoziaistvennye kursy," p. 473.

[91] S. F. Tret'iakov "K voprosu ob izmeneniiakh pochvy," pp.168–78.

[92] Data from a variety of experimental stations across European Russia led at least one prominent agronomist in the 1920s to generalize that green fallow was viable in the non-black earth zone (but not elsewhere) (Vorob'ev, *Rol' faktorov urozhaia*, p. 7).

[93] Kliuev, *Chto nado znat' o pochve*, pp. 59–60.

[94] Turn-of-the-century ethnographers studying Russian settlers in Siberia also noticed the tendency to retain agricultural traditions for hundreds of years after transplantation to dissimilar climates had rendered them obsolete or even deleterious. See the review of Aleksei Makarenko's *Sibirskii narodnyi kalendar' v etnograficheskom otnoshenii*, St. Petersburg 1913, written by "Vl. B." *Russkie Vedemosti*, March 12th, 1914, p. 7.

[95] Demidov, *Zhizn' Ivana*, p. 82. Written in 1916–17, this work describes life in Tula province, northwest of Tambov. The boy Van'ka's initiation to tilling with the *sokha* is on pp. 173–175, mowing on pp. 177–179.

[96] The best evidence I have encountered on the division of agricultural labor by gender and age comes from a survey in Riazan province, on Tambov's northwestern border: Persidskii, "Razdelenie truda," pp. 14–25. The survey registered the virtual exclusivity of male work in tilling, harrowing sowing, carting of manure, meadow scything, and crop scything. Crop sickling, in contrast, was almost exclusively female work, as was weeding and sheave tying. These gender divisions blurred only where large numbers of men left the village in summertime to work elsewhere. A number of sources discuss such cases. L'vov offers useful and concise comments on places where women took responsibility for all fieldwork (*Vospominaniia*, pp. 147–149). A literary rendering of a woman undertaking plowing and scything appears in Garin-Mikhailovskii's "Akulina" from the cycle *Derevenskie panoramy*, in his *Sobranie sochinenii*, p. 313. On the other hand, it should be noted that plenty of men worked with the sickle before the days when the scythe became popular for use on field crops (for a source from Tambov see, e.g., Filipchenko, "V zashchitu serpa," p. 356; or Skrebitskii, *Krest'ianskoe delo*, pp. 364–366; and Lavrent'ev, "Ob uborke khleba," p. 893). In some places men were sickling all the way to the end of the Old Regime (*Tseny na rabochie ruki v sel'skom khoziaistve Chernigovskoi gubernii*, p. 6).

[97] These harrows tended to weigh less than 18 pounds (Trostianskii, "Khoziaistvenno-statisticheskoe opisanie," p. 238). Preobrazhenskii (*Opisanie Tverskoi gubernii*, pp. 158–9) contains a valuable discussion of other sorts of peasant harrows, none of which played a meaningful role in Tambov.

[98] Deilidovich, "Ocherk sel'skogo khoziaistva," p. 358.

[99] Dmitriev, *Opyt prakticheskikh zamechanii*, chast' 1, p. 37.

[100] Mertvyi, *Sel'skokhoziaistvennye vospominaniia*, pp. 36, 59; and Osipov, "Kak ia khodil v narod," p. 493.

[101] It was not unknown for peasants with an extra horse and harrow to double the pace of the work by leading two horses with harrows at once. Skrebitskii, p. 358. A footnote on p. 360 explains that two-horse work was not as common as the table on p. 358 implies.

[102] The simple wooden harrow was not in itself an obstacle to cross-furrow work. The first pass could be along the furrows, and then the wooden harrow could cope with the perpendicular direction. Kliuev, *Chto nado znat' o pochve*, p.77. V. E. Postnikov, for one, noted cross-furrow harrowing in south Russia (*Iuzhno-russkoe krest'ianskoe khoziaistvo*, p.223).

[103] Harrowing at a rapid pace is only appropriate when the idea is to break up surface clods while leaving the rest of the soil unworked. Kliuev, *Chto nado znat' o pochve*, p.76.

[104] Interviews; Kliuev, *Chto nado znat' o pochve*, p.73. GATO, f. R-956 op. 1 d. 124 p. 10 comments that a couple of *volosts* did two passes, while making no mention of the number of passes anywhere else.

[105] Kliuev, *Chto nado znat' o pochve*, p. 77.

[106] Interviews.

[107] Deilidovich, "Ocherk sel'skogo khoziaistva," pp. 359–360.

[108] Kliuev, *Chto nado znat' o pochve*, p.72. See also, e.g., Roth, *Agriculture and Peasantry of Eastern Russia*, p. 34. Not every peasant had the skill to put a harrow together properly, noted Selivanov (*God Russkogo zemledel'tsa*, p. 37). The same was true of the *sokha*, as we will see in our comparison of the *sokha* and the plow, below.

[109] Kochetkov, "Sel'sko-khoziaistvennye besedy," p. 7.

[110] N. M., "Besedy o krest'ianskom khoziaistve," p. 464.

[111] N. M. Vasil'ev, *Kak obrabatyvat' parami*, p. 8. Vasil'ev was not alone in noticing peasants' over-harrowing. See for example Morshansk agronomist K. N. Khodnev, who noted "5–10, even 15 passes after the raising of fallow" (as cited in Iu. Eremeeva, "Ustroistvo krest'ianskogo khoziaistva," p. 5). "... the work performed is abominable" despaired another observer of chronic over-harrowing, in Samara province (Roth, *Agriculture and Peasantry of Eastern Russia*, p. 34).

[112] Ermolov even located some sayings (not from the black-earth region) advising farmers to raise dust when harrowing (for buckwheat) (Ermolov, *Narodnye primety na urozhai*, p. 123).

[113] Vasil'ev, *Kak obrabatyvat' parami*, pp. 11–16; see also Bruk, *Kak naladit' krest'ianinu*, e.g.

[114] The single source I have seen testifying to this application of harrows implies that only the most capable farmers did so, and only after weeds came up through the crust (*SSS*, Elatma, pp. 37–38). Of course after the appearance of agronomists peasants might begin harrowing after rains (*Statisticheskii ezhegodnik 1907 g.*, p. 125, e.g.).

At least two more sources note harrowing as standard procedure after rains in one particular situation—subsequent to spring sowings (Selivanov, *God Russkogo zemledel'tsa*, p.36; Baranovich, *Materialy dlia geografii i statistiki Rossii*, p. 181). This harrowing was an integral part of spring sowing methods, rain or no rain (see the discussion of *lomka* below). These two sources do not reflect an advanced understanding of soil structure, therefore, but rather a concern to facilitate the sprouting of the seeds.

[115] Bauer, *Ukhod za parom*, pp. 55–56; L. A. Pel'tsikh, *Trekhpolka ili mnogopol'e?*, pp. 37–38. Even an iron harrow is alright for this job. Landlords in Tambov were becoming aware of the benefits of spring harrowing of rye in the first half of the nineteenth century (see, e.g., a discussion in *Zapiski Lebedianskogo Obshchestva Sel'skogo Khoziaistva za 1850 god*, Moscow 1851, p. 357).

[116] Preobrazhenskii, *Opisanie Tverskoi gubernii*, p. 242. For similar resistance in Tambov, see e.g. *Otchety uchastkovykh agronomov za 1911 god*, p. 5. One peasant in Tambov *uezd* reported marvelous results when he tried harrowing his rye in the spring on the advice of *zemstvo* agronomic aid posters (Sazhin, "Boronovanie ozimykh posevov vesnoiu," pp. 234–236). An agronomist working in Voronezh estimated the typical advantage in yields from this operation to be 10–15% (N. M. Chebalak, *Sbornik statei*, p. 28).

[117] Vasil'ev, *Kak obrabatyvat' parami*, pp. 11–16.

[118] Beketov's review of agriculture in Voronezh province suggests as much. He estimated no more than 5% of the landlords were harrowing at the right times. Beketov, *Voronezhskaia guberniia v sel'skokhoziaistvennom otnoshenii*, p. 54.

[119] Chelintsev, *Opyt izucheniia organizatsii*, pp. 370–71.

[120] *Ibid.*, p. 370.

[121] The first twelve volumes of the series *Sbornik statisticheskikh svedenii po Tambovskoi gubernii* treat the peasant economy, one *uezd* per volume. While one man, N. Romanov, wrote most of the text in these volumes, their coverage is not fully uniform. Four of the volumes specify that peasants observed substantial delays before harrowing raised fallow (Borisoglebsk, Prilozhenie 1, p.27; Lebedian, p.46; Tambov, p.9; Elatma, p.37). Volumes for two other *uezds* mention lesser delays, or even immediate harrowing (Usman, p. 31; Shatsk, p. 45).

   Plenty of sources confirm long delays before harrowing at other times and places in the black-earth zone. For the 1920s in Tambov, for example, see Vakar, *Rezul'taty obsledovaniia tekhniki*, p. 6, or Pel'tsikh, *Trekhpolka ili mnogopol'e?*, pp. 29–31; for pre-war Voronezh, Kotov, *Opyt issledovaniia tekhniki*, p. 368; for Samara province, *Sam sebe agronom*, 1926 no. 44, pp. 1405–6; for Saratov, *Materialy dlia otsenki zemel' Saratovskoi gubernii. Vyp. 5*, p.47. One suspects that delayed harrowing was standard practice in most of the black-earth zone into the 1920s and even beyond.

[122] I. Shleining, in *Sel'sko-khoziaistvennyi listok*, 1912, no. 7, p. 14.

[123] Vakar, *Rezul'taty obsledovaniia tekhniki*, p. 6. A note on this source: while Vakar conducted this study in the mid-1920s, it should be clear that the findings related in this and subsequent citations reflect practices and attitudes of long-standing in the province.

[124] SSS Borisoglebsk, Prilozhenie 1, p.27; Anonymous, "Pyrei", *ES*, vol. 50, pp. 895–896.

[125] Anonymous, "Pyrei", *ES*, vol. 50, pp. 895–896.

[126] An English agriculturist who spent two years in the countryside of Samara province made the same argument: "An attempt is made to exterminate the twitch. During the hot days shortly before sowing, the sokha is sent through the land; an operation which certainly destroys some of the twitch, but which, at the same time, so thoroughly dries the soil that the seed when put in will lie for weeks without germinating." Roth, *Agriculture and Peasantry of Eastern Russia*, p. 36.

[127] *Zhurnaly soveshchaniia zemskikh agronomov ... 30–31 avgusta i 1–2 sentiabria 1911 goda*, p. 85.

[128] This is my own rough estimate. I know of no studies on the issue. It is not clear how many landowners delayed harrowing. Some tillage contracts from 1880 confirm that landowners also subscribed to delays (SSS, Borisoglebsk, Otdel 1, p.65). But attitudes may have changed by 1914.

[129] Kotov, *Opyt issledovaniia tekhniki*, p. 36.

[130] For grazing after the raising of fallow, see, e.g., *Zhurnaly soveshchaniia zemskikh agronomov* (August–September 1911), p. 85; and Vakar, *Rezul'taty obsledovaniia tekhniki*, p. 6.

[131] Kotov, *Opyt issledovaniia tekhniki*, p.35. More than 90% of Voronezh uezd farms were tilling and harrowing fallow only once before sowing.

[132] *k otsenke*, Lebedian, pp. 65–6; Borisoglebsk, p. 43; Usman, p. 36; Lipetsk, pp. 45–51.

[133] GATO, f. R-956, op. 1, d. 124, pp. 10–11; Vakar, *Resul'taty obsledovaniia tekhniki*, pp. 6–7.

134 Kotov, *Opyt issledovaniia tekhniki*, pp.40–41. At one point the text erroneously reads 81.1 in place of 82.1.

135 The Tambov agricultural experimental stations never did any work on *dvoenie*, since the practice was so well established by the time these institutions began to function.

136 Vakar, *Resul'taty obsledovaniia tekhniki*, p. 7.

137 Kotov, *Opyt issledovaniia tekhniki*, p. 36. Kuznetsov has found *dvoenie* to have been deeper than the raising of fallow in provinces to the north of Tambov (*Traditsii russkogo zemledel'tsa*, p. 60).

138 Some agronomists recommended waiting at least two weeks after tillage to sow (Bauer, *Ukhod za parom polem*, p. 40; and I. E. Lapovok, in *Sam sebe agronom*, 1926, no. 20, pp. 616–17), while Vasil'ev insisted on three or four weeks (*Kak ukhazyvat' za parami*, pp. 11–16).

139 See *k otsenke*, Kozlov, p.36 for landlords doing *dvoenie*. *k otsenke*, Lebedian, p. 65, shows 93.5% of estates doing *dvoenie* there.

140 Quite a few sources explicitly connect *dvoenie* to the clearing of weeds—not to the maintenance of a healthy soil structure *per se*. The best exposition can be found in SSS, Temnikov, p. 74. See also: *ibid.*, Kirsanov, pp. 47–48; Roth, *Agriculture and Peasantry of Eastern Russia*, p. 25. A source connecting *dvoenie* to the weed growth following manuring is *k otsenke*, Temnikov, pp. 80, 86. Judging from Kuznetsov's work, *dvoenie* originated in northern Russia as a method of drying out dense subsoils that lay close to the surface of sandy topsoil (*Traditsii russkogo zemledeliia*, pp. 57–58).

141 Kotov, *Opyt issledovaniia tekhniki*, p. 36.

142 The Russian historian Milov asserts that peasants undertook *dvoenie* after noticing crops growing better near the ends of strips, where tools turned around and so worked the soil more thoroughly (Milov, *Velikorusskii pakhar'*, p. 97). Indeed, this might have prompted some peasants to till and harrow more often. But there is no direct evidence of this connection. Be it noted here that Milov does not use the term *dvoenie* in the standard nineteenth- and twentieth-century way. He uses it to describe a second tillage of a field, even if that tillage is done at the time of sowing.

143 Indeed, a *zemstvo* study in Saratov province registered places where peasants actually abandoned *dvoenie* after the land became softer, presuming that the land no longer needed *dvoenie* (*Materialy dlia otsenki zemel' Saratovskoi gubernii. Vyp. 5*, p. 46).

144 So found Kotov in Voronezh, at any rate (*Opyt issledovaniia tekhniki*, p. 36). Soviet Commissariat of Agriculture correspondents in Tambov and nearby areas reported yield increases of 25–35% thanks to *ziab* in 1925/26 (RGAE, f. 478, op. 5, d. 3719, pp. 139–140).

145 *k otsenke*, Borisoglebsk p. 43; Lebedian, p. 65–66.

146 Ibid, Lipetsk pp.45–51. The breakdown of 135 communes was as follows: 53 were doing *dvoenie*, 38 were not, 44 had many *dvors* who were doing it. *Ibid.*, Kozlov, p. 37 shows 78 communes not doing it, 68 doing it, 29 straddling.

147 Ibid., Kirsanov, p. 61.

148 Chelintsev, *Opyt izucheniia organizatsii*, p. 368.

149 *k otsenke*, Kozlov, p. 37.

150 Naturally they would try to till about as deeply as they could in this case—usually about 2–2.5 *vershki*. Harrowing would sometimes be intensive as well—three instead of the usual two passes (Kotov, *Opyt issledovaniia tekhniki*, p. 42). The general practice with oats included a supplementary tilling and harrowing a few

days later, after the sprouts had come up (ibid, p. 41). This technique, known as *lomanie*, or *lomka*, will be discussed together with methods of sowing.

151 Vakar, *Rezul'taty obsledovaniia tekhniki*, pp. 9–10.

152 Kotov, *Opyt issledovaniia tekhniki*, p. 41. A note on this source: located just to the south of Tambov, the growth of population density in Voronezh lagged behind the southern *uezds* of Tambov throughout our period. Thus conditions in Voronezh in 1914 corresponded closely to those in southern Tambov a generation or so earlier.

153 *K otsenke*, Lebedian, p. 66; Kirsanov, pp. 61, 67–8. Many communes in Morshansk were also doing this (*k otsenke*, Morshansk, p. 47). In Borisoglebsk land appraisers found a transitional technique, wherein the stubble was harrowed once in spring prior to sowing. *k otsenke*, Borisoglebsk, p. 43.

154 *Ibid.*, Kozlov, pp. 37–8.

155 Chelintsev, *Opyt izucheniia organizatsii*, pp. 372–3.

156 Pel'tsikh, *Trekhpolka ili mnogopol'e?*, pp. 19–20; KSE, vol. 4, pp. 326–28. The increase was 25–35% in 1925 (Kostrov and Tarasov, *Ocherki po tekhnike sel'skogo khoziaistva*, p. 7).

157 In the meantime the unharrowed furrows would collect much of the spring run-off (Garin-Mikhailovskii, "Neskol'ko let v derevne," in *Sobranie sochinenii*, vol. 3, p. 28). If the winter snow cover was particularly heavy it could pack the soil down so much that tillage would have to be repeated in the spring (Kliuev, *Chto nado znat' o pochve*, p. 90).

158 *Ziab* allowed farmers to sow as much as two weeks earlier (Dmitriev, *Opyt prakticheskikh zamechanii*, chast' 1, p. 32). The historian Milov maintains that peasants adopted *ziab* as a measure to uproot weeds (Milov, *Velikorusskii pakhar'*, p. 65). He does not provide any evidence, however.

159 Kotov, *Opyt issledovaniia tekhniki*, p. 44. Unfortunately Kotov presents contradictory data, so I cannot be any more precise.

160 Sources occasionally document grazing requirements obstructing the implementation of *ziab* (for example, Engel'gardt, *Ocherk krest'ianskogo khoziaistva*, p. 56).

161 Ibid, pp.44–45; *k otsenke*, Lebedian, p.75. I have seen no evidence of *ziab* among peasants in Tambov before 1880, but some probably practiced it, judging from evidence from neighboring provinces. Thus, according to a manuscript dating from the 1840s, *ziab* was quite common then in Balashov *uezd* (Saratov province), on the southeastern border of Tambov [as discussed in *Materialy dlia otsenki zemel' Saratovskoi gubernii. Vyp. 5*, p. 56]. Some peasants in Penza *uezd* were doing *ziab* in mid-century as well (A. Gorizontov, "Khoziaistvenno-statisticheskoe opisanie Penzenskogo uezda," no. 3, p. 219). We know that a minority of landlords in Tambov was trying *ziab* before emancipation, even in the eighteenth century (M. S. Kishkin, "O zemledelii," pp. 20–21; and Milov—citing an account from Voronezh in the 1760s—*Velikorusskii pakhar'*, p. 64).

162 *K otsenke*, Kozlov, p.37.

163 Chelintsev, *Opyt izucheniia organizatsii*, pp. 372–3.

164 Kotov, *Opyt issledovaniia tekhniki*, pp. 42–44; Chelintsev, *Opyt izucheniia organizatsii*, pp. 373–4. In the *k otsenke* volumes there are no data directly devoted to this question, and so it is difficult to determine whether or not anyone was still sowing on the stubble. It is clear that at least 75% in Kirsanov and Lebedian *uezds* were *not* (Kirsanov, p. 61, Lebedian p. 65).

165 Kotov, *Opyt issledovaniia tekhniki*, pp. 42–44; Chelintsev, *Opyt iszucheniia organizatsii*, pp. 373–4.

[166] Kotov, *Opyt issledovaniia tekhniki*, p. 44; Pel'tsikh, *Trekhpolka ili mnogopol'e?*, pp. 19–20.

[167] Kotov, *Opyt issledovaniia tekhniki*, pp. 42–44; *k otsenke* Kozlov, p. 38; Chelintsev, *Opyt izucheniia organizatsii*, pp. 373–4.

[168] An important summary report from a neighboring province adamantly credits landowners for stimulating peasants' awareness of *ziab* (*Peremeny v zemledel'cheskoi tekhnike*, p. 34).

[169] Chelintsev, *Opyt izucheniia organizatsii*, p. 369.

[170] *Ibid.*, p. 371.

[171] Vakar makes this point (*Rezul'taty obsledovaniia tekhniki*, p. 7). The rye harvest tended to begin already in the first or second week of July in the south, but only from about July 20th in the north.

[172] The 1914 budget study found this occasionally, as did Kotov (Chelintsev, *Opyt izucheniia organizatsii*, p. 371; Kotov, *Opyt issledovaniia tekhniki*, pp. 36–7). A chart in *k otsenke*, Lebedian, p. 65, gives a similar impression. On the other hand, *dvoenie* without a subsequent harrowing was said to be standard among peasants in neighboring Saratov province (Kharizomenov, Lentochnaia obrabotka polia," p. 8).

[173] *k otsenke*, Borisoglebsk, p. 43. Rusov notes an area of Chernigov province where peasants were generally convinced that harrowing was no longer necessary if the field was tilled twice over the summer! (*Opisanie Chernigovskoi gubernii*, p. 360.)

[174] Chelintsev, *Opyt izucheniia organizatsii*, p.373; KSE, vol. 4, pp. 325–8. See also *Sam sebe agronom*, 1926, pp. 997–999. Note that the advantages of early *ziab* dissipate in the drier areas to the southeast of Tambov. KSE, vol. 4, pp. 329–34. Exactly here, curiously, one source establishes some cases of early *ziab* (*Materialy dlia otsenki zemel' Saratovskoi gubernii. Vyp. 5*, p. 61).

[175] During our period Russian experimental stations were working out a possible solution to the labor calendar obstacles, which precluded early *ziab*. This technique, known in Russian as *lushchenie*, was a light tillage done just after carting home the harvest. There is no evidence of peasants trying it.

[176] *Peremeny v zemledel'cheskoi tekhnike*, p. 26.

[177] Vakar, *Rezul'taty obsledovaniia tekhniki*, pp. 9–12. Likewise, researchers in Shatsk *uezd* in the 1880s noted peasants tilling *ziab* for millet, but not for oats (SSS, Shatsk, p. 47). Kotov found some cases of this in Voronezh as well (*Opyt issledovaiia tekhniki*, p. 45). For peasants failing to harrow *ziab*-tilled millet land in the spring, and thereby allowing the soil to harden, see RGAE, f. 478, op. 5, d. 3494, p. 40.

[178] *Sam sebe agronom* 1926, no. 11, pp. 329–332.

[179] Pel'tsikh, *Trekhpolka ili mnogopol'e?*, pp. 35–6; Kotov, *op. cit.*, pp. 44–45; *k otsenke*, Lebedian, p. 75; Chelintsev, *Opyt izucheniia organizatsii*, pp. 372–4.

[180] Vasil'ev, *Kak obrabatyvat' parami*, pp. 11–16; Bruk, *Kak naladit' krest'ianinu*, p.10.

[181] *Proekty*, p. 504; and, from Simbirsk province, Berezovskii, "Zapiska," pp. 251–252. Bunin characterized peasants as performing *dvoenie* by rote in a poignant passage in his well-known work *Derevnia* (Bunin, *Sobranie sochinenii*, vol. 3, Moscow 1994, p. 102).

[182] *Sam sebe agronom*, 1926, no. 20, pp. 616–7. Although the Shatilov station confirmed this in the 1920s, some if not most Russian agronomists had presumed it before the turn of the century. See, e.g., Sobichevskii, "Vspashka," pp. 409–414.

[183] A *sokha* cost about 1.25–4 rubles at the turn of the century. Plow prices were two to three times as high. See, e.g., Vorontsov, *Progressivnye techeniia*, p. 244; or *1913 god v sel'sko-khoziaistvennom otnoshenii*, vyp. 6, St.Petersburg 1914, p. 255. First-

class European equipment could range up to 25 rubles (Vasil'ev, *Kak ukhazyvat' za parami*, p. 1). Plow prices had been higher in the 1880s, 8–9 rubles minimum (Zubrilin, *Chem obrabatyvat' zemliu*, p. 12). Then they came down as supply increased.

[184] Regarding the capabilities of local blacksmiths, see the discussion of new tools in Part V.

[185] Trostianskii, "Khoziaistvenno-statisticheskoe opisanie," p. 228.

[186] This observation on the relationship of the *sokha* to manure from agronomists Sabo and Zubrilin (GATO, f. 51, op. 1, d. 168, p. 51; Zubrilin, *Chem obrabatyvat' zemliu*, p. 10].

[187] This point has been made many times (e.g., Zubrilin, *Chem obrabatyvat' zemliu*, p. 11). However, many authors have exaggerated the physical demands of using the *sokha* (for example, Zelenin, *Russkaia sokha*, pp. 35–37, 124; and Milov, *Velikorusskii pakhar'*, pp. 79, 194, citing sources). I found the tool tiring, but not frightfully so. A decisive confirmation of my perception, from a contemporary, is S. D., "Po povodu konkursa odnokonnykh plugov," p. 449.

[188] Kharchenko, P., "Obrabotka para—kak ona obychno vedetsia i kak ona dolzhna vestis'," p. 904. This is from Elets *uezd*, on Tambov's western border.

[189] Adaptations could strengthen the *sokha* for deeper work. Sources attesting such adaptations in the central black-earth region include SSS, Borisoglebsk, Prilozhenie 1, p. 27; Posashev, "Ob obrabotke zemli sokhoi i plugom," p. 91; and Zelenin, *Russkaia sokha*, pp. 45–47. Strengthened *sokhas* were becoming the norm in Saratov by the early 1900s (*Materialy dlia otsenki zemel' Saratovskoi gubernii. Vyp. 4*, pp.1–2). Fedor Lokhin recalls tilling with such a *sokha* in the 1920s.

[190] Miklashevskii, "Soznatel'nyi vybor krest'ianskogo pluga," p. 6.

[191] Zubrilin, *Chem obrabatyvat' zemliu*, p. 11.

[192] On this, see, e.g., Miklashevskii, "Soznatel'nyi vybor krest'ianskogo pluga," pp. 7–8. Because of the weakness of commercial networks in Russia, one-horse plows were not available everywhere. Where they were, peasant horses might have trouble pulling them (see, e.g., Maslov, *Plugi i drugie uluchshennye orudiia*, p. 22). In many places peasants had no inkling of the existence of one-horse plows [judging from, e.g., *Materialy dlia otsenki zemel' Saratovskoi gubernii. Vyp. 5*, pp. 22, 26–27].

[193] Novikov, "O nekotorykh zakonomernostiakh," p. 464.

[194] Deilidovich, "Ocherk sel'skogo khoziaistva," p. 357.

[195] Kliuev, *Chto nado znat' o pochve*, p. 62; Vasil'ev, *Kak obrabatyvat' parami*, pp. 11–16.

[196] Vorontsov, *Progressivnye techeniia*, p. 66

[197] Zubrilin, *Chem obrabatyvat' zemliu*, pp. 11–12.

[198] Vorontsov, *Progressivnye techeniia*, pp. 51–2.

[199] Zubrilin, *Chem obrabatyvat' zemliu*, p. 13.

[200] Vorontsov, *Progressivnye techeniia*, p. 51.

[201] This is a peasant's account, recounted in Zubrilin, *Chem obrabatyvat' zemliu*, p. 13.

[202] *k otsenke*, Lebedian, pp. 63–64; Lipetsk, pp. 45–51.

[203] *k otsenke*, Usman, p. 35; Kirsanov, pp. 59–60.

[204] Chelintsev, *Opyt izucheniia organizatsii*, p. 205. Data from Saratov province established a powerful correlation between households holding three or more draft animals and the replacement of *sokhas* with plows (*Materialy dlia otsenki zemel' Saratovskoi gubernii. Vyp. V*, pp. 26–27).

[205] *Zhurnaly soveshchaniia zemskikh agronomov ... 30–31 avgusta i 1–2 sentiabria 1911 goda*, p. 84.

[206] Beketov is adamant about this (*Voronezhskaia guberniia v sel'skokhoziaistvennom otnoshenii*, p. 36).

[207] According to A. S. Ermolov, who knew a great deal about farming conditions all over Russia, plows could be used on couch grass, provided only that *dvoenie* was done with the *sokha*. See his footnote in Sovetov, *O chernozemnoi polose*, p. 22; and likewise Cherniaev, "Sel'sko-khoziaistvennye mashiny," p. 544.

[208] One source explicitly citing this opinion from peasants is SSS, Borisoglebsk, Prilozhenie 1, p. 27. I have quoted another such source at length below.

[209] Vakar, *Rezul'taty obsledovaniia tekhniki*, p. 6.

[210] *Zhurnaly* ... (August–September 1911), p. 84.

[211] In the central *uezds* 61.5% used the plow before oats, which clearly meant *ziab*, with few exceptions. But only 40.5% plowed fallow. In the south the corresponding figures were 42.1% and 20% (Chelintsev, *Opyt izucheniia organizatsii*, pp. 369, 373). Plows went unused on fallow land on many gentry estates too (e.g. *k otsenke*, Tambov p.41, Kirsanov pp. 59–60).

[212] Interviews.

[213] Abramenkov interview. A general rule holds that doubling the depth of tillage quadruples the draft requirement, other conditions being equal.

[214] *k otsenke*, Lebedian, pp. 72–3.

[215] *k otsenke*, Lebedian, pp. 72–3; Miklashevskii, "Soznatel'nyi vybor krest'ianskogo pluga," p. 6. It will be recalled that this is the same number of furrows per *sazhen* as was customary with the *sokha*.

[216] See, e.g., Miklashevskii, "Soznatel'nyi vybor krest'ianskogo pluga," pp. 5–6.

[217] Zubrilin, *Chem obrabatyvat' zemliu*, pp. 15–21. Liphardt was a Moscow-based firm, but I have not uncovered its origin or ownership (N. P. Semenov Tian-Shanskii *Rossiia*, vol. 2, p. 289). Other manufacturers having some success selling plows in Tambov included Votkin Factory, Riazan Association, Prince Vasil'chikov's private factory (all three Russian), and Ransome (from England) (*Sel'skokhoziaistvennye statisticheskie svedeniia po materialam, poluchennym ot khoziaev. Vyp. XI*, p. 43). On the eve of the war a Ministry of Agriculture publication insisted that the quality of Russian-made plows was improving each year, but admitted the Sack plow's superiority (Artsybashev, "Semidesiatiletie russkogo sel'sko-khoziaistvennaia mashinostroeniia," pp. 23–24).

[218] See V. Miklashevskii, "Soznatel'nyi vybor krest'ianskogo pluga," pp. 7–8; Vasil'ev, *Kak obrabatyvat' parami*, p. 1; and Zubrilin, *Chem obrabatyvat' zemliu*, pp. 22–3. Glowing reports on the Sack plow from all over Russia appear in *Selskokhoziaistvennye statisticheskie svedeniia po materialam, poluchennym ot khoziaev. Vyp. 11*, pp. 57–58 (the reports from Tambov appear in chast' 2, p. 44). The same source also registers great praise for Ransome plows.

[219] Lokhin interview. This testimony stands in sharp contrast to peasants' complaints about earth sticking to the shares and moldboards of other manufacturers' plows (see, e.g., Maslov, *Plugi i drugie uluchshennye orudiia*, p. 24).

[220] *Otchety uchastkovykh agronomov za 1914 god*, p. 170; Vasiliev, *Kak obrabatyvat' parami*, p. 1; Zubrilin, *Chem obrabatyvat' zemliu*, pp. 22–3.

[221] Miklashevskii, "Soznatel'nyi vybor krest'ianskogo pluga," pp. 7–8; Lokhin interview.

[222] I located them in Umet *raion*, Tambov *oblast'*, summer 1993.

[223] Kuprianov, "O vliianii tipa pluga," p. 66.

[224] *Trudy 8-ogo soveshchaniia zemskikh agronomov Tambovskoi gubernii*, pp. 10, 66.

[225] See, e.g., Kuprianov, "O vliianii tipa pluga," pp. 65–8, 8–12; Miklashevskii, "Soznatel'nyi vybor krest'ianskogo pluga," pp. 1–8.

[226] *Trudy 8-ogo soveshchaniia zemskikh agronomov Tambovskoi gubernii*, pp. 8–9.

[227] Kuprianov, "O vliianii tipa pluga," p. 66.

[228] Miklashevskii, "Soznatel'nyi vybor krest'ianskogo pluga," pp. 1–8; *Trudy 8-ogo soveshchaniia zemskikh agronomov Tambovskoi gubernii*, pp. 8–12, 65–8. 90% of the plows that Kotov found in Voronezh *uezd* in 1914 were two-shared (*Opyt issledovaniia tekhniki*, pp. 35, 37); Mozzhukhin found about the same ratio in the black-earth corner of Tula province (Mozzhukhin, *Zemleustroistvo v Bogoroditskom uezde*, pp. 219, 222).

[229] These inventories often included imitations of popular models or original designs produced by small firms in the region (see, e.g., *Sel'skokhoziaistvennye statisticheskie svedeniie po materialam, poluchennym ot khoziaev. Vyp. 11*, pp. 43, 48).

[230] Biriukovich, *Sel'sko-khoziaistvennaia tekhnika*, p. 165; Zubrilin, *Chem obrabatyvat' zemliu*, p. 4.

[231] As recommended in, e.g., Dmitriev, *Opyt prakticheskikh zamechanii*, chast' 1, p. 39. While at least one, eighteenth-century source presents this method of sowing as typical (as cited in Milov, *Velikorusskii pakhar'*, p. 133), later sources almost never mention it.

[232] One estate manager complained he could not find any peasants capable of casting grass seeds evenly at all (Posashev, "Sel'skoe khoziaistvo v Eletskom i Dankovskom uezdakh," pp. 13, 23). See also P. Morozov, "Otchet po selu Pantsyrevke," p. 140. L'vov recalls how all the most skilled sowers were hired for grass sowing on his family's estate (*Vospominaniia*, pp. 176–178). His account of grass sowing is by far the most detailed I have encountered.

[233] A.S., "Sev i seialki," *ES*, vol. 63, p. 324; Evans, *Ask the Fellows Who Cut the Hay*, p.88. Two handed sowing is attested in one source from Tambov (*SSS*, Shatsk, p. 52). According to a couple of sayings from A. S. Ermolov's collection (*Narodnaia sel'sko-khoziaistvennaia mudrost'*, vol. 2, pp. 251–6, 275–6), peasants tried to sow rye and oats at a faster pace than other crops. This makes sense, given the shorter period of time in which conditions for the sowing of these crops are ideal.

[234] Dmitriev, *Opyt prakticheskikh zamechanii*, chast' 1, p. 39.

[235] Final interview in Nosiny, Shatsk *uezd*. For further confirmation of sowers' carefulness not to spray their seeds onto neighbors' lands, see, e.g., Grabovskii, *Kak pereiti na shirokie polosy*, p. 4.

[236] Anonymous, "Zapiska o vozdelyvanii," p. 45; Deilidovich, "Ocherk sel'skogo khoziaistva," p. 363; A.S., "Sev i seialki," p. 325.

[237] For testimony that peasants ordinarily did this, see e.g. *TMK*, Podol'sk, p. 925.

[238] Ermolov, *Narodnaia sel'sko-khoziaistvennaia mudrost'*, Vol. 2, pp. 251, 269.

[239] See also A.S., "Sev i seialki," p. 323.

[240] Ermolov, *Narodnaia sel'sko-khoziaistvennaia mudrost'*, Vol. 2, pp. 268–9, 277.

[241] *KSE*, vol. 5, pp. 475–482.

[242] *KSE*, vol. 5, pp. 475–482; and A. S., "Sev i seialki," p. 323.

[243] Ermolov, *Narodnaia sel'sko-khoziaistvennaia mudrost'*, Vol. 2, pp. 251–6. *SSS*, Borisoglebsk, otdel I, p.68, laments that this saying was alive and well in the area.

[244] See Vakar, *Rezul'taty obsledovaniia tekhniki*, p. 9; *Proekty*, p. 459, e.g. Interestingly, critics from provinces to the west and northwest of Tambov complained that peasants there sowed oats too late (Brzheskii, *Ocherki agrarnogo byta krest'ian*, p. 49).

245 Posashev, "Sel'skoe khoziaistvo v Eletskom i Dankovskom uezdakh," p. 8; Pel'tsikh, *Trekhpolka ili mnogopol'e?*, Tambov n.d., pp. 28–29. Pel'tsikh ran the province's agricultural experimental station in the 1920s.

246 This failing summoned a flood of complaints from agronomists. See, e.g., *Proekty*, pp. 375–76; *Otchety uchastkovykh agronomov za 1914*, pp. 105–06; *Otchety uchastkovykh agronomov za 1911 god*, pp. 82, 128; RGAE, f. 478, op. 5, d. 3494, p. 40.

247 RGAE, f. 478, op. 5, d. 3494, p. 40, e.g.

248 Koshelev, "Ob urochnykh rabotakh," pp. 114–115.

249 *k otsenke*, Lebedian, p. 231.

250 On the other hand, sources do record instances where the entire village completed rye sowings in just a few days following a heavy rain (e.g., *Otchet ob agronomicheskoi deiatel'nosti*, p. 80; and *Otchet o deiatel'nosti agronomicheskogo personala za 1912 sel'sko-khoziaistvennyi god*, p. 87). Conversely, in drought conditions peasants might wait as long as until the end of October for a rain heavy enough to warrant sowing (*Otchet ob agronomicheskoi deiatel'nosti*, p. 2).

251 Lokhin interview #2. Some printed sources also mention three periods of rye sowing (e.g., the prolific agricultural specialist of the eighteenth century, A. T. Bolotov, as cited in Milov, *Velikorusskii pakhar'*, p. 119). Presumably some characteristic of the land or the seeds governed the division. According to an anonymous mid-nineteenth-century commentator relief was the issue—they would sow the highest lands first, the low-lying areas last ("Zapiska o vozdelyvanii i sbyte khlebov," p. 43). Dmitriev reports sowing lands in ascending order of quality, which differs little from relief, in practice (*op. cit.*, p. 38).

252 Peasant Kozyrev, cited in Brzheskii, *op. cit.*, p.53. Ribbon-like distribution of seeds was inevitable where peasants declined to do harrowing after *dvoenie*. Most of the seeds would fall into the *sokha*'s furrows. Kharizomenov, *op. cit.*, *loc. cit.*; Dmitriev, *op. cit.*, p. 30.

253 Ia. Rudnev, "O sistemakh zemledeliia v zaorenburgskom krae," pp. 268–269.

254 Kishkin, *op. cit.*, p. 23. On the other hand, the most skilled peasants were said to be able to spread seeds as accurately as broadcast sowing machines, or even more so (Terpigorev, *Oskudenie*, in *Sobranie sochinenii*, p. 70; L'vov, *Vospominaniia*, p. 62). Interviews confirm that families ordinarily had a designated sower.

255 Preobrazhenskii, *op. cit.*, pp. 212–213.

256 A. S., *op. cit.*, p. 324; A. A. Zubrilin, *Chem obrabotyvat' zemliu*, pp. 25–27. Garin-Mikhailovskii estimated that in some villages increased sowing densities prompted by tardy sowing cost peasants more than state taxation ("Neskol'ko let v derevne," *op. cit.*, pp. 28–29).

257 *KSE*, vol. 5, p. 482.

258 On the other hand, *zemstvo* statisticians usually managed to find one or more peasants in each village who would report how densely they sowed crops per *desiatina*, usually in volume measurements (one *chetvert'* of rye per *desiatina*, for example) (*Proekt obshchikh osnovanii*, p. 19). Moreover, I am told that some survivors can still recount sowing norms for the principal crops of their family farms, in *puds* per *desiatina*. Whether these were village norms or merely family norms I cannot say. When statisticians and agronomists reported sowing norms they invariably gave a figure meant to be taken as an average for the given locality. But it does not necessarily follow from this that the *village* had any established sowing norms. Surely the statisticians gathered this information either in conversation with the farmers, or by measuring seeds in a few farmers' *lukoshka* as sowing

commenced. Most farmers probably kept count of the number of "bags" of each grain they sowed in each year (see e.g., *Peremeny v zemledel'cheskoi tekhnike*, p. 8). Then by recalling which strips of land they sowed with a particular crop they could give a rough estimate of how many *puds* they sowed per *desiatina*. Meanwhile, a peasant diarist from Vologda province does appear to have reckoned his expenditures of seed grain in *puds* per strip (*Dnevnik Totemskogo krest'ianina A. A. Zamaraeva*, pp. 64, 167). At any rate, there is no clear answer as to the influence of the village on sowing norms.

[259] Milovskii, "O poseve khlebov", p. 4. Milovskii appears to have landlords as well as peasants in mind here.

[260] *Sel'sko-khoziaistvennye statisticheskie svedeniia po materialam, poluchennym ot khoziaev. Vyp. 8*, pp. 3–4. An eighteenth-century lament on the same tendency is Olishev, "Opisanie godovoi krest'ianskoi raboty," pp. 121–122. A predictable extension of the tendency to sow more densely on better lands was the habit of sowing the best quality seeds on the best lands. I have only seen this in one source, I concede: Potekhin, "Krest'ianskie deti," p. 285.

[261] Zubrilin, *op. cit.*, pp. 25–26.

[262] *Ibid.*

[263] A. S., *op. cit.*, p. 324. Lodged grain can take two to three times longer to reap with manual tools than unlodged grain (Koshelev, "Ob urochnykh rabotakh," pp. 115–116).

For the sake of simplicity the discussion in this section has not covered all of the nuances involved in determining the appropriate density of sowings. Some observers, for instance, recorded inefficiencies in the sowing of important crops like flax and potatoes. Peasants were said not to perceive the advantages of adjusting the density of flax sowings when intending to sell the seeds for oil processing instead of using the plant for fiber (A. Gorizontov, "Khoziaistvenno-statisticheskoe opisanie Penzenskogo uezda," no. 3, p. 223). Likewise they were not necessarily aware of the option to cut potatoes in half before planting (e.g., V. Korostovetz, *Seed and Harvest*, pp. 86–87).

[264] For samples of statistics, see G. Ermolenko, "O semenakh i podgotovke ikh k posevu," p. 294; and Bubrin, "Posevnoi material," pp. 682–683. In the most striking result, seeds just 20–25% bigger than small seeds gave thrice the yield (Koval'kovskii, *Znachenie sortirovki i ochistki*, pp. 6–7). The advantage of big seeds over medium-sized seeds was not nearly so large (Bubrin, *op. cit.*, p. 683).

[265] *KSE*, vol. 5, pp. 466–73.

[266] See, e.g., Naidich "Orudiia i sposoby molotby i veianiia," pp. 94–5. Naidich cites only one source testifying to peasants' segregation of the largest grains for sowing, Preobrazhenskii's mid-19th-century account of agriculture in Tver province. Many more could be found, however. One from Tambov is Trostianskii, "Khoziaistvenno-statisticheskoe opisanie," pp. 237–238. From Kaluga (anonymous), "Prodolzhenie opytnykh zamechaniia," pp. 51–52. Or, citing an eighteenth-century source from Tver, Milov, *op. cit.*, p. 148.

[267] Ermolov, *op. cit.*, vol. 2, pp. 241–243.

[268] GATO, f. 51, op. 1, d. 235, p. 150. This report came from Griazi sector. Agronomists in Kozlov *uezd* seconded this opinion, "Doklad Upravy ob agronomicheskoi pomoshchi," p. 550.

[269] Ermolenko, "O semenakh i podgotovke ikh k posevu," p. 291.

[270] *Otchety uchastkovykh agronomov za 1911 god*, p. 87. Local agronomist M. A. Bogoslovskii of Usman *uezd* reported more or less the same findings (*Zhurnaly ...* August–September 1911, p. 109). Many, perhaps even most, peasants were equally

indifferent to segregating potatoes by size for sowing purposes (*Sel'skokhoziaistven-nye statisticheskie svedeniia po materialam, poluchennym ot khoziaev. Vyp. 7*, p. 23). There is one indication of peasants of trying to reduce the presence of weeds in their sowing material by choosing a relatively weed-free field from which to thresh seed grain (Trostianskii, "Khoziaistvenno-statisticheskoe opisanie," p. 237).

[271] *Proekty*, p. 401. This from Muchkap sector. A mid-nineteenth-century observer in Morshansk *uezd* also noticed peasants' unwillingness to send seed grain through sieves, except for secondary crops intended for sale (Trostianskii, "Khoziaistvenno-statisticheskoe opisanie," pp. 237–238). Counterindications, of peasants using sieves to prepare seed grain, do appear in the sources (e.g., *Otchet ob agronomicheskoi deiatel'nosti*, pp. 56, 80; Iudin, "Ochistka i sortirovanie semian," p. 1). P. Maslov in Samara province recorded the use of sieves among only the more conscientious farmers ("O semenakh i podgotovke semian k posevu," no. 3, p. 48).

There must be evidence of indifference to seed grain all over Russia. Take, for example, this comment, from Pskov: "... as in many other places in Russia, local peasants adhere to a strange conviction that the quality of seed grain exerts no influence on the yield. Thus they always employ more or less the worst of their grain as seed ..." (Zinov'ev, "Borokskaia obshchina," p.320; likewise Neruchev, "Istochniki sel'skokhoziaistvennogo znaniia v narode," p. 117; Sovetov, "Kratkii ocherk agronomicheskogo puteshestviia," p. 374; and, with respect to buckwheat alone, Posashev, "Sel'skoe khoziaistvo v Eletskom i Dankovskom uezdakh," pp. 9–10). Overviews from an *uezd* in Khar'kov province noted that peasants tended to sow grains of below average or bottom quality—except for wheat destined for sale (*Ocherk ekonomicheskoi zhizni krest'ianskogo naseleniia*, pp. 149–150; and *Statisticheskii ezhegodnik 1907 g.*, pp. 46, 47). The unfortunate habit of using sieves only for grain destined for the market was not confined to Tambov. See, for instance, Bauer, *Ukhod za parom*, p. 53; Krasil'nikov, "Kakim zernom nado seiat'," pp. 22–23; and Arnol'd, *Obshchie cherty agronomicheskoi tekhniki*, p. 12. Provocative parallels to this practice can be found in other branches of peasant technology. Describing agricultural life in Tver province in the middle of the nineteenth century, Preobrazhenskii noted that peasants would feed well only those cattle they were sending to market (Preobrazhenskii, *op. cit.*, p. 345). Likewise, according to an observer of horse-breeding practices in Tambov, peasants sought to improve the genetic quality of horses only when they intended to sell them (Levashev, "Sovremennoe sostoianie krest'ianskogo konevodstva v Tambovskoi gubernii," p. 695). I suspect Levashev is exaggerating a bit.

[272] Sev, "Sortirovka semian," p. 76. An agronomist from another *uezd* in Samara was equally critical of peasants' handling of seeds (Maslov, "O semenakh i podgotovke semian k posevu," no. 3, pp. 40–41). A great many more sources could be found, from all over Russia. Both Sev and Maslov do note a slowly increasing awareness of the significance of the size of seeds among younger farmers (p. 77, pp. 40–41, respectively).

[273] Average annual prices for rye, 1893–1899, in kopecks per *pud*. Elets was a big grain-trading center, on Tambov's western border.

	Largest seeds	Medium	Light
Elets	50.5	48.8	41.8
Lebedian	48.5	46.8	39.8

Source: k otsenke, Lebedian, p. 96

[274] Paduchev, "Iz Kozlova, Tambovskoi gubernii", pp. 1773. A Polish peasant's memoir paints a similar picture of negligence on the issue of the replacement of seed grain and many other technical issues (Slomka, *From Serfdom to Self-Government*, the chapter "Getting a Living").

[275] Ermolov, *op. cit.*, vol. 2 pp. 241–243.

[276] As Preobrazhenskii put it, "The thought never occurs to our peasants that yields suffer from the deterioration of the quality of seed grain, and that better seeds should be acquired in replacement" (*op. cit.*, p. 241). See also P. Maslov (*op. cit.*, no. 5, p. 67), who reports that peasants would go 20–30 years without changing seeds; F. Nikonov, "Byt i khoziaistvo malorossov v Voronezhskoi gubernii," pp. 169–170, who noted Ukrainian peasants paying much more attention to the cleaning and replacing of grain than their Russian counterparts in Voronezh province; Garin-Mikhailovskii, "Neskol'ko let v derevne," in *Sobranie sochinenii*, vol. 3, p. 72; and Pelevin, "Sortirovanie semian i ego pol'za," p. 69. Pelevin, a peasant farmer himself, provides interesting testimony regarding peasants' ignorance of the connection between the quality of grain sown and the quality of the grain in the subsequent harvest. He notes how he, like other peasants, believed that special sorts of land produced exclusively the bigger seeds they sometimes saw for sale (*ibid.*, p. 69).

[277] Klopov, "Posevnoe zerno rzhi i ovsa v Belorussii," pp. 117–118, 127.

[278] Borodavkin and Kamenskii, *Krest'ianskaia rozh' Bronnitskogo uezda*, p. 6. A large study in Khar'kov province registered similar findings (Baraboshkin, *Issledovanie i kharakteristika semennogo materiala*, pp. 90–97).

[279] Klopov, *op. cit.*, pp. 113–114. Compare in particular the figures for Valuisk uezd (Voronezh province) with those of the Khar'kov station.

  Be it noted here that many sources testify to farmers' awareness of the usefulness of replacing their seeds periodically. The historian Milov cites a few from the eighteenth century, but it is not entirely clear if these sources refer to landlords' or peasants' practices (*op. cit.*, p. 112). Kuznetsov presents evidence of seed replacement on peasant farms in our period in Vladimir and Iaroslavl provinces (*op. cit.*, p. 66), as does Vorontsov, from several provinces (*Progressivnye techeniia*, pp. 17, 63–64). The evidence on this question is therefore not unanimous. We can be sure that peasants recognized the unsuitability of seeds below a certain quality threshold. This threshold was diseconomically low, however, among many or even most farmers. It might take a rapid deterioration of seeds' quality to catch their attention. See, for instance, the comments on buckwheat seeds in *Peremeny v zemledel'cheskoi tekhnike*, pp. 5–6.

[280] In Morshansk *uezd*, for example, "seeds and methods of sowing" was the main theme of all travelling lectures in the second winter of the agronomic aid campaign, 1911–1912 ("Doklad Upravy o deiatel'nosti agronomicheskoi organizatsii v 1912 godu," pp. 9, 11).

[281] It is tempting to posit a parallel between peasants' indifference to the quality of seeds and their scepticism concerning the value of controlled breeding of livestock. At least a significant minority of peasants did not believe in the property of inheritance in animals. The many indications pointing towards this conclusion include *Konevodstvo v Kazanskoi gubernii*, pp. 53–54; Mikhel'son, "O sredstvakh k uluchsheniiu skotovodstva," p. 118; Pridorogin, "Zhivotnovodstvo v Tambovskoi gubernii," p. 33; Pridorogin, "Zakliuchenie professora," p. 835; "Otchet o deiatel'nosti praktikantki po ptitsevodstvu A. P. Verzilovoi," in *Otchety uchastkovykh agronomov za 1914 g.*, p. 317; and RGAE, f. 478, op. 2, d. 233, pp. 13–19. The last

source includes some evidence from 1917 suggesting a slowly growing awareness on peasants' part of the value of mature bulls for breeding purposes. See Kerans, "The Workhorse" for a preliminary discussion of breeding issues and practices with respect to horses.

282 *KSE*, vol. 5 pp. 459–61. Interestingly, Bauer disagrees with this generalization (*Ukhod za parom*, p. 52).

283 Once peasants had chosen their seeds they did not prepare them in any special way. In the late nineteenth century European agriculturalists were experimenting with soaking seeds in urine or mixing them with powdery fertilizers. These attempts yielded no positive results, and were discarded before Russian agronomists set out to introduce new methods into peasant practice. A.S., *op. cit.*, p. 322. On the other hand, for Tver province Preobrazhenskii notes that "everyone, from old times" preferred year-old seeds to new ones (*op. cit.*, p. 212).

284 "Predstoiashchii posev ozimykh khlebov," pp. 257–261.

285 *Ibid.*

286 Quote from *ibid.* As one astute observer pointed out, peasants ought to have been less concerned with the age of the seeds than with their quality. Fresh rye was not necessarily better, especially if the spring and summer had been cold and rainy. Dmitriev, *op. cit.*, pp. 22–25.

287 A. S., *op. cit.*, pp. 325–6. The best results are usually obtained with slightly shallower coverage. Deeper coverage can also expose incompletely decomposed manure (Dmitriev, *op. cit.*, chast' 1, p. 40).

288 The employment of rollers on freshly sown land became more common for the same reason (on which, e. g., *Peremeny v zemledel'cheskoi tekhnike*, p. 21; or *Sel'skokhoziaistvennye statisticheskie svedeniia po materialam, poluchennym ot khoziaev. Vyp. XI*, p. 42). The efficacy of harrowing rye seeds was a disputed question. According to the only experiment I have ever uncovered, levelled soil gave slightly higher rye yields (Sokovnin, "Zemskaia khronika," pp. 952–953). On the other hand, some agriculturalists insisted on the superiority of *sokha*-tilled, unharrowed sowings. According to their reasoning, the *sokha* lifted most of the seeds up a bit, leaving the seeds more room to send roots down quickly into the soft soil below. Harrows, on the other hand, levelled the ground and left the seeds closer to the unworked subsoil. See, e.g., the report of a man named Rudnev, in *Zapiski Lebedianskogo Obshchestvo Sel'skogo Khoziaistva za 1850 god*, Moscow 1851, esp. pp. 365–366. Rudnev's concern might apply more to areas with hard clay subsoils than to other areas.

289 Vakar, *op. cit.*, pp. 13–14; k otsenke, Lebedian, pp. 66, 76; Chelintsev, *Opyt izucheniia organizatsii*, p. 374.

290 Kotov, *Opyt issledovaniia tekhniki*, p. 44.

291 Chelintsev, *op. cit.*, pp. 372, 374. No data exist for earlier periods.

292 A turn-of-the-century survey in Tambov registered depths up to 2.5 *vershki* for rye, while 1.5 *vershka* should suffice (*Sel'skokhoziaistvennye statisticheskie svedeniie po materialam, poluchennym ot khoziaev. Vyp. XI*, p. 46). Brzheskii cites one observer complaining that peasants were doing post-sowing tillage even more deeply than pre-sowing tillage (Brzheskii, *op. cit.*, p. 53).

293 Agronomist V. Milovskii of Balashov *uezd* (on Tambov province's eastern border) commented that the majority of farmers in his area paid a steep price for this error in one particular year (Milovskii, "O poseve khlebov", p. 5).

294 Anonymous, "Pol'za i vred prinosimie boronoi", p. 6.

[295] Chelintsev, *op. cit.*, p.387. See also *k otsenke*, Lebedian, p. 69, for a rare statistical survey of various post-sowing tillage techniques.

[296] This conservative estimate is from *KSE*, vol. 5, pp. 473–474.

[297] For a conservative estimate, and some other figures, see Minin, "Sel'skoe khoziaistvo," p. 107; and *Proekty*, pp. 39–40. Tests suggested that crops did a bit better in rows arranged north-south than in east-west rows. Sunlight found the plants more evenly with a north-south orientation, and dry eastern winds were better-blocked (Mezentsov, "Doklad V. I. Mezentsova po punktu M," p. 130).

[298] See, e.g., *Zhurnaly zasedanii Sel'sko-khoziaistvennoi komissii Tambovskogo uezdnogo zemstva, 1909–10 gg.*, p. 47; or *Proekty*, pp. 38–44.

[299] See, e.g., *Proekty*, pp. 372, 420.

[300] *Otchety uchastkovykh agronomov za 1911 god*, p. 13.

[301] *Ibid.*, p. 49.

[302] *Proekty*, p. 413.

[303] *Otchety uchastkovykh agronomov za 1911 god*, p. 13.

[304] *Proekty*, p. 49.

[305] *Ibid.*, pp. 44–45.

[306] *Otchety uchastkovykh agronomov za 1911 god*, p. 91.

[307] *Otchety uchastkovykh agronomov za 1914*, pp. 163–164.

[308] See, e.g., *Otchety uchastkovykh agronomov za 1914*, pp. 170, 202, 312.

[309] *Proekty*, p. 280.

[310] "Kartinki Volyni," in *Sobranie sochinenii*, vol. 4, p. 110.

[311] Some of the details in this paragraph come from Iurlov, "Neskol'ko slov o zhnitve," pp. 23–24; Koshelev, "Ob urochnykh rabotakh," p. 108; Potekhin, "Krest'ianskie deti," pp. 291–293; Afrosimov, "Opyt otsenki rabot v dvorianskikh pomest'iakh po uezdam," p. 884; Filipchenko, "Variatsii vo rzhi nyneshnogo urozhaia," p. 555; Verbov, *Na vrachebnom postu v zemstve*, pp. 108, 110; and Chaev, "Poslushnitsa," p. 819. In general, diseases thrived more in the autumn and winter than in summer. Figures of registered diseases in Tambov at the turn of the century can be found in Shidlovskii, *Kratkii obzor glavneishikh ostrozaraznykh zabolevanii.*

[312] *Broken Earth*, p. 94.

[313] As attested in, e.g., *1882 god v sel'sko-khoziaistvennom otnoshenii*, St.Petersburg 1882, Otdel II, p.60; and Garin-Mikhailovskii, "Na khodu," in *Sobranie sochinenii*, vol. 3, p. 255. In addition to dislodgment losses, tardily reaped grain was more susceptible to spoilage in case of rainy weather after reaping, because the casing of fully ripe grain is less waterproof than less mature grain (Lavrent'ev, "Ob uborke khleba," p. 894).

Dislodgment was not quite as severe on grain cut with the sickle instead of the scythe, primarily because the sickler held the stem of the grain during cutting. Peasants were favoring scythes over sickles almost everywhere in Tambov by the end of the nineteenth century. They might have been a bit hasty in foregoing the sickle, however. The tool had a number of subtle advantages over the faster-working scythe (the finest comparison of the two tools I have seen, from a Tambov landlord, coincidentally, is Filipchenko, *op. cit.*).

Millet is more vulnerable to dislodgment than other grains. To begin with, millet does not grow inside ears, and so is not sheltered from wind. Secondly, millet grains ripen earlier in the upper portions of the plant than the lower. While the farmer waits for the lower grains to ripen, the upper are already over-ripening. A hard wind could knock out 25–35% or more of a millet crop even before reaping began (*Proekty*, p. 456). Lastly, millet stalks remain quite green even as the lower grains become ripe. After reaping, the plant cannot be bound into sheaves until the stalks dry out, about two days later. Otherwise the stalks will quickly begin to rot. By the time the crop can be bound, a substantial portion of the grains are falling off the plant (all of this from agronomist Iudin, "Kak vybrat' vremia uborki khlebov," pp. 1–2).

The dangers of dislodgment can be still more serious with oil plants than with grains. Families with a lot of land in the south of the province relied on sunflowers as a cash crop, and so would have extra incentive to buy a reaping machine. Oats suffers only very moderately from dislodgment, unless it is subjected to an overnight freeze—after which it dislodges much faster than rye (Firsov and Kiseleva, *Byt velikorusskikh krest'ian-zemlepashtsev*, p. 42; Preobrazhenskii, *op. cit.*, p. 249).

[314] Toren, "Sposoby uborki khlebov", p. 76.

[315] Sovetov, "Zhatva", *ES* vol. 22, p. 729. This rule was known in cruder forms as far back as Roman times, at least to some people (Buromskii, "Protsessy sozrevaniia pshenitsy," p. 203).

[316] SSS, Borisoglebsk, otdel 1, p.48; *ibid.*, vol. 16. *Chastnoe zemlevladenie Kirsanovskogo uezda*, p. 225. The former source discusses one estate, the latter generalizes about landlords' practices. Significantly, a chart distilled from reports of the Ministry of Agriculture's correspondents in 1896 notes no diference between peasants and landlords concerning the dates when reaping of rye ordinarily began (*Svod statisticheskikh svedenii. Vyp. III*, p. 90—the restriction of the data to the year 1896 is mentioned at the outset of section XI. Although this suggests a widespread preference among peasants for reaping at the yellow ripeness stage, it is neither clear nor definitive evidence.

[317] Selivanov, *God Russkogo zemledel'tsa*, p. 67; and Shostak, "Zamechaniia o sel'skom khoziaistve v Khersonskoi gubernii," p. 10.

[318] Pel'tsikh, *Trekhpolka ili mnogopol'e?*, pp. 37–38. For the same criticism, from Orel province at the turn of the century, see Brzheskii, *op. cit.*, p. 53).

[319] Sovetov, "Zhatva," p. 727. Emphasis added.

[320] The peasant was from Elets *uezd*, Orel province. Cited in Brzheskii, *Ocherki agrarnogo byta krest'ian*, p. 53. Other testimony on peasants' waiting for grain to reach full ripeness before beginning reaping includes Deilidovich, "Ocherk sel'skogo khoziaistva," p. 365; estate manager F. Posashev—who specifies that he reaped at yellow ripeness, while peasants preferred to wait for full ripeness— "Sel'skoe khoziaistvo v Eletskom i Dankovskom uezdakh" (respectively, Orel and Riazan provinces), pp. 5, 10, and, from his later experience in Voronezh province, "Razvedenie probshteiskoi i shampanskoi rzhi," p. 704; I. Mal'nev, "Rezul'taty vol'nonaemnogo truda v Borisoglebskom uezde v 1864 godu," p. 54; B. Borisov, "Leto 1871 goda v Ekaterinoslavskoi, Khar'kovskoi i Kurskoi guberniiakh," p. 269; I. I. Sontsov of Kursk ("O nailuchshem vremeni kos'by i zhatvy khlebov," pp. 860–861; agronomist A. Iudin of Balashov *uezd* in Saratov province ("Kak vybrat' vremia uborki khlebov", pp. 1–2); Ia. Rudnev from Orenburg, "O sistemakh zemledeliia v zaorenburgskom krae," p. 267; agronomist A. Vagin from St. Petersburg province ("O nekotorykh priemakh povyshenii urozhaev," p. 7); and Ivanitskii, *Materialy po etnografii Vologodskoi gubernii*, p. 37. Sontsov and N. A. Pavlov (*Zapiski zemlevladel'tsa*, p. 224) insist most landlords were making the same mistake. Agronomist A. A. Bauer of Vladimir province also implies that peasants there tended to reap tardily (Bauer, *Ukhod za parom*, pp. 62–63). Surely many more sources could be found.

Some sources explicitly indicate or imply properly timed reaping. Preobrazhen-skii (in Tver, in the 1850s) notes that unevenly ripening fields would be reaped before the whole field was ripe, and that "reaping in our area always commences before the grain is fully ripe" (pp. 248–249). Likewise, the writer Potekhin depicts a peasant fully competent in judging the readiness of grain for reaping ("Krest'ian-skie deti," p. 290). Additionally, Milov cites one eighteenth-century source de-scribing timely reaping (op. cit., p. 144), and a mid-nineteenth-century Tambov landowner's comments on the selection of seed grain imply the same (Kishkin, op. cit., p. 32—he says farmers preferred to select seed grain from the latest reaped rye, that grain being the ripest [consequently most rye was reaped a bit earlier]). These testimonies are competent and valuable, but no more so than the many sources establishing late reaping.

Peasants' timing of meadow mowing often came in for similar criticism to grain reaping. According to a number of observers peasants would mistakenly delay mowing their meadows until the grass had finished growing. They did not appre-ciate how much nutritional value was lost during the final period of growth (from Tambov, Uchety uchastkovykh agronomov za 1911 god, p. 5; Kostroma province, Dmitriev, Opyt prakticheskikh zamechanii, chast' 2, p. 19; Tekushchaia sel'sko-khoz-iaistvennaia statistika Kurskogo gubernskogo zemstva. 1899 god. Kniga 1-aia, p. 69; Opyt sel'skokhoziaistvennogo obzora, p. 40). A Voronezh province agronomist's critique of related inaccuracies, in the reaping of sunflowers, is Braslavskii, Sel'sko-khoziaistvennye besedy, pp. 10–11.

[321] Iudin, op. cit., loc. cit. Other sources noted peasants appraising ripeness according to the color of straw (Deilidovich, op. cit., loc. cit.; anonymous, "Zapiska o vozde-lyvanii i sbyte khlebov," p. 46; V. Ber, "Ob uborke khlebnykh rastenii," p. 93).

[322] P. Karamzin, "Ob uborke zernovykh khlebov i poteriakh ot nee proiskhodiash-chikh," p.54. Further reinforcement for Sovetov's and Karamzin's criticism of the landowners on this issue comes from an observer in Kharkov province, who noted that the landowners began to hire peasants to reap their grain v prozelen' (before it all went yellow) only after experiencing difficulty in finding a sufficient number of hands for hire at what they considered to be peak reaping time (Sel'sko-khoz-iaistvennye i statisticheskie svedenii po materialam, poluchennym ot khoziaev. Vyp. 1, p. 94).

[323] Lavrent'ev, "Ob uborke khlebov," p. 894. It is true that grain reaped quite prematurely and also improperly dried can transmit fungal diseases if these are already present in the grain ears (Matossian, "Climate, Crops, and Natural In-crease," p. 461). This might be the rot to which peasants in Lavrent'ev's article were referring. Early sources do offer one more explanation for tardy reaping. Farmers might allow fields to reach full ripeness so as to seed the land for the next year all by itself with the shattered grain (Anonymous, "O sostoianii sel'skogo khoziaistva v iuzhnoi Rossii v 1851 g.," p. 52). This practice pertained only in the southern steppes, where labor was at a premium, and where the system of farming foresaw sowing the same crop on a unit of land year after year, to soil exhaustion. Since this motivation for tardy reaping is specific to extensive systems of farming prevailing before the three-field system, I do not sense that tardy reaping in our time and place derived from it. On the other hand, an inspection of landlord farming in Voronezh province in 1893 registered this variant of late reaping there (Beketov, Voronezhskaia guberniia v sel'skokhoziaistvennom otnoshenii, p. 49).

[324] Karamzin, *op. cit.*, p.54. A peasant from neighboring Elets *uezd*, Orel province, also noted peasants' inattentiveness to grain dislodgment during the binding of sheaves in dry weather (Brzheskii, *op. cit.*, p. 53).

[325] Karamzin, *op. cit.*, pp. 61–63.

[326] In the 1860s the Free Economic Society's journal did report the findings of German and French studies confirming Hannam's discovery (*TVEO*, 1864, vol. 4, vyp. 3, pp. 220–221). There may well have been other reports available to those who kept up with the agronomic literature.

[327] *Ibid.*, pp. 74–84.

[328] Karamzin cites a number of contemporaries' impressions on ths issue (*op. cit.*, p. 59). Some of the agriculturalists in Tambov who corresponded regularly with government statisticians in St. Petersburg estimated losses of 20–40% of the rye in 1882, e.g. (*1882 god v sel'sko-khoziaistvennom otnoshenii*, St.Petersburg 1882, Otdel II, p. 75, and reports of nearly 50% losses, from Kursk, p. 60).

[329] A. N. Skosyreva, "Khod sozrevaniia ozimoi rzhi," p. 112.

[330] A day's wait was standard in some places (Kotov, *op. cit.*, p. 48).

[331] SSS, Spassk, p. 29; Toren, "Sposoby uborki khlebov," p. 78; D. P. Semenov, "Promysly i zaniatiia naseleniia," p. 214.

[332] Sovetov, "Zhatva," p. 729.

[333] V. P. Semenov-Tian-Shanskii, *op. cit.*, pp. 214–215; Sovetov, "Zhatva," p. 729. Rarely, the crosses would be made of 17 sheaves (SSS, Elatma, p. 39; Kuznetsov, *op. cit.*, p. 49). This was most likely to happen with small sheaves.

[334] Selivanov, *op. cit.*, p. 57. A discussion of alternative methods of building stacks is Bekhteev, "Ukladka kopen."

[335] Kotov, *op. cit.*, p. 48.

[336] The inconvenience of horizontal drying is especially marked for scythed crops, where the straw is much longer and the sheaves less tidy. Scythed sheaves are not very stable when stood up against each other. Filipchenko, *op. cit.*, p. 356.

[337] Toren, *op. cit.*, pp. 82–3.

[338] These are 1920s reports, from GATO, f. R-2786, op. 1, d. 22, p. 1; ibid, d. 25, p. 1. Statistical data isolating losses from rains coming while reaped crops lay in the fields are very rare. However, the provincial *zemstvo* did publish collations of reports from *volost'* administrations and a large network of voluntary agricultural correspondents during the final years of the Tsarist regime. Here we can find striking confirmation of the havoc wreaked by untimely storms, and the ineffectiveness of *krestsy* in rainy weather. In the years 1914–1916, 78–89% of the reports indicated that either fall or spring grains (usually both) suffered from rains while drying in the field (*Kratkii sel'sko-khoziaistvennyi obzor Tambovskoi gubernii za 1914 god*, p. 32; ... *za 1915 god*, p. 30; ... *za 1916 god*, p. 33). In the rainiest years as much as 70% of the grain might be lost in some localities (Konovalov, "Derevenskie kartinki," p. 4). In recognition of the gravity of the problem, a Provincial Agronomic Conference in 1918 included artificial grain drying in its list of priorities for improving the state of agriculture in the province: GATO, f. R-956, op. 1, d. 38, p. 35.

[339] Selivanov, *op. cit.*, p.55.

[340] Kishkin, *op. cit.*, p. 13.

[341] Fortunatov, "Mertvyi inventar' v russkom krest'ianskom zemledelii" pp. 582–3.

[342] Korinfskii, *Trudovoi god russkogo krest'ianina*, vyp.7, "Snopovoz", p. 13; *k otsenke* Lebedian, p. 81. The oversized cart was called *rydvan* in Tambov (Trostianskii, "Khoziaistvenno-statisticheskoe opisanie," p. 248). Judging from Selivanov (*op.*

cit., p. 58), farmers did not load up their carts with so many sheaves in clear weather. Of course the number of sheaves per load depended on the size of the sheaves. Smaller sheaves, from sickled rye, or oats (the sheaves of, which were smaller than rye sheaves—Selivanov, *op. cit.*, pp. 58–59) could be more tightly packed, allowing a heavier load in case of bad weather. A useful selection of data on the pace and labor requirements of carting appears in Skrebitskii, *Krest'ianskoe delo*, pp. 386–391.

[343] Breakdowns in village grazing regimes could force peasants to accelerate carting, although not as urgently as storms. One example from Khar'kov province is illustrative. Here the villagers themselves dismantled the fencing that limited livestock's access to the fields. The animals got loose on the nearest rye field, breaking up the *kopny* and compelling peasants to cart home the rye when they wished to be reaping their spring grains. Sumtsov, *Ocherki narodnogo byta*, p. 19.

[344] Zinov'ev, "Borokskaia obshchina," p. 319. The other sources alluded to include Karamzin, *op. cit.*, p.75; Preobrazhenskii, *op. cit.*, pp.253–254; Brzheskii, *op. cit.*, p.53. An eighteenth-century source from northern Russia insists that some of the sheaves of grain tended to lie in contact with carts' wheels, leading to more losses in transit as the wheels threshed the sheaves (Olishev, *op. cit.*, pp. 122–123). Milov cites other eighteenth-century laments on carting losses (*op. cit.*, p. 142). An overview from the end of our period estimates carting losses to have reached 10% in some cases (*Osennye sel'sko-khoziaistvennye raboty*, p. 69). The highest estimate I have encountered of carting losses, "... up to 50%," comes from Simbirsk province, where the distance from farm to fields was very high (M. F. Odinokov, "Kindiak-ovskaia ekonomiia E. M. Persi-French," p. 54). Odinokov might have lumped reaping and carting losses together. He does, however, specify early reaping on this estate.

Some peasants—we cannot know how many—were careful to lay a canvas in the cart bed during transport (N. O. Osipov, *op. cit.*, p. 488; N. V. Uspenskii, "Propazha," p. 37). Another source implying the use of canvases is Shaternikov, *Otchego v krest'ianskom khoziaistve semena plokhi*, p. 12.

[345] SSS, Shatsk, p. 55; Anonymous, "Zapiska o vozdelyvanii i sbyte khlebov v Lebedianskom uezde," p. 47; Zinov'ev, *op. cit.*, pp. 319–320; Preobrazhenskii, *op. cit.*, p. 254; Selivanov, *op. cit.*, pp. 59–60; A. Gorizontov, *op. cit.*, no. 3, p. 223. The sacred trinkets are mentioned in Ivanova, *Zhizn' i pover'ia krest'ian Kupianskogo uezda*, p. 166; and Ivanov, "Verovaniia krest'ian Orlovskoi gubernii," pp. 116–117. Selivanov and the first source cited here describe proper methods of constructing platforms for grain stacks. Plenty more detail appears in P. Iurevich, "Agronomicheskie puteshchestviia po Rossii," pp. 84–85. The best known expert in late Imperial Russia on this and other questions concerning agricultural structures was I. Strakhov (*Sel'sko-khoziaistvennaia arkhitektura*). Strakhov estimated mice took as much as 1/8 of the grain harvest in some years (it is not clear if this is a regional or national estimate) ("Khranenie sel'sko-khoziaistvennykh produktov," *ES*, vol. 74, p. 605). His estimate might also include grain lost to mice in the fields. An observer in Tambov in the 1920s estimated mice got 30% of the millet crop in one year (Iakovlev, *Nasha derevnia*, pp. 46–47). A vivid description of mice making grain storage holes in the fields appears in *Sel'sko-khoziaistvennyi obzor Nizhegorodskoi gubernii za 1894*, pp. 14–15.

[346] The following information on the *ovin* is gathered from Korolev, "Zernosushil'nia," pp. 571–73, and Saburova, "Sel'sko-khoziaistvennye postroiki dlia obrabotki i khraneniia zerna," pp. 99–110.

[347] This calculation is based on a normal yield of 9 *kopen* (a *kopna* is a stack of four *krestsy*, or 52 sheaves) per *desiatina. Proekt obshchikh osnovanii*, p. 20.

[348] It should be noted here that a simpler version of the *ovin*, the *riga*, began to replace the *ovin* in some parts of the central black-earth region in the middle of the nineteenth century (Saburova, *op. cit.*, p. 107). The distinctions between the two structures can be omitted here, since they do not affect any part of the analysis.

[349] Estimates of the added time required to thresh air-dried grain ranged from 20–50% (Skrebitskii, *Krest'ianskoe delo*, pp. 368–370).

[350] According to one source, certain experiments concluded that as much as 20% of the grain can be lost in *ovin* drying (Preobrazhenskii, *op. cit.*, p.130). I have never come across evidence to confirm or amend this assertion, however.

[351] See, e.g., V. P. Semenov-Tian-Shanskii, ed., *Rossiia. vol. 2*, pp. 50–51.

[352] *Ibid.*, Vakar, *Rezul'taty obsledovaniia tekhniki*, p. 15, is another of the numerous sources citing peasants complaining that the climate had become drier.

[353] Kviatkovskii, "Zernosushilki," p. 38.

[354] *Proekt obshchikh osnovanii*, p. 39

[355] Far and away the best literary rendering of threshing is the story "Molot'ba," by the Mordvinian peasant writer from Saratov province, Stepan Anikin (reprinted in Anikin, *Plodnaia osen'*).

[356] Korinfskii, *Trudovoi god russkogo krest'ianina*, vyp.8, "Zamolotki", p. 15; (anonymous) "Opytnye zamechaniia o molot'be," p. 45; Zinov'ev, "Borokskaia obshchina," p.320; *Otchety uchastkovykh agronomov i instruktorov Morshanskogo zemstva za 1913 god*, p.86; Smith, *Peasant Farming in Muscovy*, p.35; Milov, *op. cit.*, p. 149; and Gromyko, *Trudovye traditsii krest'ian Sibiri*, p. 64 for further confirmation. Winter threshing was not without drawbacks. The quality of the grain deteriorated in the dampness (Filipchenko, *op. cit.*, p. 356).

[357] Selivanov, *op. cit.*, p. 60.

[358] Evans, *Ask the Fellows Who Cut the Hay*, p. 96.

[359] The texts of some threshing songs appear in Ivanova, *Zhizn' i pover'ia krest'ian Kupianskogo uezda*, pp. 143–146. On the other hand, according to one ethnographer Russians did not like to sing much during threshing (Bers, "Rol' ritma v zhizni narodov," p. 130). On a more general level, sources give a mixed picture of the frequency of singing during work in rural Russia. Some noted very little singing, even during haymaking and on walks home (e.g., F. Nikonov, "Byt i nravy poselian-velikorussov," p. 148). Others, more numerous, reported just the opposite (e.g., L'vov, *Vospominaniia*, pp. 148, 153–154, and elsewhere).

[360] Kliuss, "Molot'ba," p. 667; "Thrashing," *Encyclopaedia Britannica*; interviews. I wish to thank Russian ethnographer S. V. Kuznetsov for alerting me to the importance of rhythm to flail threshing. A written source mentioning the rhythm of threshing is Solov'ev, *Rodnoe Selo*, Part 2, p. 61.

[361] Smith, *op. cit.*, p.36; "Thrashing," *Encyclopaedia Britannica*. There are other, significantly higher estimates. See, e.g., A. Ryshkov, "O molot'be," p. 5.

[362] "Thrashing," *Encyclopaedia Britannica*.

[363] Kliuss, "Molot'ba," p. 667; and Karamzin, "Ob uborke zernovykh khlebov," p. 77.

[364] Karamzin, *op. cit.*, p. 77.

[365] *Ibid*, pp. 77–84. Peasants' chickens would find much of the scattered grain, but so too would wild birds. A good discussion of this and many other aspects of poultry raising among peasants in the central black-earth area is Kazantsev, "Domashnee ptitsevodstvo v chernozemnykh uezdakh Orlovskoi gubernii."

[366] Interestingly enough, stone rollers were never used for threshing in Tambov, although this technique was not uncommon in nearby provinces to the east and south (P. L., "O molot'be khlebov katkami", p.495). The fullest description I have seen of rail beating is Potekhin, "Krest'ianskie deti," pp. 294–300. Good descriptions of animal trampling include Rudnev, "O sistemakh zemledeliia," pp. 265–266; Ryshkov, "O molot'be," and Kordatov, "Chernukhinskaia volost', Nizhegorodskaia uezda," pp. 20–21. A photograph of rail beating appears in Kushner, ed., Russkie, p. 89.

[367] Bauer, Ukhod za parom, pp. 53–4.

[368] Ibid.

[369] Naidich, "Orudiia i sposoby molotby i veianiia," p. 88.

[370] Preobrazhenskii offers some commentary on this (op. cit., p. 258). Peasants might just pick up the soiled straw and feed it to the horses straight away (Moshkov, "Gagauzy Benderskogo uezda," p. 69). Mention of the trampling of millet in Tambov appears in P. L., "O molot'be," p. 496.

[371] Naidich, "Orudiia i sposoby molotby i veianiia," pp. 89–90; Kliuss, "Molot'ba", p. 667. An estate manager in Simbirsk province pointed out how easy it was to protect the grain from the horses. He lay the sheaves on the threshing floor with the ears on the floor, covered by the straw. The contact of the ears with the floor speeded the threshing and saved the grain from the horses at the same time. Peasants were stubbornly resistant to this improvement, he complained. A. Klements, "Zametka o konnoi molot'be v privolzhskom krae," pp. 9–11.

[372] Bunin, I. A., "Apple Fragrance," in Light Breathing and Other Stories, p. 34.

[373] Naidich, "Orudiia i sposoby molotby i veianiia," pp. 91–3; and k otsenke, Lebedian, pp. 84–88.

[374] Larger, more expensive models on some landowners' estates could thresh three times as much per day (given the presence of a dozen horses and 25–30 workers). Sbornik statisticheskikh svedenii po Oboianskomu uezdu, p. 68.

[375] Threshing machines are thought to have led peasants to abandon ovins in large numbers in Moscow and Vladimir provinces: Vorontsov, Progressivnye techeniia, pp. 234, 246. Together with the perceived alteration of the climate, they were responsible for the same phenomenon in Tambov.

[376] See Naidich, "Orudiia i sposoby molotby i veianiia," pp. 91–3.

[377] Sel'sko-khoziaistvennye mashiny i orudiia, pp.68–69; Trudy Tsentral'nogo Statisticheskogo Upravleniia. Tom 5, vyp.2, pp. 120–121. Judging from the 1920 tool census, hand-powered models became much more widespread sometime after 1910 (RGAE, f. 478, op. 5, d. 2012, p. 146).

[378] This arrangement was known as propusk in the region. See k otsenke, Lebedian, pp. 84–88, and Kirsanov, pp. 77–78.

[379] Proekt obshchikh osnovanii, p.37. See also k otsenke, Kozlov p. 43, Usman pp. 44–45, Borisoglebsk p. 53.

[380] Klopov, op. cit., pp. 115–116 (citing other studies). Some studies achieved slightly better performance, especially if the straw was sent through the machine a second time (e.g., Zalenskii, "K metodike ucheta urozhaia," pp. 9–12).

[381] According to data from Poltava province, 9.3% of all threshing machine injuries were fatal on the day of the event, if not instantaneously (as reported in Zhurnaly zasedanii Kurskogo Gubernskogo Zemskogo Sobraniia, Ocherednoi sessii 1901 g., Kursk 1902, p. 628).

[382] A diagram and some commentary on this technique appears in Koval'kovskii, Znachenie sortirovki, p. 11.

[383] Naidich, "Orudiia i sposoby molotby i veianiia," p. 95.

[384] Karamzin, "Ob uborke zernovykh khlebov," p. 84. Spreading a large cloth on the ground would minimize losses. But I have encountered only one source reporting this tactic, from the environs of Samara: Burnaby, *A Ride to Khiva*, pp. 57–58.

[385] Naidich, *op. cit.*, pp. 95–96.

[386] See, e.g., *Proekty*, p. 401, as quoted earlier.

[387] Sieves turn up very infrequently in Tambov agricultural sources for our period. *k otsenke*, Lebedian, pp. 84–88, mentions landlords tending to use sieves, but peasants not. Naidich also asserts that this tool was rare in this area ("Orudiia i sposoby molotby i veianiia," p. 98). We know, on the other hand, that some peasants in Kozlov *uezd* developed improved, complex forms of sieves. They carried these around the province and beyond, cleaning grain for a fee. Soimonov, "Kozlovskaia gorka;" and Beketov, *Voronezhskaia guberniia v sel'skokhoziaistvennom otnoshenii*, p. 75.

[388] Naidich, "Orudiia i sposoby molotby i veianiia," pp. 96, 98.

[389] *Ibid.*, p. 96.

[390] *Proekty*, pp. 639, 642; and Maslov, *Plugi i drugie uluchshennye orudiia*, p. 26. Village artisans were probably producing the cheaper machines mentioned in these sources.

[391] Lindeman, "Chrezzernitsa," pp. 393–398.

[392] Bauer, *Ukhod za parom*, p. 54. As we saw in our discussion of peasants' selection of seed grain, many peasants excluded the very largest grains from sowing material. But of course many did not. One expert from the time recommended sowing medium-sized seeds along with large seeds, so as to minimize the extent of *chrezzernitsa* (Shaternikov, *op. cit.*, pp. 14–16).

[393] *KSE*, vol. 5, pp. 466–473. A reasonably thorough overview of the history and variety of sorting machines up to the end of the Imperial period is Koval'kovskii, *op. cit.*, pp. 14–31.

[394] *Otchety uchastkovykh agronomov za 1914 god*, p. 170.

[395] Arnol'd, M. F., "Posevnye semena krest'ianskikh khoziaistv Bezhetskogo uezda," (Tver province—D.K.) pp. 189–190.

[396] *KSE*, vol. 5, pp. 463–6. Also Bauer, *Ukhod za parom*, p. 52. According to the scattered statistics I have found on this question, the cleanest rye in the Imperial period was an average of about 91%, in Voronezh province, 1911–1913 (Voronov, ed., *Naselenie i khoziaistvo Voronezhskoi gubernii*, pp. 392–393).

[397] Respectively: *Doklady Tambovskoi gubernskoi zemskoi upravy … po agronomicheskomu otdelu*, p. 18; *Proekty*, p. 38. A source for Tambov *uezd* in 1912—*Otchet o deiatel'nosti agronomicheskogo personala za 1912*, p. 83—claims that peasants' spring crop seed grain was up to 15% impure.

[398] Ermolenko, "O semenakh i podgotovke ikh k posevu" p. 293.

[399] *KSE*, vol. 5, pp. 463–6.

[400] *Ibid.*, pp. 471–2.

[401] *KSE*, vol. 5, pp. 471–472.

PART TWO

TOWARDS
A HISTORY AND UNDERSTANDING
OF AGRONOMIC APTITUDE

The point is that most peasants have their own way of thinking regarding the cleaning and sorting of seeds. Many of them assert that yields do not depend on the condition of the seed grain:

Well, fine. We can sow store-bought [cleaned and sorted—DK] oats, or maybe rye. And they'll grow. But what of it? ... If God wills it they grow, so picking out certain seeds to sow is pointless.

What can you say in response? Choose your saying: 'from poor seeds come not fine offspring', or 'as ye sow, so shall ye reap', etc.

The peasant hears you out for all this and much more, paying full attention. And then...[sic] and then he blurts out his usual, traditional, and, of course, decisive and peremptory: "Our grandfathers before us lived without these new-fangled ideas of yours, and didn't go hungry. We'll get by as they did."[1]

It is hard to imagine a more telling illustration of peasants' indifference and complacency towards science and agricultural improvement than this conversation between a peasant and an agronomist in Moscow province in the 1920s. As we shall see in our discussion of the first years of the agronomic aid programs, this attitude generated a wave of despair among the community of agronomic specialists. It became clear that most peasants' mental approach to their craft differed sharply from the agronomists'. The specialists were not prepared for this, and so it would take time for representatives of the two camps to arrive at a common language.

What was the peasantry's mental approach to agriculture, where had it come from, and how was it developing in our period? How had it shaped their agronomic aptitude, and how did it affect their reception of science? To cope with these questions, we must start from an analysis of their conceptualization of the central elements of their agricultural life—land and tillage. On the basis of our previous discussions of tillage, we now attempt to characterize the features and limitations of peasants' understanding of soil and tillage in its historical development. Let it be noted that the presentation below is schematic. Peasant farmers' understanding of soil and tillage could evolve at a local or even individual level, so the countryside never presented a fully uniform picture in this regard.

The Peasant Farmer and Soil:
The Four Stages of Comprehension

Stage 1
Tillage as a Mixed Blessing

Simply by virtue of the fact that they tilled the soil, the peasantry had advanced beyond the most primitive level of agronomic knowledge. Every farmer was aware of the connection between tillage and yields. It is possible to sow land without any tillage, and under extraordinary circumstances many peasants did this on some strips. They might have been too poor to rent a horse at a certain time, or they might have lived in communes with some arable lands located at such a great distance from the village that tillage was simply too much trouble. And everyone could see what happened to the land of drunkards and misfits who missed spots when tilling their strips. Crops grew poorly on such lands, and people knew it.[2]

So tillage was necessary. But Russian peasants acquired a deep and lasting ambivalence towards tillage as they settled the grasslands of the black-earth region in the eighteenth and nineteenth centuries. Here they quickly recognized that long-standing grasslands gave better yields when plowed up than did continuously cropped lands. They also noticed that a dense mass of steppe grass roots accumulated if the land was left unplowed over the course of a decade or more.[3] Evidence from a late-nineteenth-century study in Tsaritsyn *uezd* in Saratov province, to the southeast of Tambov (where peasants still practiced shifting cultivation of grasslands), confirms that steppe farmers readily connected these two observations: "The Tsaritsyn peasant's impression of the 'strength' of land is inseparably connected to the 'stoutness' of the land [from the grass roots—D.K.]."[4] Farmers noticed, moreover, that tillage broke down the root system in the soil's surface, and surmised that this process weakened the land. Therefore they sought to minimize their tillage regimes. They plowed once in the fall for spring crops (wheat whenever possible), and then sowed rye straight on to the same land immediately after the harvest, with no tillage apart from a single session of harrowing to cover the seeds.[5]

If peasants at this stage of understanding of the soil suspected tillage of wearing the land out, how did they assess the effect of crops? Remarkably, when asked how many years they cropped their land and how many years they let it rest, they counted rye years as rest, because no tillage went on during rye's tenure![6] For the same reason they even maintained that "rye fertilizes the land."[7] Thus peasants in this system of farming did not properly appreciate the demands crops put on soil resources. They made tillage the prime culprit for soil fatigue and exhaustion. Since, moreover, soil fertility was associated with a dense network of grass roots, the only prescription for tired soil was rest from tillage. Further, peasants advocated herd grazing on fields at rest precisely because, and only because, the animals would pack down the surface of the soil.[8] And so peasants at this stage were nearly blind to the benefits of applying manure to their fields.[9] Having noticed the flourishing of weeds on manured land, they associated manure with stimulating weed growth rather than with restoring soil fertility.[10]

Stage 2
Working the Surface of the Soil

Once population densities exceeded certain limits, shifting cultivation systems of farming were no longer feasible. Most or all lands suitable for raising crops were plowed up and brought under continuous cultivation. This process, which was virtually complete everywhere in Tambov province by the middle of the nineteenth century, required a sharp shift in peasants' conceptions of the soil. The rich, "stout" soil of the grasslands became an unrealizable ideal, to farmers' deep and enduring regret.[11] At a loss as to how their soil might be improved without the customary, multi-year periods of replenishment with grass roots, peasants could experience a certain degree of disorientation and dejection. "Well, what kind of strength has the land got left? It's nothing but dust now, ash," said peasants comparing continuously tilled land to the grasslands they remembered plowing up a generation earlier.[12]

Naturally peasants at this stage realized that a year of rest (fallow) protected the soil and helped to restore its fertility. But how did they interpret this protection? Was the soil resting from tillage, or from crops, or from both? Neither agronomists, nor ethnographers, nor agricultural historians ever posed this question. Yet it is indispensable both for understanding how peasants conceived of their work in the early stages of the three-field system, and for evaluating their responses to the economic and demographic pressures of the late Imperial period.

Could it be that the early steppe farmers' ambivalence towards tillage—"Stage 1" in the present analytical scheme—survived into the period marked by continuous cultivation? So it would seem from an expression not infrequently encountered in areas where the three-field system had been in operation for a couple of generations or more: namely, that the land was "tilled out."[13] But the meaning of this expression is not as clear as it appears at first glance. It does not in fact isolate the consequences of tillage in particular from the consequences of crop raising in general. Peasant usage of the expression, "the land is resting" is more precise in this regard. In three-field agriculture we find this expression employed exclusively with respect to the fallow period, when tillage does take place.[14] It is never employed in regard to the year when rye grows to maturity and is harvested, *when no tillage goes on at all.*

Peasants at this stage of understanding of soil had therefore reversed the early steppe farmers' conception of the influence of crops and tillage on soil fertility. As far as they were concerned crops tired the soil, not tillage. They now associated tillage with improving the land. As one of the most careful observers of Russian agriculture declared, when characterizing peasant attitudes to tillage: "It is well known that the softer and looser the land is made, the higher will be the yield."[15] Those among them who did not bother to till their land were outcasts: "He who is lazy with the *sokha* will suffer hardship for a whole year," went one saying; "Whether it will grow or not, one must till," went another.[16]

Certainly the overcoming of earlier prejudices against tillage represented a very important step in peasants' agronomic aptitude. But this step was not sufficient by itself for peasants to develop advanced tillage techniques. Being unaware of the capillary structure of soil and the manner in which soil acquires and loses moisture, their understanding of the connection between soil moisture on the one hand and the timing or depth of tillage on the other hand was very faint. As far as they were concerned, soil moisture depended on rain, not on the way in which the land was worked. Consequently, none of them sensed the full significance of keeping the upper layer friable. Instead, farmers at this level of understanding of soil—the huge majority until at least the turn of the century—rested content *so long as the surface of the land had been tilled, once.* As we saw in Part I, they would not harrow their fallow after a hard rain (which would compress the surface and create a crust after drying). They might dismiss the suggestion of *dvoenie,* insisting that it would produce crops without grain in the ears.[17] Some would not even bother to harrow their land after raising fallow, unless weeds were proliferating![18]

Thus, even though peasants' recognition that crops could tire out the land was an important step beyond the stage 1 understanding of soil, they were slow to shed the Stage 1 prejudice against tillage. They did not yet perceive the advantages of periodic tillage, nor did they come across them through trial-and-error. The following comments (the first two from local agronomists, the third from a peasant), encapsulate peasant attitudes to the timing of tillage in Stage 2:

> When asked "Why don't you do fall tillage?" [ziab—D.K.] almost everywhere they give one and the same answer: "We've got only so much land, we'll manage in the spring".... they simply do not imagine all of the advantages of fall tillage, and calculate: "Let he who has a lot of land and cannot cope with it all in the spring till in the fall. We can handle it in the spring."[19]

> ... The peasants are holding adamantly to their conviction in the uselessness of fall tillage.[20]

> Before the arrival of the local agronomist...no one in our village had any idea what ziab tillage was, or that early fallow would be better than late fallow.[21]

To anyone familiar with the literature on agricultural improvements in late Imperial and early Soviet Russia, these citations may appear unrepresentative. The ordinary explanation for peasant resistance to early fallow and fall tillage concerns the impositions of the communal grazing regime. Thus peasants ordinarily rebuffed agronomists' suggestions for early fallow by insisting that their herds depended on fallow land for grazing at this time of the year. Indeed the herds did depend on fallow land for grazing, but this reasoning is far less logical and complete than it appears. We know, for instance, that many communes held chunks of arable land separated at some distance from their core holdings, and inaccessible to their herds. Farmers could have raised fallow early on these lands, but by all indications they did not.[22] Similarly, communes could have organized their herds' grazing regimes in such a way as to leave a portion of their fallow free to be raised earlier.[23] The only known cases of this, however, followed agitation from agronomists or landlords.[24] As we saw earlier (in discussions of green fallow, and harrowing) peasants were more alert to attacking the visibl threat of weeds on fallow land than to defending themselves against the dangers of hardened soil. They were quite comfortable with allowing their herds to "beat out" the soil until June and then having the sun "burn it out" in between the raising of fallow and the first harrowing. As we saw earlier, sometimes they even continued to maintain that herd grazing on fallow helped the soil!* We can be confident therefore, that for quite a long time after advancing to the three-field system the great mass of peasants had little inkling of the importance of early tillage, either in the fall (ziab) or in the spring (early fallow).[25] Surely it is no accident that contemporary compilers of agricultural folklore never found any sayings advocating early tillage.[26]

Peasants at this stage of agronomic understanding were just as indifferent to the depth of tillage as they were to its timing. As we have already seen, two-shared plows often gained favor over one-shared plows simply because they worked more quickly. The ability of single-shared plows to till more deeply was of no import to peasants who felt obligated merely to work the surface of the soil. Indeed, agronomists sometimes noted that many who purchased plows were not tilling any deeper with them than they had with their sokhas. And others were buying cultivators so as to work an even shallower layer than they had with the sokha![27]

The failure to comprehend the fundamentals of soil moisture also impeded farmers' awareness of the dangers to their crops from weeds. In contrast to their concern with killing off weeds before sowing, peasants could be astonishingly indifferent towards weeds growing amidst their crops. In sharp contrast to folklore in Germany (to take a known example), Russian sayings actually counseled farmers to disregard weeds so long as grain could grow amongst them.[28] An English farmer who spent a year in Samara province in the late 1870s recounted that "Many agriculturalists [gentry and peasant alike—D.K.] will deny the presence of weeds in their fields, but whenever I went to look, I found them simply choking the corn [all grains—D.K.]."[29]

Certain features of local agronomists' reports confirm that indifference to weeds lived on in Tambov up to the time of the revolution. The best evidence to this effect arises from analysis of peasants' handling of broadcast-sown millet and ribbon-sown crops. Millet was the crop most vulnerable to weeds. If its sprouts came up at all slowly, or if weather conditions were unfavorable, weeds could overcome millet, and there

---

*See Part I, section "Green Fallow and Other Shortcomings," for expressions of this sentiment after the imposition of the three-field system.

was no alternative but to mow the strip down as hay. As we saw in our treatment of sowing techniques, it was this threat from weeds that motivated peasants to do *lomka* tillage of millet after sowing. But once the survival of the sprouts was assured, peasants weeded millet "very stingily and sparingly."[30]

The same attitude surfaced after the appearance of seed drills. Earlier, in analyzing peasants' mistakes in applying seed drills, we noted their indifference towards inter-tillage of row-sown crops. Farmers could usually be persuaded to inter-till millet, since they were at least familiar with the idea of weeding millet. But agronomists had to nag them repeatedly to inter-till rye, because *they could not see any point to weeding a crop that was not about to be suffocated.*[31]

At this stage of soil understanding, therefore, peasants remained unaware of the fact that weeds suck out soil moisture from the soil and accommodate the multiplication of a wide range of pests. They minded weeds only insofar as they took surface space away from their crops. For rye, their most important crop, they took a variable degree of interest in clearing weeds from fallow land before sowing. That was all: "Walking through the fields, you can always tell the peasants' lands from the landlords' by the tufty yellow weeds blossoming all over them."[32]

Inevitably then, peasants at the second stage of soil understanding appraised land improperly: "Peasants judge [any given unit of] land based on the yields it has given in the past few years, which can depend on various factors, while agronomists evaluate land according to its quality."[33] Unable to see the real connections between tillage and yields, peasants thirsted all the stronger for the landlords' lands. If the *barin's* yields were better, it had to be because his land was better.[34]

Stage 3
First Steps to Intensify Tillage

At this stage the peasant farmer began to adopt more intensive techniques of working the soil, thereby elaborating on the conception of tillage's ameliorative capacity gained in Stage 2. With a greater or lesser degree of conviction, he accepted one or more of the notions that the depth, the timing, or the frequency of tillage could improve crop yields. In addition to the simple requirement to till the surface, the farmer now wished to do *dvoenie*, or to till deeper or earlier than before.

As we saw in the section "The Evolution of Tillage Regimes," the preference for increased frequency of tillage made the fastest head-way—*dvoenie* becoming a standard practice across almost the whole of Tambov by 1914. No doubt peasants' fixation on the immediate and visible threat of weeds to their sowings accounts for the speed with which *dvoenie* caught on. Insofar as this was their motivation in performing *dvoenie*, the technique did not reflect a refined understanding of the soil. Nevertheless, the sources do allow us to detect a more sophisticated motivation for *dvoenie*, at least among some farmers. When peasants said of *dvoenie* that "the land likes it," this surely testified to a belief in tillage as beneficial in its own right.[35] The preference they now acquired for "fluffy" soil indicates the same belief.[36]

Peasants were slower to adopt earlier tillage than they were to increase tillage frequency. We have seen, however, that by 1914 perhaps as many as one half of Tambov's households were tilling in the fall on lands to be sown in the spring with oats.[37] And we have good reason to believe that interest in early raising of fallow was steadily rising in Tambov, thanks to some unique data on this question from a similar province.[38] So peasants were slowly acquiring sympathy with the idea of tilling earlier than traditionally. It could be the case that much or even most of this interest reflected the propagandizing efforts of Russian agronomists. The agronomic community focused heavily on the timing of tillage throughout black-earth Russia. In some areas of Tambov early tillage was quite common among landlords, whose example might also have piqued peasants' curiosity.[39] But surely much of peasant interest in earlier tillage represented a natural, indigenous development of their understanding of the soil.[40]

Peasants' understanding of the soil was not advancing very far, however. Tillage regimes were evolving, yes. But the sources show that the growing numbers of peasants who reached Stage 3 were having a lot of trouble in executing intensified tillage operations. They simply tacked new instructions onto the established tillage paradigm without any awareness of the logic underlying them. Not knowing the manner in which soil moisture is gained or lost, they did not understand the circumstances that made intensified tillage practices desirable or disadvantageous. Hence, while they might indeed till earlier, more deeply, or more frequently, they might also commit serious errors. Many of those purchasing plows began tilling too deeply too soon, bringing up "dead" soil which harmed their crops.[41] Meanwhile, those who tilled strips of fallow land early, in May or even April, tended to leave these strips unharrowed for the customary 1–2 week period after the first tillage.[42] Similarly, they almost always left their early fallow unworked for a long time after the first harrowing.[43] By raising fallow early they were putting their soil in better shape, creating marvelous conditions for weed growth. Still unaware of the fundamentals of soil moisture, they did not yet understand the need to keep the upper layer of soil friable, and the weeds off, in the months before sowing.

Stage 4
Theoretical Understanding of Soil Structure

As we shall see in Part V, one of the primary goals of the agronomic aid effort was to give farmers a professional understanding of soil structure. Only then would they know the real rules of the game, so to speak, which would enable them to make sound decisions under variable weather and labor conditions. Clearly this entailed nothing short of a cultural revolution. In essence, this would be a transformation of the peasant farmer into the agronomist, with whose approach to questions of tillage and soil we are fully familiar. Without the scientists' help, however, peasants had little hope of reaching this stage.

Profit Maximizing, Utility Maximizing, or Something Else?

In proposing the existence of contrasts between peasants' and agronomists' approaches to technological and economic issues we are encroaching on territory that is very familiar to twentieth-century scholars of peasantries. For our purposes here, the most important contributions these scholars have made concern the distinct character of peasant farmers' decision-making strategies. Here they have established that the economic logic of actors on, or close to, the subsistence margin does not conform to the crude but common conception of *Homo economicus* as a profit maximizer akin to a capitalist entrepreneur. As so many development agencies have been disappointed to find out, subsistence-, or near subsistence-level farmers will not necessarily respond to opportunities for profit.[44] When and where the farmer declines to maximize profits, he does so for at least one of the following reasons:

1) *Risk Aversion.* In some cases innovations that promise to raise yields in an average year may also increase the fluctuation of yields. If a farmer perceives that troughs in bad years could drop him below the subsistence line, he will likely eschew the innovation in question.

2) *Satiety, or Drudgery Aversion.* If one is fully content with one's standard of living, and sees no need to build up more reserve wealth, then one is not likely to seek more profits.

3) *Fatalism.* If one has reason to believe that nothing can be done to raise one's standard of living—that surplus wealth will dissipate or be expropriated, for instance—then one will not attempt to raise productivity or seek higher profits.

4) *Non-economic Imperatives.* For any individual or firm, a variety of cultural norms, social pressures, and personal preferences can attract resources that might otherwise be invested in production. Peasants are more susceptible to such non-productive allocation of resources than are modern capitalist entrepreneurs.

Instead of a profit maximizer, therefore, we must look at the peasant farmer as a utility maximizer. This appears to be a very safe perspective—indeed the idea of *Homo economicus* as a utility maximizer (and not necessarily a profit maximizer) lies at the heart of neo-classical microeconomic theory.[45] Many scholars and observers have proceeded to conclude from this, however, that the peasant farmer was "the rational man of the land," or "the optimizing peasant," who shrewdly navigated through tricky technological and economic waters to make the most of his limited material possibilities.[46] This conclusion has been so widely shared that it is almost impossible to locate any critical study of peasant agricultural technology written by an historian.[47]

Yet it does not follow from the distinction between priorities of profit maximizing and utility maximizing that peasant farmers (or anyone else) were maximizing what we might call "material utility." In other words, we cannot assume *a priori* that non-economic imperatives did not significantly constrain peasants' *material* well-being. Moreover, even when peasants were pursuing material utility, we cannot assume that they successfully oriented among the technological options open to them, however hard they may have been trying. The faltering evolution of peasant farmers' comprehension of soil discussed above testifies quite plainly to this. If and where cultural imperatives or technological inaccuracies carried substantial material costs, it would be misleading to term peasant farmers "the rational men of the land."

The task before us, therefore, is to evaluate the degree to which peasants maximized material utility. This evaluation is indispensable both for appraising the performance of peasant farmers and for understanding the agrarian problem as a whole. Only on its basis can we assess the significance of peasant culture and technological aptitude to the agrarian problem. With these issues in mind, we now proceed to investigate the influence of peasant culture on economic and technological matters. Along the way, we shall have occasion to raise doubts not only about peasants' attainment of material utility, but even about the degree to which the routinization of work compromised utility maximizing behavior itself—behavior which standard microeconomic theory implicitly assumes.

Agriculture and the Magico-Religious World View

The most visible obstacles to economic efficiency on the Russian peasant farm issued from the interweaving of religious and superstitious elements with agricultural practice. Any observant visitor of a Russian village in the spring or summer would notice that work was scheduled around holidays, accompanied by rituals, and guided by superstitions. Thus the village assembly would forbid many or all kinds of fieldwork on Sundays and certain holidays throughout the year. When farmers began or ended work sessions they would turn towards the east, or a church, or an icon, cross themselves and recite certain prayers.[48] Depending on the job and the circumstances, they might include additional rituals, anything from saving the first and last sheaves of the harvest for ceremonial purposes, to tilling a furrow around the village (to ward off epidemics), or sprinkling themselves with water before leaving the house, or selecting an elderly woman to lead the cattle out of the village on the first day of grazing.[49] Throughout the year, meanwhile, they would try to anticipate weather, yields, and other phenomena by means of a large repertoire of proverbs and omens.[50] Immersion in the world of agricultural rites and superstitions began early in childhood. Even before they were old enough to work peasant youngsters were taught to imitate the rituals that the adults were performing in the fields.[51]

Much of this lore was indispensable to the work process. As we pointed out in the analysis of grain sowing, many of the proverbs and sayings by which peasants oriented during the agricultural year were unsound. But most of them were quite useful expressions of agronomic wisdom, the fruit of generations, or even centuries, of popular experience. Meanwhile, many of the accompanying rituals and superstitions were relatively innocuous. Individually, most of the beliefs, rituals, and superstitions probably came at little or no material cost, at least most of the time. The more broadly one studies the phenomenon, however, the more apparent becomes the grip in which the supernatural world held Russian peasants. We must investigate, therefore, the degree to which looking at the world through this prism affected peasants' economic behavior and material well-being.

Here we must begin by pointing out that the body of folklore was never uniform anywhere in the black-earth zone. Because of the irregular pattern of colonization of the region, individual beliefs or practices could vary substantially from one village to the next.[52] Yet everywhere the network of superstitions and religious injunctions was so rich as to be virtually all encompassing. The sun, water, fire, lightning, and even the wind had metaphysical content: "Don't curse the wind—that's a sin" a peasant might tell his son.[53] Mirages on the horizon were reflections of devils at work.[54] At least in some areas, peasants would never consider making a sale or a trade after sundown, in the absence of the sun's benevolent presence.[55]

Meanwhile, peasants peopled the terrestrial world with a variety of goblins and spirits. Field fairies (*polevye babushki* or *polevye rusalki*), water sprites (*vodianye* or *rusalki*), and forest demons (*leshie*) lurked in their respective domains, while minions of the devil or other dark forces in various guises (werewolves or witches, for example), threatened to appear in the village in disguised forms at any time. Perhaps most important of all was the house goblin—the *domovoi*—who would signal his wishes to the head of the household through dreams, noises, or afflictions cast on horses.[56]

Furthermore, peasants considered themselves potential carriers or negotiators of supernatural forces. Villagers might suspect one or more of their number to be sorcerers, counter-sorcerers, healers, or possessed. A host of instructions were available on neutralizing "the evil eye," or spells cast on one's grain fields, and so on. Magic, good, or evil was even attached to certain places—a copse of bushes amid plowland, a certain lake, a particular grove of trees, or a boulder.[57]

In whatever manner the mixture of beliefs and practices varied as between individual villages, it is clear that the invisible, supernatural world was ever present. Peasants accepted the existence of this world unconditionally. While conducting research in the 1870s, Sartor ethnographer A. N. Minkh recorded how the faces of young and old were equally captivated by the teachings of elderly peasants on these matters.[58]

The tenacity of superstitions was all the greater for their being so deeply intertwined with the rhetoric of Orthodoxy. Russian peasants were notable for the readiness with which they invoked Orthodox saints for protection from dark forces in everyday affairs.[59] As a traveler through Orel province on the eve of the First World War found out, peasants knew the saints' domains in daily matters—including their roles in the many branches of farming and livestocking—like they knew the backs of their hands.[60] Peasant religion rested on a synthesis of supernatural forces, both Christian and folkloric. So it was no accident when an ethnographer in Tambov noticed how peasants would become very distressed if anyone expressed a measure of disbelief with respect to their constellation of spirits, ghosts, and forces.[61]

The ubiquitousness of the supernatural world meant that all manner of movements and incantations could be prescribed, while other movements, actions, or words were proscribed. When the young Ivan Vol'nov mentioned the possibility of the family horse's demise, his father burst out: "You're bringing down evil, you little devil! Don't talk like that anymore!" He spit on the ground three times and incanted: "Lord, Jesus Christ. Away! Away! Away!"[62] And so peasants might cross themselves and recite a prayer almost at every undertaking.[63] "Every holiday, every day, even every step was accompanied by some sort of gesture," noted an ethnographer in Byelorussia.[64]

The potency and abundance of village beliefs and rituals inevitably spawned swarms of idiosyncratic or petty superstitions, many of them carrying deleterious economic consequences. Convinced, for example, that fires caused by lightning were expressions of God's will, peasants in many areas would refuse to extinguish these fires with water.[65] They would try to douse some of the flames with milk, if anything—rain, after all, being "milk from the sky cows."[66] And so huge villages would sometimes burn to the ground.[67] Other sources record peasants' superstitious prohibition on cleaning seed grain if it had been purchased, or their refusal to take measures against pests that had been seen (by someone) to descend from the clouds (as punishment for the peasants' sins).[68] Preying on widespread peasant ignorance regarding horses, horse dealers constantly fooled peasants into buying unsound animals.[69] When the horses subsequently failed, the deceived peasants would assume that the *domovoi* had taken a disliking to them.[70] Meanwhile, peasants often considered selective breeding of horses a sin; when and where selective breeding was condoned, they might avoid it with any livestock whose barns were at a slightly lower altitude than their own.[71]

A superabundance of holidays added still more to the economic cost of peasants' belief system. In the late Imperial period Russians celebrated more holidays than any other European nation.[72] Many of the holidays were not encouraged by the Church or the State. In honor of a cult of Fridays, for instance, many villages would forbid tillage and carting work, or any work that raised dust, or even all kinds of field work altogether, on that day of the week.[73] Naturally many holidays fell during quiet periods in the agricultural year, and others, such as those during the reaping season, served as vitally needed respites during long stretches of backbreaking labor.[74] But many other holidays delayed

time-sensitive operations, such as reaping, or spring tillage and sowing—the Easter holiday could last a week or more.[75] The economy did
not benefit, meanwhile, from the fact that holidays provided convenient excuses for heavy drinking, organized fighting, brawling, and domestic violence.[76] What is more, the number of holidays was growing,
as peasants established ever more local holidays. From an average of
95 holidays in the 1850s, there were 105 in the 1870s, and 123 by
1902.[77] Beyond the injuries and expenses associated with holidays, the
surplus of holidays in Russia above the quantities then observed in
America was costing the Russian peasantry a colossal amount of labor
time—as many as 4.1 billion man-work days per year at the turn of the
century.[78]

The Ebbing—and Returning—Tides of Ritual and Superstition

The countryside's world of beliefs, rites, rituals and superstitions was
too complex and inconsistent to remain static over time or uniform
over space. Moreover, from the last third of the nineteenth century
onward it was increasingly vulnerable to the trickle down influence of
science. It is not surprising therefore that most of the ethnographers
who recorded rural beliefs and behavior simultaneously noted that
certain of these features were fading out. Rituals of various kinds were
becoming empty motions or amusements as peasants forgot their
original motivations. The rites or ceremonies might live on for a while,
especially if they performed a social function by bringing co-villagers
together. Alternatively they might soon disappear.[79] In many places
holidays were less well observed by the turn of the century than they
had been earlier (sometimes, at least, thanks to recognition of the
economic costs[80]).[81] Some farmers admitted their doubts about the
usefulness of religious processions through the fields; others were citing
omens less frequently, or giving less credence to reports of magical or
miraculous events.[82]

A coordinated ethnographic study of popular superstitions in dozens
of provinces in the 1890s confirmed the breadth of the trend towards
skepticism. While the study found seers, witches, and faith healers to
be more or less omnipresent in the countryside, it also registered a
gradual remission of popular trust and belief in such characters. People
were becoming less interested in the predictive and explanatory powers
of the local gurus, because "nowadays there are lots of learned folk, who

can tell you when the southern wind is coming, or when there's gonna be rain."[83]

However inevitable might have been the appearance of skeptical challenges to traditional supernatural beliefs in the countryside after the arrival of literacy and education,[84] the struggle for pre-eminence between the two mentalities would partly depend on economic progress. As Russian ethnographers A. Maksimov and L. A. Tul'tseva have noted, so long as poverty held the bulk of the peasantry close to the margins of subsistence, periodic crises would serve to regenerate their accustomed reliance on the supernatural world.[85] Prayers, incantations, religious processions, and consultations with "knowers" (faith healers, generally speaking) offered hope to people chronically subject to economic uncertainty and psychological stress.[86] Further, peasants could deftly absorb or harmonize evidence of science's predictive power into their supernatural world view with the simple reflection, "People have become cleverer than the devil."[87] Finally, the traditional culture included something akin to its own safeguard against erosion from unbelievers—namely, injunctions such as "one can be happy only insofar as one follows the ways of one's ancestors."[88] Little wonder, then, that ethnographers and other observers kept finding so many vestiges of the superstitious and supernatural worlds in the countryside, decade after decade, right up to collectivization.[89]

The stubborn persistence of magic carried clear consequences for the maturation of "the optimizing peasant." The cultural climate was only very slowly becoming receptive to the scientific conception of nature as passive, and deductively knowable. Habits of experimentation, for instance, could only develop insofar as peasants accepted this conception of nature. This is a topic to which we shall return below.

Intellectual Consequences
of the Magico-Religious World

While in the short term the interpenetration of the natural and supernatural worlds in peasant mentality carried substantial economic costs, in the long term the intellectual consequences were still more costly. The overabundance of superstitions and rites that grew out of peasants' understanding of supernatural forces inevitably hobbled their perception of terrestrial causes and effects. How easily could a farmer perceive the connections between his methods of work and his results when so many of his culture's teachings sought to explain those results either on the basis of fate, or on the basis of behavior that—to the scientific eye—had nothing to do with work?

Peasant culture offered a bewildering array of explanations for meager or failed crops. If an individual family's yield was poorer than the village average, might that not be because they had failed to observe certain customs? Had the man heading out to sow his land failed to return home after seeing a woman, or after crossing paths with a neighbor?[90] Had he begun sowing with the bucket of seeds the priest blessed on the second day of Easter?[91] Had they sown the crop whose raw grains had risen to the top of a ceremonial loaf of bread?[92] Had they buried a container of holy water in the field?[93] Had they mixed a handful of earth with some millet seeds immediately upon seeing the first crane fly by, so as to ensure that the grain would grow well?[94] Was the husband not properly devout?[95] Had he offered the appropriate prayer after tillage?[96] Had the family properly observed Good Friday?[97] Had lightning burned a swathe through one of their strips of grain (the feared *perezhin*), or had the grains' ears been lighter than normal? Both cases were clear evidence that a local witch or sorceress had cursed them.[98] Had the ears of their grain been devoured by a pest and gone black—a bad omen known as *chernyi zazhin*?[99]

Peasants readily employed supernatural explanations for village-wide crop failures as well. Often, but not always, they perceived God's personal will here. He could withhold rain or send pests in punishment for people's sins.[100] Threatening droughts produced a variety of desperate and drastic measures, ranging from religious processions through the fields, to the uncovering of witches presumed to have cast spells to drive away the rainclouds, to the disinterment of suiciders from the village burial grounds (suicide being considered a very serious sin).[101] Folklore also offered a rich menu of markers to predict yields, any one of which could be employed as a retrospective explanation of a crop failure. If a particular crop failed, might that have been because a certain weather pattern, bird, or plant had not appeared on a particular winter day?[102] If meadow grass was growing weakly in the spring, might that not be because someone had left a harrow out in the rye field after a day of work in the previous summer?[103]

And so we can be certain that the supernatural explanatory matrix blurred peasants' vision of terrestrial causation. Further, we can be just as certain that this malady could at times acquire a more advanced form—namely, that peasants would stop looking for terrestrial causation. Thus one particularly observant ethnographer noted that peasants favored interpreting each others' results in supernatural terms even when technological explanations were immediately at hand: "If a co-villager's crop fails because he sowed too sparsely or used shriveled seeds, spoiled in grain drying, the peasants ascribe this, as with livestock diseases, to sorcery."[104] Here was the mind-set that could easily produce a stubborn, intransigent indifference to technological innovations. As a peasant character of Tolstoy's said to Prince Nekhliudov (as Tolstoy renamed himself in a story based on his personal experiences) in response to the suggestion that he do more manuring: "Again, what can I tell you, your grace? It is not manure that grows the grain. It is all God's doing."[105]

Levels of Material Optimizing—
Active Experimentation vs.
the Passive Accumulation of Experience

It should not surprise us that the combination of a weak grasp of technology and a world view heavily reliant on supernatural forces constantly threatened to routinize peasants' attitudes to agricultural work, or at least to many agricultural operations. The consequences of this kind of routinization are perhaps less apparent. They include the underdevelopment of two critical mechanisms in peasant farmers' intellectual repertoire—empirical learning and the experimental ethos. In investigating these aspects of the mental world of the Russian village and measuring them against the yardstick of "the optimizing peasant" construct, it will be best to begin with the phenomenon of experimentation.

Many studies have identified sophisticated, systematic experimentation within traditional agricultural communities, even among illiterate peasants. Allen W. Johnson, the scholar who did the most to collate these studies, concluded not only that the propensity to experiment is intrinsic to human beings, but also that "experimentation is probably as natural as conformity in traditional communities."[106] These conclusions underlie very sanguine estimations of the capacity of indigenous populations to refine agricultural technologies and adapt them to changing circumstances if need be.[107] Folk agricultural wisdom, in this view, is experimental as well as empirical—farmers do not merely notice and reflect on the results they achieve each year, but greatly accelerate the learning process by designing and conducting experiments of various kinds. Folk agricultural wisdom is therefore potent, vital, and evolving. So it appears to be in many traditional agricultural societies, at any rate.

How are we to know if this general picture obtained among the peasantry of the central black-earth region? Experimental practices are very difficult for the historian to measure, since even literate farmers are unlikely to record or publish many of the trials or experiments that they carry out. Nevertheless, sufficient data exist for us to establish a picture of some important aspects of experimental practice in the area of the Russian countryside in question.

The evolution of peasants' conceptions of soil and tillage provides an important window on experimentation. Consider the perspective of the peasant farmer at the second stage of soil understanding, where the folk paradigm required him merely to work the surface of the land a single time. What kind of experimentation could there be in such circumstances, where crop failures and successes could only be explained by forces lying outside of farming technology? In the absence of meteorological science, it appeared to peasants that God gave rain, if and when He chose. Drought or pestilence meant that witches and sinners had betrayed the village.[108] Tillage techniques were certainly not to blame. Indeed, there was no question of examining tillage work with an eye to improving it. "In our village no one uttered a single word about any kind of improvement of our farming."[109] And so there was no conceptual room for the kind of trial-and-error experimentation that might have provided practical methods of defense against drought even without the attainment of a theoretical understanding of the fundamentals of soil moisture. The rule of superstition was pervasive as regarded tillage.

Agronomic improvements could and did take hold in this mental climate. Thus peasants purchased plows, or attached metal teeth to their harrows. Likewise, with respect to other field operations, they replaced sickles with scythes, hired threshing machines, etc. But these technical advances shared the common goal of making labor go faster or easier. People accepted the new equipment on account of the fact that it worked faster, not because it worked better:

> In the last few years the plow has begun to replace the *sokha* on peasant farms. Threshers, reapers, and other agricultural machines are also appearing. But the new equipment does little if anything to improve working of the land. In acquiring new equipment the peasant's first concern is to increase labor pro-

> ductivity, with threshing or reaping machines for example. When choosing a plow they want to know how fast a model will work, not how well. Hence in this area [Sosnovsk sector, Morshansk *uezd*] they purchase only two-shared plows.[110]

With population density rising, and land per capita of the agricultural population rapidly shrinking, this approach was decidedly unpromising. The only way out of poverty and hunger lay in additional application of labor, not labor conservation.

Might experimentation be more apparent at the third stage of soil understanding, where farmers took steps to intensify tillage roughly along the lines which agronomic science would recommend? As they did so, a large space opened up for a critical attitude towards work, for doubt, and for experiments. How much deeper should I till? How much earlier? But it seems that peasants did not dwell on such matters. The transformation of methods of labor did not trigger more inquisitiveness or curiosity. Spirited debate would arise only if exceptional weather conditions caused a new technique to backfire.[111] Thus there is almost no evidence of systematic trials with various tillage techniques. First a few peasants would intensify tillage (*dvoenie*, or *ziab*, for instance) after working on landowners' estates. Then—perhaps—the rest of the village would copy the new technique and that would be the end of it. Note how one local agronomist summed up the attitudes of peasants towards technological improvements (in an area where tillage regimes had intensified in the last two generations):

> The majority of the peasants distrust the idea that it is possible to raise yields with improved tillage. The weather alone is important to them: if the rains come, so will the harvest. They consider it unprofitable to expend labor and resources on improving tillage.[112]

To be sure, tillage regimes did intensify in several ways during the last three to four decades preceding 1914. But the very pace of the change exposes the faintness of experimental practice in the villages. As noted in the section "The Intensification of Tillage Regimes," a striking fact in the evolution of tillage techniques in Tambov was the speed with which certain alterations took place. *Dvoenie* in particular would have arisen much earlier and spread much more slowly if peasants in the more densely populated sectors of the province had been tinkering with alternative methods.[113]

More thorough information concerning attitudes towards experimentation comes from peasants' handling of new strains of crops. To a certain degree, peasants had always been aware of distinctions between strains of crops.[114] Thus we know that they generally assigned names to particular strains, and could adjust cultivation practices to suit perceived properties of strains. Peasants in Saratov province are known to have been aware of three botanical categories of millet, for example, each of which thrived in particular soil and climate conditions. They preferred to keep these categories of millet separate so as to capitalize on these strain-specific properties.[115] Someone, at sometime—perhaps initially a peasant, or a local landowner, or a priest—must have keenly observed the differences between strains, and perhaps even conducted experiments with them. We can be sure, moreover, that some peasants undertook rudimentary trials with new species of crops or techniques. Some data have survived directly verifying this type of experimentation.[116]

Much of the information regarding peasants' attitudes towards strains of crops, however, testifies to a remarkable degree of indifference to distinctions between strains and the opportunities biological diversity offered for experimentation. Peasant terminology for strains of grains was often so indistinct as to permit the mixing of widely varying biological material. Thus, "ordinary," "local," "Russian," and "peasant" were commonly encountered names for strains.[117] Sunflowers might be called merely "striped" or "gray," for instance, on the mistaken assumption that these characteristics sufficed to identify biological properties.[118]

A detailed study of varieties of grains in Saratov province (on Tambov's southeastern border) in 1912/13 that was repeated in 1924 provides valuable elaboration on peasant attitudes to strains of crops. Although the study did not produce a uniform picture, some of its findings were startling. Thus, peasants would often employ one name for many varying strains of a particular grain.[119] Alternatively, they would continue to call their grain by a given sort name long after the grain had become a mixture of many sorts and the sort in question had ceased to predominate.[120] Peasants would not necessarily test new strains of grain versus old strains. Unless instructed, moreover, they were not likely to take any pains to keep the newly acquired variety separate from their old grain.[121] Such habits could not be further removed from the ethos of experimentation. And let it be recalled that the peasants participating in these studies were among the more advanced in agrotechnical matters. Co-villagers were even less inclined to experiment.[122]

In conclusion, it seems that the spirit of the empirical method developed feebly in the Russian village. This was no accident. In addition to the fact that a worldview permeated with supernatural forces interfered with the development of technological acumen among peasants, the economic geography of central and southern Russia long precluded the same development. From the initial settling of the open spaces of the huge black-earth region to the last decades of the nineteenth century, land was always abundant relative to labor. This relationship dictated that farmers concentrate all of their energies on the extension of sown area, not on yield-boosting refinements, which would have almost always involved the intensification of labor. The economic and demographic pressures of the late nineteenth and early twentieth centuries escalated at great speed, far more quickly than the farming population could reverse their long-ingrained orientation towards extensification. Thus experimentation remained a low priority. Villages in black-earth Russia never set aside certain plots of land for experiments, as agricultural communities in some other nations have been known to do.[123] As one observer in the central black-earth region had remarked before emancipation, "The peasantry learns through experience, not experimentation."[124] He could have put it nearly the same way half a century later.

Self-Reliance and the Overcoming of Traditional Sources of Knowledge

Like most Durnovka men he could only repeat the old simple wisdoms, confirming what has been known to everyone for ages and ages.

—Ivan Bunin, *The Village*, 1910[125]

When a thoughtful, intelligent person takes a look at work of typical peasants, he is struck by the amount of time and effort the peasant usually manages to waste. The shame is that they work only with their hands, leaving their brains at rest.

—Ia. G. Apsit, 1915[126]

Even if experimentation generally failed to take strong root, we can be certain that peasants were always learning about agriculture through experience. It could not be otherwise. But here too the "rational man of the land" construct would be a somewhat misleading rendering of the peasant farmer's behavior. Routinization penetrated peasant agricultural thinking very deeply, and in many ways. In the cultural environment of the village the process of learning through experience was never so simple or unobstructed—and therefore never so potent—as one would intuitively assume.

In investigating the manner in which peasant farmers learned from experience we can begin by considering the traditional sources of agricultural knowledge in the village. The peasant had five separate sources of knowledge to guide his agricultural decisions, four of which bound him to established practices and discouraged independent thinking. First, he had a rich lore of folk sayings from which to draw—"sow oats in mud, and you will be wealthy," etc. Then there were the old local village traditions—"when the trees in the last hollow dress themselves [i.e., take leaves], begin tillage on that field." Third, the village elders were there to give their opinions, on the basis of their lifetime of personal experience. The widespread custom of a few older men congregating to determine the proper time to begin the sowing or reaping of particular crops testifies to the great weight of this sort of knowledge in the community—on these specific questions, at any rate.[127] Fourth, some families had their own traditions—"we harrow until the clods are fully broken up," or "we sow twelve baskets of oats on this strip, but less densely on that one," etc. In an atmosphere of paternal domination, such traditions could easily solidify. The father certainly exerted the strongest influence on young peasants' agricultural education. Finally, the farmer could fall back on his own experience and judgment, informed in some cases by what he had seen on landlords' farms or while traveling through other territories. "I remember weather like this. I say we reap now, no matter what the neighbors say." "I think we should do *dvoenie*," "I think we need a plow," etc.

Folk agricultural wisdom would remain vital and growing so long as peasants took care to exercise their individual judgment. But the rich network of sources of knowledge discouraged them from developing this faculty. These sources of knowledge preserved traditions and precedents, thereby protecting the individual and the community from the dangers (and the opportunities) of technological deviation. It is true that farmers would often weigh farming decisions individually, from the perspective of their household, and would sometimes decide to execute labor operations differently from the bulk of their neighbors. A household might not be able to afford to sow as much oats as its neighbors, and so would opt for cheaper millet seeds instead. A family's horse might be lame, precluding fall tillage. In years where the hay mowing looked like overlapping with the ripening of the rye, some peasants would want to make hay before commencing reaping, or vice versa.[128] But this sort of decision-making did not amount to a rethinking of established technological methods or paradigms. That could only arrive via a different route.

In peasant practice, individual *judgment*, as opposed to individual *calculation*, tended to begin only where technological lore ended, in situations where precedent could not provide the farmer with any clear guidance. It has been argued that such situations turn up frequently and inevitably in traditional agriculture, because: 1) agricultural folk wisdom is not all-encompassing; 2) the uncertainty of the technologies employed generates disagreement within communities on technological questions; 3) each plot of land is a bit different from the next, and is changed by those who work it in ways noticeable only to them; and 4) folk wisdom often enjoins the farmer to employ his or her knack for the craft. All of these circumstances, the argument goes on, force peasant farmers to learn and think on their feet much of the time, which constantly generates and refreshes folk agricultural wisdom in individual farmers.[129]

However potent this process might be in other settings, its influence on peasant grain farming in black-earth Russia was quite weak. The broad, flat expanses of relatively homogeneous soil and vegetation here did not warrant much attentiveness to microclimatic variation. Most villages did possess a small assortment of soil types, and descriptions of land redistribution practices testify that they were aware of these types.[130] But the variety of soil conditions was very limited, such that farmers were unlikely to encounter situations where the folk agricultural canon could not provide them with guidance. Where neither the traditional Russian, nor village folklore foresaw a localized problem, farmers could observe how respected elders or other neighbors in the village handled it. Even when a peasant faced a problem individual to his own farm, he did not always have to think it through in isolation. Family traditions already accounted for many such situations: "We sow more densely on this strip of land than on that one," for instance.

Thus, in grain farming operations, at least, the black-earth peasant rarely faced unforeseen circumstances that forced him to think on his feet and devise new responses. Nature could certainly produce phenomena unanticipated in the cultural lore, and peasants might diagnose these phenomena individually. But most novel phenomena would be inconsequential curiosities that would not require technological responses or prompt further investigation—thus we have an account of peasants disagreeing over why rye began to turn yellow in the fields prematurely. Was a cold spell to blame, or the warm weather that had preceded the cold?[131] Only a significant danger or opportunity, like the appearance of a new tool, a drought, or the imposition of a new tillage regime, could force peasants to make a technological decision uninformed by precedent.

Given all the transformations in grain-farming operations we documented in Part I, it must be admitted that many stimuli of this nature did reach individual farmers in the half century following emancipation. And these stimuli often prompted them to think on their own: researchers in Saratov province, for example, found villages where farmers were divided into three groups on particular questions of harrowing in preparation for millet sowings.[132] Observers in other provinces noted what short periods of drought could do to peasants' unanimity on certain technical questions. For example:

> ... in the absence of subsequent rains, fallow raised in June has been left unharrowed and *dvoenie* has not been done. Weeds are flourishing. Now rains have come, but no one knows exactly what to do. Is it best to do *dvoenie*, or to sow straight away? Therefore everyone is doing as he thinks best—some are doing *dvoenie*, some are sowing.[133]

Other reports testify to peasants' inveterate inquisitiveness whenever they encountered new tools or new ways of work. As one local agronomist remarked:

> ... during work, when conducting a demonstration in the field with some tool or machine from the lending point—be it a plow, a seed drill, or whatever—a group of 10–15 curious peasants working on neighboring strips always gathered around to watch, and discuss ...[134]

The fact that unexpected stimuli forced peasants to think in new ways and that they habitually displayed great curiosity regarding new tools or methods of work is very significant to our appraisal of the vitality of folk agricultural wisdom. It would clearly be wrong to characterize this aspect of peasant culture as dormant or inert. At the same time, it would be equally wrong to base our evaluation of peasants' technological inquisitiveness on the example of the rather thin layer of farmers whose efforts constantly renewed the community's understanding of agricultural phenomena or drove this knowledge forward.

The natural and predominant tendency among peasant farmers was not to develop individual judgment on technological or meteorological questions, but rather to follow the example of a few leaders in the village.[135] Witness, for instance, the Tambov writer Alexander Ertel's account of a controversy over the timing of the sowing of rye. Here Ertel is talking to a peasant named Vasilii Mironich, the wealthiest, most respected peasant in his village:

> "Bad fortune this fall, wouldn't you say, Vasilii Mironich?"
> "What can you do, its God's will!"....
> "The rye sprouts are rotting, it seems."
> "It couldn't be otherwise, yes, they're rotting. Should have known, it would have been better to sow later."
> "Yes, but I can't make out Vasilii Mironich, what was the point of hurrying? Why, you yourself finished sowing your rye before First *Spas* [August 1st, old style—D. K.]"
> Vasilii Mironich smiled smugly. "You can't guess? It's clear, we guessed that the earlier we sow, the richer will be the growth of the rye sprouts, and the more the animals will have to graze on when the first frosts come. But it didn't turn out in our favor. And now everyone is blaming the failed sowing on me."
> "Who is?"
> "Our co-villagers. We had never sown before Assumption [August 15th, old style—D. K.], not ever. And now I—is it a sin?—start sowing before First *Spas*, and everyone copies me. So now look. What a mess."
> "Well, what are you to blame for?"
> "I'll tell you. Do you know that fellow Trofim?"
> "You mean Trofim Kuz'kin?"
> "Yeah, that's the one. He finished his sowing around Ivan *Postnyi* [August 29th, old style—D. K.]. 'Like our forefathers sowed, so shall I,' he said. 'They weren't any more stupid than we are.'"
> "And it turned out well for him."
> "Yes it did turn out well for him!" laughed Vasilii Mironich. "His sprouts barely covered the ground, and so they aren't rotting. The peasants have all gone over to his side now. But you know what the peasant is, don't you? The peasant is a fool. Whichever way the wind blows, he goes with it."[136]

The imitation of successful and respected neighbors' work methods could make perfect sense—but not when carried too far. Blind, reflexive imitation could be very dangerous, as Ertel's account demonstrates. Preobrazhenskii's discussion of the manner in which peasants would

determine the appropriate time to sow helps to flesh out the extent of
the influence of a few farmers over the rest:

> The selection of the time to sow depends a bit on [weather]
> conditions, and a bit on omens. But to a far greater degree it
> depends on the example of neighbors. "Well, people are sowing,
> so it's time to sow" says the peasant, reaching for his seed bucket.
> *Rare are the farmers who choose the time for sowing on the basis of
> weather conditions.*[137]

This kind of passivity created an unhealthy climate for the cultivation of folk agricultural wisdom. Local knowledge could not grow as
quickly as demanded in the period under study through the efforts of
a mere handful of farmers in each village. What is more, relying on the
judgment of others could easily become an insidious habit among
peasants, hobbling their mastery of the arts of husbandry. Surely this
concern underlay scathing verdicts on the passiveness of peasant
farmers' agricultural acumen, from Engel'gardt, the writer Bunin, and
a *zemstvo* agronomist:

> If, on the one hand, the complete fool is a rarity, then only
> slightly less rare is the particularly competent farmer. Average
> people predominate; through imitation of others, most within
> their ranks have learned to do their work reasonably well, but
> are *incapable of running a farm independently. They are incapable
> of working without following someone else's example.*[138]

> [a man who grew up as a peasant, speaking to his brother, about
> the peasants:] Just think, they've been tilling the soil for a
> thousand years—what am I saying, more!—and no one, not a
> single soul, knows how to do it properly! It's their only job, yet
> they don't know how to do it! They don't know when it's time
> to start tilling, when to sow and when to mow! "We do like
> people do," they say, and that's that! Hear that? "We do like
> people do"![139]

> In the commune all work proceeds as if by inertia. The bell
> rings—time to make hay, or till. Every member of the commune
> takes a more nonchalant approach to farming than the next,
> placing all their hopes on "smart Gerasim" or "experienced
> Peter."[140]

Issuing from the village's traditional networks of knowledge and the
public character of work—in the sense of the visibility of everyone's

field work regimes—the unconscious, indifferent, routine, herd-like approach to work to which all of these quotations attest represented a serious limitation on peasants' ability to refine their technologies in response to the rapidly changing economic and demographic conditions of the period under study. Progress through the second and third stages of comprehension of the soil, for instance, demanded that farmers abandon the first four of the five traditional sources of knowledge. The farmer would have to comprehend the fundamentals of soil science and exercise his own judgment in applying them to his individual circumstances. Only on this basis could he decide what portions of the folkloric canon to retain. And tillage was not the only operation in need of rethinking. Our treatment of the other labor operations has demonstrated the breadth and depth of agronomic ignorance, and it is clear that farmers would have to adopt a critical attitude to traditional sources of knowledge if they were to correct these flaws as well. Most important, they would need to acquire a minimal understanding of the basics of reproduction and inheritance if they were ever to sow stronger seeds and breed stronger animals.[141]

Technical vs. Allocative Inefficiency

The peasant has a mind, for sure, only he lacks knowledge, and the compass within which he applies his mind is far too narrow...
—A. N. Engel'gardt, 1876[142]

While self-reliance and the refining of folk agricultural wisdom could raise the level of technical efficiency in the fields, the material well being of the peasantry would also depend on improvements in farmers' organizational or "allocative" efficiency. "Allocative efficiency" is a measurement of the efficiency with which economic actors select inputs so as to generate desired outputs. Russian peasants always faced difficult choices in juggling limited resources of land, labor, and capital to produce and dispose of agricultural goods. Were they coping with these challenges effectively in the late nineteenth and early twentieth centuries?

The limited development of self-reliance among peasants with respect to technical questions alerts us to the likelihood that they were not meticulously weighing and selecting their inputs. We can begin to test this impression by investigating peasants' habits of calculation. Calculation is obviously essential to the efficient allocation of resources, and we know that peasants did cultivate their powers of calculation to a certain extent. In the decades following emancipation an ever-increasing portion of peasants, especially young males, learned some mathematics as part of basic schooling. Many sources confirm that numeracy, arithmetical skills, and an impressive capacity for remembering transactions were common attributes of Russian peasants in this period (at least among men).[143] Since market relations do so much to promote these skills, and since they were spreading rapidly in the countryside after 1861, we can be sure that numerical skills were advancing among the rural population.[144]

We can be just as sure, however, that habits of applying calculation developed much earlier and more quickly with respect to economic negotiations (at the marketplace, or among neighbors) than to farm organization. As strange as it may seem, agronomists found that even the more literate farmers had no idea of the value of keeping farming accounts:

> Does the peasant know a lot about his farm? He keeps something in his head, he forgets some of it, and about the rest he hasn't got the faintest idea. If you ask a peasant how much he made or lost on his farm, how much it costs him to produce a unit of rye or milk, how much of his production he converted into money, how much he spent, or how much property he has, he won't be able to give you any answers.[145]

Nor did farmers keep any records of the weather.[146] At least as late as the 1880s, it appears that many peasants resented the very notion of measuring their own grain. They would even laugh at landlords who did so.[147] Researchers in Tambov in the 1890s reported that peasants could recite precise crop yields only for the past 2–3 years.[148] According to one *uezd*-level summary report, they would not count serious drought years when giving assessments of average yields.[149] Many peasants, moreover, could not even arrive at a reliable estimate of their current yields. They would find out only when they sold a wagonload at the bazaar.[150]

Of course peasants could raise yields and accumulate resources without undertaking managerial accounting. But they would not make full use of economic opportunities until they did keep good accounts. To take a basic example, how else were they to know what to do with root crops? Should they use them as fodder in order to increase their livestock holdings, should they sell them to starch factories or distilleries, or should they eat them? The quantity of calculations required to answer this and other common organizational questions was too complex to handle without recourse to pencil and paper.[151] In the sequel, accounting practices trailed far behind the adoption of other innovations. Apart from very rare exceptions, peasants began to keep accounts only in the 1920s, after the Soviets started calibrating progressive taxes to the income of individual households.[152]

Peasants' inattentiveness to accounting generated very costly inaccuracies in farm organization. A simple example of this concerns the use of manure. In Tambov, as elsewhere in Russia, the commune's periodic redistribution of arable land was said to have stifled peasants' incentive to apply manure. Why, asked peasants (and the legions of commentators who mimicked them) should anyone expend the effort and resources to care for his land if it might soon be taken away from him?[153] As logical as this argument appears, it was the fruit of miscalculation—or non-calculation. Indeed, in just one average year the boost in grain yields from manure would more than compensate farmers for the labor expended in applying it.[154] Shortages of manure and agronomic ignorance do more to explain peasants' reticence to use manure than do land tenure relationships.[155] We shall encounter other organizational inaccuracies in Part III.

The tardy and limited employment of calculative powers to farm organization suggests that economic acumen of other kinds developed slowly among the peasantry. Many observers, for example, recorded remarkable carelessness towards risk among peasants. We have already seen that peasants did not try to weigh the risk of drought by keeping records of the weather. The magnitude of the threat of drought remained, therefore, very uncertain to them. In the face of this uncertainty it is quite surprising that peasants did not do more to cultivate the habit of accumulating resources so as to safeguard themselves against the possibility of droughts and partial crop failures. Many observers insisted that peasants avoided work in the winter months not because they had good reason to feel secure about the coming year, but because they were too shortsighted to appreciate the benefit of earning some income in anticipation of need.[156]

As some contemporaries saw it, peasants were careless about risk because they generally operated on a diseconomically short time-horizon and manifested an "inability to project plans and expectations far into the future."[157] Notice how a good farmer addressed his neighbors on the subject of winter preparations for the upcoming work year:

> ... it is most important to think ahead, but we are only good at hindsight. Each of us sits at home beside the stove all winter picking our nose until spring comes, and we say "Oh no, there isn't enough of this, nothing left of that, and now I can't go get anything because the roads are impassable."[158]

The quotation is from the peasant writer Sergei Semenov, who adds that all of the peasants listening to the speaker conceded the justice of the accusation. Russian peasants' refusal to glean harvested fields lends further credence to the portrayal.[159]

Does it then follow that peasants were diseconomically lazy? It is interesting to note that the theory of rationality underlying neoclassical economic theory precludes our posing this question. For virtually all contemporary economists human behavior is eminently rational, in the sense that our individual decisions concerning resources are products of our calculations on how to maximize utility. If a peasant chose not to do more weeding, for example, that meant that the value he placed on doing some other task, or simply on resting, was higher than the expected return from more weeding. Similarly, if he chose to follow the example of a neighbor in determining the appropriate time to sow his millet, that merely implied that he did not expect much utility value to come from the time and effort it would require for him to think the issue out for himself. For an economist, therefore, a peasant farmer is a rational economic actor, just like everyone else.

But this concept of rationality—commonly termed the theory of revealed preferences—is eminently unrevealing. It is a tautology, as Gary Becker virtually concedes in his manifesto "The Economic Approach to Human Behavior."[160] Economists have wrestled with the weaknesses of the theory of revealed preferences in many ways.[161] With respect to the problem of the routinization of work and its consequences for technological thinking, the most pertinent ideas have come from the maverick economist Tibor Scitovsky.

One of Scitovsky's fundamental points is that we often make decisions without informing ourselves of our options. It follows, therefore, that we cannot automatically equate subjects' freely chosen decisions with their rational self-interest.[162] He reaches this position by proposing that we have two sources of pleasure: comfort (rest, food, etc.), and stimulation—meaning novelty that requires "culture" (by which he means background) for its enjoyment. He then argues that most people are easily bewitched by comforts, and are prone to neglect the pursuit of stimulations that require "culture". Further, as the economist Amartya Sen has interpreted Scitovsky:

> If constructive stimulation is neglected in actual behavior, this is not because people have examined the alternatives and the range of choices that are in fact within their command, and have come to the considered conclusion that they really do want comfort rather than stimulation....
>
> Scitovsky's theory turns to a considerable extent on our unwillingness or reluctance to examine the real options we have. Another way of understanding Scitovsky's thesis, then, is to see it as the identification of the need for more *self-examination* of what it is that we really want, rather that considering it simply as an external diagnosis that what people will profit from most is stimulation rather than comfort....
>
> Scitovsky's theory of rationality does not, ultimately, involve denying the necessity—for rationality—of attempting to get what one really wants, but this wanting is considered, as it were, at a higher level. *A person may really want creative stimulation—without being reflectively clear that this is what she does want—and then mistakenly pursue a life style that does not promote what would most satisfy her.* In this sense, Scitovsky's thesis can be seen as being broadly within the conventional framework of rationality in terms of what a person *really* desires: much of the sophistication of the concept takes the form of providing a deeper characterization of what is really desired.[163]

In asserting the inadequacy of the conventional characterization of rational behavior, Scitovsky's work is a direct challenge to the theory of the optimizing peasant. His notion of comforts luring people away from cultivating the skills requisite to the enjoyment of stimulation mirrors the relationship most peasants adopted towards technological culture. They rested content on the legacy of agronomic folk wisdom, and ceded the terrain of technological investigation to a few leaders in the village. In so doing, they narrowed the sphere of options within their purview. Quite apart from the possibility that they forfeited a certain amount of enjoyment (stimulation) intrinsic to technological exploration, they suffered painful material consequences for succumbing to the comfort of avoiding the responsibility to cultivate a critical attitude towards work. Insofar as this was true, they were not behaving in their own best interests.

Apart from undermining the assumption that peasants conformed to the popular "poor-but-efficient" portrayal, what can Scitovsky's psychological, "bottom-up" explanation of human behavior tell us about the question of inefficiency in peasant agriculture? Are not all of us just as prone to inefficiency? Is the pursuit of stimulation equally elusive in all environments? Answers to these questions depend on our interpretation of the "top-down" influence of specific cultural values and economic pressures that do so much to shape attitudes and behavior.[164] Could it be that in the village these values and pressures posed inordinately high obstacles to efficient economic behavior, and thereby drove the peasant farmer ever deeper into the trap of "comfort"/routine? Our analysis of the magico-religious world and the network of traditional sources of knowledge have already pointed our interpretation in that direction. Continuing now with a treatment of fatalism in the Russian countryside, we can explore how far this road will take us.

Fatalism

The fact is, [the peasants] really do not much care what happens to them. This spirit is a product of history; as an able Liberal said to me, "if you never see your pay coming, you lose interest in your work."
—Sir Bernard Pares, 1907[165]

Fatalism comes in many guises. People who are convinced that they cannot improve their material standard of living will not attempt to do so, whether they 1) believe in divinely pre-ordained fate, 2) perceive material advance to be economically impossible, 3) succumb to pressures to conform to community norms, or 4) fear expropriation from more powerful people in their midst. Observers, commentators, and memoirists in peasant Russia focused much more on the last two styles of fatalism than on the first two. Thus the sources are not rich enough to allow us individually to weigh the influence of each of these dimensions of fatalism on the conceptualization and application of agricultural technologies. At the same time, the sources do reveal some of the mechanisms at work in the village that discouraged the application of intellect to technological questions.

Perhaps the most important of these mechanisms was peer pressure, which could take many forms. While all humans feel pressure to conform to community norms, the absence of anonymity in the village intensified this pressure. Anyone experimenting with new tools or procedures had to be prepared to face ridicule or even hostility from his neighbors. Gossip was an ever-present lever imposing conformity. "The women love to make small talk, and choose whatever subject comes closest to hand and lies closest to their heart—that is, they pass judgment on their friends and neighbors' behavior, no matter what they have been up to."[166] "Each and every one keeps an eye on each other, on where they have gone, what they have done, what they have bought, what they ate, drank."[167] While many sources reported that peasants feared ridicule, one of the most astute observers, a long-serving Tambov administrator named Alexander Novikov, sensed that their anxiety before the court of public opinion was extraordinarily strong:

> Generally speaking, fear of ridicule is deeply entrenched among the people. They fear evil much less than being laughed at. Often one hears them decline sound advice on this account—"they will laugh at us." Sending a girl to school is out of the question—"that is not done; they will laugh at us." Those leaving school try to unlearn proper grammar, for fear of being laughed at.[168]

Other accounts leave no doubt that these anxieties extended to technological behavior: "So often, hidden behind a peasant's outward indifference and skepticism, lies a fear of becoming a laughing-stock to co-villagers for having jumped at an innovation ..."[169]

If twitting or derisive gossip did not suffice to maintain traditional standards of behavior, direct intervention could follow. In some cases a peasant might attempt to punish an individualistic neighbor on his own, out of envy or jealousy. He might, for instance, try to sabotage the offender's crops in the field.[170] In other cases "justice" was collectively imposed. The peasant writer Sergei Semenov noted that communes might forcibly restrain co-villagers from tilling their lands in uncustomary places or at uncustomary times, not on account of any material conflict of interest, but simply as a leveling measure: "How dare you stir up trouble in the commune! You'll give others ideas."[171] Witness, moreover, how some peasant acquaintances explained the force behind peer pressure to a *zemstvo* doctor:

> In the village it isn't Princess Marya Alekseevna [the local landowner—D. K.] who maintains order, of course, but certain "people." And they are stricter than any Princess could ever be. "What will people say?", and especially "people will laugh"—no

one in the village will dare to struggle against this. Just you try—those "people" might not limit themselves to words and laughs.[172]

Other sources attest that collective violence in the name of conformity was at the very least a latent feature of village life throughout Russia.[173]

And so social pressures could certainly constrain non-conformity of any kind, including the pursuit of technological innovations. Neighbors would likely confront the aspiring innovator: "Oh, so you want to be smarter than the fathers, is that it?... You wanted to be smarter than us?" "So you thought the grandfathers were stupid, didn't you."[174] Moreover, fatalism could afflict families who were entirely obeisant to community norms. Leveling measures could befall any family that noticeably improved its economic standing, for the price of success was often envy and animosity from one's neighbors. A telling, although extreme, case of this is F. E. Romer's story of a man driven to suicide by co-villagers' hounding of him after he unexpectedly acquired wealth.[175] According to the peasant writer Pod"iachev, villagers genuinely enjoyed seeing their neighbors fall: "... everyone hates each other to a surprising degree of ferocity. Hardship or woe for one is a joy to the rest, an inexhaustible subject for conversation."[176] Pursuit of a higher material standard of living was not easy in such an atmosphere.[177]

Partial expropriation could come from many other directions. Upon the mere appearance of a bit more wealth, such as with the purchase of new tools, for instance, co-villagers might expect higher dowries from a family.[178] Peasant officials at the village or *volost'* level who harbored personal grudges would pounce on the same symptoms of wealth to demand more in taxes from such a family. Newly appointed, inexperienced Land Captains determined to follow the letter of the law and squeeze out all tax arrears as quickly as possible would pursue the same course.[179] The depredations of lower-level officialdom in the countryside were a well chronicled, much lamented sore in Russia.[180] And some well-informed commentators insisted that peasants' fatalism and dissipation stemmed first and foremost from the helplessness of the individual before the commune and other officials.[181]

In sum, then, we can conclude that social relations in the countryside constantly generated a degree of economic fatalism among the peasantry, and that this fatalism must have exerted a long-lingering pull over economic behavior in the countryside. We can, moreover, reasonably hypothesize that this behavior, in turn, exerted a dulling influence on peasants' agronomic acumen. Insofar as people rejected the practicability of innovative methods of work, they would become less attuned to locating alternative technologies.

At the same time, statistical indications of economic behavior reveal that social relations were not so oppressive as to deaden peasants to the lure of gain. A significant layer of families rose well above the modest material level at which the bulk of the villagers lived. They held much more land, more horses, and more livestock than they needed for subsistence.[182] They had large, visible stacks of grain in reserve, drove in nice carriages, wore nice leather boots, purchased factory-made clothing, built large brick homes, put up iron roofs, had fine stallions, acquired new tools and leather harnessings. These were ubiquitous symbols of status in the countryside, to which most peasants aspired, and to which many always strove, regardless of the jealousies or other complications that might arise. Symbols of economic success brought respect to the household, and meant enhanced opportunities for their children. Generally speaking, young men and women could not aspire to marry into significantly wealthier families.[183] As the historian Stephen Frank has noted, customs segregated wealthier and poorer peasant youths even at evening gatherings.[184]

In sum, fatalism was an inevitable and ubiquitous denizen of the village, but it was just one element of a broader worldview. A *zemstvo* doctor working on the southeastern border of Tambov just before the First World War uncovered this relationship for himself when treating epidemics with preventative medicine. He found that while the people looked on diseases fatalistically, as God's will, they readily agreed to preventative medicine in the form of vaccinations.[185] In reality, God's will—or any other variant of fatalism—left plenty of space open for man's will.

The Work Ethic in Rural Russia

While we can confidently assert that the pursuit of status protected the countryside from the stranglehold of fatalism, the connection between the pursuit of status and technological culture is not so clear. Several issues require investigation here. How much status accrued to those who knew a lot about agricultural technology, to those who were inquisitive about technology, to those who worked hard, and to those who worked skillfully and precisely? Taken together, these issues will help us to form a picture of the work ethic in rural Russia, and to sense the manner in which this ethic molded peasants' attitudes towards their craft.

Certainly the men who appeared to know the most about agriculture enjoyed respect in the village. Neighbors readily followed the lead of "smart Gerasim" or "wise Peter," as we saw above. Membership in an informal council of elders that deliberated on agrotechnical or other issues was an honor.[186] Some sources attest, moreover, that a certain amount of esteem accrued to peasants whose fieldwork technique was especially precise or skillful. One observer, at any rate, recorded that the appearance of plows disturbed the peasants who tilled most skillfully with the *sokha*. The plow threatened to deprive them of the esteem they derived from their technique.[187]

There are some indications, furthermore, that villagers acknowledged those among them who worked especially hard—"hard work pleases God," as they might sometimes put it.[188] We know, at any rate, that peasants commonly disdained several varieties of neighbors who did not work hard, or worked poorly. These varieties included the least capable farmers in their midst; anyone who might shirk work on days when the mass of the village was in the fields; those who were last out to the fields in the mornings; the young men who resisted performing agricultural labor after working in the city; those who could not keep their farms going and became hired laborers; and those who were simply poor—who wore the same dirty shirt day after day.[189] "Everyone tries not to lag behind the others in work, so as not to be considered a poor farmer by the village ... peasants are quite good at distinguishing a businesslike farmer, and respect him, even if he be poor," noted one observer in Tula province.[190]

Finally, and most importantly, peasants might attach real honor to a man who explored the environment in search of deeper understanding. The writer Alexander Ertel' offered a wonderful portrait of this type of man—the character Semion in the stories "*Moi domochadtsy*" and "*Serafim Ezhikov*," who stares at the sky and the fields whenever he gets the chance, cultivating his talents at divining the weather, recalling or composing stories and sayings related to nature and farming.[191]

Peasant society did therefore attach some status and approval to technological prowess. At the same time, it is far from certain that community approbation was strong enough to stimulate technological culture. The ethnographer Fenomenov's breakdown of peasant attitudes towards work is very instructive in this context.

In the first place Fenomenov identified a sizeable minority of peasants who truly enjoyed "the poetry of agricultural work," in the manner of the writer Gleb Uspenskii's famous character Ivan Ermolaevich in the 1880 piece *Krest'ianin i krest'ianskii trud* (*The Peasant and Peasant Labor*).[192] Men of this kind faithfully followed the dictates of agronomic folk wisdom, and drew great aesthetic satisfaction from a task well executed. They did not, however, think in terms of refining methods of work or experimenting with innovations. These concerns were the domain of a second type of farmer. These men were good, energetic farmers who never complained about the arduousness of agricultural work, who were relatively well-off materially, and who were reflective and inquisitive about their craft. According to Fenomenov, these people were a minute minority—likewise, the knowledgeable Engel'-gardt estimated them to be no more than 1–2 men per village.[193]

In contrast to these groups, Fenomenov found the majority of the peasants to be wholly indifferent to agriculture. They expressed little curiosity in their work, and derived little enjoyment from it. As another observer remarked:

> Peasants never pose questions concerning the life of plants or animals, or of the inner workings of nature. They do not like to read on such topics either, being convinced that "everything comes from God, but it is not so in books." Of trees, for instance, they reason: they've always grown, so they will always grow.[194]

These were the people who would sow good quality seeds only for a crop they intended to sell, not for themselves.[195] They worked because they had to, because other people did, or because their father told them to. They regarded peasant labor as very hard, harder than any other.[196] As far as they were concerned work was "God's punishment."[197] And they attached little if any value to work in and of itself. As remarked another ethnographer, from Riazan province "The peasants' lack of respect for hard work is remarkable. 'Him? He digs in the field like a beetle from morning to night'!"[198]

It followed to many peasants, therefore, that work was to be avoided if possible. Indeed, historian Boris Mironov has recently characterized Russian peasants as beholden to a "minimalist" work ethic common to all pre-capitalist societies, and defined by an indifference or antipathy to work.[199] His discovery of peasants' success in expanding the number of holidays per year in the late Imperial period makes the thesis especially persuasive.*

---

*See above, section "Agriculture and the Magico-Religious World View."

In some sense the unambitious, non-acquisitive, "minimalist" work ethic must have been weakening by the end of the nineteenth century, as industrialization began providing windows of social mobility. Nevertheless, newfound social mobility would tempt many energetic peasants away from agriculture, not towards it. The great majority of peasants continued to see agricultural work as unbecoming to anyone who could avoid it.[200] Once villagers saw a neighbor rise out of the village and escape the hard, "doggish" lot of the peasant, then many of them wanted their sons to follow this example.[201] Unless they had a realistic chance of acquiring a quantity of land large enough to live comfortably and prestigiously in the village, peasants with ambitions to social climbing usually aimed "to become 'someone'," be it a successful trader, a skilled worker, or a low-level functionary for the state or the local landlord.[202] Those who did get out of agricultural labor—even if only for a few years of service in the army—tended to look down on those who had not. They would often drop identifiably peasant manners of speech, and refer to their own relatives as "dark peasants."[203]

The indifference to work among a wide layer of peasants influenced agricultural performance in important ways. It must have affected the quality of work, at least to some degree. Of course peasants took pride and satisfaction in a job well done, be it a well-tied sheaf, a well-sharpened scythe, or a well-harrowed strip of land.[204] And so most peasants probably performed fieldwork tasks reasonably well.[205] "Our business is to till the land. Till it properly, without missing any spots, and you'll get grain."[206] But fieldwork was not an arena for the pursuit of excellence. We search the sources almost in vain for indications of status devolving to individuals on account of the precise execution of tasks: "Rare is the man who loves to till, and who shows off his work, the way he sets up the *sokha,* and the manner in which he chooses a horse," noted Engel'gardt.[207] In contrast to some other societies, Russian peasants do not appear to have toured the fields in groups after plowing, inspecting each man's tillage and establishing a hierarchy of peers based on the precision of work.[208]

Surely the average peasant—in any country—was more impressed by shows of strength and speed in the field than by accurate or innovative work. Vivid images in Russian culture remind us of the fact.[209] Literary descriptions of agricultural labor regularly describe peasants urging each other or themselves not to fall behind the pace at which others work.[210] The writer Ertel' even maintained that one of the most common types of peasant were those men who evaluated their peers *exclusively* in terms of physical strength, as manifested in fieldwork or in ritual, group fist fights.[211] As a Voronezh province peasant related:

> Generally the best fighters enjoy great honor and respect, much more respect than the best men in public affairs. Such a fighter is a real hero—people talk about him, bow low to him on the street, and address him formally.[212]

In contrast to the status accorded to physical prowess, the village rewarded technological inquisitiveness very stingily. Thus, one peasant who successfully pursued seed selection and sowing innovations found that his co-villagers eventually did come to respect him and look to him for guidance and advice. But he had to endure several years of ridicule and discouragement before they adopted this attitude to him.[213]

At some level, therefore, most peasants were sufficiently open-minded to recognize and appreciate technological inquisitiveness. But other values almost always enjoyed a much higher priority and profile. So long as this remained the case, the work ethic in the countryside would not stimulate a critical attitude towards methods of work, and men like Ertel's Semion described above would remain exceptional. The character of the rural work ethic was an important obstacle to the steady achievement of technological refinements and innovations.

The Consequences of Cultural Condescension

> It is eerie and frightening to live in that ocean of [rural] humanity.... Millions live "just like others do," each one sensing and recognizing that "in every respect" he is as worthless as a dried sardine, and that he has meaning only as part of a clump ...
>
> —Gleb Uspenskii, 1883[214]

In uncovering the roots of routine we can and must look beyond the terrain of social relations and the spectrum of values in peasant culture to locate very different kinds of influences shaping peasant economic mentality. To begin with, we can consider the manner in which the wider cultural world affected peasants' self-perception as economic actors. Here the work of contemporary American sociologists is immediately relevant.

Studies of minority populations in the U.S.A. suffering from discrimination and negative stereotyping have demonstrated that to an identifiable extent these populations buy into the condescending perceptions and portrayals of them from without. They underinvest in education and training, and thus help to perpetuate their subordination.[215] Cultural condescension towards peasants in Imperial Russia was widespread and deep-seated, as a wealth of contemporary sources attested.[216] Were inferiority complexes regarding learning and education commonplace among peasants? If so, this feature of the psychological climate would not bode well for the development of technological and economic aptitudes.

Naturally we cannot hope to establish a scientific measurement of inferiority complexes among peasant farmers relative to other sections of Russian society. The sources do, however, allow us some fruitful insights into this aspect of peasants' psychological world. We can examine, for instance, the legacy of serfdom. Nearly half of the peasants in Tambov were enserfed in the mid-nineteenth century. Serfdom did not ordinarily relieve peasants from the responsibility of running their own farms. Nevertheless, it must have served to routinize agricultural work to some extent. "Serfdom created a repressed peasant personality, and made it intrinsic to the breed," as one commentator lamented.[217] It is very difficult to measure the long-term influence of serfdom on work, however, since the sources for the late Imperial period do not often identify villages according to their status as ex-state or ex-serf. In any event, direct influences of serfdom on agricultural practice must have faded over the post-emancipation decades.

One visible and significant holdover from the era of serfdom was the self-deprecating language peasants employed before landlords or other authority figures: "Of course, we are dark people; your grace would know better, your mind sees further," to take a poignant example.[218] On the one hand, such expressions tended to be part of a calculated "language of subordinate status," as perceptive serfowners were always aware.[219] But on the other hand, it is reasonable to raise the possibility that many or most peasants internalized the deferential language and obsequious behavior they and their neighbors were compelled to display before authorities. "Humility inevitably degenerated into self-abasement," to paraphrase Maurice Hindus.[220]

Cultural condescension and attendant inferiority complexes did not stem exclusively from peasants' relationships with landlords and officials. The average peasant experienced subjection from other directions as well. Being chronically cheated by merchants in town could induce a sense of helplessness, for instance.[221] More important, a strongly defined cultural hierarchy often developed between villages or portions of villages. The large villages which were so typical throughout the black-earth region tended to consist of several sub-units, in one of which were concentrated the homes of the wealthier families, the church, the village officials, and the stores.[222] Families living in the other sub-units would tend to be culturally marginalized, and they could become victims of derogatory stereotyping—one neighborhood being known for producing horse thieves, another for carpenters, a third for drunkards, etc.[223] Moreover, villages in privileged locations tended to exercise cultural leadership over other villages. The presence of a railroad station or a periodic bazaar, for example, gave a village a great deal of authority in the formation of public opinion in the surrounding area.[224] In the geographically privileged villages peasants were said to exhibit "*a significantly better developed sense of self worth.*"[225] Here peasants, especially the younger males, were shedding some of the traditional culture, on account of which they looked down on other villages as backward.[226] "We are simple people of the soil," outlying peasants would say by way of contrasting themselves with the lead villages.[227]

> Kovernino [a village of this kind—D. K.] is not only a bazaar center. It is also the center of the non-material life of the region. Peasants ask anyone returning from the bazaar: 'Well, what's new? What are they saying there?', and all believe the stories of the 'bazaar goers.' They listen to them with rapt attention.[228]

The authority of the leadership villages even extended to the question of translating political disaffection into open rebellion.[229] To a significant extent, therefore, these villages must have been leaders in technological matters as well. While waiting for the example of these privileged villages, the bulk of the peasants elsewhere would be less likely to cultivate doubts on established agricultural practices.[230]

Geography, Climate, and Technological Acumen

Very few Russians, including agronomists, ever evidenced an awareness of the micro-geography of cultural and technological life in the countryside. The macro-geographical perspective, on the other hand, was a much more popular topic. Here we encounter a range of reflections concerning the influence of the steppes on folk life and culture, all of which boil down to a hypothesis of the drawbacks of homogeneity.

Quite a few observers, for example, expressed concern over the monotony of the peasantry's economic life in the black-earth region, as compared to the more diversified economy of the northern half of the country. They posited that the shortage of non-agricultural activities restricted peasants' contact with merchants and other townsmen and deprived them of intellectual stimulation. The dearth of topographical variety (in the form of forests and elevations) even robbed them of important sensory experiences, the argument continued.[231] A dull peasant character developed in these circumstances. Black-earth peasants were said to be less talented, resourceful, clever, energetic, and keen-witted than their counterparts in other regions.[232] The character of their thinking was "… not adroit, but rather inflexible and confused. They have difficulty making sense of things and subjects."[233]

After visiting the Caucasus region with its sprinkling of small ethnic enclaves, moreover, the writer Gleb Uspenskii mourned that the huge expanse of Russia exacerbated the peasantry's cultural isolation and carried more lamentable consequences. He proposed that in cultural terms the Russian peasant lived more as a collective person than an individual. The peasant could assimilate most of the riches of folk culture, yes, but he could not create them, or even comprehend all of them. Peasants' individuality was stunted, they succumbed to violence, and they accepted this state, "because we are unlearned people."[234]

We need not be so naive as to take the economic–geographical critiques of peasant intellect and personality at face value. Individual personality developed in the central black-earth region just as it must in every human community. Authors from Turgenev and Leskov at the beginning of our period to Prishvin and Vol'nov at the end of it energetically demonstrated the richness of emotions and personalities among the central black-earth peasantry. At the same time, observers who were well acquainted with various regions of Russia did consistently remark on the backwardness and crudity of peasant life in the central black-earth provinces relative to other regions (or in steppe areas relative to remaining forested areas within the central provinces). They found central black-earth peasants' homes to be remarkably filthy, and their clothing to be shoddier than expected.[235] Mothers did not keep their children as clean as elsewhere.[236] The repertoire of songs was limited, and drinking was more dominant as a form of entertainment.[237] They did not stand up for themselves against officials as actively as peasants in other areas, they were less hostile to authority, and their whole attitude was simply more downtrodden.[238] Peasants living in more wooded zones themselves considered steppe-dwelling peasants to be culturally and intellectually inferior.[239]

Although peasant culture may truly have been more coarse and uncouth in the central black-earth region than elsewhere, this need not have affected the evolution of agricultural technologies. To locate the influence of geography on technology we must turn away from broad cultural trends to consider the specific relationship of climate to technological awareness. From this perspective what strikes the observer's eye is the tremendous contrast between the variability of the weather on the one hand, and the repetitiousness of the work from year to year on the other hand. Annual rainfall fluctuated wildly in the more southern and eastern zones of European Russia, wreaking havoc with grain yields. For Tambov province as a whole, the grain harvest in good years was as much as five times that in bad years. Local level results varied much more, of course.

Meanwhile, notwithstanding the steady evolution of agricultural techniques over the last half-century before the First World War, peasant farmers were performing virtually the same operations year after year. They naturally traced the fluctuation of their yields first and foremost to the timing and quantity of the rainfall. One observer noted that "The steppe peasant sees fluctuations in yields as stemming exclusively from weather."[240] "The sky grows the grain," went a common saying in black-earth Russia.[241] This sort of reasoning made the intrinsically elusive task of deciphering the connections between tillage techniques, water retention in the soil, and yields even more difficult. It is easy to see, therefore, how semi-arid conditions could stunt peasants' minds as to the importance of the quality of their work to the final result. A critical attitude towards work could not easily develop in such circumstances. Likewise, it was difficult for farmers to feel in control of their own futures—a state of mind that must have amplified existing fatalistic predilections.[242]

Language Acquisition, and Childrearing Practices

Having investigated a variety of religious, social, and geographic–climatic constraints on the free functioning of ethnoscience, we are now in position to confront directly some of the issues of peasant psychology that have cropped up throughout the present discussion of technological acumen. The natural point at which to begin is childhood. Did certain, typical features of childrearing and childhood in peasant society exercise an identifiable influence on the formation of intellectual character?

Peasant children began with a significant intellectual handicap by virtue of the limited vocabulary of their parents. Modern studies of the communication environment surrounding infants and young children have posited some startling connections between the manner in which language is learned and the development of mental character. Of central concern in this context are three natural (but not necessarily ubiquitous) features of the imparting of language in pre-literate or largely illiterate agrarian societies: 1) the weak vocabulary of the adults who form the child's speech community;[243] 2) the adults' avoidance of "baby talk;" and 3) adults' tendency to speak *to* or *at* infants and very young children rather than to engage in empathetic, interactive conversation ("highly child-centered conversation") with them.[244] As any anthropologist would be quick to point out, this style of language imparting serves to impose respect for parental authority, to instill obedience, and to emphasize the value of harmony. In turn, these features function as a survival mechanism—they contribute to ensuring the vital coordination of family effort at stressful periods of the year.[245]

On the other hand, linguistic and psychological research has shown that this survival mechanism comes with a price. A communication environment enriched with articulate adults, "baby talk," and highly child-centered conversation yields many returns in a child's development. As they mature, children from such environments display substantially higher than average levels of articulateness and "rhetorical sensitivity" (the ability to listen effectively to others, and to be sensitive to their points of view). They engage in more self-directed learning, and show superior cognitive development as well.[246] The import of these qualities with respect to technological and economic aptitudes demands no elaboration.

While evidence concerning vocabulary and language-imparting practices among the Russian peasantry is scarce, what we do know is consistent with the pattern attributed to agrarian societies and outlined above. All studies found young peasants' vocabularies to be smaller than urban youngsters'.[247] Nine- and ten-year olds were said to be unable to differentiate between the words "hello," "thank you," and "good-bye" in their polite forms.[248] One observer recorded adult peasants not knowing the words "north" or "south," and confusing the terms "east" and "west," or "Christian" and "peasant."[249] A pair of studies in the 1920s confirmed that peasants were far less acquainted than urban workers with the vocabulary employed in newspapers of the day.[250] Peasant speech was described as being less abstract and relying more on concrete examples than that of educated men.[251] Peasants' dependence on obscenities also implies small vocabularies. By all accounts swearing was ubiquitous among the men, among children already from a very young age, and even among some women.[252] Swearing was of real interest to peasants. It provided the indispensable spice of conversation, and extended to unlikely categories of inanimate objects.[253] Youths could acquire a measure of peer respect from exceptional talent in cursing.[254]

Secondly, available evidence suggests the possibility that peasants made relatively little use of baby talk. From a very young age children were addressed more or less as adults. The populist writer Zlatovratskii, for one, was struck by this difference between the city and the country. Whereas in towns he would speak to children aged 10–13 "in kids' talk," he did not have to adjust his tone when speaking to their counterparts in the countryside.[255]

Thirdly, it appears that peasants spoke more commandingly and harshly to their children than did townspeople. Witness, for example, one peasant girl's first impressions of her schoolteacher:

> "At first her way of talking was strange to us. We were accustomed only to crude, harsh speech. The adults never wasted their breath on us kids; more often than not they would simply shout at us while attending to something else. But she spoke calmly, even endearingly, such that we didn't even consider disobeying her."[256]

Bunin noticed the same tendency of adults to speak to children as inferiors, although he situated the divide between Russians and other nationalities, not between village and town.[257] In sum, Russian peasant children did not generally have what anthropologists call "conversational peer status." They had fewer opportunities to initiate and lead conversations than do children in most contemporary industrialized nations.[258]

It is likely that the climate of stern parental authority in the peasant household reinforced the harshness of the speech community in hampering peasant childrens' intellectual development. Many psychologists have posited a link between parental-instilled obedience and stern discipline during childhood with helplessness and indecisiveness in adulthood.[259] Were peasants raised in a stifling authoritarian atmosphere?

Children are in a dependent position in any family culture, of course. The hierarchical nature of relations in the traditional peasant family accentuated this dependence, however. The head of the peasant household answered to the village community for all members of the family, so he controlled all major economic decisions, and adjudicated internal disputes. Agricultural life required absolute obedience to the head of the household, as outside observers and peasants themselves agreed—"There is no other way," "So it must be," explained a farmer to the writer Gleb Uspenskii.[260] Women in the household controlled subsidiary branches of the farm, such as poultry, some of the livestock, and a small section of land on which to grow hemp or flax which they would then process and dispose of.[261] And grown sons of the head of the household might have a consultative voice in farming and other decisions from which women were almost completely excluded, as a rule.[262] But ultimate authority always rested with the head of the household, unless he became manifestly unsound. Children occupied the bottom positions in the hierarchy, and were almost completely powerless. What is more, socialization processes outside the home often served to reinforce youngsters' status as completely subordinate to the group. So, at least, argued a student of peasant games, some of which appeared tailor-made to crush individual boys' pride and force them to submit to the group.[263]

Contemporaries were less disturbed by the authority of peasant parents over their children than by the abuse of that authority through acts of violence. The comments of a peasant from Saratov province capsulize one wing of opinion:

> From a young age parents do not raise their children as they should. They teach them through the ugly example of their own lives, through their drunkenness, quarreling, and cursing. They

> do not teach them to follow reason or good. In fact our children
> get no oversight at all—"do whatever you want to do." The only
> teaching comes from a stick or a knout, and often for no cause
> at all—parents beat them simply because they bothered them a
> bit, or because they feel riled.[264]

Townspeople had long since learned to "educate" their children (and each other) with persuasion or example, and not blows or tyranny, lamented prominent, well-informed observers of peasant life.[265] Such commentators were clearly worried that overcoming the culture of violence would be a painfully slow process for the peasantry.

However well-informed these observers were, the picture they painted of rampant, arbitrary child abuse could not have been fully representative. Plenty of sources attested that parents would patiently hold back from beating their children, and were not cruelly disposed towards them.[266] Punishments were said to be careful, enlightened, measured, and didactic.[267] Other sources insisted that important changes took place in family relations in the decades following emancipation. They maintained that although parents might have been habitually abusive earlier, they were treating children less roughly by the turn of the century.[268]

It is very clear, moreover, that the father's despotic powers in the household were slowly receding in this period. Fathers retained great power and authority, undoubtedly. Often they would deprive children of rights to inheritance, and would take them to village authorities to be whipped or intimidated if they did not want to do this at home.[269] But sons began to assert themselves more strongly in various matters, such as selecting a bride, leaving the village temporarily to search for a paying job, or even insisting on separating from the household altogether.[270] Many contemporaries attributed this assertiveness to the rise of off-farm employment and military service among young men. The simple experience of being under the control of another boss, be it a non-commissioned officer in the army or a foreman, could do a great deal to instill a spirit of independence from their fathers in peasant youth.[271]

The domestic life of the peasantry was changing. But for our purposes the important points concern that which remained the same. Notwithstanding the growing assertiveness of the young men, the size of the average family in Tambov remained stable at 6.6 for the last three decades before the World War.[272] Parents retained ample control over their children. Even the teenagers might be forbidden to speak during mealtimes.[273] Violence could never have been far from the child's mind. According to the ethnographer Fenomenov, who was very experienced and acutely observant, even the most tender mother would sometimes deem it necessary—"just in order to confirm her authority"—to thrash children as young as three or four years of age with rods, or whatever else was at hand.[274] Moreover, mistreatment and even beating of elderly members of the family was not uncommon, and served further to poison the psychological climate at home.[275] What is more, there is strong evidence that violence was more serious and more persistent in the central agricultural provinces than elsewhere. These provinces ranked very high relative to other regions in officially registered cases of beatings and fights.[276] The percentage of army recruits from Tambov who had lost bone tissue in their noses was 38% above the national average.[277] And the same Fenomenov, who had spent a lot of time in Orel province, noted that intra-family quarrels among the peasants he studied in Novgorod province (in the Northwest of European Russia) were relatively tame compared to the center of Russia, where adults would torment children, and husbands would "not rarely beat their wives 'to death'."[278]

This is precisely the kind of atmosphere psychologists worry about. Most social commentators in late Imperial Russia were concerned that cruel peasant parents were succeeding only in passing on their moral decay to their children. What concerns us is the real possibility that they were limiting the mental development of their children.[279] This perspective cannot be ignored in an analysis of the agrarian problem in its technological dimension.

The Unavailability of Schooling and Literacy

> Nowhere is there exhibited a closer connection between elementary education and national prosperity than in agricultural improvement.
>
> —A. I. Chuprov, 1907[280]

It remains for us to consider the significance for the evolution of agronomic aptitude of illiteracy and the unavailability of school education in rural Russia. Scholars have interpreted the influence of literacy on methods and habits of thought in a variety of ways. On one extreme, theories asserting a direct causal link between literacy and particular cognitive capacities have been sharply contested. On the other hand, theories dismissing the possibility of literacy having any effect on the character or habits of thinking are extreme in their own right. The middle ground that has recently emerged sees literacy as meaning something different in each society. In this view literacy carries "implications" for mentality rather than guaranteed effects.[281]

Important perspectives on the possible implications of literacy and schooling on thought patterns have come from the two American scholars Sylvia Scribner and Michael Cole, together with their adherents. In one especially important article published in 1983, Scribner and Cole summed up a range of anthropological studies on the connections between schooling and cognitive behavior.[282] The studies indicate that while the ability to reason, generalize and conceptualize is common to all culture groups, different methods of education produce very different patterns of application of these capacities. Informal education tends to consist of teaching by example, of learning by imitation—as peasants traditionally learned farming.[283] In informal education the verbal component of both the learning and the teaching is far less than with school education. School-educated children are taught to think systematically, and to be aware of their thinking path in solving problems. They are far more likely to ask "why" questions, and to weigh information independently of the status of the person imparting it.

As another scholar of literacy has explained these and other findings, the point is not that education generates logical resources outright. Instead, education enhances our awareness of these resources, and makes it easier for us to use concepts we already have.[284] Thus in their own research Scribner and Cole found that school-educated people were much more able to cope with certain sorts of logical problems than unschooled people were.[285] Unschooled people dealt almost equally well with fully abstract syllogisms, but performed relatively poorly when the syllogisms were presented in familiar terms (when the elements in the problems included animals or tools, for instance, in place of logical symbols). Those who had attended school, in other words, had gained facility with applying a school-related discourse of logical, abstract thinking to concrete situations. A facility with shifting between abstract and concrete understanding of phenomena was precisely the sort of capability that could assist peasants engaged in the re-examination of established technological paradigms. Perhaps it was no accident that agronomists found young, school-educated men to be the quickest to think abstractly about soil and plant processes, and that they grasped guiding agronomic concepts far more easily than any other group.[286]

Many peasant children were attending school. By the turn of the century more than half of the Russian population aged 8–11 was enrolled in primary schools (in the countryside as well as the towns), and attendance rates hovered around 90%.[287] Just 30 years earlier only one-fourth to one-third as many children had been enrolled.[288] In Tambov the primary school network filled in quickly in the late Imperial period—over 2,600 village schools were operating by 1914, just 740 short of the *zemstvo's* final target.[289] Whereas the literacy rate among rural men in Tambov had been just 9% in the early 1880s, it reached 24% by 1897.[290] Data on army recruits show that literacy was advancing still further among young men, who would sooner or later take charge of family farms. 35% of the recruits from Tambov were registered as literate in 1894, 58% in 1911.[291]

Surely it would be naive to propose that schooling was automatically generating a new mental awareness in Russian peasant schoolchildren. Literacy can come in very different guises. Its effects must be minimal where pupils learn little more than the ability to connect printed symbols with words in their vocabularies. Children in Russian primary schools tended to get a very short and spare education, and the schooling did not necessarily encourage independent thinking or a critical attitude towards regnant practices and values.[292] Even where teachers might encourage alternative points of view—on topics like meteorology, demonology, and hygiene, for example—there was no guarantee that their pupils would really listen. The gap between pupils' and teachers' preconceptions on scientific topics was very wide, so the children could have filtered and processed much of what they heard into forms divergent from the intent of the instruction.

Nevertheless, in late Imperial Russia, the peasant's education was more than a thin veneer. Surveys confirmed that impressive majorities of pupils, including those who did not graduate, retained or improved the basic skills of reading, writing, and mathematics after leaving school.[293] The importance of educational programs, moreover, did not lie in the direct transformation of the mass of peasant children into energetic experimenters devoted to dissecting the material environment. The re-examination and refinement of established agricultural technologies did not require an army of local scientists. Schooling could be an effective lever if it stimulated but a small fraction of the student body to explore and embrace contemporary agronomic science. This, as we shall see below, is precisely what happened.

Finally, it is important to note that the spread of literacy would affect popular attitudes towards science in subtle, indirect ways. Much, even most, of the reading material available in the countryside in the last three decades before the First World War attempted to reshape certain aspects of peasant culture. The blossoming agricultural press, for instance, energetically challenged peasant agricultural methods. Even though studies of peasant reading habits tended to register the unpopularity of agronomic and other "self-help" literature, peasant letters to agronomic journals and local agronomists' testimony confirm that they had readers in the villages.[294] As early as 1893, in fact, a summary of agricultural correspondents' reports in Nizhnyi Novgorod province (on Tambov's northern border) rated the printed word the second most important stimulus to innovations among peasants.[295]

More importantly, the historian Jeffrey Brooks has pointed out that the popular literature that began to reach the countryside in substantial quantities by the late nineteenth century was filled with positive images of science and reason overcoming the charlatanry, stupidity, or silliness of sorcerers, witches, and faith healers.[296] Authors of stories and tales for mass consumption—many of them from the countryside themselves—explicitly, purposely, and consistently encouraged readers to shed superstitions in favor of a more scientific outlook. The ongoing commercial success of this literature testifies to its contribution to the erosion of belief in supernatural forces in the late Imperial period, which we noted earlier.

Slowly but surely, directly and indirectly, schooling would play a large role in the evolution of the agrarian problem in Russia. Schooling could play the same role in raising agricultural performance in Russia as it has in other countries.[297]

Conclusion
From Faith in Routine to Belief in Agency

The eternal "We do as people do" not only travels from mouth to mouth, but seems to be in the air they breathe.
—Alexander Fet, 1862[298]

He who has not seen the villages lately cannot imagine the changes that have taken place in the last fifteen to twenty years in the farmer's intellectual appetite.... There is no doubt that a peasant intelligentsia is forming.
—Fedor Shcherbina, 1899[299]

The Faith in Routine

Having examined the primary constraints on technological thinking in rural Russia, we are now in position to view peasant agronomic aptitude in sharper focus. To begin with, it is clear that village culture produced relatively few individuals with an inclination to technological exploration and experimentation. Insofar as such personalities did arise, furthermore, they faced greater obstacles to cultivating their talents in the rural world than in the urban. As the rural observer and writer Garin-Mikhailovskii remarked concerning one peasant who persistently strove to educate himself and escape from the peasant world, "He who knows the village knows what force of will was required to manage this in the deaf, school-less village. The labors of Lomonosov pale before his achievement."[300] The features of village culture we have traced in Part II made it very difficult for farmers to escape from routine, even as economic opportunities and imperatives beckoned.[301]

The entrenchment of routine is not intrinsic to traditional smallholder agriculture. As indicated earlier, an ethos of experimentation and innovation has thrived in many peasant milieux (at least in the late twentieth century, and perhaps earlier). But several circumstances set the Russian case apart in this respect. First, up to the end of the nineteenth century the magico-religious world of the Russian village remained unmediated by any awareness of the accomplishments of science in manipulating nature. Even relatively remote and largely illiterate peasant populations cannot remain completely unaffected by science in the second half of the twentieth century, when scholars have been documenting the vitality of their ethnoscience. As we saw earlier, the very notion of man's agency vis-à-vis nature was perceived weakly and shallowly in the Russian village.

Second, the semi-arid conditions of southern Russia presented peasants with especially difficult tasks in divining tillage principles. The combination of semi-arid conditions and rapid population growth made the proper understanding of soil and tillage tremendously important. But it proved almost impossible for peasants to understand the capillary structure of the soil without direct or indirect guidance from agronomists. This was a frustrating situation, in which it was not easy for peasants to see where to look for technological innovations and refinements.

Third, opportunities for cultural borrowings were quite limited in rural Russia. Borrowing is a powerful lever of technological progress in all endeavors, periods, and places.[302] It is always easier to borrow a practice or method than to create it. The very presence of foreign examples stimulates creativity as well. In explaining the technological backwardness of French agriculture in the seventeenth–nineteenth centuries, the historian Fernand Braudel pointed to the relative isolation of most of France, distant as most of it was from the sea, and separated from its neighbors by mountain and river barriers.[303] What might we say of Russia in this regard? No area in Europe was farther away from the centers of the agricultural revolution in northwestern Europe—The Netherlands, England, and later Denmark—than black-earth Russia.

Fourth, the economic and cultural gulf separating peasant farmers from private landowners was wider in Russia than elsewhere. With respect to the evolution of agricultural technology the main problem was not the well-known legal and administrative discrimination against the peasant estate. The paucity of smaller, progressive landowners was of greater importance. These were the people who had the education, the inclination, and the resources first to research new tools, methods, and systems, and then to demonstrate how they might be adapted to local conditions. The layer of these farmers was much smaller in Russia than in other European lands. In the late nineteenth century, below 2.5% of the land was held in units of 10–100 *desiatinas*. In Tambov the figure was 3.1%. The corresponding layer held 29% of the land in France, 35% in Baden, 38% in Prussia, and 62% in Norway, for example.[304] Russian peasants had far fewer opportunities to view innovations in action on local farms than did peasants in these countries.[305]

Finally, as we pointed out in our analysis of experimentation in peasant agriculture, the huge expanse and fertility of the black-earth zone carried inevitable and long-lasting consequences in the formation of popular attitudes towards technological exploration. "It seems to me that nature played a cruel trick on our people," a schoolteacher in Tambov province remarked to me one day.[306] He had in mind the way in which the abundance of high-quality land had encouraged many generations of farmers in the black-earth zone to favor extensive over intensive measures to raise production. Until the second half of the nineteenth century it was always easier for farmers to expand their sowings or move onto new lands whenever they needed to produce more. "The conquest of nature went wide and not deep" as Trotsky expressed this tendency in his masterful piece "Peculiarities of Russia's Development."[307] Indeed, until the middle of the nineteenth century it would not have made much sense for farmers in the black-earth regions to expend significant effort on discovering yield-boosting technologies. Fundamental features of nineteenth-century Russian economic geography bore a much closer relationship to contemporary Spain or the United States than to northwestern Europe— or, for that matter, western Africa or southeast Asia in the twentieth century. Economic geography created work habits that took deep root in the Russian peasantry.

The routinization of attitudes towards work does not lend itself very well to quantification or comparative measurement, but the Russian case must have been relatively severe. Research on technical inefficiencies in smallholder agriculture provides indirect confirmation of the fact. A survey of recent studies located a sharp divide with respect to efficiency between smallholders in stable economic environments and those farming in rapidly changing conditions. Predictably, farmers in stable environments tend to come much closer to practicable levels of efficiency than do farmers in unstable environments. Whereas crop yields among the former were found to be fairly close to the realistically attainable, the latter were reaching only 70% of the attainable, on average.[308] In the turbulent times of late Imperial Russia significant technical inefficiencies were to be expected. As we saw in Part I, however, peasants in Tambov were underachieving by extremely wide margins. Their yields were below 50% of the realistically attainable.

The persistence of glaring inefficiencies testifies to the unrelenting grip of routine on the farming population. At the same time, the persistence of routine poses a vexing question to the historian: how could a mechanical approach towards work survive among people who, as we saw in Part I, were so thoroughly transforming their methods of work? There is no simple answer to this riddle. It must be remembered, however, that the cultural conditions which did so much to shape peasant attitudes towards work and technology remained firmly in place as agricultural methods evolved. The mere alteration of a practice in the field did not necessarily unsettle peasants' impression of the sanctity of their technological repertoire. "Considering themselves born agriculturalists, some peasants think that they are doing all that is possible to raise high yields, and that there is no room for improvement ..." remarked an agronomist in Voronezh province in 1915.[309]

Through the action of a subconscious psychological mechanism the German sociologist Georg Elwert has termed "nostrification," many peasants must have reinterpreted change as tradition. In other words, instead of perceiving new technological methods and cultural forms as recent borrowings or inventions, peasants maintained a strong tendency to conceive of their present body of practices as traditional and indigenous.[310] Of course, at some level almost all peasants must have understood that the times were changing. We know, for instance, that ethnographers of the period regularly recorded peasants' impressions and opinions concerning cultural changes in the decades since emancipation. But, in technological matters, at least, it appears that peasants commonly did interpret novelties as traditions. The sources are certainly filled with peasants announcing—incorrectly—that they were working just as their fathers and grandfathers before them had always worked.[311] The notion of "nostrification" thus helps us to understand how a remarkable blindness to technological possibilities could survive in a time of relatively rapid technological turnover: "Criticism and a conscious attitude to the running of the farm is absent almost everywhere"— stated an inspector of agriculture in a region where agriculture was changing even more quickly than in Tambov.[312]

The Rise of a New Type in the Village

If the regnancy of routine in the village had so much to do with the broad cultural background of peasant society, then a prospective take-off into agricultural growth would depend to some extent on transfor-

mations in that background. Among the many developments in peasant culture in the second half of the nineteenth century, some trends
were serving to open up avenues for the reshaping of attitudes to
technology. In particular, a number of currents at work in this period
were widening the interpersonal, private spaces in peasant society. In
these spaces could grow the stronger spirit of individuality and self-as-
surance requisite for farmers to explore technological alternatives and
see them through the difficulties of a trial period.

As regards the expansion of private space in peasant society, we have
already noted that young men who left the village in search of seasonal
labor often became less submissive to patriarchal authority upon their
return home. Service in the army performed a similar function. Since
the army did not maintain soldiers year-round until at least 1906, many
of the enlisted men sought out wage labor during their term of service.[313]
25–30% of young peasant men entered military service in the last
quarter of the nineteenth century.[314] Inevitably, some of them brought
back new, progressive ways and ideas to the village on a variety of
matters, ranging from hygiene to political consciousness.[315]

Off-farm employment, army service, and schooling all contributed
to what the historian Stephen Frank has called "a growing assertion of
self by peasant youth in late nineteenth century village society."[316] The
enhanced spirit of independence and personal dignity was particularly
visible in the behavior of women. With increasing frequency, peasant
women shed encumbering traditional clothing, adopted diverse styles
of clothing, insisted on being called "miss," arranged their own entertainment season independently of adults and precedents, defied arranged marriages, sought redress for grievances at the *volost'* courts,
and kept their homes cleaner.[317]

The processes reshaping peasants' social and intellectual character
had taken root by the turn of the twentieth century. The reformation
of human capital in the Russian countryside was only a matter of time.
At this point national politics intervened to accelerate the changes
already underway. The combination of the Russo–Japanese War, the
revolution of 1905, the agrarian revolts of 1905–06, the harsh repres-
sions of these revolts, and the dismissal of the first two Dumas,* served
to intensify peasants' awareness of politics to an unprecedented extent.
The consequences quickly made themselves apparent in matters of
daily and local life. Peasants became hungrier for, and better acquainted

---

*The Duma was the national parliament, to which Tsar Nicholas conceded in 1905
in order to weather the revolutionary storm of that year.

with, the written word.[318] Parish priests in Tambov noticed a marked decline in religiosity among males in the years 1905–1908. In subsequent years they observed how young peasant men were departing the era of unquestioning obedience to their elders.[319]

As far as the technological realm is concerned, the ascendance of the secular and the individual in peasant life expressed itself most clearly in the growing cohort of young men who embraced science as a perceived antidote to the beliefs of the traditional magico-religious world.[320] After throwing off many of the popular superstitions and beliefs this cohort pressed to employ alternative methods of work, thereby provoking a fierce generational conflict in many families. A letter to an agricultural journal from one of these young peasants captures the spirit of the conflict:

> Take any 100 older men, say age 50 or so, and you'll find maybe three who can read, at the most five. Now take a hundred younger men, and you'll find maybe five who can't read. And so the old are locked in struggle with the young. For instance, the son and the father are under the same roof. The father is 50 years old, from the stone age, you might say, and runs the farm accordingly. The son is 25 to 30, and the father blocks him in everything. He can't try out any new crop; he can't sow clover or any other new plant. Nor can he buy some new equipment from the *zemstvo*, like a plow or a seed-drill, because his uneducated father forbids all these dreams with a wag of his crooked finger. And so the old ways reign, and the son must wait, until such time as he becomes the boss under his own roof....
>
> The angry old men grumble to everyone that "Some sort of andronomists [sic] have shown up, something new is brewing. But we lived fine before without any of that, and are living now!" They speak out against the agronomists, and sometimes curse the schools too: "They only make the kids go soft."[321]

The man who wrote this letter spoke for many more like him. The ranks of a new peasant intellectual elite were taking shape in the final decade and a half before the World War. In 1907–10 the Valuisk *uezd* *zemstvo* (in Voronezh province, just to the south of Tambov) set up a network of *volost'*-level agricultural councils, the plenary sessions of which included an elected representative from every village. Often not understanding the purpose for which they were sending representatives, many of the villages elected dull, lifeless members to the councils. But many sent another kind of man:

The contemporary countryside displays a wide gradation of types— from the dim and the mentally broken to people of great competence and worldly development.... in every council there are several people interested in all kinds of innovations. They are fully intellectual, reading agricultural newspapers and journals. In short, they are an intellectual aristocracy of the countryside.[322]

Dissatisfied with the explanatory poverty of folk wisdom, and aware of the existence of agronomic science, a growing cohort of intellectually curious farmers was waiting for someone to explain this science to them. These farmers would be the pioneers, through whose example new approaches would spread to other peasants. The initial reports of the local agronomists who began work in Tambov in 1910 verify the presence of inquisitive, intelligent farmers in a large majority of the villages. Furthermore, the reports show that the bulk of the other farmers were genuinely interested in hearing agronomic lectures. The traditional folk wisdom's hold on most peasants was not unbreakable. It would be the local agronomists' job to lead the way in rethinking it.

Notes

[1] Zubrilin, *Chem obrabatyvat' zemliu*, p. 41.

[2] See, e.g., the various sayings counseling peasants not to leave spots of land untilled, in Ermolov, *Sel'sko-khoziaistvennaia mudrost'*, vol. 2, p. 211.

[3] The amount of time required to complete this process was rarely less than twelve years (Ermolov, *Organizatsiia polevogo khoziaistva*, pp. 108–123). Some peasants felt that a far shorter time-span sufficed, however (*Materialy dlia otsenki zemel' Saratovskoi gubernii. Vyp. III*, p. 5).

[4] *Ibid.*, p. 26.

[5] This technique is not without some agronomic justification. If stubble is left above the rye seeds it will collect more snow cover than will bare land in winters with light snows. In such years rye under bare soil will freeze (*Sbornik statisticheskikh svedenii po Samarskoi gubernii. vol. 6*, pp. 47–49). In other years, of course, the farmer pays the price for this kind of insurance.

It is possible to locate cases where peasants employing shifting cultivation systems in the steppes did till the land before sowing rye. But peasants resorted to this tillage only in the face of a superabundance of weeds. In addition to the fact that avoiding tillage economized on labor, their agronomic instinct was to sow rye on the wheat stubble (*ibid.*).

[6] *Materialy dlia otsenki zemel' Saratovskoi gubernii. Vyp. III*, p. 26.

[7] *Ibid.*

[8] Explicit testimony to this effect appears in the anonymous report, "O sostoianii sel'skogo khoziaistva v iuzhnoi Rossii v 1851 g.," pp. 51–52.

[9] Data from the Kharkov *zemstvo*'s network of agricultural correspondents—the great majority of whom were themselves peasants—offer perhaps the clearest confirmation of the slowness with which steppe farmers came to understand manure. In the south and east of the province, where shifting cultivation systems of farming still prevailed at the time of this study in 1907, almost half of the correspondents reported that farmers were still ignorant of the usefulness of manure (*Statisticheskii ezhegodnik 1907 g.*, p. 10). Interestingly, experimental stations in the southern steppes of European Russia determined that manure was of dubious value there, at least in some places. Manure was clearly beneficial in typical conditions of Khar'kov, however. A presentation of regional data appears in Vorob'ev, *Rol' faktorov urozhaia*, p. 8.

[10] *Sbornik statisticheskikh svedenii po Samarskoi gubernii. Vol. 2*, p. 92; ibid, *Vol. 5*, p. 53. Many late-nineteenth-century sources record skepticism or ambivalence towards manure among Tambov peasants (one example is *SSS, Usman*, pp. 42, 44). Similar sources from neighboring provinces include: for Balashov *uezd*, Saratov province,

Ionson, "O sel'skom khoziaistve v Rossii. Putevye zametki o raznykh guberniiakh." pp. 28–30; from Voronezh, Nikonov, "Byt i nravy poselian-velikorussov Pavlovskogo uezda, Voronezhskoi gubernii," p. 71; from Orel, Sovetov, "Kratkii ocherk agronomicheskogo puteshestviia," p. 385. A fairly detailed discussion of the evolution of the use and understanding of manure among peasants in one province is *Materialy dlia otsenki zemel' Saratovskoi gubernii. Vyp. III*, ch. 9.

[11] *Materialy dlia otsenki zemel' Saratovskoi gubernii. Vyp. III*, pp. 5–6.

[12] *Ibid.*, p. 26.

[13] "*Vypakhalas'*," in, e.g., *ibid.*, pp. 96, 144–147, and elsewhere.

[14] For one example, see *Proekty*, p. 400.

[15] Selivanov, "God Russkogo zemledel'tsa," p. 36. Selivanov was writing in the mid-nineteenth century, but the area he was describing in Riazan province had long since adopted three-field agriculture and tillage. Further, as remarked an agricultural specialist in Kursk province in 1899, where shifting cultivation of the grasslands must have disappeared in favor of continuous cultivation around the middle of the nineteenth century: "Peasants have long since considered tillage mandatory." *Tekushchaia sel'sko-khoziaistvennaia statistika Kurskogo gubernskogo zemstva. 1899 god. Kniga I*, p. 68.

[16] Ermolov, *Narodnye primety na urozhai*, p. 150; Ermolov, *Sel'sko-khoziaistvennaia mudrost'*, vol. 2, p. 212.

[17] Gil'tenbrandt, A., "Sel'sko-khoziaistvennye zametki po puti ot g. Starogo Oskola," p. 278.

[18] Kotov, *op. cit.*, p. 36; Erpulev, *op. cit.*, p. 12; Chebalak, *op. cit.*, p. 26.

[19] *Proekty*, p. 399.

[20] *Proekty*, p. 322 (Muchkap sector). Garin-Mikhailovskii noted the same opinion among peasants in Samara province. When he probed them on it, they expressed the mistaken conviction that *ziab deprived* the soil of moisture (the same attitude appears in *Peremeny v zemledel'cheskoi tekhnike krest'ian Nizhegorodskoi gubernii*, p. 26). The example of Garin-Mikhailovskii's own farming slowly weaned them of this prejudice. Garin-Mikhailovskii, "Neskol'ko let v derevne," in *Sobranie sochinenii*, vol. 3, pp. 49–50.

[21] Gorelkin, "Selo Verkhne-Spasskoe, Tambovskogo uezda," p. 142.

[22] Some explicit statements of this, from agronomists in Orel province and a landowner in Voronezh, are A.A. Trifonov, *Pochemu neobkhodimo podnimat' par rano?*, pp. 28–29; *Agronomicheskii otchet (za 1911–1912 g.)*, p. 68; and D. Ermolov, "Iz Bobrovskogo uezda (Voronezhskoi gubernii)," p. 8. There is no reason to believe that conditions were any different in Tambov. The twelve-volume study of the peasant economy in the early 1880s (SSS, vols. 1–12) gives detailed accounts of arable lands not subject to grazing, but mentions only a few communes in one *uezd* raising fallow early (*ibid*, Shatsk, p. 45).

[23] Some landlords in Tambov were employing this technique (Fon-Gagen, "Iz Usmanskogo uezda, Tambovskoi gubernii," p. 403). Alternatively, peasants could simply have rented more grazing lands for their herds from nearby landowners (as an agronomist in St. Petersburg province recommended: Sharkov, "Obrabotka krest'ianskoi pashni," p. 6). Such lands were available for most villages, at costs below the value of the additional production of rye that would accompany early fallow.

[24] For example, *Zhurnaly* ... (March 1911), p. 7; *ibid.* (August–September 1911), p. 70; or Solov'ev, "Urozhai glavneishikh khlebov na pokazatel'nykh poliakh," p. 11. A landowner in Saratov province, N. A. Pavlov, himself persuaded eighteen

commutes to set aside a portion of their fallow land for early tillage (*Zapiski zemlevladel'tsa*, p. 209).

25 Writing in 1915, an agronomist in Voronezh *uezd* noted that peasants had only lately come to recognize the hazards of green fallow (Chebalak, *Sbornik statei po sel'skomu khoziaistvu dlia krest'ian*, p. 26). Perhaps the most thorough data on this question comes from Khar'kov province, to the south and west of Tambov. Quite a few of the Khar'kov provincial *zemstvo's* agricultural correspondents (80% of whom were peasants) stated explicitly that peasant farmers in their areas had no understanding of the significance of early fallow. *Statisticheskii ezhegodnik 1907 g.*, p. 6; *Statisticheskii ezhegodnik 1908 g.*, table 35. As late as 1910 over half of the correspondents were reporting that peasants were taking no interest in early fallow (*Statisticheskii spravochnik po Khar'kovskoi gubernii*, pp. 32–33). Where early fallow was making inroads, the statisticians attributed it to agronomists' agitation (*Statisticheskii ezhegodnik 1907 g.*, pp. 6–7, 43).

26 The collections I have cited in this work by Ermolov are the most complete, but ethnographers produced quite a few others, usually in article or chapter form. I have located only one saying, from Kiev province, advocating early fallow (Ermolov, *Narodnye primety na urozhai*, p. 122). Elsewhere Ermolov maintained that peasants were too wedded to allowing their herds onto fallow land to envision any other fallow than green fallow (*Sel'sko-khoziaistvennaia mudrost'*, vol. 2, p. 222).

27 *Proekty*, pp. 49–50; Karev, "Iz Bolkhovskogo uezda, Orlovskoi gubernii," pp. 403–404. According to Karev, peasants feared the possibility of plows ruining their land by bringing up inferior soil lying below the black earth on the surface. He goes on to report how peasants jumped to acquire plows a year later, after seeing landlords' results with the new tools.

28 Ermolov (*Narodnye primety na urozhai*, p. 147). The only clear indications of peasants showing concern that weeds could deprive nearby crops of soil resources that I have ever found come from Moscow province (*Statisticheskii ezhegodnik Moskovskoi gubernii za 1889 god*, Moscow 1889, p. 176, and *ibid. za 1906 god. Chast' pervaia*, p. 70).

29 Roth, *Agriculture and Peasantry of Eastern Russia*, p. 25.

30 *Proekty*, p. 457.

31 *Proekty*, pp. 44–45, 527; *Otchety uchastkovykh agronomov za 1911 god*, pp. 48–49, 91; *Otchet o deiatel'nosti agronomicheskogo personala za 1912 sel'sko-khoziaistvennyi god*, p. 84; Ovchinnikov, "O lentochnom poseve prosa," p. 250; Khurtin, "Moi opyty s podsolnukhom," p. 527. Incomplete understanding of the significance of inter-tillage was probably quite common among landlords as well. See, e.g., Anonymous, "Pravil'naia obrabotka propashnykh rastenii," pp. 230–232 (reprint from the journal *Khutorianin*).

32 Mozzhukhin, *Zemleustroistvo v Bogoroditskom uezde*, p. 108. Most peasants surely did not understand that weeds and other seeds could lie dormant beneath the surface for several years or more before germinating. This ignorance accounts for the mass of superstitions regarding the transformation of crops—the belief, in other words, that rye once sown could turn into darnel grass, or oats into rye. See, e.g., Shaternikov, *op. cit.*, pp. 4–5.

33 *Proekty*, p. 69.

34 *Proekty*, p. 563. Another source testifying to peasants' errors in appraising the quality of land (in Iaroslavl province) is Iur'evskii, *Vozrozhdenie derevni*, p. 10.

35 This comment from Samara province (*Sbornik statisticheskikh svedenii po Samarskoi gubernii. Vol. 2*, p. 90).

[36] See discussion in the section "Green fallow and other shortcomings." "Fluffy" soil was derided at an earlier stage, when peasants were giving up shifting cultivation systems of farming and getting used to the three-field system. See the comments in *Materialy dlia otsenki zemel' Saratovskoi gubernii. Vyp. III*, pp. 149–150, 164.

[37] See treatment of this in the section "The Evolution of Tillage Regimes."

[38] The data are from Khar'kov province, where most of the regional zemstvo's agricultural correspondents felt that peasants understood that early fallow was preferable to late, green fallow (*Statisticheskii ezhegodnik 1907 g.*, p. 6; *Statisticheskii ezhegodnik 1908 g.*, table 35). In 1910 almost half of the correspondents reported that peasants were interested in early fallow (*Statisticheskii spravochnik po Khar'kovskoi gubernii*, pp. 32–33). This percentage would have been higher in Tambov, given the higher population density there (portions of Khar'kov were yet to adopt a three-field system; in those areas farmers could hardly have been concerned with early fallow).

[39] Sources testifying to widespread fall tillage or early fallow on estates in Tambov include: *SSS, vol. 16, Chastnoe zemlevladenie Kirsanovskogo uezda.* p. 223; *k otsenke*, Lipetsk, pp. 45–51; Kozlov, pp. 36–37; Borisoglebsk, p. 43; Kirsanov pp. 59–60. Some technologically inquisitive landlords in Tambov became aware of the advantages of early fallow much earlier (e.g., N. Bunin, "Vedemost' o zemledel'cheskikh rabotakh," p. 388). Surely many landlords decided on early fallow as a means of securing cheap labor—it could be difficult, after all, to hire peasants to till fallow if they were busy with the same task simultaneously. An indication of this line of reasoning among landlords is Posashev, "Razvedenie probshteiskoi i shampanskoi rzhi," p. 704.

[40] It is conceivable that peasants arrived at an understanding of early fallow's benefits to the soil through what we might term "forced experimentation." Local agronomists in Tambov occasionally noticed peasants raising fallow earlier than normal in dry years, when grazeable vegetation on the fallow died out (e.g.: agronomists Gudvilovich, in *Zhurnaly ...* (1911), pp. 84–85), and N. M. Vasiliev, in *Otchety uchastkovykh agronomov za 1914 g.*, p. 107). The original motivation behind this was probably to work the land before it became too parched and hard for the *sokha*. If farmers thereupon noticed an unexpectedly good yield, they might associate it with the timing of the raising of fallow. This hypothesis remains unsubstantiated by direct evidence. We cannot be certain how peasants came to value earlier tillage.

[41] *Proekty*, pp. 49–50; *Zhurnaly...* (August–September 1911), p. 84; *Peremeny v zemledel'cheskoi tekhnike*, p. 38.

[42] *Proekty*, pp. 451–52, 493–94. Sources from bordering provinces corroborate that this was a typical failing: *Polevoe khoziaistvo Penzenskoi gubernii*, p. 36; Kostrov and Tarasov, *op. cit.*, pp. 19–21; Trifonov, *Pochemu neobkhodimo podnimat' par rano?*, (1929), pp. 22, 26–27 (this source pertains primarily to Orel, Tula, and Riazan provinces).

[43] *Proekty*, pp. 31–32; *Agronomicheskii otchet (za 1911–1912 g.)*, p. 68; *Otchety uchastkovykh agronomov za 1914 god* (hereafter *Otchety 1914*), p. 104; *KSE*, vol. 6, p. 387. Similarly, peasants doing ziab before a late-sown spring crop like millet might leave their land unharrowed in the spring. The soil would settle and become nearly unusable by the time they were ready to sow (GATO, f. 478, op. 5, d. 3494, p. 40).

[44] According to a summary of the relevant studies, changes in the prices of agricultural products have generated "an incredible diversity of price reactions [among peasant farmers—D. K.], from none, to perverse, to expected, for different crops, regions, and periods." John Adams, "Peasant Rationality: Individuals, Groups, Cultures," p. 275.

45 See, e.g., Becker, *The Economic Approach to Human Behavior*, p. 5.

46 For an overview of the theory of "the optimizing peasant" see Ellis, *Peasant Economics*, chs. 4–8. Innumerable works have shared this perspective. Two of the best known are: James Scott, *The Moral Economy of the Peasant*, pp. 2–3; and Eugen Weber, *Peasants Into Frenchmen: the modernization of rural France, 1870–1914*, Stanford 1976, pp. 126, 128.

In Russia the term "rational man of the land" goes back at least as far as M. E. Saltykov-Shchedrin's mid-nineteenth-century story by that name ("Khoziaistvennyi muzhichok," in *Melochi zhizni*), and was borrowed by Cathy Frierson to characterize a common perception of the peasant in late Imperial Russia (*Peasant Icons*, ch. 4). The most recent overview of scholarship on the Russian peasantry, by historian David Moon, reflects the exclusivity of the optimizing peasant approach in Russian studies. Moon's summary amounts to a blanket defense of peasant technology, and is permeated with skepticism about notions of improvement, advance, and progress with respect to this technology. Moon had no alternative literature to synthesize. *The Russian Peasantry*, pp. 126–133, 155. Recent discussions of peasant technology from historians in Russia take the same line (see, for example, the most high-profile works on the topic, Goriushkin et al., *Opyt narodnoi agronomii v Sibiri*, esp. p. 11; and Milov, *Velikorusskii pakhar'*, esp. pp. 109, 205).

47 In recent years quite a few local studies of contemporary agriculture in developing countries have cast doubt on the efficiency of small farmers. For an overview, see Ali and Byerlee, "Economic Efficiency of Small Farmers in a Changing World." The only historian I have seen expressing disbelief in the optimizing peasant paradigm was Jerome Blum ("Michael Confino's *Systemes agraires*," p. 497). He did not attempt to back up his doubts with evidence, however.

48 For examples, see, e.g., the story "Molot'ba," in Anikin, *Plodnaia osen'*, pp. 125, 127; A. I. Ertel', "Muzhichok Signei i moi sosed Chukhvostikov" (from the cycle *Zapiski stepniaka*), in *Sobranie sochinenii*, vol. 1, p. 104; Mashkin, "Byt krest'ian Kurskoi gubernii Oboianskogo uezda," p. 83; Iakushkin, "Nebyval'shchina" and "Muzhitskii god," in *Sochineniia*, St. Petersburg 1884, p. 131 and p. 157, respectively; Fet, "Iz derevni," p. 593; Zernova, "Materialy po sel'sko-khoziaistvennoi magii v Dmitrovskom krae," p. 25; Podgorskii, "Na pashne," p. 58.

49 The rituals with sheaves appear in quite a few sources, including Vsevolozhskii, "Ocherki krest'ianskogo byta Samarskogo uezda," pp. 33–34; and Zolotarev, "Etnograficheskie nabliudeniia v derevne RSFSR (1919–1925 gg.)," p. 153. Many sources note or describe tilling a furrow around the village ("*opakhivanie*"). From Tula province: P. Troitskii, "Selo Lipitsy i ego okrestnosti," p. 92; a short anonymous overview of reports on the practice is "K voprosu ob opakhivaniia," pp. 175–178. The sprinkling of water is from A. N. Trunov, "Poniatiia krest'ian Orlovskoi gubernii o prirode fizicheskoi i dukhovnoi," p. 13. The source for selecting a herd leader is Tul'tseva, "Obshchina i agrarnaia obriadnost'," pp. 54–55.

50 Perhaps the best collection of sayings from the central black-earth region in our time period is G. Iakovlev, "Poslovitsy, pogovorki, krylatye slova."

51 Tul'tseva, *op. cit.*., pp. 58–59. The most thorough data on the ages at which boys and girls began to participate in various farming operations come from a survey in Ranenburg *uezd* of Riazan province (Ranenburg bordered Tambov's Kozlov *uezd*) in the 1920s by Ia. S. Stepanov, "Trud derevenskikh rebiat," which might not have been published. N. Rybnikov relates much of Stepanov's data in his *Krest'ianskii rebenok*, esp. pp. 13–18. The age at which peasant children began working might

have been declining in the late nineteenth century, as families strove to intensify labor. The same intensification could have worn them out earlier and shortened their labor careers. So maintained one very well-informed ethnographer in Khar'kov province (V. V. Ivanov, "Sovremennaia derevnia v Khar'kovskoi gubernii," p. 2).

[52] So remarked the finest folklore compiler of Saratov province (Minkh, "Kolenskaia volost'," p. 100).

[53] Vol'nov, *Povest' o dniakh moei zhizni*, p. 39.

[54] Ogloblin, "Razval," pp.168–169.

[55] Sumtsov, *O tom, kakie sel'skie pover'ia i obychai v osobennosti vrednye*, pp. 20–22.

[56] A great many sources mention the *domovoi*. Good discussion from the black-earth zone is in Minkh, *op. cit.*, pp. 102–103, and Zvonkov, "Ocherk verovanii krest'ian Elatomskogo uezda Tambovskoi gubernii," pp. 76–78.

[57] Examples of this include Zvonkov, *op. cit.*, pp. 74–75; Zimin, *op. cit.*, p. 14; L'vov, *Vospominaniia*, p. 43; V. N. Ladyzhenskii, "Neokonchennye vospominaniia," in *Zemstvo*, 1995, no. 1, p. 12. In contrast to some other peasant societies, Russian peasants appear to have excluded plants and soil from personification. They did not revere plants or perceive them to possess supernatural will. For cases of this in western Africa, see Amanor, *The New Frontier*, p. 116.

[58] Minkh, *op. cit.*, pp. 104–105. There are indications that some peasants harbored doubts about the presence of supernatural forces in which others around them believed, even before the filter-down influence of science began to erode traditional belief in these forces. Chekhov, for instance, describes such a skeptical peasant in his "Muzhiki" (*Sobranie sochinenii*, vol. 8, p. 227–228).

[59] V. A. Federov, "Kul'tura i byt poreformennoi srednevolzhskoi derevni po materialam etnograficheskogo biuro," in Iu.I. Smykov, ed., *Krest'ianskoe khoziaistvo i kul'tura derevni srednogo povolzh'ia*, Ioshkar-Ola 1990, p. 98.

[60] F. Kriukov, "Mel'kom (Vpechatleniia proezzhego)," in *Russkoe Bogatstvo*, 1914, no. 8, p. 174.

[61] Zvonkov, *op. cit.*, pp. 70–74.

[62] Vol'nov, *op. cit.*, p. 38.

[63] M. M. Zimin, *Koverninskii krai*, pp. 20–21. Note as well, for instance, the behavior of a man in Chekhov's story "V ovrage" in *Sobranie sochinenii* (1962), vol. 8, p. 443.

[64] G. Klodnitskii, whose work was inserted in an article of Animelle, "Byt Belorusskikh krest'ian," p. 235.

[65] From Tambov: Amelia Lyons, *Among the Gentry*, p. 59. From other provinces: Sumtsov, *op. cit.*, pp. 18–20; Korinfskii, *V mire skazanii*, pp. 114–115; Kolchin, "Verovanie krest'ian Tul'skoi gubernii," p. 13; Tarachkov, *Putevye zametki*, p. 132; Neustupov, "Verovaniia krest'ian Shapshenskoi volosti," p. 118; Ivanova, *Zhizn i pover'ia krest'ian*, p. 165.

[66] Sumtsov, *op. cit.*, *loc. cit.*; Kolchin, *op. cit.*, *loc. cit.*; Neustupov, *op. cit.*, *loc. cit.*; Ivanova, *op. cit.*, *loc. cit.*; A. I. Ivanov, "Verovaniia krest'ian Orlovskoi gubernii," p. 112; Korostovetz, *Seed and Harvest*, p. 154. The idea of rain being milk from "the sky cows" appears only in Sumtsov. The writer Ivan Bunin also noted gentry preparing bowls of milk when thunder sounded (in the story "Sukhodol," *Sobranie sochinenii*, vol. 3, p. 173).

[67] Tarachkov, *op. cit.*, *loc. cit.*

[68] Respectively, Zernova, *op. cit.*, p. 25; M. Neruchev, "Istochniki sel'sko-khoziaistvennogo znaniia v narode," p. 117.

[69] A wealth of sources discuss peasants' astonishing ignorance concerning horses. Many more sources than those cited here discuss each failing. Regarding errors in evaluating and purchasing horses, Miasoedov, "Nastavlenie o tom, kak osmatrivat' pri pokupke loshad'," pp. 92–97; on common errors in feeding, V. Manzhin, "Kormlenie loshadei v neurozhainye gody'" pp. 57–63; on inaccurate shoeing, Veber, "O kovke loshadei," pp. 637–638; on inattentiveness to, or ignorance of, diseases, *Doklad Bogorodskoi uezdnoi zemskoi upravy po veterinarnoi chasti*, p. 10; and "Sleduet li doveriat' konovalam," in *Ezhegodnik Cherdynskogo uezdnogo zemstva*, pp. 187–191; on inveterate blood purging, Ekonom, "O vrede, proizvodimom na domashnykh zhivotnykh ot nesvoevremennogo krovopuskaniia," pp. 61–64. One good source in praise of ordinary peasants' knowledge of equine diseases, and also of horse healers' talents, is G. I. Uspenskii, *Krest'ianin i krest'ianskii trud*, pp. 392–393. Uspenskii equivocates later, however, when he portrays a horse healer as a charlatan (*ibid.*, pp. 445–446). Horse traders' chicanery is well attested. Examples include Khatunskii, *Okolo volosti*, pp. 190–191; Roth, *op. cit.*, p. 48; Miasoedov, *op. cit., loc. cit.*

[70] Khatunskii, *op. cit., loc. cit.*; Animelle, *op. cit.*, pp. 255–256; Preobrazhenskii, *op. cit.*, p. 346; A. I. Ivanov, "Verovaniia krest'ian Orlovskoi gubernii," p. 86. Curiously, Ivanov found peasants tended to call the *domovoi "khoziain"* (head of the household). A teacher in Kursk reported the same (Rezanova, "Derevnia Salomykova," pp. 104–105).

[71] Respectively, *Konevodstvo Kazanskoi gubernii*, pp. 53–54; Animelle, *op. cit.*, p. 259.

[72] One turn-of-the-century compilation records Russia as celebrating 98 holidays per year, England 87, Spain 75, France 63, Prussia 60 ("Prazdniki," *ES* (Brokgauz-Efron), vol. 48, p. 942). But this count is appropriate only for international comparison. It is far too low for Russia. It includes State holidays, Sundays, and other official Church holidays, but not the many local holidays villages observed—especially the *khramovye prazdniki*, holidays in honor of the saint or event for which the local church was named (Preobrazhenskii, *op. cit.*, p. 100; "Soobrazheniia o nuzhdakh," *TMK* Vilna, pp. 27–28). These *khramovye prazdniki* were often big affairs extending for several days and attracting peasants from nearby villages (M. S. Semenov, "Vo khmeliu;" Anonymous, "Doklad po voprosu ob umen'shenii kolichestva prazdnichnykh dnei," pp. 388–389; L'vov, *Vospominaniia*, pp. 204–205).

[73] Tul'tseva, *op. cit.*, pp. 52–53; Zlatovratskii, *Derevenskie budni*, pp. 244, 506; Korinfskii, *V mire skazanii*, pp. 80–86. Ermolov relates that the peasantry had many sayings advocating or forbidding certain actions on particular days of the week. He left them out of his compilation of folk wisdom because they were purely superstitious, and had no scientific merit (Ermolov, *Narodnye primety na urozhai*, p. 132).

[74] For an excellent discussion of an exhaustion-induced holiday, see Zlatovratskii, *op. cit.*, pp. 348–350.

[75] According to Boris Mironov's calculations, 62% of the holidays fell during the 58% of the days of the year in the agricultural work season, from April to October (*Sotsial'naia istoriia*, vol. 2, p. 309). Kiselev recorded 13 holidays during a 36 day period at the height of the reaping season, from July 14th to August 18th ("Tochnoe opredelenie prazdnikov," p. 1017). Traditionally, Easter tended to delay work for 7–9 days (e.g., from Tula province, L'vov, *Vospominaniia*, pp. 50–51; and from Tambov, N. Bunin, "Khoziaistvennye zapiski i vedemosti g. Bunina," pp. 27–28).

[76] Laments on drinking and domestic violence during holidays were very common. The best known is a literary rendition, in Chekhov's story "Muzhiki" (*Sobranie*

sochinenii, vol. 8, p. 228). See also Iur'evskii, *op. cit.*, pp. 89–91. An excellent source on organized, ritualized fist-fighting in the central black-earth region is Fomin, *Kulachnye boi v Voronezhskoi gubernii.* For the connection between holiday drinking and brawling, see Christian, *Living Water*, pp. 76–79. The evolution of the rural clergy's attitude towards holiday drinking is not clear to me. One early source, however, from Riazan province, complains of priests encouraging drunkenness, on the grounds that, since alcohol is given by God, it would be sinful not to drink it (Protas'ev, "O poroke, svoistvennom krest'ianam," p. 5). Peasant women were quick to register their thanks for the peacefulness of holidays after the government prohibited alcohol in 1914 (*Kostromskaia derevnia v pervoe vremia voiny*, p. 32).

[77] Mironov, *Sotsial'naia istoriia*, vol. 2, pp. 306, 308. Figures available for the central black-earth region fit this picture. Count Petrovo-Solovovo, who held estates in southern Tambov, reported 97 non-working days in the mid-nineteenth century—52 Sundays and 45 holidays, including local holidays (*Sel'skoe blagoustroistvo*, 1858, kn. 3, otdel II, p. 39). A study just to the south of his location, in Voronezh province, registered 120 holidays as of the turn of the century (Shuvaev, *Vymiranie i vozrozhdenie derevni*, p. 62).

It seems the Church hierarchy's attempts to limit or reverse the increase in holidays foundered against the opposition of local clergy, who wished to avoid friction with peasants (Mironov, *Sotsial'naia istoriia*, vol. 2, pp. 312–313).

[78] So computed Mironov (*Sotsial'naia istoriia Rossii*, vol. 2, p. 311). It is important to note that we cannot be sure for exactly how long work was prohibited on holidays. While plenty of sources establish that holidays were observed for the entire day, at least one fully reliable witness insists (for her region, anyway) that peasants were free to work as usual after lunch time (P. V. Ivanova, *Zhizn i pover'ia krest'ian*, p. 2). Wherever this was so, the diseconomic effects of holidays were not so large. In all likelihood, half-day observance of holidays was a step towards non-observance. So reported another ethnographer from the same province (V. V. Ivanov, "Sovremennaia derevnia v Khar'kovskoi gubernii," p. 13).

[79] Federov, "Kul'tura i byt srednevolzhskoi derevni," p. 98; Vsevolozhskii, *op. cit.*, pp. 33–34; Zolotarev, *op. cit.*, p. 154.

[80] Tul'tseva, *op. cit.*, pp. 52–53; Semenova-Tian-Shanskaia, *Village Life in Late Tsarist Russia*, p. 113; *Opyt sel'sko-khoziaistvennogo obzora Saratovskoi gubernii za 1886 g.*, chast' 2, p. 15. The last source contains a reprint of a landowner's chronicle of weather and agricultural work. The chronicle mentions that in this year peasants cut short their observance of Easter so as to continue with weather-delayed sowings.

[81] Bondarenko, "Ocherki Kirsanovskogo uezda," p. 74; Gorev, *Agronom priekhal*, pp. 26–27; Korinfskii, *V mire skazanii*, p. 81; V. V. Ivanov, "Sovremennaia derevnia v Khar'kovskoi gubernii," pp. 11–13; Anonymous, "Doklad po voprosu ob umen'shenii kolichestva prazdnichnykh dnei," p. 388.

[82] Zlatovratskii, *op. cit.*, pp. 320–321; Gorev, *op. cit.*, pp. 26–27; Chekhov, "V ovrage" in *Sobranie sochinenii*, vol. 8, pp. 450–451.

[83] Ushakov, "Materialy po narodnym verovaniiam velikorussov," p. 165.

[84] Modern science (as conveyed by literacy and education) need not be the only stimulus of skepticism towards supernatural beliefs. Some scholars have argued that the segregation of social roles in a modernizing economy works to undermine magic all by itself. They point out that social relationships are depersonalized because people begin to play single-stranded roles instead of multi-stranded roles in each other's lives. Georg Simmel might have been the first to sense the

connection between social segregation and traditional beliefs, in his essay "The Metropolis and Mental Life," in *The Sociology of Georg Simmel*, pp. 324–339. See also Obelkevich, *Religion and Rural Society*, pp. 311–312.

[85] Maksimov, "Narodnye sredstva bor'by s epidemiiami," p. 6; Tul'tseva, *op. cit.*, pp. 48–49. The writer Garin-Mikhailovskii made more or less the same point in the 1890s ("V sutoloke provintsial'noi zhizni," *Sobranie sochinenii*, vol. 4, pp. 367–368).

[86] Indeed, scholars of seventeenth–nineteenth-century England and France have even speculated that broad transformations associated with modernization might have increased the role of magic and superstition in the lives of common people in this period. As the argument goes, the growing alienation of the Church and its clergy from the masses allowed the creative powers of the latter freer rein than before. In the English case, the alienation is traced to the clergy's adoption of a more mechanistic view of the world; in France, to the marginalization of the Church after the traumas of the revolutionary period. See, respectively, E. P. Thompson's review of two books, one of them Keith Thomas's *Religion and the Decline of Magic: studies in popular beliefs in sixteenth- and seventeenth-century England*, London 1971; and Weber, "Religion or Superstition?," in *My France*, p. 122. I have not sufficiently researched the Russian case to offer an opinion on its similarity.

The most vivid accounts I have encountered of icon processions through the fields are in Solov'ev, *Rodnoe Selo*, Part 1, pp. 70–73; and Demidov, *op. cit.*, pp. 86– on. For a more ceremonial procession, from Kursk province in 1854, see Aksakov, *Pis'ma iz provintsii*, pp. 348–351. Village priests derived much needed income for services of this nature, so they were not rushing to encourage peasants to embrace agronomists' attitudes to meteorology (see, e.g., Anonymous, "Doklad po voprosu ob umen'shenii kolichestva prazdnichnykh dnei," p. 389; and Nefedov, "Ivan voin," p. 126).

[87] A. I. Ivanov, "Verovaniia krest'ian Orlovskoi gubernii," p. 118.

[88] The ethnographer P. Troitskii reported this as a standard opinion among peasants (*op. cit.*, p. 103). One of Garin-Mikhailovskii's characters goes so far as to stigmatize technological change as sin ("Babushka Stepanida" from the cycle *Derevenskie panoramy*, in his *Sobranie sochinenii*, vol. 3, Moscow 1957, p. 306). For more sayings enshrining the imperative of living according to traditional sayings, see Ermolov, *Narodnye primety na urozhai*, pp. 3–4. Horror tales also served to enforce conformity to traditional rites and rituals. See, e.g., a short tale recorded in P. V. Ivanova, *Zhizn i pover'ia krest'ian*, p. 146.

[89] See, e.g., research on agricultural superstitions in Orel province in the years 1928–1930 in Zernova, "Materialy po sel'sko-khoziaistvennoi magii;" or Ogloblin, "Razval," pp. 168–169; Zolotarev, *op. cit.*, pp. 152–154; and A. Putintsev, "Iz etnograficheskikh vpechatlenii i nabliudenii," p. 44. Although he reported observance of canonical religion to be in retreat, even among the traditionally more devout sectarians, Ogloblin sensed no decline of superstitiousness among peasants. While both Zolotarev's and Putintsev's articles discuss the continued hold of various superstitions, their greatest value lies in their recording of new elements in peasant culture during the period of revolution and civil war.

[90] Zernova, *op. cit.*, p. 25; Animelle, *op. cit.*, p. 257.

[91] Solov'ev, *Rodnoe selo*, Part 1, p. 18.

[92] P. V. Ivanova, *Zhizn i pover'ia krest'ian*, p. 83.

[93] *Ibid.*

[94] *Ibid.*, p. 137.

[95] As the wife of peasant writer S. P. Pod"iachev accused him (*Zhizn' muzhitskaia*, pp. 23–4). Hindus records a nearly identical incident (*Broken Earth*, pp. 138–139).

[96] Garin-Mikhailovskii, "Neskol'ko let v derevne," *Sobranie sochinenii*, vol. 3, p. 39.

[97] Korinfskii, *V mire skazanii*, p. 84.

[98] Sumtsov, *op. cit.*, pp. 8–9; Trunov, *op. cit.*, pp. 16–17.

[99] "Zavoroshka," in Prishvin, *Sobranie sochinenii*, vol. 1, p. 681.

[100] For one of a great many sources on this, see Bondarenko, *op. cit.*, pp. 74–75. For a case of peasants perceiving witches to be behind drought, see, e.g., from Tula province, D. I. Uspenskii, "Tolki naroda," pp. 184–5. Other deities often shared the credit with God for good weather. Chief among them were Saint Nicholas the Miracle Maker, and, less frequently, Ilia the Prophet and Saint George the Dragon-slayer. Ermolov, *Narodnye primety na urozhai*, p. 150.

[101] One good discussion of a religious procession through the fields is Zlatovratskii, *op. cit.*, pp. 320–321. For a witch-hunt in connection with a drought, see *Otchety 1914*, p. 172. On attitudes to suicide and suiciders, Sumtsov, *op. cit.*, pp. 9–10; Bondarenko, *op. cit.*, pp. 86–87. Garin-Mikhailovskii also mentions disinterment of the worst sinners (or of drowned people) during droughts, in "Neskol'ko let v derevne," *Sobranie sochinenii*, vol. 3, pp. 39–40; and "V sutoloke provintsial'noi zhizni," *ibid.*, vol. 4, pp. 435–436.

[102] The first Minister of Agriculture, Ermolov, devoted an entire book to the topic (*Narodnye primety na urozhai*). For a thorough collection of yield-predicting sayings from Khar'kov province, see "O predskazanii pogody," in *Khar'kovskii kalendar na 1887 god*, pp. 612–618. Many of the yield-predicting sayings were agronomically sound, but many were not (as both Ermolov and the Khar'kov compiler pointed out—respectively, p. 150, p. 614).

[103] Meshcherskii, "Pervaia stupen'," pp. 233–234.

[104] Animelle, *op. cit.*, p. 216.

[105] Tolstoi, "Utro pomeshchika," in *Sobranie sochinenii*, Vol. 2, p. 361. Garin-Mikhailovskii encountered the same intransigence among peasants (and a landlord as well) on exactly the same issue ("Neskol'ko let v derevne," and "Pod vecher. Ocherk." in *Sobranie sochinenii*, vol. 3, p. 66 and p. 213, respectively). Ermolov, for one, insisted that this fatalistic sentiment lay very deep in the Russian peasantry (as reflected in sayings like "If God doesn't give rain, the land will not give crops," or "Not the land, but the weather grows the crops"). See his comments in *Narodnye primety na urozhai*, pp. 149–150.

[106] Johnson, "Individuality and Experimentation in Traditional Agriculture." This article collates studies demonstrating systematic experimentation in a wide range of traditional agricultural communities. The quotation appears on p. 156. On experimental behavior, see also Paul Richards, *Indigenous Agricultural Revolution*, esp. pp. 26–33, 71, 97–98, 109, 149; Louk Box, "The Experimenting Farmer," esp. pp. 90–91; and Amanor, *The New Frontier*, esp. pp. 206–212.

[107] Paul Richards, *op. cit.*, is probably the best known exponent of this position.

[108] For a concise overview of these trends, see N. F. Sumtsov, *op. cit.* See also *Otchety 1914*, p. 172, for a witch-hunt undertaken against an agronomist on the occasion of a drought.

[109] Volosatov, "Selo Tugolukovka," p. 346.

[110] *Otchety uchastkovykh agronomov za 1911 god*, pp. 131–32.

[111] On this, see the valuable comments in *Peremeny v zemledel'cheskoi tekhnike*, pp. 23, 26.

[112] *Otchety uchastkovykh agronomov za 1911 god*, p.131. For more on peasants' igno-rance and indifference regarding care for fallow land, in Kursk province, see Erpulev, "K voprosu ob uluchsheniiu," pp. 11–14.

[113] Furthermore, we may note that the rapid adoption of *dvoenie* and other important techniques testify to the incautiousness of many adopters. It is fairly clear that not all peasants were carefully weighing the decision to innovate. This supposition squares quite nicely with the conclusions of an Asian study to the effect that what passes for considered innovation among peasants is in some cases nothing more than blind, unreflective imitation: Pomp and Burger, "Innovation and Imitation," pp. 423–431. The authors found that about 70% of cocoa plant adopters had no idea of the price or yield of cocoa when they adopted it. The most frequently stated reason for adoption was "because other people do so too" (pp. 425–426).

[114] Many sources must attest to this, albeit laconically. Thus we can see that at the turn of the century a good portion of the Samara *zemstvo*'s peasant correspondents were keeping separate track of yields from two sorts of wheat (*Razmery posevnoi ploshchadi*, pp. 10–24). A pre-emancipation source from Penza explicitly recorded peasants distinguishing between the sorts of oats landlords were then importing into the region (A. Gorizontov, "Khoziaistvenno-statisticheskoe opisanie Penzenskogo uezda," no. 3, p. 220). Peasants were aware of strains of vegetables as well. Sources recording strains of vegetables include Goppe, "Razvedenie repchatogo luka na poliakh," pp. 8–9; and Bobovich, "Puti agrotekhnicheskogo progressa," p. 63.

    In his work on the eighteenth century Milov relates the enormous repertoire of sorts of fruits and vegetables cultivated in Russia (*op. cit.*, chapter 8, esp. pp. 277, 283). It does not follow from this, however, that all or even most peasants were keenly aware of the existence of different sorts of grains. Appearance and taste distinctions between strains of fruits and vegetables are much more obvious than with grains. Further, most of the variety of fruits and vegetables arose in or adjacent to cities and towns, as Milov himself emphasizes. Finally, Milov is a very diligent and well-informed scholar, but he presents little evidence of peasants (as opposed to landlords) deriving, searching, or maintaining specific sorts of grains. Indeed, investigations of peasant practice revealed awareness of sorts of fruit and vegetables to be wanting (see, e.g., G. Kositsyn, "Doklad instruktora-sadovoda," p. 47; or, with respect to tobacco, a discussion of peasants' complete indifference to sorts, in RGAE f. 478, op. 2, d. 235, pp. 26–28).

[115] Meister, ed., *Svodka rezul'tatov*, pp. 66, 78–79.

[116] Vorontsov chronicled a range of experiments in his *Progressivnye techeniia v krest'ianskom khoziaistve* (pp. 62–68). Both he and Vikhliaev detail how peasants in Moscow province commonly conducted trials of clover grass in out-of-the-way corners of the fields (respectively, *Progressivnye techeniia*, p. 197; and *Vliianie travoseianiia*, pp. 43–44). Agricultural correspondents noted the same sort of trials with corn when that crop first appeared (*Statisticheskii ezhegodnik 1907 g.*, p. 21; Ivlev, "Malenkaia proba," pp. 265–266). A rare source identifying a thin layer of peasants aggressively pursuing experiments is Bel'skii, *Novaia zemledel'cheskaia Rossiia*, p. 111. Bel'skii notes elsewhere (pp. 21, 27) that experimentation was much more common among peasants who separated from the commune and set up consolidated plots according to the provisions of the Stolypin reform (on which see Part IV).

[117] See, e.g., Meister, *op. cit.*, p. 66.

[118] Troitskii, "O kul'ture maslichnogo podsolnechnika," p. 8.

[119] Meister, *op. cit.*, p. 43. This particular failing was very common in one *uezd* (Vol'sk), less so in others.

[120] *Ibid,* esp. p. 46.

[121] *Ibid.*, pp. 53–54. On almost 7,000 *desiatinas* of sowings registered as sort-specific in Saratov province in 1927, only 26% of the grain was judged to be at least 95% sort-pure; 49% of the grain was 80–95% sort-pure, while the remaining 25% was described as "foul" (N.V. Orlovskii, "Kratkii ocherk razvitiia semenovodstva v Saratovskoi gubernii," in Meister, ed., pp. 10–12). On a similar note, some of the peasants voluntarily conducting trials with new methods or new strains of crops under local agronomists' direction would neglect to measure yields on the trial plots separately from their other plots (see, for example, GATO, f. 51, d. 235, p. 168).

[122] Sequential data from Moscow province likewise implies that the layer of peasants interested in trying out new varieties of seeds was very thin, at least until the turn of the century. In the 1880s quite a few of the Moscow *zemstvo*'s agricultural correspondents noted rising interest among peasants in new, distinct varieties of grains. In a variety of ways, some peasants began taking up new varieties, and kept track of them (*Statisticheskii ezhegodnik Moskovskoi gubernii za 1889 g.,* pp. 176–179). Yet for a long time this kind of inquisitiveness was not contagious: the 1906 edition of the same source reveals very little interest in new varieties. Since 13% of the 1906 correspondents noted interest in *either* sorts *or* new spring-sown crops, the proportion perceiving some degree of interest in sorts must have been below 10% (*ibid. za 1906 g. Chast' pervaia*, pp. 43, 195–196).

It might be argued that peasants' indifference to imported sorts of crops represented a healthy wariness of the dangers of biological diversity. New sorts of crops can cause serious problems if they cause pathogens to hybridize or mutate in ways that allow them to attack hitherto resistant plants. Apart from the absence of evidence demonstrating peasants' awareness of such a danger, their continuous cultivation of a limited genetic base created dangers of its own. Pathogens can multiply in a soil if crops appear there repeatedly. On these topics, Christensen, "Diseases of Wheat," pp. 693–696. Proper use of fungicide can minimize the danger of contagion from imported seeds, as Russian agronomists understood before 1914 (Garshin, *O semenakh dlia poseva,* for example). On the other hand, fungicides were not readily available in Russia (as K. Matseevich pointed out in a book review in *TVEO*, 1912, no. 1–2, p. 25).

Interest in sorts did rise throughout Russia in the last years before the First World War. Agricultural bulletins and periodicals of this period are littered with advertisements for varieties of seeds, and *zemstvo* agronomic aid programs encouraged peasants to investigate new strains. A layer of proselytizing landlords and clergymen were equally potent in stimulating peasant interest in seed strains, among other technical refinements (for discussion of their roles, and the significance of the agricultural press, see, e.g., *Peremeny v zemledel'cheskoi tekhnike*, pp. 16, 18, 19, 32, 34–35, 37, 38, 39, 41, 43.). It seems, however, that most of the trade in specific varieties of seeds was in the hands of unscrupulous local dealers who diluted their products with admixtures of foreign material and non-germinating seeds (judging from a report from St. Petersburg province, at any rate: Pravikovskii, "O pokupke novykh sortov semian," pp. 7–8).

[123] See, e.g., Johnson, *op. cit.*, p. 155. I have not found any evidence of black-earth region villages arranging experimental plots before the arrival of local agronomists (Vorontsov reported some instances of this in the northern half of European Russia—*Progressivnye techeniia*, pp. 177, 197). Other opportunities for experimen-

tation were going wasted. Thus peasants did not try sowing spring crops together in various mixes—a promising technique, according to data from other countries (for foreign data, see, e.g., Vorob'ev, *Rol' faktorov urozhaia*, pp. 6–7). Nor did peasants experiment with sequences of crops in particular parts of the spring section of the three-field system (the significance of this will become more clear after the discussion of field systems, in Part III). On this see, e.g., explicit comments in Trostianskii, *op. cit.*, p. 235. To be fair, a few observers did detect this practice: Kotov, *op. cit.*, p. 32; and Milov cites one source, *op. cit.*, p. 48. It should be noted at this point that Russian landowners demonstrated little more proclivity to experiment than peasants in the late nineteenth century. See, e.g., A. P. Mertvyi's comments in *op. cit.*, pp. 202–203. One Tambov landowner who did undertake plenty of experiments was Prince L. D. Viazemskii. He achieved marvelous results. Rye yields on his estate "Lotarevo" in Usman *uezd* averaged 173 *puds* per *desiatina* in the first decade of the twentieth century, which was more than twice as high as the average among landlords in the *uezd*, and more than three times the peasant average (from the report "Ob organizatsii opytnykh uchrezhdenii v Tambovskoi gubernii," *ZhTGZS ocherednoi sessii 1910 goda*, p. 525). According to this source Viazemskii was one among quite a few Tambov landlords closely engaged in agricultural experimenting at this time.

[124] Stakhovich, *Istoriia, etnografiia i statistika Eletskogo uezda*, p. 33.

[125] Bunin, "Derevnia," *Sobranie sochinenii*, vol. 3, p. 102.

[126] Apsit, "Kak nado rabotat'," p. 805.

[127] For example, Engel'gardt, *Iz derevni*, pp. 103, 309.

[128] Rare documentation of cases of this appears in *Statisticheskii ezhegodnik Moskovskoi gubernii za 1889 god*, pp. 102, 112, and elsewhere.

[129] Johnson, *op. cit.*, pp. 151–154.

[130] Lengthy discussion of soil types and peasant land redistribution practices is included in the first twelve volumes of the series *SSS*. This information appears in the opening sections of each volume with the exception of volume 1, devoted to Borisoglebsk *uezd*, which is organized differently.

[131] *Statisticheskii ezhegodnik Moskovskoi gubernii za 1889 god*, p. 97.

[132] *Materialy dlia otsenki zemel' Saratovskoi gubernii. Vyp. III*, p. 96.

[133] *Tekushchaia sel'sko-khoziaistvennaia statistika Kurskogo gubernskogo zemstva. 1900 god. Kniga IV.*, Kursk 1900, p. 64. This must have been a rather common story. It appears again in *Sel'sko-khoziaistvennyi obzor Samarskoi gubernii za 1898–1899*, pp. 18, 27–28; and (in a somewhat different context, for oats this time) in *Statisticheskii ezhegodnik Moskovskoi gubernii za 1899 god*, p. 48. Surely other sources could be found.

[134] *Otchety uchastkovykh agronomov za 1911 god*, p. 46. A similar comment appears in a local agronomist's report from Borisoglebsk *uezd* (*Proekty*, pp. 561–562). Likewise, in Samara province the English agriculturalist H. L. Roth was struck by peasants' inveterate interest in new tools and machines: "The peasant carries the seed of improvement within him: he is exceedingly inquisitive, is always craving for information about foreign countries, and an explanation of some new machine affords him immense satisfaction." (*op. cit.*, p. 79).

[135] A. I. Ertel' offers a valuable presentation of a peasant named Semion who does cultivate his talents for divining weather in the stories "Moi domochadtsy" and "Serafim Ezhikov" (from the cycle *Zapiski stepniaka*), in *Sobranie sochinenii*, vol. 1. Ertel' indicates how unusual or even rare this type of man is, and how the other peasants respect him for his talent.

[136] A. I. Ertel', "Iz odnogo kornia" (from the cycle *Zapiski stepniaka*), in *Sobranie sochinenii*, vol. 1, pp. 52–53.

[137] Preobrazhenskii, *op. cit.*, p. 245 (emphasis added).

[138] Engel'gardt, *op. cit.*, p. 308 (emphasis added).

[139] Bunin, "Derevnia" in *Sobranie sochinenii*, vol. 3, p. 125. Garin-Mikhailovskii (who had even more experience with peasants than Bunin) passed a similar judgment on peasant farmers' ignorance and apathy concerning agronomic knowledge. "Neskol'ko let v derevne," in *Sobranie sochinenii*, vol. 3, p. 29.

[140] *Zemstvo* agronomist Kuznetsov of Iaroslavl province, as quoted in Iur'evskii, *op. cit.*, pp. 8–9.

[141] For discussion of breeding practices among peasants, see Kerans, "The Workhorse."

[142] Engel'gardt, *op. cit.*, p. 217. Zlatovratskii came to a similar formulation. After recounting how peasants properly identified and energetically defended their personal interests in communal affairs (such as land redistributions), he reflected: "It is a separate question, of course, how broadly peasants apply their rational self-interest ..." (*op. cit.*, p. 317).

[143] See, e.g., Engel'gardt, *op.cit.*, pp. 214–218; or Arkhangel'skii, "Selo Davshino," pp. 46–47. Alexander Ertel' found these qualities to be significantly more developed among "kulaks" than in the mass of the peasantry ("Iz odnogo kornia," *op. cit.*, pp. 52, 59). While almost all peasants could do arithmetic, far fewer could handle multiplication and division—at least in part, no doubt, because they never bothered to keep accounts (see, e.g., Firsov and Kiselev, *op. cit.*, p. 172). The same source describes the relative weakness of mathematical skills among women (*ibid.*). It seems that peasants retained arithmetic skills better than literacy (Eklof, "Peasant Sloth Reconsidered," p. 374).

[144] Wrote Ol'ga Semenova-Tian-Shanskaia, studying peasants in Riazan province in the years 1898–1902: "Until recently, some peasants could not distinguish one type of paper money from another, count money correctly, or figure out the prices for manufactured goods. But now every peasant has a billfold, and he knows how to manage properly his tax records and to calculate his accounts with the landlord or storekeeper." (*op. cit.*, p. 146). A mid-nineteenth century literary rendering of peasants' difficulties with numerical operations is Nikolai Uspenskii's story "Oboz," *Povesti, rasskazy i ocherki*, pp. 165–172. A. N. Antsiferov noticed the same difficulty commonly obtaining among peasant women in central Russia during the First World War (*The Cooperative Movement*, p. 282). A similar indication, applying to men, is Zimin, *Koverninskii krai*, p. 6.

[145] Bruk, *Kak naladit' krest'ianinu*, p. 49. "We don't count or measure anything," a peasant in Moscow province flatly informed the poet A. Fet just after emancipation. Fet estimated that peasants in his home region of Orel were paying a bit more attention than that to quantities, albeit not to accounting or record keeping (Fet, "Iz derevni," p. 579). Further testimony to the absence of farm accounting comes from *Sam sebe agronom*, 1926, no. 47, pp. 1485–86; and personal interviews.

It should be pointed out that the neglect of accounting on peasant farms was not at all unique to Russia. Peasants elsewhere in Europe behaved similarly (see, e.g., Obelkevich, *op. cit.*, p. 49). Still, by the early twentieth century many German colonists in southern Russia were keeping detailed accounts (Bel'skii, *op. cit.*, p. 53; and the chapter discussing yields in Postnikov, *Iuzhno-russkoe krest'ianskoe khoziaistvo*). Traditionally those peasants who bothered to keep track of certain transactions used tally sticks (*birki* in Russian) (Selivanov, *op. cit.*, p. 61; Nebol'sin, *Okolo muzhichkov*, p. 17; Ertel', "Vizgunovskaia ekonomiia" (from the cycle *Zapiski stepniaka*), *Sobranie sochinenii*, vol. 1, p. 139; Vol'nov, *op. cit.*, p. 169). They might also make charcoal marks on a wall in their homes (Reshetnikov, "Tetushka Oparina," p. 94).

Landowners were not much ahead of peasants with respect to accounting. At the time of emancipation the huge majority of landowners in Tambov were ignorant of accounting and commercial practices that were then routine in western Europe (Terpigorev, *Oskudenie*, in *Sobranie sochinenii*, pp. 17–18; and, for neighboring *uezds*, Posashev, "Sel'skoe khoziaistvo v Eletskom i Dankovskom uezdakh," pp. 1–2, 20–21). Things did not change much over the next few decades. See, e.g., the assessment in *SSS, vol. 16*, pp. ii, 143, 226; Mertvyi, *op. cit.*, pp. 246–247; and *Otchet o deiatel'nosti pravitel'stvennoi agronomicheskoi organizatsii v Orlovskoi gubernii za 1912 god*, p. 2. Nevertheless, quite a few counter-indications testify that landlords were acquiring habits of accounting. A source from early in our period is Anonymous, "O vliianii krest'ianskoi reformy na khlebnuiu proizvoditel'nost' v Voronezhskoi gubernii," pp. 383–387. See also "Oblastnoi s"ezd sel'skikh khoziaev v g. Khar'kove v 1886 g.," in *Khar'kovskii kalendar na 1887 god*, pp. 482–483; or Garin-Mikhailovskii, "Neskol'ko let v derevni," in *Sobranie sochinenii*, vol. 3, p. 20. One source mentioning the appearance of record-keeping among some literate peasants is Golubev, "Vliianie gramotnosti," pp. 117–118.

[146] In his literary portrait of a village on the Volga, K. N. Solov'ev does mention a deacon who recorded storms' characteristics for decades (*Rodnoe Selo*, Part 1, p. 75).

[147] *Sel'sko-khoziaistvennye i statisticheskie svedeniia, po materialam poluchennym ot khoziaev. Vyp. 1*, pp. 2–3.

[148] *K otsenke*, Lipetsk, p. 31; Tambov, p. 61; Morshansk, p. 67, Borisoglebsk, p. 62.

[149] *K otsenke*, Lipetsk, p. 33. Be it noted that the same report accuses landlords of the same behavior (*ibid.*).

[150] Solov'ev, "Sravnitel'naia urozhainost'," p. 7. Solov'ev does note that peasants were becoming more attentive to yield measurement at this time, in part out of a desire to measure the effectiveness of innovations. Peasants might count their yields in 100s of sheaves, or in numbers of *kopny* (Fenomenov, *Sovremennaia derevnia*, chast' 1, p. 91).

[151] For a literary rendering of the frustration these calculations could cause peasants, see Garin-Mikhailovskii's "Akulina," from the cycle *Derevenskie panoramy*, in *Sobranie sochinenii*, vol. 3, pp. 322, 328.

[152] A 1926 report of a *volost'* party secretary in Borisoglebsk *uezd* is the only source I have ever uncovered that explicitly mentions peasants keeping accounts in significant numbers. The source identifies taxation as the stimulus to keeping accounts (PATO, f. 840, op. 1, d. 3385, p. 38). The attention individual taxation aroused among peasants in the early 1920s is attested in B. V., "Pis'ma s dorogi," p. 24. Before the 1920s villages divided their tax burdens among member households crudely, without generally attempting to gauge incomes in any direct way. The number of separate taxes made it difficult for illiterate peasants to keep track of how much they owed (see, e.g., Garin-Mikhailovskii, "Na sele," from the cycle *Derevenskie panoramy*, in his *Sobranie sochinenii*, vol. 3, p. 377).

[153] The number of primary and secondary sources relating this argument is so large as to excuse citation. The only historian I have noticed discussing how communes tried to accommodate manure use within the framework of periodic repartitions is Esther Kingston-Mann ("Peasant Communes and Economic Innovation." Kingston-Mann exaggerates communes' performance in compensating families for the

loss of manured strips during repartitions (p. 45, e.g.). Judith Pallot notes other cases of this practice (*Land Reform in Russia*, p. 82). A multitude of sources testify that communes avoided giving this sort of compensation (see, e.g. Mosolov, "Pis'ma zemleustroitel'ia," pp. 92–93).

[154] For one calculation from Tambov, see *Proekty*, pp. 54–55.

[155] Several circumstances could condition shortages of manure, including shrinking livestock holdings, the use of manure as a heat source (a nearly inevitable accompaniment of the deforestation that plagued central and southern Russia from the mid-nineteenth century on), and increased application of manure to the garden plot. Regarding peasants' ignorance of the usefulness of manure, see above, endnotes 9–10. Eventually peasants almost everywhere must have recognized manure's effectiveness—even where they refrained from applying manure to their fields, they used it in the garden plots (with rare exceptions). In Tambov manure use slowly worked its way down into the central and southern *uezds* from the 1880s on. For analysis and discussion, see Kerans, "Agricultural Evolution ...," Part I.

[156] In the nineteenth century Russian peasants were accused of sloth at least as often as other peasantries. See, e.g., Pares, *Russia Between Reform and Revolution*, p. 365; Roth, *op. cit.*, p. 74 [elsewhere (p. 80) Roth notes that peasants were getting a bit more farsighted in this respect]; *Ocherk ekonomicheskoi zhizni*, p. 151; Semenova-Tian-Shanskaia, *op. cit.*, p. 145; Daragan, *Mysli sel'skogo khoziaina*, pp. 70–72.

[157] Semenova-Tian-Shanskaia, *op. cit.*, p. 139. This was certainly not a rare opinion, about landlords as well as peasants. Another discussion is Kozlov, "Khoziaistvennyi otchet," pp. 169–170.

[158] S. T. Semenov, *Dvadtsat' piat' let v derevne*, p. 154.

[159] Gleaning was standard only in Russia's western borderlands. Elsewhere it was considered shameful (*Osennye sel'sko-khoziaistvennye raboty*, pp. 69–70). See also Preobrazhenskii, who lamented the grain peasants were forfeiting by not gleaning (*op. cit.*, p. 251). Further testimony to wasting of gleaning opportunities appears in Anonymous, "Zapiska o vozdelyvanii i sbyte khlebov v Lebedianskom uezde," pp. 53–54. This source records how peasants would take care to pick up stray ears only with wheat. Gleaning was much more common in Western Europe. Communities would assign 5–7 days for gleaning after the sheaves were cleared from the fields. So, at any rate, reports one summary of early English agriculture (Ault, *Open-Field Husbandry*, pp. 14–15).

[160] In Becker, *op. cit.*, p. 7. As Becker rightly insists, "the economic approach" is very successful in predicting a wide range of behaviors, and has therefore yielded many important theorems (*ibid.*).

[161] See, e.g., discussion in Amartya K. Sen, "Rational Fools," esp. pp. 91–94.

[162] See, e.g., the summary of his work in Friedman and McCabe, "Preferences or Happiness? Tibor Scitovsky's Psychology of Human Needs," pp. 471–480.

[163] Sen, "Rationality, Joy and Freedom," pp. 485–486. Underlined emphasis added.

[164] Scitovsky is quite aware of the importance of "top-down" influences on behavior. A reshaping of child-rearing practices and educational reforms are prominent among his policy proposals, for instance (Scitovsky, "My Own Criticism of *The Joyless Economy*," pp. 601–604; Friedman and McCabe, *op. cit.*, p. 475). I have borrowed the "top-down" "bottom-down" perspective on Scitovsky from Thomas More's discussion of *The Joyless Economy* (in *The Journal of Leisure Research*, vol. 25, 1993 no. 3, pp. 317–318).

[165] Pares, *Russia Between Reform and Revolution*, p. 95.

[166] Arkhangel'skii, "Selo Davshino," p. 48.

[167] Pod"iachev, *Zhizn' muzhitskaia*, p. 21.

[168] Novikov, *Zapiski zemskogo nachal'nika*, p. 60. Wives could be as sensitive to gossip as their husbands. See, for example, S. Maslov, *Mirskoi chelovek*.

[169] Kochetkov [an agronomist working in Nizhegorod province, just north of Tambov], "Sel'sko-khoziaistvennye besedy," p. 8. See also Shatsk *uezd* agronomist V. S. Sabo's description of peasants' reticence to participate in agricultural exhibitions for fear of ridicule (*SKhZh*, 1912/13, no. 1, p. 53); or A. I. Ertel's description of a Samara village where peasants were afraid even to plant trees near their homes for shade, lest they be singled out for ridicule ["Samarskaia derevnia (fotografiia)," p. 131]; and Garin-Mikhailovskii, "Neskol'ko let v derevne," in *Sobranie sochinenii*, vol. 3, pp. 72, 103. Likewise, peasants might try to shame co-villagers who evidenced an interest in reading, or learning to read (see, e.g., Anonymous, "Lozhnyi styd," pp. 13–15; and Karonin's story, "Uchenyi"). This kind of badgering could slow, but not halt, the spread of literacy, as we shall see below.

[170] See, e.g., Bel'skii, *op. cit.*, p. 164. See also an episode in Ertel's story "Iz odnogo kornia" (from the cycle *Zapiski stepniaka*—in *Sobranie sochinenii*, vol. 1, p. 55) where a shepherd declines to protect the crops of a non-conformist co-villager from trespass by some of the grazing animals. Likewise, a co-villager killed half of the peasant writer Pod"iachev's bees one night after he did some work on a holiday (*Zhizn' muzhitskaia*, pp. 19–21).

[171] S. T. Semenov, *op cit.*, pp. 247–248.   •

[172] Verbov, *op. cit.*, p. 101. The quote comes from a conversation that took place only a few miles southeast of Tambov province, in Balashov *uezd* of Saratov province, just before the First World War.

[173] Garin-Mikhailovskii's short story "Volk" ("Wolf") is an unforgettable saga of a commune ostracizing and punishing an ambitious, individualist co-villager for years on end (in *Sobranie sochinenii*, vol. 4, pp. 535–558). Ivan Vol'nov's autobiography provides a gripping account of mob violence (in this case, kulak-mobilized) against a family whose son is perceived as betraying arrogant ways when returning home after getting an education (*op. cit.*, pp. 167, 179–185). For more on the same theme, see the discussion of the Stolypin reform in Part IV.

[174] Garin-Mikhailovskii, "Na nochlege," in *op. cit.*, vol. 4, p. 142; and Meshcherskii, *op. cit.*, p. 233.

[175] Romer, "Schastlivchik."

[176] Pod"iachev, *Zhizn' muzhitskaia*, p. 22. The writer Viacheslav Shishkov described the prevalence of precisely the same sentiments among peasants in a small Siberian village (*Taiga*, in his *Sobranie sochinenii*, vol. 1, pp. 20–21). Whether or not Shishkov was making a general statement on the Russian peasantry, this is how his book was received. For further attestation of envy in the villages, consider Animelle's comments: "Envy is a very strong emotion among the peasantry. If a peasant sees that a neighbor's grain is growing better, or his livestock is doing better, etc., then he speaks to his family about it with deep anxiety, and hopes somehow, so long as it is clandestinely, to inflict damage on his neighbor". (*op. cit.*, p. 252). Hard times, such as famines or the period after the revolutionary upheavals of 1905–06, exacerbated these kinds of antagonisms. See, for instance, Korolenko, *V Golodnyi god*, p. 20; and Konovalov's vivid articles "V derevne" and "Budni sovremennoi derevni."

[177] Historians David Ransel and David Moon have recently emphasized another explanation of Russian peasants' leveling behavior. Endorsing an idea traceable primarily to anthropologist George Foster, Ransel and Moon propose that peasants

understood the aggregate wealth of the village as fixed, as a "limited good" (Ransel, "Introduction," pp. xxvi–xxviii; Moon, *The Russian Peasantry*, p. 274; Foster, "Peasant Society and the Image of the Limited Good"). It follows that peasants would resent other households who held surplus resources, surpluses representing over-appropriation of scarce community goods. Directly or indirectly, the less well-off would pressure neighbors to redistribute some of their accumulated wealth.

The notion of "limited good" as a motivation governing leveling behavior in villages looks reasonable at first glance. But its applicability to Russian peasants in the late Imperial period is dubious. To begin with, plentiful evidence illustrates peasants' awareness of the variability of the wealth available to the community. Harvests could fluctuate wildly. Three or four good harvests in succession could substantially raise the material standing of any village. The Samara writer Karonin devoted a series of works to a village experiencing the opposite, thanks to fires, a steady decline in yields, and other calamities (e.g., "Kuda i kak oni pereselilis'"). Sources commonly recorded peasants who sensed a steady deterioration of their soil (e.g., *Statisticheskii ezhegodnik 1907 g.*, pp. 46–47, ibid. *1908 g.*, p. 54). They might explain this in various ways—God was sending the apocalypse, or the sun was giving less heat (Trunov, *op. cit.*, pp. 5–6). Peasants did consider measures to raise the wealth of the community. The commune could buy land, sell forests, convert pastures to arable, set aside land for orchards, etc. (see, e.g., comments from local agronomist Dlugokanskii in *Otchet o deiatel'nosti agronomicheskogo personala za 1912 sel'sko-khoziaistvennyi god*, pp. 101–102). Peasants were fully aware of the variability of non-agricultural earnings as well. And, as we shall see below, they had some sense of who among them were sub-standard farmers, or drunks. It is not likely they ascribed the poverty of these people to neighbors' "(wrongful) private appropriation of a community good," to borrow Ransel's wording.

Foster's conception has come under criticism from other angles. See, e.g., Sutti Ortiz, "Reflections on the Concept of 'Peasant Culture'." pp. 328–330.

[178] Vnukov, *Protivorechiia staroi krest'ianskoi semi*, pp. 7–8, 12.

[179] For an insider's discussion of peasant officials' and Land Captains' behavior in this respect, see, Matveev, "V volostnykh starshinakh," *Russkoe Bogatstvo*, 1912, no. 2, pp. 93–94. Until 1903 the law held peasant communes collectively responsible for some taxes. In principle, therefore, wherever the commune had tax arrears surplus wealth was always vulnerable to confiscation. Contemporaries insisted that this vulnerability deprived peasants of all incentives to improve farming (see, e.g., A. V. Sheremet'ev's comments to a government commission in the 1870s, cited in Volin, *A Century of Russian Agriculture*, pp. 54–55). In practice, of course many peasants did safely accumulate surpluses. Collective responsibility was not uniformly enforced, as the growth of tax arrears attests. Even before 1903 the government abandoned it with respect to insurance and food loans (*TMK*, Tambov, p. 345). One commentator in Tambov in 1902 declared collective responsibility to be nearly a dead letter by then ("Doklad A. D. Briukhatova ob osnovnykh prichinakh, tormoziashchikh rost' i razvitie krest'ianskoi sel'skokhoziaistvennoi promyshlennosti," in *ibid.*, p. 465). Families who failed to meet tax obligations faced a variety of sanctions, including expropriation of land (see, e.g., SSS, Borisoglebsk, Otdel 2, p. 11, Prilozhenie 1, pp. 22–23).

[180] The State's repression of the peasantry and the rest of society tended to be under-reported, since the press was often instructed not to chronicle officialdom's

transgressions (Stepniak, *The Russian Peasantry*, p. 132). A brief overview is *ibid.*, pp. 128–140.

[181] One national overview containing this conclusion is Rittikh, *Zavisimost' krest'ian*, pp. 185–186. For one of many local counterparts, see Kordatov, "Chernukhinskaia volost'," p. 32.

[182] 10.9% of the households in Tambov held five or more horses in 1888. 3.6% had this many in 1912. *Voenno-konskaia perepis' 1888 goda*, St. Petersburg 1889, pp. 8, 80–81; *Voenno-konskaia perepis' 1912 goda*, Petrograd 1914, pp. 14, 134–135.

[183] On which see, e.g., Vsevolozhskii, *op. cit.*, p. 5; Matveev, *op. cit.*, p. 77; and K. N. Solov'ev's novel *Rodnoe selo*.

[184] Frank, "'Simple Folk, Savage Customs?'," pp. 717–18.

[185] Verbov, *op. cit.*, p. 101.

[186] Peasants could recognize wisdom in relatively younger men too: "You don't measure brains by the beard," as a saying went (Sokolov, *Tambovskii fol'klor*, p. 307). A peasant character in one of Bunin's stories expresses his pride over the fact that the older men sometimes come to him for technological advice ("Budni," in *Sobranie sochinenii*, vol. 3, p. 363).

[187] Engel'gardt, *op. cit.*, p. 208. Another case (from Tambov province) of a peasant expressing appreciation for precise work (albeit for her own work in this instance) appears in the oral history collection *Golosa krest'ian*, p. 85.

[188] So declares a hired laborer in G. I. Uspenskii's "Krest'ianin i krest'ianskii trud," p. 428. Engel'gardt too relates that peasants valued strength and hard work more than capital (*op. cit.*, p. 326).

[189] For example, see, respectively, Vol'nov, *op. cit.*, p. 231; Engel'gardt, *op. cit.*, pp. 291–292; K. N. Solov'ev, *Rodnoe Selo*, Part 2, p. 58; *Statisticheskii ezhegodnik Moskovskoi gubernii za 1906 god*, Chast' 1, p. 206; Engel'gardt, *op. cit.*, pp. 300–301, and Meshcherskii, "Pervaia stupen'," p. 241; Ertel', "Moi domochadtsy" (from the cycle *Zapiski stepniaka*), in *Sobranie sochinenii*, vol. 1, p. 201.

[190] E. M. Iakushkina—from Tula province—in Barykov et al., *Sbornik materialov*, p. 200.

[191] Ertel', "Moi domochadtsy" and "Serafim Ezhikov" (from the cycle *Zapiski stepniaka*), in *Sobranie sochinenii*, vol. 1.

[192] It should be noted here that in Uspenskii's opinion the huge majority of Russia's peasants still conformed to this type at the time of writing (the close of the 1870s) ("Krest'ianin i krest'ianskii trud," pp. 408–409). He suspected—and lamented—that the infiltration of urban influences would dilute the traditional work ethic of this type.

[193] Fenomenov, *Sovremennaia derevnia*, vol. 2, pp. 93–94; Engel'gardt, *op. cit.*, p. 326. A. I. Fenin, an industrial boss in the Donbass region in the 1890s and 1900s, came to a similar formulation regarding peasants' attitudes towards work. Fenin maintained that only a minority of the peasants who came to work in the mining industry had the talent and temperament to become skilled workers. The rest lived in material and psychological squalor. "This type of miner exhibited all the defects of Chekhov's or Bunin's *muzhik*: a depressed imagination, a dull brooding frame of mind.... They were incredibly ignorant.... if not empty, at least they were not touched by anything, living more by instinct than reason." Fenin, *Coal and Politics in Late Imperial Russia*, pp. 49–50.

[194] Firsov and Kiselev, *op. cit.*, p. 175. Elsewhere, the same source records observers' impressions to the effect that peasants derived little aesthetic satisfaction from nature (ibid, p. 168). This is an interesting and unexplored thesis, for which it is

possible to find both support and counter-indications (see respectively, e.g., Seli-vanov, *op. cit.*, p. 50; and Rybnikov, *op. cit.*, p. 39; versus S. T. Semenov, *op. cit.*, p. 54).

[195] *Ocherk ekonomicheskoi zhizni*, pp. 149–150.

[196] Fenomenov, *Sovremennaia derevnia*, vol. 2, pp. 93–94.

[197] Fenin, *op. cit.*, p. 54. A character in Bunion's *"Sukhodol"*—a migratory peasant, admittedly, no longer a farmer—goes as far as to declare agricultural work "inde-cent and boring" (*op. cit.*, p. 174). Similarly, the peasant Savka in Chekhov's *"Agaf'ia"* chooses penury over farm work (*Sobranie sochinenii*, vol. 4, pp. 48–49). It is possible to find entirely contrary appraisals of peasants' attitudes to agricultural work—namely, that peasants loved this work. See, e.g., Potekhin, "Krest'ianskie deti," p. 287; and the Samara province peasant-turned-writer Neverov, who recalled himself at the age of 10–12 being enthralled by agricultural labor (*Sobranie sochinenii v chetyrekh tomakh*, vol. 1, p. 10). This must have been so, in some sense at least. But early twentieth century surveys provide powerful evidence of antipathy to agricultural labor. A survey of attitudes among peasant youths in Samara province in the 1920s registered the low popularity of agricultural work there. Only 14% responded that they liked this kind of work, versus 31% who disliked it (Rybnikov, *Krest'ianskii rebenok*, p. 22). When asked what profession they would like to pursue, just 1% of peasant kids in a 1913 study answered "agriculture" (*ibid.*, p. 66).

[198] Semenova-Tian-Shanskaia, *op. cit.*, p. 150. On the physical pain of work and the resentment it could inspire among peasants, see Pod"iachev, *Zhizn' muzhitskaia*, p. 16; or Stepniak, *The Russian Peasantry*, pp. 170–171. Some sources reveal peasants singling out manure work as especially distasteful (Semenova-Tian-Shan-skaia, *op. cit.*, p. 148; *Statisticheskii ezhegodnik Moskovskoi gubernii za 1910 god*, p. 121). A pejorative characterization of Russian peasants' attitude to work, as compared to the relative enthusiasm of Mordvinian and Votiak peasants living in proximity to them in Kazan province, is Sboev, *O byte krest'ian v Kazanskoi gubernii*, p. 28. On the other hand, a commendation of Russian male peasants' work habits, as compared to Moldovan men's, is Aksakov, *Pis'ma iz provintsii*, p. 276.

[199] Mironov, *Sotsial'naia istoriia*, vol. 2, pp. 305–317.

[200] See, e.g., Ivan Vol'nov's rendering of a village's confused and angry reaction to a young peasant who comes home from the nearby town where he is pursuing his education and participates in manuring work, (*op. cit.*, pp. 166–168). In a similar vein, the historian Barbara Engel notes that men who earned livings outside the village would frequently decline to do any agricultural work during stays back home ("The Woman's Side," p. 70). Ertel' depicted a character of this type in "Zhadnyi muzhik" (in *Volkhonskaia barishnia*, pp. 193–194).

[201] Ivan Vol'nov drew this picture very clearly (*op. cit.*, esp. pp. 152, 155, 191), as did Pod"iachev (*Zhizn' muzhitskaia*, p. 42).

[202] This expression ("*vybrat'sia v 'liudi'*") appears in Fenin, *op. cit.*, p. 49. Valuable discussion of the relationships between occupation and status in the villages appear in V. V. Ivanov, "Sovremennaia derevnia v Khar'kovskoi gubernii," pp. 5–15. While insisting that prosperous non-agricultural peasants garnered the highest status, Ivanov is careful to present the manner in which the most successful farming peasants maintained their pride by deriding these wealthy neighbors. Peasants did not unanimously concede the ascending hierarchy of hired laborer–independent farmer–prosperous farmer–non-agricultural peasant. But most peasants probably did see their society through the prism of this hierarchy. Bernard Pares, for one,

mentions some of the more literate peasants disdaining field work and aspiring to clerical jobs (*op. cit.*, pp. 365–66). For an interesting literary rendering of a young woman's dreams of escaping agricultural life so as "to live like shopkeepers or suburban tradesmen," see Muizhel, *Khutor No. 16*, p. 31. Observers sometimes noted a "brain drain" away from agriculture among the gentry as well (one source from Tambov is Lipetskii zemlevladelets, "Iz Lipetskogo uezda," p. 15).

For illustration and discussion of the status acquired by peasants doing clerical or organizational work for landlords in estate administration, see Ivan Turgenev's "Kontora" (from *Zapiski okhotnika*), in *Polnoe sobranie sochinenii*, vol. 4, p. 162; or Engel'gardt, *op. cit.*, p. 39. Villagers' respect for estate or peasant officials was always mixed with some fear, even for the lowliest watchmen of the landlords (as Prishvin described in "Zavoroshka," *op. cit.*, pp. 693–694).

Peasants' preparation of workhorses for contests at agricultural exhibitions provides a curious reflection of the striving to avoid labor. Insofar as they could, owners of show horses would often pamper the animals shamelessly. They would spare them from work, keep them in stalls, and give them so much rich fodder that the horses were completely unfit for work. They had glorious coats, but were incapable of hauling their owners' carts from home to the exhibitions (Blank, "Po povodu predstoiashchei," pp. 874–875).

Of course many peasants dreamed of starting a big farm in Siberia. A peasant writer from Saratov province, S. Anikin, reported interesting conversations with migrants on their way to Siberia with this goal in mind ("Chego prosit derevnia," p. 732). Nevertheless, the example of those who did leave the village for other occupations exerted an ever-increasing temptation on peasant youth. By the 1920s these aspirations would be stronger than ever (Rybnikov, *Krest'ianskii rebenok*, p. 33).

203 Novikov, *Zapiski zemskogo nachal'nika*, p. 212; Nemirovich-Danchenko, *With a Diploma*, pp. 42–43; Engel'gardt, *op. cit.*, pp. 301–302; *Statisticheskii ezhegodnik Moskovskoi gubernii za 1906 god*, Chast' 1, p. 206.

204 Ermolov did locate a couple of sayings exhorting farmers to harrow thoroughly (Ermolov, *Narodnye primety na urozhai*, p. 123).

205 Such, it will be recalled, was Engel'gardt's assessment (*op. cit.*, p. 308, as quoted above).

206 A peasant in Viatka province, 1860, quoted by Iakushkin, "Putevye pis'ma. Iz Vetliuzhskogo uezda," in *Sochineniia*, p. 278.

207 Engel'gardt, *op. cit.*, p. 207. Likewise, as indicated above in the discussion of attitudes towards inter-tillage, farmers did not compete to keep their rye fields especially free of weeds. An indication of peasants competing to perform a standard operation as early as possible (spring sowing) appears in *Peremeny v zemledel'cheskoi tekhnike*, p. 28. Prince L'vov does describe the high esteem accorded one peasant who worked especially well and accurately. It seems, however that this respect issued more from the L'vov family than from fellow peasants (*Vospominaniia*, p. 45).

208 See, for instance, Evans, *The Crooked Scythe*, pp. 49–53. I have heard of the same practice from a Palestinian farmer, Mohammed Abu Latefa. One story of Russian peasant life contains such a scene, but the conversation is directed mostly at disparaging a poor job of tillage. Certainly no hierarchy of quality of work is established. Potekhin, "Krest'ianskie deti," pp. 288–289. Broadcast sowing might have been an arena where accuracy was prized, at least within the circle of the family. As noted in the discussion of sowing in Part I (section "Agronomist's Criticism of the Timing and Technique of Sowing"), families might select one

person to do all of the sowing. A case of a peasant in Orel province expressing his appreciation for accurate broadcasting appears in Konovalov, "Na khutorakh," no. 1, pp. 59–61. The farmer Konovalov described truly loved the nuances of agriculture. He valued good work very highly. At the same time, he complained of widespread indifference to work among other peasants.

[209] Consider, for example, the mowing contest in Dovzhenko's film "Earth," or the writer Ivan Bunin's peasant character Zakhar Vorob'ev, who once held a horse by its forelegs and lifted it off the ground at a fair ("Zakhar Vorob'ev" in *Sobranie sochinenii*, vol. 3, p. 321).

[210] Examples include Potekhin, "Krest'ianskie deti," p. 293, 304–305, 308; A. F. Pisemskii, "Leshii," from the cycle *Ocherki iz krest'ianskogo byta*, in *Sobranie sochinenii*, p. 262; and Demidov, *op. cit.*, pp. 228–229.

[211] See his priceless portrait of the character Mikhailo, in the story "Moi domochadtsy" (from the cycle *Zapiski stepniaka*, in *Sobranie sochinenii*, vol. 1, pp. 217–218).

[212] Fomin, *Kulachnye boi*, p. 5.

[213] Pelevin, "Pol'za sortirovaniia semian," pp. 51–52; and his "Sortirovanie semian i ego pol'za," pp. 69–70).

[214] G. I. Uspenskii, "Iz putevykh zametok," p. 260. The fish Uspenskii mentions is actually the Caspian Roach.

[215] See, e.g., Glenn C. Loury, "Incentive Effects of Affirmative Action," in *Annals of American Academic Political and Social Science*, 523, September 1992, pp. 19–29 (as cited in Becker, "The Economic Way of Looking at Behavior," p. 5).

[216] For abundant examples from the central black-earth region, see Astyrev, *V volostnykh pisariakh*; Novikov, *Zapiski zemskogo nachal'nika*; Stoliarov, *Zapiski Russkogo krest'ianina*; Ertel', "Barin Listarka" (from the cycle *Zapiski stepniaka*), in *Sobranie sochinenii*, Vol. 1, pp. 170–196; Iakushkin, "Chisti zuby, a to muzhikom nazovut!" in *Sochineniia*.

[217] Mertvyi, *op. cit.*, p. 8. Iur'evskii seconds this insight (*op. cit.*, pp. 67–68). Works blaming serfdom specifically for entrenching sloppy work habits include Harold W. Williams, *Russia of the Russians*, London 1915, pp. 344–345; and Roth, *op. cit.*, pp. 73–81.

[218] From Ertel', "Zhadnyi muzhik," in *Volkhonskaia baryshnia*, p. 188. Contact with German settlers in the southern belts of the black-earth zone could produce similar, derogatory self-perceptions among Russian and Ukrainian peasants there. See, e.g., Garin-Mikhailovskii, "Kartinki Volyni," in *Sobranie sochinenii*, vol. 4, pp. 101–102. The same author describes the condescension Russian peasants might express towards less materially advanced peoples, like the Tatars ("Na khodu," in *ibid.*, vol. 3, p. 254).

[219] See, for instance, the pointed comments of Iu. F. Samarin, "O krepostnom sostoianii i o perekhode iz nego k grazhdanskoi svobode," in *Sochineniia*, p. 24. Samarin equated peasants' self-deprecating language before serfowners to the latters' language before higher government officials. According to at least one observer (in a black-earth province on the Volga), peasants spoke and acted much less deferentially towards landlords once they learned of the Emancipation Decree in 1861. They referred to themselves as children and their lords as fathers less often; they doffed their caps less readily (Vodovozova, "Zakholustnyi derevenskii ugolok," p. 135). Some sources reported a similar rejection of deference, this time towards Land Captains and lesser police officials, after the experiences of 1905–06 (e.g., Konovalov, "Derevenskie kartinki," pp. 1–2). Nevertheless, deferential behavior towards authorities never disappeared.

[220] *Broken Earth*, p. 279.

[221] See, e.g., two sources cited earlier, in connection with peasants' difficulties in counting money or calculating measurements: Zimin's discussion of peasants being cheated at a market, in *Koveminskii krai, op. cit.*, p. 6; and N. V. Uspenskii's 1860 story "Oboz," *op. cit.* See also the treatment of the late-nineteenth-century economic conjuncture in Part I (section "An Agrarian System under Stress").

[222] Verbov, *op. cit.*, p. 84; V. V. Ivanov, "Sovremennaia derevnia v Khar'kovskoi gubernii," p. 19; Vol'nov, *op cit.*, pp. 7–8; Rezanova, *op. cit.*, p. 5; Garin-Mikhailovskii, "Na sele," from the cycle *Derevenskie panoramy*, in *Sobranie sochinenii*, vol. 3, p. 379. See also the memoirs from Tambov and Saratov provinces in *Golosa krest'ian*, pp. 78, 137. At least one observer insisted that "village patriotism" was much weaker in the black-earth zone than in the north of Russia, where the villages were much smaller, and were isolated from each other (Sokolovskii, "Istoriia odnogo khoziaistva i Krest'ianskii Bank," pp. 335–336).

[223] Vol'nov, *op, cit., loc. cit.* Judging from one recent study, individual identities of sub-units within villages remain to this day in Russia (Tkachenko, "Prostranstvennaia identifikatsiia sel'skikh zhitelei," p. 163).

[224] A village with a school or a church could probably play the same role for neighboring villages that were too small to have these institutions. Before the appearance of railroads the proximity of villages to roads could account for substantial cultural differences. A mid-nineteenth-century researcher in Smolensk province attributed ethnic Russian peasants' greater industriousness, resourcefulness, and ambitiousness (relative to Belorussian peasants) to the Russians' practice of placing their villages along through roads. Byelorussians were frequently unable even to count, he reported. Ia. A. Solov'ev, *Sel'sko-khoziaistvennaia statistika Smolenskoi gubernii*, p. 94 (as cited in V., "Literaturnaia letopis'," pp. 15, 21).

[225] Ganeizer, "V Tambovskoi Manchzhurii," p. 150. Emphasis added. Garin-Mikhailovskii describes a similar dynamic among villages nearby his estate in Samara province. In this case one village's sense of its superiority stemmed from the emancipation, when it received much more land than its neighbors. "Neskol'ko let v derevne," in *Sobranie sochinenii*, vol. 3, pp. 61–62. Solov'ev's *Rodnoe Selo* is set in a village of the kind under discussion.

[226] I. Kallinikov, "O sobiranii skazok v Orlovskoi gubernii," p. 353. Not rarely, of course, leadership villages would have schools, and a relatively high literacy rate. Research in several *uezds* of Voronezh province at the turn of the century found literacy in large villages to be about 50% higher than in small villages (Voronov, *Materialy po narodnomu obrazovaniiu v Voronezhskoi gubernii*, pp. 128–129).

[227] Kallinikov, "Skazochniki i ikh skazki," p. 255.

[228] Zimin, *op. cit.*, p. 11.

[229] See, e.g., Ganeizer, *op. cit.*, p. 166.

[230] Of course the presentation of village interrelationships in this discussion is simplified. Various circumstances could dilute the influence of leadership villages over their neighbors. The legacy of serfdom was particularly significant in this respect. Village practices developed around whatever administrative system their landlord imposed. This contributed to the formation of long-lasting village identities, which could stand in the way of cooperation, borrowings, and mutual respect between villages. Some perceptive comments on this topic appear in Luginin, "Volostnye sudy," pp. 388–389. On the other hand, even the bitterest inter-village animosities arising out of serfdom could recede within a few decades after emancipation. Thus, state peasants and serfs are said to have been on the worst of terms in Khar'kov

province (for example) before emancipation, and to have come to terms with each other by the 1890s. By that time the former serf villages were looking up to their neighbors, and imitating their cultural leads. Valuable comments on this topic appear in V. V. Ivanov, "Sovremennaia derevnia v Khar'kovskoi gubernii," pp. 3–4.

[231] A zemstvo statistician working in Orel province remarked how all the villages just blended into each other after a while, so indistinct were they from each other (Belokonskii, Derevenskie vpechatleniia, pp. 37–38).

[232] Sharing this perspective were, e.g.: Ertel', "Stepnaia storona" (from the cycle Zapiski stepniaka), in Sobranie sochinenii, vol. 1; Baranovich, Materialy dlia geografii i statistiki Rossii, esp. pp. 134, 384–6; Astyrev, op. cit.; and Tarachkov, Putevye zametki, p. 131.

[233] Baranovich, op. cit., p. 134.

[234] G. I. Uspenskii, "Iz putevykh zametok." See esp. pp. 258–9, 261–2. The "father of Russian Marxism" G. Plekhanov in large part agreed with Uspenskii's derogatory characterization of peasants as culturally inert and herd-like (Sotsial-Demokrat, 1888, no. 1, as cited in G. I. Uspenskii, Polnoe sobranie sochinenii, vol. 8, p. 621).

[235] Tarachkov, op. cit., p. 131; Kriukov, "Mel'kom," pp. 189–90, 201, 202. At least one saying enshrined indifference to sanitary conditions in the home: "not the cleanliness of the walls makes the hut beautiful, but the richness of the food" (Z-n, "O prichinakh izmel'chaniia i boleznennosti naroda," pp. 22–23). Presumably attitudes towards cleanliness began to evolve later in our period, thanks in part to the army (see below).

[236] So remarked a very experienced Siberian physician, who singled out the filthiness of children of mothers who had migrated from Tambov and Voronezh provinces (Krasen chelovek uchen'em, p. 19). Hygienic negligence had limits. Judging from a Tambov writer's story, mothers who left babies unwashed for weeks at a time incurred derision (Levitov, "Dvorianka," in Stepnye ocherki, p. 165).

[237] Kallinikov, "O sobiranii skazok," p. 357; Astyrev, op. cit., loc. cit.

[238] Novikov, Zapiski zemskogo nachal'nika, pp. 41–42; Fenomenov, Sovremennaia derevnia, vol. 1, p. 236. The writer Ertel', who had a great deal of experience in estate administration, recorded the general conviction among estate officials in Samara province (a sparsely populated province in the southeast of European Russia, along the Volga river) that peasants there were much more hostile towards authority than peasants in Tambov ("Samarskaia derevnia" pp. 132–133). The rash of agrarian disturbances in the region from 1905 on does not invalidate earlier characterizations of the population.

[239] Troitskii, "Selo Lipitsy i ego okrestnosti," p. 95.

[240] Bel'skii, op. cit., p. 94. The peasant saying recurs in, e.g., Iur'evskii, op. cit., pp. 115–116. This conviction did not reign only in semi-arid lands. Leo Tolstoy and Keith Thomas found very similar formulations in Tula province and England, respectively (Tolstoi, "Utro pomeshchika," in Sobranie sochinenii, vol. 2, p. 361; Keith Thomas, Religion and the Decline of Magic, p. 664).

[241] Iur'evskii, op. cit., pp. 115–116; also Bel'skii, op. cit., p. 94. Ermolov found similar sayings, from Khar'kov province (Narodnye primety na urozhai, p. 126).

[242] So noted Sutti Ortiz, a scholar of Thirld World peasantries: "A farmer can formulate an expectation of his harvest only if he can have a mental picture of the outcome and if he has any confidence about the likelihood of his prognosis....it should not surprise us that as uncertainty decreases farmers are less likely to express their prospects in terms of fate or supernatural events" (in Teodor Shanin, ed., Peasants and Peasant Societies, pp. 330–331).

243 For an analysis of the differences between "oral-based" and "literate-based" language, see Ong, *Orality and Literacy*.

244 On the prevalence of this sort of speech community in agrarian societies (and in other circumstances), see Elaine Slosberg Andersen, *Speaking with Style*, pp. 20–21.

745 Further, parents enforce behavioral norms on children in the interest of socialization. Those adolescents who conformed to local standards of behavior could expect much better marriage prospects and social standing than those who did not. See, e.g., Garin-Mikhailovskii's "Akulina" from the cycle *Derevenskie panoramy*, in his *Sobranie sochinenii*, vol. 3, pp. 328–329.

246 For an overview of the relevant studies, see Shachtman, *The Inarticulate Society*, pp. 23–36.

247 Rybnikov, *op. cit.*, p. 47. Rybnikov does not cite these studies individually. One of them estimated the average adult peasant's vocabulary at a mere 800 words (Hindus, *Broken Earth*, p. 29). Hindus never gives his sources.

248 Novikov, *Zapiski zemskogo nachal'nogo*, p. 12. Novikov was very experienced in the Tambov countryside, so his observation is valuable. But it is hard to say if he is not exaggerating here. In a story by Chirikov, for instance, a peasant mother teaches her children to say "thank you" ("Dobryi barin," p. 184). Vol'nov recounts that children beginning at school did not know the word "surname" (*op. cit.*, p. 53).

249 Nebol'sin, *op. cit.*, p. 94. The confusion between "Christian" and "peasant" is reported as ubiquitous in P. I. Astrov, "Ob uchastii sverkhestestvennoi sili," p. 50. The two words sound very similar in Russian.

250 Ia. M. Shafir, *Gazeta i derevnia*, Moscow 1924; and his *Voprosy gazetnoi kul'tury*, Moscow 1927, as cited in Comrie and Stone, *The Russian Language in the Twentieth Century*, pp. 196–7.

251 G. I. Uspenskii, "Krest'ianin i krest'ianskii trud," p. 468; Rybnikov, *op. cit.*, p. 47.

252 On the frequency of swearing, see e.g., Bondarenko, *op. cit.*, p. 79; V. P. Semenov-Tian-Shanskii, *Rossiia. vol. 2*, p. 183; Kallinikov, "O sobiranii skazok," p. 355; Chekhov, "Muzhiki," in *Sobranie sochinenii*, vol. 8, p. 211. On swearing among children and women, Kosogorov, "Russkoe narodnoe vospitanie," pp. 73–4; Bunin, "Sukhodol," p. 166.

253 Kallinikov, *op. cit., loc. cit.*; Bondarenko, *op. cit., loc. cit.*; V. P. Semenov-Tian-Shanskii, *op. cit., loc. cit.* The last source also notes that the central black-earth provinces eclipsed all other regions in the number of court cases registered under the heading "insults to honor"—which can serve as a very rough and indirect measure of obscenities.

254 Pod"iachev, *Moia zhizn'*, pp. 32, 40.

255 Zlatovratskii, *Derevenskie budni*, p. 273.

256 Glukhikh, "Iz nevedomogo mira," p. 73.

257 Bunin, "Derevnia," p. 62.

258 One study of this contrast is Ben G. Blount, "Parental Speech and Language Acquisition."

259 For a classic statement with reference to historical trends, see Alice Miller, *For Your Own Good*.

260 G. I. Uspenskii, "Krest'ianin i krest'ianskii trud," pp. 415, 420.

261 Fet, "Zametki o vol'no-naemnon trude," p. 235; Kishkin, "Dannye i predpolozheniia po voprosu ob uluchshenii byta krest'ian v Kirsanovskom uezde," p. 233; SSS, Borisoglebsk, Prilozhenie 1, p. 22; Vnukov, *op. cit.*, p. 5; Federov, *op. cit.*, p. 132; Semenova-Tian-Shanskaia, pp. 102, 125–6; Reshetnikov, "Tetushka Oparina," p. 109. At the same time, some ethnographers reported that heads of

households would not allow their wives to sell even a chicken or a dozen eggs without permission (e.g., G. A. and A. M. Kalashnikov, "Selo Nikol'skoe," p. 205).

262 Federov, *op. cit.*, p. 131. An agronomist in Samara province lamented how peasants regarded women "... as members of the family who understand absolutely nothing, with whom it is virtually useless even to talk about the family economy." P. Maslov, "Nuzhna li krest'ianskoi zhenshchine gramota," p. 56.

263 See esp. Balov, "Rozhdenie i vospitanie detei," pp. 90–114.

264 Kurbatov, "O derevenskikh detiakh," p. 3.

265 See, e.g., Tarachkov, *Putevye zametki*, pp. 11–12. The historian B. N. Mironov has recently made the same point ("Semia," p. 236). Other prominent discussions of violence towards peasant children include G. I. Uspenskii, "Iz putevykh zametok," pp. 261–2; Chekhov, "Muzhiki," p. 213; Bunin, "Derevnia," p. 84; Fenomenov, *Sovremennaia derevnia*, vol. 2, p. 25; and Semenova-Tian-Shanskaia, *Village Life in Late Tsarist Russia*, p. 5.

266 Ivanitskii, *Materialy po etnografii*, p. 56. The two best-known peasant autobiographies from the central black-earth region complement this view. Stoliarov mentions nothing but kindness from his parents, and Vol'nov points out that the utter callousness with which his father invariably treated him was not typical among other fathers. They would caress their sons and play with them (Stoliarov, *op. cit.*; Vol'nov, *op. cit.*, p. 21).

267 Arkhangel'skii, "Selo Davshino," p. 48.

268 Kosogorov, "Russkoe narodnoe vospitanie," p. 74. A very experienced ethnographer in Siberia made the same observation (Krasnozhenova, "Rebenok v krest'ianskom bytu," pp. 12–13).

269 So noted Bondarenko in Tambov in the late 1880s ("Ocherki Kirsanovskogo uezda," p. 6). Fathers might beat grown daughters as well, and savagely, in case of insubordination (see, e.g., Levitov, "Dvorianka," in *Stepnye ocherki*, p. 152). A valuable depiction of a woman defending harsh discipline for children appears in Reshetnikov, "Tetushka Oparina," p. 108. For a literary rendering of village elders intimidating an adolescent boy into conforming to village ways, see Garin-Mikhailovskii's "Akulina" from the cycle *Derevenskie panoramy*, in his *Sobranie sochinenii*, vol. 3, pp. 325–327.

270 See, e.g., V. P. Semenov-Tian-Shanskii, p. 181; Novikov, *Zapiski zemskogo nachal'nika*, p. 212; Frierson, "*Razdel*: the Peasant Family Divided," pp. 77–8, 83–4. Citing studies of family divisions in the early nineteenth century, Frierson points out (p. 78) that in many areas the extended patriarchal family must have begun to weaken well before emancipation. The rapid downward adjustment of the size of the average family immediately after 1861 supports this conclusion. In Tambov at the time of emancipation the average serf *dvor* was 8 people, the average state peasant *dvor* 9.9 (Frierson, p. 80). By the early 1880s the provincial average was only 6.65 (*Sbornik ocherkov*, p. 33). A useful, brief overview of the erosion of patriarchal authority is Federov's summary of unpublished sources from the Tenishev archive, "Kul'tura i byt srednevolzhskoi derevni," esp. pp. 131–2. A literary rendering of adolescents' growing disrespect for their elders in the 1870s is Ertel's "Zemets" (from the cycle *Zapiski stepniaka*), in *Sobranie sochinenii*, vol. 1. A recent historical discussion, based primarily on analysis of evening gatherings among peasant youth, is Frank "'Simple Folk, Savage Customs?'." The combination of growing adolescent defiance and the persistence of stern parental control in our period is well captured in peasant youths' repertoires of songs and ditties (on which,

see, e.g., the brief summary of a very active compiler of this aspect of peasant culture, B. Kabanov, "Zabytaia mysl'," p. 2).

[271] So insisted, for example, R. Vnukov (*op. cit.*, p. 4); and Novikov (*op. cit.*, *loc. cit.*). Vol'nov's autobiography traces the same development in his own life (*Povest' o dniakh moei zhizni*). Famines probably accelerated the process. As Tul'tseva has pointed out, after the failed 1891 harvest huge numbers of young people headed for towns in search of income (*op. cit.*, p. 47). Sons also expressed their growing sense of independence from their fathers by spending the money they earned in off-farm work on themselves before they ever returned home. Traditionally they were meant to bring home as much of their earnings as possible (see, e.g., *Ocherk ekonomicheskoi zhizni*, p. 151; and G. I. Uspenskii, "Krest'ianin i krest'ianskii trud," p. 425).

Young women also took part in the rising spirit of assertiveness among peasant youth. See the conclusion to Part II, below.

[272] *Sbornik ocherkov*, p. 33. According to official statistics, on the eve of emancipation the average family was about 8 people among serf peasants, 10 among state peasants (Frierson, "Razdel," p. 80). This would indicate a great wave of family divisions in the first twenty years after the abolition of serfdom. The pre-emancipation figures are inflated, however. The Ministry of State Domains was in favor of larger families, so peasants often divided households surreptitiously. For discussion, including comments on Tambov, see Chernenkov, *K kharakteristike krest'ianskogo khoziaistva*, esp. pp. 37–39, 47–48.

The late Imperial figures might be also be inflated, however. Family splits required the approval of the village assembly. Village assemblies could be unwieldy, especially in the large settlements so common in Tambov. Since the assembly might require a costly amount of vodka before giving its consent, many families must have split up *de facto*, but not *de jure* (e.g., K. P. Chernyshev, "Doklad," p. 429; on the other hand, some villages left decisions on family splits in the hands of sub-assemblies composed of heads of households from a portion of the village—*SSS*, Borisoglebsk, Prilozhenie 1, p. 19). The size of the average household in Tambov did drop quickly after 1917, reaching 5.9 in 1920 (*Sbornik ocherkov*, p. 35). The most vivid illustration of a village assembly's thirst for vodka is the Tambov writer Levitov's story "Rasprava," in *Stepnye ocherki*. A great many sources corroborate the importance of vodka to village assemblies.

[273] So reported, at any rate, M. Skubak, a village schoolteacher from Khar'kov province (published in P. V. Ivanova, *Zhizn' i pover'ia krest'ian*, pp. 148–149).

[274] Fenomenov, *Sovremennaia derevnia*, vol. 2, p. 25. Maurice Hindus recorded even more startling observations of mothers' cruelty to children, from a city-bred woman who had resettled in the village during the civil war (*Broken Earth*, p. 245). The writer A. A. Potekhin traced the fearful callousness of peasant women to the dulling, exhausting requirements of the work they performed, especially sickling ("Krest'ianskie deti," p. 307). Recently an historical geographer has generalized that ages 7–10 saw the harshest discipline for peasant children, as parents prepared them to participate in domestic and field tasks (Listova, "Traditsii trudovogo vospitaniia v derevne," p. 126). Listova's article provides a good overview of the steps by which children acquired work skills (through games imitating work operations, and by using undersized hand tools when starting out).

[275] Novikov insists that mistreatment and violence towards the elderly within peasant families was typical, at least where the family economy was not very successful and the patriarch did not retain a strong grip on his power (*op. cit.*, pp. 18–20). Many

authors described peasants' callousness towards the elderly (see, e.g., Prishvin, "Zavoroshka," in *Sobranie sochinenii*, vol. 1, pp. 643–44; or Tolstoi, "Utro pomesh-chika," in *Sobranie sochinenii*, vol. 2, pp. 371–374).

276 Semenov-Tian-Shanskii, *op. cit.*, p. 183.

277 Bliokh, *Sravnenie material'nogo byta i nravstvennogo sostoianiia naseleniia*, Table 51. This for the years 1879–1882 (no other data available).

278 Fenomenov, *Sovremennaia derevnia*, vol. 2, p. 25. Likewise, the well-known physician and ethnographer D. N. Zhbankov described women of the black-earth regions as "oppressed pariahs ... who are frightened of saying a word in the presence of their masters." He contrasted them to the more "independent, self-reliant, and self-assured" women in areas further north, where many of the men earned their livings outside of the village (as quoted in Barbara Engel, "The Woman's Side," pp. 73–4). A vivid description from Samara province of a husband torturing his wife (with his father's help) appears in Garin-Mikhailovskii, "Akulina," from the cycle *Derevenskie panoramy*, in *Sobranie sochinenii*, vol. 3, pp. 332–335.

After spending some time in Orel province the traveler F. Kriukov was surprised at how softly peasants further to the north treated their children ("Mel'kom," no. 9, p. 164). To the south, meanwhile, in Voronezh province, the cleric ethnographer F. Nikonov rated Russian fathers much more explosive and tyrannical than Ukrainians living in the same province. He also noted how much more respect Ukrainian peasants paid to women, relative to Russian peasants. Nikonov, "Byt i khoziaistvo malorossov v Voronezhskoi gubernii," p. 331. It is perhaps significant that sources describing peasant wives beating their husbands pertain to Ukrainians, not Russians (Nikonov, *op. cit.*, *loc. cit.*; Josephine Calina, *Scenes of Russian Life*, p. 165).

279 In the opinion of the well-known literary critic N. A. Dobroliubov, peasant parents beat down their childrens' inquisitiveness with the intention of producing subjugated intellects and personalities. The purpose, to Dobroliubov's mind, was not so much to enforce parental supremacy as to protect the children from the disappointments and dangers of aspirations in a society which discriminated against them. He did not think parents were entirely successful in this purported aim. Dobroliubov, "Features for the Characterization of the Russian People," in *Selected Philosophical Essays*, pp. 480–482.

280 Chuprov, *Melkoe zemledeliia i ego osnovnye nuzhdy*, St. Petersburg 1907, p. 138 (as cited in Volin, *op. cit.*, p. 64, and Morachevskii, *Agronomicheskaia pomoshch' v Rossii*, p. 34).

281 A recent, concise appraisal of the state of the relevant debates is Finnegan, "Literacy," pp. 336–339.

282 Scribner and Cole, "Cognitive Consequences of Formal and Informal Education," pp. 553–9.

283 Information on Russian peasants' teaching methods for agricultural tasks is very sparse. Interviews and existing sources do emphasize the role of demonstration/imitation. Thus Fedor Lokhin recalls his father teaching him how to till with the *sokha* without any words at all. "He said, 'Here Fedya, you go.' So off I went down the furrow. 'Good job!' he said, and walked off to take a nap." Demidov painted a similar picture (*Zhizn' Ivana*, pp. 178, 216). Examples of peasants giving clipped instructions on how to use certain tools appear in Tolstoi's *Anna Karenina* (Part III, ch. 4, in *Sobranie sochinenii*, vol. 8, p. 294); Prishvin, *Dnevniki*, p. 341; and *Golosa krest'ian*, pp. 182–183.

284 I am paraphrasing Olson, *The World on Paper*, pp. 35, 38–39.

285 See the discussion in *ibid*, pp. 39–43.

286 Kochetkov, "Sel'sko-khoziaistvennye besedy," pp. 11–12; *Zhurnaly* (August–September 1911), pp. 90, 109.

287 Eklof, "Peasants and Schools," pp. 121–23.

288 Bogdanov, *Gramotnost' i obrazovanie*, p. 91.

289 *Kratkii obzor sostoianiia narodnogo obrazovaniia*, pp. 1–4. 57% of the school-aged children were enrolled by 1914, 78% of the boys (*ibid.*, p. 22).

290 Early 1880s figure is from Bogdanov, *op. cit.*, p. 24. 1897 figure from *Pervaia vseobshchaia perepis'*, pp. 12–13.

291 V. I., "Deiatel'nost' zemstv v oblasti narodnogo obrazovaniia," p. 213. For the Empire as a whole, not including Finland and Poland, the literacy rate among rural men aged 9–49 (i.e., those who were or would soon be participating in the management of family farms) was 35.5% in 1897, rising to 67.3% by 1926 (Bogdanov, *Gramotnost' i obrazovanie*, p. 91).

 Army regulations rewarding recruits for schooling must have raised peasants' attentiveness to education. In the late nineteenth century soldiers could reduce their term of service by two or three years if they had graduated from primary school (Fursova, "Rasprostranenie gramotnosti i obrazovaniia," pp. 23–24).

292 Nationwide, only 10% of the peasant pupils completed the three-year primary school program (Eklof, "Peasants and Schools," p. 123). In Tambov this figure exceeded 30% by 1914 (*Kratkii obzor sostoianiia*, pp. 24–25).

293 For data and discussion, see Eklof, "Peasants and Schools," pp. 124–30. Surveys of *zemstvo* agricultural correspondents (who were largely or even mostly peasants themselves) registered a range of interesting contrasts between the literate and the illiterate in village life. See V. Golubev, *op. cit.*, pp. 112–121; *Vestnik Pskovskogo gubernskogo zemstva*, 1902, no. 6, pp. 75–76; and also *Rasprostranennost' trakhomy v Kazanskoi gubernii*, Kazan 1914, p. 73.

294 Eklof has surveyed some of the studies of reading habits (Eklof, "Peasants and Schools," p. 126). Some observers insisted that agricultural literature was very popular in the villages (one example is Kalashnikov, "Selo Nikol'skoe," p. 176).

295 *Peremeny v zemledel'cheskoi tekhnike*, pp. 34–35. The same source cites several cases (pp. 19, 27, 37). The primary stimulus, according to this summary, was the example of landowners and clergymen.

296 Brooks, *When Russia Learned to Read*, ch. 7.

297 Most, but not all, contemporary studies locate a positive correlation between education on the one hand and agricultural know-how and performance on the other hand. For a review of recent work, see Lockheed, Jamison, and Lau, "Farmers, Education, and Farm Efficiency: A Survey," pp. 37–76; Ali and Byerlee, "Economic Efficiency of Small Farmers in a Changing World," pp. 17–18.

298 Fet, "Zametki o vol'nonaemnom trude," p. 265. Fet was not directly discussing peasant attitudes towards agriculture in this passage, but he extended the same sentiments to their technological thinking later in the same piece (p. 273). The "We do as other folk do" sentiment spread beyond the ranks of the peasantry. "As other folk do, I do" resignedly declares an inefficacious landowner in Nemirovich-Danchenko's *With a Diploma*, p. 51.

299 In Voronov, *Materialy po narodnomu obrazovaniiu v Voronezhskoi gubernii*, pp. vi–vii.

300 Garin-Mikhailovskii, "Na nochlege," *op. cit.*, p. 142.

301 Our discussion of the obstacles to mental development in the village is not complete. For example, smoke inhalation during the long winters in peasant huts

might have affected children's brain development on a wide scale. Professor Richard Hellie raised this consideration to me privately.

302 The recent work of Italian genetic archeologist Luigi Luca Cavalli-Sforza challenges this notion with respect to pre-historic agriculture. Cavalli-Sforza found the adoption of wheat spread out across Europe no faster than the migration of the people introducing it (Ridley, "How Far From the Tree?," p. 14). However much Cavalli-Sforza's findings may reverse our understanding of innate proclivities to imitation, the importance of imitation in recent centuries cannot be denied.

303 Braudel, *The Identity of France*, pp. 283–285.

304 The data and the idea underlying this paragraph come from Lintvarev, "Doklad," esp. p. 377. The figure from Tambov pertains to individually owned land, including land purchased by individual peasants. Units of land purchased by communes or associations are excluded. Computed from *Statistika zemlevladeniia 1905 g.*, pp. 10, 26.

305 There was a wave of urban-educated, technologically inquisitive landowners coming to the countryside from the 1880s on. They brought humanitarian values as well as technological innovations, and managed to improve the social and economic atmosphere in some areas. But their influence did not extend far beyond St. Petersburg and Moscow provinces. On this, see N. Sokolovskii, "V odnom iz zalokhust'ev," esp. pp. 88–90, 92–94. The bulk of rural Russia was suffering an extended "brain drain," as talented people sought careers in the cities, especially St. Petersburg and Moscow.

306 Mikhail Ivanov, Znamenskii raion, Tambovskaia oblast', May 1993, personal conversation. This sentiment was familiar in the late Imperial period. "The peasant expects everything from the land, which he takes no trouble to improve" wrote Bernard Pares in 1907 (*Russia Between Reform and Revolution*, p. 365).

307 Leon Trotsky, *The Russian Revolution*, p. 1.

308 Ali and Byerlee, "Economic Efficiency of Small Farmers in a Changing World," pp. 12–13.

309 Chebalak, *Sbornik statei po sel'skomu khoziaistvu dlia krest'ian*, pp. 3–4.

310 Elwert's idea appears in his paper "Social Transformation as an Endogenous Process Dealing with Strangers: A Comparison of Three African Rural Communities." Elwert is not alone in detecting an illogical psychological mechanism among peasants. A tantalizing passage in Garin-Mikhailovskii's "Babushka Stepanida" describes how villagers invented—and believed in the reality of—all sorts of metaphysical adventures for an old woman who lay unconscious for a couple of days (from the cycle *Derevenskie panoramy*, in *Sobranie sochinenii*, vol. 3, p. 309). Be it noted that neither Garin-Mikhailovskii nor Elwert labels these mechanisms as peculiar to peasants. This is a separate question, irrelevant to the present argument.

311 Interestingly, it might be possible to find significant instances of the converse, where peasants interpreted resurrections of traditional practices as novelties. These cases could arise when farmers returned to an old technique they had discarded and forgotten. Quite a few sources over the years record peasants deciding to sow rye earlier, after suffering bad results from later-sown rye. Did this lesson need re-learning every once in a while? *1882 god v sel'sko-khoziaistvennom otnoshenii, po otchetam poluchennym ot khoziaev. Period II—letnyi*, St. Petersburg 1882, Otdel II, p. 88; *Sel'skokhoziaistvennye i statisticheskie svedeniia, po materialam, poluchennym ot khoziaev. Vyp. 1*, p. 90; *Otchety uchastkovykh agronomov za 1911 god*, p. 146. From the 1920s: RGAE, f. 478, op. 5, d. 3494, p. 52; GATO, f. R-956, op. 1, d. 465, p. 23.

³¹² *Podvornoe i khutorskoe khoziaistvo v Samarskoi gubernii*, p. 109—pertaining to Stavropol *uezd*.

³¹³ Bushnell, "Peasants in Uniform," pp. 104–5.

³¹⁴ *Ibid.*, p. 102.

³¹⁵ Sources indicating progressive influences of returning soldiers in a general way include Vsevolozhskii, "Ocherki krest'ianskogo byta Samarskogo uezda," p. 1; Sokolovskii, "Istoriia odnogo khoziaistva i Krest'ianskii Bank," p. 335; and Muizhel, "Khutor, No. 16," in *Khutor No. 16 i drugie rasskazy*, pp. 1–20. A specific indication of heightened hygiene consciousness in a returning soldier appears in Vol'nov, *Povest' o dniakh moei zhizni*, pp. 207–209. Regarding seditious attitudes among peasant soldiers, as revealed in their letters home, see Federov, "Kul'tura i byt poreformennoi srednevolzhskoi derevni." On the role of returning soldiers as prototypes of "the rational hero" in popular literature, see Brooks, *When Russia Learned to Read*, p. 255. As in Germany, the Russian government did eventually sponsor agricultural education programs for soldiers. In the last years before 1914 somewhere between 50,000–100,000 soldiers would have heard lectures by agronomists (judging from limited data in Morachevskii, *Agronomicheskaia pomoshch' v Rossii*, pp. 335–336).

The historian John Bushnell has argued that soldiering did not "civilize" or "modernize" young peasants in any direct or appreciable way, because life in the army largely replicated their experiences of subordination to landlords and other authorities. Bushnell himself recognizes, on the other hand, how many peasants were uprooted by army service. I maintain that the uprooting by itself was significant. See Bushnell, *op. cit.*, pp. 101–114. Alexander Novikov offered a very insightful and very concise discussion of the influence of army service on peasants in his *Zapiski zemskogo nachal'nika* (pp. 211–214). Novikov saw army service as accentuating pre-existing traits among individual peasants. In his opinion service raised both efficacious and destructive personalities to new levels.

³¹⁶ Frank, "'Simple Folk, Savage Customs?'," p. 716. Boris N. Mironov has echoed this characterization ("The Peasant Commune after the Reforms of the 1860s," p. 28).

³¹⁷ On new, diverse styles replacing traditional clothing, see, e.g., E. Trubetskoi, "Novaia zemskaia Rossiia," p. 72. For peasant women demanding to be called "miss," Semenova-Tian-Shanskaia, *Village Life in Late Imperial Russia*, pp. 55, 142. On youth arranging festivities in new and independent ways, Frank, "'Simple Folk, Savage Customs?'," pp. 715–16. On women resisting arranged marriages, see, e.g., B. Kabanov, "Zabytaia mysl'," p. 2. Arranged marriages remained rather common at the turn of the century, especially among poorer peasants (see, e.g., Tul'tseva, *op. cit.*, p. 47; and Vol'nov, *Povest' o dniakh moei zhizni*—the fate of the sister Motia). Regarding the readiness of women to appeal to the *volost'* courts, see, e.g., Vsevolozhskii, *op. cit.*, p. 26; and Farnsworth, "The Litigious Daughter-In-Law," pp. 89–106. On improvements in the cleanliness of homes, see the interviews in Pares, *Russia Between Reform and Revolution*, pp. 360, 366, 371.

³¹⁸ E.g., Pares, *op. cit.*, p. 364. A wonderful survey of reading habits and politicization in the countryside appears in *Statisticheskii ezhegodnik Moskovskoi gubernii za 1906 god. Chast' 1-aia*, Moscow 1907, pp. 209–219.

³¹⁹ Orlova, "Religioznyi faktor demograficheskogo povedeniia," p. 111.

³²⁰ Observers explicitly describing young peasants' "strong faith in science" include A. I. Ivanov, "Verovaniia krest'ian Orlovskoi gubernii," pp. 68–69; and *Statisticheskii ezhegodnik Moskovskoi gubernii za 1906 god*, Moscow p. 196. Other sources noticing the general trend of young, literate peasants leading the way in distancing

themselves from the traditional belief structure are Minkh, *op. cit.*, pp. 100, 108, 112; and Vsevolozhskii, *op. cit.*, pp. 33–34.

321 Murav'ev, "Shkol'noe obrazovanie," pp. 68–69. Although witnesses like Murav'ev offer invaluable depictions of generational conflicts, they tend to be weighted towards the perspective of the young. Judging from some other sources, the "angry old men" might have had some legitimate, concrete concerns about the characteristics of the new village youth. It could be, for example, that the increasingly independent peasant youth was distracted away from cultivating traditional skills to established standards. Near the end of the nineteenth century at least two well-informed observers insisted that central black-earth region peasants were becoming significantly less skilled in particular agricultural tasks (P. D., *Russkii sotsializm i obshchinnoe zemlevladenie*, p. 160; Brzheskii, *Ocherki agrarnogo byta krest'ian*, p. 41). For interesting comments on literate youth rejecting established beliefs and stoking the sharp generational divide in this period, see the interviews in Pares, *Russia Between Reform and Revolution*, pp. 368–69, 371–72).

322 Frankovskii, "Odin iz vidov agronomicheskoi pomoshchi naseleniiu," p. 567.

PART THREE

THE THREE-FIELD SYSTEM
AND BEYOND

As analysts of technology pointed out long ago, the organization of work can be just as important to the character and efficiency of a production process as the tools and techniques employed. A factory that has too little or the wrong kind of machinery, a hotel with too many beds and not enough refrigerators, or a farm with three workhorses but no cows—all are clear examples of an inefficient organization of resources or technology. The organizational challenges facing the Russian peasant farmer were not as numerous or complex as the questions connected to the technology of field work. The primary issues concerned the allocation of the family's labor units to each day's tasks, the acquisition or relinquishing of farm animals (or household members), the system of farming (the field system), and the selection of crops to sow. Part III focuses on the last three—livestock holdings, crop sowings, and field systems, with the aim of uncovering the ways in which the three-field system did or did not evolve in our time period.

Before proceeding any further, however, it will not be amiss to provide a short introduction to systems of agriculture and systems of farming, two related concepts which must underlie any evaluation of the organization of agriculture. This discussion will demonstrate the pivotal position of the three-field system in the intensification agriculture. It will also help to reveal why this system was so resilient, and so difficult to overcome.

Systems of Agriculture, Systems of Farming, Crop Rotations. Delineation of Terms

The term "system of agriculture" denotes the main orientation of a farm's production. In early-twentieth-century Russia the most common production orientation was grain growing, followed by livestock raising, dairy farming, and "industrial crop" growing (sunflowers, sugar beets, flax, tobacco, potatoes—in short, crops destined for sale to industries that reprocess them). Thus a peasant growing only enough grain to feed his family and a large landowner raising large quantities of grain for export on international grain markets both fall under the same category of a grain-growing system of agriculture. The system of agriculture often finds reflection in the farmer's proportions of different categories of land. A livestock-raising system, for example, tends to demand a huge area of pasture lands for the herds, whereas a dairy farm might demand less. A grain-growing farm will naturally devote most of its territory to tilled land.

Whatever the system of agriculture on a farm, the system of farming denotes the manner in which the farmer organizes his tilled land. Not all agriculturists have a system of farming. Livestock raisers, for instance, may have 100% pasture land, and dairy farms can be very large and productive without having a significant farming component. For most scholars, the key determinant of the system of farming is the way in which the selection and distribution of crops restores fertility to the soil. On this basis arose the following evolutionary scheme of systems of farming:[1]

1) *Primitive "Slash and Burn" Farming.* Here a section of forest or scrub is cleared, and its trees and shrubbery are burned to enrich the soil with their ashes. Tillage then goes on for as many consecutive years as the soil gives satisfactory returns (rarely more than 5–6 years). At this point the land is abandoned, without any attempt to restore its fertility.

2) *Shifting Cultivation ("long fallow", zalezhnaia sistema, perelog).* This system represents an advance beyond the slash and burn system, in that

the land is not abandoned after it becomes exhausted. Instead, the farmer lets the land rest for many years (usually 10–25 years, but sometimes less), until the action of the air restores all or most of its fertility. At this point the cycle begins again. While each patch of exhausted land is recovering, several other patches are employed, such that anywhere from 2/3 to 5/6 of the tilled land is always resting.

3) *Grain-Fallow System (2-field or 3-field system; 4-field system of this family is often unstable)*. Here the soil is allowed one year of rest for every one, two, or three years of crop raising. Three years of crops to one year fallow tends to be too hard on the soil. Fertilizing, if practiced at all, is not yet sufficient to allow for dispensing with the need for fallow. Fallow systems allow for 1/2 to 3/4 of the tilled land to be sown each year—a significant advance in productivity over shifting cultivation.

4) *Balanced Farming (plodosmen, 4-field dystem, Norfolk system, 4-gield plus fodder grass field, etc.)*. This system of farming applies a calculated rotation of crops to the soil in order to maintain its fertility. Fallow is dispensed with, or nearly so. Instead, crops that deprive the soil of indispensable nutritive elements and properties alternate with different crops that enrich the soil with the nutrients or properties extracted by the preceding crop. Further, crop diversity in balanced farming systems introduces crops whose root structure addresses different layers of the soil, and who compete with weeds and pests in new ways.

5) *Industrial Farming*. This system represents the highest stage of farming, where the farmer possesses the requisite knowledge and means to employ sophisticated fertilizing techniques in order to protect the soil while growing whatever crop the market may demand in the current year.

Crop Rotations

Crop rotations are the various sequential combinations of crops which farmers sow. Naturally there are many practicable crop rotations within each system of farming, and the farmer must weigh his choice carefully. In the shifting cultivation system, for example, a careless sowing of winter grains year after year will provide immediate cash returns, but will also exhaust the soil much more quickly than a less strenuous rotation including spring grains or fodder grasses. In balanced farming, to take another example, the various crops stand in a delicate balance relative to each other. A nitrogen-accumulating crop like clover grass must follow a nitrogen-depleting crop like rye or wheat.* If this proves impractical in the given conditions of climate, soil, labor, or technology, then an appropriate fertilizer will have to be applied in conjunction with the substitute crop.

Naturally this neat scheme of systems of agriculture, systems of farming, and crop rotations is of limited use in assessing the characteristics of individual farms. Real farms tend to present a more complex picture. It is not always easy to determine which system of agriculture a farm employs. Many farms may market a variety of products, any one of which can provide the lion's share of the income in any given year. Sometimes a farmer may find it best to employ one system of farming on one portion of his land and another system elsewhere. He may perform operations that seem to overlap the characteristics of two or more of the systems of farming which we have just described. He may have no system whatsoever!

Nevertheless, the concepts of systems of agriculture and systems of farming can be valuable tools for the study of agriculture and its history. Theorists of the late nineteenth and early twentieth centuries waged pitched battles over the significance of these concepts, and succeeded in greatly enhancing our understanding of agricultural evolution in several ways.[2]

1) *There Is No Hierarchy of Systems.* All attempts to establish the universal superiority of any one system of agriculture or system of farming for all farms failed. The viability of various systems of agriculture is self-evident—there is a place for dairy farmers, grain farmers, etc. As regards systems of farming, however, the great contribution of balanced farming systems to the agricultural revolution in England led to much speculation that this system was the panacea for all farmers. Indeed, the scheme of systems of farming given above does correspond to the historical evolution of farm organization. And it is tempting to interpret the scheme as a hierarchy of progress, where each successive system represents an inherently superior organization of farming. The farmer's dependence on the natural environment decreases with each successive system, and the intensity of farming increases: the amount of land left fallow or abandoned declines, labor and capital inputs per unit area of land increase, and crop production per unit area also rises.

---

*The leaves of clover grass accumulate nitrogen from the air, and deposit this nitrogen in their roots, which remain in the soil after the harvest. Clover is the crop most famous for this property, but there are many others.

Additionally, the relatively more intensive systems are more complex to organize, and require more agronomic knowledge (the farmer must know how various categories of crops influence each other in a balanced farming rotation, and he must know which types of fertilizers best supplement any given crop in an industrial system).

Thus to an agronomist, to an historian, or to the state—which tends to be in favor of maximizing production, and increasing tax collections—the more intensive systems do reflect an ascending perfection of the agricultural art. But no farmer of any kind is interested in maximizing production at all costs. They will not increase capital or labor inputs unless the return promises to compensate them adequately for the resources invested. To take an example, in sparsely populated areas it is much more expensive to hire a large work force than in overpopulated areas. A large landowner in a sparsely populated locale would be foolish to try a farming system with maximum labor intensity. A more extensive system would be more appropriate. Similarly, peasants and other family farmers are naturally reluctant to intensify their farming systems beyond a certain point, since they themselves are doing the labor. Such farms could of course increase their capital inputs. They could purchase advanced equipment or artificial fertilizers, for example. But they do not necessarily have the money to do this, even if such investments promise good returns. Less intensive systems are sensible for them.

There is, therefore, a major divide between farmers and authorities in the approach to questions of farm organization. As we shall see in our examination of the first efforts to reorganize agriculture in Tambov, both the state agents of the Stolypin reform and the *zemstvo* agronomists were slow to recognize that peasant farmers were very reluctant to accept farming systems with maximal labor intensity. This was not a failure on the agronomic authorities' part to understand "peasant mentality." Rather it was a fundamental miscalculation of basic principles of farm organization: farmers would not take on more work simply so as to increase production. Until they foresaw significant returns on the proposed extra work, they would not perform it. As a result, agronomic aid programs would waste scarce resources—and time, which we now know was also in short supply in the final years before the World War and forced collectivization—in efforts to eliminate the three-field farming system from the countryside. This is an issue to which we shall return in a later section.

2) *There Is No Single Yardstick to Measure Agricultural Intensity.* There is no definitive procedure to measure the intensity of all agricultural

enterprises. The intensity of a farm's or enterprise's *farming operations* can be measured to a reasonable degree of accuracy, by calculating the quantities of labor and capital expended per unit area. But of course the farming operations—the system of farming—only exist within the context of a given system of agriculture. For example, a relatively extensive system of farming, producing large quantities of hay, can very effectively coincide with a capital- and labor-intensive dairy goods system of agriculture. There is no certain yardstick to measure the intensity of such an enterprise relative to an intensive grain-growing farm, or to a sugar-beet-growing and -processing enterprise. We can of course measure the intensity of, for instance, grain-growing farms relative to each other. But comparisons of enterprises engaged in different systems of agriculture are inherently complex, and any such calculation will inevitably involve subjective or arbitrary elements.

3) *There Can Be No Definitive Agricultural Regionalization.* From the above it follows that there can be no definitive agricultural regionalization. A regionalization based on systems of agriculture would not be very informative. As we have seen, the term itself is quite imprecise, and some systems of agriculture (especially livestock raising and grain growing), are to be found both among primitive peasant societies and complex capitalist enterprises. In principle, a regionalization based on systems of farming is equally unattractive, since farming plays an entirely subordinate role in many agricultural systems.

4) *The Causation of Intensification.* A long series of debates, extending to the present day, concerned the reasons for the evolution of increasingly intensive systems of farming. The great divide in these debates was the relative importance of population pressure on the one hand and market forces on the other hand.[3]

For Russian Marxists and the main body of German agricultural economists, the growing influence of market forces was the decisive factor impelling farmers to increase their production per unit area. By the term "market forces" they understood both opportunities to sell agricultural produce for profit and the necessity to sell so as to meet monetary obligations. Market opportunities grew apace with industry, which demanded raw materials from agriculture like sugar beets, potatoes, and flax, and with urbanization, which demanded large quantities of food for the population of the cities. Taxation and the rising cost of land and agricultural equipment, meanwhile, forced the farmer to exchange ever more of his production for money.

For other scholars, most notably the Russian populists, demographic forces were the decisive factor in agricultural intensification. They argued that substantial rises in rural population density (a trend we have already noted for Tambov and the rest of Russia's black-earth zone in our period) forced farmers onto smaller and smaller plots of land, forcing them to reorganize their system of farming along more intensive lines.

A definitive conclusion on the causation of the evolution of systems of farming has proved to be very elusive. But in Russia some degree of reconciliation between the two camps in this debate was achieved by the mid-1920s. In the first decades of the twentieth century the growing influence of market forces on all aspects of the agricultural economy became ever more difficult to deny, and in 1924 the leading populist theorist of agricultural evolution, N. P. Oganovskii, conceded that population pressure could not promote the intensification of farming beyond the stage of grain-fallow systems. He pointed out that *once this stage of farming is established, further increase of population density creates a crisis which cannot be resolved in the absence of large urban and industrial markets.*[4] The success of more intensive systems of farming (balanced farming, or the industrial system) is predicated on the marketing of large quantities of crops and animal products which the peasantry itself does not need—sugar beets, flax, potatoes, dairy products, sunflowers, etc.

From this discussion of systems of agriculture it follows that grain-fallow systems represent a threshold in the evolution of "natural" or "pre-modern" farming in two respects. First, so long as the action of air, rainfall, and tillage remains the only means of restoring soil fertility, grain-fallow systems maximize the productivity of the land. Barring the availability of unrealistic quantities of manure, fallow cannot be eliminated or contracted any more than in grain-fallow systems without either the application of chemical fertilizers or the employment of a finely tuned "balanced farming" rotation of crops. In other words, until they become aware of certain scientific advances, peasants have little chance of implementing any system more intensive than a three-field system.

Second, the dependence of multi-field systems on the marketing of diverse farm products implies the dependence of an agricultural revolution on the appearance of complimentary transport networks and industries. The importance of this conclusion to Russia's agrarian problem is clear. If in the short run the refinement of individual labor operations determined the fate of peasant agriculture, in the long run the pace and pattern of industrial development would weigh just as heavily. As the density of population rose, the character of the agrarian problem would acquire new features that lay beyond the reach of peasants or agricultural administrators to control. Even if their leading officials had understood the importance of particular industries complimentary to multi-field systems, neither the Tsarist nor even the Soviet Ministry of Agriculture ever had much influence over patterns of industrial development.

In general, and as we shall see below with respect to Tambov, late-Imperial Russian industrialization was not catering to the agricultural sector. In the absence of a conductive infrastructure, agronomists tried to concoct hybrid systems that would carry the village as far down the road to an agricultural revolution as economic conditions allowed. Although the heyday of these systems came in the 1920s, we must discuss them here in Part III. For they formed an important landmark in the terrain of farm organization, and their potential as stepping-stones between grain-fallow and multi-field systems will certainly affect our understanding of the agrarian problem.

Oganovskii's observation concerning the interconnection between agricultural intensification and industrialization is particularly poignant for Tambov and many other areas of Russia in the early twentieth century, where the three-field system predominated and the rural population was rising fast. Unless the volume and accessibility of industrial and urban markets for agricultural production blossomed on the one hand, and urbanization absorbed some of the surplus population in the countryside on the other hand, the rural crisis in central Russia could assume more dangerous forms...

The Fodder Crisis:
Decay of the Three-Field System?

Having traced the evolution of labor practices in response to economic and demographic pressures, it is now time to analyze the corresponding evolution in the feeding and care for domestic animals. Naturally, these developments meant more to the animals than to the peasants! But, as will become clear below, the viability of peasant agriculture depended in no small part on the facility with which communes and families could intensify farming while maintaining delicate balances between the feed requirements of their animals on the one hand and the dividends they offered—in the form of food, labor, wool, etc.—on the other hand.

The Elements of the Fodder Crisis

Fallow is raised late so as not to deprive the herds of their only serviceable pastureland in the late spring. But what kind of pasture does this land present? In dry years especially..., [in the last days before fallow is raised] only *smiataia polyn* [wormwood] remains on the fallow. The starving cattle rip out grass roots and swallow them together with earth and dust. But, sooner or later, the peasants must till the fallow. Then, with the hay grasses usually still drying on the meadows, the literally starving herds have no alternative but to scramble for scraps of anything edible on the beaten-down pastures, in the gullies, even along the roads. Their summer trials over, winter confronts the animals with hunger anew. Hay shortages leave them on a straw diet. In most peasant households the animals have to survive all winter on straw, and not only spring crop straw, but often rye straw as well [oats and millet straw are much better feed than rye straw—D.K.].... only the horse has the privilege of eating some oats or other grain in the winter and spring. By the springtime animals who have passed the entire winter on straw diets are

> frightful to look at [the stall-feeding period in Tambov was never
> less than five months—D.K.]. Only their remarkable hardiness
> keeps them from dying *en masse*.
>
> —N. Brzheskii, 1908[5]

In the voluminous agronomic literature of early-twentieth-century Russia, few issues generated as much unanimity among specialists as the fodder question in three-field communal farming. According to the regnant logic, under conditions of rising population the three-field farming system dug its own grave by stimulating farmers to convert their pasture and meadow lands into arable, on which they could grow more grain crops. The conversion of the pastures and meadows, the logic continued, undermined the livestock sector, and restricted animal holdings to a bare minimum. In consequence, manure supplies fell, and grain yields fell with them, once the soil began to fail under the strain of repeated grain sowings. Terse explanations of this vicious cycle, the so-called "crisis of the three-field system," can be located almost everywhere in the literature of the day. From this paradigm agronomists and agricultural administrators concluded that the three-field system had outlived its day, and must cede place to systems which would produce fodder sources on arable land.[6]

The standard treatment of the fodder question is a ferocious condemnation of the three-field system. But which elements, if any, of this standard interpretation will stand up to empirical verification? How was the "crisis of the three-field system" developing in Tambov? And what was the outlook for the animal branches of the peasant economy as of 1914?

Winter Fodder

Speaking generally, it is fair to say that the amount and composition of fodder resources available on the farm determine the features and parameters of livestocking in peasant agriculture. As we shall see in the conclusions to this section, under very favorable circumstances farmers would purchase concentrated fodder for their livestock. But for most · farmers, in Tambov and elsewhere, this was never a realistic or even a conceivable option. Smaller farms would have to purchase some straw to help their cows get through the year, but the great mass of fodder for all farms came from their own lands.[7]

In an earlier discussion we saw how most of those lands which exclusively supported the animal population in Tambov, namely meadows and pastures, were tilled up and converted into permanent arable land during the first three-quarters of the nineteenth century. Moreover, the quality of the remaining pastures and meadows was naturally very low. Pastures were notoriously poor, since the best pasture lands were the first to be converted into arable. The same was true for many of the meadows. Some communes were fortunate enough to retain meadows of top quality, especially in the northern *uezds*, where the climate was not so dry, and much less of the territory had soils suitable for exploitation as arable land. But even the best meadows gave only meager yields in comparison to their potential. With precious few exceptions, nowhere in Russia—Tambov included—had farmers learned to sow, harrow, irrigate, drain, weed, or fertilize their meadow-lands [Table 3.1].[8] As often as not, *peasant* meadows yielded a bit less hay than these general figures indicate, because communes sent their herds out to graze on meadows early in the spring.[9] After touring

Table 3.1. Hay Yields, Tambov vs. Germany and America

	Meadows as % of allotment land, 1917	Average yield in *puds* per *desiatina* of meadow, 1896–1910	
		Steppe	Lowland
Temnikov	14.2	80.4	117.6
Elatma	17.0	103.3	141.7
Spassk	11.2	103.8	158.7
Shatsk	6.3	112.5	140.5
Morshansk	7.2	104.9	143.1
Kozlov	4.3	97.7	126.8
Tambov	3.1	75.4	122.2
Lipetsk	3.5	97.4	124.1
Lebedian	3.2	85.4	135.9
Kirsanov	4.1	91.4	138.1
Usman	3.3	82.4	114.8
Borisoglebsk	3.1	64.8*	108.1
Total	5.3	88.4	132.2
Average		104.7**	
German meadows	—	205	
American meadows	—	236	

*Source corrected.
**Average yield for all meadows, for the years 1901–1910.
Sources: Column 2 from *Sbornik ocherkov*, p. 45. Yields from *Urozhai khlebov, trav, i proch.*, pp. 68–74. Average yield for all Tambov meadows computed from Oganovskii, *Sel'skoe khoziaistvo Rossii v XX veke*, p. 274. Yields for German and American meadows from Pokrovskii, "Doklad," p. 467.

Shatsk *uezd*, for example, a special *zemstvo* instructor on meadows and fodder grasses reported that peasant meadows were all in such a state of disrepair that they were giving less than one-third of the yields possible with proper care and exploitation.[10]

The shortage of meadow grass forced peasants and landlords alike to find substitutes for hay as winter fodder. Even in the very south of the province, grazing could not begin before mid-April, nor continue past early November (all dates new style). Few if any families had enough hay to last the five to six month stall-feeding period. The detailed *zemstvo* animal husbandry study of 1912 found that hay was virtually non-existent in some *volosts*.[11] Indeed, the peasants of entire *uezds* were more or less without hay from their own lands [Table 3.2]: Even though these figures come from a year that was quite poor for meadow grass (1911), they are shockingly low. Farmers collecting but

Table 3.2. Meadow Hay Collected (in *puds* per *desiatina* of land in agricultural use on all peasant farms)

Kozlov	0.48
Lipetsk	0.94
Lebedian	0.75
Tambov	1.04
Usman	0.48
Kirsanov	1.42
Borisoglebsk	0.74

Source: *Materialy po raionnomu kachestvennomu obsledovaniiu zhivotnovodstva*, vol. 2, pp. 258, 270, 274, 278, 282, 286, 290.

one *pud* of hay for each *desiatina* of land in agricultural use would need well over 100 *desiatinas* of land per cow, were they to give the cows a diet high in hay!

The natural substitutes for hay were straw and chaff. According to the only complete data, for the relatively poor grain years 1906–1910, rye gave about 1.4 times as much straw as grain, while oats and millet gave about 1.25 times as much straw as grain.[12] Straw and chaff are less nutritious than hay, but they could nevertheless keep the animals alive until the spring.* Their abundance after each harvest meant that they

---

*Four units (by weight) of oats or millet straw are worth about three units of simple meadow hay. Each are equivalent to about five units of rye straw (*Sam sebe agronom*, 1926, no. 9, p. 270).

Table 3.3. Stall Feeding: Grain and Its By-Products vs. Hay (all figures in *puds*, as given to all animals combined, per farm, for the entire stall-feeding period)

	North	Center	South
Straw and chaff	322	478	499
Hay	109	88	23
Potatoes	59	95	17
Grain and flour	66	*146*	*169*

Source: Chelintsev, *Opyt izucheniia organizatsii,* p. 305.

eclipsed hay in animals' stall-feeding diets [Table 3.3]: The figures in italics demonstrate the complete dependence of the livestock sector on grain production. They also explain the tenacity with which peasants stuck to sowing grain crops—a problem we shall examine more closely later, in connection with the prospects for the implementation of more intensive systems of farming.

Naturally the horses got the best of the available feed. According to standard norms of the day, workhorses needed about 40 *puds* of oats per year. Only the bigger farms in the black-earth portion of Tambov could consistently afford such a ration.[13] As we saw in Part I, the peasantry was selling off prodigious quantities of oats to meet various obligations. For most of our period workhorses in Tambov probably received less than half of the recommended ration of oats.[14] Still less remained for the rest of the livestock. The horses were swallowing more than half of the grain available for fodder, so they tended to receive roughly 50–100% more nutrition than cows during the stall period.[15]

Hay and grain shortages were certainly not the only weakness of winter feed regimes. Since they failed to keep any accounts of their resources, peasants could not properly plan ahead. They did not necessarily even know how many *puds* of straw were in a stack of grain. Therefore they could not optimize their decisions on when to keep, sell, buy, or slaughter animals.[16] Among a minority of the farming population, inattentiveness to reconciling fodder resources with animal holdings could result in gross errors, forcing the sale or slaughter of livestock late in the winter.[17]

Moreover, existing feed norms might have been very wasteful. Feed norms varied by locality and the acumen of the women making the decisions, but most of them probably thought that a ration of about one *pud* of hay or straw per day per cow was alright. Unfortunately, this was significantly more than the animals could properly digest, even if they did bother to eat it all.[18] Veterinary researchers found cows that needed 17 fodder units per day getting 27; those needing 14 were getting 20.[19] There is nothing to suggest that these cases were rare exceptions.[20] Animals also suffered from under-diversified diets. Proper feed combines straw or hay with concentrated fodder and root crops like potatoes or beets. As we shall see below, it was necessity rather than learning that eventually prompted peasants to broaden the composition of stall feed.

No attempt was made to keep feed clean. No one built feed troughs—fodder was simply thrown on the floor for the animals to scrounge up on their own. Inevitably, in this way some of the precious fodder was wasted. Finally, at least one agronomist noted with respect to hay that "[peasants] confuse bulk with nutritive value."[21] As noted in the discussion of the timing of grain reaping in Part I, many peasants preferred to mow grasses after they grew to their maximum volume, when in fact by this time the grass was over-ripe. They probably dried hay incorrectly as well, which will surprise no attentive reader of this book.[22] As if all of these blunders were not enough for the animals to suffer through, how can we best describe the atrocious hygienic conditions and cold temperatures to which they were exposed all winter? Well, perhaps this is better left to the reader's imagination...[23]

Summer Fodder

As the long passage quoted at the outset of this section illustrated, fodder problems were no less severe in the summer than in the winter. Pasture lands were never sufficient to hold the herds for more than a month or so. Sheep could graze on these lands intermittently throughout the year, but cattle and horses inevitably spent most of their time elsewhere. In late July or so, after the hay was mown, dried, and carted home (or otherwise safely stacked), the herds would graze on the meadows' grass stubble. But this too could not last them long. Meadow grass stubble usually provides about 7–15% of the quantity of hay mown. But it gives less when the meadow is tardily mown, as was usually the case throughout Russia.[24] Therefore, in every village, without exception, the herds had to graze for much of the time on the arable land.[25]

The typical grazing sequence for cattle went something like this: from mid-April to early July they stood on the green fallow, perhaps spending a week or two grazing on the meadows beforehand.[26] From early July to early August they were on the pastures and then the meadows, from early August to early November on the stubble. In the southern *uezds*, and, less so, in the central *uezds*, the herds also grazed on the rye sprouts for two or three weeks in October.[27] Here we should explain that there was nothing wrong *per se* with allowing the animals onto the rye sprouts. Whether the herds grazed there or not, winter frosts would wipe out the portions of the plant above the surface. The key was to wait until frosts hardened the ground before sending the animals onto the rye. Most survivors insist that they did wait, but the sources testify to the contrary—all too often, the animals went out onto wet ground, chewed up the soil with their hooves, and threatened the rye's root structure.[28] "A barbaric habit!" cried one ranking agronomist.[29] It might have cost peasants as much as 25% of their rye yield, according to one farmer's estimate.[30]

For a long time this common grazing regime served the communes very well. Even after arable land replaced almost all of the pasture and meadow land, the animals could find a lot to eat on fallow and crop stubble. A typical *desiatina* of meadow would give about 100 *puds* of hay and 7 *puds* of grazeable grass per year, or 321 *puds* of feed over three years. If this land was good enough to till, then as arable it would still give more than one-half this much fodder: 25* *puds* of green fallow weeds, 70 *puds* of rye straw (much of which, admittedly, was employed as a heat source or for roofing), perhaps 20* *puds* of rye stubble, 50 *puds* of oats or millet straw, another 20* *puds* of spring crop stubble, and 30 *puds* of oats grain as well. This comes to 215 *puds*, not counting chaff or rye sprouts.

In practice, arable land was providing ever more fodder over the decades that concern us, 1880–1914. Grain yields rose, bringing chaff and straw yields up with them. Land rental and purchasing increased the peasants' sown area, bringing in still more grain, chaff, and straw. Meadows were being rented too. Thus it appears that there ought not to have been any fodder crisis at all. But the amounts of animals per capita were dropping, and quite sharply, as we saw in Part I. How could this have happened?

The most important key to this puzzle lies in the timing of fodder availability. Hay, grain, chaff, and straw are all stall feed. So are potatoes. Green fallow, pastures, meadow stubble, crop stubble, and rye sprouts had to hold the herds for one half of the year. But, *unlike winter fodder sources, the summer fodder sources could not rise alongside increased*

---

*In hay equivalent. Note that these are high estimates of the hay equivalent to be found on green fallow and crop stubble.

crop yields.* The extension of land available to the peasant sector by an estimated 12% from 1882–1912 meant an increase of about the same 12% in their traditional summer fodder sources.[31] That is all.** With population increasing by 47% for the same period, there was really no way for animal holdings to remain stable per capita.

Thus the fodder crisis was in fact a summer fodder crisis, occasioned by rising population density. To feed all of the new mouths, peasants needed to till a larger share of their land. And, since population increased so much faster than landholdings, *they needed to maintain more livestock per unit area.* By boosting grain yields (and, to a much lesser extent, by sowing fodder crops, like potatoes) peasants could and did increase supplies of winter fodder. But they were helpless to augment supplies of grazeable summer fodder, and so livestock holdings rose much slower than population [Table 3.4]:

Table 3.4. Peasant Animal Holdings, 1880/84 vs. 1912

	1880/84		1912	
	Total	Per 100 capita	Total	Per 100 capita
Horses	629,000	30.0	603,000	19.5
Cattle	588,000	28.0	831,000	26.9
Pigs	487,000	23.2	334,000	10.8
Sheep	2,883,000	137.5	2,600,000	84.1
	1880/84	1912	% Increase, 1880/84–1912	
Total # of Animals*	1,554,000	1,727,400	11.2	

*For the purposes of this calculation pigs and sheep have been equated to 1/10 of a large animal, as in the Tambov *zemstvo*'s 1912 study of farm animals. Other ratios (such as 1/8) are also valid, but would not alter the picture in any significant way.
Sources: See Appendix "Nutrition and Mortality in Tambov, 1880–1914."

*Technically speaking, this is not true. If pastures are cared for and sown with optimal grasses, they will produce more. Likewise, arable land can be sown with grazeable grasses, in a three-field or other alignment. But neither of these cases were real alternatives for peasant farmers, for reasons which will probably not escape an attentive reader of this book.
**Strictly speaking, summer fodder sources per *desiatina* of arable land were actually shrinking. Potatoes' increased share of spring field sowings on the one hand, and the gradual deterioration of the soil on the other hand both made for less forageable weed growth on green fallow. On the other hand, arable land provided more forage per *desiatina* than either meadow or pasture. Renting and purchasing slightly boosted the amount of arable land as a percentage of all peasant land, so the quantity of summer fodder available probably rose at the same pace as land holdings.

At first glance, the final figure in this chart appears to serve as a striking confirmation of the dependence of animal holdings on grazing sources. As we have just seen, the amount of grazeable fodder available to peasant animals, as measured by the amount of land to which peasants had free access (allotment land, purchased land, and a bit of their rented lands),* rose by approximately 12% in this period. However, we have yet to consider two important features of summer fodder regimes in the province: rental of grazing privileges, and the development of stall feeding in the summertime.

Summer fodder shortages hit all communes collectively. The grazing of herds in common meant that all families shared in the these shortages as virtual equals. Communes had but two alternatives to deal with the problem—either collectively to rent grazing privileges from neighboring landlords, or individually to supplement forage with stall feed.

1) *Rental of Grazing Privileges.* If the data on arable land rental are much weaker than we would like, they are incomparably better than the information on rental of grazing privileges. *Zemstvo* statisticians failed to collect any information on the quantity of land involved in such deals. Consequently, this type of land rental left no trace in any statistical treatment of land renting.

When communes bargained with a neighboring landlord to acquire grazing access for their herds, ordinarily they did not arrive at a purely monetary settlement. They agreed to perform some quantity of agricultural labor for the grazing privileges, often in addition to a cash payment. The land-appraisal studies of the late 1890s record many representative deals, complete with estimates of the cost of the grazing rights were they to have been resolved exclusively by means of monetary transactions. But the statisticians had no clear idea of the quantity of land involved in all such deals put together. Thus it is difficult even to estimate the cost of these grazing privileges to the average commune. Figures ranging from 20–50 kopecks per *desiatina* of green fallow, meadow stubble, or crop stubble seem to have been the most common.[32]

What does emerge from the land-appraisal studies' discussions of the rental of grazing privileges is the rampancy of these deals. Knowing that the terms of emancipation sharply reduced the rights of peasants in the central provinces to send their animals out onto landlords' lands, we can safely assume that deals for grazing privileges must have been commonplace right away after 1861.[33] While not every commune

*See endnote 31.

rented grazing privileges, it appears that every commune wanted to do so. Many villages simply had no landlords to whom to turn for such deals. For these communes, as well as any other commune that faced summer fodder shortages despite gaining access to some additional grazing territory, the only way to maintain animal holdings was to undertake stall-feeding in part of the summer.

2) *Summer Stall Feeding.* So long as population density remains below a certain level, in the summertime farmers will always prefer to let their animals forage for food rather than to expend labor on feeding them. In shifting cultivation systems of agriculture this is never a problem, since grasses growing on the portion of the arable land that is unsown offer superior grazing. In grain-fallow systems of farming the situation can become more complex. So long as a large portion of land remains uncultivated, as full-time, high-quality pasture, then the grazing regime inherited from the shifting cultivation system demands no alteration. But once most of the pastures are tilled up, then the summer fodder balance gets tighter.

What happens when, as in Tambov and elsewhere, nearly all of the pastures are tilled up? In the climatic conditions of Tambov and the surrounding region, where cattle cannot graze more than about 6½ months of the year, a cow and a horse together need approximately 300 *puds* of hay equivalent during the grazing period.[34] Assuming a scant, low diet of 25 *puds* per month, it is clear that grazing on arable land alone could not support the animals required for the farming population. A single horse and a single cow together would need to forage for 300 *puds*. If we estimate each *desiatina* of arable land to provide 25 *puds* worth (from green fallow, rye stubble, spring crop stubble, and rye sprouts), then a family would need 12 *desiatinas* of arable land to support these two animals alone. Unfortunately, few and far between are horses able to cope with 12 *desiatinas* of three-field system arable land per year. Even a very strong horse on a compact farm could not easily handle more than 8 or 9 *desiatinas*, in my opinion.

It follows then that communes had to overcome their reliance on grazing as the only source of summer fodder once arable lands outnumbered pasture lands by a substantial margin.[35] The purchasing of grazing privileges from local landlords was only an expensive, stop-gap measure. The real solution lay in stall feeding. No information of any kind exists on summer stall feeding in Tambov before the 1914–15 budget study. The budgets establish that stall feeding was by that time prevalent everywhere in Tambov, and that it was predominant in the more fully tilled, black-earth majority of the province.[36] The critical periods came in April, when little if anything was growing on the ground, and in June, after the raising of fallow. At these times large majorities of *dvors* were supplementing grazing with at least some stall feeding [Table 3.5]:

Table 3.5. Percent of Farms Stall Feeding, in Addition to
(or in Place of) Grazing, 1914 (dates old style)

	April	May	June	July, 1st half	July, 2nd half	Aug.	Sept.	Oct.
North	50.4	29.2	12.5	12.5	6.7	4.1	6.7	—
Center	77.5	62.5	77.3	60.0	42.5	35.0	37.5	—
South	76.2	71.4	76.2	61.9	52.4	57.1	43.3	33.3

Source: Chelintsev, *Opyt izucheniia organizatsii*, p. 328.

While these data confirm the importance of the relief offered by crop stubble in late July–early August, they also indicate that even then the crisis was not over for many villages.

Unlike the rental of grazing privileges on landlords' estates, the effectiveness of summer stall feeding depended on each *dvor* individually. Farms with more land per capita had fewer animals per *desiatina*, consequently they had more fodder resources per animal, and could provide more feed in the summer (and in the winter too, naturally).[37] The smaller farms either had to restrict their animal holdings or purchase low-grade fodder from a neighbor or a landlord.[38] But it does not necessarily follow from this that the larger farms were not concerned about the shortage of grazing lands. As we shall see in our discussion of the considerations involved in transitions from grain-fallow systems to balanced farming systems, the larger farms always faced uncomfortable shortages of labor during the harvest period. While the smaller farms had more labor than they could employ even during these months, to the larger farms any expenditure of labor on stall feeding from July to early September (o.s.) was particularly irritating.[*]

Conclusions and Consequences

In summary, our inquiry into the fodder crisis allows us to draw a number of important conclusions. Firstly, it is clear that almost all communes were experiencing serious shortages of grazing land. Rental of grazing privileges from landlords could solve this problem for a time,

_____

[*]We shall return to this topic more than once, especially in Part IV.

but not for long, if the size of animal herds continued to rise. Secondly, as herds outgrew the capacity of grazing lands to support them, farmers were being forced to stall feed their animals in the summertime. Both the prevalence and the intensity of summer stall feeding were rising inexorably. Thus, summer fodder supply was the weak link of the fodder problem in Tambov. On the positive side, the mandatory employment of grain (including rye) in feed rations effectively improved the quality of fodder. As the share of grain in stall feeding rose, milk output per cow would also rise. This trend became very visible by the mid-1920s, when a lot more grain went to the cows, out of necessity.[39]

Thirdly, we can induce that fodder shortages haunted a large percentage of farms that had no shortages of food for family members. According to Chelintsev's rough calculations, farms in the center and south of the province (with typical family compositions and animal holdings) sized 10 desiatinas or more had grain surpluses, whereas only larger farms, of 12 or more desiatinas, had surpluses of both grain and straw.[40] The fodder problem, taken as a whole, appears to have been more critical than the food problem in Tambov.

Fourthly, standard impressions of the fodder crisis in peasant farming (as outlined at the beginning of this section) are rather misleading. It is certainly true that the conversion of top quality pasture lands into arable instigated the fodder crisis, by eliminating the best sources of fodder for the months before the harvest. In these months green fallow did not provide anywhere near as much grazing as did healthy, untilled grasslands.[41] The conversion of meadows into arable, on the other hand, did not instigate or accelerate any crisis of the three-field system of farming, at least not in this area of Russia. Meadow conversions did reduce the quantity of fodder available overall, but this consequence was of little significance to the fodder crisis in practice, because supplies of summer fodder were not thereby reduced. To the contrary, green fallow and crop stubble provided about three times as much summer feed as meadow stubble.* Of course the disappearance of meadows had some effect on the fodder problem, by depleting reserves for summer stall feeding.

Furthermore, the fodder crisis in Tambov was not spiraling in the way that the standard treatments imply. To begin with, manure supplies did not play a significant role in field husbandry in Tambov, or anywhere

---

*Three desiatinas of meadow stubble would offer about 21 puds of grass, whereas one desiatina of green fallow and two of crop stubble would give about three times as much fodder, in hay equivalents. To this calculation we could also add rye sprouts.

else in the black-earth zone. Nor were they destined to do so in the future—the timing and techniques of tillage would remain the most important factors here. There was, therefore, no strong connection in practice between livestock holdings and crop yields. Moreover, animal holdings *per desiatina* were actually rising throughout our period. Manure supplies were not shrinking. All of which is not to say that the fodder crisis was a mirage. It was real, and it was deepening. But it was not as desperate as one might believe from simplistic accounts.

Fifthly, and most importantly, we must confront the fact that the animal sector was expanding at a slower rate than the fodder supply. From 1880/84–1912 the grazing area increased by well over 12% (12% plus the rental of grazing rights on private lands), and additional fodder sources were expended in the stalls in the summer to keep the animals alive. But animal holdings increased by only 11%. The obvious conclusion is that peasants were passing their economic hardships on to the animals. Farm surpluses and non-agricultural income together were not sufficient to pay taxes, keep the family fed, and maintain the accustomed quantities of animals per person. This was the dynamic behind the declining standards of per capita nutrition that we demonstrated in Part I.

Sixthly, until such time as multi-field systems did establish themselves in Tambov, the question remains as to how farmers could get enough fodder to halt or reverse the decline of animals per capita. There were three possibilities:

1) Improvements in grain yields could produce huge amounts of fodder in the not distant future. Considering how primitive agrotechnical standards were, further increases in straw and grain yields were almost a foregone conclusion. But how quickly would this happen? In large part, progress would depend on the educational efforts of the local agronomists.

2) Alternatively, the by-products from enterprises processing potatoes or sugar beets (such as distilleries, starch factories, or sugar-processing factories) could provide a lot of fodder. The network of processing industries expanded substantially in the last two decades before the World War, and villages located near these factories were already leaning heavily on them for fodder.[42] But there is no reason to think that processing industries would affect a large portion of the peasantry anytime soon. This is a topic to which we shall return, at the end of Part V.

3) The last option was to sow fallow land with fodder crops. As with the raising of grain yields, the success of this rather advanced technique, "sown fallow," or "employed fallow" would depend on the work of the local agronomists. We will return to this topic below.

Finally, as the role of grazing relative to stall feeding continued to decline, most of the communes in the region were nearing the time when the larger, influential farms in their midst would lose one of their primary objections to the transition to a multi-field farming system. The elimination or near elimination of grazing on the arable land in favor of stall feeding is a key feature of most multi-field systems of farming. Families with large amounts of arable land would not tend to welcome this transition, since they saved so much labor by letting the animals forage on their own for food. But, once large farms were already stall feeding their animals for the greater part of the summer, they would find it less traumatic to do without arable grazing altogether.

The nuances and significance of this point will become clearer once we have analyzed the circumstances involved in transitions to multi-field systems. For the moment, we can only remark that an accurate evaluation of peasant agriculture's prospects in Tambov (and elsewhere) as of the close of the Tsarist period requires a thorough assessment of the prospects for the successful adoption of multi-field systems.

A System Despised

By the late nineteenth century the three-field system was dominant everywhere in Tambov, and covered all but the extremities of European Russia.[43] Sowing grain on two-thirds of the arable land was obviously more productive than any shifting cultivation or two-field fallow system, and it did not strain the soil as much as would sowing grain on three-fourths or more of the land. But virulent antipathy for the three-field system was snowballing among educated Russians by this same time. The agricultural revolution in Europe had taken place in the format of more intensive farming systems. In Holland, Belgium, England, and Denmark in particular, variations on balanced farming systems had led to tremendous increases in production and income. German agriculture was intensifying very rapidly in the second half of the nineteenth century. Thanks to the combination of root crops (such as sugar beets and potatoes, grown for industrial processing into sugar, alcohol, and starch) and artificial fertilizers, by the early twentieth century the so-called "industrial" systems of farming became more common in Germany than anywhere else in the world.[44]

All across northern and western Europe the three-field system was becoming rare. Fallow land was minimized; fodder crises were solved; grain yields rose.[45] The region experienced a simultaneous and sustained growth of population, yields, and labor productivity—an unprecedented triad, which has been labeled "the most 'revolutionary' development in European agriculture in the last two thousand years."[46] Agriculture generated ever-increasing surpluses to feed the burgeoning cities. The countryside provided the cities' textile factories, distilleries, and other processing industries with both the raw materials and the labor force needed to fuel further industrial expansion.

Comparisons of the agricultural performance of their own country to that of the more advanced European countries shamed many Russians. In seeking to explain the backwardness of Russian agriculture their attention inevitably turned to the three-field system and the organizational framework which was thought to have entrenched it, the peasant commune. From the 1880s on, the three-field system bore the brunt of an avalanche of polemical abuse and professional criticism.

The idea that the backwardness of the Russian peasant economy stemmed in large part from the retention of the three-field system beyond its day became—and remains—an article of faith. Intensification *within* the three-field system certainly contributed to rising yields in many places in Europe, and could do so in Russia, as we demonstrated in Part I. The room available for technological improvements within the traditional system was not widely perceived at the time, however—neither in Russia nor in Europe, where the intensification had proceeded very gradually.[47] And so loathing for the three-field system extended to absurd lengths: "If only we could get to improved tillage, by moving beyond the three-field system"; or "only by abolishing the three-field system can we rid ourselves of droughts" [of droughts, not of the consequences of droughts!—D.K.].[48]

Critics harped primarily on four drawbacks of the three-field system: green fallow's depletion of soil fertility, abandonment of one-third of the arable land each year under fallow, inadequate summer fodder resources, and the insufficient production of winter fodder.[49] They promised salvation in the form of multi-field systems, which would lead Russian agriculture along trails blazed in Europe. Unfortunately, until the turn of the twentieth century Russia was very short on both empirical and theoretical knowledge of multi-field systems applicable to the huge black-earth zone. The great advances in European agriculture had taken place in very different soil and climatic conditions. As late as 1909, well-informed Russian analysts of agrarian problems could complain that they had not come across any knowledge, or even practical suggestions, on multi-field systems for the black-earth zone.[50] The vacuum of uncertainty lasted until about 1910–1912, by which time the idea of a special sort of four-field system quickly acquired tremendous popularity in the agronomic community.[51] This was the *propashnaia* system, to which we now turn.

Propashnaia Farming Systems

With rural population growth far outstripping the increase of non-agricultural employment in most of black-earth Russia, the key element to the successful reorganization of the farming system appeared to be the introduction of crops that were both more labor-intensive and more productive per unit area than grains. Potatoes, sugar beets, fodder beets, corn, carrots, peas, lentils, and turnips were the most widely mentioned candidates. Ideally, these crops could be inserted into the three-field system's crop rotation after rye, creating a four-field system. The candidate crops, along with sunflowers, all shared the characteristic of inter-tillage (they were sown in well-separated rows, allowing for weeding and cultivation between the rows with *sokhas* or smaller hand-operated weeding tools during the growing season).* The action of inter-tillage on the soil wiped out weeds, improved soil structure, and maintained soil moisture much better than was the case with grain crops. Inter-tillage was often compared to fallow in regard to its influence on the soil. Thus a system which included inter-tillage crops in between rye and spring grains in the crop rotation was not a simple four-field fallow system. It was a nascent form of a *balanced farming system*, which would not put anywhere near as much strain on the soil as would a standard four-field *fallow system* (fallow–rye–spring wheat–oats, to take an example often found in areas to the south and east of Tambov). For identification purposes, in this study we will call the four-field rotation with an inter-tillage crop between rye and the spring grain by the Russian name for the section occupied by inter-tillage crops—*propashnaia*.

The *propashnaia* system had much to recommend it. Firstly, the amount of land left fallow would decline from 33% to 25%. Secondly, the influence of the inter-tillage crop on the soil would improve the yield of the spring grain crop. Some studies found yield increases of 20% or more.[52] Thirdly, and correspondingly, the improved care for the soil would render crops less susceptible to droughts. Inter-tillage crops needed only about 50–70% of the moisture that grain crops needed.[53] Fourthly, more labor could be profitably applied than with the three-field system. There would be more work, more income, and less of a labor crunch at harvest time, since the inter-tillage crops all ripen later than grains. Finally, productivity per unit area would permit farms to accumulate more fodder for their animals. This fodder would sustain more animals, who would provide more food, more income, and more manure.

The *propashnaia* system was not without shortcomings, some of which would delay its acceptance in the villages. But we will postpone

---

*In traditional practice, peasants neither sowed sunflowers in proper rows nor weeded them as they ought to have, thanks to which yields remained very low (Borisoglebskoe uezdnoe zemstvo, *Proekty*, p. 45; *KSE* vol. 6, p. 440). In a correctly run *propashnaia* system the sunflowers would become a more labor-intensive crop.

our examination of these shortcomings until after we have traced the organizational underpinnings of the traditional three-field system. For now, suffice it to say that the advantages of the *propashnaia* system were so many, so powerful, and so apparent, that most of the agronomic community all over the black-earth zone embraced it wholeheartedly.

The Organization of the Three-Field System

The waves of polemical hatred and hostile agronomic scholarship directed against the three-field system would do much to shape Tsarist and Soviet agricultural policies and agronomic aid programs up until the time when mass collectivization effectively abrogated peasant farming. Most agricultural administrators and agronomists alike considered the overcoming of the three-field system to be the primary goal of their work. But the three-field system proved to be remarkably resilient in the face of this pressure. It survived. It is the task of this section to begin to explain how and why this was so.

Part I has already acquainted us with the wide range of productivity which farming in the three-field system can embrace. At first the twin pressures of population growth and monetary obligations prompted peasants to extend their land holdings rather than to alter their farming techniques in any way. But later, when further extension was not practicable, families were compelled to intensify their farming operations. They adopted *dvoenie*, and *ziab*. They harrowed more. They used manure. We have also seen how much room was still left within the framework of the three-field system for further intensification. Manure use could be extended, seeds sorted, seed drills employed, etc.

There was a lot of slack within the system, and methods of labor were being transformed to take advantage of this. But, did the transformation of methods of labor justify the retention of the system? For all the speed with which labor practices evolved and new tools appeared, the percentage of failing and vulnerable farms continued to rise. At this point we must ask ourselves what was preventing farmers from adopting more intensive systems. After all, the adoption of intensive systems would not in any way impede the evolution of individual labor operations. There was no reason why productivity could not rise thanks to both systemic transitions and the evolution of methods of labor.

In order to decide if and why the three-field system made sense in early-twentieth-century Tambov, we must delve into the organizational structure of the system as it functioned in practice. This task is not easy.

The many elements of peasant farms hung in delicate and varying balances relative to each other. Inevitably, the heterogeneity of the farms themselves will belie any simplistic attempt to explain the mechanisms which determined the organization of farming. The size of families, the ratio of "eaters" (the young or unfit) to "workers", the size and composition of animal holdings, the amount of arable land, the quality of the soil, the size of the village, the distance to market, the level of grain prices—these are but a few of the many features that distinguished farms from one another, and lent to each village and each family its own set of concerns, motivations and possibilities. Nevertheless, it is possible to identify the logic behind the three-field system with respect to each of the main groups—large-, medium-, and small-sized farms.

Two notes should be made at this point. Firstly, students of Russian peasant sociology might be tempted to dismiss out of hand any attempt to probe farm organization preferences among different groups of peasant households. According to the notion of cyclical mobility among peasant households that Alexander Chaianov systematized and popularized in the 1920s, families' economic strength and organizational priorities shifted with the inevitable changes in their demographic structure (children were born, grew to maturity, then left the family to set up their own households or join others).[54] Further, calamities or unanticipated births could complicate the family composition at any time.[55] It might seem to follow, therefore, that farmers could never form stable organizational preferences. In practice they did, as our analysis of the fate of the three-field system both before and after the First World War will show.

Secondly, here and elsewhere in Part III, by categorizing farms according to size we intend not merely to segregate the farms by the amount of land they held. Families with more land tended as a rule to have more land per capita. Many studies all over Russia established this pattern, apparently without exceptions.[56] As far as the topics in Part III are concerned, the most salient consequence of this fact was the relative shortage of both human and horse labor per unit area on the larger farms.[57] Of course smaller farms could also be short on labor, especially when afflicted with a large ratio of children to adults. This ratio is perhaps the surest indicator of farms' distress, as Vasil'chikov's path-breaking work argued as early as 1881.[58] But we can safely stick to our division of farms according to landholding, because surfeits of children over adults appear to have occurred rather evenly across the spectrum of small to large farms.[59]

Farm Organization in the Three-Field System:
Crop Choices in the Commune

As strange as it may seem to many readers familiar with standard treatments of the peasant commune, farmers were relatively free to choose the disposition of their crop sowings on the arable land. Since communes divided arable land into strips and doled it out to all member households in piecemeal fashion, each family's strips of land were interspersed with the strips of other families. According to common presumption, the subordination of the inter-stripped lands to communal herd grazing forced farmers to homogenize crop sowings on each large unit of land. Otherwise, the theory continues, the animals would consume any crops still standing when they came through.

The logic of the standard perception of the organization of sowings within the commune will make more sense with the help of a concrete example. Consider Figure 3.1, which depicts the late springtime, before

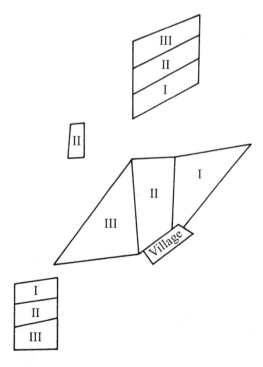

Figure 3.1. A Division of the Arable Fields into Three Sections

the raising of green fallow. In the three-field system, all fields marked with the Roman numeral "I" might lie fallow, lands marked "II" would be reserved for winter grains, and lands marked "III" would comprise the spring field. Surely no one would try to grow a crop on the green fallow fields, since the animals are foraging there. Then consider the situation in late July, after the rye harvest, but before the spring crops have fully ripened. If anyone had sowed a spring crop among the rye, it would now be devoured as the herds came onto the rye stubble. Finally, picture the spring fields after they are harvested. If anyone sowed a late-ripening crop like corn among early ripening plants, like oats, then the animals will now eat this too. Above and beyond these disincentives to heterogeneous sowings, farmers are said to have feared impurities in their fields that would result from the broadcast sowing of unlike crops. Since some broadcast-sown seeds will spray onto neighbors' strips, peasants are said to have enforced homogeneous sowings within each large field.

In consequence, it is often assumed that the commune essentially dictated the pattern of fieldwork in the village.[60] As Westphalian Baron von Haxthausen put it in a very influential passage on the Russian commune:

> Perfect order, one could almost say military discipline, charac-
> terizes the work in the fields. On the same day and at the same
> hour everyone sets out to plow and harrow and they all return
> at the same time.[61]

This has been the typical perception of open-field agriculture ever since.[62]

In fact, very little of this "logic" applied in practice. To begin with, our discussions of seeds and sowing in Part I have illustrated peasant farmers' indifference to the purity of seed grain on the one hand, and the tendency for sowers to take care not to spray seeds onto neighbors' strips. After all, seeds are grain; they are valuable. Why throw them around wastefully, instead of bending down a bit to keep them all on one's own land? We cannot know how many peasants sowed carefully and how many did not. But we can safely assume that farmers did not feel threatened by the possibility of foreign seeds straying onto their land.[63] Peasant innovators themselves indicated that the proximity of unlike sorts of crops on neighboring strips did not deter them from experimenting.[64] And a survey in 1910 and 1911 comparing open-field farming practices with newly consolidated plots found no difference between the two groups in the percentages of farmers who had adopted "improved" seed grain.[65]

The drawbacks to sowing crops on green fallow land are quite clear, and it is difficult to imagine this happening.* But we should be aware that in an unspecifiable minority of communes the herds did not have access to all of the fallow lands. Cases where some arable land units were inaccessible or too far away to permit grazing were not entirely rare, as many sources attest.[66] More importantly, there were rarely any restrictions on crop choices below the division into winter and spring crops for the winter and spring fields, respectively. Because crops always stood drying in the fields for a period of time after reaping, families never had to reap their fields contemporaneously. A week's difference in the timing of reaping, or the ripening of a crop, never caused any conflicts.[67] The important moment was when the family got around to bringing the sheaves home.[68] In the spring field the time at which one's crops ripened mattered even less than in the winter field. By the time spring crops were ripe, the herds had already begun grazing on the winter field stubble, taking the edge off of the cattle's hunger.[69] Grazing on the spring field crop stubble was not really mandatory until September, when all but the latest-ripening crops, like potatoes, beets, and sunflowers, would have been harvested.[70]

Additionally, the quality and relief of each unit of soil often governed crop choices for everyone. If, for example, oats or potatoes (the earliest- and the latest-ripening of the standard spring field crops, respectively) tended to grow poorly on a particular field, then they would not be sown there, and conflicts as to the time to begin grazing would not arise. Similarly, peasants preferred to sow labor-intensive crops like potatoes on the nearest available lands. It so happens that the most labor-intensive crops were all late ripening. Among them, only millet was reaped before September (old style). Thus many of these sowings would end up together, in which case shepherds could rather easily keep the herds away from them.[71]

All the same, all types of spring crops typically grew side by side in the spring field, at least on a significant portion of it:

> In the ordinary peasant three-field ... [the spring field] contains all manner of plants: oats, millet, lentils, sunflowers, potatoes, and others. In such a catch-all field crops are intertwined without any rhyme or reason. But it would be much better if the

---

*Yet there were in fact cases of this. See below.

disposition of spring field crops was put into order, such that crops demanding equivalent care would be grouped together in one place.[72]

Many other sources confirm peasants' sowing of early- and late-ripening crops nearby one another in spring section fields.[73] Since potatoes were the most important of the late-ripening crops in Tambov, we might expect that the communal herds were allowed onto these mixed-up fields to graze on the early-ripening crops' stubble before the potatoes were harvested. After all, yields of root crops do not decline by very much if their tops are trampled within a couple of weeks before they have ripened.[74] But sunflowers also ripen late, so communes in the southern *uezds* (where sunflower sowings were concentrated) must have taken steps to keep the animals away until such time as the sunflowers were harvested.[75]

What about the winter field? Here the parcelization of land confronted innovation-minded farmers with a special problem. Apart from the possibility of the village herd trampling any late-ripening crop, the requirement of the rye plant for pollination from airborne spores of other rye plants restricted opportunities for experimentation. Because rye pollination involves an airborne exchange of genetic material, imported sorts of rye usually degenerated within a few years, becoming almost indistinguishable from local rye. Farmers (and most agronomists) were not aware of cross-pollination, and some of them did try out new sorts of rye. They often reported satisfaction with the results.[76]

Cross-pollination did limit the open-field farmer's freedom to experiment with rye. But was rye the only crop in the winter field? Judging from our earlier analysis of the summer fodder crisis in Part III, we would certainly not expect to find any spring crop sowings in the winter field. In most villages fodder resources were expended by the time of the winter crop harvest, in July, so the animals had to be put on the rye stubble at the first opportunity. But did this circumstance really exclude spring crops from the winter field? Not entirely. Sometimes horseless *dvors* would not manage to till and sow some of their strips in the winter field. They would have to sow something on these strips in the spring. Additionally, in common cases where the rye failed in the fall, froze in the winter, or rotted during the thaw, peasants could re-sow their rye strips in the spring (with spring crops, naturally). Not all would do so, but some would.[77]

Overall, we must conclude that common grazing and the inter-stripping of land posed few obstacles to crop choices within the framework of the three-field system. As we saw throughout Part I, work regimes varied widely within villages—the "perfect order" or "military discipline" of which Haxthausen spoke was an exaggeration.[78] So long as they kept off the fallow section, farmers were free to select their sowings as they saw fit. In fact, small numbers of farmers sometimes managed to overcome the resistance of the village to sowings on the fallow section.[79] Peasants had plenty of room to experiment, and to respond to market opportunities—if only they were willing to take the initiative in tinkering with or departing from standard patterns of labor and farm organization.

Subsistence Farming and Market Forces

A strong tendency in peasant farming is the priority families place on producing enough to keep themselves and their animals fed, and entering voluntarily into market transactions only after securing their own survival. Thus peasant communities do not tend to specialize into rye growers, sheep raisers, horse breeders, etc. In an age of increasing market opportunities and monetary obligations, this principle can be undermined. "Cash crops" or other market-directed commodities can generate a lot of income, with which the family can buy foodstuffs. Sunflowers, horses, potatoes, eggs, pork, lentils, flax, sugar beets, and tobacco were the most important options of this kind in Tambov. But even in the face of these market opportunities, peasant farmers will not easily part with the subsistence principle. This is a very old observation, which a medievalist recently put very well:

> The peasant's relation to the market ... differs from that of a capitalist farmer. We might characterize his position as market involvement without market orientation. Although few peasants dwell in economies entirely innocent of money, prices, and exchange, and though few remain utterly separate from the market sector, they tend not to structure their economic activity around the market. The goal is rather maximum self-sufficiency ... and entry into the market only to obtain the minimal cash required for money dues or the purchase of the few consumption items ... that could not be raised or fabricated at home.[80]

Scholars of various backgrounds have correctly contested the universal applicability of the subsistence ethic for the understanding of peasant societies. Probably the best-known insight in this respect concerns the propensity of some peasants to "gamble" or invest, in the hope of reaching a higher level of security or status (by acquiring a horse, securing a prestigious and potentially lucrative marriage, etc.).[81] As we shall see below, however, for most peasants in Tambov the emphasis on sowing consumption crops retained most of its strength even after market opportunities arose and monetary obligations increased. From the peasant's point of view, the advantages of producing enough grain to feed oneself were not difficult to see. The grain was procured at "wholesale" prices, so to speak, not at market prices. One could monitor the quality of the grain. In the case of a bad year, one could eat grain, but not the money received from cash crops.

With rye being the exclusive crop in the winter field, all of the cash crops in Tambov were spring sown.[82] Thus these crops all competed for the limited space in the spring field. Each farmer tried to gauge how much oats or millet or potatoes the family might need in the coming year, and distributed his sowings accordingly. Only the larger farms had the luxury of raising cash crops like sunflowers or hemp, which could not be consumed.

A second principle of peasants' crop selection is their tendency not to calculate their own labor as an expense. The peasant family is at once proprietor and laborer. A proprietor by himself will evaluate the merits of a particular crop according to the net income he expects to receive from it—gross production minus material expenses, including the wages paid to his labor. On a family farm, however, laborers are not salaried. Instead, they simply appropriate all of their own production. Paramount to them, therefore, will be gross income, not net income. Take, for example, a case where they could grow crop "X" at minimal estimated labor expense (say 10 rubles, if such labor were hired), producing 50 rubles worth of crop. Or they could grow crop "Y" at 30 estimated rubles worth of effort, producing 55 rubles worth of crop. Generally they will choose to grow crop "Y", since labor expense is not only "free", but labor unused is simply wasted. At the same time, people will not expend extra effort if the anticipated rewards are insufficient. If they truly need the food, or the money, they will work much harder to produce. If they do not feel such a strong need, then they will grow a less labor-intensive crop.

While analyzing the history and geography of sowing patterns in Tambov, we must keep in mind the relative labor requirements and market values of gross production per *desiatina* of the primary crops. This chart is compiled from the budget study of the year March 1914–March 1915 [Table 3.6]. A *desiatina* of sunflowers, for example, usually brought in more cash than a *desiatina* of its major competitors

Table 3.6. Labor and Reward, per Crop

	Male labor days, per des. Female and adolescent labor included at a lesser rate[a]	Average yield per des.[b]	Market price, in rubles per pud[c]	Market value of gross production, in rubles per des.[d]
Rye	20.9 (22.4)	46.7	0.80	37.4
Millet[*]	28.2 (39.5)	36.3	0.65	23.6
Oats	14.9 (15.4)	41.7	0.71	29.6
Potatoes	53.2 (81.5)	426.3	0.18	76.7
Hemp, and flax for fiber)	80.5(164.4)	—	—	91.5
Sunflowers[**]	18.7 (NA)	59.2	1.18	69.9

[a]Figures in parentheses are offered for the sake of comparison. They are borrowed from a budget study in neighboring Penza province in the 1920s (Studenskii, Problemy organizatsii krest'ianskogo sel'skogo khoziaistva, p.135).
[b]Sources: RGAE, f. 478, op. 2, d. 237, pp. 13–20. Sunflower statistics for the years 1912–1914 only.
[c]Sources: For rye and oats, Mironov, Khlebnye tseny, tables 11 and 14, for the years 1911–1914; for potatoes, the year 1912–13, in Sbornik ocherkov, p. 186. Millet and sunflower prices are for an unspecified period of years before 1914, from Noarov, "Krest'ianskie biudzhety Tambovskoi gubernii," Prilozhenie.
[d]Value of straw and chaff not included.
[*]This crop was a little more difficult to grow in the north of Tambov.
[**]Sunflowers were a lot more difficult to grow in the center, impossible in the north of the province. The minimal amount of labor expended on sunflowers reflects peasants' primitive cultivation techniques. For sources on this matter, see the outset of the section "Propashnaia Farming Systems" above. The labor intensity of this crop was subject to increase sharply if it were sown in wide rows and cared for properly.
Source: Chelintsev, Opyt izucheniia organizatsii, p. 345.

in the spring field. So the larger farms in the South sowed them [Tables 3.7–3.9]:

How did sowing patterns within the three-field system evolve under the influence of population pressure and economic conditions? Firstly, we have seen that farms got smaller over time, because population grew much faster than new lands were acquired. From this we would expect to find less area devoted to oats—traditionally the primary marketed crop in Tambov—and more area devoted to consumption crops like millet and potatoes. At the same time, however, the intensification of labor was mitigating the pressure of population by generating higher yields. Thus, in effect farms were not shrinking as much as landholding statistics imply. Nevertheless, as we saw at the outset of Part I, consumption declined after the mid-1880s because of taxation and other monetary obligations, such as land acquisitions, etc. And so many

Table 3.7. Crop Choices in the Spring Field (budget study data, 1914; all figures represent percentage of entire sown area devoted to the crop in question)

Size of farm (in *des.*)	NORTH				
	< 5	< 8	<11.5	<18	> 18
Potatoes	19.4	08.8	09.3	06.4	–
Millet	10.9	10.5	14.5	3.2	–
Oats	20.0	28.2	22.1	**43.0**	–
Lentils	0.0	1.8	0.7	0.5	–
Sunflowers	0.0	0.0	0.0	0.0	–

Size of farm (in *des.*)	CENTER				
	< 5	< 8	<11.5	<18	> 18
Potatoes	7.6	5.4	5.3	3.5	3.2
Millet	18.0	16.4	14.0	10.7	9.9
Oats	26.6	27.7	**32.8**	**34.3**	37.3
Lentils	0.8	0.0	0.0	1.1	0.0
Sunflowers	0.0	0.4	0.0	0.0	0.0

Size of farm (in *des.*)	SOUTH				
	< 5	< 8	<11.5	<18	> 18
Potatoes	–	2.5	1.8	1.5	1.3
Millet	–	13.3	10.0	9.4	9.3
Oats	–	27.0	25.2	27.6	26.9
Lentils	–	2.0	2.4	**4.3**	5.8
Sunflowers	–	4.1	12.8	10.3	17.4

Source: Chelintsev, *Opyt izucheniia organizatsii,* pp. 286–288.
Note: Here the bold figures indicate the most obvious cases of production for market, not for consumption. In the case of oats, surplus production often went to young horses being raised for sale.

Table 3.8. Market Significance of Individual Crops (% of harvest sold; Tambov budget study data, 1914–15)

		NORTH	CENTER	SOUTH
Winter field	Rye	10.9	11.4	13.9
Spring field	Millet	3.6	5.4	4.8
	Potatoes	7.6	4.6	1.4
	Oats	15.3	34.4	33.8
	Sunflowers	–	–	97.0*

*The source mistakenly reads 79%.
Source: Kostrov, Nikitin, and Emme, *Ocherki organizatsii krest'ianskogo khoziaistva,* p. 76.
Note: Here we see the significance of sunflowers and oats as marketed crops. Rye and potatoes (in the north, near distilleries and starch manufacturing enterprises) play a secondary role, millet being the least marketed.

Table 3.9. Sales of Crops vs. Amount Consumed (accumulation of reserves
and potato feeding to animals is not included. Amount consumed is taken as 100,
figures in chart represent relationship of sales to this consumption total)

Size of farm (in *des.*)	NORTH				
	< 5	< 8	<11.5	<18	> 18
Rye	0	0	8	111	–
Millet	0	0	0	19	–
Potatoes	9	11	24	67	–
Oats	67	110	40	30	–
Sunflowers	0	0	0	0	–

Size of farm (in *des.*)	CENTER				
	< 5	< 8	<11.5	<18	> 18
Rye	29	28	60	32	54
Millet	10	0	15	0	22
Potatoes	0	2	9	0	57
Oats	177	159	78	185	231
Sunflowers	0	0	0	0	0

Size of farm (in *des.*)	SOUTH				
	< 5	< 8	<11.5	<18	> 18
Rye	–	9	55	20	53
Millet	–	7	0	0	28
Potatoes	–	0	0	0	1
Oats	–	87	184	64	76
Sunflowers	–	940	2,110	1,990	3,530

Source: Chelintsev, Opyt izucheniia organizatsii, pp. 294, 296, 298.
Note the almost complete sale of sunflowers, the high marketing of oats, the high
marketing of rye and potatoes in certain circumstances.

families did need to grow more millet and potatoes. Statistics bear this
out: the sown area of these two crops was 28% higher in 1901–1910
than in 1883–1887. While in the first period they occupied 14.5% of
the sown area, in the second period they occupied 18.6%.[83]

The extension of consumption sowings left less room for cash crops.
At the same time, industrial and commercial growth at both the national and local levels after the turn of the twentieth century began
providing a greater variety of market opportunities than ever before.
While the smaller farms concentrated on consumption crops, the larger
farms retained the requisite flexibility to take advantage of these
opportunities. They rented land on their own, and grew large amounts
of oats or sunflowers for sale.

Up to this point in our discussion, the contrasts between larger and smaller farms with respect to sowing patterns are not complex, and they offer us no surprising insights as to the organization of peasant farming. Only when we consider sowing patterns in the light of fodder balances and marketing conditions does the story begin to take unexpected turns. With these angles in mind, let us now focus more closely on the mid-size and smaller farms.

Mid-Size Farms. The budget data clearly establish that the typical farms were harvesting and selling large amounts of grain. They were doing well enough not be concerned with the threat of starvation, and could afford to devote some of their spring-field sowings to valuable market-directed crops. Instead, they stuck to their traditional grain sowings[Table 3.10]:

Table 3.10. Destination of Mid-Sized Farms' Grain

	Center	South
Sizes of farm, in *desiatinas*	8–11.5	8–11.5
Grain harvested, per farm, in *puds*	461	394
% of harvest sold	20%	34%
% fed to animals	39%	35%
% reserved for sowing	12%	13%
% eaten	25%	32%
Grain sold, in *puds* (minus grain purchased, presumably)	92.2	135.5
Labor-intensive, marketable crops sown		
(potatoes, flax, and hemp)	6.1%	4.5%
Labor-extensive cash crop sowings (sunflowers)	0%	12.8%

Source: Chelintsev, *Opyt izucheniia organizatsii,* pp. 288, 292.

Several circumstances prevented these farms from growing more cash crops to take advantage of market opportunities. Firstly, the characteristics of the fodder crisis in the three-field system served to restrict sowings of crops that could not contribute to animal feed. Sunflowers, flax, hemp, and tobacco do not provide any straw for livestock, and *straw was at more of a premium than grain for the mid-sized farms.* Here we see how the animals' needs could exercise a strong degree of control over farmers' crop choices and flexibility in responding to the pressures and opportunities of markets. At the given level of grain and straw yields, and in the absence of high quality pasturelands, a large percentage of farms were hamstrung by the fodder crisis. They could not allot any more space to cash crops without becoming dependent on market transactions to provide money with which they could then buy fodder.

The fodder crisis did not tie the mid-sized farmer's hands completely, however. Some crops, like potatoes and beets, can function as fodder, human food, or cash crop. If the mid-sized farms' high ratio of grain to non-grain sowings was diseconomic, we must ask what was preventing them from planting more of these root crops. Because this question is even more pertinent to our analysis of the organizational flaws of the smaller farms, we shall treat it in the section, which now follows.

Small Farms. The smallest farms could only produce so much grain on their smaller allotments. Their grain surpluses above human consumption needs were very small, and they had no chance to produce adequate amounts of straw. Thus they had to buy more straw, selling a little grain and potatoes, and doing some non-agricultural work to generate cash. So they were in money trouble as well as fodder trouble. Additionally, as Table 3.11 shows, not having enough fodder, they were feeding animals as high or higher a percentage of the grain they grew

Table 3.11. Grain Production for Livestock

Location and size of farm, in *des.*	Grain harvested per farm, in *puds*	% fed to animals	Grain harvested per farm, in *puds*	% fed to animals	Grain harvested per farm, in *puds*	% fed to animals
	North		Center		South	
0–5	74	37	163	32	—	—
5–8	164	29	256	40	239	38
8–11.5	178	43	461	39	394	35
11.5–18	361	36	533	27	584	37
18+	—	—	1,684	26	931	30

Source: Chelintsev, *Opyt izucheniia organzatsii,* p. 292.

*I have intentionally simplified the "small farms" category in what follows. This category could easily be divided into two: those who had large livestock and the 19% of the province's households (as of 1912) who had neither a horse nor a cow. As has been pointed out before, the latter group had no immediate fodder requirements, and so might have very different priorities from the former. They might especially resent proposals for any field system entailing a reduction of the amount of land devoted to growing grain (*Sel'sko-khoziaistvennye i statisticheskie svedeniia, po materialam poluchennym ot khoziaev. Vyp. 12,* p. 38—citing correspondence from Tambov). At the same time, many of the farms without livestock surely wanted to re-acquire them. These people would be interested in increasing fodder resources. I will focus only on those small farms with aspirations to maintain or acquire at least one horse or cow.

than were the middle and larger farms (which did not mean that the smaller farms' animals were eating better, however).

The preponderance of consumption-directed grain sowings was, therefore, even more diseconomic for the smaller farms than for the mid-sized farms. Cash crops made perfect sense for the small farms. Of course, the more area they devoted to cash crops, the more food and feed they would need to purchase on the side. But, so long as they remained within the framework of the three-field system the small farms could not avoid taking this plunge into market relations. The mid-sized farms, on the other hand, could still hope to boost grain and straw yields through various technical improvements, which would alleviate their fodder crunch and expand their options to grow other crops for profit. If they made progress along such a path, then they would avoid becoming dependent for their survival on the vagaries of the market.

And so the mid-sized farms could avoid reorganizing their farms along the lines of a multi-field system. As we shall see subsequently, peasants had no understanding of multi-field systems. They were no more comfortable with the idea of reorganizing their system of farming than they were with becoming dependent on market relations. All multi-field systems entailed reducing the area sown to rye. Rye had always kept the family alive, and so they were naturally very reticent to reduce rye sowings, even if in so doing they could undertake various measures (such as early fallow tillage) that promised to boost yields by as much as the area sown to rye declined.

The smaller farms, on the other hand, could not realistically hope to reach a subsistence plateau within the three-field system. To recall our rough calculations in the section "The Fodder Crisis," farms holding less than about 10 *desiatinas* of land (all land, not just arable land) could not expect grain farming ever to produce enough fodder to support a horse, a cow, and some lighter stock. Consider a farm with 5 *desiatinas* of arable land. Unless they could double their grain yields, how could a family with this much land pay its taxes, feed itself, and feed its animals? They had to find off-farm employment, or take to sowing special fodder or cash crops. It is true that our presentation of the technological shortcomings of grain farming in Part I established that yield increases of 100% or more were well within the reach of peasant farmers. But the peasants themselves did not understand this. They were only dimly aware of the low quality of their own work, and were not prompted to search for ways to improve it. Even when they did become more aggressive in this regard, the single most effective step towards improving grain yields—timely tillage—was in large part blocked to them. As a rule communes would not allow anyone to till strips in the fallow field until such time as the herds had exhausted the grazing there.

Given the limitations of non-agricultural employment in Tambov, how were the smaller farms responding to their predicament? In essence, they had two options from which to choose—market gardening on their private plots, or the cultivation of root crops on the arable land. As we shall see, the economic conditions of the period did not encourage farmers to pursue either of these alternatives. At the same time, we shall also see that peasant farmers were not paying particularly close attention to economic circumstances.

Market Gardening

In isolated spots, peasants were doing very well with cash crops like onions, cabbages, raspberries, tobacco, etc. But across most of the province, *peasants did not even understand that these crops could bring in cash*.[84] Raspberries, for example, brought tremendous profits to one village in Lebedian *uezd* fully 60 *versts* away from the town of Elets.[85] 60 *versts* is a long way to transport raspberries. Literally dozens of villages could have participated in this market alone, but they did not.[86] Similarly, tobacco plots popped up in small groups of villages in Kozlov and Usman *uezds* during the last decades of the nineteenth century. The tobacco trade could bring in reasonably good income, as could fruits and vegetables. But interest did not quickly spread to other villages, despite the presence of buyers who traveled around the countryside purchasing eggs, poultry, and other secondary products.[87]

Perhaps peasants' general ignorance of the market opportunities for specialized cash crops should not surprise us, given the limited size and reach of these markets throughout Russia. The villages immediately surrounding provincial capital cities adapted themselves to meeting the obvious dietary demands of the non-agricultural population. They easily and cheaply supplied all of the milk, butter, eggs, and vegetables that the small urban population could consume, while the rest of the countryside focused on grains.[88] Urban demand for agricultural products was especially low in Tambov, where seven of the twelve *uezd* towns actually declined in size from 1863–1897.[89] In the overwhelming majority of villages no one could even foresee the circumstances in which any crops other than grains, sunflowers, or potatoes would generate substantial income. In any event, the peasantry of the Central Agricultural Region would remain remarkably unaware of the their opportunities on national and regional markets well into the 1920s.[90]

Root Crops

In these conditions, and within the confines of the three-field system and communal herd grazing on the arable land, the key to any successful reorganization of small peasant farming lay in potato and sugar beet cultivation. These crops demanded an awful lot of labor. They had to be hand planted—which obviously took much more effort than broadcast sowing of grain—they needed to be weeded two or three times during the growing season, and they had to be dug out of the earth at harvest time.

In return for all of the labor they demanded, potatoes and sugar beets could reward farmers of our period with much more income per unit of land than could grain crops. Table 3.6 (in the section "Subsistence Farming and Market Forces") illustrates this relationship, but also indicates that rye and oats were giving more of a return per day of labor expended than were potatoes. Thus families holding large amounts of land were quite correct in concentrating their attention on grain crops. With respect to the smaller farms, on the other hand, the work required for the cultivation of grain crops could never occupy all of the families' labor reserves. Root crops provided them with the opportunity to put idle hands to productive use.

As farm sizes shrank over the course of the late nineteenth century, Tambov peasants began to plant potatoes in increasing amounts. Maps 3.1 and 3.2 establish both the slow ascent of potato cultivation over time and the heightened popularity of this crop in the more land-hungry northern and northwestern uezds.[91] That peasants embraced the potato in response to need is indisputable. But why, we must ask, were potatoes so much more popular in the northern uezds than they were in the south? The sowing patterns shown in Tables 3.7 and 3.9 (in the section "Subsistence Farming and Market Forces") clearly indicate that the smaller and mid-sized farms in the central and southern uezds (and to a lesser extent, even in the north) were sowing less of their territory to potatoes than would appear to be economically desirable. How, then, are we to explain farmers' fidelity to oats and millet in the face of the obvious advantages of potatoes?

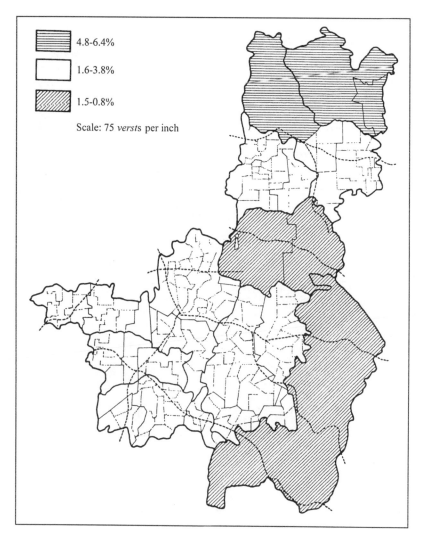

4.8-6.4%

1.6-3.8%

1.5-0.8%

Scale: 75 *versts* per inch

Map 3.1. Percent of Peasants' Sown Area Devoted to Potatoes, 1883–1887
(*Source*: Chelintsev, *Opyt izucheniia organizatsii krest'ianskogo khoziaistva*, p. 64)

In solving this riddle, we must begin by pointing out that potatoes were not only onerous for peasants to produce, but were also very expensive to transport and awkward to sell. Demand for potatoes within the province was quite limited. Processing plants (such as industrial and liquor-producing distilleries, or starch factories) were functioning in only about one *volost'* in eight on the eve of the World War, and the great majority of them were very small-volume opera-

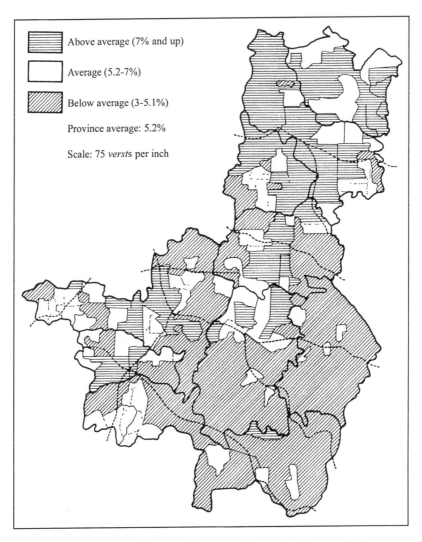

Map 3.2. Percent of Peasants' Sown Area Devoted to Potatoes, 1912
(*Source:* Chelintsev, *Opyt izucheniia organizatsii krest'ianskogo khoziaistva*, p. 61)

tions.[92] They did not have to look far to acquire all the potatoes they needed, and they got them very cheaply.[93] Since peasants and landlords in nearby villages provided the potatoes, most other villages had no accessible market for potatoes. Sugar beets were even less marketable, there being only a few sugar factories in operation during the whole period.

Theoretically, peasants could have used the railroads to get potatoes or sugar beets to the bigger cities of Russia. But, as we saw with our example of tobacco earlier, the market networks of the province were not yet arranged for this. No one was buying industrial volumes of potatoes at local rail stations.[94] Thus, until such time as dense industrial and commercial networks developed in Tambov, potatoes and beets could not serve as cash crops for the great majority of the peasantry. Of all the potatoes produced in Tambov in 1913, only 24% were sold to distilleries or exported out of the province. Even if we include deliveries to starch factories, perhaps no more than 31% of all of the potatoes were converted into cash, and about two-thirds of this was from non-peasant farms.[95] Peasants were converting no more than about 10–15% of their own potatoes into cash.

For Chelintsev the dearth of markets explained the retardation of potato sowings in Tambov. A decade later, another formidable agrarian scholar, G. A. Studenskii, essentially repeated Chelintsev's argument when confronted with the same retardation of potato sowings in neighboring Penza province during the 1920s.[96] Chelintsev's reasoning seems all the more sensible when we consider that the bulk of the potato processing enterprises were located in the northern *uezds*, where potato sowings had in fact risen to their highest levels in the province.[97]

But the idea that the scarcity of markets restricted the rate of adoption of potatoes is not convincing. Potatoes can serve not only as a cash crop, but also as food for man or animal. Why were farmers not growing more potatoes with the aim of alleviating their fodder problems? A concrete example should clarify this question.

Consider the hypothetical case of a family in the middle of Usman *uezd* (a nondescript area, with black-earth soil, not close to marketing points—very representative of most of the southern half of the province). This family is sowing four *desiatinas* of land each year, two in the winter section, and two in the spring section. If they typically divide their spring section sowings between millet and oats, this gives them approximately one *desiatina* of each of these crops in each year. About 50% of the oats will be converted into cash, the rest saved for the horse.

What was to prevent this family from replacing all or most of their millet sowings with potatoes? The average yield of millet in this area was 59.6 *puds* per *desiatina*—or 57.6 *puds*, subtracting two *puds* for seed. To this we must add the straw, at an average of 49 *puds* per *desiatina*. Potatoes were much more productive in comparison. The average potato yield on peasant lands in the center of Usman *uezd* was 403 *puds* per *desiatina*, excluding the seed requirement. Setting aside 250 *puds* to compensate family members' diets for the loss of millet grain (and this is a very generous conversion rate for millet), the farm would be left with 153 *puds* of potato for fodder. By weight, potatoes have roughly the same fodder value as millet straw, so this works out to a surplus of over 100 *puds* of potatoes![98] Of course this might be too many potatoes. In light of the difficulty of storing or selling potatoes, the surplus might go entirely to waste. All of the extra labor expended to raise the potatoes would be lost. But all this indicates is that the family ought to sow 2/3 or so of a *desiatina* with potatoes, and reserve the final 1/3 for more oats, which can always be stored, sold, or fed to the horse.

In some cases extenuating circumstances prevented farms from planting more potatoes. In the northern *uezds* of the province the budget study revealed that the smaller farms usually diverted a lot of labor to off-farm work, even during the spring and summer months.[99] If one or two of the men in the family were occupied in non-agricultural trades, then the remaining members might be unable to cope with the extra labor requirements of potato cultivation. Conversely, when families found profitable market access for potatoes and hoped to sow an ever increasing area to them, the commune's enforcement of the three-field system stopped them from extending potato sowings at the expense of fallow land. But for the most part there was no objective reason for the small and medium-sized farms to be sowing so much millet and so little potatoes. Potatoes were more productive than millet, and their yields were more reliable.

Knowing that peasants were growing potatoes in response to need, we can nevertheless concede that some lag in the extension of potato sowings made sense. It was natural for middle-sized farms to look for ways to increase grain yields rather than grow potatoes. Doing *dvoenie* or an extra harrowing was a lot less arduous than cultivating potatoes. They probably did not want to eat a lot of potatoes either, and no one wanted to over-produce potatoes and be stuck with a useless, rotting surplus.

But once peasants ran out of ways to boost grain yields, the potato deserved their full attention. To say that the budget study revealed sowing patterns that were sub-optimal in this regard would be putting it lightly. That peasants' acceptance of the need to grow more potatoes tended to lag so long deserves criticism.

All too often, peasant farmers were not thinking their organizational problems through. This attitude cannot be explained away as just another of the inevitable growing pains the peasantry had to experience in making the transition from subsistence to market-oriented farming.

The routinization of attitudes to methods of labor we observed in Parts I and II affected farm organization as well. As the government and *zemstvo* agronomists would quickly find out, the dissemination of agronomic science and the promotion of an agricultural revolution among such farmers would be a long and difficult struggle.

Multi-Field vs. Three-Field Systems

With ever-increasing numbers of peasant farms slipping into economic difficulties in the decades leading up to the First World War, most agronomists, administrators, and other educated observers of the economy in predominantly agricultural regions like Tambov were very concerned about the possibility of famines and social disorders. The conjunction of poor harvests in 1905 and 1906 (in 1906 peasants' oats and rye yields *averaged* only 14.9 and 23.5 *puds* per *desiatina*, respectively)[100] with the rebellions of those tumultuous years only exacerbated this concern. Once the government established that under no circumstances would there be any expropriation of privately-owned lands in favor of the peasantry—no "second emancipation"—only one alternative seemed to remain. The rate at which the productivity (per unit area) of peasant agriculture was increasing would have to accelerate through the implementation of multi-field systems. This conclusion fueled much of the enthusiasm for the Stolypin reform: surely, went the common logic, if the communal restraints on peasant farmers' individual initiative were lifted, then more intensive systems of farming would flourish.

The multi-field system that gained great and lasting popularity in circles endeavoring to reorganize peasant agriculture in the black-earth zone was the four-field *propashnaia* system, described at the outset of Part III. Despite the many recommendations of this system, it would not prove to be widely applicable in practice. In investigating the reasons for this we will clarify many of the technical obstacles and social divisions standing in the way of a reorganization of peasant agriculture along more intensive lines.

Weaknesses of the *Propashnaia* System

The primary theoretical attraction of the *propashnaia* system, the 25% of the sown area devoted to inter-tillage crops, often functioned as the primary drawback of the system in farmers' eyes. Few of the medium- or large-sized farms had the labor power required to care for so much land sown with labor-intensive crops like potatoes or beets. We have already seen how the larger farms could not easily cope even with stall feeding of their livestock during the summer months. The *propashnaia* system entailed not only stall feeding, but also an increase of the sown portion of the arable land to 75% (as opposed to 66% under the three-field system), and the devotion of 25% of the arable land to labor-intensive crops![101]

In practice, families unable to cope with the work load involved in growing potatoes on a large area tried sowing less labor-intensive crops in the inter-tillage section of the *propashnaia*.[102] But this was rarely an effective solution to their difficulties. If, for example, they sowed millet or oats, then they were effectively retreating to a four-field grain-fallow system, which both put excessive strain on the soil (three successive crops before fallow in place of the two crops in the three-field system) and entailed sowing spring grain crops two years in a row (spring grains do very poorly if sown in succession). They could try sowing more sunflowers in the inter-tillage section of the *propashnaia*, but only if they were in range of a marketing point for sunflower seeds. Moreover, spring grains do poorly if they come right after sunflowers in the crop rotation, and sunflowers provide no fodder. Few farms really wanted or needed to sow a large area to sunflowers.

Above and beyond the *propashnaia* system's prodigious labor require-ments, farmers employing this system were almost certain to face difficulties in disposing of their production. The fodder crisis was very serious in Tambov, as we have seen. But extending the sown area to 75% of the arable land and growing high-yielding crops on 25% of the land would generate far more fodder than most *dvors* needed. If a distillery, starch factory, sunflower oil-processing plant, sugar factory, or some other such processing enterprise were located nearby, then farmers could simply and profitably market the excess production. Likewise, those living in the immediate vicinity of towns could convert the extra fodder into increased cow or pig holdings for sale to the non-agricultural population. But the large majority of Tambov's villages were not so favorably located. As we have already seen in our treatment of the geography of the province's grain markets at the turn of the century, relatively few villages had markets or railheads nearby. The network of enterprises processing agricultural products remained very sparse and weak throughout our period.

The *propashnaia* system's emphasis on labor-intensive crops would also be troublesome for the many communes with arable lands situated more than a few miles away from the village. We have already noted how farmers quite naturally preferred to concentrate their sowings of the more labor-intensive crops on those lands located closest to the village. But this was not possible in the *propashnaia*, where the inter-tillage crops had to rotate through all of the arable lands once every four years. Thorough statistics on the distance of Tambov villages from their arable lands do not exist, but information from the budget study of 1914 throws some light on this subject. The average distance from the center of villages to their most distant lands was 3.6 *versts* in the northern *uezds*, 5.5 in the center, and 5.7 in the south.[103] Raising intensive crops became prohibitively inconvenient at a distance of roughly three *versts*.[104] How many families could do all of the requisite work and cart home the harvest if they sowed inter-tillage crops on their farthest-off land?

Further difficulties arose from the reduction of the area of land sown to rye in the *propashnaia* system. Rye was the peasant's staple crop, which kept him fed, covered his roof, provided bedding for the animals, and brought in some cash in good harvest years. It served many functions in the peasant economy, and its yields were also the most stable of all crops in this climatic zone. Peasants in central black-earth Russia—and elsewhere—were always very leery about reducing rye sowings, and rightly so. Additionally, in the ever-extending areas suffering from deforestation, rye straw had become an essential source of heat for the peasants. In the absence of other sources of heat a larger than average sized peasant hut could require up to 5 *desiatinas* worth of rye straw per winter.[105] One astute agronomist pointed out that peasants in forest-deficient areas were rejecting the *propashnaia* system first and foremost because of their need for rye straw (as a heat source, for roofing, for stall bedding, etc.).[106]

The contraction of summer fodder sources in the *propashnaia* was another cause for concern. In a standard three-field system all of the arable land is available for herd grazing at some point during the year, either as green fallow or crop stubble. But in a *propashnaia* system 25% of the arable land, the potatoes, sunflowers, or beets of the inter-tillage section, cannot provide any grazeable stubble. The system obviously presumes a lot more stall feeding than most peasants were used to, especially if the commune wished to preserve soil moisture by earlier tillage of the fallow field.

Thus the *propashnaia* system met peasants' needs only in certain circumstances. The system made sense where a lot of labor per unit of arable land was available, where a market or processing enterprise was nearby, where a substantial area of supplemental grazing land (either pastures or the local landlord's arable land) was accessible, and where all of the arable land was reasonably close to the village. In other circumstances, it would not be warmly welcomed, especially by the larger farms.

Before the Revolution as well as in the Soviet period, agronomists and administrators voiced concern over the possibility that the larger, wealthier farms would obstruct communal adoptions of multi-field systems out of a selfish desire to keep their neighbors in a weakened, easily exploitable state.[107] Peasants themselves often shared this concern, as evidenced by an indignant protest from a large group of peasants from a village in Kozlov *uezd* concerning an intra-communal conflict over the transition to a four-field *propashnaia* system. When some of the larger farms found a pretext to block the transition, other peasants complained to the authorities that "our transition to a *propashnaia* system has been wiped out by *a clique of rich people*, to whom such a transition is unwelcome."[108]

But this analysis is one-sided, if not erroneous. The present discussion has underscored the agrotechnical basis for the larger farms' desire to remain within the three-field grain system. They generally did not stand to gain from labor-intensification of farming, and they understood this with perfect clarity. If they actively discouraged their neighbors from seeking to install a *propashnaia* system, they had much more than exploitation on their minds. The larger farms were working at or near full labor capacity during the peak times of the growing season—spring tillage and sowing in April–May, fallow tillage, weeding, and hay making in June, harvesting and fall sowing in July–August, and carting and threshing in September. If we divide the six-month period April–September into twelve two-week stanzas, and we include all agricultural and non-agricultural labor actually performed, we see that the larger farms were working under a much greater strain than were the smaller farms [Table 3.12]: The numbers in bold face indicate the

Table 3.12. Amount of Time at Full Labor Capacity, Large Farms vs. Small Farms
(the figures indicate the number of two-week periods
from April through September during which all labor was used)

	Male labor			Female labor		
	North	Center	South	North	Center	South
Small farms	6.8	**1.7**	3.8	2.0	3.3	1.0
Large farms	6.5	4.0	5.2	4.8	2.6	1.5

Source: Chelintsev, Opyt izucheniia organzatsii, p. 269.

farms with the most excess labor, while the rest indicate the farms working under the heaviest load.*

The labor strain shouldered by the larger farms forced them to resort to the hiring of labor at key moments during the year. They did not want to do this, since hired hands had to be paid in some fashion, and they had to be supervised. But there was no avoiding it. On the largest farms, hired hands were performing anywhere from 9–16% of the agricultural work throughout the year.[109] The men of the larger farms were simply too busy to leave any time for caring for the animals, which were left in the hands of the women and children.[110] In these circumstances the large farms—and a good portion of the medium-sized farms as well—stood to lose a great deal from any curtailment of common grazing. They did not have the time to gather, transport, store, and serve fodder to their animals. The more time the animals could spend in the village herd under the supervision of a hired shepherd, looking for food on their own, the better it would be for the larger farms. Thus these farms would oppose not only the propashnaia, but any system that impinged on common grazing.

At this point we might well ask what would prevent the larger farms from adjusting to the abolition of common grazing, with more hiring of labor. These farms were the wealthiest, so it would seem that they could easily find the means to hire some more help. Furthermore, if grain and other crop yields stood to rise in multi-field systems thanks to more timely tillage and superior crop rotation, those holding the most land would seem to profit most of all.

---

*Lest Table 3.12 appear misleading, we should note here that the labor intensity of the farms in the northern uezds was not so much higher than the figures here imply. The larger farms in the center and south had much more territory sown to grain, which entailed a huge expenditure of labor at a few key moments. And non-agricultural employment opportunities were greater in the north.

But the situation was not so simple. The significant labor intensification concomitant to multi-field systems would drive up both the required amount and the cost of hired labor. Consider the position of a farmer with a relatively big farm, say 15 *desiatinas* or so. Think how much extra work he would have to do in a more labor-intensive system. How would he get it done? Once the neighbors have their own work to do, whom would he be able to hire, and at what price?[111] In the end he might make some more money on the year, if he could find someplace to sell his surplus of potatoes. But why would he wish to go through all of this? He was not living so poorly with the three-field system. He did not need a lot more headaches and an awful lot more work for some uncertain profits. Thus the larger farms, and a substantial portion of the medium-sized farms as well, had no reason to leave the three-field system at least until such time as market opportunities for root crops, meat, or dairy products appeared nearby their villages.[112]

Unfortunately, neither administrators nor agronomists were quick to realize the shortcomings of the *propashnaia* system. By the mid-1920s the GZU (*Gubernskoe Zemel'noe Upravlenie*—Provincial Department of Land Administration—a Soviet governmental institution responsible for all matters concerning land and agriculture) of Voronezh province recognized the system's drawbacks and ceased propagandizing it.[113] But the reputation established for the system before the Revolution was so strong that it continued to influence the education of young agronomists throughout the 1920s. The records of Tambov agronomic conferences show that many agronomists continued to support the *propashnaia* all the way up to collectivization.[114]

Employed Fallow
and Improved Three-Field-Based Systems

Quite independently from the *propashnaia* system, a family of alternative systems arose from attempts to improve the three-field system by sowing fodder crops on the fallow field, a technique called "employed fallow" (*zaniatyi par* or *zaniatoi par* is the Russian term).* The idea was to sow a fast-maturing grass like vetch on the fallow land as early as

---

*Of course any time crops are sown on a unit of land it is inaccurate to call such land fallow. But in discussions among farmers or agronomists the term "employed fallow" helped to clarify the unit of land in question (an employed fallow crop was on the fallow section of the arable land, and nowhere else) and never caused any confusion.

possible in the spring, then cut it down for hay in June.[115] This left
enough time to till the field and to do *dvoenie* before sowing the rye at
the usual time, in early August. The soil would suffer no more from this
treatment than it did from green fallow, and in a typical year the farmer
would accumulate an extra 100–200 *puds* of high quality hay per
desiatina of employed fallow.[116]

The major drawback to employed fallow was the loss of grazing space
for the herds in the period April–June, which was a critical period for
most peasant livestock. Because the roving herds would devour any
unprotected grass growing on strips in the fallow section, no one could
even experiment with the technique until a majority of the commune
acceded to the exclusion of a specified portion of their fallow section
from the grazing regime. Many agronomists were quick to recommend,
communes set aside a portion of their fallow section each year for
employed fallow. After all, they might as well produce some hay or till
their fallow early if they did not need all of it to be grazing land. Furthermore, those communes planting a substantial amount of potatoes
in a contiguous portion of the spring section nearest the village had
nothing to lose from establishing employed fallow on these locations,
since green fallow was so barren after potatoes.[117]

Considering the meager pickings available to herds grazing on green
fallow, it might seem logical for peasants to try employed fallow for
grazing purposes, not for the production of hay. Experimental stations
would eventually recommend such a strategy, pointing out that sown
grasses could generate four or more times as much fodder as green
fallow.[118] This was a bright alternative, but it was not as simple to effect
as it appears at first glance. Firstly, none of the available sown grasses
could mature to a grazeable condition until the start of May, and the
most popular choice of all, vetch, took a month longer than that.[119]
Thus stall feeding could not be avoided until the grasses were ready.
Secondly, how would herds behave once set loose onto rich fields of
sown grasses? They would of course swarm all over the field, trampling
and spoiling much of their own luxury meal. And if the grass was
primarily clover or alfalfa, they would also run a good risk of dying from
bloating.[120] In England and Scotland these considerations prompted
farmers to "fold" livestock across rich grass fields in pens that allowed
them access to a very limited space at any one time, but few if any
Russian peasants were aware of that technique.

Naturally the introduction of employed fallow—or any other measure requiring communal consent—would be more difficult in the large
villages so commonly found in Tambov and elsewhere in central and

southern Russia. As we shall see in our treatment of land reorganization and the Stolypin reforms, both the sheer numbers of households involved and their greater economic disparities in the larger villages made concerted action more difficult to achieve there. But at this point it is appropriate to note that large villages often contained more than one commune. Other historians have emphasized the presence of "split" communes, where the members of two or more communes resided in one large village.[121] 18.5% of the villages in the nearby provinces of Voronezh, Orel, and Kursk (combined) housed more than one commune. The figure for the one province most similar to Tambov, Voronezh, was 6.9%.[122] Estimating roughly, up to 12% of Tambov's communes might have been of the "split" variety.

Additionally—and this is a point that historians have not yet emphasized—large *communes* often allowed sub-sections (called *povytki*, in southern Tambov) to handle purely agricultural matters.[123] A village of 800 *dvors* could be broken down into 8–10 *povytki*, for example, each *povytka* composed of families whose strips of arable land formed coherent units in the fields. Since the *povytka* would periodically conduct its own agricultural meetings (*sotennye skhody*) to organize its grazing regime (the grazing of its members' animals on their own lands) or decide other farming questions, it could arrange to try employed fallow, for example, independently of the rest of the commune. Unfortunately, data concerning *povytki* do not exist, since in such cases the commune, not the *povytka*, remained the legal entity. They might not have been very common. But, at least for a substantial minority of the largest villages, reform of the communally controlled elements of the agricultural system was not as difficult as it might have been without "split" communes and *povytki....*

The combination of the slow but inexorable trend among peasants towards more stall feeding of animals in the spring, the rising fodder crisis, and the agronomic community's justifiable hostility towards green fallow made employed fallow extremely attractive to agronomists concerned with raising the productivity of peasant agriculture. Many of them would enthusiastically push it on peasants. As Part V will show, they got some response. While employed fallow made sense as an improvement within the confines of the three-field system, it also recommended itself as a step towards multi-field systems. Quite a few closely related systems could evolve from a three-field system with employed fallow, the most important of which we will now examine.

Before doing so, however, it bears noting that these new systems or arrangements do not fit neatly into the evolutionary scheme of systems of farming we presented above. They can be interpreted as improvements within the confines of the grain-fallow system, or they can be construed as forms of balanced farming. But their theoretical classification is not important to us in the present context. The point is that these proposed arrangements could increase productivity per unit area, regardless of what category of system of farming they should be attached to.

1) *Voronezh Six-Field System.* First promoted by Boris Bruk, the director of the Voronezh agricultural experimental station, this system was certainly the simplest multi-field system for peasant communes to implement. It required dividing the fallow section into two parts, so as to set up two parallel three-field systems. A certain amount of fallow land located nearby the village would be sown with fodder grass, as employed fallow, while the remainder of the fallow would remain as green fallow. In the two subsequent years, equivalent amounts of the sections of land slated for use as fallow would be sown with fodder grass, thereby establishing an "infield-outfield" three-field system, in which the infield rotation would be: employed fallow–rye–spring crop (ideally a labor-intensive, high-yielding crop suitable for the arable lands nearest to the village, like potatoes). The outfield rotation would remain: green fallow–rye–spring grain.

Strictly speaking, this simple system is not a six-field system, since the six sections are not necessarily equal in size, and the infield and outfield crop rotations do not cycle through each other's lands. The system is actually a double three-field system. But the arrangement is extremely flexible in allowing for the gradual extension of the infield as the commune grows accustomed to employed fallow and stall feeding on the one hand, and wishes to grow more labor-intensive crops on the other hand. As an additional convenience, the infield area would also tend to include the manured lands. Given the natural evolution of stall feeding, potato growing, and manuring in central Russia as peasant population density continued to rise, the Voronezh Six-Field was an ingenious plan.

2) *Advanced Six-Field System.* If a the majority of farms in a village could completely forego arable land grazing from April to July—either because the village had a large amount of pasture lands or because families felt ready to commit themselves even more fully to stall feeding—then the Voronezh Six-Field system could easily evolve into a true six-field system with two fields of employed fallow: employed fallow–rye–spring grain–employed fallow–rye–inter-tillage crop (pota-

toes, beets, sunflowers, e.g.). Here we have six fields, both fallows are employed, one spring field has inter-tillage crops. Such a system would retain most of the advantages of the Voronezh Six-Field system versus the *propashnaia*, albeit at a slightly higher cost in labor, because of the reduction of grazing lands. Indeed, in this system the grazeable portion of the arable land is reduced to only 50%!

3) *An Improved Three-Field System with Early Fallow.* While employed fallow would not bring rye yields down below levels achieved after green fallow, it would not raise them either. Unlike early fallow, employed fallow did not preserve soil moisture so as to protect the rye crop against drought. Thus rye yields after employed fallow would always remain both lower and more susceptible to fluctuations than after early fallow. And so agronomists tried to devise improved three- or six-field systems that would include early fallow. Since early fallow produced no fodder of any kind, it did not make sense for many villages to substitute early fallow for employed fallow in the Voronezh Six-Field system outlined above. A bit of the employed fallow might be sacrificed for early fallow, but this would not be enough early fallow to provide much protection against drought. The Tambov agronomist E. A. Rolofs eventually developed a better plan.

Rolofs proposed to introduce early fallow on about two-thirds of the fallow section of the three-field system. The other one-third of the fallow would remain green fallow, but to treble its fodder value this land would be sown with grass in the preceding year. On the one hand, this arrangement would reduce spring grain sowings by the one-third of the spring section which would be sown with grass. On the other hand, the farm would harvest a greater than compensatory amount of rye in typical conditions, thanks to the influence of early fallow. The grain harvest would also be more stable, and the one-third of the spring section devoted to grass would dramatically reinforce hay reserves.

4) *A Six-Field System with both Employed and Early Fallow.* Finally, communes that became acquainted with both employed and early fallow could include them both in a simple six-field system. All this required was to divide the fallow field into two parts each year, one part being tilled in April (early fallow), and the other part being employed fallow. According to plan, the units of land under early fallow in one year would be employed fallow the next time they would fall in the

---

*Like the Voronezh Six-Field detailed above, this system was also identified in some of the agronomic literature as the "Voronezh Six-Field system". The two systems are very similar, and Voronezh agronomists did much to popularize both of them, so the confusion was natural.

fallow section of the rotation (three years later). Correspondingly, the lands sown with fodder grass would be early fallow three years later. In this system the winter and spring sections remained unchanged from the traditional three-field. Like the "Advanced Six-Field system" discussed above, this system would do away with arable land grazing before July. But those communes capable of introducing it would reap the rewards of both employed and early fallow.

5) *A Combination of Employed Fallow and the Propashnaia System.* Finally, one six-field system managed to combine the *propashnaia* system and employed fallow into a single crop rotation: employed fallow–winter grain–employed fallow–winter grain–inter-tillage crop–spring grain.[124] The elimination of spring-time grazing and the reduction of spring-grain straw were obvious drawbacks to this system. But it seemed to offer an attractive alternative to a total commitment to the *propashnaia* system.

Conclusion

In contrast to the four-field systems, a wonderful feature of the family of systems related to employed fallow was the gradual pace at which they could be introduced. Labor intensification could be altered without any land redistribution at all, simply by exchanging one such system for another. Under no circumstances could a single system ever appeal to all members of even a medium-sized commune, since families' labor, livestock, and land holdings varied over a wide range. But as long as the commune could easily modify its field system, the peasants would be able to adjust to fluctuations in population density, the appearance of a processing enterprise, or the construction of a new railroad station.

Thus there were many ways for peasant communes to intensify production per unit area without diving into the complications of a four-field *propashnaia* system. Employed fallow was a very flexible first step towards multi-field farming, and, as we shall see in our treatment of the agronomic aid effort in practice, the local agronomists did encourage peasants to adopt it. But, until the 1920s, agronomists themselves only faintly foresaw the various systems into which employed fallow could develop. Scholarship, experimentation, and propaganda regarding these systems were virtually non-existent before the First World War. When agronomists before the 1920s recommended employed fallow they rarely had anything more in mind than a stop-gap improvement of the three-field system, until such time as the farmers could manage to arrange a *propashnaia* system.

Certainly the tardiness of the agronomic community in investigating multi-field systems that could arise out of employed fallow stemmed from the sub-optimal grass yields that such systems could provide. It was well known by this time that grasses gave much better results when they were allowed to grow on a piece of land for several years in succession.* Employed fallow and any multi-field systems that might

---

*For an agronomic explanation of this, see the discussion below.

arise on its basis assigned grasses only a single season before they were plowed up, and did not allow for a second growth of the grass later in the year, since the field had to be tilled in preparation for the rye sowing. Thus, when agronomists did sense the imperfection of the *propashnaia* system in not providing fodder, they did not instinctively look for solutions involving employed fallow. Instead, they sought to increase the applicability of the *propashnaia* by attaching multi-year grass sowings to it. To these and other experiments with multi-year grasses in multi-field systems we now turn.

Systems with Multi-Year Grasses

The sowing of fodder grasses on arable land was one of the key features of the agricultural revolution in Europe in the eighteenth and nineteenth centuries. Grasses not only provided large yields of high quality fodder. Many of them also enriched the soil by accumulating reserves of nitrogen from the air and storing them in their roots, where they acted as fertilizer for subsequent crops. Nitrogen accumulation was what primarily attracted agronomists and farmers to grass sowings in most of Europe and the northern half of Russia, where arable lands tended to be short of nitrogen. In the black-earth zone, however, most lands were not nitrogen-deficient, even well into the 1920s.[125] Here grasses could perform other important functions. Their dense growth choked out weeds, and, when allowed to grow and develop for several years, grass roots helped to rejuvenate the structure of soils turning dust-like from over-tillage. Grass roots also go deep into the soil, pulling up phosphate and potassium from depths, which grain roots cannot reach.[126] Moreover, most grasses gave their best yields not in their first season on a plot of land, but in the subsequent two to four years. If esparcet would give about 200 *puds* per *desiatina* when sown on employed fallow, it could give over 370 *puds* when grown to maturity on a separate plot and cut down twice per year. Clover and alfalfa yields rose in similar fashion.[127] These circumstances explain the preferability of multi-year grass sowings to grasses sown for only a single season.

Unfortunately, since employment of multi-year grasses had to allow for the grass's remaining on one spot for periods of anywhere from four to six years, multi-field systems that included such grasses were difficult to organize in conditions of peasant farming. Assume, for instance, that 20% of the arable land will be devoted to multi-year grasses every year.

If the grass has a maturation period of five years, then the crop rotation would extend to twenty-five years in length. Peasants could easily get confused in trying to run such a long rotation, as experience with shorter rotations in the northern half of Russia had already shown.[128] Moreover, multi-year grasses could provide such good yields that most farmers would not want to assign so much of their arable land to them. They simply would not need so much winter fodder. If, however, they reduced the area sown to multi-field grasses, then the crop rotation would become even longer. Additionally, the longer became the period between which grasses were not sown on any particular piece of land, the less effective would be the grasses' ameliorative affect on soil structure.

Thanks to the moister climate in the northern half of Russia, the introduction of fodder grasses and the rise of balanced farming systems could skirt some of these obstacles and proceed more easily there than in the southern half. Clover grass, the best known of all of the fodder grasses involved in the European agricultural revolution of the eighteenth and nineteenth centuries, could accomplish all of the agronomic tasks demanded of a multi-year grass crop within the space of three or even two years. This allowed for shorter, more streamlined, versions of balanced farming than could be devised with slower-developing grasses. Such systems acquired popularity in the Baltic provinces of the Russian Empire as early as the first half of the nineteenth century, and slowly gained ground among Russian peasants from the 1880s on, reaching the northern *uezds* of Tambov in the 1920s.

But clover does not cope well in dry or drought-prone regions like the black-earth zone.[129] If well manured, it could serve on employed fallow (see discussion above). But it was not so attractive as a multi-year crop. In black-earth Russia the most famous multi-field systems, like the "Norfolk system", or the "Iaroslavl Four-Field system" could not apply. Since an administrative reform assigned Tambov's northern *uezds* to other provinces early in 1923, the present study will not treat the history or the nuances of the many multi-field systems developed for climatic conditions north of Morshansk *uezd*. Indeed, no attempt will be made to cover all of the proposals or attempts relevant to the remaining three-fourths of the province. Instead, we shall focus on what we shall call "the Four-Field + Grass system", which, for all practical purposes, was the only multi-field system with multi-year grasses to be propagandized and to appear on peasant farms in the area.

Four-Field + Grass System

This system was the natural answer to some of the major shortcomings of the *propashnaia* system. It entailed dividing the arable land into five even parts, running a four-field *propashnaia* system on four of the fields while leaving the fifth field free for multi-year grass sowings. This fifth field would be effectively withdrawn from the rotation for as long as the grass grew well on it. Then it would be plowed up, and one of the other four fields would be sown with grass and removed from the rotation.

Obviously the insertion of sown grasses in this system bolstered fodder production versus the pure *propashnaia* system. And the reduction of the area devoted to inter-tillage crops from 25% to 20% of the arable land would likewise be a welcome adjustment to many farms. At the same time, the retention of the *propashnaia* system on 80% of the arable land meant that most of the drawbacks to that system remained unresolved.

Moreover, the Four-Field + Grass system added a few problems of its own to those of the *propashnaia* system. Firstly, it reduced the area sown to rye even more than its parent system did—down to only 20% of the arable land. Secondly, the system could not provide optimal results unless the grass section was retained for a period of exactly five years. As we saw above, multi-year grasses tend to give increasingly good yields for a few years before tapering off, at which time farmers instinctively seek to replace them with another crop. An inter-tillage crop should precede the grass, and a spring grain should follow it.[130] But if the grass were plowed up after four or six years, then the alignment of the fields would fall temporarily out of whack and the system would demand band-aiding. Finally, grass yields would be very uneven in this or any other system that included multi-year grasses. In its first and last years on any particular plot of land the grasses would give far less hay than in their best years. Coping efficiently with such fluctuations would not be easy for farmers who had never kept accounts.[131]

In practice, the Four-Field + Grass system would prove to be more widely applicable than the *propashnaia*, since it did not emphasize inter-tillage crops so heavily. But it was not as well suited to peasant agriculture as the improved three- and six-field systems discussed above. Nor were any of the many other multi-field systems with which various agronomists and landlords were experimenting in the first decades of the twentieth century. Up to the eve of collectivization of agriculture in 1929, Tambov peasant farms never flirted with any multi-field system other than those in the present discussion.

Before concluding our comparisons of the multi-field systems that would be available to peasant farmers in our period, we must consider the consequences of two systems coexisting in a single commune. As we saw earlier, the large gap in labor intensity and marketing requirements between the three-field on the one hand and the *propashnaia* or Four-Field + Grass systems on the other hand could discourage peasants from making the transition from the former to the latter. But the gap between systems could be decreased if communes combined two field systems. The four-field system could occupy the nearer lands, with the three-field remaining in place on lands further away.

Both before and after the revolution agronomists would occasionally propose combining two systems (Voronezh's Boris Bruk being the most prominent example in the central black-earth region),[132] but few if any villages ever experimented with this. The problem was not that communes were incapable of running two separate field systems on their lands. Cases of infield-outfield arrangements were not uncommon in areas with a lot of land per capita.[133] But these cases always involved a grain-fallow system (such as the three-field system) on the infield and a less structured, or even totally unregulated, system on the outfield.[134] Communes capable of running separate infield-outfield systems of that variety were not necessarily willing or capable of organizing a four-field system at all, let alone in conjunction with a three-field system. Apart from the complexity of administering a pair of systems, the redistribution of land strips required to set them up would be especially tricky. And once the two systems were in place any desired extension of the four-field in response to population or other pressures would create a tremendous land redistribution chore. Thus it should come as no surprise that few agronomists embraced the idea of partial introductions of the *propashnaia* or Four-Field + Grass systems with any enthusiasm [Tables 3.13–3.20].

Table 3.13. The Three-Field System

Year / Fields	#1	#2	#3
1	Green fallow	Winter grain	Spring grain
2	Winter grain	Spring grain	Green fallow
3	Spring grain	Green fallow	Winter grain

Table 3.14. Propashnaia System

Year / Fields	#1	#2	#3	#4
1	Green fallow*	Winter grain	Inter-tillage crop	Spring grain
2	Winter grain	Inter-tillage crop	Spring grain	Green fallow*
3	Inter-tillage crop	Spring grain	Green fallow*	Winter grain
4	Spring grain	Green fallow*	Winter grain	Inter-tillage crop

*Early or employed fallows can also be tried.

Table 3.15. Voronezh Six-Field System

Year / Fields	Fields nearest to the village		
	A	B	C
1	Employed fallow	Winter grain	Spring grain
2	Winter grain	Spring grain	Employed fallow
3	Spring grain	Employed fallow	Winter grain

Year / Fields	Fields farther away		
	A	B	C
1	Green fallow	Winter grain	Potatoes
2	Winter grain	Potatoes	Green fallow
3	Potatoes	Green fallow	Winter grain

Table 3.16. Advanced Six-Field System

Year/ Fields	# 1	# 2	#3
1	Employed fallow	Winter grain	Spring grain
2	Winter grain	Spring grain	Employed fallow
3	Spring grain	Employed fallow	Winter grain
4	Employed fallow	Winter grain	Inter-tillage crop
5	Winter grain	Inter-tillage crop	Employed fallow
6	Inter-tillage crop	Employed fallow	Winter grain

Year/ Fields	# 4	#5	# 6
1	Employed fallow	Winter grain	Inter-tillage crop
2	Winter grain	Inter-tillage crop	Employed fallow
3	Inter-tillage crop	Employed fallow	Winter grain
4	Employed fallow	Winter grain	Spring grain
5	Winter grain	Spring grain	Employed fallow
6	Spring grain	Employed fallow	Winter grain

Table 3.17. Improved Three-Field System

Year/Fields	#1	#2	#3
1	Early fallow Green fallow	Winter grain	Spring grain Sown Grass
2	Winter grain	Spring grain Sown grass	Early fallow Green Fallow
3	Spring grain Sown grass	Early fallow Green fallow	Winter grain

Table 3.18. Six-Field System with Employed and Early Fallow

Year/ Fields	# 1	# 2	# 3
1	Employed fallow	Winter grain	Spring grain*
2	Winter grain	Spring grain*	Early fallow
3	Spring grain*	Early fallow	Winter grain
4	Early fallow	Winter grain	Spring grain
5	Winter grain	Spring grain	Employed fallow
6	Spring grain	Employed fallow	Winter grain
Year/ Fields	**# 4**	**# 5**	**# 6**
1	Early fallow	Winter grain	Spring grain
2	Winter grain	Spring grain	Employed fallow
3	Spring grain	Employed fallow	Winter Grain
4	Employed fallow	Winter grain	Spring grain*
5	Winter grain	Spring grain*	Early fallow
6	Spring grain*	Early fallow	Winter grain

*An inter-tillage crop could also be tried at this point in the rotation.

Table 3.19. Combined Employed Fallow and *Propashnaia* System

Year/ Fields	# 1	# 2	# 3
1	Employed fallow	Winter grain	Employed fallow
2	Winter grain	Employed fallow	Winter grain
3	Employed fallow	Winter grain	Inter-tillage crop
4	Winter grain	Inter-tillage crop	Spring grain
5	Inter-tillage crop	Spring grain	Employed fallow
6	Spring grain	Employed fallow	Winter grain
Year/ Fields	**# 4**	**# 5**	**# 6**
1	Winter grain	Inter-tillage crop	Spring grain
2	Inter-tillage crop	Spring grain	Employed fallow
3	Spring grain	Employed fallow	Winter grain
4	Employed fallow	Winter grain	Employed fallow
5	Winter grain	Employed fallow	Winter grain
6	Employed fallow	Winter grain	Inter-tillage crop

Table 3.20. Four-Field + Grass System

Year/Fields	# 1	# 2	# 3	# 4	# 5
1	Green fallow	Winter grain	Inter-tillage crop	Spring grain	
2	Winter grain	Inter-tillage crop	Spring grain	Green fallow	
3	Inter-tillage crop	Spring grain	Green fallow	Winter grain	
4	Spring grain	Green fallow	Winter grain	Inter-tillage crop	
5	Green fallow	Winter grain	Inter-tillage crop	Spring grain	
6	Winter grain	Inter-tillage crop		Green fallow	Spring grain
7	Inter-tillage crop	Spring grain		Winter grain	Green fallow
8	Spring grain	Green fallow		Inter-tillage crop	Winter grain
9	Green fallow	Winter grain		Spring grain	Inter-tillage crop
10	Winter grain	Inter-tillage crop		Green fallow	Spring grain
11	Inter-tillage crop		Spring grain	Winter grain	Green fallow
12	Spring grain		Green fallow	Inter-tillage crop	Winter grain
13	Green fallow		Winter grain	Spring grain	Inter-tillage crop
14	Winter grain		Inter-tillage crop	Green fallow	Spring grain
15	Inter-tillage crop		Spring grain	Winter grain	Green fallow
16		Spring grain	Green fallow	Inter-tillage crop	Winter grain
17		Green fallow	Winter grain	Spring grain	Inter-tillage crop
18		Winter grain	Inter-tillage crop	Green fallow	Spring grain
19		Inter-tillage crop	Spring grain	Winter grain	Green fallow
20		Spring grain	Green fallow	Inter-tillage crop	Winter grain
21	Spring grain	Green fallow	Winter grain		Inter-tillage crop
22	Green fallow	Winter Grain	Inter-tillage crop		Spring grain
23	Winter grain	Inter-tillage crop	Spring grain		Green fallow
24	Inter-tillage crop	Spring grain	Green fallow		Winter grain
25	Spring grain	Green fallow	Winter grain		Inter-tillage crop

Note: The blank areas are for multi-year grass.

Notes

1 Although theorists have offered many competing schemes, very few differ substantially from that presented here. A concise overview in English is Grigg, "Ester Boserup's Theory of Agrarian Change."

2 The most detailed overviews of these debates are Knipovich, *Sel'sko-khoziaistvennoe raionirovanie*; and Krokhalev, *O sistemakh zemledeliia. Istoricheskii ocherk*. Short, clear, and able introductions from the turn of the century include Fortunatov, "Sel'skokhoziaistvennaia ekonomika;" Karyshev, "Zemledelie (ekon.);" and Sovetov, "Sevooborot."

3 The best-known English-language survey of this scholarship is Grigg, *Population Growth and Agrarian Change*.

4 Kondrat'ev and Oganovskii, *Perspektivy razvitiia sel'skogo khoziaistva SSSR*, pp. 40–41. Some Russian landlords came to this conclusion much earlier, although they did not enunciate it as clearly. They encountered difficulties in intensifying agriculture beyond grain-fallow systems in the absence of nearby markets. Some nineteenth-century discussions are *Zapiski Lebedianskogo Obshchestva Sel'skogo Khoziaistva za 1849 god*, Moscow 1850, pp. 14–96; Tarnovskii, "O pol'ze sveklosakharnykh zavodov v Rossii v vidakh uluchsheniia khlebopashestva;" and "Oblastnoi s"ezd sel'skikh khoziaev v g. Khar'kove v 1886 g.," in *Khar'kovskii kalendar' na 1887 god*, esp. p. 483.

5 Brzheskii, *Ocherki agrarnogo byta krest'ian*, p. 56. Note that Anfimov (*Krest'ianskoe khoziaistvo*, p. 103) cites the very same passage, but from VSKh, 1903, no. 27, p. 4. Brzheskii possibly failed to cite someone else.

6 An agronomist in Poltava province, K. S. Ashin, is the only one I have found who questioned the validity of this reasoning. He accused agronomists of chronically assuming the centrality of fodder problems without ever bothering to establish them in fact. See his *Obshchestvenno-agronomicheskie etiudy*.

7 See Chelintsev, *Opyt izucheniia organizatsii*, p. 306 for data on this question.

8 Kliuss, "Luga," p. 68. Some sowing of meadows can be traced in Tambov at the turn of the century. Apparently only a handful of such cases involved peasants, however (*k otsenke*, Kirsanov, p. 138; Merinov, "K voprosu ob uluchshenii senokosov," pp. 658–661).

9 *k otsenke*, Kirsanov, p. 138.

10 *Zhurnaly ...* (30–31 August and 1–2 September 1911), p. 119.

11 *Materialy po raionnomu kachestvennomu obsledovaniiu zhivotnovodstva*, vol. 2, table XLII.

12 *Urozhai khlebov, trav, i proch.*, pp. 8–9, 20–21, 32–33, 44–46. Chaff weighed about 10% of grain with rye and millet, 17% with oats.

[13] Budget study figures show such farms feeding their horses up to 70 *puds* of oats in a year (Chelintsev, *op. cit.*, p. 218).

[14] According to Kaufman, the national average at the turn of the century was 23.6 *puds* of oats per horse (*Agramyi vopros v Rossii*, p. 52). A budget study in several *uezds* of Voronezh province in the 1880s produced similar figures to Tambov's—18 *puds* of oats per horse on peasant farms (as cited by L. N. Maress, "Proizvodstvo i potreblenie khleba" p. 15).

[15] Chelintsev, *op. cit.*, pp. 219, 424.

[16] For a poignant discussion of this problem by a peasant from Tula province, see *Sam sebe agronom*, 1926, no. 47, pp. 1477–1481.

[17] So Selivanov noted in the mid-nineteenth century, among both peasants and landlords ("God Russkogo zemledel'tsa," p. 52). More reports of the same problem appear in, e.g., *Statisticheskii ezhegodnik Moskovskoi gubernii za 1906 god. Chast' pervaia*, p. 48.

[18] See articles by the famous agronomists A. A. Zubrilin and S. I. Fridolin in *Sam sebe agronom*, 1926, no. 39–40, pp. 1221–1228, and no. 48, respectively. For further evidence of the one-pud-per-day-per-cow norm, from Spassk *uezd*, see ibid, no. 32, p. 1023.

[19] RGAE, f. 478, op. 5, d. 2011, p. 37.

[20] Agronomists found over-feeding of livestock to be very common among well-off Latvian farmers in Novgorod province, for example (V. Vasil'ev, "Kursy po sel'skomu khoziaistvu," pp. 31–35.) For more on the prevalence of over-feeding of hay and straw, see *Sam sebe agronom*, 1926, no. 9, p. 270.

[21] *Otchety uchastkovykh agronomov za 1911 g.*, p. 5. Kliuss also notes peasants' chronic tardiness of mowing, but does not attribute it to ignorance ("Luga," p. 68).

[22] For a discussion of this, see *Sam sebe agronom*, 1926, no. 24, pp. 743–746.

[23] Information on these matters is not hard to find. See for instance V. P. Semenov-Tian-Shanskii, *Rossiia*, vol. 2, pp. 227–228, and *Materialy po kachestvennomu obsledovaniiu zhivotnovodstva*. In part, poor care for livestock reflected peasants' disrespect for attentiveness towards farm animals (with the exception of horses). A Kursk landowner lamented the difficulty in finding able workers to fill responsible positions in barns. Peasants would beg to be assigned somewhere else: "They will laugh at me," "I'm capable of more" (L. O'Rurk, "O skotovodstve v sele Khokhlovke," p. 42). It should be pointed out that landlords in the black-earth zone did not traditionally take much better care of their animals than peasants. In 1902 a study of 1,728 landlords in Saratov province found only about 10% to be observing even elementary rules of care. Only 20–30 were model husbandmen in this respect (Kostritsyn, "Iz nabliudenii nad mestnogo skotovodstva," pp. 14–15). Matters surely improved in the next decade. In 1910 about half of the landlords holding animals in Tambov and Saratov provinces were moving to raise imported breeds of livestock (Berezov, "Nazrela-li dlia iugo-vostoka potrebnost' v zootekhnicheskom opytnom uchrezhdenii?," p. 5).

[24] Ianovskii, "Vygon," pp. 482–485; Kliuss, "Luga," p. 68.

[25] I have never found a single exception to this rule. Every village involved in the 1914–1915 budget study conformed to the pattern (Chelintsev, *op. cit.*, pp. 323–327).

[26] The hardest period for the livestock was usually June, when green fallow grazing was pretty well expended, and the meadows had not yet been cut. Research in Moscow province established that cows might lose 70–150 pounds of weight in June, and might give no milk for much of June and July (*Stenograficheskii otchet 3-go*

Vserossiiskogo soveshchaniia zemorganov, p. 261). Cattle could sometimes be so weak in June as to be unable to walk home (Pestrzhetskii, "O nedugakh khoziaistva," p. 271).

[27] Chelintsev recites many characteristic grazing sequences (*op. cit.*, pp. 323–327). See also *Proekt obshchikh osnovanii*, p. 18, which confirms the ubiquity of meadow grazing after hay making.

[28] Many sources testify to this. The most explicit condemnation is in GATO, f. R-946, op. 1, d. 5420, p. 9.

[29] Cited in Mozzhukhin, *op. cit.*, p. 109. This from Tula province. It is not without interest that Ermolov managed to find sayings warning against grazing on rye stubble in Poland, but not in Russia (*Narodnye primety na urozhai*, p. 146).

[30] An agriculturist/correspondent in Khar'kov province (*Statisticheskii ezhegodnik 1907 g.*, p. 47). A three-year test in another black-earth province registered a 20% difference, on average (Anonymous, "O vrede past'by skota po ozimiam"). There were places in the central black-earth region where peasants allowed their livestock onto the rye field in spring as well, costing themselves even more (Pestrzhetskii, "O nedugakh khoziaistva" p. 271).

[31] Here allotment lands are taken as a stable 3,000,000 *desiatinas*. Peasants had purchased about 200,000 *desiatinas* of non-allotment land by 1882, 622,000 by 1912 (Oganovskii, *Sel'skoe khoziaistvo Rossii v XX veke*, p.55; *Podvornoe obsledovanie zhivotnovodstva*, prilozhenie 1). This yields an increase of 13%. The calculation is more complex, however, because peasants were renting large amounts of land as well: 533,000 *desiatinas* of non-allotment land in the early 1880s, and about 500,000 in 1912 (*Sbornik ocherkov*, pp.42, 53; *Podvornoe obsledovanie zhivotnovodstva Tambovskoi gubernii v 1912 godu, Prilozhenie I*. The figure in the later source, for 1912, required adjustment, because it includes nadel land rental). If we include these lands in our calculation, then the territory accessible to peasants rose by just 10% from the early 1880s to 1912. But neither would this figure be accurate, for rental of arable land did not generally include grazing privileges. So explains the only comment I have ever seen on the matter, at any rate (Romanov, *Selo Kamenka i Kamenskaia volost'*, p. 153). Hence I have estimated the rise in summer fodder territory at 12%. 80–84% of all registered land rental in the province throughout our period was for arable land, from the limited data available (*Sbornik ocherkov po voprosam ekonomiki i statistiki Tambovskoi gubernii*, Tambov 1922, pp. 42, 53; *Kom Tsentra*, vol.1, p. 118; *Podvornoe obsledovanie zhivotnovodstva Tambovskoi gubernii v 1912 godu, Prilozhenie I*).

[32] See *k otsenke*, Lipetsk, e.g., pp. 73–75. Plenty more information on the variety of deals to rent grazing lands appears in SSS, vol. 12, pp. 130–140.

[33] See Ivaniukov, "Krest'ianskoe khoziaistvo Tambovskoi gubernii," pp. 9–10; and Ianovskii, "Vygon," pp. 482–485. There were of course estates where peasant livestock was forbidden to trespass on the lord's fields (e.g., Lachinov, "Otchet chlena-korrespondenta," pp. 76–77).

[34] Chelintsev, *op. cit.*, p. 321.

[35] It is simply not possible to be more precise as to the ratio of arable to pasture land at which reliance on grazing alone would no longer suffice. Many standard accounts claim that the three-field system begins to degenerate once arable lands exceed pasture and meadow lands combined, if not earlier (e.g. Pavlovsky, *Agricultural Russia*, p. 84; R. G. Nol'dshtein, "Chto dokazyvaet 'Opyt ekonomicheskoi otsenki' A. N. Minina," p. 35; Shil'der-Shul'dner, *Krest'ianskie nadely*, p. 13; Ivaniukov,

"Krest'ianskoe khoziaistvo Tambovskoi gubernii," p. 7). But, for reasons I will not go into here, I find such general rules to have little if any value.

[36] Families gave the animals more or less the same kinds of feed as in the winter, only in summer they could include grasses from the garden plot and weeds cleaned off their millet strips (Chelintsev, *op. cit.*, p. 325).

[37] Chelintsev, *op. cit.*, p. 326. Figures from the same source (pp. 309, 311) establish that middle-sized farms provided their animals with more hay than smaller or larger farms, while the largest farms fed them a lot of grain. The smallest farms had little but straw and chaff for their animals.

[38] For solid data concerning the purchase and sale of fodder resources within villages, see Chelintsev, *op. cit.*, pp. 306–307.

[39] For statistics, see RGAE, f. 478, op. 5, d. 3719, pp. 127–128.

[40] Chelintsev, *op. cit.*, p. 310.

[41] Kliuss, "Luga," p. 68 (statistics for "novaia stepnaia luga"). If 120 *puds* of mown hay was considered a good yield from grasslands in Borisoglebsk *uezd* (SSS, Borisoglebsk, Prilozhenie 1, p. 28), then such lands would have provided around 150–200 *puds* of fodder during the summer grazing period (mowers leave some of the grass as stubble, and the grass continues to grow after mowing).

[42] Chelintsev, *op. cit.*, p. 312 shows how much of feed was *barda*.

[43] See, e.g., the map in Pallot and Shaw, *Landscape and Settlement*, p. 130.

[44] For an overview, see Perkins, "The Agricultural Revolution in Germany, 1850–1914."

[45] In England the percentage of arable land lying in bare fallow fell to about 20% by 1800, 4% by 1870; in Sweden, from about 45% in 1800 to about 15% in 1900 (Grigg, *The Transformation of Agriculture in the West*, pp. 18, 86). In France, from 34% in the late eighteenth century to 13% in 1892 (Grigg, *Population Growth and Agrarian Change*, p. 198). In Germany fallow dropped from an estimated 25% in 1800 to 15% by 1878, and to about 8% already by 1900 (Blum, *The End of the Old Order in Europe*, p. 200; Perkins, *op. cit.*, pp. 79, 91).

Grain yields rose rapidly with the spread of multi-field systems and chemical fertilizers in Germany. Wheat and rye yields increased about 50% from 1880 to 1910 (Perkins, *op. cit.*, p. 109). In England yield increases from the introduction of multi-field systems largely predated the reliable recording of yields. Yields continued to rise in the nineteenth century, perhaps by as much as 50% for wheat between 1820 and the 1880s (Grigg, *Population and Agrarian Change*, p. 36).

[46] Overton and Campbell, "Productivity Change in European Agricultural Development," p. 44.

[47] The paucity of statistics before the final third of the nineteenth century has made it difficult for historians of European agriculture to establish precisely how much intensification went on within the framework of the three-field system there. An overview of the main lines of intensification (the sowing of fodder crops on the section of land ordinarily kept fallow, and the planting of potatoes and other root crops) is Blum, *The End of the Old Order in Europe*, ch. 12. Grain yields in open-field farming doubled or even tripled over the course of several centuries in the pre-modern period (see B. H. Slicher van Bath, "The Yields of Different Crops (Mainly Cereals) in Relation to the Seed, c. 1810–1820," in *Acta Historicae Neerlandica*, vol. 2, 1967, pp. 26–106—as cited in David Grigg, "Ester Boserup's Theory ...," p. 74). A recent discussion of technological advance within the three-field system on open fields is Allen, "Enclosure, Farming Methods, and the Growth of Productivity in the South Midlands." Allen concludes that grain yields

in the South Midlands approximately doubled over the period 1450–1750. Composite statistics for Germany, Switzerland, and Scandinavia show grain yield increases of about 25% between the turn of the eighteenth century and the early nineteenth century—before the wide adoption of multi-field systems (Grigg, *The Transformation of Agriculture in the West*, p. 34).

[48] Cited in Guliaev, *Perspektivy mnogopol'ia v chernozemno-rzhanykh raionakh povolzh'ia*, p. 3.

[49] Leading the campaign against the three-field system was the famous Moscow *zemstvo* agronomist A. A. Zubrilin. He summarized his views in many articles (see, for instance, "Nedostatki trekhpol'ia;" and *Sam sebe agronom* 1926, no.36, pp. 1143–1146).

[50] Erpulev, "K voprosu ob uluchsheniiu krest'ianskogo zemlepol'zovaniia v chernozemnom polose;" and Chuprov, *Melkoe zemledelie i ego osnovnye nuzhdy*, pp. 125–126. Naturally many people were working on these topics, and were publishing their thoughts. But reliable information on multi-field systems in the black-earth zone did remain very scant, especially as concerned small-scale farming. A couple of examples of discussions from the turn of the century are the work of V. G. Frankovskii in *Tekushchaia selsko-khoziaistvennaia statistika Kurskogo gubernskogo zemstva. 1900 g. Kniga IV*, Kursk 1900, otdel II, pp. 7–26; and Trube, "Doklad," pp. 371–375. Apparently, recommendations for farming in the vicinity of sugar-beet- or potato-processing plants were easier to come by than recommendations for the great majority of areas more distant from such marketing points (Khvostov, "Doklad," pp. 513–516). Significant numbers of central-black-earth-region landlords had been experimenting with multi-field systems before the emancipation. See especially the roundtable discussions from the Lebedian Agricultural Society (which served Tambov and neighboring provinces) in ZhMGI, 1849, ch. XXXI, otd. 1, pp. 39–51; or N. Strekalov, "Udobnyi perekhod iz trekhklinnogo polevodstva v plodosmennoe mnogopol'e." Many more could be added.

[51] The work of the Bezenchuk experimental station in Samara province in the first two decades of the new century did the most to legitimize the *propashnaia* system (Guliaev, *Perspektivy mnogopol'ia*, p. 4).

[52] KSE, vol. 6, p. 442. The Tambov experimental station reported that when following potatoes in a *propashnaia* system, oats yielded 8% more grain and 4% more straw than when it followed rye in the three-field system. Pel'tsikh, *Propashnoi klin, gibel' trekhpolki*, p. 3.

[53] KSE, vol. 6, p. 441.

[54] The classic statement is Chaianov, *Organizatsiia krest'ianskogo khoziaistva*.

[55] The latest rendering of this perspective is Robert E. Johnson, "Family Life-Cycles." Johnson portrays peasant families' economic status as chronically fragile (p. 726).

[56] Shanin, *The Awkward Class*, pp. 63–65.

[57] Labor calendars from budget studies in Tambov and neighboring Penza province confirm that the larger farms were relatively short on both human and horse labor. See the labor calendars in A. N. Chelintsev, *op. cit.*, pp. 269–272; Studenskii, *Problemy organizatsii krest'ianskogo sel'skogo khoziaistva*, pp. 75, 94. Another breakdown from Tambov is Noarov, "Krest'ianskie biudzhety Tambovskoi gubernii v 1923–1924 gody," p. 42. On the relative shortage of human and horse labor on larger farms in Chernigov province, G. A. Kushchenko, "K dinamike krest'ianskogo khoziaistva," esp. pp. 52, 55. For Tula, *Materialy dlia otsenki zemel' Tul'skoi gubernii*, pp. 193–194.

[58] Vasil'chikov, *Sel'skii byt' i sel'skoe khoziaistvo v Rossii*.

[59] On which see, e.g., Lukin, "K voprosu vvedeniia sevooborotov v zemel'nykh obshchestvakh," pp. 38–40. It is plausible to propose that the relative economic strength of larger farms allowed them to support higher fertility (or simply lower infant mortality), and thus have higher ratios of children. In this case the relative labor shortage of the larger farms would be all the greater. Data from Voronezh province and a recent study of a locality in late Imperial Tambov confirm the lower infant mortality on the larger farms (respectively, S. D. Morozov, "Demograficheskoe povedenie sel'skogo naseleniia," p. 102; and Avrekh, D'iachkov, and Kanyshev, "Sotsial'nye i fiziologicheskie aspekty," p. 37).

[60] The best-known overviews presenting work regimes as rigidly uniform in the manner here described are Slicher Van Bath, *The Agrarian History of Western Europe, A.D. 500–1850*, pp. 61–62; and Blum, *op. cit.*, p. 123. Both of these authors offer judicious qualifications to their generalizations, but it appears that only the most recent work in the history of European agriculture has appreciated that open fields did not generally imply common sowings for all households (Eric Kerridge—who treats the continent as well as England—in *The Common Fields of England*, esp. pp. 110–111).

[61] Haxthausen, *Studies on the Interior of Russia*, p. 94. Haxthausen went on to say that the commune did not directly impose conformity to the work regime—"... elders issue no rules ... the undertaking functions by itself." For him the regulation of work was indirect, but stringent nevertheless (see *ibid.*). Haxthausen's work in the 1840s was very important in opening educated Russians' eyes to the idea that the peasant commune was the key to understanding their country's peculiarity vis-à-vis Western Europe.

In Western Europe perception of a common work regime in open-field villages predated Haxthausen. According to Marc Bloch, the Frenchman De Verneilh was the first to describe the phenomenon of "compulsory crop rotation," in 1811 (*French Rural History*, p. 40).

[62] The most recent rendering—from one of Russia's most knowledgable agrarian historians, no less—is V. V. Kabanov, *Krest'ianskaia obshchina i kooperatsiia Rossii XX veka*, p. 49. Kabanov follows countless others.

[63] It is possible to find contemporaries, even agronomists, who assumed that farmers were concerned about unlike sowings on adjacent strips (see, e.g., Borisov, "Klever, korneplody i kartoshka pri mnogopol'i," p. 382). But never is any evidence or argumentation adduced.

[64] *Statisticheskii ezhegodnik Moskovskoi gubernii za 1889 g.*, p. 178.

[65] For the six provinces of the central agricultural region, 79 of 160 reports indicated that open-field farmers were adopting improved seeds. 5 of 12 reports noted the same for consolidated plots. I. V. Chernyshev, *Obshchina posle 9 noiabria 1906 goda*, p. 162.

[66] See, e.g., Bruk, *Organizatsiia obshchinnogo sevooborota*, pp. 13, 15, or Trifonov, *Pochemu neobkhodimo podnimat' par rano?*, (1925), pp. 28–29. Pershin's *Zemel'noe ustroistvo dorevoliutsionnoi derevni* devotes a lot of attention throughout to the problem of inaccessible or overly distant arable lands. See also the discussions of land organization in Part IV.

[67] An explicit discussion of non-contemporaneous reaping (on account of rainy weather and differences of opinion on the danger of cut grain rotting) appears in *Sel'sko-khoziaistvennyi obzor Nizhegorodskoi gubernii za 1894 god*, p. 25. Alternatively, dry years could also cause staggered reaping. See note 70.

68 Families who reaped late had to rush before the herds came through. One peasant's lament on this matter appears in *Statisticheskii ezhegodnik 1907 g.*, p. 51.

69 Where the commune had substantial quantities of meadowland, the summer-fodder crunch ended as soon as the meadows were cut. Communes would send cattle out on to some portion of the meadows right away, before any re-growth would occur (see, e.g., the discussion of grazing regimes in *Statisticheskii ezhegodnik Moskovskoi gubernii za 1910 g.*, pp. 220–223). Of course for most villages in Tambov this was a very short-term option, since they had so little meadow land.

70 Local chronicles of the agricultural year printed in a Moscow *zemstvo* publication provide some interesting information on this topic. They note, for instance, that families were carting their sheaves off the spring fields on their own schedules. They did not fully clear the spring fields until the end of September. *Statisticheskii ezhegodnik Moskovskoi gubernii za 1889 g.*, pp. 98–99.

A couple of counterindications (where oats was cleared quickly, within 6–9 days) appear in *Statisticheskii ezhegodnik Moskovskoi gubernii za 1910 g.*, p. 167. At the same time, this same source notes that in many places both the winter and the spring fields were cleared very slowly, over the course of 4–6 weeks (pp. 172, 174). Communes could hold the herds away from portions of the spring field, if need be. If late rains broke drought conditions, then many dormant oats seeds would sprout, as late as early July (a phenomenon called *podgon* in Russian). We have explicit evidence that some farmers—but not all—would wait for the *podgon* oats to ripen, fully a month after the initial oats ripened. Communes permitted them to reap late. *Statisticheskii ezhegodnik po Simbirskoi gubernii za 1911 god*, pp. 20–21; and *Tekushchaia selsko-khoziaistvennaia statistika Kurskogo gubernskogo zemstva. 1900 g. Kniga IV*, Kursk 1900, p. 39. Alternatively, in drought-like conditions some families might re-sow on top of a failing early-sown spring crop. This too would require late reaping, which the commune allowed (*ibid*, p. 38).

71 Data collectors for the budget study noted that when potatoes were planted on arable land (as opposed to garden plot territory) they were always on the nearest strips (Chelintsev, *op. cit.*, p. 391).

72 Pel'tsikh, *Propashnoi klin—gibel' trekhpolki*, pp. 3–4.

73 The phenomenon was general. Examples from Tambov include *Proekty* , p. 48; and *SSS*, Spassk, p. 30. For other areas, or general observations, see, e.g., *Materialy dlia otsenki zemel' Saratovskoi gubernii. Vyp. III*, p. 125; *Orlovskaia guberniia v sel'sko-khoziaistvennom otnoshenii 1890 g.*, otdel II, p. 11; *Statisticheskii ezhegodnik po Moskovskoi gubernii za 1889 g.*, Moscow 1889, pp. 50–51; *ibid.*, *za 1910 g.*, p. 85; Chuprov, "Obshchinnoe zemlevladenie," p. 143. Alternatively, in drought-like conditions some families might re-sow on top of a failing early-sown spring crop. This too would require late reaping, which the commune allowed. *Tekushchaia sel'sko-khoziaistvennaia statistika Kurskogo gubernskogo zemstva. 1900 g. Kniga IV*, Kursk 1900, p. 38; Barykov et al., eds., *Sbornik materialov dlia izucheniia sel'skoi pozemel'noi obshchiny*, esp. pp. 314, 363–64, 392. Bernard Pares's description of peasant fields implies the same (*Russia Between Reform and Revolution*, p. 75).

For instances of alternative crops within the winter field (wheat alongside rye), see *Statisticheskii ezhegodnik po Moskovskoi gubernii za 1889 g.*, p. 177. For spring crops in the winter field, see below.

A unique pre-revolutionary color photograph of unlike crops in adjacent strips (in Moscow province) appears on in Prokudin-Gorskii, *Photographs for the Tsar*, p. 64.

74 Sobichevskii, "Botva," pp. 496–97.

[75] Communes often announced that certain portions of the spring field would be grazed later than others (Chuprov, "Obshchinnoe zemlevladenie," *op. cit.*, p. 145).

[76] For example, Ponomarev, "Uluchsheniia v krest'ianskom sel'skom khoziaistve," p. 267; Dmitriev, *op. cit.*, p. 26; *Statisticheskii ezhegodnik po Moskovskoi gubernii za 1889 god*, pp. 176–179; Monin, "S miakotnykh zemel' Voronezhskogo uezda. Rezul'taty poseva rzhi shampanskoi, ivanovskoi, i prosto-mestnoi," pp. 977–978; A. Petrov, "Zametki i nabliudeniia sel'skogo khoziaina," pp. 205–206. The fullest contemporary discussion of the issue of cross-pollination I have encountered is Shaternikov, *Otchego v krest'ianskom khoziaistve semena plokhi*.

[77] Almost every annual overview of agriculture mentions this variant of unlike sowings. A few examples: *Statisticheskii ezhegodnik 1907 g.*, Khar'kov 1908, p. 97; *ibid.*, *1908 g.*, otdel 2, p. 2; *Statisticheskii ezhegodnik po Moskovskoi gubernii za 1895 g.*, pp. 6–7, 37–38; *ibid.*, *za 1910 god*, p. 41; *Sel'sko-khoziaistvennyi obzor Vologodskoi gubernii*, pp. 51–52. More rarely, some families preferred to sow spring wheat, barley, or other crops instead of rye. They might, for instance, have rented off most of their strips in the spring section, leaving them potentially short of spring-sown crops. Alternatively, they might not have had any confidence in the quality of certain strips of land, and decided to sow cheaper seeds, like millet, on that land. Whatever the motivation, they simply waited until spring, and sowed their chosen crop right in the middle of the rye. The best discussions and descriptions of this are *Materialy dlia otsenki zemel' Saratovskoi gubernii. Vyp. III*, pp. 141–143; and SSS, Borisoglebsk, prilozhenie I, p. 5. Other indications include Troitskii, "Iz nabliudenii nad kul'turoi ozimykh khlebov," p. 4; Zinov'ev, "Borokskaia obshchina," p. 314; and Vermenichev, Gaister, and Raevich, *710 khoziaistv Samarskoi derevni*, p. 129.

[78] Another historian of Russia who has pointed to a degree of freedom in peasants crop choices in the open fields is Judith Pallot (*Land Reform in Russia*, pp. 84–85). We should point out that a few sources do testify to imposed work regimes. Thus a couple of peasants from Smolensk province complained about the village assembly forbidding anyone to manure, till, sow, mow, or reap ahead of schedule (in Chernyshev, *Krest'iane ob obshchine*, pp. 5–7). This sort of regimentation was more likely where strips and the pathways leading to them were especially thin. No one wanted a neighbor walking over his land or crops. See, e.g., Dmitriev, *op. cit.*, p. 8.

[79] In some places the strain of hunger and debt eventually impelled poorer farmers to sow crops on green fallow land that their communes ordinarily used for grazing (e.g., SSS, Tambov, p. 45; *ibid.*, Kirsanov, p. 39). Meanwhile, a number of peasants interested in growing fodder grasses on fallow land (a technique to be described below) in one village in Tambov *uezd* concentrated the grass sowings on one edge of the fallow and paid the village shepherds 14 rubles to protect the crop from the herds (Bilibin, "Doklad Upravy o deitel'nosti uezdnogo i uchastkogo agronomov," p. 47). Although it is not clear how peasants in other cases arranged to safeguard their sowings in the fallow section from the herds, it is clear that the pressure of poverty could break down the very limited role the commune played in the agricultural system. In a poor region of southwestern Russia, for example, the encroachment of fallow-land sowings was said to be chronic already by 1900, notwithstanding the obvious threat this posed to the livestock sector and the inevitable opposition of co-villagers (Chikhachev, "Dokladnaia zapiska," p. 916; Iozefi, "Osoboe mnenie Mirovogo Posrednika," pp. 924, 928, TMK Podol'sk). Plenty more reports of the degeneration of the three-field system into fallowless farming in land-short areas appear in *Statisticheskii ezhegodnik 1907 g.*, pp. 49–50;

KSE, vol. 6, pp. 389, 439—describing Poltava and Khar'kov; and Bruk, *Obshchinnoe travoseianie na chernozeme*, p. 4. Many more could be found.

In conclusion, the common grazing of the herds was a flexible feature of openfield farming. Manipulation depended on power relationships in the village, and on courting the shepherds (whose role in peasant agriculture remains unexplored).

[80] Hoffmann, "Medieval Origins of the Common Fields," pp. 28–29.

[81] Samuel Popkin, for one, points this out in *The Rational Peasant*, pp. 28, 33.

[82] Among peasants, market-directed winter-wheat sowings were never of any significance anywhere in the province throughout our period. The cultivation of winter wheat was far too risky after green fallow. Rye fares much better on poorly prepared land than does wheat. The peasantry's exclusive reliance on rye was entirely sensible, and would last right through collectivization.

[83] *Srednyi urozhai v Evropeiskoi Rossii za piatiletie 1883–1887 gg.*, pp. 32–33, 40–41; *Sbornik statistiko-ekonomicheskikh svedenii po sel'skomu khoziaistvu Rossii i inostrannykh gosudarstv. God desiatyi.*, pp. 66–67. It should be borne in mind that these statistics slightly overstate the increase, since some land devoted to potatoes escaped registration until 1893 (see notes to Appendix Table 1 "Nutrition and Mortality in Tambov, 1880–1914").

[84] Chelintsev, *op. cit.*, pp. 352, 354. A similar observation from Kursk province appears in *Tekushchaia sel'sko-khoziaistvennaia statistika Kurskogo gubernskogo zemstva. Kniga I*, Kursk 1901, pp. 85–86. A national overview offering the same opinion is Masal'skii, *Iavleniia progressa v sovremennom krest'ianskom khoziaistve*, pp. 45–46.

[85] *K otsenke*, Lebedian, p. 119.

[86] Other observations of peasants forfeiting opportunities to grow berries (for instance) for sale are, e.g., Stepanov, "Razvedenie zemlianiki i klubniki na priusadebnykh zemliakh;" and Kishkin, *op. cit.*, p. 48.

[87] Urusov, "Issledovanie sovremennogo sostoianiia ptitsevodstva," pp. 637–639; Nikolaev, "O iaichnoi torgovli," p. 220. These dealers and other peddlars could be important sources of information for villages on a wide range of topics. See the illustration in Nefedov, "Ivan voin," pp. 127–132.

[88] Kotov (*op. cit.*) provides discussion of the evolution of farming in the immediate vicinity of Voronezh up to the revolution. The small *uezd* towns in the black-earth region were nearly self-sufficient in dairy and meat products up to the end of our period. Thus, *uezd* towns in Saratov province had about 1,000 head of cattle each, which was plenty (N. Kozhevnikov, "Bych'i sluchnye punkty gorodov," pp. 10–11). Even Saratov, a provincial capital with a population of 220,000 (five times the size of the city of Tambov), was supplying one-third of its own milk as late as 1911. At the turn of the century it had supplied about two-thirds. Anonymous, "Molochnoe stado v gorode Saratove," p. 11.

[89] Chermenskii, *Ot krepostnogo prava k Oktiabriu*, p. 41.

[90] RGAE, f. 478, op. 5, d. 3719, p. 220.

[91] The maps are from Chelintsev, *op. cit.*, pp. 63, 64, 61, respectively.

[92] Chelintsev, *Opyt izucheniia organizatsii*, pp. 35–45; RGAE, f.478, op. 2, d. 236, pp. 4–6, 38–39.

[93] See, for instance, Semushkin, "Kartofel, kak korm dlia skota", pp. 121–122.

[94] By contrast, peasants in a few spots in Voronezh province just to the south of Tambov, were exporting large quantities of potatoes on the railroads in this period. But this was exceptional in Voronezh, and was yet to develop at all in Tambov. Chelintsev, *op. cit.*, p. 351; *KSE*, vol. 6, p. 434.

[95] Distilleries processed 13.6 million *puds* of potatoes in the last year before the war, while starch factories were processing 4.4 million *puds* at the same time. Another 0.6 million *puds* were exported out of the province (computed from RGAE, f. 478, op. 2, d. 237, p. 17, and Veber, *Ocherk sel'skogo khoziaistva Tambovskoi gubernii*, pp. 27–28). Distilleries' own lands provided 58% of the potatoes they needed, with landlords and peasants delivering the rest (computed from RGAE, f. 478, op. 2, d. 237, p. 17).

[96] Studenskii, *Problemy organizatsii krest'ianskogo sel'skogo khoziaistva*, pp. 134–136.

[97] For the geography of all varieties of industrial enterprises, see *Sbornik ocherkov*, pp. 113, 115.

[98] Calculated from *Urozhai khlebov, trav i proch.*; *Proekt obshchikh osnovanii*, pp. 20–21. Fodder conversions from *Sam sebe agronom*, 1926, no. 3, p. 40.

[99] Chelintsev, *op. cit.*, pp. 268–269.

[100] *Urozhai khlebov, trav i proch.*, pp. 9, 21.

[101] For the amounts of labor typically required to raise some of these crops, see Table 3.6.

[102] GATO, f. R-2786, op. 1, d. 14, pp. 4–5; Guliaev, *Perspektivy mnogopol'ia*, pp. 10–12.

[103] Chelintsev, *op. cit.*, p. 384.

[104] Pershin, *Zemel'noe ustroistvo dorevoliutsionnoi derevni*, pp. 200–201.

[105] SSS, Borisoglebsk, Prilozhenie 1, pp. 11–12.

[106] Guliaev, *op. cit.*, p. 17.

[107] N. B., "Bol'noi vopros", *SKhZh*, 1914, no. 13; GARF, f. 1235, op. 1, d. 1139 [letters to the newspaper *Krest'ianskaia gazeta*], p. 96 (from Lipetsk *uezd*); *Stenograficheskii otchet II-ogo Vserossiiskogo agronomicheskogo s"ezda*, p. 177 (a representative from Leningrad); GATO, f. R-2786, op. 1, d. 14, p. 4 (Kozlov okrug, Sosnovskii raion, 1928); GATO, f. 51, op. 1, d. 168, p. 136.

[108] GATO, f. R-956, op. 1, d. 466, p. 20. Emphasis added. S. T. Semenov also notes larger farms' tending to oppose multi-field systems (*op. cit.*, pp. 257, 261–262). Social antagonisms between the better-off and the weaker households over the issue of multi-field systems could have surfaced via one more route. Village-wide transitions to multi-field systems did not generally involve a quantitative redistribution of land between households. When going to a multi-field system, or when acquiring more arable land, communes tended only to undertake a reassignment of land between households (*zhereb"evka*) (Vorontsov, *Progressivnye techeniia*, p. 116; A. A. Zubrilin in *KSE*, vol. 6, pp. 397–398; and Zyrianov, *Krest'ianskaia obshchina Evropeiskoi Rossii 1907–1914 gg.*, p. 172. When arranging a six-field system they could often manage to avoid any reassignments, simply by dividing each of the three field sections into halves (Brutskus, *Agrarnyi vopros i agrarnaia politika*, p. 165). Yet in some villages discussion of a transition beyond the three-field system must have aroused opinion in favor of a full redistribution of land from scratch. This would be a threat to households whose landholdings exceeded their per capita share (they would have to forfeit some of their land). In these cases the well-off families must have resisted the multi-field system with extra effort.

[109] Chelintsev, *op. cit.*, p. 274.

[110] For statistics, see Chelintsev, *op. cit.*, p. 271. In the wintertime men took over feeding duties (*ibid.*, p. 272).

[111] The cost of hired labor rose steeply where conversions to multi-field systems were widespread. In Kaluga province, for example, the portion of communes with multi-field systems jumped from 1 in 75 in 1908 to 1 in 6 in 1913. The cost of hiring

a woman laborer at harvest time rose from 25 kopecks per day to 40 kopecks per day over the same five years. Trubetskoi, "Novaia zemskaia Rossiia," p. 71.

[112] For statistics on the plight of labor-short farms in multi-field systems in practice (from Moscow province), see Lukin, "K voprosu vvedeniia seveoborotov v zemel'nykh obshchestvakh," pp. 38–40.

[113] Guliaev, *op. cit.*, pp. 15–16.

[114] See, for example, GATO, f. R-2786, op. 1, d. 14, pp. 1–10.

[115] Opinions varied sharply on the best grass or mixture of grasses to sow on employed fallow in the central black-earth region. For example, experimental stations published conflicting conclusions on the ability of one important candidate, alfalfa, to stand up to drought weather (*KSE*, vol. 4, pp. 354, 374). Mixtures of clover and esparcet might give excellent yields, but the clover demanded both manuring and a lot of moisture, and the esparcet needed soil rich in lime (Bruk, *Obshchinnoe travoseianie na chernozeme*, pp. 6–7; *KSE*, vol. 4, pp. 352–354). Vetch-oats mixtures, meanwhile, could give the best yields of all, as much as 320 *puds* per *desiatina*—provided that the land was well manured first (*ibid.*; Trifonov *Zaniatoi par v severochernozemnom khoziaistve*, p. 5). But this mixture did not enrich the soil with nitrogen like clover or alfalfa did (concerning this property, see the section on multi-year grasses), nor could it be harvested and taken off the fallow field to allow for tillage as early as esparcet, or even clover. Thus the ensuing rye yield would be sub-optimal after vetch-oats. Selecting grasses for employed fallow was obviously not a simple task, and remember that we have not even considered here alternative crops which could be grown for fodder on employed fallow, such as peas, or an oats–lentil mixture. For most farms, ideal solutions would have involved a complicated combination of grasses, each assigned to the portions of the arable land most appropriate for it. The best scientific overview of employed fallow for the central black-earth region is I. D. Rogoza's "Zaniatye pary v lesostepi."

[116] It is not possible to be any more precise than this in generalizing about yields on employed fallow, since so many variables were involved, including the type and condition of the soil, manuring, the timing of harvesting, the weather, and the crop involved. For what it is worth, a seven-year comparison of employed fallow yields on un-manured land in Chernigov province found that esparcet, vetch, and clover gave average yields of 199, 155, and 129 *puds* per *desiatina*, respectively (*KSE*, vol. 6 p. 288). Yields on peasant lands would stand to be lower, of course.

[117] I owe this insight to Bruk's *Obshchinnoe travoseianie na chernozeme*, p. 12. The marriage of employed fallow to potatoes led Bruk to devise the "Voronezh Six-Field system", described below.

[118] Pel'tsikh, *Trekhpolka ili mnogopol'e?*, Tambov, n.d., pp. 31–32; *Sam sebe agronom*, 1926, no. 11, pp. 327–329.

[119] Pel'tsikh, *Trekhpolka ili mnogopol'e?*, Tambov, n. d., pp. 40–42; *Sam sebe agronom*, 1926, no. 11, pp. 327–329; *KSE*, vol. 4, pp. 371–378.

[120] *KSE*, vol. 4, p. 376.

[121] Split communes could arise in several ways, such as the division of a village between a landlord's heirs, or on the peasants' own initiative. V. Vorontsov discussed this issue in his *Krest'ianskaia obshchina*, as does Moshe Lewin's article, "The *Obshchina* and the Village," pp. 20–21.

[122] Pershin, *Zemel'noe ustroistvo dorevoliutsionnoi derevni*, p. 171.

[123] SSS, Borisoglebsk, Prilozhenie 1, pp. 11, 15–19, 38, 42–43; Dobrosel'skii, "Byt' ili ne byt' obshchine," p. 444.

124 As discussed by Tambov's L. A. Pel'tsikh in *KSE*, vol. 6, pp. 439–440, and in his *Propashnoi klin—gibel' trekhpolki*, p. 5. It was doing well in some spots in Voronezh in the 1920s.

125 *Sam sebe agronom*, 1926, no. 33, p. 1050; *ibid.*, no. 39–40, p. 1267.

126 *Sam sebe agronom*, 1926, no.39–40, p. 1268.

127 *KSE*, vol. 6, p. 290. About two-thirds of the yield came from the first cutting.

128 Rolofs, *Mnogopol'e na chernozeme*, p. 14.

129 While there were some prominent dissenting voices, most agronomists decisively rejected clover as a candidate for the black-earth zone. See, e.g. *KSE*, vol. 6, pp. 430–431. However, many agronomists in the central *uezds* of Tambov (and even in Voronezh province to the south) continued to consider clover at least potentially viable right up to the eve of collectivization (GATO, f. R-2786, op. 1, d. 160, p. 13, e.g.; for Voronezh: Bruk, *Obshchinnoe travoseianie na chernozeme*, p. 52).

130 Such is Guliaev's view, anyway (*op. cit.*, p. 26). Other opinions can be found on this question (see, e.g., B. V. "Rol' kormovykh rastenii v krest'ianskom khoziaistve", pp. 353–355; or *Otchet o deiatel'nosti agronomicheskogo personala za 1912*, p. 116). The disagreements do not bear on the point I am making.

131 To address this problem, agronomists did develop systems with staggered grass sections. Such adjustments made for almost prohibitive complexity, however.

132 Bruk, *Organizatsiia obshchinnogo sevooborota*, Voronezh 1922.

133 Marc Bloch recorded many such areas in France, for instance (*French Rural History*, p. 28).

134 See, e.g., *Materialy dlia otsenki zemel' Saratovskoi gubernii. Vyp. III*, pp. 75–77.

PART FOUR

GOVERNMENT'S SOLUTION TO THE AGRARIAN PROBLEM: THE STOLYPIN REFORM IN TAMBOV

What was the Stolypin Reform?

From the mid-nineteenth century up to the 1900s, a powerful current of opinion within the Tsarist regime remained steadfastly concerned about the dangers of large-scale migrations of the peasant population into the cities. Ever since the French revolution, urban and proletarian mobs in Europe had periodically demonstrated the threat they could pose to authoritarian, oligarchic societies. If Russia had thus far been spared traveling this historical road, then, so the thinking went, this was in no small measure thanks to the leveling mechanisms of the peasant commune. By periodically redistributing its lands among households the commune supposedly saw to it that all of its members could scratch out a satisfactory living. So long as peasants could get by on their farms, they would not seek to relocate to the cities.

In the spirit of this reasoning, the government sought to bolster the commune's role in the organization of the countryside. Even before the emancipation of the serfs in 1861, the commune had functioned as an intermediate administrative link between the state (or the landlord) and peasant families. Emancipation legislation formalized this link by explicitly attaching various administrative responsibilities to the commune, and protected the existence of the communes by forbidding the alienation of communal lands into the hands of non-peasants. This was the division of lands into the categories "allotment" and "private" (or "non-allotment") land, which we encountered in Part I.

As Russia entered the twentieth century the regime appeared to be set in a long-term alliance with the peasant commune. But appearances were deceiving. This alliance would not survive more than half a decade. As we saw at the outset of Part III, the rebellions of 1905–1906 jolted the government's attitude towards the peasantry and the nation's agrarian problems. The commune's egalitarian redistribution of land was thought to have stunted the masses' respect for private property, and the communal gathering was seen as a ready-made tool for the concentration and coordination of rebellious activities. Indeed, attacks on private estates acquired the most serious dimensions in the Volga and central black-earth regions, where peasant allotment lands were held almost exclusively in redistributional tenure. For most of the year 1906, before the shock of the disorders and the repression that halted them wore off, a great variety of schemes involving the expansion of peasant allotment lands at the expense of privately owned lands dominated public and official discussions of agrarian reform. By late 1906, however, the regime felt strong enough to dismiss all talk of alienating private lands, and moved instead to reorganize peasant land-holding on a non-communal basis.[1] The first decree, on November 9th, 1906, was the beginning of what has since come to be known as "the Stolypin reform," after the Prime Minister who did so much to shape and to promote the movement.

To be sure, the disorders of 1905–06 did not by themselves undermine the government's faith in the commune. The government's and educated society's awareness of the commune's place amid the tensions in rural Russia grew at a fast pace throughout the decade and a half following the traumatic crop failure of 1891.[2] Official commissions set up in 1899, 1901, and 1902 deliberated on the character and seriousness of these tensions to growing publicity.[3] Recommendations to abolish one or another feature of the peasantry's communal organization excited opinions throughout the provinces. Would the peasant economy benefit from the abolition of its right periodically to redistribute arable land? Would the parcelization of arable land also have to go? What about collective responsibility for certain taxes, or the separate courts for the peasant estate?* The proceedings of local committees composed of landlords, zemstvo officials, and provincial administrative personnel in 1902 record the state of opinion among educated society. As Map 4.1 indicates, disaffection with the commune was very widespread at this time.[4]

The first few years of the 1900s did witness limited reforms faintly presaging the spirit of the Stolypin reform. In the sphere of justice, volost' courts* were prohibited from sentencing peasants to corporal

---

*Russian society was divided into five estates (sosloviia): the clergy, the gentry (or "nobility"), the merchants, the townsmen, and the peasantry. The peasantry was specifically excluded many rights, including coverage by the civil code. Civil disputes among peasants were resolved according to local traditional customs in volost' courts. This exclusion of the bulk of the nation from the civil code occasioned a prolonged debate in pre-Revolutionary Russia. See Frierson, "The Volost' Court Debate, 1870–1912;" and her "'I Must Always Answer to Law...'."

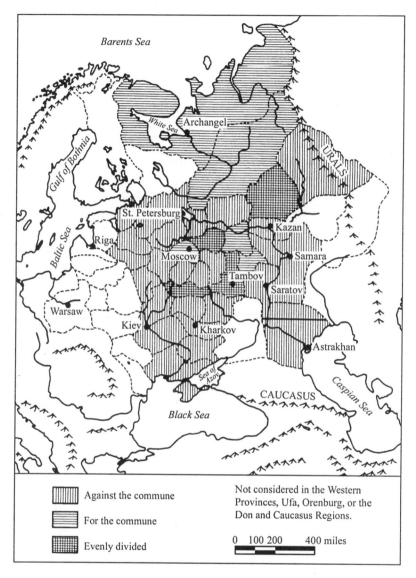

Map 4.1. "Witte Commission" Committees' Attitudes towards the Commune
(*Source:* Oldenburg, *The Last Tsar,* vol. 2, p. 19)

punishment in 1904.[5] Also abolished were peasants' collective responsibilities for certain taxes, wherein the solvent members of communes
had been saddled with their poorer neighbors' arrears.[6] Further measures akin to the Stolypin reform might have followed. We cannot say
for sure what the government might have undertaken in the absence

of the ferocious experience of 1905–1906. It is certain, however, that the revolts spurred the government into quick action, and shaped the Stolypin reform's deeply anti-collectivist character.

The Stolypin reform's fundamental legislation came out in the November 1906 decree, with subsequent elaborations in laws of 1910 and 1911. The reform allowed individual farms to separate from the commune in two ways.

1) At the time of a full redistribution of land anyone could now petition for hereditary title to their existing strips. This would protect their land from alienation at any future redistribution, be it full or only partial. Before 1906 a family could only accomplish this if they had paid off all of the redemption dues for their land, and even then they had to convince the commune to consent to the change in tenure. Communes had always been unenthusiastic about releasing any of their land from future redistributions, but after the 1906 decree it was very difficult for them to prevent determined heads of households from acquiring personal title to their strips. If a majority in the commune denied a request, the applicant could set the matter before the Land Captain* on appeal.

Of course families that had decreased in size, and thus stood to lose land upon the next repartition, were natural customers for this aspect of the 1906 decree. The decree did stipulate that families in this category would compensate the commune for the excess land they took out of repartitional tenure, but the size of this compensation was fixed at very low prices, based on assessments taken at the time of the emancipation operation. Additionally, in communes that had not undertaken a general repartition in the previous 24 years, even this compensation was waived.

2) More boldly, any farm could petition for the consolidation of their arable land into a unified plot, a process that before the 1906 decree had been even less of a realistic option than acquiring private tenure on one's existing strips. A unified holding would be easy to secure against grazing from the communal herds, so communes were predisposed against granting such requests. They were, however, obliged to arrange unified plots on all standing requests at the moment of a general repartition. Since repartitions were not frequent events, communes

*Established in 1889, the Land Captains were officials responsible to the Ministry of the Interior with broad administrative powers in rural, and especially peasant, affairs. In 1907 there were 81 of them in Tambov, each responsible for a number of *volosts* (*Spisok lits sluzhashchikh po vedomstvu MVD*).

could effectively stall requests for consolidation. In response to this tactic, the law of 1910 forced communes to arrange consolidated plots at any time, unless they could convince the *uezd* Land Organization Committee* that the formation of unified plots would present acute difficulties for the commune. Moreover, any large group of households (either one-fifth of the commune's membership, or 50 families, whichever was smaller) could compel the commune to arrange consolidated plots immediately, without any avenue for stalling. So as to ensure that communes did not cheat consolidators in any way, the Land Organization Committees were authorized to resolve any frictions arising during the arrangement of unified plots.

Apart from individual farms' separation, the reform also allowed for entire communes, or large portions of them, to renounce communal land tenure. By a two-thirds vote, the commune could impose personal property rights to their land on the heads of households, and abolish all land repartitioning. By the same two-thirds majority, the commune could opt to rearrange its land into consolidated plots.[7] In such cases, the dissenting minority could retain its rightful amount of land under the old repartitional tenure system. They would in effect become a separate commune. A further nuance in promotion of village-wide consolidations concerned communes that had already voted to accept personal property. If, on any subsequent occasion, such communes voted to form consolidated plots, then the consolidated plots were mandatory for all households. The law of 1911, moreover, reduced the requirement for this variant of commune-wide consolidation from a two-thirds majority to a simple majority.

The 1910 law introduced another twist, this time in favor of commune-wide conversions to personal property. Its 1st article declared the repartitional mechanism dead in communes which had not undertaken any full redistribution of land since they received this land under the terms of the emancipation operation that began in 1861. By this stroke of the pen the government changed the form of land tenure of about 35% of the repartitional communes, according to an official estimate.

*Established at *uezd* and provincial levels in 1906, the Land Organization Committees contained a broad collection of rural notables, including representatives from the Ministry of Agriculture, the Ministry of the Interior, the *zemstvos*, and the nobility, as well as some peasants. Despite this motley composition, they were under the supervision of the Governor, and so would tend to support the government line on the various land organization issues they adjudicated. These committees were responsible also for the distribution of loans and subsidies to peasants consolidating their plots. See Atkinson, *The End of the Russian Land Commune*, pp. 64–67.

A study of 36 provinces estimated that over half of the affected communes were actively practicing redistributions of land, but only on a partial basis (minor readjustments of strips, not full repartitions).[8] This blow to the repartitional commune did not hit the Tambov area very hard, however, since in the black-earth center full land repartitioning was the general rule.[9]

The primary and most evident goal of the Stolypin reform was to stimulate farming improvements in two ways. First, it was presumed that farmers obtaining full property rights to their strips of arable land could then proceed to manure and otherwise care for that land, without worrying about the prospect of losing it to a neighbor in the next redistribution. The second path pertained to those receiving a consolidated plot. Embracing the same logic as many European governments that undertook measures to eliminate the open fields of peasants' arable land in the nineteenth century, the Russian government expected that the consolidation of plots would free farms from the constraints of the common grazing regime, allowing them set up multi-field systems and undertake other innovations without suffering interference from the rest of the commune. Additionally, consolidated farms would recoup the labor time previously expended on transit between their often far-flung strips.

For the first couple of years of the reform, the government did not place the strongest emphasis on the formation of consolidated plots. In the wake of the revolts of 1905–06, the first item on the agenda was to instill in as many peasants as possible the ethos of private property in land. The obvious intent of the first article of the 1910 law (that prohibited redistribution of land in communes not having undertaken a general redistribution for 24 years or more) was to exorcise the redistributional mechanism from Russia as quickly and as widely as possible. It was this element of the Stolypin reform—the notion that by compelling heads of households to accept property rights the peasantry would cease to thirst for opportunities to expropriate the landlords—that generated some of the most biting criticism of the reform. It seemed to some observers that instead of being given the land the peasant was to be educated not to want it.

Beginning late in 1908, the emphasis of the reform shifted dramatically in favor of the formation of consolidated plots.[10] The government now rested its hopes for a resurrection of the peasant economy squarely on the backs of the most progressive, innovative, and aggressive peasant farmers. The idea was for them to acquire a consolidated plot and lead the way for others like them to follow. This was what Stolypin called "the wager on the strong", which by implication anticipated the failure and immiserization of the weak. Certainly every effort was to be made to encourage and cajole maximum numbers of peasants into participating in this aspect of the reform. But no one expected all of them to succeed as individual farmers. The towns, industry, and Siberia would have to absorb those portions of the peasantry that could not keep the pace.

Results and Limitations of the Stolypin Reform

As is well known, in numerical terms the Stolypin reform made striking progress in rearranging peasant land tenure during the decade before the revolution in 1917. By late 1915, the Land Organization Committees had set up approximately 1.3 million of the estimated 15 million peasant farms in European Russia on consolidated plots on allotment land.[11] Meanwhile, of an estimated 11.5 million families that were living in what had been repartitional communes in 1905, about 2.5 million had acquired hereditary tenure to their arable land, either through individual or commune-wide conversion of tenure (the 2.5 million figure includes those who had gone on to acquire unified plots).[12] Additionally, somewhere in the neighborhood of 1.7 million more households (estimates range very widely, reaching as high as 3.5 million or more) now resided in communes that had lost the right to redistribute land, according to the provisions of the 1910 law.[13] They still considered themselves to be living in repartitional communes, and in some cases they even managed to perform land repartitions.[14] But it was only a matter of time before the authorities would catch up to them and enforce the 1910 law. All told, therefore, about one-third of those farms that had held their arable land in communal tenure in 1906 no longer did so by the time of the revolution. Moreover, the Peasant Land Bank[*] had negotiated peasant purchases of another 260,000 consolidated plots on private and state-owned lands by mid-1913.[15] Behind these impressive figures lay cause for concern. After reaching a peak in the years 1908–1909, appropriations of hereditary title slowed down.[16]

---

[*]Formed in 1883, the Peasant Land Bank played a critical role in financing peasant land purchases throughout the final decades of Tsarist Russia. It became a lever of the Stolypin reform after 1906, when its terms were heavily biased in favor of individual families purchasing land in prepared consolidated plots. A convenient summary is Atkinson, op. cit., pp. 67–70.

Table 4.1. Formation of Consolidated Plots in European Russia, by Years
(Data cover 47 of the 50 provinces.)

1907	1908	1909	1910	1911	1912	1913	1914
8,315	42,350	119,380	151,814	206,723	122,522	192,988	203,915

Source: Dubrovskii, *Stolypinskaia zemel'naia reforma*, p. 244.

Consolidated plot formations reached their height in 1910–1911, after which their numbers leveled off [Table 4.1]. Various difficulties in executing peasants' requests go far to explain the deceleration. Peasant applications for consolidations actually continued to increase into 1912, but the Land Organization Committees and the specialists involved in land reorganization were overwhelmed by the volume of applications for all kinds of projects, and certain features of the 1911 law made their work more complex.[17] Meanwhile, the Peasant Land Bank had sold off most of its more attractive properties in a relatively short time. It could not continue to supply peasants with as many purchasing opportunities as it had in the first years of the reform, since the wave of panic that had prompted landowners of all varieties to sell off their properties after the 1905–06 revolts had subsided by 1908.[18]

The presence of these obstacles cannot hide the fact that peasant enthusiasm for the movement was not snowballing at the pace or in the locations the government had hoped. As Map 4.2 shows, those regions that supposedly needed consolidated plots the most, the central black-earth, Volga, and southwest, were among the least active in the reform movement. These were the most overcrowded regions, where peasant–landlord conflicts were the most tense.

Additionally, critics of the land reform insisted that official statistics charting the progress of the reform did not reflect genuine enthusiasm for individual farming on peasants' part. They claimed that systematic coercion on the part of the Land Captains and the Land Organization Committees artificially induced conversions of tenure and consolidated plot formations, and they questioned the longevity and even the authenticity of some of the individual farms that had been set up. A brief look at these accusations will be useful to us before we begin to examine the course of the reform in Tambov.

Unfortunately, it is difficult to say how much and how effectively local officials pressured individual peasants, communal assemblies, and village officials into participating in the Stolypin reform. Coercion from the authorities could take many forms, such as the threat to sell to

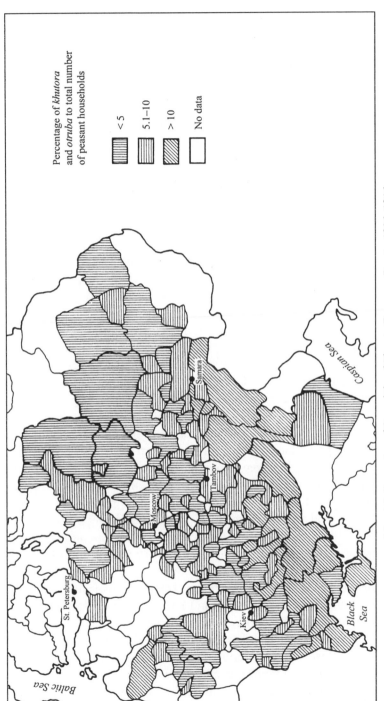

Percentage of *khutora*
and *otruba* to total number
of peasant households

< 5

5.1–10

> 10

No data

Map 4.2. Formation of Consolidated Plots in European Russia, 1906–1916

Baltic Sea

St. Petersburg

Moscow

Tambov

Samara

Kiev

Black
Sea

Caspian Sea

immigrants from other regions private or state lands that had traditionally been rented to locals, unless the locals contracted to purchase these
lands in the form of consolidated plots.[19] Likewise, Land Organization
Commissions and Land Captains could arrange to grant the commune's
best lands to the first families applying for consolidated plots (a tactic
calculated to scare the rest of the families into accepting unified plots
before all of the top quality land was gone).[20] This was probably the
most common lever of coercion. Strictly illegal measures are more
difficult to uncover.[21]

Arm pulling and scheming on the part of local officials should not
surprise us, for, as we shall see in our treatment of the course of the
Stolypin reform in Tambov, their superiors exerted intense pressure on
them from 1909 on to push through the reform. By the same token, we
would expect coercion to have played much more of a role in some
areas than others. Extra-legal methods might have been more common
in the Volga and central agricultural regions, where the peasantry was
least inclined to form consolidated plots on its own initiative. Much of
course depended on the forcefulness of the administration in each
province. Judith Pallot's search of the archives reveals complaints about
administrative coercion to have particularly common in five provinces:
Tambov, Taurida, Samara, Kiev, and Ekaterinoslav.[22]

Apart from the issue of extra-legal coercion, we must take into
account that some large proportion of peasants who accepted consolidated plots did so only for short-term financial reasons. To take a simple
example, what would we expect a peasant to do if a representative of
the Peasant Land Bank offered him a long-term loan of 150 rubles, with
no interest, if only he agree to purchase a consolidated plot on Bank-
owned land? What if a member of the *Uezd* Land Organization Committee promised a village subsidies of 60 rubles per farm, plus new
equipment, and access to some more forest land, if only they agreed to
form consolidated plots? Of course peasants would respond to this kind
of persuasion (or trickery—some of the more lavish promises employed
to bait peasants were not fulfilled).[23]

Unwilling consolidators also appeared on the statistical rolls, thanks
to the strategies of the Peasant Land Bank. The Bank heavily biased
the terms of purchase of its land in favor of buyers of consolidated plots,
so much so that it effectively refused to sell its lands to groups of
peasants that would use the land in communal fashion.[24] Unless officials
policed consolidated farms set up on such land with periodic inspections, these farms were prime candidates to resume communal-style
agriculture, as we shall see below.

We are not asserting that all or even a large percentage of consolidations came about because peasants were outwitted or squeezed into
accepting them. But it is clear that the initiative in the formation of
consolidated plots often came from outside the village. We will treat
this issue more thoroughly in our focus on the reform in Tambov. For
now, we merely wish to emphasize that the inevitable result of coerced
or cajoled consolidations was the creation of a substantial mass of un-
successful individual farms. As the statistics regarding arrears to the
Peasant Land Bank attest, purchasers of consolidated plots tended to
fall very quickly into a desperate financial condition, unable to relocate
their buildings, pay for their plots, and reorganize their farming operations at the same time.[25]

Finally, we may note that statistics on consolidated plots could not
uncover instances of fake or temporary individual farming. The Peasant
Land Bank often sold large units of land pre-divided into consolidated
plots around a new village site. But the peasants would not necessarily
honor their pledges to farm these plots individually. They could set
up their sowings in such a way as to allow for common grazing, subdivide their plots into strips when arranging family splits or inheritance, and even undertake land repartitions with their neighbors as
they had in the commune. Documented cases of these practices are
plentiful enough to suggest that they were becoming increasingly
common events.[26] Furthermore, a certain minority of those families
who purchased consolidated plots on non-allotment land retained their
inter-stripped allotment lands thereafter.[27] According to the statistics
they appear to be individual farmers, but, as historian Judith Pallot has
observed, is it really appropriate to categorize them in this way?[28] After
all, many peasants had purchased some private land before 1906, and
there had never been much characterization of them as the vanguard
of the agricultural revolution.

If the tone of the present discussion has given a pessimistic view of
the reform, we must emphasize that the picture was not gloomy
everywhere and in all respects. We shall not attempt here to offer a
thorough review of the many issues relevant to a balanced evaluation
of the reform. A couple of indicative comments will have to suffice. For
example, as George Yaney has pointed out, the common generalization
of Land Captains forcing peasants into participating in the Stolypin
reform is very unfair. Notwithstanding the pressure that their superiors
put on them, the Land Captains' performance in the field was far from
uniform. Even those who did seek to accelerate peasant involvement
in the reform were not necessarily able to force anything through

against determined peasant resistance.[29] As a rule, therefore, neither the Land Captains nor any other officials mandated the reform on the countryside, by any means. As we shall see in our discussions of the motivations that lay behind peasant involvement in the reform, many peasants had quite a few reasons to volunteer their participation.

Additionally, interpretations of the Stolypin reform must account for geographic variation. In the northwestern provinces, where the move towards consolidated plots and advance systems of farming had begun before 1900, the Stolypin reform fell on fertile ground. So too, in the great grain belt of the southeast, did substantial percentages of farms find it expedient to part with communal land relations. Over most of the rest of the country farming continued as if unaffected. Or did it? It will be the main task of Part IV to explain whether and to what degree this was so, on the basis of an examination of the progress of the reform in Tambov.

The Stolypin Reform in Tambov

Peasant Land Organization in Tambov

Ever since the late eighteenth century, analyses of European peasant-ries' parcelization of arable land into strips have generated a good deal of confusion and impassioned debate. Scholars have offered swarms of insights and conclusions regarding the motivations behind the open fields, many of which have overlapped or contradicted each other.[30] In order to minimize the confusion, the present discussion will be confined to three key questions concerning the open fields in Tambov. How badly splintered were the strips at the turn of the century? Was splintering getting worse? What were the advantages of retaining or abandoning open fields?

Those familiar with the literature on the open fields, will immedi-ately note that our selection of topics avoids one of the more complex riddles facing agricultural historians, the problem of the origins of the open fields. For all the interest that the problem of origins may provide, it would take us too far afield to put it on our agenda. We know that parcelization and common grazing antedated the three-field system.[31] Thus the open fields had been ubiquitous in the province for many generations before the period we are studying, and the circumstances and calculations that had motivated their introduction were not nec-essarily operative by the turn of the twentieth century.

What interests us are the motivations that lay behind the system in our period. Once the provisions of the Stolypin reform permitted communes or individual families to consolidate their plots, why might they wish to do this? Why might they resist? Was parcelization efficient for the commune as a whole? For certain farms? For no one at all? To answer these and other questions, we begin with an examination of the state of land parcelization within communes at the turn of the century.

Land Parcelization within Communes

Probably as early as the middle of the nineteenth century, arable land parcelization became ubiquitous in Tambov. A small percentage of communes in which each farm held one unified plot of land could still be found in neighboring Voronezh province at the end of the century. But these were always in villages that had yet to install three-field fallow systems of farming.[32] As population pressure mounted, and as common grazing on the arable land became mandatory, everywhere the peasants parcelized the land.

Before strips could be assigned to individual households, the arable land had to be divided into chunks. Two variables governed this division—the quality of the soil and the distance of the field from the village. With very rare exceptions, communes categorized land into two or three zones by distance, so most of the scattering issued from qualitative distinctions.[33] Soil quality was the most apparent distinction between fields, but others could play just as big a role. Ravines or hollows running through the village's allotment land could split up an otherwise even plain into many separate fields, as could streams, or patches of trees. Once the land was segregated into chunks (known as *delezhy*, *sorta*, *iarusy*, *kony*, or by other words; the most common English word for this is furlong), then each family would receive a strip of land in each chunk. Nuances and exceptions to this rule were common, particularly in the large communes located on the steppes. Here the furlongs were very large, and were traced into columns before distribution to households. Likewise, the larger communes had far too many families to allow for splitting their smaller furlongs up among all households. As we saw in Part III, these communes often broke themselves up into sub-communes for all agricultural affairs, including land repartitioning. This somewhat simplified view of repartioning practices will suffice for our present purposes. Readers in need of a more precise and detailed picture can turn to Pershin's work.

How many strips did a farm tend to have? By all indications, the number of strips declined from north to south in the province. Soil quality was more variable towards the north, where the land was also less flat and more forested. The simplicity of the landscape along Tambov's southern belt kept the number of furlongs to a minimum there. Villages with three or six strips per farm (one or two in each section of the three-field system) were not at all uncommon there, while 11–16 strips was said to be typical in the center.[34] Among the farms participating in the budget study, the average number of strips varied from 28 in the north, to 16 in the center, and only 14 in the south.[35]

Judging from these figures, Tambov farmers do not appear to have faced any major problems with the width of their strips. Even a smallish farm holding four *desiatinas* of arable land in twenty-eight strips could not have complained of having extremely thin strips. Taking the average field in the north of Tambov to be 70 *sazhens* long,[36] this would make the average strip for such a farm about five *sazhens* wide. Still more encouraging is the evidence from other provinces indicating that communes were sometimes careful to prevent strips from shrinking below a certain area, such as one-fourth, one-sixth, or one-ninth of a *desiatina*.[37] Considering the comfortable size of strips in many Tambov villages, it is conceivable that some communes in the province were learning to regulate the open fields in this manner. This practice must have been very uncommon, however, since there is no evidence of it.

Other sources cast different light on the picture of thin strips. In Spassk *uezd*, for instance, strips are said to have been no more than three *sazhens* wide, meaning that our four-*desiatina* farm would have had about 45 strips.[38] For proper statistics concerning strips, we must turn to the neighboring provinces of Orel and Voronezh [Table 4.2]:

Table 4.2. Degrees of Land Parcelization

	% of communes in which average farm had # of strips				
	1–5	6–10	11–20	21–40	41+
Orel (*uezd*)	13.1	13.8	27.3	33.9	14.9
Voronezh (province)	22.8	25.7	35.7	15.0	0.8

Source: Pershin, *Zemel'noe ustroistvo*, pp. 209, 212–213.

As the data demonstrate, extreme fragmentation was not at all rare in the central black-earth region. Farms in about one-half of the communes in Orel *uezd* had more than 20 strips. Even on the prairies of Voronezh, peasants in 16% of the communes had more than 20 strips. Researchers even found extreme cases of farms with upwards of 100 strips.[39]

When we come to discuss the disadvantages of land parcelization below, it will be useful to have an idea of the width of the strips in typical and abnormal cases. In the absence of statistical measurements on the width of strips in Tambov, we can safely borrow data from Voronezh.

Here we find that strips varied in width from one-third of a *sazhen* to more than fifty *sazhens* wide. In the typical commune the average width was in the neighborhood of five *sazhens*, which is not very wide at all, and the thinnest strips tended to measure only 1–2 *sazhens* wide.[40]

In interpreting these numbers, we must keep in mind that in the great majority of communes farms would receive strips in widths commensurate to their family size. Thus the larger, more economically powerful families would not face the inconveniences of thin strips to the same degree as their neighbors. When we come to discuss these inconveniences in detail, we will see what consequences issued from the unequal width of strips.

The Evolution of Land Parcelization

Our first point relates to the large and growing size of communes' landholdings in Tambov. The more land a commune held, the more time peasants were losing in transit across space from strip to strip. Compare, for instance, two farms holding eight strips in each section of a three-field system. Assume now that the first farm belongs to a relatively small commune of about 75 families, but the second farm

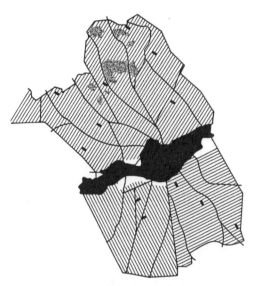

Figure 4.1. Distribution of Land Units and the Strips of a Single Household in Taly, a Village in Voronezh Province. The short black lines indicate the location of one farm's arable land strips. (*Source:* A. Minin,"Zemlepol'zovanie i. Zemleustroistvo," p. 95)

lives in a large commune of 400 families. If, as would constantly happen, conditions demand work on more than one strip in the space of a single day, members of the first farm will almost always have less distance to travel than will members of the second farm. The accompanying diagram of the open fields of a large village illustrates the problem [Figure 4.1]. Note how far apart are the shaded strips, which belong to a single household. They have 14 strips, the closest located 2½ *versts* away, the farthest 10 *versts*.

Now, we have already seen how large the communes in Tambov were, especially in the central and southern *uezds*. Conditions for the parcelization of land had never been ideal in Tambov, and they were getting ever more dubious as time went by. As we saw in Part II, communes were steadily acquiring more arable land, either through conversions of supplementary lands into arable, or through rental or purchase of non-allotment land. Communes were simply getting bigger, with more furlongs, and land at greater distances from the village. In recognizance of the growing inconvenience, groups of families would sometimes agree with the village assembly to relocate to a suitable spot. There they would set up a new village, and run their farms more or less independently from their old neighbors. But this solution was costly, and demanded a location with satisfactory access to water, meadows, and forests. By 1900 or even earlier, peasants had already taken what opportunities there were for relatively painless relocation.[41] Any subsequent formation of new villages would be expensive. Thus new village formations were rare events until the last few years before the World War, when the *zemstvos* stepped in to encourage and assist large villages in arranging them.

Secondly, population pressure on the land served to exacerbate the worst features of the open fields. The number of families in Tambov was increasing faster than the amount of land in peasant possession. With more families per furlong of arable land, strips stood to get thinner.[42] Moreover, as demand for land intensified, peasants jealously and maximally enforced equality of landholdings, which made strips thinner still.[43] Where the number of furlongs was changing, it was growing, not shrinking. Communes were unable to control the leveling impulse, which lay at the heart of the open fields. They would even align strips downslope, consciously consenting to rapid soil erosion so as to avoid the inequality between strips that would result if strips were aligned perpendicular to the slope![44]

Thirdly, even when the hazards of over-parcelization became abundantly clear, communes proved to be incapable of reducing parceliza-

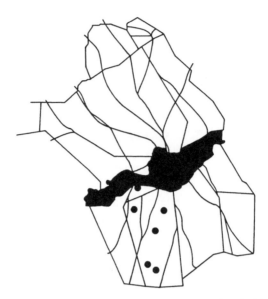

Figure 4.2. Improved Distribution of Land Units in Taly. The black dots
indicate the location, but not the shape of one farm's arable lands
(*Source:* A. Minin, 'Zemlepol'zovanie i Zemleustroistvo," p. 97)

tion. Returning to our previous example, this commune ought to have
rearranged its lands something like this [Figure 4.2]: For land distribution purposes, the village has broken up into nine smaller communes.
The black dots mark the locations of our sample family's new strips.
Instead of 14 strips they now have only 6. While previously the average
distance from home to the strips was 6¼ *versts*, it is now 5 *versts*.[45]

The repartitional mechanism gave Russian peasants every opportunity to redistribute land in wider strips. They could have reduced the
precision of their qualitative evaluation of land (i.e., reduced the
number of furlongs).* But cases of this were extremely rare, and not

*To avoid confusion among readers familiar with the literature on land repartition-
ing in Russia, we should contrast the reduction of the number of furlongs with a very
different practice, often called the *perezhereb'evka*. While the former reduced parcelization by lowering the number of categories into which land was divided before being
sliced into strips, the latter reduced parcelization by unifying all of a household's strips
within each furlong. The *perezhereb'evka* did not reduce the number of strips any further
than would a new repartition. It simply improved the arrangement of strips, without
altering farms' quantities of land to reflect changes in family composition. Over a period
of years after a full land repartition, farms would end up with extra strips in some of
the furlongs after acquiring strips of families that had migrated out of the village, failed
to keep up tax payments, or died out, etc. A good description of *perezhereb'evki* in
Tambov appears in *SSS*, Borisoglebsk, otdel II, pp. 24–27.

only in the central black-earth region.[46] When we examine what became known in the literature as "group land reorganization" (*gruppo-
voe zemleustroistvo*), we will see that without the assistance of government specialists communes were rarely able to reform the technique
of land repartitioning so as to widen their strips. Until they did learn
how to do this, their strips would gradually get thinner. In the meantime, farms with the narrowest strips tried hard to swap strips in such
a way as to wind up with fewer but wider strips.[47]

The Disadvantages of Open Fields

Having become acquainted with the state of the open fields in Tambov,
we can now proceed to analyze its consequences for peasant agriculture. We shall begin by assessing the many real or purported disadvantages parcelization posed.

1) *Time Wasted in Transit between Strips.* This is by far the most
heralded of the many criticisms of the open fields, but it is not easy to
substantiate with statistics. Indeed, in a well-known article analyzing
the problem with respect to medieval England, Donald McCloskey has
argued that the amount of time farmers wasted was more or less
negligible.[48] We shall relate the sequence of his argument before addressing its relevance for the case of central Russia.

To begin with, McCloskey points out that in medieval England the
number of strips per family was not as large as opponents of communal
agriculture were wont to maintain. Thus he characterizes a farm with
forty-four strips as an "extreme case." Furthermore, village landholding
diagrams show that individual families' strips were often separated by
minimal distances, thereby reducing the number of strips for practical
purposes. Next, he indicates that peasants' nominal strip holdings did
not necessarily conform to their actual holdings. Through rental or
unregistered swapping of strips, families could and did reduce the
effects of multiple strips. Finally, he cites sources establishing that strips
were often one-day's plowing in size, which relieved the need to travel
between strips during the course of the day. He concludes, therefore,
that time lost in transit from strip to strip was not a drawback of the
open fields.

Whatever the viability of this conclusion for medieval England, the
data cast some doubt about it for the case of central Russia. As we have
just seen, families were often saddled with absurd numbers of strips.

Forty-four strips per farm was an atypical but by no means extreme case. Perhaps families' strips tended to be close enough together as to erase any inconvenience? We cannot say for certain. But the average villages in Tambov and Voronezh encompassed (respectively) about three and four times as much territory as the average English village.[49] The

Table 4.3. Time Wasted Because of Strips (the numbers indicate days of labor (in male labor equivalents) expended per *desiatina* on farming operations, including transit time)

Average size of farm's strips in *desiatina*	Soil zones	
	Non-black-earth	Black-earth
< 0.2	29.1	—
0.2–0.4	28.8	22.1
0.4–0.8	20.9	21.7
0.8–1.2	—	16.6
1.2 >	—	12.6

Source: Studenskii, *Intensivnost' i pseudo-intensivnost' v krest'ianskom sel'skom khoziaistve,* p. 15.

Russian farmer was certainly treading many more extra miles per year than had the Englishman. Table 4.3, compiled from a 1920s budget study in Penza province (on Tambov's eastern border) is the best confirmation of our suspicion that narrower strips meant wasted time. Transit time losses were real. While this might not seem significant in an over-populated, labor-rich setting, let us recall our discussions of the harvest period, when all hands worked at an exhaustive pace, and the spring tilling, when the land could dry out very quickly. Thus it is no surprise that peasants sometimes voiced their displeasure at traveling around to various strips during the course of a day, harnessing animals and tools repeatedly.[50]

Before leaving the issue of the transit time costs associated with the open fields, we may also question McCloskey's dismissal of the possibility of a consolidated plot saving much transit time. He bases the assertion on the grounds that the daily trek from village to plot always accounted for the lion's share of distance traveled. This is quite true, but it overlooks the fact that peasants with consolidated plots located several miles away from their dwelling would camp on the site during the crucial harvest period, when they could not afford to lose time in transit.[51] To be fair, McCloskey explicitly states his arguments in reference to English villages, which were much smaller than their Russian counterparts. But the point remains that land parcelization was costing many Tambov peasants time that they could have used to advantage.

2) *Space Wasted on the Borders between Strips.* Along the side of each strip farmers left a furrow or so untilled, so as to delineate the borderline between their strip and their neighbor's. Where plows were employed, the border would be either a hump or a ditch, depending on whether the tillage tool was directing the soil out towards the next strip or in towards the tiller's strip. The humps would tend to grow a little bit over time, taking up slightly more space between the strips.[52]

Naturally the amount of arable land forfeited under borders depended on the width of the strips. The thinner the strips in any given field, the more land was lost to borders. Taking an estimated average strip width of 4.5 *sazhens*, and a typical plowing norm of eight furrows per *sazhen*, the two furrows lost to the border equal 5.6% of the land. Our estimate might be a bit high, but it corresponds closely to an official study in the 1920s, which put the space lost at 7% for the entire Russian republic.[53] Given our knowledge of the economic condition of the population, this was clearly a lot of land to forfeit. Peasants themselves regretted the land thus thrown away.[54]

Or was this land really thrown away? McCloskey insists that the amount of output lost to borders was far below the percentage of the land allotted to them, since the humps could be mown for hay, and the animals could also graze on them.[55] But what kind of nourishment grew on the borders? Virtually nothing at all grew where ditches separated strips.[56] On humps or untilled borders "... nothing grew but *polyn* [wormwood], which could be used only to make a rather noxious liquor."[57] Weeds on the borders surrounding large blocks of strips also appear to have been unpalatable to the animals:

> It is clear that the poorer the population is, and the narrower are their strips, then the denser and fuller grow the weeds on their borders. This is especially obvious after snowfalls, when it is easy to take this growth for hedges.[58]

No one had any use for the weeds growing on the borders. They were much more of a hazard than a help, as our next point maintains.

3) *The Borders Were a Breeding Ground for Pests and Weeds.* As the previous quotation attests, peasants were all too often lax in caring for their borders. As a result, the borders became fertile breeding grounds for weeds and pests that would continuously assault whatever crops farmers were trying to raise. Most peasants did not fully appreciate the

fact, but it cost them inestimable quantities of production, year after year.[59] This consideration alone is enough to condemn the idea that strips were harmless to peasant agriculture. But we have several more points to make.

4) *The Humps and Ditches Accompanying the Open Fields Created Puddles and Shadows.* Uneven moisture and sunlight complicated many of the farmer's tasks and lowered yields.[60]

5) *Plows, and Other Tools Were Very Difficult to Use on Thin Strips.* It is hardly difficult to imagine the impossibility of employing large machines like reapers on thin strips, but thin strips tormented farmers when using many of the more basic tools as well. Wooden framed harrows could not turn around on the thinnest strips, and the best iron-framed models needed about twice as much room. Simple plows can turn at just about as tight a radius as a *sokha*, but the more stable wheeled plows need much more room. Row seeders also demanded wide strips. Border violations during tillage and harrowing operations generated untold quantities of fistfights and legal protests.[61] Furthermore, on all but the very widest strips of 15 or more *sazhens*, cross-tillage was out of the question. Peasants do not appear to have had any inkling of the benefits of cross-tillage, but, as they came to appreciate its potential, the open fields would prohibit it.[62]

Strips of thin or even moderate width created a special obstacle to plowing. As we saw in our discussions of tillage, plows create twice as many "dead furrows" (either humps or ditches) as do *sokhas* (see Figures 1.5 and 1.6 "Styles of Plowing" in Part I). The most common style of tillage was *v sval* ("gathering"), where a sizeable hump remained down the center of the strip. Harrowing could wear down most of the hump, and some grain would survive on it. But over a period of years the hump would grow, as would the consequences stemming from it. Grain growing on the center of the strip would ripen earlier than the grain around it, and work with row seeders might not be possible (row seeders required a flat surface).[63] Of course farmers could try to keep their strips as flat as possible by alternating tillage *v razval* with tillage *v sval*. But it appears that few plowholders in Russia or elsewhere in Europe understood or bothered to do this.[64] For many farms holding plows, therefore, the *sokha* retained its value for at least some of their strips. It was up to the individual to decide what width of strip warranted plowing.

6) *"Neighborhood Effects."* The mere proximity of each family's land to the land of many other families created opportunities for interference of many kinds. Indeed, the primary motivation behind the humps and

ditches marking strip borders was to prevent neighbors from encroaching on one another's land by tilling an extra furrow along their own strip's edge.[65] Borders, however, could not stop thieves from filching some sheaves of grain drying unattended on adjacent strips.[66]

For the smaller farms, land parcelization often brought them an extra headache. As we noted earlier, the smaller farms would tend to get thinner strips than their neighbors. As if this was not bad enough, "Observation confirms that when land is repartitioned the small farms' tiny strips are, not rarely, grouped amidst the thicker strips of the larger farms."[67] Once the small farm tried to work a thin strip, if their harrows or tillage tools strayed over the border their neighbor would loudly protest. By means of protests over border violations, wealthy families could effectively prevent their weak neighbors from working their strips. The small farm would have no recourse to sell or rent off such strips to the wealthy neighbor, for virtually nothing.[68]

The Advantages of Open Fields

In the face of this litany of drawbacks to land parcelization, it is incumbent on us to explain why peasants continued to inter-strip their land, and did not enthusiastically rush to unify their plots when the Stolypin reform so strongly encouraged them to do so. We can cite two substantive advantages to open fields.

1) *Land Holdings Were Equalized to a Degree.* This is the most obvious advantage of the open fields, the one that virtually all analysts focus on. The common assumption that parcelization *originated* from collective egalitarian sentiments is difficult to accept, as we saw above. And more than a few scholars have scoffed at the idea that egalitarianism *ever* played any kind of role in peasant land relations.[69] But a degree of egalitarian spirit with respect to land did exist in the Russian peasantry. The periodic redistribution of land was the most obvious expression of this spirit. But peasants also perceived parcelization *in and of itself* as an egalitarian arrangement. During the late Tsarist and early Soviet periods, countless observers attested that peasants favored land parcelization as a guarantor of everyone's right to receive some of the best land in the village. "Every farmer is certain that the quality of the land varies from spot to spot, and that (when land is repartitioned) one should not be deprived of one's fair share from each spot."[70] Peasants themselves would declare that land "is parceled up among all [households], as is

just."[71] Of course this attitude does not by itself demonstrate the existence of principled egalitarian sentiments among peasants. After all, an individual's insistence that everyone in the group share in a divisible resource is just as likely to stem from that individual's fear of not getting any (when the group does divide it) as it is to stem from genuine concern for the welfare of the others in the group.

But the methods by which villages redistributed land in the central black-earth region do establish the development of a degree of egalitarianism after emancipation. Under serfdom, landlords sought to ensure that their serfs could manage to work the demesne and grow at least enough on the side to subsist. Landlords therefore enforced land repartitioning to individual families according to their labor capacity. In apportioning quantities of land to each household, labor capacity was measured by the number of marital pairs contained in them (po tiaglam). Thus a farm with three marital pairs would stand to get three times as much land as a farm with only one pair. Although households' equipment and draft horse holdings did not figure directly in po tiaglam calculations, in practice this method of land apportionment did roughly reflect farms' labor capacity. For landlords took pains to restrain the growth of economic differentiation among their serfs, including taking measures to preserve roughly equal livestock and draft horse holdings among all households.[72] Since the range of available tools and equipment available before emancipation was so limited, differentiation of labor capacity could only develop so far under serfdom.

After the emancipation, repartitions po tiaglam disappeared in favor of other methods. By the late nineteenth century, two methods were clearly dominant. The first, both chronologically and numerically, segregated farms according to the number of males (repartition po nalichnym dusham muzhskogo pola, not to be confused with a method that counted only males of working age, repartition po nalichnym rabotnikam muzhskogo pola). The second method simply assigned land according to the number of mouths to feed in each household (repartition po edokam).[73] The second method was obviously the more democratic, but even the first, which predominated in Tambov and the rest of the central black-earth region all the way up to the end of Tsarist Russia,[74] represented a very long step on the road to egalitarianism. The preoccupation with households' labor capacity so evident in repartitions po tiaglam receded. All males got a share of land; a farm could have no horses, and no tools, but if it had males, it got land. As we saw in Parts I and II, equipment holdings were growing unevenly between

families, while horselessness was growing rampantly. Over time, therefore, the number of males in a household was an ever less accurate
measure of labor capacity. Apportioning land on this basis was a very
clear sacrifice of productivity in favor of equality.

Again, it might be a stretch to label these new methods of land
repartitioning as proof of egalitarianism. As so many accounts have
emphasized, the Russian village was no paradise of equal rights for
all households.[75] The wealthier families could finagle or pressure the
commune into decisions on all kinds of questions, matters of land
distribution included. Many families must have supported the new
repartitioning rules out of fear that either in the present or the foresee-
able future they would do worse under the old rules. And, after all, the
equalizing spirit of the new rules applied only to land, not to tool or
animals, and it extended no further than the commune's borders. In
no case would a well-landed village offer to give up some of its land to
a less well landed village nearby.

At any rate, whether we call this egalitarianism or not, we do see
that communes were willing to sacrifice productivity for a certain brand
or element of equality. Equality was a good thing. And equality was
interpreted very literally: "Every farmer is certain that the quality of
the land varies from spot to spot, and that (when land is repartitioned)
one should not be deprived of one's fair share from each spot." What
could be more equal than that?! Unified plots could never offer that
much equality.

2) *The Attractions of a Common Grazing Regime.* In standard discussions of peasant attitudes towards the merits of common grazing on arable land, historians have drawn a contrast between the
larger and smaller farms based on the proportion of animals each
group grazed. In some cases they assert that the larger farms held the
lion's share of the animals, and so they would inevitably fight any
motion to curtail the common grazing regime.[76] In other cases we
read that the smaller farms held more animals per unit area of arable
land, since most peasant families would try to keep a cow and a
horse even if they did not have a lot of land.[77] If and where this was
true, the thinking goes, the smaller farms would try to enforce common grazing. Alternatively, both the largest and the smallest farms
are represented as holding relatively more animals than land, prompt-
ing both groups to oppose the desires of "middle peasants" to abolish
common grazing.[78]

Our analysis of the organization of farming in Tambov reveals that
there was no ground for conflicts between larger and smaller farms on

the issue of common grazing. As we noted in our discussion of the *propashnaia* system, common grazing was a tremendous benefit for the large farms because it economized on labor. All farms large enough to be working at or above their labor capacity for a large part of the growing season would unequivocally support common grazing. On the other hand, it might seem that small farms with surpluses of labor even at peak times had nothing to lose, and much to gain, if the village parted with common grazing. But the equation is not that simple. While the weaker farms, smaller land allotments did not permit them to produce the fodder resources necessary to maintain animal holdings as large per capita as the larger farms, the weak farms did have more animals per unit of arable land, thanks again to the fact that their allotments were so much smaller. Constantly faced with fodder shortages, the smaller farms depended on common grazing to keep their animals alive. Unless and until they found a multi-field system that promised to supply them with large quantities of summer fodder, these farms too would always support the open fields, because of the common grazing that would not be practicable otherwise.

How many families can we expect to have been in favor of the abandonment of common grazing? Perhaps all farms holding somewhere between 4–10 *desiatinas*? Maybe even a wider range? In fact, we would be a lot closer if we guessed that *no one at all wanted to abandon common grazing*. The labor common grazing saved was obvious to everyone, but the benefits of parting with it were visible only to two categories of peasants. The first were the poor households who had lost almost all of their livestock but somehow managed to continue farming. They had no use for grazing lands. They were the peasants we noticed in Part III (section, "Farm Organization in the Three-Field System: Crop Choices in the Commune") pushing crop sowings onto the fallow section of the open fields.

The second category liable to oppose common grazing on the arable lands were the farmers who understood the advantages of timely tillage or a multi-field system. We need only recall Part II of this study to sense how few farmers fell into this category. Of course, times were changing, and the population's awareness of agronomic science and farm economics would develop quickly as agronomic aid programs gathered momentum. But, as we shall emphasize on more than one occasion later, neither the government nor the *zemstvos* had started any serious measures of agronomic aid by the time that the Stolypin reform began.

As far as the great mass peasantry was concerned, therefore, common grazing was a wonderful feature of the open fields.*

While it seems clear why various farms preferred common grazing to stall feeding, we have yet to establish what objections they might have had towards tethering animals on their strips. Firstly, and most obviously, the weak who suffered so acutely from fodder shortages needed to graze on more land than they themselves had. They would always favor common grazing over tethering. Secondly, tethering would involve more inconveniences than common grazing. Families maintained quite a few grazeable animals, if we count all cattle, pigs, sheep (who are problematic to tether, since they can eat rope), and their young. That is a lot of tethering. And the animals would need periodic escort to watering holes; in any case, animals can only graze for so long within the range of a rope short enough to contain them on a 10–20-foot-wide strip of land. The 1914 budget study in Tambov included one farm that was forced to pasture their animals in this fashion after their village abolished common grazing (in connection with the formation of unified plots). "In this family ... the 10-year-old boy and the 11-year-old girl had to shepherd the cows all day from 4–5 AM to 8–9 PM, all the way from May to August. In September and October they pastured the cows for about one-fourth of each day."[79]

Furthermore—and this is perhaps the most important, yet least known, point—grazing on tethers is an inefficient use of fodder. When confined to a small area, cattle trample out more of the edible growth than they do when allowed to graze freely:

> Every farmer knows that as a grazing area shrinks, its fodder value declines not proportionally but progressively. If, for instance, a pasture of 100 *desiatinas* can support 100 head of cattle for a certain amount of time, then 50 *desiatinas* could hold not 50, but about 40. 10 *desiatinas* would suffice for about 5 head, 3 *desiatinas* for just 1.[80]

Finally, as McCloskey points out, what was to prevent fodder-short farms from tethering inaccurately, so as to allow their hungry animals

---

*We might also note here the irrelevance to peasants of another common criticism of common grazing—the uncontrolled animal breeding it allowed. Peasants were almost completely indifferent to refined methods of livestock breeding. On the other hand, farmers were concerned with horse breeding, so by the turn of the century many villages began arranging to keep stallions away from mares. For discussion, see Kerans, "The Workhorse in Late Imperial Russia."

to stray a bit onto neighbors' strips?[81] Peasants would obviously prefer common grazing to tethering.

Having treated the advantages of the open fields, at this juncture we must discuss one of the primary disadvantages of any scheme designed to abolish it. The abandonment of land parcelization would involve prodigious transaction costs. All too often, agronomists, even the very best of them, recommended that communes seeking to abandon or reduce parcelization (by reducing the number of furlongs) could compensate families receiving poorer or more distant lands with additional quantities of land. Modern scholars have repeated the argument.[82]

But this is far from an ideal solution, especially in the large villages that were so common in Tambov. If a farmer were offered two parcels of far-off, low-grade land (that averaged maybe 40 *puds* of rye per *desiatina*) for his top piece of nearby black-earth (averaging perhaps 65 *puds* per *desiatina*), would he want them? He might very well not, once he counted up how much extra work he would be forced to do on all that inferior land. The commune might offer him still more, but the more they offer, the more extra work he would be taking on. Quantity-for-quality compensations were possible, but they were not simple transactions at all.[83] The complexity rises even more in drier regions, such as the southern portions of Tambov. Here the distance of land from the nearest water source can be a paramount consideration, but it is nearly impossible to calculate. It was certainly difficult for communes to allot land in consolidated plots. Indeed, as we noted earlier, they were almost never able to arrange a reduction of the number of furlongs without seeking help from government land organization specialists.

Purported Advantages of Open Fields for Purposes of Farming in Particular

To these two reasons in favor of the open fields scholars have added six more. All six are arguments contending that parcelization was beneficial to farming in particular. Before we draw any conclusions as to the viability of land parcelization in Tambov during our time period, we must acquaint ourselves with these arguments as they relate to our subject matter.

1) It has been argued that holding land of varying qualities allowed farms to space out their labor more effectively during the year.[84] Since lands do not all reach readiness for tillage at the same time, crops do not all ripen at the same time, and so forth, families with diversified holdings would not face such a labor crunch at peak moments as they would with unified plots.

This argument seems to make perfect sense. Or does it? Firstly, it takes no account of villages dividing uniform land into two, three, or even four grades, according to its distance from the village. This aspect of parcelization aimed at equality, not productivity.

Secondly, and more importantly, the argument is irrelevant for all operations related to the spring section, since very few households sowed only one spring crop there. Nor does it have anything to do with winter grain tillage or sowing, since some imprecision in the timing of these operations was usually permissible. Rain could prompt a bit of a rush with rye sowing, but in that case the farmer would certainly prefer to have all of his land in one place, since he would have to sow it all in short order. With respect to the ripening and harvesting of winter grain, on the other hand, a farm would stand to benefit from a dispersion of strips—*provided only that growing conditions on these strips varied by a considerable margin.* This would allow the family to reap the strips sequentially as the grain ripened. But we have no reason to suspect that communes entertained such considerations in selecting the manner in which to allot their land to households. Even in the uniformly black-earth flatlands of the south, where growing conditions did not vary from spot to spot, they divided up the land into strips. Moreover, as we saw earlier in Part I, their understanding of the relationship of grain ripening to reaping was very primitive. We can be certain, therefore, that central Russian peasants did not have the labor calendar in mind when dividing land into strips.

2) According to a very old and popular argument, strips offered valuable insurance against localized crop failures from scattered afflictions such as pests or droughts. This idea too makes some sense. But did peasants really think that way? This passage comes from an informed observer in Shatsk *uezd,* in northern Tambov:

> There are people [i.e., not peasants—D.K.] who contrive to find advantages in parcelization: they say that the scattering of each farm's strips all over the landscape somehow "insures" them against complete harvest failure, since not all of the strips will be battered by hail or devoured by pests. Likewise, they

maintain, during a drought rain will sprinkle on some or another spot. These arguments are so weak and frivolous to any farmer that they are hardly worth refuting. Such "insurance" is terribly expensive, entailing as it does wasting large amounts of time and labor ... [thanks to the inefficiencies of scattering—D.K.]. And we might well ask to what extent this "insurance" actually functions, since hail and drought ordinarily visit wide areas, not the odd one-eighth of a *desiatina*.[85]

How many farmers believed that pests would show up in one spot and not travel to another? How many believed that droughts would be visited on one portion of a village's land, but not another?[86] This can of course happen, if some land is low-lying, marsh-like, or prone to flooding. But then why did communes not give everyone some land at varying moisture levels, and leave the parcelizing at that? And if insurance is what peasants wanted, why did they not just diversify their crops a bit more? That would offer them incomparably more insurance than land scattering ever could.[87]

Perhaps in some villages Russian peasants truly perceived some insurance value in land parcelization. McCloskey, for one, cites sources from other countries testifying that peasants held this position explicitly.[88] Should we concede that avoidance of risk was an attraction behind parcelization? If so, then only very tentatively. When farmers in Tula province were asked to identify drawbacks to unified plots as opposed to strips, only 1 of 163 mentioned the insurance value of strips.[89] The Tambov farmer favored the open fields because of the convenience of common grazing and the access parcelization gave him to some of the best soil. The sources do confirm this. In explaining their rationale for not wanting to consolidate their lands they never mentioned the insurance value of strips.[90]

3) According to another old argument, we hear that strips could easily be arranged to a size appropriate for a single day's plowing, thus eliminating the problem of time supposedly lost in transit between strips.[91] Beyond the point that the amount of time wasted in transit was not the main drawback to the open fields, this argument is entirely worthless. As we have already seen, the sizes of strips varied dramatically from village to village, field to field, and family to family. Nowhere was any attempt made to correlate the sizes of strips to a day's tillage. And quite rightly so. As our treatment of tillage operations in Part I demonstrated, the pace of work was highly variable.

4) It has been argued that the ditches marking strip borders were useful, and necessary, for drainage.[92] Drainage ditches could be an advantage elsewhere, but not in black-earth Russia. With their soil too poorly cared for to absorb what moisture it received from rainfall and the spring thaws, farmers were not concerned with drainage.

5) As McCloskey inquires, if strips were in fact detrimental to farming, why did no one try to buy up or rent strips in such a way as to form a unified plot? He confidently declares that farmers did not arrange to unify their plots in England, despite the presence of a market in land.[93] While this might have been so in England, it was not necessarily so in Russia. To begin with, wealthier peasants certainly did try to buy up or rent strips located alongside of their own—a tactic sometimes called *okruglenie*.[94]

We must note here that *okruglenie* served only to widen strips, not to unify them. *Okruglenie* testifies merely to farmers' preference for a very small number of strips, not for consolidated plots. But the reasons that families do not appear to have striven fully to consolidate their plots had nothing to do with any purported advantage of open fields over consolidated plots for farming purposes. The obstacle here was common grazing, which would force holders of unified plots to leave their land unsown one year in three, when that area had to lie fallow. This explanation for the limits to *okruglenie* does not satisfy McCloskey:

> The usual explanation [for why peasants held on to land in each of the sections of the crop rotation—D.K.] is that it was necessary to have land in all three fields because each year one of the three lay fallow: a peasant who held all of his land in West Field would starve in the year in which the village decreed that it must lie fallow and open to grazing livestock. The plain statement of the argument is enough to reveal its weakness, for a peasant with a more consolidated holding could raise a larger crop in one year, sell the excess to his neighbors, and buy food with the accumulated sum in the year in which his land lay fallow. There is little doubt that a market in grain inside or outside the village existed in medieval times, and no doubt whatever that it existed in a highly developed form in modern times.[95]

To borrow a phrase, the plain statement of McCloskey's argument is enough to reveal its weakness. Anyone without sowings for a year ran a terrible risk in the case of a poor harvest. Grain prices would rise dramatically, and it would be very difficult to buy enough food to keep oneself fed. Conversely, it must be admitted, a farmer with all of his land in one section of the crop rotation could raise a surplus even in a drought year for that crop. He could strike it rich. But peasant farmers were very averse to this type of gambling. More than a few times in this study we have noted how poorly—and, more amazingly, how rarely— they coped with various economic and agricultural calculations. We have also noted their reticence to make organizational adjustments that would increase their dependence on market exchanges. None of them would ever want to go a full year without sowings.

Perhaps more importantly, at least in contemplating this issue with respect to Tambov, McCloskey's reasoning overlooks the fact that only the better-off families would be able to arrange a unified plot in the midst of the commune's lands. How could these farms possibly cope with the labor demands of a rye harvest on land three times the area of their accustomed territory?! This is a huge problem, which cannot be properly solved by resorting to hiring labor on an amplified scale. Hired labor in the Russian village was no replacement for one's own.[96]

Moreover, and this is perhaps the most salient point of all, just what would these farmers do with themselves during the year that all of their land was left fallow? McCloskey proposes that they could hire themselves out to work for other peasants or a landlord. It is safe to say that successful Russian farmers would never consent to do this, even if wages for agricultural labor had been higher than their miserably low levels.[97] In sum, the fact that no one arranged to rent strips in such a way as to create a unified plot on communal land is not evidence of the superiority of open fields over consolidated plots for crop raising purposes.

6) Historians have defended parcelization by pointing to the lack of evidence that consolidated plots brought in larger rents or cost more to purchase.[98] If the price of a consolidated plot was not any higher, the argument goes, then individual farms' crop raising operations must not have benefited from consolidation. The argument is an empty one. As we have just seen, no one wanted a consolidated plot on land subject to common grazing. In Russia after 1906, when the Stolypin reform allowed families to consolidate their land and withdraw it from the common grazing regime, many of them recognized the advantages this presented for their crop raising operations. From then on, consolidated plots did in fact sell for substantially more money than inter-stripped land.[99] Badly splintered holdings were next to worthless, in extreme cases selling for as little as one-tenth the price of other lands![100]

Parcelized Holdings vs.
Consolidated Plots: Conclusions

Much of what gave the scattering of strips a bad name all over Europe was the perception that it was responsible for peasants' inertness to multi-field systems. Surely this is what fired critics of the open fields to exaggerate their shortcomings and ignore their advantages. In Part III we saw that the absence of multi-field systems in the central black-earth region had nothing to do with open fields. Excepting villages located very close to the few towns, prevailing conditions simply did not allow for multi-field systems, especially the highly touted *propashnaia* system.

Does this mean that land parcelization was economically rational so long as the three-field system remained well suited to the economic and agrotechnical conditions? Certainly strip scattering did not maximize grain yields, as Fenoaltea has argued so unconvincingly. The open fields were indeed detrimental to crop-growing operations. But dividing up each farm's land into *only a few strips* per section in the three-field (or any other) system was a very small price to pay in return for the benefits of common grazing. To everyone, except for farms that possessed the fodder to stall feed their animals, the labor to get this fodder to the animals, and the experience or education to appreciate the potential of timely tillage, the combination of common grazing and mildly scattered strips was certainly preferable to unified plots.

But this is an endorsement of well-organized open fields. Theorists weighing the merits of parcelization versus unified plots never stop to question the accuracy with which villages organized open fields.[101] In practice, the peasantry's stewardship of its landholding system sometimes evolved in a manner befitting the censure contemporaries heaped upon it. As the demand for land intensified, the mass of peasants embraced the egalitarian implications of parcelization, and they often enforced the subdivision of arable lands to a diseconomic extent. The aligning of strips downslope and the division of village land into a greater number of furlongs clearly restricted the productivity of the village's lands.

Some communes tempered this leveling tendency, either by resisting periodic repartitions of land (repartitions that would create more furlongs) or, more rarely, by undertaking partial redistributions designed to widen strips. Others, meanwhile, diffused the consequences of rampant egalitarianism by arranging to form new, smaller villages a handful of miles away. All too often, however, communes were incapable of controlling the splintering of strips. Sometimes, in fact, strips were so thin that communes gave up sections of their land:

> ... in the summer of last year, while conducting a preliminary investigation for land reorganization in a large village not far from a town, I had the chance personally to witness the absurdities, the improper use of what land communes do possess, to which parcelization into thin strips can lead. The village rents out a portion of their allotment land to peasants of a neighboring village at a very low price, only because, as the peasants themselves explain, "it simply is not worth our while to work such thin strips." And the land in question is black-earth soil, that would give above average yields if only they would take proper care of it.[102]

S. Kliuev, a Soviet era agronomist who cannot be accused of bias towards unified plots, claimed that thin strips were costing the worst affected villages as much as 50% of their crops![103]

Given what we have learned in this study about the open fields and the development of the peasant economy in Tambov, how should we assess the government's goal of reorganizing peasant agriculture through the formation of unified plots? Is it possible that the open fields were not worth saving in villages where they had not degenerated into thin strips, or not worth repairing where they had? Taking a long-term view from the year 1906, we can state with confidence that as population growth served gradually to shrink average holdings, and as transport and industrial networks slowly filled in, multi-field systems would become attractive to larger percentages of farms. But the common fields prevented individuals from serious experimentation with multi-field systems or other practices (such as employed or early fallow) that could lead farmers towards these systems. So long as common grazing went on, all of the farmers would have to adopt a new farming system at the same time. Unless the commune could agree to divide into two separate units, there was no way for half of the village to retain the three-field system while the rest tried a *propashnaia*. Without personal experimentation or acquaintance with multi-field systems, few farmers would be inclined to support the introduction of a new system. Moreover, the power of large, wealthy farms to manipulate village assemblies would allow them to oppose the introduction of multi-field systems. We might, therefore, argue that land parcelization was destined to exercise an increasingly deleterious influence on the peasant economy, even if it were lessened.

On the other hand, there was, and remains, room for a different point of view on this issue. When *minorities* of families on land with common grazing wished to convert to a different farming system, then common grazing (and, by extrapolation, the open fields) did pose an insurmountable obstacle. But once a *majority* arose in favor of a change, and once this majority overcame the resistance of the wealthier families who opposed change, then the open fields became something of an ally in the spread of new farming systems. According to the law, in communal assemblies two-thirds of the heads of households constituted a majority sufficient to undertake all manners of land reorganization projects, including the rearrangement of field systems. While a farmer on a consolidated plot could introduce any number of innovations, he could only lead by example. The peasant commune, by contrast, had the potential to impose advanced farming systems *en masse*. As we shall see in Part V, it was this feature of the commune as an agent of technological change that lay at the heart of the competing vision for the reorganization of peasant agriculture which the *zemstvos* and their agronomists counterposed to the Stolypin reform.[104]

The Stolypin Reform
and the Configuration of Peasant Lands

Distant Lands and Inaccessible Lands

The parcelization of land is the feature of village land organization that has drawn the most attention, both from contemporary analysts and historians of peasant agriculture. To peasants themselves, however, the distance or convenience of access to their land was often a more important problem.

As we noted during our examination of the *propashnaia* system, the 1914 budget study established that most communes possessed arable lands located at a great distance from the village. In the northern, central, and southern *uezds*, the most distant patches of land were 3.6, 5.5, and 5.7 *versts* away from the village, respectively. Thorough statistics on this question from *uezds* bordering Tambov to the south and west suggest that the villages selected for the budget study were probably a bit more fortunate in this regard than typical villages. In Elets *uezd*, on the eastern edge of Orel province, bordering Tambov's Lipetsk and Lebedian *uezds*, 21% of the communes had land at five or more *versts* away. In Voronezh *uezd*, on Tambov's southern border, 29% of the villages had such land, with 16% having land at distances of ten *versts* or more.[105]

The long distances peasants had to travel to some of their lands was an inevitable consequence of the great breadth across which villages held land. The paucity of water sources had conditioned the formation of large villages along rivers, and as population grew communities had little choice but to extend their croplands further and further out into the prairie. The further out they went, the more difficult it became to maintain farming operations at customary levels: "Transit to and from far-off strips chews up a mass of time, tires horses, compels hurried and careless tillage, and greatly delays both tillage and the collection of the harvest."[106] According to one calculation, land located 9.2 kilometers away required twice as much time to work as land 1.4 kilometers away.[107] Hauling home the harvest from distant fields was an arduous task all by itself. A farmer with a *desiatina* of rye located 10 *versts* from the village would need five complete days of work to cart home an average yield.[108] Moreover, it is not difficult to imagine the extent of the weed problem on distant lands, or the consequences for yields. Rotting and theft of unattended sheaves after reaping was certainly commonplace out there. What were the chances of such land receiving manure? One observer estimated yields on distant lands to be about 30% below yields on other lands.[109]

Sub-optimal configurations of villages' lands served to amplify the hazards of distant fields:

> ... the most typical and widespread defect in the layout of peasant lands is the extension of the territory away from one side of the village. The fields of commune #1 of the village Sosnovka, formerly the property of Count Benkendorf, begin one and a half *versts* from the village and stretch out for 15 *versts*. The most distant fields, moreover, are the widest, while the nearest are but 90 *sazhens* wide. The narrow fields belonging to the village *Ot'ias* extend for 12 *versts*; the village must position the sections of its crop rotation sequentially, one behind the other at greater distances from the village.[110]

Awkward, ribbon-like configurations of land were especially likely to occur among villages clustered together along one side of a river or stream. According to one estimate, fully half of the 300,000 peasants in Kirsanov *uezd* lived in such villages along the Vorona river. Their fields stretched out into the steppe for 20 or more *versts*.[111] This malady was not rare throughout Tambov's central and southern *uezds*, and indeed over much of black-earth Russia.[112]

More common was the interspersion of communes' lands with landlords' or other communes' lands. Most often, this interspersion arose out of the haste with which government officials registered communes' land holdings after the emancipation decree in 1861. Rather than conduct complicated surveying operations to delineate each individual commune's lands, officials frequently preferred to assign large units of land to groups of neighboring villages.[113] They left it to the peasants themselves to divide up the lands between them. Communes often did so in the fashion of intra-communal land repartitions—they split up the land according to quality and category (arable, pasture, meadow, etc.) and assigned each commune disconnected portions of land.[114] As late as 1905 24% of peasant lands in Tambov remained registered in multi-communal tenure; disconnected holdings, distant lands, and animosities between villages were typical consequences.[115]

Alternatively, interspersed land holdings arose out of the emancipation, when landlords insisted on keeping the best lands on the estate for themselves. They did not wish to part with the demesne's top quality fields, even if these fields were stuck in the midst of lands allotted to the peasants. Moreover, under serfdom some landlords had sought to boost serfs' labor productivity by including the arable lands closest to the village in the demesne. They retained this arrangement in the emancipation contracts, leaving the village with a variable number of plots elsewhere.[116]

Unlike some of the neighboring provinces, the *zemstvos* in Tambov did not undertake any statistical studies of interspersed holdings. The best we can do is to present the results of such studies from *uezds* bordering Tambov [Table 4.4]: In extreme cases in the region, in Kursk

Table 4.4. Communes with Interspersed Holdings
(at the turn of the twentieth century)

	% of communes holding land in # of parcels		
	2	3–5	6 or more
Elets (Orel)	11.0	4.2	0.2
Zadonsk (Voronezh)	17.5	4.1	0.0
Voronezh (Voronezh)	17.3	9.1	0.3
Bobrov (Voronezh)	8.9	1.3	0.0
Novokhopersk (Voronezh)	13.6	3.8	0.0

Source: Pershin, *Zemel'noe ustroistvo,* pp. 175–177.

province, some communes were saddled with 100 or more separate units of land.[117] But, as the chart indicates, only a moderate proportion of villages faced any hardship from land interspersion.

Those communes that did have multiple units of land faced special difficulties in escorting their herds to the fields for grazing. The threat of legal complications if the animals damaged the crops or hayfields of a landlord or other village on the way to the fields more or less forced peasants to rent some of this land if they were ever to take their herds out to isolated fields. When communes declined to pay for the privilege of livestock passage, they collided with an entirely different malady. Farmers abused land not subject to common grazing:

... the primary reason for unregulated farming on some units of land is the inconvenient configuration of villages' land allotments.... On so-called *pestropol'e** units of land only a few farmers ever leave strips fallow, while the majority simply sow grain year after year, which badly exhausts the soil. Peasants themselves attest that yields are always lower on *pestropol'e* land than under the three-field system—both grain and straw yields are low, and the grains themselves are small.[118]

Land Configuration and Consolidation of Plots

At least in the early stages of the Stolypin reform, officials envisioned the consolidation of plots as a cure for the poor configuration of peasant lands as well as for strip parcelization. Everyone recognized that in villages with land spread out over large areas the unification of strips into consolidated holdings would not by itself spare the farmer from tremendous expenditures of time and effort on transit to and from his land. This concern prompted the government to push for peasants to relocate their dwellings onto their newly created unified plots. For administrators, the farmstead (*khutor* in Russian land organization terminology) thus became the panacea for all the deficiencies of peasant land organization. Simple unified plots onto which peasants did not relocate their homes (known as *otrubs*) were less desirable. The central authorities, therefore, pushed local officials to arrange *khutors*, not *otrubs*, wherever possible.[119]

Unfortunately, conditions in Tambov and most of the rest of black-earth Russia were not favorable to the formation of *khutors*. Water sources were too sparsely distributed, as were meadows, forests, and villages themselves. Peasants did not wish to move away from accustomed water sources, churches, schools, and companionship.[120] Moving to a *khutor* was expensive, especially when we consider that this would force families to trade away their most valuable land of all, the garden plot.

Regardless of these unpropitious conditions, provincial administrations in Tambov and other black-earth provinces were under just as much pressure to form *khutors* as administrations elsewhere. Parroting the government line in favor of *khutors*, many local officials in Tambov

---

**Pestropol'e* denotes systemless cropping on land not subject to common grazing. Agronomists all over the black-earth zone constantly complained about farmers' tendency to overexploit such lands.

did initially pass this pressure on to the peasantry.[121] In addition to whatever extra-legal coercion they devised, they might offer substantial financial assistance above and beyond aid from central institutions to cover the costs of reconstructing their dwellings and garden plots on the new sites.[122] Their efforts went unappreciated; peasants quite correctly avoided *khutors*. Research revealed that many of those who did purchase *khutors* from the Peasant Land Bank did so only because nearby villages that had always rented the land in question declined to buy them.[123] Land-hungry "outsiders" thus unexpectedly got their hands on some extra land. The Peasant Land Bank's *khutors* were the less attractive for the crudity with which they were set up; the Bank often divided estates into *khutors* without proper combinations of categories of lands or adequate access to water sources.[124]

In the last years before the World War the government gradually came to recognize the inefficacy of insisting on *khutors* over *otrubs*.[125] The provincial administration in Tambov came to the same conclusion as early as the end of 1909.[126] From then on, the Land Organization Committees tried to redesign Peasant Land Bank lands into small communities in the center of a number of *otrubs*.[127] And so *otrubs* predominated over *khutors* in the province from then on. This did not signify, however, that the government had given up on reducing the consequences of distant and inaccessible lands. As we shall see in our treatment of group land organization, peasants and enlightened administrators managed eventually to shift the focus of the Stolypin reform away from the formation of consolidated plots. The new emphasis fell primarily on projects designed to eliminate interspersed land holdings and arrange micro-villages on distant lands.

The Stolypin Reform in Action

The Administration Takes the Initiative

Before we examine the intra-village relationships that did so much to shape the direction of the Stolypin reform, we must be aware that the government did not simply issue the law of 1906 and stand by to observe peasants' reactions. It is true that in Tambov, at any rate, pressure from St. Petersburg does not appear to have filtered down to local officials very powerfully before 1909. Some of the Land Captains virtually ignored the reform up to this time, burying themselves in other duties.[128] Inspectors from St. Petersburg touring Tambov in 1909 found villages where no one had even heard of the Stolypin reform.[129] But by then Stolypin and company were losing patience with the sluggish pace of the reform throughout the nation, and they instructed the provincial Governors to step up the pressure on peasant communes to form consolidated plots.[130] Beginning in 1909 the administrative climate in Tambov changed markedly.

When directives from St. Petersburg to encourage consolidations reached him, Tambov Governor N. P. Muratov quickly organized a series of meetings with Land Organization Committees, the Land Captains, and all other pertinent administrative personnel to discuss the matter. The records of one of these meetings, perhaps the most important one of all, have survived.[131] These records starkly reveal the substance and style of the pressure the administration exerted on local officials and peasants in order to further the Stolypin reform. The meeting in question took place in Tambov from the 21st to the 23rd of September 1909. In attendance were all of the most important personnel from Kirsanov, Kozlov, and Tambov *uezds*, as well as from the provincial level.

On September 21st, 1909, under the approving eye of Governor Muratov, Vice-Governor N. Iu. Shil'der-Shul'dner delivered a strongly worded opening speech to the assembled Land Captains, Land Organization Committee members, *zemstvo* officials, and other administrative ranks.[132] He insisted that privatization of land tenure must replace the repartitional commune, and that consolidated plots must replace the open fields. In conjunction with subsequent measures of agronomic aid, this path, and only this path, would save the peasantry from deeper impoverishment and famine:

> ... every day, every hour, and everywhere, all agronomic aid personnel must energetically explain to the peasant farmer that he has no future outside of the new form of land organization.[133]

Shil'der-Shul'dner then appealed to his audience to devote maximum energy to the fulfillment of the reform. He emphasized the administration's conviction that the law of 1906 had put all of them in the front lines of what he cloudily termed "a general battle for historical necessity." In keeping with this spirit, the Governor had already authorized the Land Captains to drop all of their commitments in the oversight of peasant legal matters for all but eight days per month. He was now considering relieving them of such duties altogether. This would allow the Land Captains to focus almost entirely on pushing through the reform. Beyond this, the Governor announced that he had allocated "significant funds" to be awarded to those Land Captains who put forth the greatest effort in carrying out the Stolypin reform.[134]

But how were they to go about doing this? Shil'der-Shul'dner instructed them thusly:

> Almost all of your administrative activity should consist of visits to villages, convoking village meetings, deciding matters on the spot. Categorically we demand that you actively pursue the implementation of the law of November 9th [the decree of 1906], a task which is entirely within your capabilities....[135]

Shil'der-Shul'dner also reassured the Land Captains that they were not to harbor any anxieties about putting pressure on peasants in the interests of furthering the reform. He did not, on this occasion anyway, endorse strong-arming communes into forming otrubs en masse. He asked instead for the Land Captains to exert "constant moral pressure" on the peasants, to "agitate" for commune-wide consolidations. And he promised to support their efforts to the fullest:

> In order to work productively and successfully, you must first of all have firm soil under your feet. I consider it our sacred obligation, as the highest organs of state power in the province, to secure for you, Land Captains, this chief guarantor of success. Anyone senseless enough to seek to undermine your authority,

which is so important to your work, will get an appropriate rebuff.[136]

The Vice-Governor was giving the Land Captains his word that anyone daring to agitate against or obstruct the Stolypin reform would be silenced. Many people among the educated community in the province were not well disposed towards the Stolypin reform, and were speaking out against it.[137] Most prominently, but not exclusively, these were members and sympathizers of Russia's young socialist parties, like the Socialist Revolutionary party and the social-democratic parties.

The administration in Tambov sensed that the main sources of opposition, however, resided within the peasantry and local official-dom. They feared that the largest and most influential farms in the villages would influence village officials and the local police to obstruct the formation of consolidated plots. As we saw in our analysis of the attractiveness of open fields to various sizes of farms, these fears were not groundless. The larger farms had good reasons not to want their villages to form unified plots. But so did almost all other farms! It comes therefore as no surprise to learn that Land Captains and *zemstvo* officials at the conference denied the existence of any campaign on the part of wealthy peasants to enlist the collusion of village and police officials in stopping consolidations.[138] Whatever the true extent of local officials' opposition to consolidations may have been, Governor Mura-tov was sufficiently concerned to insist that he be personally informed regarding any local official suspected of hindering the progress of the reform. Even passivity or sluggishness in the processing of consolidations warranted such oversight.[139]

Overall, the message from the provincial leadership to its Land Captains and other intermediate ranks was clear. The Stolypin reform would be reform from above, with the Land Captains and Land Organization Committees leading the charge. No one was asking them to coerce peasants in any way. But at the same time, no one was warning them to temper their approach to encouraging consolidations. It is difficult to tell how many of the assembled officials agreed with their leadership's approach to the reform. The presence of the Governor and the Vice-Governor probably intimidated anyone who might have had misgivings about prematurely pushing peasants into consolidations. At any rate, in the discussions that followed Shil'der-Shul'dner's address only the two highest-ranking *zemstvo* officials (whose positions were semi-autonomous from the Governor's control) and one Land Captain attempted to soften the leadership's approach to the reform.[140]

The Peasantry's Response
to the Stolypin Reform

Aquisitions of Hereditary Title to Land

Officials in Tambov could not have been displeased about the quantities of peasant households that sought to acquire hereditary title to
their allotment land. Almost as soon as news of the reform reached the
villages a great wave of families rushed to take advantage of this
opportunity. According to official statistics, by September 1st 1914,
communes had received 134,560 requests for transfer of land to personal title. This is a very large figure, representing 28% of all households
registered as members of communes in the province.[141] But, in the face
of intra-village hostility, 2,736 farms (2% of the requests) withdrew
their petitions before the village assembly put the issue up for discussion. Village assemblies approved only 10% of the remaining requests,
automatically transferring the other 90% to the Land Captains' offices
for appeal. Appeals were virtually guaranteed success, since Land
Captains were under instructions to approve transfers of land into
personal title. But local animosities obviously dissuaded many peasants
as they waited for the Land Captains to process their acquisitions of
personal title. 7.5% of the households reaching this stage withdrew
their requests before processing was complete. By September 1914
90,936 households—19% of all households in the province*—had
received private title to their land.[142] Over 34,000 of these deals were
complete in the first two years of the reform, the pace slowing thereafter.[143] In addition, the Ministry of Internal Affairs estimated that about
15,000 more households should be considered to hold their land in
personal tenure, in accordance with the 1st article of the law of 1910
(that abolished communal tenure in any commune not having performed a full land repartition since the emancipation).[144]

While these numbers must have pleased the government, they did
not enchant the majority of the peasantry. Several factors fueled
villagers' animosity towards those of their members who applied for

*The 90,000 who acquired personal tenure represented 18.9% of all peasant
households, or 19.4% of all households residing in communes that had held their
allotment in communal tenure (as opposed to hereditary household tenure) before the
Stolypin reform began. Only 3% of the province's peasants lived in communes with
hereditary tenure as of 1905 (Dubrovskii, *Stolypinskaia zemel'naia reforma*, prilozhenie 1).

private title. To begin with, any transfer of land out of communal tenure reduced the commune's reserves of its most valuable commodity, land. The land that these families took away would never again be available to those who remained as full-fledged participants in the commune, or to their children.[145] The commune could even lose herd-grazing rights on these lands, if the owner subsequently elected to petition for a consolidated plot.

Village assemblies' indignation will be easier to understand once we identify the kinds of people who were requesting personal title. One very astute observer of the Stolypin reform in practice, V. P. Drozdov, characterized those most commonly petitioning for personal title thusly:[146]

1) Families preparing to leave the village for full-time work in the cities or relocation to Siberia. This was a significant portion of the population—in the period 1906–1914 about 4% of all peasant families in the central black-earth region migrated to Siberia alone.[147]

2) Families who had left the village long ago, but had remained registered as members of communes. They had been renting their land to neighbors; now they sought title to the land so as to sell it. Drozdov notes cases of Tambov peasants returning to their villages to demand personal title after absences of 30–40 years!

3) Households that had shrunk since the previous land repartition, and so stood to lose land upon the next repartition. A family that had lost one of its two males, for instance, stood to lose half of its land—without any compensation.

4) Peasants obtaining title as protection. They could sell the land quickly in case they might need some cash sometime in the future.

A survey of peasant attitudes towards the Stolypin reform taken in 1910–11 more or less confirms the accuracy of Drozdov's picture for Tambov.[148] The average size of privatized holdings, only 4.1 *desiatinas*, likewise testifies to the preponderance of weaker farms among the privatizers.[149]

Considering the kinds of people that were requesting personal title, it is easy to understand their neighbors' hostility. In peasants' eyes, households belonging to categories 2) and 3) in the above scheme had no moral right to take land away from the commune:

> ... in our village families are acquiring personal property for land allotted to members that have since died. We find this extremely offensive; the dead get land, while the living do not ...[150]

> It is quite clear why people seek personal tenure. Those who
> have non-agricultural jobs wish to sell their land and leave the
> village, while others—loafers—sell off their land and drink the
> proceeds, leaving their children landless forever.[151]

Households in the first category, meanwhile, presented a subtler
problem. These people obviously intended to sell their land to the
highest bidder, who would of course be one of the richer members of
the village.[152] The commune could attempt to buy the land, and dole
it out as though the land remained in communal tenure. But the Land
Captains were wise to this defense, and could intervene to ensure that
land in personal tenure stayed out of communes' hands.[153] Drozdov
even met a Tambov Land Captain who was quite willing to allow
non-peasant speculators to purchase privatized allotment land. To
Drozdov's objection that was against the law (only peasants could own
allotment land, and in limited quantities), the Land Captain pled
ignorance.[154] Even in the unlikely event that the commune might
eventually succeed in recovering privatizers' lands, why should they put
themselves through such an ordeal? The wisest move was to deny
requests for personal tenure: "Communes are refusing requests for
personal tenure out of their own interests, seeking to keep the land in
their disposal."[155]

The government always advertised concern with agrotechnical
problems as one of its primary reasons for promoting acquisitions of
personal title. Thus, once the farmer no longer feared losing his land
in the next repartition, he would supposedly be more likely to manure
the land and otherwise take better care of it. But almost none of the
households requesting personal title had such considerations in mind.
The complete absence of any connection between privatization and
improved farming methods was impossible to deny. The Free Economic
Society's survey found no difference whatsoever between privatizers'
and communal peasants' agricultural techniques and results.[156] In final
confirmation of the irrelevance to privatizers of the supposed agrotechnical advantages of personal tenure, we may note that these households
often readily consented to shifting the location of their strips when the
remaining members of the commune performed subsequent land repartitions.[157] It was the *amount* of land that really mattered to them, not
the permanence of their strips' locations.[158]

The Formation of Consolidated Plots

As we noted in our overview of the Stolypin reform, the government did not place primary emphasis on unified plots until about 1908–09. In the absence of intensive agitation and propaganda the consolidation movement did not acquire any momentum in Tambov. According to the Governor's information, up to the middle of 1909, only 1,752 households had filed requests for individual consolidations of allotment land, while 26 communes with another 1,399 farms had voted to form consolidated plots in unison.[159] For a province with about 450,000 farms in 3,344 communes, this was a paltry showing indeed.[160] Since the Land Captains and Land Organization Committees greatly intensified their agitation after the Governor's conferences in the late summer of 1909, these numbers probably tell us more about peasants' attitudes to consolidations than do the statistics covering the whole period of the Stolypin reform. Be that as it may, the number of households consolidating their plots in 1911 was double the number in 1910, and quadruple the number in 1909.[161] The provincial Land Organization Commission reported 25,727 consolidated plots on allotment land as of the end of 1914, which represented 5.3% of all farms.[162]

The statistics regarding consolidated plots on non-allotment land are less precise. The Peasant Land Bank did not record how many purchasers of its consolidated properties also possessed consolidated plots on allotment land. Nor did they record how many of their customers purchased more than one property. There must have been some overlap. Moreover, the Peasant Land Bank's statistics were never complete.[163] Pershin calculated the amount of peasant-held non-allotment consolidated lands to be 92,716 *desiatinas* of such land, versus 178,066 *desiatinas* of allotment land consolidations.[164] Thus unified plots occupied about 6% of allotment land and about 14% of peasant-owned non-allotment land.[165] The 270,782 *desiatinas* of consolidated lands represented a little over 7% of all peasant-held lands. Given the fact that consolidated farms tended to have a bit more land than the average farm, we can estimate that somewhere between 6–6.5% of the households in the province were involved in the consolidation movement.[166]

Peasant Attitudes to Consolidated Plots

Agrotechnical Considerations

In reading through the sources relating central black-earth region peasants' attitudes towards consolidated plots, one cannot help but recognize the clumsiness of the government's attempt to reorganize peasant agriculture along individual lines. These sources confirm our conclusions presented above with respect to the advantages of arable land parcelization. The great majority of farmers did not want to unify their lands in one spot, nor did they relish the prospect of some of their neighbors doing so. At the same time, the identical sources illustrate the ambivalence many farmers felt towards their traditional communal organization of agriculture. They were aware of the drawbacks to the open fields.

When asked why they did not desire unified plots, peasants almost always insisted that they did not have enough land to allow this. The following comments all come from peasant participants in the Free Economic Society survey:

> Consolidations would be bad for our commune, because we have so little land.—Kirsanov *uezd*

> Open fields are preferable, because we do not have much land, and our consolidated plots would be too small—Kozlov *uezd*

> In our opinion, open fields are preferable ... because our allotments are so small. And besides, what kind of consolidated plot could you make out of two or three *desiatinas*, which is a greater amount of land than some of us have.—Morshansk *uezd*

> In our area there are no *otrubs* or *khutors* as of yet; all are constricted and suffering from land hunger, and are expecting some action from the government on that score.—Kozlov *uezd*[167]

At first glance these comments appear quixotic. If they had so little land then should they not have welcomed the opportunity to escape from land parcelization and the common grazing regime that prevented them from adopting some intensive farming practices? Land hunger by itself cannot explain the widespread antipathy towards unified plots.

When complaining that their landholdings were too small to allow for consolidations, peasants surely had in mind the difficulties of livestock grazing we discussed earlier, during our analysis of the relationship between common grazing and the open fields. Small, fodder-short farms relied on common grazing to keep their animals alive, while the larger farms supported common grazing so as to economize on labor. This equation also appears illogical at first glance. It does make sense that a farm of 2–3 *desiatinas* could not feed a horse and a cow unless the family managed to intensify their farming a great deal. But how could a family holding 15 or more *desiatinas* of land complain that they needed more land in order to run their farm successfully on a consolidated plot? When asked how large a unified plot would have to be before they would consider it preferable to their dispersed holdings, peasant responses varied from 8 *desiatinas* to 50 *desiatinas*![168] Why?

Much of the answer lies in the distribution of labor requirements between farming and livestocking operations in differently sized farms. As we discovered during our analyses of farm organization and common grazing in Part III, the larger farms with more than 12 or 15 *desiatinas* of land could not generally afford to expend labor on livestock during much of the growing season. They would welcome consolidation only if they had so much arable land that they could comfortably afford to leave a large portion of this land unsown. This would permit their animals to roam and forage all summer with minimal oversight. And it would leave their hands free to concentrate on crop raising.

In contrast to the large farms, most medium-sized farms (in the range of about 6–12 *desiatinas*) could cope with the labor required for tethering and extra stall feeding. And they understood that a consolidated plot would benefit their crop-growing operations.[169] All too often, however, these and other peasant families had no idea if or how a new fodder arrangement would work in practice. Many simply did not envision themselves replacing the common grazing regime with tethering or full-time stall feeding:

> Peasants do not relish the prospect of unifying their strips into
> separate plots, both because of lack of land and because this

would complicate the grazing of livestock on arable land.—
Tambov *uezd*, landowner

Otrubs just won't work for us ... what can one do on a small plot
of two *desiatinas*? Not only your horse or your cow, but even your
chickens will trample all of your sowings.—Morshansk *uezd*, a
peasant

The good side of consolidated plots is that all of the land is in
one place. But as far as the animals are concerned, well, you
can't do anything with them.—Riazan province, a peasant[170]

There were no insuperable agrotechnical obstacles preventing medium-sized farms from consolidating their holdings. But as far as these
people could tell, neither were there any over-arching advantages.
Until they came to appreciate the benefits of improved tillage or
multi-field systems more fully, they would not feel inclined to abandon
the traditional common grazing regime. Even where distant land and
narrow strips bedeviled them, cautiousness before the unknown could
hold peasants back from land reorganization:

Consolidated plots would be better, because communal lands
are spread out too far from the village—15 *versts*—and are cut
up into a large number of strips. The peasants are aware of this,
but attachment to old ways and uncertainty over how things
would work out keeps them from acting.—Kirsanov *uezd*, a
priest[171]

Intra-village relations must have dissuaded many potential consolidators. More often than not, peasants and village assemblies were ill-
disposed towards neighbors who consolidated plots. On an instinctive
level, they did not want to lose access to any of their customary grazing
lands. Since the average consolidator did in fact have more land than
the average family, consolidators probably were taking away relatively
more land from the commune than animals. In other words, their
consolidations did slightly reduce fodder sources for those who remained. Those households who had to relocate some of their strips to
make room for the formation of consolidated plots must have been
among the angriest.

Once potential consolidators made themselves known, neighbors
were not shy about issuing threats. In the opinion of Ivan Satin, Marshal
of Nobility of Tambov *uezd*, fear of arson and deliberate communal herd

trampling of crops was the primary reason for the weakness of the consolidation movement.[172] Alternatively, neighbors would promise potential consolidators that the village assembly would arrange them a plot on the worst and most distant lands, or that they would not allow them necessary freedom of access to their unified plot through communal lands.[173] Of course if their neighbors actually carried out such threats the consolidators could expect support from Land Captains and Land Organization Commissions. But not everyone would want to brave such friction. Statistics available only from 1913 on testify to village assemblies' resistance to unified plots. In 1913 and 1914 they refused to sanction consolidations 60% and 54% of the time, respectively.[174]

Other Considerations

Agrotechnical considerations by themselves cannot possibly explain all peasants' attitudes towards consolidations. Many households would not even have fit into our scheme based on farm sizes, labor reserves, and fodder balances. Families with unusual ratios of workers-to-eaters could have very different organizational features. Since the predominant criterion for land apportionment was the number of males in the household, the larger farms would certainly tend to have the highest labor capacity. But, as we mentioned earlier, families with varying worker-to-eater ratios existed all across the spectrum from smaller to larger farms. The vagaries of family composition and livestock holdings created many exceptions to our scheme separating farms according to their landholdings. Nevertheless, this scheme seems very useful in explaining the sluggishness of the consolidation movement in the central black-earth region. When we come to examine the profiles of households that did consolidate, we will see that they were indeed mid-sized farms blessed with higher than average labor capacity.

However useful our agrotechnical scheme may be, many other circumstances served to shape peasant attitudes towards consolidations. Thus most of the larger farms were strong enough to buy or rent some non-allotment land on their own, and to arrange to rent land from the weaker farms. They did not stand to benefit so much from the crop-raising advantages of a unified plot, since some of their land would remain scattered anyway. Nor would the wealthy entrepreneurial peasant be anxious to reduce his ties to the community. He might have a successful store in the village, operate a windmill or a threshing machine, or hold debts over the heads of fellow villagers. As Chernyshev put it, "the *miroed* (exploiter of fellow peasants, 'kulak') had no reason to hurry to leave the commune. The dismantling of the commune would dismantle the foundations of his wealth."[175] If such peasants wanted to experiment with better tillage they could easily do so on some of their non-allotment lands. Alternatively, they could arrange for one of the sons to separate and set up a consolidated plot. The truly wealthy could enjoy the best of both worlds:

> Most of the small, consolidated plots pass very quickly into the hands of a few well-off peasants. These latter do not separate from the commune themselves; having a lot of *otrub* land on the side, they still make full use of grazing with the communal herds.[176]

Financial incentives certainly influenced a substantial minority of families seeking consolidated plots. The Peasant Land Bank gave interest-free loans of 150 rubles to anyone who contracted to purchase a pre-prepared unified plot and agreed to move their dwelling to the spot.[177] The government gave out a large number of 100-ruble subsidies under similar circumstances.[178] And a decree of November 1906 made mortgages of allotment land accessible only to those who had consolidated that land.[179] Moreover, unified plots sold for higher prices than dispersed holdings. The Free Economic Society survey gathered information on the ownership status of only 82 unified plots, but the results are telling: 38 were working their land themselves, 22 rented it out, and 22 had sold it off in entirety.[180]

Methods of Forming Consolidated Plots on Allotment Land

Because of the unattractiveness of consolidated plots to most households and the complexity of rearranging arable lands into unified plots, very few villages elected to abandon the open fields in unison. As we noted earlier, only 26 villages made this decision before the administration devoted its undivided attention to the formation of consolidated plots in late 1909. By 1917 a total of 296 villages had petitioned for unified plots, of which 172 had completed the transition.[181] 37% of all consolidated plots in the province arose through commune-wide conversion.[182]

For the most part these appear to have been small villages with a large percentage of failing farms. Averaging only 64 households per commune, they were little more than one-third the size of the typical village.[183] They averaged less than 7 *desiatinas* of land (all categories of land) per household.[184] Indeed it is difficult to imagine the largest villages wanting to break up into unified plots, since some farms would have to accept plots at great distances away from home. A thorough study of all consolidators in Orel *uezd* in 1913 found that communes adopting unified plots in unison were poor and short of land.[185] The following passage, from a peasant letter to the newspaper *Tambovskii Krai*, is probably representative of the plight of these villages after commune-wide consolidations:

> We have nothing to smile about here, our position is pitiful. Not even a good harvest will help; very many small farms are faced with famine in the near future. I cannot see all of huge Russia from here, but I can see the large village Glukhovka, Kirsanov *uezd*. Land organization has done in the peasants of this village for good. They might as well quit farming and board an airplane for Mars.[186]

Farming on the Consolidated Plots

Since the government intended the consolidation movement to lead the peasantry down the path of agricultural revolution, any analysis of the Stolypin reform in its relationship to Russia's agrarian problems must attempt to evaluate the agricultural performance of the consolidators. Who exactly were these "pioneers," and how did they manage their farms? Who imitated their practices, and how many peasants adopted unified plots after seeing consolidators' farms in action? Answers to these questions can tell us where the Stolypin reform was headed before the period of wars and revolutions began in mid-1914.

Unfortunately, existing data are far too weak to allow for firm conclusions regarding any of these questions. With the exception of one *uezd* in Orel province, no one undertook any thorough studies of consolidated farms anywhere in the central black-earth region. For Tambov, we will have to rely on one small survey of 412 *khutors* on State lands in the southern and central *uezds* in 1912.[187] All other information is anecdotal in character.

We may note, however, that the period of time between the formation of consolidated plots and the disruptions beginning in 1914 would be too short for us to identify meaningful trends in consolidators' agriculture even if we had more data. These households almost always faced difficult hurdles in reorganizing their farms during the first few years after separating from the commune. They had to make new arrangements for animal care, which always entailed unaccustomed expenditures of labor. They had to acquaint themselves with the features of their new plot, in order to decide which crops would do best on which spots. And more often than not they had to deal with tired soil, because communes would not assign them land in fields coming out of fallow.[188] Those who purchased plots on non-allotment lands always had supplementary expenses. They had to pay a lot of money for their land, and a lot more if they moved their dwellings there. Government loans helped them to get through this period, but rarely covered more than one-third of all the expenses.[189]

Further clouding evaluations of consolidators' work is the fact that a minority of them either would not or could not entirely separate their agricultural operations from the commune's. A little-known article of the decree of 1906 permitted consolidators to graze their animals with communal herds and also to prohibit the same herds from trespassing on their unified plots.[190] If enforced, this law would have been tremendously beneficial to consolidators. But it appears to have been ignored. Instead, there is evidence that the communal herds sometimes visited separators' lands. Here is one such case:

> According to researchers, local peasants sometimes insist on sending their herds to graze on *otrubs*. Since these plots' arable land lies within one section of the communes' land, this forces farmers to leave their plots entirely unsown one year in three.[191]

Obviously consolidators facing such circumstances could never introduce a multi-field system or employed fallow. In a similar vein, we can recall how wealthy farms would often retain their communal allotments—and hence the right of their animals to participate in common grazing—while appropriating weaker households' consolidated plots. Limited evidence suggests more than half of the consolidators managed to keep at least a portion of their allotment lands.[192] For grazing purposes, some of those who had sold their allotments probably transferred some of their livestock to relatives who stayed in the commune.[193] Furthermore, as we noted earlier, farmers on connected groups of consolidated plots sometimes arranged their sowings so as to allow herd grazing on the arable land. Participation in these various kinds of common grazing relieved some consolidators of the need to reorganize farming.

A final difficulty in analyzing farming on unified plots stems from the fact that *zemstvo* agronomic aid programs penetrated the countryside in the last five years before the World War. As we shall see in Part V, the local agronomists influenced communal and consolidated farming alike. In these circumstances, it is not possible to interpret all of the technical advances we spot on consolidators' farms as reflections of the characteristics of the consolidators or as the direct consequences of land organization. After 1910 many new methods gained currency thanks only to the efforts of the *zemstvo* agronomists. Without their propaganda consolidators' farms would not have looked the way they did.

A Profile of Consolidators:
The 1912 Study of *Khutors* on State Lands

Keeping in mind that our data are very weak, we may now proceed to examine Tambov consolidators' agricultural potential. Because the 1912 study embraced only *khutors* on State Lands, its subjects must have been among the economically strongest consolidators in the province. Their plots were rather expensive, especially when taxes and the cost of transferring their dwellings and farm structures to the new plot are included.[194] Nevertheless, few of them came from the most wealthy and powerful peasant households. Judging from horse and livestock holdings, about 75% of them came from the middle peasantry or the stronger portions of the middle peasantry. Only 3% had no horse, while 61% had one horse, 33% had two or three. Just 3% came from the very large farms, with four or more horses.[195] The largest farms were participating in the consolidation movement, but they were under-represented versus their numbers in the communes. In 1912 8% of the province's households had four or more horses.[196]

Almost all of the consolidators belonged to the 5–15 *desiatina* range of farm. Their average holding, including any lands they might have retained in their communes or purchased elsewhere, totaled 12.1 *desiatinas*.[197] Throughout the growing season they were able to handle almost the entire labor load without hiring outside hands.[198] Indeed, those who had more than one horse also had enough labor capacity to rent more land.[199] These were economically strong, working families whose worker-to-eater ratio must have been above average. As a group they were probably younger and more literate than the typical household.[200] The consolidators had both the resources and the courage to attempt farming on their own, outside of the commune. Only one-third of them retained any land at all within their communes.[201] The numerical dominance of the middle and somewhat stronger than average farms among the consolidators conforms closely to the predictions of our agrotechnical scheme, and to data from many other provinces.[202] The picture Pershin and other scholars have drawn of the consolidation movement as both a symptom and a cause of differentiation in the village is not borne out in this case.[203]

Data from the *zemstvo*'s 1912 study of livestock holdings are more or less consistent with the findings regarding *khutors* on State lands. The *zemstvo* data are broader, but still very incomplete. They cover almost 5,000 consolidators, who held an average of 15.5 *desiatinas* of land. 18%

of them did not have any horses, which is far more than among the State land consolidators. But this is no surprise, since the *zemstvo* data included many poor villages that had consolidated in unison. The percentage of farms with two or more horses was 43%, 7% above the level of the State lands study.[204]

Agricultural Improvement

As far as information on consolidators' farming operations and field systems are concerned, the Free Economic Society survey can only provide us with some sketchy impressions. For the most part we must rely on scattered commentaries from the reports of the *zemstvos'* local agronomists. Unfortunately, these reports offer very uneven coverage. As we shall see in Part V, the local agronomists began work only in 1910, and there were never enough of them to meet peasant demand for their services. Moreover, since much of the expenditures on *zemstvo* agronomic specialists came from *zemstvo* taxes, the local agronomists were under orders to serve all of the agricultural population. Thus the great majority of the local agronomists worked predominantly with the communes, since communal peasants so vastly outnumbered consolidators and landlords in their districts. They did not have the time to address the particular needs of consolidators or landlords with any frequency. Nevertheless, many agronomists kept track of responses to agronomic advice among consolidators. Additionally, the Land Organization Committees managed to fund a handful of local agronomists whose primary duty was to work with consolidated farms. These agronomists' reports help to fill in some of the gaps in our knowledge of the consolidators' agricultural performance.

Participants in the Free Economic Society survey did detect increases in grain yields and improved care for livestock on consolidated farms. Table 4.5 includes all responses from the central agricultural and Middle Volga regions. But the survey data do not tell us the extent to which grain yields were rising; nor do they give us much of an impression as to how consolidators achieved these results. Both for Tambov and the whole of the two regions concerned, it does not appear that consolidators encompassed in the survey were improving tillage regimes or adopting multi-field systems.[205] Nor were they acquiring improved tools or equipment at a faster rate than their neighbors in the communes.[206] If consolidators truly did manage to increase their grain

Table 4.5. Agriculture on Consolidated Farms vs. Communal Farms,
1910–1911 Survey (all figures indicate % of response)

	Increased yields	Decreased yields	Increased #s of livestock	Decreased #s of livestock	Improved care for livestock	Care for livestock worse
Communal peasants	15	9	19	14	14	14
Consolidators	42	0.4	28	28	52	23

Source: Chernyshev, Obshchina posle 9 noiabria 1906 g., pp. xxiv–xxv.

yields in the first couple of years on their new plots, this was only a function of the innate advantages of unified holdings over open fields. But it is possible that many survey correspondents mistook consolidators' *superior* yields for *improved* yields. As we shall see below, consolidators tended to be stronger households in the first place. Most of these families must have been achieving above average yields even before they acquired unified plots.

Sources from the last few years before the World War give us a fuller and more positive view of farming improvements among consolidators than does the Free Economic Society survey. The 1912 State lands study found plows on 42% of the khutors, as opposed to just 10% among peasants overall in the same uezds.[207] Early fallow and ziab tillage appear to have been typical practices on these khutors.[208] From local agronomists' reports we also know that consolidators all over the province were conducting supervised trials of early fallow, employed fallow, and even mineral fertilizers. As a very rough estimate, perhaps half of the consolidators made improvements to their tillage regimes, in the form of early fallow and ziab.[209]

It was common knowledge among agronomists in Tambov that consolidated farmers were much more receptive to their advice than were peasants remaining in the communes.[210] In the only seven uezds for which such statistics exist, approximately 80% of the demonstration plots* belonged to consolidators.[211] Likewise, in Tula province, Mozzhukhin found that about one half of the consolidators he studied in 1912 had consulted directly with an agronomist.[212] A substantial portion of the consolidators were interested in multi-field systems; at

---

*Demonstration plots were small units of land, usually a single strip or even a portion of a strip, on which a farmer volunteered to experiment with a particular agrotechnical innovation under the guidance of a local agronomist. The idea was to persuade the experimenter and his neighbors of the usefulness of the new technique.

least a couple of agronomists found this to be a standard disposition among them:

> I see that consolidators pay close attention to my suggestions that they change their system of farming.—agronomist Gudvilovich, Tambov *uezd*

> Conversations with consolidators show them to be fully prepared to improve their farms; the selection of a new system of farming is much easier for them than for communal farmers.
> —agronomist Lysov, Usman *uezd*[213]

Interest in multi-field systems did not always translate into practice, of course. Very limited data from Tambov and neighboring provinces suggest that 15–20% of the consolidated farms managed to implement multi-field systems by 1914.[214] Systems with employed fallow were extremely rare, since so few agronomists were aware of them at this time.[215] Most of the time they tried the *propashnaia* system, thanks to agronomists' enthusiastic agitation in its favor. Additionally, astute agronomists often noticed consolidators' willingness to experiment with fodder grasses so as to ease the fodder shortages they suffered while trying to make new grazing arrangements for their animals. They parlayed this interest into the implementation of Four-Field + Grass field rotations on unified plots.[216]

Above and beyond our sense that consolidators tended to be younger, braver, and better educated than the typical villagers, the rate of agrotechnical improvements on their farms allows us to speculate that the experience of running farming operations under new conditions often stimulated their inquisitiveness, initiative, and self-confidence. In Mozzhukhin's opinion, consolidation "developed a thirst for progress in the peasant psyche."[217] Others went so far as to claim that they could identify consolidators by their purposeful stride and demeanor as they walked across the fields.[218] However exaggerated these impressions may have been, the consolidators were an avant-garde in rural society.

Having done all we can to uncover the identity and agricultural performance of the consolidators, we would like to address the final two questions on our agenda: how many communal farmers imitated their farming practices, and how many peasants adopted unified plots after seeing consolidators' farms in action? Unfortunately, we have no data whatsoever with which to answer these questions. As we shall see in Part V, demonstration plots played a key role in spreading all kinds of agrotechnical improvements among communal farmers. Some con-solidators must have exercised a positive influence in this way.[219] Likewise, well-run consolidated farms must have convinced some wavering households that separation from the commune could be profitable.

Conclusion

In its original form, the government's plan to reorganize peasant agriculture along the lines of individualized farming was not an appropriate solution to the agrarian problem in most of central and southern Russia. No matter how many households might eventually value the advantages of a unified plot over the conveniences of common grazing, the scarcity of water sources in the black-earth zone precluded the formation of consolidated plots on a wide scale. The best way to reduce the handicaps of the open fields was to help communes to reduce the number of furlongs on their arable land—a technique identified by the word *komassatsiia* in the Russian terminology. *Komassatsiia* would serve both to widen strips and to permit the retention of a common grazing regime. Meanwhile, the best way to ease the burden of distant and inaccessible lands was to organize and subsidize the formation of out-settlements from the larger communes. Whether these new settlements were arranged as groups of unified plots or not, the proximity of the peasants to their land would certainly improve the quality of farming.

Yet projects designed to improve land organization within the framework of the commune (so-called "group land organization")* represented a threat to the Stolypin reform [Map 4.3]. Key officials at the top of the Ministry of Agriculture and the Ministry of Justice's land survey section were staunchly opposed to such projects.[220] An administrator in Orel province expressed their concerns very clearly:

---

*"Group land organization" was a catch-all term for a wide range of land organization projects involving groups of peasants, but not including village-wide consolidations. Typical projects included the formation of out-settlements from over-sized communes (which could involve the formation of unified plots around the new dwellings), the delineation of property lines between neighboring communes and private landowners, and *komassatsiia*.

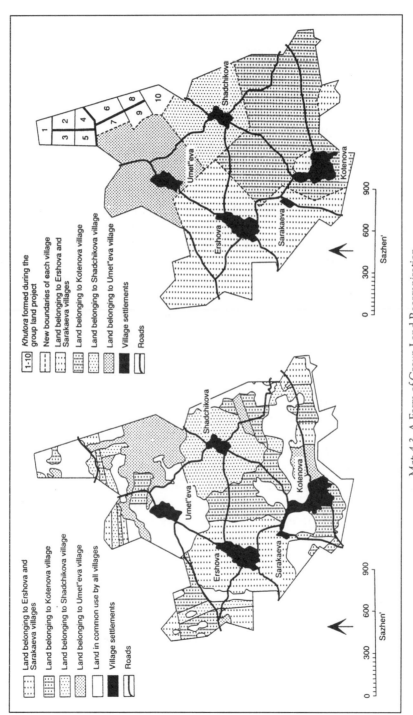

Land belonging to Ershova and Sarakaeva villages
Land belonging to Kotenova village
Land belonging to Shadchikova village
Land belonging to Umet"eva village
Land in common use by all villages
Village settlements
Roads
Umet"eva
Shadchikova
Ershova
Sarakaeva
Kotenova
0
300
600
900
Sazhen'
1-10
Khutora formed during the group land project
New boundaries of each village
Land belonging to Ershova and Sarakaeva villages
Land belonging to Kotenova village
Land belonging to Shadchikova village
Land belonging to Umet"eva village
Village settlements
Roads
1
2
3
4
5
6
7
8
9
10
Umet"eva
Ershova
Shadchikova
Sarakaeva
Kotenova
0
300
600
900
Sazhen'

Map 4.3. A Form of Group Land Reorganization.
The separate units of land belonging to each village are unified, as much as possible. *Source:* Pallot, *Land Reform in Russia, 1906–1917*, pp. 202–203.

> ... it is not desirable to help communes to clean up their land entanglements, since any such help would constitute a half-measure, satisfying peasants for another decade or so and complicating the task of persuading them to improve their land organization [to abandon the commune in favor of consolidations—D.K.]. Communal petitions for help in widening strips or eliminating interspersed holdings testify to peasants' consciousness of the shortcomings of their current land organization. With subsequent prodding, it is relatively easy to convince these communes to accept consolidations.[221]

In spite of the regime's declared resolve to push through consolidations, awareness of the drawbacks of the Stolypin reform galvanized opposition in the *zemstvos* and within the Ministry of Agriculture. In 1909 and 1910 *zemstvos* all over Russia held firm against Stolypin's repeated requests that their agronomic aid programs be targeted towards consolidators.[222] From 1911 the Ministry of Agriculture began to break the Ministry of Internal Affairs' pressure to emphasize consolidations. In that year the Ministry of Agriculture supported the *zemstvos* for insisting on providing services to communal farmers as well as consolidators. The Ministry declared that it would subsidize all agronomic aid programs for those *zemstvos* that insisted on universal coverage.[223]

Zemstvo leaders in Tambov moved swiftly to establish their preference for group land organization over consolidations. In March 1912 the provincial agronomic conference passed a resolution encouraging all agronomists to agitate for group land organization projects where villages suffered from narrow strips or interspersed lands.[224] Then provincial agronomist D. M. Shorygin issued his instructions for all personnel to work only with communes and cooperatives, and to avoid expending energy on individual farms.[225] Neither the *zemstvo* boards nor their agricultural committees took any action to direct their specialists' attention back towards the consolidators.

By 1913 the Ministry of Agriculture was willing to advertise the fact that they were often giving priority to group land organization projects over consolidations.[226] Then a 1914 Ministry of Agriculture circular instructed all provincial administrations not to allow work on consolidated plots to slow down work on the formation of out-settlements or other projects aimed at improving communal land organization.[227] Even though very little group land organization work actually got done before the outbreak of war, the regime's commitment to consolidations had splintered.[228]

The turn towards group projects did not represent a renunciation of the government's long-term goals. The offensive against the commune was not called off. The numbers of households with personal property to their land continued slowly to grow, as did the number of consolidated plots. In the field the pressure to form consolidations did not abate even after 1914, despite the Ministry of Agriculture's avowed opposition to it during wartime.[229] If the government had tried hard enough and long enough to erase the peasant commune, it might well have succeeded.

But the rewards might not have been worth the effort. As we shall see in Part V, the surest route to agricultural modernization lay through the peasant commune, not around it. Technical innovations and systemic transitions could snowball more quickly within the commune than on individual farms. Despite the dynamism displayed by about one half of the consolidated farms, therefore, it would be precipitous to argue that the Stolypin reform was carrying the peasantry forward to an agricultural revolution. Instead, it is entirely reasonable to propose that the consolidation movement slowed down the momentum of change building up within communes. The departure of consolidators removed many of the boldest and most energetic people from the village assemblies.[230] According to their social profile, after all, these were the farmers most open to learning from the agronomists who began to penetrate the countryside at this time. If these peasants had not been allowed to leave the communes, communal agriculture would have developed more quickly than it did. The success of the agronomic aid effort in Tambov in the late 1920s—including collectively introduced innovations such as early fallow, *ziab*, and multi-field systems—testifies to this.

Suffice it to say that defective land organization was not the main obstacle to increased agricultural productivity. The intellectual underdevelopment of the countryside we outlined in Part II had far greater ramifications for the future of rural society than did inaccuracies in the arrangement of land. Improvements in land organization could certainly help peasant farming. So would the transfer of privately owned lands into peasant possession, as the Tsarist regime's liberal and radical opponents insisted throughout the decades preceding 1917. But substantial increases in productivity were simply not possible without a revolution in peasants' approach to their craft.

Notes

[1] The best treatment of the ministerial and court politics taking the government down this path is Macey, *Government and Peasant in Russia, 1861–1906*.

[2] It is customary to label this crop failure a famine. Yet it is not so clear that mass starvation ensued, as a cholera epidemic might well account for the jump in mortality in 1892. See, e.g., Robert Bideleux, "Agricultural Advance under the Russian Village Commune System."

[3] The first commission, instructed to analyze the impoverishment of the central black-earth region provinces, was established in 1899, under the direction of an official from the Ministry of Finance, V. I. Kovalevskii. This commission was expanded two years later, and put in the hands of V. N. Kokovtsov. An extremely prominent inter-ministerial commission ("The Special Conference on the Needs of Agriculture") was established early in 1902 under the chairmanship of Sergei Witte. A commission within the Ministry of Internal Affairs studying legislation concerning the peasantry also began work in 1902 [Oldenburg, *Tsarstvovanie Nikolaia II-ogo*, pp. 161–163; Meisi (Macey), "Zemel'naia reforma i politicheskie peremeny," pp. 7–8].

[4] Oldenburg, *The Last Tsar*, Gulf Breeze, Fla., 1977, vol. 2, p. 19.

[5] Robinson, *Rural Russia under the Old Regime*, p. 150.

[6] This law covered most of the country in 1903 (Robinson, *op. cit.*, p. 209). As we saw in Part II, the manner and consistency with which it was applied in practice over time and space is a complex question which still awaits detailed treatment.

[7] This right had existed for repartitional communes since 1861. The 1906 law extended it to villages holding their land in hereditary tenure (B. D. Brutskus, *Agrarnyi vopros i agrarnaia politika*, p. 166).

[8] K. R. Kachorovskii, *Russkaia Obshchina*, St. Petersburg 1900, cited in Oganovskii, "Zemleustroistvo," p. 563.

[9] A survey by the Free Economic Society in 1910–1911 found that over 80% of the communes in the Central Agricultural and Volga Regions had performed full land repartitions after emancipation. Only one in ten did not repartition land in any fashion (Chernyshev, *Obshchina posle 9 noiabria 1906 goda*, p. xx).

[10] This periodization is George Yaney's (*The Urge to Mobilize*, see pp. 285, 321–322, for example).

[11] Atkinson, *op. cit.*, p. 79.

[12] *Ibid.*, p. 81.

[13] *Ibid.*, pp. 76–77; Oganovskii, "Zemleustroistvo," p. 563.

[14] Atkinson, *op. cit.*, p. 77.

[15] Oganovskii, "Zemleustroistvo," p. 266.

[16] Atkinson, *op. cit.*, pp. 75–76, 89.

[17] Oganovskii, "Zemleustroistvo," p. 566.

[18] *Ibid.*, p. 566; and Atkinson, *op. cit.*, p. 68.

[19] Drozdov, *Okolo zemli*, pp. 22–23.

[20] Pallot, "The Stolypin Land Reform," pp. 177, 180; and Pallot, *Land Reform in Russia*, pp. 117–126. After a tour through parts of Tambov and Tula provinces in 1910, one observer insisted that land organization officials commonly—and illegally—enforced this tactic even in villages where all the land was already converted to private property (Konovalov, "Derevenskie kartinki," pp. 5–9).

[21] Here I have in mind tactics such as accusing outspoken critics of consolidation of obstructing the functioning of village assemblies, or simply throwing the critics in jail on some other pretext. They might also arrange unified plots on land other peasants had already sown. See e.g., *Krest'ianskoe dvizhenie v Rossii iiun' 1907 g.—iiul' 1914 g.*, pp. 113–114; or Pallot, *Land Reform in Russia*, pp. 135–136; 142–146.

[22] Pallot, *Land Reform in Russia*, p. 143.

[23] These examples are all taken from Alekseev, "Ocherki novoi agrarnoi politiki," pp. 211–213. Many sources describe similar events.

[24] For an overview, see Atkinson, *op. cit.*, pp. 67–70.

[25] *Ibid.*, pp. 97–98.

[26] See, for example, Drozdov, *op. cit.* pp. 24–29; I. A. Konovalov, "Budni sovremennoi derevni," pp. 285–288; I. Solov'ev, "O krest'ianskikh pastbishchakh," *SKhVIuV*, 1913, no. 13, pp. 11–13; Alekseev, "Ocherki novoi agrarnoi politiki," p. 208; Atkinson, *op. cit.*, p. 88; Pallot, "The Development of Peasant Landholding," pp. 93–94, 103, 105. With respect to the arrangement of sowings so as to facilitate common grazing, Mozzhukhin's meticulous account of an *uezd* in Tula province—not far to the northwest from Tambov—insists that this was not consolidators' normal response (*Zemleustroistvo v Bogoroditskom uezde*, p. 234). Astute observers of village reality had warned decades earlier that reversions to traditional practice would follow premature consolidations (Vorontsov, *Progressivnye techenii*, pp. 102–103).

[27] Drozdov, *op. cit.*, p. 35. For a few statistics on this, see Pallot, "The Development of Peasant Landholding,", pp. 105–106.

[28] Pallot, *op. cit.*, pp. 105–106.

[29] See the discussion in Yaney, *op. cit.*, pp. 288–306.

[30] One of the most recent treatments is Eric Kerridge's *The Common Fields of England*. Conceding merit in a number of explanations for the rise of common fields, Kerridge argues that the motivations varied from place to place (p. 4).

[31] Vorontsov, *op. cit.*, p. 117. For a good English-language discussion of the appearance of strips before the three-field system, see Hoffman, "Medieval Origins of the Common Fields."

[32] Pershin, *op. cit.*, pp. 208–209.

[33] *Ibid.*, p. 208.

[34] *Ibid.*, p. 211.

[35] Chelintsev, *op. cit.*, p. 384.

[36] SSS, Spassk, pp. 8–15.

[37] Pallot, *op. cit.*, p. 96. Pallot's evidence is from Tula province around the turn of the century.

[38] SSS, Spassk, pp. 8–15. Researchers found farms broken up into as many as 54 strips in Kozlov *okrug* in the late 1920s (GATO, f. R-2786, op. 1, d. 14, p. 4).

[39] Pershin, *op. cit.*, p. 208.

[40] *Ibid.*, p. 218.

[41] Pershin, *op. cit.*, pp. 164–167.

[42] For a good account of how this tended to happen in practice, see *ibid.*, p. 223. In his analysis of parcelization in England McCloskey maintains that inheritance did not thin out strips (*op. cit.*, pp. 102–113). He asserts that families would arrange to inherit coherent strips rather than split them up even thinner. This certainly was not the case in central Russia, where inheritance arrangements did reduce strip widths (see Pershin, *op. cit.*, pp. 213, 220).

[43] Scholars stating this explicitly include Studenskii and Pokshishevskii (respectively, *Intensivnost' i psevdo-intensivnost'*, p. 13; and *Tsentral'no-chernozemnaia oblast'*, p. 42). In places, communes were performing qualitative (not quantitative) adjustments of the lands each household held nearly every year (*perezhereb'evki*—see footnote on p. 324). See, e.g., *TMK*, Khar'kov, p. 391.

[44] Sources disagree on how frequently communes did this. Brutzkus declares the practice ubiquitous in the black-earth zone (Brutskus, *Agrarnyi vopros i agrarnaia politika*, pp. 164–5). A German agricultural official who traveled to Russia during the Stolypin reform period felt that arranging strips downslope was common in the black-earth zone (Aukhagen, *Kritika russkoi zemel'noi reformy*, p. 28). Likewise Mozzhukhin (*Zemleustroistvo v Bogoroditskom uezde*, p. 92). Grabovskii and Eremeeva (respectively *Kak pereiti na shirokie polosy*, p. 6, and "Agronomicheskaia pomoshch' naseleniiu," p. 57) say it happened, but do not specify how commonly. Bilimovich also mentions it (Bilimovich, "The Land Settlement in Russia and the War," p. 316). Stebelsky (citing V. Masalskii, *Ovragi chernozemnoi polosy Rossii, ikh rasprostranenie, razvitie, i deiatel'nost'*, St. Petersburg 1897) also says strips were arranged downslope, but does not indicate how commonly ("Agriculture and Soil Erosion in the European Forest-Steppe," p. 56). The only counter-indication I have seen, reporting peasants taking care to arrange strips cross-slope, is Shlippenbakh, "Sredstvo protiv vymochki ozimei," p. 123.

[45] Minin, "Zemlepol'zovanie i zemleustroistvo," pp. 94–97.

[46] Pershin, *op. cit.*, pp. 226, 228; Brutskus, *op. cit.*, p. 165; Posnikov, *Obshchinnoe zemlevladenie*, pp. 143–144. Judging from a recent Russian work, communes in the northern half of Russia fared little better in this regard (Zyrianov, *Krest'ianskaia obshchina Evropeiskoi Rossii 1907–1914 gg.*, p. 57). Some observers in the black-earth center did see villages keeping down the degree of parcelization ("Doklad o formakh krest'ianskogo zemlepol'zovaniia," p. 416).

[47] Pershin, *op. cit.*, p. 226.

[48] McCloskey, "The Persistence of English Common Fields." His arguments on this issue appear on pp. 75–79.

[49] McCloskey (*op. cit.*, p. 79) gives 9.6 square kilometers as above average for an English village. According to figures in Pershin (*op. cit.*, p. 149) the average village in the central and southern *uezds* of Tambov held 21.5 square kilometers, while in Voronezh the area climbed to 27.2.

[50] For example, Chernyshev, *Krest'iane ob obshchine*, pp. 12–13; Reynolds, *My Russian Year*, p. 103. It is possible to find counter-indications. Thus one observer insisted that farmers paid no attention to time lost in transit between strips (Krasovskii, "Undorovskaia obshchina. Simbirskaia guberniia," p. 363).

[51] See, e.g., Obolenskii, "Ocherki khutorskoi Rossii," p. 42; Konovalov, "Na khutorakh," no. 2, p. 7; and B. Iur'evskii's discussion of Samara, in his *Vozrozhdenie derevni*, pp. 95–131.

[52] The area lost to humps and ditches can be controlled by alternating the style of tillage—plowing *v sval* in the first year, *v razval* in the next year, and so on (see "Styles of Plowing" Figures 1.5 and 1.6 in Part I). Surviving farmers admit to not having done this, however.

[53] Danilov, *Rural Russia Under the New Regime*, p. 133. Surely the many farmers without plows tilled border furrows with a *sokha*, which would economize a bit on land lost to borders. An official study in Iaroslavl province, in the northern half of European Russia, estimated land borders to occupy 14% of the allotment land there (Mosolov, "Pis'ma zemleustroitel'ia," p. 92). Another figure, from Samara, put the territory at 3.3% (N. Selivanov, *Obshchinniki*, p. 26).

[54] Grabovskii, *op. cit.*, p. 4.

[55] McCloskey, *op. cit.*, p. 80.

[56] Interviews; Posnikov, *op. cit.*, pp. 138–140; Grabovskii, *op. cit.*, p. 5; and S. S. Bekhteev's comments in Gosudarstvennyi Sovet. Sessiia 5-aia, *Stenograficheskii otchet*, p. 1441.

[57] Pares, *My Russian Memoirs*, p. 218. Animals did not like to eat wormwood (V. P. Semenov-Tian-Shanskii, *Rossiia. vol. 2*, p. 228).

[58] Ermolenko, "Sornye travy," pp. 219–227. P. Maslov affirms that peasants would not bother to mow these useless weeds, so they would grow to maturity and flourish ("O semenakh i podgotovke semian k posevu," no. 3, p. 47). Note also Bunin's description of wormwood going uneaten by livestock and standing on field borders in the fall, in the story "Poslednoe svidanie" (*Sobranie sochinenii*, vol. 3, p. 345). Pares made the same observation (*My Russian Memoirs*, p. 218).

[59] For a case of peasants complaining about the costs of weeds on borders, and recognizing that landlords did not have to suffer from the same problem, see N. Selivanov, *Obshchinniki*, p. 24.

[60] S. Kliuev is one of *many* agronomists who complained of this (*Chto nado znat' o pochve*, p. 63). The notion Judith Pallot advances of uneven fields acting as a form of insurance (raised portions profiting in wet years, lowered portions in dry years) is not convincing (Pallot, *Land Reform in Russia*, p. 81). Peasants did not have the luxury or intention of wasting land in this way. Interviews confirm their preference for lowering humps with the harrow.

[61] Pershin, pp. 224–225; Mosolov, "Pis'ma zemleustroitel'ia," p. 91.

[62] I did find one survivor who did cross-tillage on inter-stripped land, but this was in a small commune with wide strips, in the 1920s.

[63] Grabovskii, *op. cit.*, pp. 4, 7.

[64] Survivors in Tambov concede that they did not, as mentioned earlier. Jerome Blum characterizes strips in Europe as ridged, typically (*The End of the Old Order in Europe*, p. 122).

[65] Grabovskii, *op. cit.*, p. 3.

[66] Grabovskii, *op. cit.*, p. 8; Pares, *My Russian Memoirs*, p. 218.

[67] Pershin, *op. cit.*, p. 225.

[68] *ibid.*, pp. 224–226.

[69] P. N. Zyrianov is the latest Russian scholar in this camp. Like so many others, he traces it to Populist ideology that was desperate to interpret the peasant commune as the germ of a future socialist society in Russia (*Krest'ianskaia obshchina*, pp. 42, 53, and elsewhere). McCloskey's article (*op. cit.*) recounts scholars apart from himself who reject the role of egalitarianism in the medieval European village.

[70] Grabovskii, *op. cit.*, p. 10.

[71] Mosolov, *op. cit.*, p. 94. See also Chernyshev, *Krest'iane ob obshchine*, pp. 36–37.

[72] See Hoch, *Serfdom and Social Control in Russia*, pp. 115, 117–118. Hoch's information on this point is not limited to Tambov. At the same time, stratification could advance very far on some estates. See, e.g., the description of an estate in Spassk province in *Krest'ianskoe dvizhenie v Rossii v 1796–1825 gg.*, p. 654).

[73] The assumption is that repartitions *po edokam* entailed each family receiving land in accordance with the number of mouths they had to feed. But in practice *po edokam* might not always have worked so simply. In determining families' sizes for purposes of land allotment, peasants could apply a formula weighting individuals according to work capacity. Thus Zyrianov cites a case of a land repartition *po edokam* where men were weighted at three times women (Zyrianov, *Krest'ianskaia obshchina*, p. 45).

[74] *Ibid.*, pp. 54, 194–195.

[75] For an elegant overview of the levers by which richer families oppressed their neighbors in European peasantries (including Russia), see Blum, "The Internal Structure and Polity of the European Village Community," pp. 549–552.

[76] Hilton Root is one who emphasizes this consideration (*Peasants and King in Burgundy*, pp. 139, 153). Root is also aware of poorer peasants' dependence on common grazing.

[77] Examples include Grigg, *Population Growth and Agrarian Change*, p. 200; and Blum, *The End of the Old Order in Rural Europe*, p. 269.

[78] See, for example, Koefoed, *My Share in the Stolypin Agrarian Reforms*, pp. 83–84. Koefoed believed that the largest and smallest farms would always and everywhere favor common grazing.

[79] Chelintsev, *op. cit.*, p. 273.

[80] Iozefi, "Osoboe mnenie Mirovogo Posrednika," p. 926. See also Iudin, "Ob ukhode za sel'sko-khoziaistvennymi zhivotnymi," p. 7. To the given point we may add that some animals would take poorly to tethering. Pares reported that cows unaccustomed to tethering might express their distress loudly and at length (Pares, *My Russian Memoirs*, p. 222).

[81] McCloskey, *op. cit.*, p. 84.

[82] *Ibid.*, p. 112.

[83] As an observer in Simbirsk province recounted, "Peasants are not keen on trading good land for a larger quantity of poorer land" (Krasovskii, "Undorovskaia obshchina," p. 363). Some communes in Tambov arranged exchanges of strips every year because of the difficulty of quantity-for-quality appraisals (*SSS*, Usman, pp. 20, 24). Quite a few sources do report peasants devising simple bidding schemes to resolve potential frictions on this score (*SSS*, Temnikov, p. 31; Shustikov, *Plody dosuga*, Iaroslavl 1900; Koefoed, *My Share in the Stolypin Agrarian Reforms*, pp. 38–40; Pares, *My Russian Memoirs*, p. 219; Pallot, *Land Reform in Russia*, pp. 87–88). Alternatively, the commune might ask a government land surveyor to assign quantity-to-quality ratios himself, after they told him how many varieties of land they had (Pares, *op. cit.*, *loc. cit.*). For good data on quantity-for-quality compensations as practiced during the Stolypin reform in Tula province, see Mozzhukhin, *op. cit.*, pp. 161–164.

[84] McCloskey (*op. cit.*, p. 94) traces this idea to Charles Parain, in Postan, ed., *The Cambridge Economic History of Europe*, p. 138. Stefano Fenoaltea accepts the idea ("Transaction Costs, Whig History, and the Common Fields").

[85] Mosolov, *op. cit.*, pp. 91–92.

[86] In fact, as at least a few reports related, some peasants were concerned that hail could affect small areas of land ("Doklad komissii po punktu Ch," p. 360; Iak-

ovlevich, "Novoe i staroe v Russkom sel'skom khoziaistve," p. 13; and the comments of a Saratov peasant quoted in Bel'skii, *Novaia zemledel'cheskaia Rossiia*, p. 95, as cited in Pallot, *Land Reform in Russia*, p. 76).

[87] See on this: Cheredeev, "Odno iz sredstv obezpecheniia urozhaev v nashem uez- de," p. 5; also Pel'tsikh, *Trekhpolka ili mnogopol'e?*, p. 8.

[88] McCloskey, *op. cit.*, p. 114.

[89] Mozzhukhin, *op. cit.*, pp. 277–278.

[90] The Free Economic Society survey of attitudes towards the Stolypin reform did not record anyone advocating parcelization for insurance purposes (Chernyshev, *Obshchina posle 9 noiabria 1906 g.*). One rare case of this opinion appears in "Doklad komissii po punktu Ch," p. 360.

[91] Stefano Fenoaltea is the most recent scholar to take this argument seriously (*op. cit.*).

[92] Fenoaltea, *op. cit.*

[93] McCloskey, *op. cit.*, pp. 93–95.

[94] SSS, Tambov, p. 60; Chuprov, "Itogi obshchninnogo zemlevladeniia," in *Rechi i stati*, vol. 1, pp. 419–420; Pershin, *op. cit.*, pp. 224–226; Zyrianov, *op. cit.*, p. 191; Vorontsov, *op. cit.*, p. 120.

[95] McCloskey, *op. cit.*, p. 93.

[96] For good statistics on the inferiority of hired labor, see Voronov, *Effektivnost' uslovii i sposobov obrabotki krest'ianskoi pashni*.

[97] This follows from the discussion of status and values presented in Part II, and was confirmed in an analysis of peasant farms in Chernigov and Poltava provinces. There economist V. Vorontsov found peasants preferring to rent land rather than to do hired labor, even if materially they stood to do significantly better as laborers (cited in Zverev, "N. F. Daniel'son, V. A. Vorontsov," p. 160).

[98] Fenoaltea, *op. cit.*

[99] Kofod, *Russkoe zemleustroistvo*, pp. 127, 171; Brutskus, *op. cit.*, p. 192. Bilimovich generalizes that consolidated plots fetched prices about 50% higher than stripped land (*op. cit.*, p. 342). There are indications of peasants' appreciation of the value of unified plots before 1906. A committee in Orel province reported peasants (presumably those purchasing or renting non-allotment lands) rating unified plots at about twice the value of parcelized land ("Doklad o formakh krest'ianskogo zemlepol'zovaniia," p. 419).

[100] Pershin, *op. cit.*, p. 226; Bushinskii, "Vozrazhenie," p. 928.

[101] I have never encountered this, at any rate.

[102] Mosolov, *op. cit.*, pp. 93–94.

[103] Kliuev, *Chto nado znat' o pochve*, p. 67.

[104] This was a rather commonly encountered opinion. Early and influential exponents included Vorontsov and Chuprov (respectively, *Progressivnye techeniia*, pp. 172–173; and *Stati i rechi*, vol. 2, p. 547).

[105] Pershin, *op. cit.*, pp. 201, 203.

[106] SSS, Lipetsk, p. 28 (as cited in Pershin, *op. cit.*, p. 206).

[107] Danilov, *op. cit.*, p. 139. This is a 1920s calculation from Balashov *uezd*, Saratov province, on the eastern border of Tambov's Kirsanov and Borisoglebsk *uezds*.

[108] This calculation is derived from comments in Kozlov, "Zapiska po voprosam," p. 166.

[109] Brzheskii, *op. cit.*, p. 65.

[110] SSS, Morshansk, p. 72 (as quoted in Pershin, *op. cit.*, p. 196).

[111] Dashkevich, "Likvidatsiia Bankovskikh zemel' i zemleustroistvo v Kirsanovskom uezde," p. 754.

[112] Pershin, *op. cit.*, p. 190.

[113] *Ibid.*, p. 168.

[114] *Ibid.*, pp. 167–168.

[115] *Ibid.*, pp. 167–169; SSS, Spassk, pp. 25–26.

[116] All information in this paragraph from Pershin's work (*op. cit.*, pp. 172–190).

[117] *Ibid.*, p. 179.

[118] SSS, Lipetsk, p. 27.

[119] Pallot, "Khutora and Otruba in Stolypin's Program of Farm Individualization," pp. 243–244, 249–252.

[120] A wealth of sources recorded peasants' reservations on this score. For a selection of comments from Tambov, see Chernyshev, *Obshchina posle 9 noiabria 1906 g.*, pp. 50–55. Land organization reformers elsewhere in Europe ran into the same sort of reticence among peasants to part with nuclear villages (Blum, *The End of the Old Order in Europe*, p. 269). An illustration in literature of peasants struggling to adjust to the social isolation imposed by life on a farmstead appears in Muizhel, *Khutor, No. 16*, pp. 33–34. The isolation was said to be especially hard on children (Konovalov, "Na khutorakh," no. 2, pp. 11–12, 15–16).

[121] GATO, f. 51, op. 1, d. 168, p. 137; Dashkevich, "Likvidatsiia Bankovskikh zemel' i zemleustroistvo v Kirsanovskom uezde," pp. 747–753.

[122] GATO f. 51, op. 1, d. 168, p. 95.

[123] Iurin, *Khutora i otruba v Tambovskoi gubernii*, pp. 7–8.

[124] Drozdov, *op. cit.*, pp. 16–19.

[125] Pallot, "Khutora and Otruba," pp. 254–255.

[126] GATO, f. 51, d. 168, p. 137.

[127] Drozdov, *op. cit.*, pp. 18–19.

[128] GATO, f. 51, op. 1, d. 168, p. 138.

[129] Yaney, *op. cit.*, p. 277.

[130] On which see, e.g., Matsuzato, "The Fate of Agronomists in Russia," pp. 181–182.

[131] GATO, f. 51, op. 1, d. 168, pp. 131–155.

[132] *Ibid.*, pp. 131–134.

[133] Quoted in Bobynin, "Agronomicheskaia pomoshch' naseleniiu Tambovskoi gubernii," *SKhZh*, 1915, no. 18–19, p. 494.

[134] GATO, f. 51, op. 1, d. 168, pp. 133–134.

[135] *Ibid.*, p. 133.

[136] *Ibid.*, pp. 133–134.

[137] *Ibid.*, pp. 132–134.

[138] *Ibid.*, p. 138.

[139] *Ibid.*, pp. 138–139.

[140] *Ibid.*, pp. 135–136. The dissenters hoped to see the reform move at the peasants' pace, and they hoped to avoid fomenting antagonisms within the villages between separators from the commune and non-separators. Where communes could not agree on the desirability of unified plots, they advised Land Captains to leave them alone and concentrate instead on other communes that might agree by a two-thirds vote to form consolidated plots.

[141] 482,024 *dvors* resided in the province as of 1914 (RGAE, f. 478, op. 2, d. 236, p. 75).

[142] All statistics from Dubrovskii, *op. cit.*, 1963, prilozhenie 4. These transfers of title went almost exclusively to individual members of the commune—commune-wide

conversions to personal tenure (by a two-thirds vote) were extremely rare (Chernyshev, *Obshchina posle 9 noiabria 1906 g.*, p. 37).

143 GATO, f. 51, op. 1, d. 168, p. 133. Acquisitions of personal tenure dropped off sharply throughout the country beginning in about 1910 (Oganovskii, "Zemleustroistvo," p. 556). In Tambov a final total of 96,805 households received personal title by 1917 (Dubrovskii, *op. cit.*, prilozhenie 3).

144 Simonova, "Ekonomicheskie itogi Stolypinskoi agrarnoi politiki," p. 33.

145 Chernyshev, *Obshchina posle 9 noiabria 1906 g.*, p. 167.

146 Drozdov, *op. cit.*, p. 57.

147 Simonova, *op. cit.*, p. 37.

148 Chernyshev, *Obshchina posle 9 noiabria 1906 g.*, pp. 41–43, 47–49. As of mid-1909, only a little over 10% of privatizers were registered as having sold off their land in toto (GATO f. 51, op. 1, d. 168, p. 133). But, as Drozdov notes, peasants were past masters at concealing sales of allotment land. They rented this land to neighbors for long terms, informing only the village *starosta* and a few other witnesses (Drozdov, *op. cit.*, pp. 67–68). Oganovskii estimated that up to one-third of allotment land sales escaped official registration (Oganovskii, "Zemleustroistvo," p. 560). The Free Economic Society's survey data correspond nicely to these insights. Out of 402 indications, privatizers are said to have worked their land 69% of the time, while 19% sold it (in full) and 11% rented it out. The rising wave of privatizers selling off their land so as to give up agriculture caught the administration in Tambov by surprise. Vice Governor Shil'der-Shul'dner tried in vain to blame this on subversive socialist propaganda among the weaker peasants (GATO, f. 51, op. 1, d. 168, pp. 132–133).

149 Dubrovskii, *op. cit.*, prilozhenie II. Personal title generally applied only to arable land and the house plot (Chernyshev, *Obshchina posle 9 noiabria 1906 g.*, p. 46). If these families' access to meadows and pastures could be included, they would not appear quite so small.

150 Chernyshev, *Obshchina posle 9 noiabria 1906 g.*, p. 47.

151 *Ibid*, p. 48. Privatizing households were supposed to pay an artificially fixed price for any land they took beyond what the next repartition would give them. But most of the time they got away without paying anything at all (*ibid*, p. 50).

152 The evidence indicates that peasants rarely sold their land to the commune (*ibid.*, pp. 55, 57). Presumably, wealthy neighbors would give a higher price. Right from the outset of the reform rich villagers began accumulating unlawfully large quantities of allotment land (e.g., GATO, f. 51, op. 1, d. 168, p. 150).

153 Alekseev cites reports of this in Tambov and other provinces (*op. cit.*, pp. 232–233).

154 Drozdov, *op. cit.*, p. 66. Drozdov insists that non-peasant purchasing of allotment land was not rare (p. 66).

155 Chernyshev, *Obshchina posle 9 noiabria 1906 g.*, p. 47.

156 *Ibid.*, pp. 43–46. To be fair, one survey correspondent from Orel province did observe privatizers increasing their attention to manuring (*ibid.*, p. 175). It is true that in a survey of privatizers in the Volga province of Simbirsk 15% claimed to have sought personal title with the aim of improving their farming operations. But this survey (and a similar one conducted on a national scale, which yielded almost identical results) lumped consolidators together with households who privatized but did not subsequently request a unified plot (Oganovskii, "Zemleustroistvo," p. 557).

157 Zyrianov, *op. cit.*, p. 183.

[158] Counterindications do exist, but they are indirect. Thus, studies in Kazan and Samara provinces (but not in Voronezh) found greater interest in privatization of tenure in areas near marketing points. This would imply the intention to improve care for the land. Keller and Romanenko, *Pervyi itogi agrarnoi reformy*, p. 97.

[159] GATO, f. 51, op. 1, d. 168, p. 135.

[160] The number of communes from *ibid.*

[161] Kofod, *op. cit.*, pp. 116–117.

[162] This figure comes from Ministry of Agriculture data in *Statisticheskii ezhegodnik Rossii, 1915 g.*, VI otdel, pp. 6–11 (as cited in Dubrovskii, *op. cit.*, p. 582). Unfortunately, available statistics vary widely regarding the number of consolidators on allotment lands. On the low side, in 1923 the provincial department of agriculture reported that a total of 17,724 had existed on January 1st 1914. This would be just 3.7% of all households registered at the time (RGAE, f. 478, op. 2, d. 236, p. 75). On the high side, Pershin's 1928 work cites 24,991 consolidated plots by January 1917 for the eight central and southern *uezds* alone. This would be 6.7% of all households registered in those *uezds* in 1916 (Pershin, *op. cit.*, pp. 430–433). I do not know if the figure I have placed in the text is the most accurate.

[163] Pershin, *op. cit.*, p. 244.

[164] Cited in Dubrovskii, *op. cit.*, p. 585. Dubrovskii used Pershin's 1922 monograph *Uchastkovoe zemlepol'zovanie v Rossii*, pp. 46–47. The somewhat lower figures in Pershin's 1928 work pertain to the post-1923 boundaries of the province (*Zemel'noe ustroistvo*, p. 245).

[165] Judging from the landholding statistics in the 1912 *zemstvo* survey (*Podvornoe obsledovanie zhivotnovodstva*, Prilozhenie 1).

[166] Pershin's higher estimate refers to Tambov's post-1923 borders (*op. cit.*, p. 245).

[167] Chernyshev, *Obschina posle 9 noiabria 1906 g.*, Part I, p. 50–52.

[168] Chernyshev, *Obschina posle 9 noiabria 1906 g.*, p. 54. The same source cites peasants from Voronezh and Riazan offering the same opinion (*ibid.*, p. 170).

[169] *Ibid.*, pp. 52, 54, 169, e.g.

[170] *Ibid.*, pp. 51 , 50, 169.

[171] *Ibid.*, p. 52.

[172] GATO, f. 51, op. 1, d. 168, p. 135.

[173] Chernyshev, *Obschina posle 9 noiabria 1906 g.*, as cited in Pershin, *op. cit.*, p. 243. This case is from Voronezh province.

[174] Pershin, *op. cit.*, p. 253.

[175] Chernyshev (his own words), *Obschina posle 9 noiabria 1906 g.*, p.167. Administrators were well aware of these circumstances (GATO, f. 51, op. 1, d. 168, p. 138).

[176] Pershin, *op. cit.*, p. 260, and also p. 263. Both cases from Voronezh.

[177] Alekseev, *op. cit.*, p. 211; also an announcement in *SKhZh*, 1914, no. 2, p. 98.

[178] Chernyshev, *Obschina posle 9 noiabria 1906 g.*, p. 55.

[179] Atkinson, *op. cit.*, pp. 69–70.

[180] Chernyshev, *Obschina posle 9 noiabria 1906 g.*, p. 43.

[181] Rossiiskii Gosudarstvennyi Arkhiv Ekonomiki (RGAE), f. 478, op. 2, d. 236, pp. 74–75 (a 1920s report on the consolidation of farms in Tambov, 1906–1916).

[182] Dubrovskii, *op. cit.*, p. 589.

[183] RGAE, f. 478, op. 2, d. 236, pp. 74–75. For average village size see Part I of the present study.

[184] *Ibid.*

[185] Pershin, *op. cit.*, p. 257.

[186] Alekseev, *op. cit.*, p. 216.

[187] Iurin, *Khutora i otruba v Tambovskoi gubernii*, Tambov 1913.

[188] *Doklady ob agronomicheskoi organizatsii*, p. 62; *KSE*, vol. 6, pp. 425–426.

[189] See Iurin, *op. cit.*, pp. 12–17, for good figures on these matters.

[190] So writes Judith Pallot, *Landscape and Settlement in Romanov Russia, 1613–1917*, p. 180. The law was ambiguous, however, regarding the consolidators' rights. It was clear they could make use of forests, meadows, and permanent pastures. Their rights to arable grazing were left open to local interpretation (Pallot, *Land Reform in Russia*, pp. 120–121).

[191] Alekseev, *op. cit.*, p. 210. This example comes from Chernigov province. For another, from Tambov *uezd*, see *SKhZh*, 1912/13, no. 7, pp. 294–296. See also Alekseev, *op. cit.*, pp. 234–235, for a bloody brawl between consolidators and their neighbors over the same issue, in Kharkov province. Malevolent peasants could trespass on consolidators' fields with their carts as well (Konovalov, "Na khutorakh," no. 1, pp. 46, 48).

[192] One-third of the households included in the Tambov study of *khutors* on State lands and more than two-thirds of the consolidated farms in Shatsk *uezd* had some allotment land. Iurin, *op. cit.*, pp. 15–16; "Otchet Tambovskomu gubernskomu zemskomu sobraniiu ocherednoi sessii 1911 goda ob agronomicheskoi deiatel'nosti uezdnykh zemstv Tambovskoi gubernii za 1911 goda," in *Zhurnaly Tambovskogo Gubernskogo Zemskogo Sobraniia ocherednoi sessii 1911 goda*, pp. 812–813.

[193] Documented cases of this, from Tula province, appear in Mozzhukhin, *op. cit.*, p. 234.

[194] Iurin, *op. cit.*, pp. 11–14.

[195] *Ibid.*, p. 17.

[196] *Voenno-konskaia perepis' 1912 goda*, pp. 14, 132–135.

[197] Iurin, *op. cit.*, p. 11.

[198] *Ibid.*, pp. 25–26.

[199] *Ibid.*, p. 22.

[200] Mozzhukhin found this to be the case in Tula province (*op. cit.*, pp. 188–189).

[201] Iurin, *op. cit.*, pp. 15–16.

[202] For a selection of data from other provinces, see Mozzhukhin, *op. cit.*, pp. 193 (note in particular the figures for Efremov and Novosil'sk *uezds*), 200, 205.

[203] Pershin, *op. cit.*, pp. 263–264, 270–271; and Konovalov, "Na khutorakh," e.g.

[204] All figures from *Materialy po podvornomu obsledovaniiu zhivotnovodstva*, prilozhenie II.

[205] Chernyshev, *Obshchina posle 9 noiabria 1906 g.*, pp. xix, 45.

[206] 46% reported increased equipment holdings among communal peasants, 50% among consolidators (Chernyshev, *Obshchina posle 9 noiabria 1906 g.*, p. xxiv).

[207] Iurin, *op. cit.*, p. 28; *Sel'sko-khoziaistvennye mashiny i orudiia*, p. 68; *Podvornoe obsledovanie zhivotnovodstva*, Prilozhenie 1. The 10% figure is an estimate based on the number of plows in 1910 and the number of households in 1912. These data indicate only 8.3% as many plows as households, but of course there were fewer households in 1910 than in 1912.

[208] Iurin, *op. cit.*, p. 28.

[209] In three black-earth *volosts* of Tula province Mozzhukhin found more than 50% of the consolidators raising fallow relatively early (*op. cit.*, pp. 253, 318–319). Matters should not have been much different in Tambov, but evidence of tillage intensification is sparser. Apart from the State lands study, only two agronomists ever reported early fallow to be a general or mass phenomenon among consolidators. And one of these agronomists' districts probably encompassed many of the State

lands *khutors*. (Tambovskoe uezdnoe Zemstvo, *Otchet o deiatel'nosti agronomichesk-ogo personala za 1912 sel'sko-khoziaistvennyi god*, pp. 67–69; *Proekty*, pp. 394–395. The latter source is from the district that probably overlapped with the State lands *khutors*.)

210 Borisoglebsk *uezd* agronomist N. M. Vasiliev claimed to speak for all of his colleagues to this effect (*Otchety uchastkovykh agronomov za 1914 god*, p. 92). At least three other *uezd* agronomists conveyed the same conclusion, and the chief agronomist in the province accepted it as a general rule (I. P. Solov'ev, *Obzor agronomicheskoi pomoshchi*, p. 33).

211 I. P. Solov'ev, *Obzor agronomicheskoi pomoshchi*, pp. 34–35, 78. Tambov *uezd* was one of the *uezds* where the agronomic organization did not keep track of the category of households participating in demonstration plots. Surviving reports from the local agronomists give the same impression, however (*Otchet o deiatel'nosti agronomicheskogo personala za 1912 sel'sko-khoziaistvennyi god*, passim).
    The consolidators' share of the demonstration plots was about 80%. But this figure is a very imprecise measure of the levels of interest among the two groups of farmers, since individual households could and did offer to do many demonstration plots simultaneously. Furthermore, circumstances traceable to the Stolypin reform itself could obstruct communal peasants' implementation of new farming techniques. N. M. Vasiliev pointed out that the presence within communes of households waiting for execution of their requests for unified plots often served to delay the adoption of agrotechnical innovations in the communes. *Otchety uchastkovykh agronomov za 1914 god*, p. 162.

212 Mozzhukhin, *op. cit.*, p. 262. N. P. Blagoveshchenskii of Borisoglebsk *uezd* was an excellent example of an agronomist focusing on consolidators and getting good results. See his reports for the years 1910–1911 in *Proekty*, pp. 363–395.

213 Both as cited in Iurin, *op. cit.*, p. 30.

214 In surveyed sections of Tula and Orel provinces, around 42% of the *khutors* and 16% of the *otrubs* had multi-field systems (or regressive *pestropol'e*) of some kind (Mozzhukhin, *op. cit.*, pp. 248, 275–276). 20% of the *khutors* and 5% of the *otrubs* in Shatsk *uezd* had multi-field systems as of 1911 ("Otchet Tambovskomu gubernskomu zemskomu sobraniiu ocherednoi sessii 1911 goda ob agronomicheskoi deiatel'nosti uezdnykh zemstv Tambovskoi gubernii za 1911 goda," in *Zhurnaly Tambovskogo Gubernskogo Zemskogo Sobraniia ocherednoi sessii 1911 goda*, pp. 812–813). These numbers were surely growing gradually.

215 I have found only one instance of this family of systems, in Tambov *uezd* (Iurin, *op. cit.*, p. 30).

216 There are only a couple of known cases where large groups of consolidated farms adopted multi-field systems [I. P. Solov'ev, *op. cit.*, p. 44 (this was in Morshansk *uezd*); and *Proekty*, p. 485]. An alternative, agronomically regressive response to the novelty of consolidated plots should be mentioned here, namely the abandonment of the three-field system for rapacious grain sowings without fallow. Only one report, from Tambov *uezd* agronomist V. Bilibin in 1910, noted this development (*Doklady ob agronomicheskoi organizatsii za 1910 god*, p. 62). But one senses that it was not a rarity. A survey of consolidated farms in Bogoroditsk *uezd* (Tula province) found *pestropol'e* on one fourth of the *khutors* and almost two-thirds of the *otrubs* (cited in Pallot, "Agrarian Modernization on Peasant Farms," pp. 440–441).

217 Mozzhukhin, *op. cit.*, p. 264.

218 Kofoed, *My Share in the Stolypin Agrarian Reforms*, pp. 78–79. In this instance Kofod is relating the sentiments of a rural official, not just his own opinion. The ste-

reotypical peasant gait was "heavy, 'with a roll'" (Zasodimskii, "Ot sokhi k ruzh'iu," p. 465). Peasant women had nearly the same stride as the men, according to one observer (Winter, *The Russian Empire of Today and Yesterday*, p. 96).

[219] Perhaps the only explicit mention of such influence on communal peasants from consolidators in Tambov is in *Proekty*, p. 485.

[220] Pallot, "Khutora and Otruba," pp. 248–250.

[221] Pershin, *op. cit.*, p. 228. This statement from late 1908.

[222] Alekseev, *op. cit.*, pp. 222–223; Bobynin, "Agronomicheskaia pomoshch'," 1915, no. 18–19, pp. 482–490, no. 20–24, p. 552.

[223] Bobynin, *op. cit.*, 1915, no. 20–24, p. 558. The Ministry of Agriculture's subsidies were partial, usually covering 33–50% of all expenses.

[224] As discussed in Bobynin, *op. cit.*, 1916, no. 1–10, p. 25.

[225] *Proekty*, pp. 74–79.

[226] Yaney, *op. cit.*, p. 358.

[227] Cited in an announcement in *Shatskoe Khoziaistvo*, 1914, no. 12, pp. 285–286.

[228] In Tambov, statistics available for the central and southern *uezds* for the period 1907–1917 show that about 2% of the farms were involved in the creation of out-settlements or in the exchange of lands interspersed with neighboring property holders. Pershin, *op. cit.*, pp. 412–415.

[229] In April 1915 the Ministry of Agriculture openly declared land organization work should cease until the soldiers came home, since the peasants involved should consent to all projects (Matsuzato, "The Fate of Agronomists in Russia," p. 195). But some land organization work did continue. The Land Organization Committees initially lost about 25% of their personnel to mobilization, but quickly replenished the ranks. Sem. Maslov, "Nashe sel'skoe khoziaistvo i voina," pp. 16–17.

[230] As Stepan Anikin pointed out, many of the consolidators had been leaders in the agrarian disturbances of 1905–06 ("Chego prosit derevnia," pp. 738–739).

PART FIVE

ALTERNATIVES FOR REFORM, PROSPECTS FOR DEVELOPMENT

Russia needs an army of educated and experienced agronomists, thousands strong, plus instructors and technical specialists in all branches of agriculture behind them.

—V. V. Morachevskii (director of the Informational and Publishing Bureau of the Ministry of Agriculture), 1914[1]

Slides accompanying the agronomist's speech illustrated how to raise tubers. Miss Kondyreva's voice was assured and convincing. It was clear how weightily her words fell on the heads of those who had just been scoffing and mocking agronomists. Everyone strained to take in the novel sermon. It was obvious that no one had ever heard anything of what she was saying. Miss Kondyreva spoke and explained for a long time, then finally finished and politely parted. Tumult and argument broke out again, and tobacco smoke rose around all the peasants' heads. Only now in the din you could make out something different.

.... "Say whatever you like," cried one lanky peasant over the crowd, "but we are fools!"

—peasant Sergei Vorob'ev, 1914[2]

Introduction

The Stolypin reform portended epic and irremediable transformations in rural society, as all shades of opinion at the time conceded. Thus the reform certainly deserved the great fanfare and heated polemics it generated in the last decade of the old regime. The Stolypin reform did not, however, monopolize the field of agrarian reform. Working for the most part in the *zemstvos*, local elites all over Russia hastened to formulate agronomic aid projects designed to retain and improve open-field agriculture. Taken as a whole, these projects constituted a wide-ranging effort that cut across the designs of the Stolypin reform. The *zemstvo* agronomic aid campaigns did not have the resources to reach the peasantry as quickly or broadly as the Stolypin reform. But by 1914 they had already advanced beyond their embryonic stages, and had acquired powerful support in St. Petersburg. The agronomic aid effort was important to understanding where Tambov and the rest of rural Russia was headed in the pre-war period.

The Pre-History of the Agronomic Aid Effort

Despite the predominantly agricultural character of the economy, before the revolution of 1905 neither the Tsarist government nor the *zemstvos* ever undertook any significant measures to encourage technological progress in the agricultural sector. Characteristically, Peter the Great was the most energetic ruler in this regard. He introduced the potato and encouraged the production of silk and flax, for instance.[3] But in the century and a half between Peter and the emancipation government measures were weak, rare, and uncoordinated. A handful of agricultural schools sprang up, Nicholas I forced some peasants to grow potatoes (so as to avert famines), and German colonists were allowed into Russia in the hopes that they might exercise a positive

influence on Russian peasants.[4] The government's lethargy fully har-
monized with the contempt which the greater part of educated society
felt for agricultural matters. The following reminiscence comes from
Professor Pavlov, the editor of the agricultural journal *Russkii zemledelets*, writing in 1838:

> ... everyone can clearly recall the time not long ago when it was
> considered crude even to bring up the topic of farming among
> good company. The subject was considered to be beneath the
> concerns of genteel people.[5]

Matters did not improve in the first three decades following the
emancipation in 1861. The Ministry of State domains set up a few more
agricultural schools, established some experimental stations, and dab-
bled in agricultural education programs for adults. But on the whole
the government displayed even less activity in this period than they
had under Nicholas I.[6] An independent ministry to handle agriculture
was not even established until 1894 (the Ministry of Agriculture and
State Domains).

The government's complacency with respect to the foundation of
the country's economy would be less remarkable if the *zemstvos* had
taken up the challenge to assist agriculture themselves. But, for a
variety of reasons, the *zemstvos* expended almost no effort in this
direction. To begin with, the decline of the peasant economy became
noticeable only gradually. Moreover, neither the *zemstvos* nor anyone
else had good information on the state of the peasant economy until
the 1880s, when the *zemstvos'* statistical departments undertook their
first serious research projects (the Tambov provincial *zemstvo's* study of
Borisoglebsk *uezd* being the first comprehensive examination of an *uezd*
in Russian history).[7] Even when distress in the rural sector became
evident, the *zemstvos* could not necessarily afford to invest their limited
funds in new programs. Nor would they necessarily wish to. To many
of the landowners who controlled the *zemstvos*, the whole concept of
agronomic aid seemed superfluous. They argued that if peasants
wanted to see advanced tools and techniques, they could simply
observe farming on neighboring estates. Agronomic aid need not begin
until peasant demand for it had visibly ripened.[8]

For the most part, until the 1890s the *zemstvos* confined themselves
to organizing some savings-and-loan associations. As of 1883 none of
the 34 provincial *zemstvos* and only 6 of the 359 *uezd zemstvos* had hired
an agronomist. As of 1890 only 15 *uezd zemstvos* had formed councils

to keep tabs on agricultural matters.[9] Only a few of the *zemstvos* in the non-black-earth zone (in Perm, Moscow, Viatka, and Nizhegorod provinces) had even begun to organize some practical measures to guide peasant agriculture.[10]

The great crop failure of 1891 finally catalyzed both the government and the *zemstvos* to take some action. The Ministry of Agriculture and State Domains began functioning in 1894, and moved to set up more experimental stations and agricultural schools. They also installed a network of inspectors in the provinces, who relayed detailed reports on agricultural conditions back to St. Petersburg.[11] In the decade of work before the outbreak of the Russo–Japanese War and the revolution of 1905, however, the Ministry did little more than set the stage for the burst of activity that would accompany the Stolypin reform. Since the Ministry had no local organs, it could not maintain close contact with the *zemstvos*. Indeed, the Ministry was so pitifully funded that it could not even dream of supporting any agronomic aid programs that the *zemstvos* might arrange.[12] In the absence of financial assistance from the government, the *zemstvos* were reticent to begin hiring agronomists and setting up permanent aid networks. Most *zemstvos* were now willing to keep a single agronomist on their staffs—by 1904, 31 provincial *zemstvos* and 250 *uezd zemstvos* had hired agronomists—but they were only willing to fund token projects, such as the establishment of a couple of equipment stores or seed cleaning stations.[13]

In Tambov the *zemstvos* strongly resisted the governor's efforts to draw them into agronomic aid programs in this period. Moved by the traumas following the 1891 crop failure, and favorably impressed with *zemstvo* programs in Moscow province, at the annual meeting of the provincial *zemstvo* assembly in December 1892, Governor V. P. Rokossovskii insisted that the Tambov *zemstvos* begin agronomic aid measures. Begrudgingly, the provincial *zemstvo* assembly approved an agronomic aid plan at its next plenary meeting a year later. In accordance with this plan, in early 1894 each *uezd zemstvo* hired an agronomist, set up a tiny experimental station, and opened an equipment store. But already by the end of that same year the *zemstvo* assemblies moved to starve the plan of funds. As the landowners saw it, peasants could just as well walk over to many estates and see advanced tools and techniques in action. Many peasants themselves worked on the estates. So why should the *zemstvo* pay out large sums to agronomists, who were inevitably less well-attuned to the particular conditions of each locality than were the landowners and their estate managers?[14]

At the 1895 provincial *zemstvo* plenary sessions the executive board tried to persuade the assembly to be patient with the agronomic programs, but to no avail. Neither the provincial assembly nor the majority of the *uezd* assemblies would allocate funds in this direction. By 1897 only 5 agronomists, 4 experimental fields, and 10 equipment stores remained at work in the province. Funding even for this minimal agronomic presence was precarious in the subsequent decade.[15] By 1904–05 an influential cohort of *zemstvo* leaders in Tambov was proposing to revivify agronomic programs, but the revolution of 1905 and the outbreak of peasant revolts in the province ended all discussions of this kind. Reform-minded *zemstvo* leaders were thrown out of office in the next elections, and expansion of the agronomic aid effort was no longer an issue.[16]

The peasant revolts, the land question, and the commencement of the Stolypin reform dominated the attention of rural Russia for several years after 1905. As in Tambov, agronomic aid networks made little progress in the rest of Russia. By the year 1909 about two *uezd zemstvos* in three had an agronomist on their staffs, and the same percentage had established commissions that periodically held meetings to discuss agricultural affairs. But by the same year only 45 of the 359 *uezd zemstvos* had hired local agronomists—about 120 in all—to live and work in the villages.[17]

The agronomic aid effort began a period of explosive growth in a roundabout way, in connection with widespread disappointment in the progress of the Stolypin reform. In the initial period of the Stolypin reform the government made virtually no effort to provide consolidators with agronomic assistance. The administrators in St. Petersburg appear to have expected an agricultural revolution to take off automatically once peasant farmers set up unified plots. What funds they did assign were allocated merely to cover families' expenses in moving their dwellings onto their consolidated plots, for instance. No one paid any attention to the problem of providing consolidators with agronomic instruction, equipment-lending stations, or animal-breeding services.[18] But farmers certainly needed this kind of help, as we saw throughout Parts I and IV of the present work. Inevitably, it was not long before news of agronomic fiascoes and economic failures among consolidators began to come in from all over the country.[19]

By mid-1909, Stolypin himself was sufficiently alarmed to appeal to the *zemstvos* for help in saving the consolidation movement. On September 19th he sent all provincial Marshals of Nobility telegrams with urgent instructions.[20] At the annual *zemstvo* assemblies—which always began at the *uezd* level during autumn, and concluded at the provincial level in December–January—they were instructed to press the *zemstvos* into arranging a network of agronomic aid programs and services for consolidators. Tambov's provincial Marshal of Nobility, Prince N. N. Cholokaev, and Vice-Governor Shil'der-Shul'dner appeared at the *zemstvo* sessions and did their best to drum up support for Stolypin's proposals. But to no avail. Here and elsewhere throughout Russia, the *zemstvo* assemblies adamantly refused to focus their energies on the small minority of the population on consolidated plots. Most of the *zemstvos* were quite willing to begin agronomic aid on a broad scale, but only if their services would extend to all peasants.[21]

The government gave in to the *zemstvos* on the direction of the agronomic aid effort. In late 1910 Stolypin repeated his entreaties to the *zemstvos* to arrange special assistance for consolidated farms.[22] But to no effect. As the *zemstvos* rapidly developed all manners of programs and services aimed at lifting the agricultural performance of communal peasants, the Ministry of Agriculture gave ever-increasing funding to these programs.[23] By 1913 over 90% of the *uezd zemstvos* had installed networks of local agronomists. These *zemstvos* had 1,662 local agronomists in place in the countryside (about twice this amount if we include all agronomic instructors, specialists, and apprentices), together with 70 experimental stations.[24]

The struggle between the *zemstvos* and the government for control of agronomic aid had deeper ramifications for the Stolypin reform than first meet the eye. Having committed themselves to assisting peasant agriculture *en masse*, the *zemstvos* inevitably sought to employ peasant communes in the service of technological change. Correspondingly, they came to contest the government's goal of individualizing farming. The presence the *zemstvos* established in the countryside in the form of agronomists and supporting ranks would allow them to steer land organization towards *komassatsiia* and similar projects that supporters of the Stolypin reform so abhorred. This is exactly what happened in Tambov, as we shall see below.

The Organization and Ethos of Agronomic Aid

Everywhere, including in Tambov, the *zemstvos* organized agronomic aid along lines first established in Samara province. The lynchpin of the whole effort was the set of local agronomists, who took up residence in the countryside and undertook to assist farmers in understanding and applying the best lessons of agronomic science. The agronomist gave lectures with discussion sessions, made himself available for private consultations, managed an equipment-lending point, and supervised peasants wishing to conduct trials of certain tools, techniques, or crops on small units of their land (demonstration plots). The local agronomist was a general practitioner, a "jack of all trades" who fielded queries on all aspects of agriculture, from tillage, to bee keeping, to the management of credit cooperatives.

Above the local agronomists, loosely guiding their activities, stood the *uezd zemstvo* agronomist. Usually the *uezd* agronomist himself performed the duties of a local agronomist, in a reduced district around the *uezd* town. Most agronomists had an apprentice to help them out, at least during the busy summer months. The apprentice might or might not reside in the same village as the agronomist. The equipment-lending point would ordinarily be in the village where the agronomist stayed. Reinforcing this network, there might be a few special instructors (who would travel around to villages giving lectures and assistance in particular matters, such as poultry raising, forestry, meadow improvement, and so on), an experimental station, and a *zemstvo* credit bank (whose operations we will describe later, when discussing the cooperative movement in Tambov).

When the *zemstvos* first sent agronomists out into the countryside, it was widely assumed that formal lectures, group discussions, private consultations, distribution of agronomic literature, and the example of demonstration plots would suffice to energize the peasant economy. The agronomic aid effort began, therefore, as a purely educational campaign. The agronomists would not leverage peasant farmers with any measures of compulsion. Unlike their counterparts in the USSR in the 1920s, they played no role in taxation or other administrative undertakings, such as land surveying, statistical record keeping, or apportionment of duties-in-kind.[25]

The underlying ethos of agronomic aid was therefore quite harmonious with broad currents in Russian populism. The goal was to nurture the peasant farmer and the peasant economy, not to uproot the farmer from the village and turn him into an individualist yeoman à là the Stolypin reform. The agronomic community generally opposed the Stolypin reform's wholesale individualization of agriculture, as we saw at the conclusion of Part IV.[26] It is significant that the *zemstvo* agronomists did not make special agricultural education of peasant youth a priority. They believed they could work effectively with experienced peasant farmers.* To be sure, the agronomists were not deferential to peasant traditions and local knowledge. Their training and instructions gave them an agenda to pursue in the villages. They set out to recast peasants' understanding and application of technology. They would propagandize freely against superstitions that obstructed this goal.

---

*See below, section entitled "Agronomic Education."

The Agronomic Aid Effort in Tambov

The local agronomists began work in Tambov in 1910 and 1911. By mid-1911 40 were at work, in all twelve of the *uezds*; by 1914 the size of the network had increased to 61 (a few of which were vacant because of personnel problems).[27] As in other provinces, the network was insufficient to serve most of the peasantry. In 1914 the typical agronomist's district had anywhere from 5,000–10,000 peasant farms![28] Inevitably, the agronomists wound up focusing their energies on a dozen or two villages in proximity to their village of residence.[29]

The agronomists were young, reasonably well-trained men (three of those working in 1914 were women) from non-peasant (although not necessarily urban) backgrounds. More than half of them had higher-level agronomic education, the rest had mid-level.[30] Virtually everywhere in Russia at this time, however, agronomic institutes taught agriculture from the point of view of a capitalist enterprise, not from the economic, legal, and cultural perspective of peasants. Few of the local agronomists, moreover, would have had much practical experience in farming, let alone experience in the districts to which they were assigned.[31] They were definitely "outsiders" to the peasants they would serve.

As they began work, the agronomists were instructed to employ the same methods as elsewhere in Russia: To begin by acquainting themselves with the agricultural and economic conditions of their district, to lecture and lead discussions of agronomic issues with village gatherings, and to encourage interested farmers to point the way for their neighbors by adopting innovations on their own land. Additionally, the agronomists were to manage an equipment lending station, where peasants could borrow all kinds of advanced equipment for use at a minimal charge.

Beyond these guidelines concerning methods, the local agronomists had almost complete freedom of action. The general goals of the work were more or less identical in every *uezd*: To introduce advanced tools, encourage early tillage of the fallow field, to help peasants to arrange credit associations and other cooperatives, and, sooner or later, to lead the villages beyond the three-field system of farming.[32] But, at least until late in 1912, no one at the provincial or *uezd* level ever prioritized this menu for the specialists in the field. "Let each agronomist concentrate on whatever interests him most", said provincial agronomist Shorygin himself.[33]

Local agronomist V. Gromenko of Tambov *uezd* is the only one to have left a list of his aims as he set out to the countryside in 1910. By all indications, his colleagues shared the same long list of goals:

—To arouse popular interest in agronomy.
—To convince the peasants that he had no selfish motives, to win their trust.
—To give lectures and lead discussions on agronomic topics.
—To demonstrate new techniques (through peasant pioneers).
—To make improved tools available.
—To convince peasants to adopt multi-field farming systems, with fodder grass sowings and root crops (he seems to have in mind the "Four-Field + Grass field" system).
—To eliminate grazing on fallow land (the abolition of green fallow).
—To introduce improved breeds of cows.
—To arouse interest in beekeeping and market gardening.
—To persuade peasants to set up a credit cooperative and an agricultural society (a learning society).[34]

Clearly, both the leadership and the rank-and-file of the agronomic community in Tambov brought a very broad and flexible approach to the assistance campaign. They were not charging into the villages trying to abrogate the three-field system in one fell swoop.[35] They were willing to advise peasants on many matters, agronomic or economic, big or small.

The first season or two of work in the villages sufficed to temper the optimism of the agronomists. Their first contacts with farmers during traveling lectures revealed the breadth of the gap that separated the peasants from them. Audiences at the lectures were large and respectful, but rarely expressed much support for the agronomists. Often the peasants perceived the agronomist as an official. As one agronomist related: "... at first they did not know how to relate to me, with trust or with caution. The thought probably occurred to many of them that later they would somehow have to pay for associating with this person.[36]

Alternatively, peasants expressed indignation at the prospect of a student–teacher relationship. The agronomist could not win over his audience merely by presenting himself as a teacher or advisor. The idea that someone—anyone—could appear in their village and tell them how to run their farms deeply insulted many peasants. "Don't bother giving us advice. We know more about farming than any of you agronomists." "We have been raised on farming; our fathers and grandfathers before them have stood on this land for hundreds of years."[37] They showed up at the first meetings expecting to hear him lecture on how to till, for instance. They came for amusement, with the intention of laughing him off, not of listening to his counsel.[38]

Even when peasants recognized the agronomist as a benevolent agent, there was no guarantee that they would pay him serious attention. To more than a few agronomists, it seemed that the mass of the population held out no hope for improvements on their farms. This attitude could stem from two sources. For one, villagers were not infrequently convinced that agronomic science applied only to the landlords or the largest peasant farms. As one agronomist from Tambov *uezd* put it: "It is not so difficult to overcome peasants' distrust. The real problem is to break them of the conviction that their landholdings are too small to permit the successful implementation of any kind of innovation."[39]

Alternatively, material poverty could generate pessimism. When M. V. Solov'ev, a local agronomist in Lipetsk *uezd*, first noted his audiences' indifference and hostility, he attributed this to their "indolence" and "impenetrable darkness." Eventually, however, he decided that the weight of poverty had numbed them to the point that they could not really listen to agronomic advice. They wanted more land, or, if land was not forthcoming, they wanted cash. Solov'ev came face to face with this brand of despair so often that he considered the encouragement of credit cooperatives to be more important than any of his other duties.[40]

Sooner or later, peasants began to hear the agronomists out, and to discuss the merits of alternative tillage regimes, systems of farming, and so forth. A common language between the two sides remained far away, however, as one agronomist explained:

> The peasant is not indolent, he is simply distrustful and confused by the multitude of circumstances enmeshing him in village life. It is difficult for him to imagine how he could ever

> get out of these ties. Therefore, *when confronted with a novel proposition, he rejects it out of hand. He recites all conceivable communal and societal obstacles to the new idea.*[41]

Even when they ran out of concrete objections to a particular proposition, farmers would continue to resist. "[T]hey have one more argument in reserve, which they find extremely powerful and persuasive: 'Our fathers and grandfathers didn't do that, and they lived better than we do'."[42] Only after completing this exercise in pessimism would they begin to feel their way forward. "Little by little, following the lead of the agronomist or some of their more courageous neighbors, they look at the issue from various angles and cast off one 'insurmountable' obstacle after another..."[43]

Overall, peasant responses to the agronomists' lectures left no doubt about the size of the task facing the agronomic aid effort. The agronomists could succeed in gaining a measure of trust among the peasants. But they could not expect large numbers of farmers to pay them serious attention and follow their advice. Innovations would not sweep across the countryside as quickly as the agronomists could proselytize them. Instead the agronomists would have to recruit motivated farmers in the villages to undertake innovations on an individual basis. Diffusion of innovations would have to proceed very slowly, via imitation of work on these farmers' demonstration plots.

In almost every village the agronomists were able to locate farmers anxious to try innovations. From scattered indications, it is possible to establish a profile of these farmers. In the words of one agronomist, these were the men "... who search, who experiment, and who are not scared by hard work, disruptions, or even the possibility of occasional failure."[44] A couple of agronomists noted a strong connection between education and inquisitiveness. The "more developed, most literate" peasants, "more often than not young people who have not lost the habit of reading," made the best impression on one agronomist from Tambov *uezd*.[45] Another agronomist referred specifically to the many "peasant-intellectuals" whom he had encountered over the first year of his work. But in his experience these people were not necessarily young:

> Such a man tends to be middle-aged. He has read quite a bit from popular agricultural journals, and burns to work in new ways. "Thank God", he exclaims, "that we are beginning to use our heads, and that we are learning to live as they do in foreign countries. Thank you, *zemstvo*, for teaching us idiots."[46]

Other reports made no mention of education or literacy as a barometer of attitudes towards innovations. Four agronomists reported getting the best response in villages located nearby technologically advanced estates. Evidently peasants who worked on these estates as hired laborers grew accustomed to new tools and various ways of using them. Their acquaintance with new methods had not often led to experimentation on their own farms, but it had opened their minds to the prospect of improving their own routines.[47]

In practice, the demonstration plots served their purpose of diffusing innovations quite well. The superior appearance of crops on these plots was sufficient to impress local peasants with the validity of the innovations in question. In villages nearby the agronomic stations, small waves of interest rose up in seed drills, plows, fodder beets, or whatever else the trial plots had demonstrated.[48] After one or two sowings, when growing numbers of converts began to rush to imitate the innovations of their pioneering neighbors, the agronomists had the first proof of their influence on peasant agriculture. In many cases the equipment-lending stations could not meet peasant demand for seed drills, plows, or grass seeds, or beets for planting.

Now when agronomists made return visits to villages attendance always remained high, or even improved.[49] With each specialist giving about 20 traveling lectures per year, and the average attendance at each being about 50, the agronomists were reaching about 50,000 people each year in this manner in the last years before the First World War.[50] We should trim attendance figures downward to account for repeat listeners, but still the figures are large. Within the space of a few years the majority of farmers would have attended an agronomic lecture.[51]

Agronomists' informal contacts with peasants increased in proportion to the interest and curiosity generated at the village meetings. Once the agronomist gained some degree of acceptance as an authority, and once a number of their neighbors made use of him, the more cautious farmers felt more comfortable in approaching him. Most agronomists did not keep a close count on the number of peasants who came to see them for informal consultations, but those who reported their estimates noted a strong surge of customers after they had weathered the initial period of peasant distrust. One agronomist received about 150 visitors in his first spring on the job in 1911, then 800 in the next spring.[52] Another reported getting 40–50 visitors per day in his second spring (also 1912); he estimated he gave a total of 2,500–3,000 consultations over the course of the year.[53] The face-to-face character of these consultations made them especially effective.

M. G. Luchebul' of Usman *uezd* reported that those peasants who came in to see him always proceeded to try out certain innovations in practice.[54]

The quantities of peasants seeking informal consultations imply the fast growing popularity of trials and innovations roughly along lines suggested by the agronomists. Surely the number of officially registered demonstration plots—in the neighborhood of 2,000 in 1914—does no justice to the influence of the agronomists.[55] Demonstration plots were very time consuming for the agronomists. They could not closely supervise many more than they actually did. So farmers clearly began experimenting on their own, in unknown numbers.

Comparison of peasants' tool holdings in 1910 and 1917 provides indirect confirmation of the rising interest in technological change. The numbers are not unimpressive, especially when we consider that most of the growth must have come before war interrupted foreign trade and domestic production in 1914.[56] Although the *sokha*, the wooden-framed harrow, the scythe, and the flail still dominated the countryside in 1917, plows, seed drills, and reaping machines had become much more common sights in the space of a few short years [Table 5.1].

At the same time, these numbers overstate the degree of technological change in the villages. To begin with, in the rush to market all of the new equipment, none of the organizations engaged in the tool trade maintained adequate supplies of spare parts.[57] The effective life of

Table 5.1. Advanced Equipment Holdings on Peasant Farms, 1910 and 1917
(tools per 100 households)

	Northern *uezds*		Central *uezds*		Southern *uezds*		TOTAL	
	1910	1917	1910	1917	1910	1917	1910	1917
Plows	1.2	7.3	10.0	15.3	13.1	17.2	8.9	14.3
Iron harrows and cultivators	0.6	n.d.	2.4	n.d.	5.1	n.d.	2.8	n.d.
Seed drills	0.03	0.1	0.1	0.8	0.6	2.1	0.2	1.0
Reaping machines	0.03	0.3	0.6	2.1	1.0	2.0	0.6	1.7
Winnowing machines	1.8	1.4	4.5	5.0	6.1	5.9	4.4	4.5
Threshing machines	0.8	0.7	3.4	3.2	3.7	3.6	2.9	2.8

Source: Selsko-khoziaistvennye mashiny i orudiia, pp. 68–69; *Pouezdnye itogi Vserossiiskoi sel'sko-khoziaistvennoi i pozemel'noi perepisi 1917 goda*, pp. 114–121.

equipment was relatively short in this period as a result. Tools suffered still more from improper maintenance. *Zemstvo* mechanics attested that few peasants really knew how to take care of their tools. The absence of written instructions accompanying the tools did not help matters.[58] "Ordinarily", or at least "not rarely," peasants would leave their tools outdoors over the winter, uncleaned, exposed to the elements. They treated complex machinery like reaping machines just as callously as plows.[59] The fact that peasants often settled (or opted) for the cheapest models of tools further curtailed the effective life of the equipment.[60]

More importantly, the acquisition of new tools did not necessarily entail the ability to use them to full advantage. We have seen clear demonstrations of this fact in Part I, especially regarding the employment of plows. Agronomists knew not to count on the infusion of tools to carry the peasant economy forward by itself. Even as the local agronomists' influence began to spread across the farming population, plans were afoot to redirect the center of gravity of the agronomic aid effort. Tutelage was not generating fast results, so the *zemstvo* leaders pinned their hopes on the encouragement of self-help organizations.

The Second Phase of Agronomic Aid

When leading agronomists took stock of the agronomic aid effort in 1911 and 1912, they recognized the need to make concrete plans for a long-term cultural campaign in the countryside. Fortunately, government and *zemstvo* officials understood that the agronomists could not reshape peasant agriculture overnight. Both the Ministry of Agriculture in St. Petersburg and Tambov's *zemstvos* steadily increased funding for agronomic programs in these years.[61] Resistance to agronomic aid remained very strong in some of the *zemstvos*, but leading officials proved able to hold this resistance in check.[62] There would be no repetition of the abolition of agronomic programs in the 1890s.

With its future more or less secured, the agronomic aid effort now entered into a second, more complicated phase. Once peasants had started moving down the road to reforming their farming operations, the task was to sustain the momentum of this movement. Since the *zemstvos* could not finance more than 50–60 agronomists to serve the more than three million peasants in the province, the specialists would need help if they were to educate broader circles of farmers and to channel innovations in appropriate directions. However, so long as the numbers of reform-minded peasants remained small, peasant communes could not fulfill this intermediary role. The more conservative peasants continued to dominate almost all communes. But to whom else could the agronomists turn?

This search for an intermediary link between the peasant and the agronomist was common to the agronomic aid effort all over Russia in these years, and the proposed solution was everywhere the same. Agronomists looked to encourage forward-thinking peasants to organize into agricultural societies and various forms of cooperatives. The agricultural societies could perform educational functions while the credit associations could assist peasants in purchasing equipment and marketing their production. The great success of cooperative networks in Europe, most spectacularly in Denmark, raised hopes for the flowering of peasant initiative and an economic upsurge in Russia as well. The fact that cooperative movements in many European countries had blossomed in response to deep agricultural crises served to heighten the enthusiasm surrounding these organizations in the early twentieth century.[63]

The Development of the Cooperative Movement

The cooperative movement had not flourished in late nineteenth century Russia. The first experimentation with cooperatives began in the 1870s and 1880s, when *zemstvos* organized peasants into a small number of savings and loan associations. By all accounts, these associations soon proved to be dismal failures. Having no clear conception of the functions of financial institutions, peasants did not apply their loans to productive investments and routinely defaulted on accrued debts.[64] Inevitably, the *zemstvos* found themselves more or less helpless to oversee the associations' credit operations. *Zemstvo* officials were not able to tell which peasants were credit-worthy. Meanwhile, economic conditions of the last decades of the nineteenth century were most unfavorable to the development of credit operations. Farmers would not take out loans for productive investments if they were not convinced that they turn a profit on their production. With grain prices depressed and with little access to markets of any kind, peasants in Tambov and elsewhere had no such conviction.[65]

The great majority of the *zemstvo*-sponsored savings and loan associations faltered and disappeared before the turn of the century, and most *zemstvos* lost interest in cooperatives. But the peasantry's need for credit was so great that in the first decade of the twentieth century the numbers of credit cooperatives began to expand again, thanks in part to some assistance from the State Bank. While in 1900 there had been 798 credit or savings and loan associations in Russia, by 1909, there were 4,167. Membership in these institutions grew correspondingly, from 300,000 to over 2,000,000. The two million members represented over ten million people, once family members are included.[66]

In this period the central government did take some steps to encourage cooperative formation. Most importantly, a law in 1904 passed the reins of the cooperative credit movement to the *zemstvos*. This law permitted any *zemstvo* to form a credit bank (*kassa melkogo kredita*), which was authorized to sanction the formation of new credit associations and to procure base capital for them. The law was a good one. Firstly, it simplified the establishment of a credit cooperative. Groups of peasants could get permission to form a credit cooperative and complete the formalities involved with opening the institution more quickly through the *zemstvo* than through government offices. Secondly, the *zemstvo* credit banks could eventually perform a unifying role for credit cooperatives, coordinating the distribution of funds where they were most needed. Thirdly, the *zemstvo* could exercise supervision over the credit cooperatives' activities more easily than could the State Bank and its agents. All the while, the *zemstvo* credit banks were supposed to refrain from competing with rural cooperatives in the issuing of credit to individuals. Instead, the *zemstvo* banks were to attract private capital to themselves. They could then funnel this capital towards the credit cooperatives, in support of the latter's long-term loans, marketing operations, etc.

Unfortunately, few *zemstvos* were quick to take advantage of the opportunity to encourage and supervise credit cooperatives. Nationwide, only 56 *zemstvos* had credit banks by January of 1910, and many of these were not straining themselves to encourage the formation of more credit cooperatives in the countryside.[67] The *zemstvos*' banks were even competing with village cooperatives by offering credit directly to individuals.[68] As late as 1912 there were still only 120 *uezd* and 12 provincial *zemstvo* credit banks.[69] In Tambov the *zemstvos* made no move to help the cooperative movement before the time that the agronomic aid programs got underway.[70] The poverty and low cultural level of the province combined with the complete absence of official encouragement left Tambov and the other central provinces far behind in cooperative formation.[71] Tambov had only 85 credit cooperatives by 1909.[72]

The commencement of the *zemstvos'* agronomic aid programs prompted *zemstvo* leaders to take notice of the revitalization of the cooperative movement. In Tambov, as early as the summer of 1910, provincial *zemstvo* agronomist D. M. Shorygin and other leading specialists had addressed local agronomists on the importance of encouraging cooperatives of all kinds.[73] In 1912 Shorygin duly issued instructions to all agronomists to concentrate their activities in a few villages or sets of villages, and to work through cooperatives if they were present.[74]

Uezd zemstvo boards and their agricultural committees responded to the summons and administrative support for the cooperatives increased.[75] Eight *uezd zemstvos* had established credit banks by 1914.[76] The *zemstvos* also stopped competing with rural cooperatives by offering credit to individuals.[77] Moreover, most of the *zemstvo* assemblies and their leaders did what they could to popularize credit cooperatives, urging local agronomists and other educational personnel to encourage peasants to form them. Most of the agronomists discussed cooperatives at village meetings, some even attaching primary importance to this topic as early as 1911.[78] One analyst estimated that about 40 cooperatives opened in 1912 as a direct result of local agronomists' efforts.[79]

Overall, the *zemstvos* and their agronomists conducted a reasonably strong propaganda campaign in favor of cooperatives, focusing on credit. It is true that some of the *zemstvos* (and some individual agronomists) turned their backs on the cooperative movement. In Shatsk *uezd*, for example, the *zemstvo* board ordered its local agronomists not to enter into contact with cooperatives, insisting that the cooperatives had nothing in common with the agronomic aid effort.[80] Despite such uneven support, already by January 1st, 1914, there were 317 credit institutions, up from only 85 in 1909.[81] By 1914 212,000 individuals were registered as members of credit cooperatives.[82] This represented about 35% of the population, once family members are included, and was above the national average.[83]

In some respects the credit associations performed successfully in these formative years. Peasants could not help but notice how they immediately and substantially improved terms of credit. In place of the village money-lenders' annual interest rates of 50% or more, the credit cooperatives' rates on loans ranged from 8–12%.[84] Borrowers were somewhat less likely to default on their loans—as had been ubiquitous in the nineteenth century—because they applied their loans to productive purposes. Figures for Tambov do not exist, but a nationwide survey of rural credit associations in 1913 found that 86% of the loans were going to productive purposes.[85]

Nevertheless, the credit associations were inherently unstable. The quality of the leaders of the associations was not the root of the problem—cases of embezzlement among officials appear to have been rare, in Tambov, at any rate. The real difficulty stemmed from the distinct status of the peasant estate in Russian law. The law partially protected peasants from confiscation of property. They were always entitled to retain an amount of land and livestock sufficient to continue farming. Since many households had little more than that to begin with, they could default on loans with near impunity. On paper, the credit associations paid back loans taken from the *zemstvos* and the State Bank in exemplary fashion.[86] But, as historian Yanni Kotsonis has recently demonstrated, *zemstvos* tended to cover up insolvency in cooperatives by rolling over their loans to the associations.[87] We cannot be sure, therefore, how credit-worthy the associations really were. We can, however, say that the carefully maintained appearance of credit-worthiness was a crucial advantage for the future of the cooperative movement. This appearance gave private investors the confidence to invest in them.[88]

Both quantitatively and qualitatively, therefore, the cooperative movement was a modest success in Tambov in the years after 1910. The network of credit associations was about 40% complete in 1914, and it would not have taken too long to fill out if war had not come.[89] Indeed, in Tambov *uezd* this point had almost arrived already by 1916, when there were 58 credit cooperatives in the *uezd*'s 46 *volosts*.[90] So long as these associations continued to provide good service, the percentage of families taking part would have continued to increase.

Despite all the signs of steady progress, however, by 1914 the cooperatives did not yet have any real influence on the economy. In 1914 the average size of a credit association loan in the province was only 78 rubles.[91] Measured by peasants' needs, this was not very much—enough to rent a few of *desiatinas* of land, or to buy a good plow and another tool or two on the side. It was not generally enough to acquire a top quality horse. To make matters worse, very few cooperatives were managing to procure tools for their members at reduced prices. 16 cooperatives had fixed agricultural stores, and most of the rest appear to have been ordering some tools, either through the *zemstvos* or straight from manufacturers.[92] But until they learned to unify their purchases they would not be able to procure equipment at prices lower than those currently available from the *zemstvos* or private stores.[93]

Furthermore, simple credit operations did little to help farmers in marketing their production. In the early twentieth century Russian grain producers were squandering an estimated 100,000,000 rubles or more per year on untimely grain sales.[94] Almost every household in Tambov marketed some grain. Even if they had no surpluses they had to sell something after the harvest to meet tax payments or other debts. Well before 1910 the best-managed cooperatives in Russia were already organizing marketing and selling members' grain for 10 or more percent above what they would have got otherwise (the cooperatives gave members an advance on their grain, and sold it for them when prices improved over the winter and spring).[95] But the cooperative movement in Tambov was slow to follow this lead. By 1914 only 44 cooperatives in Tambov had begun to handle grain marketing.[96] Their share of the grain trade was microscopic.

Thus, as successful as the credit cooperatives might have been as institutions, one suspects that they were of very limited value to their individual members. To illustrate this contention, let us review the fate of members of one of the most advanced credit cooperatives in the province for the period 1910–1914.[97] On July 6th, 1909, 50 people formed the savings and loan association at Ploskoe village in Kozlov *uezd*, with a balance of 1,500 rubles. By 1914 the association boasted a membership of 1,400 families, and a balance of 137,000 rubles. The association was one of the few to arrange grain marketing—handling 50,000 *puds* of grain in 1913, which works out to a modest quantity of about 35 *puds* per family—and was the first to petition for permission to establish a union of credit associations (which they projected would encompass Kozlov and neighboring *uezds*).

Table 5.2. Four Years of the Ploskoe Credit Cooperative

Holdings of 100 members	Jan. 1910	Jan. 1914	Change
Allotment and purchased land, in *des.*	722.5	714.5	− 8
Sowings, in *des.*	764	687	− 77
Horses	188	174	− 14
Cows	127	127	0
Sheep	578	510	− 68
Value of buildings, rubles	16,294	17,835	+ 1,541
"Tools and other property"*	3,367	5,145	+ 1,788
Indebtedness to the association, in rubles	1,265	12,954	+11,689

*Sic.

Members of the Ploskoe cooperative were not doing as well as the cooperative itself, however. A concerned member, D. Gorbachev, recorded the above data for the one hundred families who had been members for four years as of January 1st, 1914 [Table 5.2].

What can we make of these data? To begin with, it is clear from the landholding and horse-holding data that these farms were of average or perhaps slightly above average strength.* And yet these farms were no better off in 1914 than they had been four years earlier. Gorbachev insisted that the loans were not squandered, but were put to productive use. So why were they not doing any better? Gorbachev's own analysis of the problem is telling:

> ... our farmers, faithful to their old ways and methods, have proven incapable of coping with contemporary economic life. The money they invest in their farms ... nets them not a profit but a loss. They cover their losses with more borrowing, and sink further into debt....
>
> Credit will only become useful when we develop and improve our employment of technology, and change our whole system of farming [he clearly has in mind multi-field systems—D.K.].

Although the evidence from Ploskoe is the only information of its kind, one suspects that the experience of the members of this savings and loan association was quite typical. This experience offers several valuable lessons on the potential of the credit cooperatives to assist the

---

*Ploskoe was a well-to-do village, located in Tiutchevskaia *volost'* in the south of Kozlov *uezd*. The village was 15 *versts* away from the nearest market and railroad station. It was the only village in its *volost'* whose peasants had not belonged to a landowner before the emancipation in 1861. In 1912 the average family in Ploskoe had approximately 12 *desiatinas* of land and 2 horses, as opposed to *volost'* averages of just 7 *desiatinas* and 1.4 horses (allotment, purchased, and rented land combined). The families in the Ploskoe savings and loan association were *sowing* 7.6 *desiatinas* of land, and held 1.9 horses each. Judging from the comparison of allotment and purchased land on the one hand and sown land on the other hand, about 2.8 *desiatinas* of the average savings and loan member's sowings would have been on rented land. Thus they were probably renting in the neighborhood of 3.5 *desiatinas* per farm, which would be quite expensive. But this was not the "hunger renting" we discussed in Part II. Families with more than seven *desiatinas* of allotment and purchased land were not suffering from land hunger. Therefore, most of the early members of the association—many of whom must have come from neighboring villages—were from the average or somewhat stronger than average farms in the area. All data from Tambovskoe gubernskoe zemstvo, *Materialy po podvomomu obsledovaniiu zhivotnovodstva*, pp. 130–145. The location of the village from *Spiski naselennykh mest Tambovskoi gubernii*, p. 7.

peasant economy. Credit could help a family to buy tools, but it could not teach them how to use them. Credit could not help peasants to improve yields and advance towards multi-field systems unless and until they knew how to do this. Furthermore, we can be certain that the lion's share of the credits never had any connection to agrotechnical improvements. Data for Tambov do not exist, but a nationwide survey of cooperatives in 1913 found peasants applying their loans in the following ways: land rental (23%), purchase of land (several %), purchase of animals (21%), purchase of fodder (9%), and non-agricultural applications (14%).[98] In all, peasants were investing well below one-fourth of their credits in tools, seeds, drainage, or other technological improvements.

The pattern of peasant investment suggests that credit was not yet playing a progressive role in most areas of Russia. Accessible credit might help failing farms to stay afloat for a while longer, and it might prop up average farms' standard of living for a time. But the credit associations and other cooperatives had to address two key issues before the economic fortunes of the agricultural sector could change. Firstly, they had to reinforce the *zemstvo* agronomists' efforts to bring agronomic science into the village. Secondly, they needed to unify their efforts at purchasing tools and marketing agricultural production.

Marketing Operations, Unions of Cooperatives, and Agronomic Education

The cooperative movement in Tambov was heavily tilted towards credit associations, so the movement as a whole began only slowly to play an educational role in the countryside. The most direct expression of this role came in the form of a few dozen local "agricultural societies" (*sel'sko-khoziaistvennye obshchestva*) that popped up in small numbers in these years, most of them in 1913 and 1914.[99] Agronomists, teachers, landowners, and sometimes priests encouraged groups of peasants to establish these societies, whose primary function was to promote knowledge and the interchange of ideas concerning agriculture.[100] According to their charters, agricultural societies were allowed to undertake marketings, purchase equipment, run stores, operate equipment-lending stations, and so on. But they did not have the base capital of credit associations, and their charters absolved members of any financial responsibility for the society's debts, which made them uncreditworthy.[101] And so they tended to be very poor and modest institutions, doing little more than holding discussion sessions with agronomists, distributing agricultural journals, and performing some experimental work on their members' lands.[102] A few of them arose alongside "parent" credit cooperatives.

Given the weak presence of agricultural societies in the province, it was inevitable that some of the credit cooperatives would begin to perform educational functions. Many local agronomists pressured the credit cooperatives into expanding their activities in this direction, in hopes of intensifying networks of lending stations, demonstration plots, etc.[103] Statistics are almost non-existent, but it appears that a rather small minority of the credit cooperatives responded. They might purchase stud animals for members' use, arrange local agricultural exhibitions, or invite agronomists and veterinarians to give series of lectures. Forty-seven are known to have set up equipment-lending stations, some of these offering grain cleaning on sorting machines.[104] But the huge majority of the credit cooperatives invested no more than a handful of rubles on educational measures. They might not even bother to subscribe to agricultural journals.

Although the credit cooperatives remained indifferent towards educational measures, their appetite to expand into marketing and purchasing activities grew with each year. As we noted above, their primary goal was to gain leverage in the grain trade, and a few dozen cooperatives were active in this trade by 1914. But cooperative and *zemstvo* leaders were aware that the cooperatives would play only a very limited role in the grain trade until such time as they managed to unify their marketing operations. And so when the provincial *zemstvo* organized the first conference of cooperative representatives in October 1913 the focus of the sessions centered on plans to create unions of cooperatives.

Throughout the year 1913 the question of unified action in the grade trade brought friction between the credit cooperatives and the agricultural societies to a head. The one large agricultural society, the provincial-wide Tambov Agricultural Society (publishers of the journal *Sel'sko-khoziaistvennaia Zhizn'*, which we have cited so often throughout this study), had tried to organize grain marketings on a non-profit basis to itself. Unfortunately, the credit cooperatives declined to participate, and they at first they remained cold to the idea of joining hands with agricultural societies at the October conference. Credit cooperative leaders did not see any reason to work together with agricultural societies. They sought to establish unions of credit cooperatives alone, which could handle all credit, purchasing, and marketing operations for the cooperative movement. The credit cooperatives could even undertake educational measures, if these really were necessary.[105] This attitude, favoring the creation of "universal cooperatives" out of the credit associations, was not peculiar to credit cooperative officials. Many agronomists favored taking the same road, and were already trying to create universal cooperatives in their districts.[106]

If the credit cooperatives had succeeded in dominating the October 1913 conference, the cooperative movement as a whole would have lost much of its potential to play a meaningful role in the agronomic education of the peasantry. As the best *zemstvo* agronomic personnel pointed out at the conference, credit cooperative directors were neither able nor willing to conduct educational programs. All too often they were not qualified even to handle complex marketing operations.[107] Nevertheless, it appears that the credit cooperatives were on the verge of squeezing other forms of cooperatives out of existence at this time. We have just seen how a current of opinion within the agronomic community favored just this. Furthermore, the *zemstvo* boards in Tambov had yet to comprehend the value of the agricultural societies and the enlightenment for which they stood. Whereas *zemstvos* in Poltava province, for example, were providing agricultural societies with healthy subsidies (1,000 rubles upon opening, and 800 more annually), the Tambov *zemstvos* rarely gave more than one-time grants of 100–200 rubles to their societies.[108] If the credit cooperatives had refused to work together with the agricultural societies, the *zemstvos* might have let the latter languish and disappear.

In the sequel, agronomists at the cooperative conference persuaded most of the credit associations' leaders that their institutions had enough work to do without trying to undertake major marketing operations. The conference agreed to unite grain marketings under a new "agricultural association" to be formed within the Tambov Agricultural Society.[109] This plan never got off the ground, presumably because of the dislocations connected with the outbreak of the war in the following summer.

Overall, therefore, by 1914 the cooperatives had managed to accomplish next to nothing with respect to the purchasing of equipment, the marketing of production, and the formation of cooperative unions. This is not to say that the movement was unimportant. It was young and growing. The cooperatives were providing peasants with credit, and as we will see, some educational work was getting done. It had some potential, but it was no quick fix for any aspect of the agrarian problem.

Agricultural Education

Notwithstanding their satisfaction with village meetings, consultations, and demonstration plots, the *zemstvo* agronomists knew all along that they could not rely on these measures alone to transform peasants into professional farmers with an analytical approach to agronomic problems. *Zemstvo* leaders hoped to provide motivated farmers with at least a rudimentary knowledge of many subjects, including veterinary medicine, meteorology, pests, crops, and, most importantly, soil science and tillage. They juggled two different approaches to this question: 1) the insertion of agricultural education into school curricula; and 2) a program of intensive agronomic education courses for adults.

1) *Agricultural Education and Schools*. In 1909, just as the agronomic aid effort was getting underway, Tambov's provincial *zemstvo* board appointed a committee to study other *zemstvos'* agricultural education measures. The committee focused its attention on the specialized agricultural schools *zemstvos* had set up in many other provinces. Virtually everywhere *zemstvos* had found these schools to be a wasted investment, since the graduates almost never returned to their villages with their knowledge. Instead they elected to leave the agricultural sector or take lucrative employment as managers of private estates.[110] Those who did return home were too young to exercise any influence on their families' farms. At their young age they did not carry any authority, and many of the techniques they learned at the specialized schools—such as early fallow or *ziab*—were inaccessible in conditions of peasant farming unless the commune gave its consent.[111]

While specialized schools did not meet expectations, attempts to insert agricultural studies into *zemstvo* primary schools had proven to be just as futile. *Zemstvo* teachers were not properly qualified to teach agronomy, and, more importantly, peasants did not want such subjects in the schools.[112] As a result, already by 1910 most of the *zemstvos* had given up on the idea of offering agricultural education to peasant youth. The *zemstvos* in Tambov wisely decided not to repeat such experiments.[113]

2) *Intensive Lecture Courses for Adults*. Instead of directing their attention at peasant youth, therefore, the agronomic community would have to re-educate adults. Once the local agronomists' sporadic proselytization at village meetings and consultations proved to be insufficient, the provincial agronomic conference in March of 1912 decided to experiment with intensive agronomic courses for small groups of

farmers.[114] The Borisoglebsk *uezd zemstvo* had begun holding such courses in 1910, and at least four other *uezd zemstvos* agreed to fund these events during the last two years before the World War.[115] The great majority of these courses fell into a single pattern resembling programs in other provinces.[116] In a village where an agronomist resided, for a period varying from one to four weeks in length, interested peasants convened every day to hear lectures, fulfill reading assignments, engage in discussions, witness advanced techniques, and take examinations. The *zemstvo* fed, housed, and covered the travel expenses of anyone who came to the courses from afar. They also reinforced the local agronomist with a couple of other specialists, such as instructors on beekeeping, fowl, dairy farming, credit cooperatives, etc.

Quantitatively, the intensive courses were next to insignificant. Even at their height, in Borisoglebsk *uezd* in 1913, there were only six courses graduating 288 students in an *uezd* with a peasant population of over 350,000.[117] In the first two-thirds of 1914 the *zemstvos* staged only eight courses in the entire province, graduating 527.[118]

Qualitatively, however, every account agrees that these courses were extraordinary successes. The best illustration of the style and the effectiveness of the intensive courses comes from an agronomist in Tambov *uezd* in 1914.[119] In February of 1914 agronomists offered a 17-day lecture course in the *volost'* village of Lysye gory. About 40 peasants registered to attend, some coming from quite far away for the privilege. At many of the sessions, however, as many as 200 more people would crowd in to listen. The majority of the students were from farms of average strength; ten were heads of households, twenty-five remained in their father's household, and three had no farm at the moment. Thus most of them were relatively young—all but two of the students at a similar course in neighboring Balashov *uezd* of Saratov province ranged from 18–33 years of age.[120] All of the students were literate, reading being a prerequisite for registration. Absolute silence reigned during the sessions; speakers very rarely had to ask for quiet. Clearly the level of interest was very high.

The lectures did not supply the students with a motley collection of farming tips, but were rather a comprehensive presentation of the fundamentals of an agronomic education. Farming, livestock husbandry, and cooperatives all received attention. The examination results testify both to the teachers' effectiveness and to the students' enthusiasm: of the 35 who finished the course, 4 or 5 performed "superbly," 11 or 12 "quite well," 11 or 12 "satisfactorily," a few poorly, and only 2 "very poorly."

These events were quite a bargain for the agronomic aid effort. The courses cost less than 200 rubles (of which the Ministry of Agriculture paid one-half), and the teaching did not distract the specialists from more productive endeavors (they had little else to do all winter). The intensive courses created at least a few farmers devoted to bringing modern science into village life. The graduates' complete acceptance of agronomy (and the other scientific disciplines included in the lectures) and their commitment to apply its lessons to their work is evident from the evaluations they wrote of the course. Every one of them wanted to see more courses offered, and most wanted them to be at least as long in duration, if not longer. Agronomists from other courses reported that many participants began to employ various innovations they had studied. Some purchased subscriptions to agricultural journals, and many began to inquire about how to organize proper accounting on their farms.[121] Some banded together to form cooperatives.[122]

For lack of evidence, we cannot know how well course graduates retained their knowledge and fulfilled agronomists' expectations for them. But all of the information indicates that the graduates had left the world of folk agronomic wisdom behind for good. Most importantly from the agronomists' point of view, graduates acquired a critical approach to their work. The following passage comes from young peasant Nikolai Kostikov, who traveled to a course with 18–20 fellows from his village after they read a couple of agronomic brochures and became curious about agronomy:

> For a long time I have known that our peasant ordinarily thinks only of how to sow as much land as possible, paying absolutely no attention to his methods of tillage.[123]

Perhaps the most heartening words of all regarding the lecture courses came from some graduates of the Lysye gory course in Tambov *uezd*. Together, their comments read like a paean to the agronomic aid effort:

> Courses are necessary, as necessary as it is to leave darkness for light.

> More such courses should be offered, of course, because they help us to understand how useful science can be to us.

> It is very, very important to organize such courses, because here light collides with darkness in a fierce struggle.[124]

Conclusion

The Achievements of the Agronomic Aid Effort

> Peasant agricultural correspondents' reports illuminate in stark
> relief the tendency to connect the spread of improvements, even
> the very idea of improvements, with the *zemstvo*.
> —Khar'kov province, 1907[125]

> ... conscious peasants have appeared in the villages more fre-
> quently in the last few years. They understand where the
> backwardness of their farming practices is leading. But up to this
> point in time we can admit without fear of contradiction that
> the great mass of the peasantry has made only the weakest
> [cultural] progress, and that all of the agronomists' and coop-
> eratives' strenuous efforts over the last few years have yielded
> very weak results.
> —Borisoglebsk *uezd* agronomist N. M. Vasiliev, 1914[126]

As with so many other nascent transformations in Russian society in
the final decade of the Tsarist regime, the outbreak of war in the
summer of 1914 and the revolutions of 1917 halted the development
of the agronomic aid programs before they had matured. In Tambov, as
elsewhere, well over half of the agronomic personnel was mobilized to
help in the requisitioning of fodder, foodstuffs, and other supplies for the
army. Budgets for agronomic aid shrank, and the momentum that had
built up over the previous years of work was gone.[127] The brevity of the
pre-war agronomic aid effort and the absence of any studies of this effort
in other provinces complicate our task of drawing conclusions on its
effectiveness. We can, nevertheless, offer a few considered comments.

The first and most obvious consequence of agronomic aid programs
was the fact that peasants had now become aware of the presence of
agronomists.[128] News of the agronomists' work spread far and wide, such
that peasants in the last established agronomic districts had heard
about their work, and were anxious to receive specialists in their own
localities.[129] The very presence of the agronomists, together with peas-

ants' awareness and acknowledgment of their work, represented a large step in and of itself for the evolution of peasant agriculture. Whether dimly or clearly, all peasants now understood that alternative methods of labor and farm organization existed *for them*, not only for the landowners. By 1914 popular recognition of this fact was irreversible, thanks to the efforts of pioneering farmers—consolidators and communal alike—who employed innovations.

Yet, beyond the peasants becoming acquainted with the agronomists, the latter did not appear to be making any meaningful progress in reforming peasant labor or field systems. Had the agronomists' work raised more than a few peasants' grain yields? The agronomists had no convincing statistical evidence of this. Were the numbers of horseless farms declining? No. Had even a single commune in the province adopted a multi-field farming system? I have not uncovered even one such case in the pre-Revolutionary period.[130] Was there any employed or early fallow within the three-field system? The local agronomists' reports occasionally record small numbers of demonstration plots. Otherwise, their silence is deafening.

For the most part the agronomists had managed to win peasants' trust. But this was only a small and preliminary step towards the reshaping of the farmer and his farming practices. Even this step was not fully behind all of the agronomists, as a local agronomist in Borisoglebsk *uezd*, D. A. Vasil'ev (no relation to the *uezd* agronomist N. M. Vasil'ev), found out in 1914:

> In concluding my report, I cannot help but relay a portrait of rural life that offers some reflection of the cultural level of the population and the conditions of agronomic work. In the struggle with the drought of this year ordinary folk methods [by which Vasil'ev means the complex of agricultural techniques, prayers, and superstitious behavior of all kinds] have proven to be entirely bankrupt. In connection with the drought, agronomic propaganda in favor of early fallow and *ziab* tillage has been refracted in the prism of popular ignorance, producing a miraculous absurdity, beside which pale all the preceding absurdities emanating from the people's darkness.
>
> An idea spread across the countryside instantaneously, like a lightning bolt, and took hold of everyone down to the smallest child. According to this idea the agronomist waves off gathering clouds with a handkerchief so as to prevent rain. The agronomist himself created the drought, in order to trick the peasants into believing that with his tillage methods crops will grow even without rain [when in fact, according to these peasants, the

agronomist uses spells to grow his own crops on some lands at the agronomic station—D.K.]. This idea is so widespread, and has so galvanized the population against me, that many people have warned me that I might meet with certain "unpleasant episodes." Many peasants are working to convene village assemblies, with the intention of demanding my removal and destroying my spells. As the rumors have it, I have already been fired from work in two other places because of my witchcraft.

I think this illustration of the conditions of agronomic work requires no commentary.[131]

The scapegoating that Vasil'ev experienced was untypical, perhaps even unique. Nevertheless, however rarely peasants might have turned against the agronomists in practice, his story demonstrates how close to the surface lay superstition and suspicion in the Russian countryside. Even while the agronomists gathered trust and authority among the population, it would be quite a few years before the latent tendencies that surfaced in this episode passed away.

Part of the blame for the sluggish progress of technological innovations in this period must fall on the agronomists themselves. All over Russia agricultural institutes were scrambling to turn out as many agronomists they could in the hectic years between 1905 and 1914. Critics noticed that the professional and personal qualities of the newly trained agronomists did not always match the requirements of the job. Being generally quite young, in their 20s, quite a few of them simply could not cope with the variety and complexity of the work.[132] Most were not intimately familiar with peasant technologies before they began work, and could not easily put themselves in the shoes of the peasant farmer.[133] They would have to learn a lot on the job.

Some of the hurdles facing the agronomists were psychological in nature. The perceptive Garin-Mikhailovskii once complained that Russian male intellectuals, including those who were populist-inclined, had trouble acquiring respect for peasants on a personal level.[134] Their intellectual sympathies for the peasantry did not necessarily coincide with empathy, in other words. The charge is surely heavy-handed, but it is sufficiently plausible to warrant attention. Establishing a communicative, trusting relationship with peasants was an integral part of the agronomic aid effort, so one of the more subtle tasks facing the agronomists was to shed some of the prejudices they might have brought with them to the village. The flexibility of youth was on their side here. Living alongside peasants for long periods and gaining familiarity with them, most agronomists probably made the necessary psychological adjustments. The gradual development of trust between the two sides certainly implies as much.

Problems of a programmatic nature were more widespread, more lasting, and more serious. At all levels of the agronomic community in the black-earth zone, questions concerning the relationship of tillage to grain yields dominated scholarly agendas, professional conferences, and practical work with peasant farmers. Russia's network of agricultural experimental stations was still very young in the Stolypin reform period, most of these institutions having just commenced operations. The main station in Tambov began work only in 1912. Inevitably, the experimental stations focused their attention on the predominant branch of agriculture in the southern Russia, grain farming. The resultant lopsidedness of research agendas would persist into the 1920s and beyond, as the Soviet state grappled with its own grain problems.

The work plans of individual agronomists and the proceedings of their conferences establish how deeply their training reflected these circumstances. We have already noted how the elimination of green fallow was the top priority of almost every agronomist. But of course it was very difficult for peasants to till the fallow field earlier, because of the common grazing regime. We have also noted how, after expending a tremendous amount of effort in trying to convince peasants to part with green fallow, the agronomists strove to introduce fodder crops of all varieties—the goal being to boost families' fodder reserves, thereby reducing their dependence on fallow grazing. When peasants proved slow to follow this detour, an agronomic conference in Tambov in 1913 even went so far as to recommend propagandizing collective cultivation and seeding of meadows and pastures, again with the aim of bolstering fodder reserves and reducing the population's dependence on fallow grazing.[135]

The agronomists' fixation on tillage questions was distracting them from other, more promising lines of agitation among the peasants. They did recommend seed drills, plows, and iron-framed harrows. They did warn peasants of the dangers of uncleaned seed grain. And, among a great many other recommendations, they did encourage farmers to pool their resources so as to access credit, to buy advanced equipment, and to market their production at optimal prices. But the fact remains that, of all the possible technological and organizational improvements they could have stressed, they almost invariably put the most emphasis on the category of improvement that was the most difficult to introduce at this point in time—reform of the tillage regime. The agronomic leadership in Borisoglebsk *uezd* even went so far as to formalize this trend, insisting in 1912 that the local agronomists make early fallow their top priority from then on.[136] Information is lacking, but one suspects that the agronomists in many other *uezds* heard—and welcomed—the same refrain.

As our treatment of peasant labor in Part I demonstrated, grain yields depended on many separate operations. Arguably, popular tillage practices were even more backward than the performance of other operations. But the agronomists ought to have worked more with peasants to improve their work in the simplest, most accessible ways. Some seemingly simple practices—the timing and density of sowing, for instance—were too deeply embedded in peasant culture for agronomic agitation to take swift effect. With respect to other operations, however, such as manure norms, the timing of reaping, and the proper selection of tools, peasant practice was much more malleable. By concentrating on issues like these, the agronomists could have helped peasants more quickly, and with less effort.

In the final analysis, we cannot judge the agronomists too harshly. Russia embarked on agronomic aid programs in great haste, without timely preparation or adequate funding. Upon arrival in their districts the agronomists had only the most general notions of how the local farmers performed their work. Not having the detailed information we presented here in Part I, it was very difficult for them to know exactly where to focus their attention for the fastest results. All of them were new to the task of reorganizing peasant agriculture, and the material conditions in which they worked were very trying.[137] Considering also the hostility they faced from the landowners in the *zemstvos* and the police in the countryside, even the limited achievements of their work in the 1910–1914 period are admirable.[138] Many left the profession because of the hardships and frustrations of the work (among the local agronomists employed in Tambov in 1914 the average length of service was about two-and-a-half years),[139] but by all available indications, those who stayed worked conscientiously.

Intervention and Its Discontents

In comparison to the achievements of the better-consolidated farmers, the lack of cultural and technical progress among communal peasants was especially disappointing. Are we then to conclude that peasant agriculture within the commune had no future? Where was the peasant economy heading in Tambov and places like it when the upheavals of war and revolution began in 1914?

Answers to these questions depend in part on an evaluation of the prospects for the Stolypin reform and the agronomic aid effort to contribute to the phenomenon we have labeled "The Rise of a New Type in the Village." The centrality of this phenomenon to the evolution of the agrarian problem cannot be overestimated. As we saw in Part II and elsewhere, a spectrum of features of peasant culture conditioned widespread, multifarious, deep-seated, and self-perpetuating technological ignorance among peasants. In the rapidly changing economic environment of the late Imperial period this ignorance was extremely dangerous to the peasant economy. Further, the increasingly heated international environment of the early twentieth century made technological backwardness dangerous for all of Russia. The government and the zemstvos were entirely justified in setting out to reshape technological culture in the countryside.

Undeniably, the Stolypin reform and the agronomic aid effort represented a civilizing mission. This in itself is enough to delegitimize them in the eyes of most contemporary scholars. Scholars carefully protect peasants and all other underprivileged groups from charges of ignorance or backwardness. This trend finds its broadest expression in the transformation of the term "cultural relativism." In its original rendering cultural relativism asked us merely to consider the cultural context of actions or attitudes. "Judge a man according to the values of his own culture," in other words. In recent times, on the other hand, cultural relativism has come to mean something quite different—the moral equality of all cultures. "Let not one culture judge another," in short. In this perspective "backwardness" and "ignorance" are simply calumnies when pronounced by one group on another. They are ideological illusions, as are the corresponding notions of "progress" and "civilization" which privileged spokesmen recommend to the disempowered. The contemporary ethos of cultural relativism leaves little room for anything resembling a civilizing mission.[140]

The field of peasant studies embraces this perspective wholeheartedly. As we saw in Part II, the model of "the optimizing peasant" rejects a critical perspective on peasant technological culture. "The views of the peasantry in all countries are worthy of respect; there is always good reason for their practices," spoke Albert Howard, a doyen of peasant studies.[141] As an adherent elaborated:

> ... cultivators have devised and perfected a host of techniques
> that do work, producing desirable results in crop production,
> pest control, soil preservation, and so forth. By constantly
> observing the results of their field experiments and retaining
> those methods that succeed, the farmers have discovered and
> refined practices that work, without knowing the precise chemi-
> cal or physical reasons why they work. In agriculture, as in many
> other fields, "practice has long preceded theory." And indeed
> some of these practically successful techniques, which involve
> a large number of simultaneously interacting variables, may
> never be fully understood by the techniques of science.[142]

It follows that agronomists' interventions in peasant technology are
fraught with pitfalls. As Paul Richards argues in the best-known defense
of this technology, the universal principles scientists offer peasants in
their "top-down" teachings often founder in the individual features of
micro-climates.[143] Richards insists agronomists should primarily support locally existing skills and initiatives, rather than imposing laboratory (or "colonial") science on peasant farmers.[144]

In Russian studies the protection of the peasant from criticism has
occupied advanced positions. In a recently published book entitled
Making Peasants Backward, historian Yanni Kotsonis diagnoses educated Russia's approach to the peasantry as ideologically jaundiced. In
his view all divisions of educated society in Russia, from the government to the many varieties of professionals who studied or worked with
peasants, inevitably (and almost invariably) shared the assumption of
peasant backwardness. Moreover, in Kotsonis's presentation these people understood backwardness in the deepest possible sense: they perceived peasants to be not just ignorant, but irrational. Further still, they
interpreted peasant inferiority as ineradicable—so long as peasants
remained peasants, at any rate. In consequence, professionals were out
to define peasants' interests for them. And they were doing so in the
interests of a grand strategy of self-promotion. They were not helping
peasant society, or even nurturing a new peasant elite, but merely
preparing the ground for a newly ordered society with themselves at
the controls.

How then are we to understand the wider meanings of the Stolypin
reform and the agronomic aid effort, given this menu of critiques of
specialist intervention in the village? Let us begin with Kotsonis.
Kotsonis arrived at his conclusions after studying leaders, officials, and
agents of the cooperative movement in Russia. The fact that he extends
these conclusions to agronomists and other ranks engaging peasant

Russia requires us to respond. Are his accusations extendable to agronomic aid and the Stolypin reform (not to mention other dimensions of elite contact with the peasantry, such as medicine and education)?

The first and most glaring problem is Kotsonis's continual conflation of the terms backwardness (or ignorance) and irrationality.[145] If anything, agronomists overestimated peasants' willingness to listen to reason. They expected a strong response to their lectures, brochures, and demonstrations of agricultural innovations. Even after encountering peasant indifference to their exhortations they did not rush to recommend the reprogramming of young peasants in specialized agricultural schools. They remained attached to adult education programs and consultations with heads of peasant households.

Surely the intellectual climate of the day did pre-program agronomists to expect peasants to be ignorant. But they understood peasant ignorance as a state of being under-informed, not in the sense of peasants lacking all knowledge. Moreover, the agronomic community did not rest on this assumption. Local agronomists and experimental stations expended tremendous energy on testing and measuring the efficacy of peasant practices against alternative methods. For Kotsonis, Russia's unprecedented effort to study traditional agriculture was part and parcel of a social engineering project, a nascent Taylorist manipulation. It had simpler motivations. Agronomists had to discover how effective peasant farmers' practices were, what they understood, what tools or advice they needed, what seeds or animals they could afford. Only on this basis could they offer valid recommendations for refinements.[146] The specialists' term "farm rationalization"—a term encountered far more often in the laboratory than among field agents, by the way—did not at all imply the irrationality of peasant farming in agrarian specialists' eyes, no more than business consultants today consider their clients irrational. Inefficiency is not irrationality.[147]

Did agronomists see peasants as too benighted to manage their own affairs?[148] Kotsonis presents this prejudice with respect to the cooperative movement. But neither the agronomic aid effort nor the Stolypin reform treated peasants in this way. The Stolypin reform originally gave farmers too much trust. As we saw earlier, the government was quite unprepared to give the consolidated farms advice on how to reorganize agriculture in their new conditions. They expected farmers to be able to work this out on their own.

What of Kotsonis's other characterizations of Russian specialists' approach to the peasantry? Did agronomists see peasants as "essential and unchanging" beings, "condemned to permanent 'darkness'"?[149] Did they evidence "little effort at enlistment of village elites, little attempt to cultivate a new elite, and little negotiation and compromise with rural populations"?[150] Did they want to define peasants' interests for them?[151] Were they self-aggrandizing professionals aiming to homogenize, hobble, and rule an inferior population? Again, all of these accusations lose much of their punch when transferred beyond the circles of the cooperative movement. Agronomists were acutely sensitive to some peasants' growing receptiveness to science. As we have seen, they looked for and encouraged such people, whom they very much wanted to become a powerful force in rural Russia. Their desire to diffuse innovations overrode intentions to give poorer peasants preferential treatment. The agronomic aid campaigns began with a dose of anti-kulak sentiment, but notions of social justice were tempered once it became clear that the stronger farms were quicker to try out innovations.[152] Cooperative agents were much more obsessed with richer peasants' exploitation of their poorer neighbors than were agronomists.[153]

Further, it is not fair to present the agronomists as defining peasants' interests without negotiation or compromise. They had to rely on persuasion and the power of example to effect change. They could not mandate agrotechnical measures of any kind. Correspondingly, military metaphors were not prominent in the language of the agronomic aid literature (as Kotsonis maintains was the case for the cooperative movement).[154]

Finally, in Kotsonis's rendering, the agrarian specialists aimed to legitimize and promote themselves by appropriating an ideology of modernization of a backward people.[155] This perspective does further injustice to the agronomists. Their primary objective was to lift and legitimize the agrarian sector of the economy, the peasant economy first and foremost. They were not ideological visionaries posing as the people's benefactors while all the time pursuing a reordering of society to smooth their own paths to power. The pragmatism required for their work deprived them of such extravagant pursuits.

Next, what do the perspectives of peasant studies tell us about the confrontation of science and folk wisdom in Russia? The peasant studies' insights we related above are indispensable correctives to the crude condescension visited upon peasant agriculture for centuries. The coercion modern states and development agencies have so often exercised on peasant agriculture deserves censure. It does not follow, however, that peasants automatically succeed in mastering nature to the limit of their capabilities. The "optimizing peasant" construct ignores fundamental barriers restricting peasant farmers' performance, as we analyzed in Parts I and II. It ignores the interference of the religious and superstitious worlds on technological comprehension. It ignores the possibility of inaccurate practices not dying out on their own. It ignores the possibility of peasants establishing inaccurate principles to guide their work—and pursuing them to dead ends. It ignores the inability of folk wisdom to orient in rapidly changing environments.[156] It ignores the mutability of cognitive capacities or habits under the influence of literacy and formal schooling. And it ignores the restrictions on inquisitiveness built into village society and childrearing practices. It follows that the agronomic aptitude of peasant cultures is not fixed across time and space. Cultural, social, economic, and geographical factors (such as those we examined in Part II) can greatly complicate peasants' efforts to understand nature.[157]

The analysis we have pursued in this study has demonstrated how low the ceilings of agronomic aptitude were in black-earth Russia in the late Imperial period. The fact that many scholars refuse to accept the slightest qualifications concerning peasant agronomic aptitude does not in any way weaken this conclusion, it merely reflects the allure of a universalizing ideology like the optimizing peasant construct.[158] There is no room to doubt the justification of the agronomists' descent on the villages, especially as state intervention had helped drive up agricultural productivity elsewhere in Europe.[159] Moreover, the Russian agronomic aid effort was not steamrollering local knowledge.[160] Agronomists certainly strove to impart general principles to peasant farmers, but they did not dictate how peasants would make use of such principles. They did not insist on farmers tilling a certain field at a certain time—as would happen after collectivization.[161] They intended simply to introduce peasants to yield-boosting and yield-stabilizing innovations. They set out to inform peasants of the effectiveness of different sizes of seeds, different types of tillage, different timings of reaping, etc. Peasants were free to combine this information with their own. They could explore alternatives by themselves, without passively waiting for technology transfers from the scientists.[162] Moreover, the agronomists came armed with empirical science not just theories based on experiments and experience in other lands. They were not promoting "colonial science," in other words. The Russian experimental stations were always careful to measure innovations against existing methods, using peasant labor and tools.

The Future, as of 1914

Neither the Stolypin reform nor the local agronomists succeeded in transforming peasant farming practices in the few years between their inception and 1914. Nevertheless, some important developments pointed unmistakably towards the blossoming of peasant interest in science. To begin with, the peasantry was gradually learning to orient within the technological marketplace. Looking back at the early days of the agronomic aid programs from the perspective of 1924, the manager of a *zemstvo* agricultural equipment store noticed a sharp contrast in this respect: "... at the beginning [peasants] made no distinctions between tools; they took whatever they came across. Nowadays they are starting to ask for good quality products, for established makes."[163]

More importantly, peasants began to read agronomic literature. The agricultural press blossomed in the last years before 1914 as provincial *zemstvos*, *uezd zemstvos*, and prominent agricultural societies established monthly journals devoted to discussing problems of agriculture and agronomic aid.[164] All of these journals devoted attention to problems of peasant agriculture, and solicited articles or letters from peasant farmers. At first most farmers—peasant and gentry alike—put no store in agronomic literature of any kind.[165] Nevertheless, even before 1914 local agronomists uniformly insisted that the brochures they gave out at traveling lectures and other meetings with peasants bore much fruit. Farmers would read the brochures and then seek out the agronomists for elaboration and discussion.[166]

The influence and popularity of the agricultural press spread slowly but surely in the villages, notwithstanding the disruptions of wars and revolution.[167] Thanks in no small part to the diffusion of science in print, by the mid-1920s experienced agronomists noticed that peasants were relating to them in a much more sophisticated way than before. Peasants no longer needed to hear explanations of basic principles of agronomy. Nor did agronomists need to justify the methods and goals of agronomic aid. Peasants confronted agronomists more actively with suggestions for alternative technological methods or wider policy proposals.[168] In 1914 a *zemstvo* doctor in Usman *uezd* lamented that peasants had responded much more deeply to the agronomists in a few years than they had to the doctors in decades.[169] Likewise, wrote agronomist M. Luchebul', in comparing the peasants of a part of Usman *uezd* in 1910–11 and 1924, "The population has awakened."[170]

In the long run, therefore, the agricultural press had great potential to assist the agronomic aid effort in stimulating a critical attitude to work in the villages. The press's influence would dovetail nicely with that of peasant pioneers. So long as pioneers experienced good results with innovations, the appetite to acquire and employ agronomic knowledge would continue to grow in the wider population. As peasant farmers acquired a familiarity with and taste for contemporary technologies, the rate at which they evaluated and implemented innovations would inevitably accelerate.

However promising the cultural and technological prospects for peasant agriculture might have been when Russia went to war in 1914, the agrarian problem could not evolve independently of its social and political–economic contexts. Could communal agriculture ever proceed to multi-field systems against the interests of the larger farms, who needed to economize on labor? We know that these families tended to carry a lot of clout in the villages. They could offer strong resistance to the implementation of multi-field systems or the intensification of tillage regimes (early fallow in particular) at the expense of common grazing. We also know, however, that the steady growth of the rural population was serving to shrink the size of the larger farms. As time went by, the percentage of farms with 10 or more *desiatinas* of arable land would have shrunk precipitously, whether there was a revolution coming or not.[171] The economic differentiation of the village was not going to disappear, but the motivation for the relatively larger farms to oppose labor-intensive systems would recede.[172]

The experience of the 1920s offers very persuasive evidence of the agronomists' potential to guide the reorganization of peasant communal agriculture through technical improvements and into multi-field systems. Beginning in 1924–25 the Soviet regime made a serious attempt to revivify the agricultural sector (in connection with the "Face to the Countryside" campaign), employing almost exactly the same methods as had the *zemstvos* fifteen years previously. In Tambov the tasks before the local agronomists in the 1920s were in many ways more difficult than the challenges the *zemstvo* agronomists had faced. The eleven-year period 1914–1925 brought terrible suffering to Tambov. Capping off the horrible sequence of World War, agrarian revolution, civil war, and peasant war (southern Tambov was at the center of the "Antonovshchina" revolt against Soviet power in 1920–21) were two gruesome famines, in 1921–22 and 1925. In 1925 55% of the peasant households in the province were without horses.[173] But within the space of a few years peasant agriculture made great strides [Table 5.3]. The

Table 5.3. Technological Advances in Peasant Communal Agriculture, 1925–1929

	% of farms in multi-field systems	% of seed grain sorted	% of farms doing *ziab*	% of farms doing early fallow
1925	4[a]	–	7[b]	–
1926	5[a]	3[c]	28[c]	34[c]
1927	8[a]	13[c]	64[c]	20[c]
1928	12[a]	45[c]	63[c]	16[c]
1929	20[d]	90[d]	51[d]	25[d]

Sources: [a]*Sakharov, Sel'sko-khoziaistvennye raiony Tambovskoi gubernii,* p.120. These figures cover the province in its 1923 boundaries. [b]GATO, f. R-946, op. 1, d. 5420, p. 8. This figure refers to Tambov *uezd* alone. [c]*Doklad i rezoliutsii 1-ogo Tambovskogo okruzhnogo soveshchaniia po povysheniiu urozhainosti,* p. 11. These figures purport to cover Tambov within its smaller *okrug* boundaries. [d]GATO, f. R-948, op. 1, d. 168, p. 46. These figures also refer to the *okrug.*

Let it be noted that some other archival sources are not fully consistent with some of the figures in this table.

progress of multi-field systems and seed sorting are unmistakable. Equally impressive are the high-water marks for *ziab* and early fallow. The decline of these techniques in certain years was attributable to uncommonly long periods of rain that delayed tillage.[174]

Agronomic propaganda did pay dividends. Nevertheless, the experience of the 1920s offers only limited predictive value for economic development in the absence of war in 1914. In the final years of the NEP period the Soviet government strongly discouraged families from farming on consolidated plots. Under Tsarist conditions, conversely, consolidated plots were a viable alternative for energetic farmers. Is it possible that the most enterprising farmers in the communes would have lost patience with their neighbors' reticence to try early fallow or multi-field systems? Would most of the pioneers have departed the commune, and left the majority of families without positive role models with respect to technological advance? This author suspects that such an exodus from the commune was not very likely. But the question is not answerable.

Further, we cannot predict how the relationship between the industrial and agricultural sectors would have developed. As we discussed in Part III, many multi-field systems depended on the presence of processing enterprises and efficient transport networks. Almost all of the multi-field systems in Tambov in the late 1920s were of just this kind.[175] Between 1905 and 1914, the Russian agronomic community suddenly became quite sanguine about the prospects for the "industrialization of agriculture." By this they had in mind not the mechanization of processes of production, but the proliferation, throughout the countryside, of industries allied to the new systems of farming. This meant enterprises that would process technical crops (especially distilleries, sugar factories, and starch factories), or convert pork, fowl, and dairy products into longer-keeping foodstuffs.[176] Would the networks that supported these systems in the 1920s have developed more quickly or less quickly if there had been no revolution? This is an open question.

Neither the government nor the private sector was investing significant resources in the central black-earth region. Development of the railroad network, roadways, urbanization, industrial enterprises, and industrial employment all lagged behind the national pace.[177] Commercial activity in the region was especially feeble.[178] Nascent networks of processing enterprises were concentrated on gentry estates, and thus exerted limited influence on the peasant economy.[179]

Could the zemstvos or the cooperative movement rescue the economy of the central black-earth region from this neglect? Could they finance the development of the region's infrastructure? Voices were sometimes raised for the zemstvo to coordinate the establishment of processing enterprises.[180] Much more ambitious were the proposals of Tambov landowner V. Snezhkov, who worked tirelessly to promote the idea of a zemstvo-led national union of agriculturalists.[181] Being burdened with enough programs as it was, the zemstvos in Tambov did not pursue any of these proposals.[182]

Cooperative networks were growing very quickly—by 1914 about 30% of the peasantry in European Russia was enrolled in credit organizations, 36% in the central agricultural region.[183] It appeared to some analysts that umbrella cooperatives could soon become powerful players in the country's economic development. By pooling the resources of the enormous peasantry they could greatly accelerate the flow of capital heading into the agricultural sector.[184] Long-term credit could be channeled to local unions of cooperatives to support the peasant economy in all sorts of ways, from the construction of grain storage facilities to the establishment of collective farms, the financing of processing enterprises, and the extension of the railroad network.[185]

In practical terms, however, the prospects for the cooperatives to marshal resources in the peasantry's interests were problematic. The emergence of cooperative unions posed economic and political challenges to ruling groups in Russia. Already by 1914 opposition to the cooperatives was swelling in many zemstvos. The cooperatives represented a growing threat to the zemstvos' commercial interests in selling tools, equipment and supplies to agriculturalists.[186]

Moreover, leading theorists of the cooperative movement were giving conservatives ample cause for concern by discussing the possibility of building "cooperative socialism." The idea might have been nothing more than a vague, utopian illusion, as the Russian historian V. V. Kabanov has recently characterized it.[187] But the political overtones were not lost to conservative and reactionary authorities. As a conservative *zemstvo* leader reportedly stated to some agrarian specialists:

> Gentlemen, you think we are stupid, and that we do not understand why after 1905 the intelligentsia has become so enthusiastic about cooperatives. You think we don't know that cooperatives are the pre-prepared cells in which popular opinion and social forces are mobilized.... You know, gentlemen, I suggest you stick to sowing fodder grasses, and not cooperatives.[188]

The Ministry of the Interior, the State Council,* and even the Ministry of Finance's Board of Small Credit (which oversaw cooperative credit organizations) had long records of suppressing cooperatives' attempts to unite effectively.[189] The political climate was not favorable to the cooperative movement.[190]

Clearly, powerful cooperative unions would be slow to arise. Even if they were eventually to make substantial resources available for peasant agriculture, would they have overcome established regional biases in investment strategies? Would they have been willing to direct resources towards industrially deprived regions like the central black-earth provinces? In the 1920s both the Soviet government and the cooperatives proved more interested in reinforcing existing centers of agriculturally related industry than in building up the infrastructure of the central black-earth region.[191]

In sum, the character of the agrarian problem in black-earth Russia was bound to change over time. As the cultural obstacles separating peasant farmers from the achievements of agronomy receded, new obstacles would take their place. First the divide between labor-poor and labor-rich farms, and then the complexities inherent in the coordination of agriculture with industry across the huge spaces of Russia would bedevil economic policymakers, be they Tsarist or Soviet. The black-earth of southern Russia has always been a tremendous natural resource for the nation. All the while, the exploitation of its riches has been a tremendous challenge.

---

*The upper chamber in Russia's constitutional monarchy during the last decade before the revolution.

Epilogue

The scope and ferocity of the revolts that shook the countryside in 1905–06 and 1917–18 leave no doubt in the historian's mind as to the centrality of the agrarian problem to the historical process in late Imperial Russia. Even while the country rushed to expand its industrial sector from the 1890s on, agriculture always remained the dominant branch of the economy.[192] Further, agriculture was supplying two-thirds of industry's raw materials, and it also provided the human material for the growing cities, factories and armed forces of the Empire, in the shape of peasant migrants.[193] The economic life of Russia, and her political fate, depended in large part on the capacity of the peasantry to function in a world becoming more industrial—with respect to tools on the farm and jobs in the cities, more commercial. By this I have in mind the growing importance and complexity of trade and financial relationships, and simply more crowded—the rural population of European Russia alone was growing by about 1,700,000 per year in 1914.[194]

It is incumbent on historians, therefore, to offer some perspectives on the manner in which peasant Russia coped with this changing world. The present study has looked at this problem through the window of agricultural life in the villages of the central black-earth region.

Notes

[1] Morachevskii, *Agronomicheskaia pomoshch' v Rossii*, p. 49.

[2] Vorob'ev, "Sel'skokhoziaistvennye kursy v selenii Lipiagakh," pp. 472–473.

[3] Morachevskii, *op. cit.*, pp. 59–61.

[4] *Ibid.*, pp. 63, 67–68.

[5] Cited in *ibid.*, p. 62, f. n. 1.

[6] For details, see *ibid.*, pp. 74–80.

[7] Kazimirov, "Zemskaia statistika," p. 16.

[8] Bobynin, "Agronomichekaia pomoshch' naseleniiu Tambovskoi gubernii," 1915, no. 13–15, pp. 361–362. These sentiments still predominated in *zemstvos* throughout Russia at the turn of the century, according to K. A. Matseevich ("K voprosu o zemskoi agronomicheskoi organizatsii v Saratovskoi gubernii," pp. 6–7).

[9] Morachevskii, *op. cit.*, p. 91.

[10] Bobynin, "Agronomicheskaia pomoshch'", 1915, no. 11–12, pp. 293–294.

[11] Morachevskii, *op. cit.*, pp. 81–85.

[12] *Ibid.*, pp. 84–85 on funding for the Ministry.

[13] *Ibid.*, pp. 91–99.

[14] All of the information in this paragraph from Bobynin, "Agronomicheskaia pomoshch'," 1915, nos. 11–12, pp. 293–304, and 1915, nos. 13–15, pp. 341–362.

[15] *Ibid.*, 1915, nos. 13–15, pp. 366–367, and 1915, nos. 16–17, pp. 426–430.

[16] *Ibid.*, 1915, nos. 18–19, pp. 481–482.

[17] Morachevskii, *op. cit.*, pp. 160, 163, 167.

[18] Alekseev, "Ocherki novoi agrarnoi politiki," p. 222.

[19] Alekseev (*op. cit.*, pp. 203–217) recounts reports of this kind from all over the country.

[20] Bobynin, *op. cit.*, 1915, no. 18–19, p. 482.

[21] Alekseev, *op. cit.*, pp. 222–223; Bobynin, *op. cit.*, 1915, nos. 18–19, pp. 482–490. In Tambov, two of the *uezd zemstvos* (Kozlov and Lebedian) originally acquiesced to arranging help for consolidators only. It was not long before they joined everyone else and agreed that assistance should go to all of the farming population (*ibid.*). A few provincial *zemstvos*—including Orel, Kazan, and Pskov—were willing to focus on the consolidators alone (Matsuzato, "The Fate of Agronomists in Russia," p. 182).

[22] *Ibid.*, 1915, nos. 20–24, p. 552.

[23] Ministry of Agriculture subsidies for the *zemstvos'* agronomic aid services rose from 171,000 rubles in 1908 to more than 5 million rubles in 1912. Thus the Ministry's share in the *zemstvos'* expenditures on these measures rose from about 5% in 1908 to about 30% in 1912 (*Sel'sko-khoziaistvennyi promysel v Rossii*, pp. 213, 244).

[24] Morachevskii, *op. cit.*, pp. 169; *Sel'sko-khoziaistvennyi promysel v Rossii*, pp. 156–166, 200–201. The *zemstvos* had had only 15 experimental stations in 1907. In the nation as a whole there were 212 of these stations in 1912 (*ibid.*).

[25] The Soviet Ministry of Agriculture ("Narkomzem") did not intend for local agronomists to engage in administrative tasks not directly related to spreading agricultural technology. It was common, however, for local officials to pressure agronomists into helping out in other matters. See, e.g., *Stenograficheskii otchet 3-go Vserossiiskogo soveshchaniia zemorganov*, pp. 165, 170, 230–235; or Safonov, "Tema izbitaia, no eshche ne izzhitaia," p. 27. Pre-Revolutionary agronomists might assist in data collection for surveys, but were not any more closely involved in administration.

[26] So maintained P. N. Pershin (*Zemleustroistvo i agronomiia*, p. 3). Pershin had been in the field researching the results of land organization work during the Stolypin reform period (B. Iur'evskii encountered him in Perm province: *Vozrozhdenie derevni*, p. 201, photograph on p, 184). I have found only one *zemstvo* agronomist in Tambov who favored consolidated plots (*Zhurnaly* ... (August–September 1911), p. 11). Judith Pallot located at least one more (*Land Reform in Russia*, p. 245).

[27] *Zhurnaly soveshchaniia zemskikh agronomov Tambovskoi gubernii pri Tambovskoi gubernskoi zemskoi uprave 5–9 marta 1911 g.* (herafter "*Zhurnaly* ... (March 1911)") p. 148; I. P. Solov'ev, *op. cit.*, p. 6.

[28] I. P. Solov'ev, *op. cit.*, pp. 9–10.

[29] A few agronomists in Tambov worked independently of the *zemstvos*. Land Organization Committees—*uezd-* and provincial-level organizations set up by the Ministry of Internal Affairs to oversee the implementation of the Stolypin reform—funded these agronomists. In 1912 they were absorbed into the *zemstvo's* agronomic organization (*Doklady Tambovskoi Gubernskoi zemskoi upravy Tambovskomu zemskomu sobraniiu ocherednoi sessii 1912 g. po agronomicheskomu otdelu*, p. 3). Government agronomic personnel did not disappear from the province after 1912. About two dozen specialists on various agronomic subjects continued to pursue research and to participate in educational campaigns in conjunction with local agronomists (a list appears in *SKhZh*, 1914, no. 4–5, p. 174). They taught courses to peasants and agronomists, they judged entries at competitions during agricultural exhibitions, and so forth.

Nationally the Land Organization Committees' agronomists played a larger role, since some peripheral provinces did not have *zemstvos*. There were 272 agronomists at work for Land Organization Committees in 1912 (*Sel'sko-khoziaistvennyi promysel v Rossii*, pp. 200–201). Dorothy Atkinson mistakenly attributes 1,600 agronomists to the Land Organization Committees (*The End of the Russian Land Commune 1905–1930*, p. 64). Atkinson's source is S. M. Dubrovskii's *Stolypinskaia zemel'naia reforma*, p. 268. Here Dubrovskii mentions 1,600 agronomists serving "in regions of land organization work," which clearly includes all agronomists at work in the very wide regions so designated, not just those serving directly under the Land Organization Commissions.

Additionally, agricultural societies or peasant cooperative organizations sometimes hired their own agronomists. Very few if any of these specialists ever worked in Tambov, where the cooperative movement was quite weak. Nationwide, however, this category of agronomist might have numbered as much as 5% of all agronomists as of 1913 (*Sel'sko-khoziaistvennyi promysel v Rossii*, pp. 200–201).

[30] I. P. Solov'ev, *op. cit.*, pp. 14–29. According to a Ministry of Agriculture handbook the breakdown was 50–50, both in 1912 and 1914. Most were in their 20s, some

were older. *Mestnyi agronomicheskii personal*, volumes for 1912 and 1914, pp. 201–209 and 351–361, respectively.

[31] Teitel', "K voprosu o podgotovke deiatelei po obshchestvennoi agronomii," pp. 8–10.

[32] See Bobynin, "Agronomicheskaia pomoshch'," 1915, nos. 20–24, p. 547. Provincial agronomist D. M. Shorygin's general instructions—composed in 1911—are published in *Proekty*, pp. 70–82. Instructions to Borisoglebsk agronomists in 1911 and then in 1912 are in *ibid.*, respectively pp. 233–234, 23–69.

[33] *Zhurnaly* ... (August–September 1911), pp. 6–7. Confirmation of the absence of prioritized instructions in *Proekty*, pp. 24, 68–69.

[34] *Otchet ob agronomicheskoi deiatel'nosti*, Tambov 1910, p. 77.

[35] Bobynin cites some rare exceptions to this generalization ("Agronomicheskaia pomoshch'," 1915, nos. 20–24, p. 563).

[36] *Proekty*, p. 444. Similar comments appear in T. K. Beliaev, "Shkola i agronomicheskaia pomoshch' naseleniiu," p. 232. Confusion of agronomists with government officials holding police powers would have been more common where agronomists wore uniforms and cockaded peak caps. The sources are nearly silent on agronomists' clothing. Two knowledgeable participants in *zemstvo* programs present conflicting testimony: Ashin says agronomists wore the hat and cockade, whereas Koval'kovskii explicitly states this was forbidden to *zemstvo* employees (respectively, *Obshchestvenno-agronomicheskie etiudy*, c. p. 195; *Zemstvo i zemskaia agronomicheskaia rabota*, pp. 65–66). Practice might have varied from province to province. The only photograph I have seen of *zemstvo* specialists (statisticians) at work in a village is inconclusive (Williams, *Russia of the Russians*, p. 352).

[37] Quoted in N. M., "Besedy o krest'ianskom khoziaistve," p. 461. For more of the same, see e.g. *Otchet ob agronomicheskoi deiatel'nosti*, p. 77.

[38] See for example the report of agronomist I. M. Baitsur, from Lipetsk *uezd* (GATO, f. 51, op. 1, d. 235, p. 151). His report also appears in *Zhurnaly* ... (August–September 1911).

[39] Local agronomist Gudvilovich of Tambov *uezd*, in *Zhurnaly* ... (August-September 1911), p. 82. The same sort of attitude is reported in *Doklady Tambovskoi gubernskoi zemskoi upravy Tambovskomu zemskomu sobraniiu ocherednoi sessii 1912 goda, po agronomicheskomu otdelu*, pp. 104–105). Similarly, another agronomist, in Usman *uezd*, found that no one in his audiences wanted to discuss anything about agronomy. All he ever heard was complaints about land shortages [*Zhurnaly* ... (August–September 1911, p. 103)].

[40] GATO, f. 51, op. 1, d. 235, p. 161.

[41] *Zhurnaly* ... (March 1911), p. 76. Emphasis added.

[42] N. M., "Besedy o krest'ianskom khoziaistve," p. 462.

[43] *Zhurnaly* ... (March 1911), p. 76.

[44] This from Samara province: Miller, "Novouzenskoe zemstvo i obshchestvennaia agronomiia," p. 52 (the full version of the cited passage appears in *Zemskii agronom*, 1913, no. 2, p. 28).

[45] *Zhurnaly* ... (August–September 1911), p. 90.

[46] *Ibid.*, p. 109.

[47] *Ibid.*, pp. 51, 53–54, 58; *Zhurnal* ... (March 1912), p. 104.

[48] Early fallow was first on most of the agronomists' lists, but farmers could not experiment with this on lands subject to common grazing. Most of the early fallow demonstration plots, therefore, belonged to consolidators.

49 *Zhurnaly* ... (August–September 1911), p. 78; GATO, f. 51, op. 1, d. 235, pp. 150, 152.

50 Even in the war year 1914 the 55–60 specialists gave about 700 village meetings, to an estimated audience of 35,000 (*Otchet Tambovskoi gubernskoi zemskoi upravy Tambovskomu gubernskomu zemskomu sobraniiu ocherednoi sessii 1912 goda. Otnositel'no agronomicheskoi deiatel'nosti uezdnykh zemstv Tambovskoi gubernii za 1912 god,* p. 12; I. P. Solov'ev, p. 31).

51 One of the best agronomists, V. I. Gudvilovich of Tambov *uezd*, claims to have spoken to 25% of the farmers in his district in the space of just one year (*Zhurnal* ... (March 1912), p. 109.

52 *Otchet o deiatel'nosti agronomicheskogo personala za 1912 sel'sko-khoziaistvennyi god,* pp. 81–84.

53 *Proekty,* pp. 426, 547.

54 *Zhurnaly* ... (August-September 1911), pp. 105–106.

55 I. P. Solov'ev, *Obzor agronomicheskoi pomoshchi,* pp. 34–35, 78. The figure given in the source is 1,269, for seven of the twelve *uezds*.

56 In 1915 Russian production of agricultural equipment plummeted to 50% of pre-war. It shriveled to just 20% and 15% in 1916 and 1917, respectively. *Snabzhenie krest'ianskogo naseleniia sel'sko-khoziaistvennymi mashinami i orudiiami,* p. 29. For the period 1911–1913 Russia imported just a shade over 50% of all agricultural tools and machines (not counting local blacksmiths' production, which went largely unregistered) (*ibid.,* p. 17. These imports all but dried up as of August 1914. A detailed breakdown of the quantities of imported equipment appears in *ibid.,* pp. 18–19).

57 Chelman, "Odna iz blizhaishchikh zadach kooperativnykh uchrezhdenii," p. 834. We may add here that there were not many village blacksmiths available to repair advanced tools. A landowner in Borisoglebsk *uezd* remarked in 1880 how difficult it was to find a good blacksmith anywhere (*SSS*, Borisoglebsk, otdel 1, p. 62). More than forty years later observers noted that only the very largest villages had good blacksmiths (Iakovlev, *Nashe derevnia,* pp. 27–29). Rural blacksmiths had difficulty repairing even plows, let alone more complex equipment (Medvedev, "Kursy sel'sko-khoziaistvennogo mashinostroeniia v Saratove," p. 5; and *Sel'skokhoziaistvennye statisticheskie svedeniie po materialam, poluchennym ot khoziaev. Vyp. XI,* pp. 42, 45, 46). To be fair, higher evaluations of local blacksmiths do exist. In Kazan province, for example, some of them are said to have been able not merely to repair or alter plows, but even to improve the tempering of shares and moldboards, and to construct new models to fit local tastes (S. L. Maslov, *Plugi i drugie uluchshennye orudiia,* pp. 19, 24). Another source, from Voronezh province, testifies to some smiths producing plows on their own there (*Sel'skokhoziaistvennye statisticheskie svedeniie po materialam, poluchennym ot khoziaev. Vyp. XI,* p. 48). Blacksmiths of this caliber must have dotted the countryside.

58 Such was the case late in the nineteenth century, at any rate. K. Beliaev (from Tambov), "Iz sel'skokhoziaistvennoi praktiki," p. 538).

59 Iudin, "Glavneishie pravila khraneniia i ukhoda za sel'sko-khoziaistvennymi mashinami i orudiiami," p. 4; Ustinov, "Ob uborke za zimu sel'sko-khoziaistvennykh orudii i mashin," pp. 467–468. Sometimes equipment owners told Iudin that they feared to leave anything valuable inside barns, which might catch fire. Iudin insisted that many of them were simply careless with the equipment. Iudin, "Kak khraniatsia mashiny i orudiia v krest'ianskom khoziaistve," p. 6.

[60] Quite a few observers commented on peasants' tendency to purchase equipment with scant regard for its quality. See, e.g., *Proekty*, pp. 50, 429, 639; and B. V., "Pis'ma s dorogi," p. 18.

[61] Thus the Provincial *zemstvo* allocated 12% of its budget to agronomic aid in 1913, as opposed to just 5% in 1911, and 0.6% in 1909 (*SKhZh*, 1912/13, no. 4, pp. 150–153). Likewise, the *uezd zemstvos* allocated just 2% of their budgets to agronomic aid in 1910, but 5% in 1911 and 5.7% in 1912 (*Otchet Tambovskoi gubernskoi zemskoi upravy Tambovskomu gubernskomu zemskomu sobraniiu ocherednoi sessii 1912 goda. Otnositel'no agronomicheskoi deiatel'nosti uezdnykh zemstv Tambovskoi gubernii za 1912 god*, p. 42). In 1914 the *zemstvos* on the one hand and the Ministry of Agriculture and the Land Organization Committees together on the other hand each budgeted a little over 300,000 rubles to agronomic aid in Tambov (*SKhZh*, 1914, nos. 4–5, p. 178).

[62] At the fall 1912 meetings of the Usman *uezd zemstvo*, for example, the majority of the deputies wanted to eliminate the local agronomists and their lending stations. Only the presence of some provincial level officials at these meetings forestalled this action. *SKhZh*, 1912/13, no. 17, pp. 635–641.

[63] Tiumenev, *Ot revoliutsii k revoliutsii*, p. 116. A detailed presentation of statistics on cooperatives in Europe and the United States on the eve of the First World War is Krasnoperov, "Sel'sko-khoziaistvennaia kooperatsiia v evropeiskikh i vneevropeiskikh stranakh," pp. 31–38. Numerically, the United States, Germany and Belgium joined Denmark as the greatest successes.

[64] Tiumenev, *op. cit.*, pp. 117–118.

[65] Khizniakov, "Zemstvo i kooperatsiia," p. 35.

[66] Tiumenev, *op. cit.*, p. 124.

[67] Baitsur, "O znachenii kooperativnykh uchrezhdenii i s.-kh. obshchestv dlia s.-kh. uluchshenii i o vzaimootnoshenii etikh uchrezhdenii," p. 178; Khizniakov, *op. cit.*, p. 36.

[68] Khizniakov, *op. cit.*, p. 36; M-ov, "Melkii kredit i zemstvo," p. 32.

[69] Bobynin, "Zemstvo i kooperatsiia," p. 164.

[70] In January 1904 the assembly of the provincial *zemstvo* did decide to encourage the formation of credit associations. But in the elections following the revolution of 1905 the most forward-thinking *zemstvo* deputies were all swept away in a tide of reaction. See Bobynin, "Agronomicheskaia pomoshch'," 1915, nos. 16–17, pp. 434–435, nos. 18–19, p. 481. Only one *uezd zemstvo*, Usman, even bothered to form a credit bank before 1911 (Shorygin, "O polozhenii zemskikh sel'sko-khoziaistvennykh skladov," p. 165).

[71] Tiumenev, *op. cit.*, p. 121.

[72] Shorygin, "O polozhenii zemskikh sel'sko-khoziaistvennykh skladov," pp. 133–134.

[73] Bobynin, *op. cit.*, 1915, nos. 20–24, pp. 549–550.

[74] His instructions were published in *Proekty*, pp. 70–82. They moved in step with the resolutions of an agricultural policy conference for the southeast of Russia, held in Saratov in September 1911 (reported in *SKhVIuV*, 1911, no. 18, p. 13).

[75] See for example *Proekty*, pp. 70–82, 499 for Borisoglebsk *uezd*. The Shatsk *uezd zemstvo*, for one, did not sanction any connection between agronomic aid measures and the cooperative movement, as we shall see below.

[76] Bobynin, "Agronomicheskaia pomoshch'," 1915, nos. 20–24, p. 546. The provincial bank was set up in 1912; Kozlov and Tambov *uezds* formed banks in 1913 and 1914, respectively (*Zhurnaly Kozlovskogo uezdnogo zemskogo sobraniia. Ocherednaia*

sessiia 1913 goda, p. 298; Kassa melkogo kredita Tambovskogo uezdnogo zemstva, *Doklady o deiatel'nosti kassy*, p. 17.

[77] Shorygin, "O polozhenii zemskikh sel'sko-khoziaistvennykh skladov," p. 155. Usman *uezd*'s bank stopped giving individuals credit already in 1910.

[78] All three of the local agronomists in Lipetsk *uezd* in 1911 agreed that without the formation of a solid network of credit cooperatives agronomists' work would not bear fruit. GATO, f. 51, op. 1, d. 235, pp. 152, 161, 166.

[79] Bobynin, "Agronomicheskaia pomoshch'," 1916, nos. 11–14, pp. 137–138. Data from Moscow province, in contrast, showed more than half of the cooperatives arising directly through the influence of local agronomists (Minin, "Odno iz reshenii konflikta: agronomiia—kooperatsiia," p. 9).

[80] *Zhurnaly* ... (August–September 1911), p. 116; Bobynin, "Agronomicheskaia pomoshch'," 1916, nos. 1–10, p. 15. Not surprisingly, Shatsk was one of the *uezd* *zemstvos*, which did not care to establish a credit bank.

[81] Shorygin, "O polozhenii zemskikh sel'sko-khoziaistvennykh skladov," pp. 133–134; I. P. Solov'ev, *op. cit.*, p. 163.

[82] I. P. Solov'ev, *op. cit.*, p. 63.

[83] A regional distribution of credit cooperatives at this time appears in Antsiferov, "Credit and Agricultural Cooperation," in *The Cooperative Movement in Russia During the War*, p. 269.

[84] Tiumenev, *op, cit.*, p. 141; Gorskii, "Kooperativnye tsentry," p. 163; *SKhZh*, 1914, no. 6, pp. 278–279.

[85] Tiumenev, *op. cit.*, p. 140.

[86] In every year for which figures are available Tambov credit cooperatives fulfilled at least 95% of their obligations to creditors (Shorygin, "O polozhenii zemskikh sel'sko-khoziaistvennykh skladov," p. 150). Shorygin had figures only for the years 1904–1908. Although I have never seen any other evidence, I expect that this story did not change in later years. National figures for the years 1908–1912 look just as impressive (see Tiumenev, *op. cit.*, p. 148).

[87] Kotsonis, *Making Peasants Backward*, pp. 177–181. Kotsonis's book provides extended analysis of the issues and debates among cooperative leaders and government officials surrounding peasants' separate status under Russian law.

[88] Private investors did respond. They had invested over 6 million rubles in *zemstvo kassy* already by mid-1910 (Shorygin, *op. cit.*, pp. 162–163).

[89] I. P. Solov'ev, *op. cit.*, pp. 63–64.

[90] Tiumenev, *op. cit.*, p. 137.

[91] I. P. Solov'ev, *op. cit.*, p. 63.

[92] *Ibid.*, p.49 has the 16 cooperatives with stores. Chelman, *op. cit.*, e.g., p. 831, states that the majority of cooperatives were buying tools.

[93] Chelman, *op. cit.*, discusses the cooperatives' inability to improve tool procurement when working in isolation.

[94] Cited in Shorygin, "O polozhenii zemskikh sel'sko-khoziaistvennykh skladov," p. 147.

[95] *Ibid.*, p. 147.

[96] Tiumenev, *op. cit.*, p. 143.

[97] The following account comes from a unique review of this association by a member, D. Gorbachev, in *SKhZh*, 1914, no. 7, pp. 332–335. Some of the details are located in *ibid.*, 1914, no. 6, pp. 284–285, and *ibid.*, 1912/13, no. 23, pp. 85–86.

[98] Cited in Tiumenev, *op. cit.*, p. 140.

99 There were 23 of these societies in 1912, 47 as of 1914. Bobynin, "Agronomicheskaia pomoshch'," 1916, nos. 11–14, p. 138; I. P. Solov'ev, *op. cit.*, p. 66. The societies fared better in some areas. There were at least 2,100 agricultural societies in the Empire (including Poland) in 1910, 1,418 of which were local in scale (Kuskov, "O sel'sko-khoziaistvennykh obshchestvakh," p. 6). In Poltava and Khar'kov provinces the agricultural societies accounted for more than 20% of all cooperatives as of 1912 (Bazhaev, "Kooperatsiia," p. 623). By 1915, 3,127 were registered in European Russia alone (Antsiferov, "Credit and Agricultural Cooperation," in *The Cooperative Movement in Russia During the War*, pp. 356–357).

100 Nationally, as of 1912, the social background of the initiators of agricultural societies broke down as follows: *zemstvo* agents 28%; peasants 24%; landowners 11%; clergy 9%; school teachers 8%; civil servants 5%; other persons or institutions 15%. 42% of the presidents and 33% of the secretaries of agricultural societies were "farmers" (primarily peasants, since landowners were listed separately). All data from *Sel'sko-khoziaistvennyi promysel' v Rossii*, p. 227.

101 For discussion, see, e.g., Kuskov, "O sel'sko-khoziaistvennykh obshchestvakh," p. 7.

102 In 1911 an investigation in Saratov province found fully half of the registered agricultural societies to be completely dormant (*ibid.*).

103 N. M., "Ob"edinenie kooperativov," no. 17, p. 624.

104 I. P. Solov'ev, *op. cit.*, p. 64.

105 N. M., "Obedinenie kooperativov," *SKhZh*, 1912/13, no. 18, pp. 646–647; N. Bobynin's account of the October 1913 cooperative conference in *SKhZh*, 1912/13, no. 23, pp. 793–805.

106 N. M., "Ob"edinenie kooperativov," no. 17, p. 624.

107 *Ibid.*, p. 622; Bobynin on the 1913 conference, in *SKhZh*, 1912/13, no. 23, p. 802; Viter, "O kreditnykh tovarishchestvakh Shatskogo uezda," pp. 159–160, 165.

108 Bobynin, "Zemstvo i kooperatsiia," p. 168.

109 *SKhZh*, 1912/13, no. 23, p. 803.

110 *Doklad sel'sko-khoziaistvennoi kommissii Tambovskogo gubernskogo zemstva*, p. 79; Morachevskii, *Agronomicheskaia pomoshch' v Rossii*, p. 279; Bobynin, "Agronomicheskaia pomoshch'," 1915, nos. 18–19, p. 495. One agricultural school in Voronezh province conceded that only 47% of its graduates remained in the province. Only 2% went back to family farms. Data from a school in Saratov province not much more encouraging ("Ekonomicheskie meropriiatiia zemstv," in *Vestnik Finansov, Promyshlennosti i Torgovli*, 1904, no. 12, p. 541).

111 *Doklad sel'sko-khoziaistvennoi kommissii Tambovskogo gubernskogo zemstva*, pp. 18–19. See also Vonzblein, "Agronomiia obshchestvennaia," pp. 10–15.

112 Bobynin, "Agronomicheskaia pomoshch'," 1915, nos. 18–19, p. 495.

113 *Doklad sel'sko-khoziaistvennoi kommissii Tambovskogo gubernskogo zemstva*, pp. 13–18, 24, 48; "Doklad Upravy o sel'sko-khoziaistvennykh kursakh dlia vzroslykh krest'ian Kozlovskogo uezda Tambovskoi gubernii," in *Zhurnaly Kozlovkogo uezdnogo zemskogo sobraniia chrezvychainykh zasedanii 4 ianvaria i 15 marta, ocherednoi sessii 30 sentiabria i 1–7 oktiabria i chrezvychainogo zasedaniia 9 dekabria 1913 goda*, p. 283.

114 *Zhurnaly ...* (March 1912), pp. 41–42, 165–169.

115 *Otchet Tambovskoi gubernskoi zemskoi upravy Tambovskomu gubernskomu zemskomu sobraniiu ocherednoi sessii 1912 goda. Otnositel'no agronomicheskoi deiatel'nosti uezdnykh zemstv Tambovskoi gubernii za 1912 god*, p. 13; I. P. Solov'ev, *op. cit.*, p. 31.

[116] Morachevskii provides a brief overview of agricultural courses for adults, both in Russia and abroad (*op. cit.*, pp. 315–327). The United States developed these programs more fully than any other country.

[117] *Otchety uchastkovykh agronomov za 1914 g.*, pp. 5, 10.

[118] I. P. Solov'ev, *op. cit.*, p. 31.

[119] A. S., "Sel'sko-khoziaistvennye kursy v Lysykh gorakh," pp. 353–359.

[120] Kostikov, "Pis'mo kursista o Gusevykh zemskikh nedel'nykh sel'sko-khoziaistven- nykh kursakh," pp. 17–19.

[121] *Otchety uchastkovykh agronomov za 1914 god*, pp. 204–205.

[122] *Ibid.*, p. 247.

[123] Kostikov, *op. cit., loc. cit.* Another source testifies that course graduates tended to become important allies of the local agronomists in spreading the word of science (*Proekty*, p. 548).

[124] Quoted in A. S., "Sel'sko-khoziaistvennye kursy v Lysykh gorakh," pp. 358–359.

[125] *Statisticheskii ezhegodnik 1907 g.*, Khar'kov 1908, p. 43.

[126] N. M., "Besedy o krest'ianskom khoziaistve," p. 462.

[127] See I. P. Solov'ev, pp. 1–5. Nationwide, more than 25% of the agronomists alone were mobilized into the army (L. B., "Iz tekushchei zemskoi agronomicheskoi deiatel'nosti," p. 12). Matsuzato has recently presented different data, demonstrat- ing more stable numbers of specialists in this period ("The Fate of Agronomists in Russia," p. 177).

[128] True, as late as 1914 there were backwaters where agronomists had yet to tread. The Lebedian, Usman, and Kirsanov *uezd zemstvos* had been particularly stingy about financing local agronomists, so many villages there remained ignorant of the specialists. In 1913 one landowner in Kirsanov *uezd* insisted that he knew the *uezd* very well, but had never seen, nor heard mention of an agronomist. N. Bogdanov, "Zapiski khoziaina," pp. 830–831. The Kirsanov *uezd zemstvo* funded only two local agronomic points until 1913. By 1914 they had five (I. P. Solov'ev, *op. cit.*, p. 16).

[129] A. V. Gorskii (Lebedian *uezd* agronomist), in *SKhZh*, 1912/13, no. 16, pp. 589–590. A survey of popular acquaintance with agronomists in Ufa province provides useful data here, since Ufa's agronomist/peasant ratio was similar to Tambov's. After 5–10 years of local agronomic aid (depending on the district in Ufa), 80% of the *zemstvo's* agricultural correspondents (most of whom were peasants) knew of agronomists. About 70% had made purchases from equipment stations, and 17% had ap- proached a local agronomist personally for advice. M. Krasil'nikov, "Chto znaet Ufimskaia derevnia ob agronomakh").

[130] Shatsk *uezd* agronomist V. S. Sabo is categorical on the absence of multi-field systems among the communes of his *uezd* as of 1914 ("Otchet o deiatel'nosti uchastkovykh agronomov za 1913–14 g.," pp. 363–365). The silence of all other agronomists on the matter speaks for itself.

[131] *Otchety uchastkovykh agronomov za 1914 god*, p. 172. D. A. Vasil'ev was working in Uvarovo district.

[132] See, e.g., Zemets, "Gubernskoe agronomicheskoe soveshchanie v g. Orle," *Zemskoe Delo*, 1913, no. 22, p. 1493; and Oleinik, "K voprosu o programmakh i itogakh obshchestvenno-agronomicheskoi raboty," pp. 3–4.

[133] For sharp criticism of agronomists in these respects (from the early 1920s, but applicable to our period as well), see a series of essays in the journal *Agronom* in 1924: Fabrikant, Po povodu zasukha i agronomov," pp. 10–11; Bystrov, "O pov- tornykh kursov dlia agronomov," pp. 13–14; Kuznitskii, "Agronomiia i krest'ian-

skoe khoziaistvo," pp. 8–9; and Savchenko, "Kakoi nam nuzhen uchastkovyi agronom?," pp. 10–11.

[134] Garin-Mikhailovskii, *V sutoloke provintsial'ni zhizni*, in *Sobranie sochinenii*, vol. 4, pp. 379–380.

[135] Bobynin, "Agronomicheskaia pomoshch'," 1916, nos. 15–17, p. 183.

[136] *Proekty*, pp. 68–69

[137] For a detailed survey of the material conditions in which the agronomists worked, see M. Solov'ev, "O polozhenii uchastkovogo agronoma v Tambovskoi gubernii," pp. 242–249.

[138] The Ministry of Internal Affairs did send out a circular asking local authorities to keep an especially close watch on agronomists (as well as land surveyors). Police and Land Captains did occasionally obstruct agronomists' work. Dubrovskii, *Stolypinskaia zemel'naia reforma*, p. 270; for limited evidence of police interference in Tambov, see *Zhurnaly ...* (March 1911), p. 86. For sharp criticisms of police suspicion and pressure on the agronomists, see Iu. S. Eremeeva, "Ob usloviiakh agronomicheskoi raboty v derevne," pp. 141–148, and the debate on this presentation, in *ibid.*, pp. 59–68.

[139] I. P. Solov'ev, *op. cit.*, pp. 14–29.

[140] On the transformation of cultural relativism, and its consequences, see Wrong, "Cultural Relativism as Ideology."

[141] Quoted in James C. Scott, *Seeing Like a State*, New Haven 1998, p. 305.

[142] *Ibid.*, p. 306.

[143] Richards, *Indigenous Agricultural Revolution*.

[144] A number of scholars have corroborated and elaborated on Richards's perspectives with respect to other colonized areas. Recent works include Van Beusekom, "From Underpopulation to Overpopulation," and Conte, "Colonial Science and Ecological Change."

[145] Kotsonis, *Making Peasants Backward*, pp. 31, 56, 101–102, 133, 135, and elsewhere.

[146] As a useful overview of the agronomic aid programs notes, there were some agronomists who began work without any clear appreciation of the economic constraints that might hinder the diffusion of innovations. But no one remained unaware of the economic context of peasant farming for long. Teitel', *Agronomicheskaia pomoshch' naseleniiu*, pp. 53–54, e.g.

[147] According to Kotsonis, professionals even "treated rural communities as disordered and irrational, and ignored evidence that these commodities had their own coherence." (p. 135). One wonders how he arrived at this conclusion. Was anyone in Russia unaware of peasants' capacity for collective action after the uprisings of 1905–07? Did specialists fail to notice peasant solidarity versus outsiders, including the specialists themselves? Were professionals not responsible for authoring literally thousands of studies of peasant communities, the huge majority of which recognized at least some redeeming, collective features inherent in the peasant commune? As we have seen, the agronomists laid their hopes for mass transitions to multi-field systems squarely on the shoulders of the peasant commune.

[148] *Ibid.*, p. 33, e.g.

[149] *Ibid.*, p. 106.

[150] *Ibid.*, p. 185.

[151] *Ibid.*, p. 35.

[152] An open admission of this tempering, from Tambov, is "Doklad Lipetskoi agronomicheskoi organizatsii," p. 115. Neutrality towards the social position of their customers appears to have been the trend among agronomists all over Russia. See,

e.g., Minin, "Agronomiia i zemleustroistvo v ikh otnoshenii k derevenskoi bed-note," and Matseevich "K voprosu ob ocherednykh zadachakh obshchestvennoi agronomii," plus discussion of these papers in author "P". "Pervyi vserossiiskii Sel'sko-Khoziaistvennyi s"ezd v g. Kieve." Japanese historian Kimitaka Matsuzato has come to the same conclusion ("The Fate of Agronomists in Russia," pp. 173–174). Local agronomists' neutrality with respect to assisting different layers of households would persist even in the Soviet period. One of many general discussions of this trend is Titov, "Uchastkovyi agronom i rasslenie derevni." Of course agronomists' sentiments were divided over the possibility of keeping the mass of peasant farms afloat. Most agronomists probably liked this idea in principle. But they were aware at the same time of the counter-argument: that some European nations were already 50% urbanized, and that Russia should not struggle in vain to keep a lopsidedly peasant social structure. See, e.g., the debate on Minin's paper in *Trudy pervogo Vserossiiskogo sel'sko-khoziaistvennogo s"ezda v Kieve*, vyp. 2, pp. 47–59.

[153] On which, see Kotsonis, *Making Peasants Backward*, pp. 149–159.

[154] Kotsonis, *Making Peasants Backward*, p. 117.

[155] *Ibid.*, pp. 133–34.

[156] Richards insists that peasants have their own notion of "research and development," and that this enables them to develop adequate responses to technological problems arising in turbulent times (*Indigenous Agricultural Revolution*, p. 149). Ali and Byerlee's summary of the state of knowledge (*op. cit.*) shows the contrary, as has the present study of Russia.

[157] Advocates of peasant technology are not entirely unaware of this. At any rate, Richards concedes the possibility of social factors such as personal conflicts and rivalries hindering progress in villages (*Indigenous Agricultural Revolution*, pp. 161–162).

[158] Even historians who are familiar with my marshalling of evidence peremptorily dismiss the idea of technological under-performance. In a professional correspondence historian Alessandro Stanziani insisted that I "... stress too much on peasant ignorance and superstition. This approach has been thrown away from historical, anthropological, and sociological approaches a long time ago." Stanziani (and many others I have encountered) would prefer I throw away the evidence along with the approach. Are the perspectives of specialists on late-twentieth-century peasantries in parts of Africa or Asia binding on scholars of all other peasantries?

[159] According to Jerome Blum, significant advances in European peasant agricultural productivity required state intervention in one form or another, in more or less coercive fashion (he stated this plainly in his review article, "Michael Confino's *Systemes Agraires*," pp. 497–498, and elaborated it in *The End of the Old Order in Rural Europe*). Recently scholars have found more evidence of yield increases on peasant farms in areas untouched by agronomic aid, enclosures, or other land reform measures (for information, see above, Part III, f. n. 47). But the efficacy of state intervention must still be acknowledged.

[160] To be fair, some advocates of peasant technology do not unilaterally reject the idea of agronomists offering assistance to inventive peasant farmers, or insist that peasant strategies will always suffice. See, e.g., Richards, *op. cit.*, p. 104.

[161] Interviews.

[162] An explicit statement of the *zemstvos'* intentions in this regard is Koval'kovskii, *Zemstvo i zemskaia agronomicheskaia rabota*, pp. 59–60. Many more could be found, as this logic was inherent in the agronomic aid campaigns. Of course *zemstvos'*

control over the local agronomists was limited, as we have seen. Many agronomists in the field must have been impatient with peasants, and wished they could compel them to adopt multi-field systems, for example. Alas, they did not have this kind of power.

The very breadth of refinements and innovations agronomists offered peasants might even have slowed the rate of technological change. As a well-known student of the comparative mentality of farmers maintains, the fewer technical and organizational improvements to which farmers are introduced, the more decisively, consciously, and accurately will they pursue new opportunities and acquire the attitudes necessary for continued flexibility (Kusum Nair, *The Lonely Furrow*, pp. 230–231).

[163] Quoted in B. V., "Pis'ma s dorogi," p. 18.

[164] As of 1914 Russia boasted 237 periodicals devoted exclusively to agriculture, and another 115 touching on it (Morachevskii, *Agronomicheskaia pomoshch' v Rossii*, pp. 344–345). The *zemstvos* alone were issuing at least 87 journals related to agriculture in 1914 (*VSKh*, 1916, no. 2, p. 18). Three agricultural periodicals arose in Tambov in 1913 and 1914: *Sel'sko-khoziaistvennaia Zhizn'*, *Shatskoe Khoziaistvo*, and *Sel'sko-khoziaistvennyi listok Morshanskogo uezdnogo zemstva* (Morachevskii, *Spravochnik po sel'sko-khoziaistvennoi periodicheskoi pechati na 1915 g.*).

[165] An interesting discussion of this is: Uvarov, "Kniga i opyt," pp. 114–115.

[166] See, e.g., the summary of the head agronomist of the Shatsk *uezd zemstvo*, V. Sabo, "Otchet o deiatel'nosti uchastkovykh agronomov za 1913/14 g.," p. 353. Agricultural correspondents in other provinces likewise testified to the influence of agronomic literature (Shorygin, "Chto govoriat korrespondenty," p. 11). Historian Kimitaka Matsuzato has recently presented interesting data from Moscow province to illustrate peasants' growing involvement in the agricultural press. The percentage of peasants among the agricultural correspondents to the statistical division of the provincial *zemstvo* rose from 2 in 1884 to 82 in 1915. Matsuzato, "The Fate of Agronomists in Russia," pp. 189–190. All of the more than 1,000 agricultural correspondents in Tambov received a subscription to the journal *Sel'sko-khoziaistvennaia Zhizn'* free of charge (Tumanova, "Sel'skokhoziaistvennye obshchestva Tambovskoi gubernii," p. 47).

[167] See, e.g., Chizhikov, "Nuzhny li pokazatel'nye uchastki," p. 79.

[168] On which, for instance, Chizhikov, *op. cit., loc. cit.*, or Luchebul', "Ozhivaiushchee delo," p. 62.

[169] Ts. "Iz sel'skoi zhizni," pp. 5–7.

[170] Luchebul', *op. cit., loc. cit.*

[171] Indeed, in 1927 only 2.77% and 3.99% of the farms were sowing more than 8 *desiatinas* in Kozlov and Tambov *okrugs*, respectively (*Tsentral'no-Chernozemnaia Oblast'. Statisticheskii spravochnik.*, pp. 160–161).

[172] In contrast to the Soviet period, after 1906 families could obstruct alteration of the commune's field system by obtaining personal title to their land. This problem was encountered early in the twentieth century in the western provinces, where open-field villages traditionally held their land in hereditary tenure (see the comments from Volynia, Kharkov, and Vitebsk provinces in *1905 god v sel'sko-khoziaistvennom otnoshenii vyp. 5*, St. Petersburg 1906, pp. 212–213). Communes could eventually bring pressure to bear on families resisting a multi-field system. In the worst case, they could always effect a village-wide consolidation of plots by a two-thirds vote, separate the dissenters from those in favor of a multi-field system, and then redraw their field layout. Alternatively, they could probably reach

compromises by imposing six-field systems with employed fallow (in which case the field layout would remain fairly harmonious with the three-field system).

[173] Sakharov, *Sel'sko-khoziaistvennye raiony Tambovskoi gubernii*, p. 161.

[174] GATO, f. R-946, op. 1, d. 5420, p. 1.

[175] GATO, f. R-948, op. 1, d. 168, p. 46.

[176] It appears that I. A. Stebut and P. A. Krapotkin were among the first agrarian specialists to proselytize this idea. On the swiftness with which the notion acquired popularity in the last years before 1914, see Iarilov, "Iz sel'sko-khoziaistvennoi zhizni i literatury," p. 20.

[177] The relevant figures appear in four handbooks: Varzar, *Statisticheskie svedeniia o fabrikakh i zavodakh po proizvodstvam, ne oblozhennym aktsizom, za 1900 g.*; Varzar, *Statisticheskie svedeniia po obrabatyvaiushchei fabrichno-zavodskoi promyshlennosti Rossiiskoi Imperii za 1908 g*; *Fabrichno-zavodskoi promyshlennosti Evropeiskoi Rossii v 1910–1912 gg*; and *Ezhegodnik Ministerstva Finansov (za 1900, 1908, 1912)*. Statistics on roadways by province are in *Rossiia 1913 god*, pp. 119–120.

[178] Thus the central black-earth region ranked dead last in the entire Empire in terms of the number of stores and shops per capita (see the chart in *Rossiia 1913 god*, p. 200).

[179] A law of 1891 granting substantial tax breaks to distilleries (the primary processing points for potatoes) of large size and owned by members of the gentry estate was partly responsible for the distribution of these enterprises (Emel'ianov, "K voprosu o kharaktere agrarnogo kapitalizma," p. 182). Chelintsev insisted that in the pre-Revolutionary period processing enterprises in the central black-earth region—especially for sugar beets and potatoes—did not arise in any coordination with the needs of the peasant economy (RGAE, f. 478, op. 5, d. 3719, pp. 81, 99). He attached a fair amount of the blame to the 1891 law on distilleries (*ibid.*, p. 34).

The same pattern prevailed in Germany. Estates or other private enterprises did as much of the crop raising as they could on their own lands, such that for a long time the economy of surrounding villages remained little affected. Perkins, "The Agricultural Revolution in Germany, 1850–1914," pp. 96–98. A brief and very interesting analysis of the same trend in Khar'kov province appeared in *Khar'kovskii sbornik*, vyp. 1, pp. 95–102 (anonymous).

[180] One example is Rall, "Doklad."

[181] His fullest statement is Snezhkov, "Sel'skokhoziaistvennyi soiuz uezdnykh i gubernskikh zemstv."

[182] Similar initiatives were likely underway in other *zemstvos*. I do not know.

[183] Antsiferov, *The Cooperative Movement in Russia During the War*, pp. 260, 265–269.

[184] N. P. Oganovskii, "K peresmotru agrarnoi problemy," in *Zavety*, 1912 kn. 5, p. 31, as cited in Vvedenskii, "Zemledeliia i kooperatsiia," p. 5. As of 1914 the nation's 14,586 rural credit cooperatives had amassed 405 million rubles in capital, and had 574 million rubles in outstanding loans (Kabanov, *Kooperatsiia, revoliutsiia, sotsializm*, p. 12). To put this figure in perspective, the central government's budgetary expenditures for the year 1913 were 3.4 billion rubles (*Rossiia 1913 god*, p. 153).

[185] The cost to establish industrial enterprises allied to agriculture varied greatly. Start-up costs for a small tomato paste operation required only about 2–3,000 rubles (Grekov, "Ob organizatsii artel'nykh tomatnykh zavodov," pp. 7–8). Construction and start-up costs for a medium-sized tool factory were about half a million rubles (Bal'shakov, "Kooperativnoe proizvodstvo sel'sko-khoziaistvennykh mashin i orudii," pp. 3–4).

[186] Minin, "Odno iz reshenii konflikta: agronomiia—kooperatsiia," pp. 9–10. Minin also points out here that corrupt village officials and locally powerful usurers ("kulaks" in the terminology of the period) shared this interest in suppressing cooperatives. They did sometimes manage to undermine credit cooperatives (*SKhZh*, 1914, no. 6, pp. 290–291).

[187] Kabanov, *Kooperatsiia, revoliutsiia, sotsializm*, pp. 49–58. In an earlier work Kabanov interpreted the Stolypin reform and the cooperative movement as working at cross-purposes to each other. He portrayed Tsarist agrarian policy as fundamentally unsound on account of its simultaneous endorsement of cooperatives and consolidated farms ("Puti i bezdorozh'ia agrarnogo razvitiia Rossii v XX veke"). The argument is far overdrawn, overlooking as it does the readiness with which consolidated farmers joined cooperatives. Statistics are very rare on this issue, but they speak clearly enough: in the mid-1920s 39% of consolidated farms were participating in cooperatives in Smolensk province, as against just 13% of non-consolidated farms. The corresponding figures in Moscow province were 90–100% versus 48%. *Stenograficheskii otchet 3-go Vserossiiskogo soveshchanie zemorganov*, p. 285.

[188] Minin, "Odno iz reshenii konflikta: agronomiia—kooperatsiia," p. 10.

[189] For an account of the manner in which these institutions suppressed the development of the cooperative movement, see Antsiferov, *The Cooperative Movement in Russia During the War*, esp. pp. 293–294, 300–301, 310–311. The handful of unions of cooperatives were helpless to coordinate their member organizations until 1911, when they were granted the right to make loans to individual cooperatives and to accept deposits from them. Cooperative leaders attained the long-sought freedom to form unions without first receiving permission from state organizations only in 1917 (*ibid.*, pp. 294–295).

[190] In early 1915 the Council of Ministers abruptly changed course and approved the formation of many cooperative credit unions. Within a year 18% of the credit cooperatives were formally registered in unions. Impending economic emergencies stemming from the war prompted the change of course. Previous to this, in 1912, cooperative leaders did manage to get permission to form a national channeling point for cooperative funds, the Moscow People's Bank. The bank's formation did not by itself unify the financial affairs of Russia's local credit networks. That would have to be worked out over time. Antsiferov, *op. cit.*, pp. 304, 308, 315–316, 328–354.

[191] In the 1920s the cooperatives were very successful in linking peasant agriculture with dairy processing enterprises in Siberia, the Urals, and the northeast of European Russia. Their achievements in this respect were not even remotely comparable elsewhere in the country, however (see data and discussion in Pupishskii, "K voprosu o rekonstruktsii sel'skogo khoziaistva cherez sel'skokhoziaistvennuiu kooperatsiiu," pp. 64–74). Furthermore, the mere appearance of processing enterprises would not assist the agricultural sector if the prices they offered for raw materials—such as sugar beets, potatoes, sunflowers, etc.—were too low to encourage peasants to raise them. This proved to be a great problem in the 1920s, because the Commissariat of Agriculture had no control over the management (or the establishment) of processing enterprises. The fullest treatment of this problem appears in an unpublished 1927 study of Chelintsev's, RGAE, f. 478, op. 5, d. 3719.

In the 1920s central-black-earth-region administrators constantly encountered discrimination from officials in charge of central budget distributions. As Riabinin of the Tambov Provincial Party Committee put it: "Our economic organs have always got the same reply when negotiating with central economic organs for credits for the development of industry: 'What do you mean, industry? What industry? You're a peasant province, you'll get agricultural recovery credits'." RTsKhIDNI, f. 17, op. 67, d. 375, p. 40. At one point in the 1920s Tambov was getting less money per capita from the Commissariat of Finance than any other province in European Russia (*ibid.*, pp. 18, 64).

[192] Economists naturally disagree on the weight of the major sectors in the economy. According to an official estimate for the year 1909–10, the value of all agricultural production was 9.1 billion rubles, versus 4.5 billion rubles for industry (Chernyshev, *Sel'skoe khoziaistvo dovoennoi Rossii i SSSR*, p. 60). Paul Gregory has computed agriculture's percentage contribution to the national product as follows (Gregory and Stuart, *Soviet Economic Structure and Performance*, p. 39):

	Agriculture	Industry, Construction, Transport, and Communication	Trade and Services
1883–1887	57.5	23.5	19.0
1909–1913	51.0	32.0	17.0

A well-known calculation from 1918 is less generous to agriculture. It assigns agriculture 45.4% in 1900, and 43.5% in 1913. Prokopovich, *Opyt ischisleniia narodnykh dokhodov*, p. 69.

[193] The proportion of industry's raw materials issuing from agriculture appears in Kondratiev and Oganovskii, *Perspektivy razvitiia sel'skogo khoziaistva SSSR*, p. 38. Approximately 4,000,000 peasants relocated to towns and cities in the period 1897–1914.

[194] Oganovskii, "Sovremennyi agrarnyi vopros i kooperativy," p. 15.

Appendix.
Nutrition and Mortality in Tambov, 1880–1914

I. Available Grain and Potatoes

Table 1. Average Harvests for the Whole Province, Less Seed Requirements,
Industrial Processing and Net Exports from the Province
(spoilage and grain expended on animals not subtracted; in *puds*/capita)

	mid-1880s	1895–1899	1911–1914
Rye and wheat	16.6	12.7	14.0[***]
Other grains[*]	5.5	5.0	4.1
Potatoes[**]	6.1	10.5	9.9
Oats (per horse)	15.9	8.6	26.3

[*]Primarily, in order of importance: millet, peas, lentils, and buckwheat.

[**]Potatoes are significantly less nutritious per unit of weight than grains. The most widely accepted conversion rate in our period was 1 unit of potatoes to 0.19 of rye (Maress, "Proizvodstva i potreblenie khleba," p. 13; Semenov-Tian-Shanskii, *Rossiia*, vol. 9, p. 245). Russian publications of the time often used a rate of 1:0.25. Until 1893 potatoes grown in garden plots escaped registration in sown area statistics, so the figure for the 1880s is an understatement (*Materialy dlia otsenki zemel' Saratovskoi gubernii. Vyp. IV*, p. 4—the adjustment pertained to the whole country, as this source clarifies). The drop in food per capita from the 1880s to the late 1890s was thus greater than the table indicates. Spoilage of potatoes could reach crippling proportions—up to 75% of the potatoes stored over the whole winter might rot (Pel'tsikh, *Trekhpolka ili mnogopole?*, pp. 13–14; RGAE, f. 478, op. 2, d. 237, p. 2).

[***]The Soviet Provincial Administration of Agriculture in Tambov arrived at a lower estimate for these years, of about 10 *puds* per capita (RGAE, f. 478, op. 2, d. 237, pp. 13–14). I do not find their calculations convincing.

Sources

Population: For 1880/4, the *zemstvo* survey of the countryside, cited by Chelintsev, *Opyt izucheniia*, pp. 33–35, adjusted upward to estimate growth to 1885, and to account for c. 8% urban population. For late 1890s, *Pervaia vseobshchaia perepis'*. For 1911–1914, *Rossiia 1913 god*, section I.

Horses: For 1885, *Voenno-konskaia perepis' 1888 goda*, p. 1 (which provides data for 1882 and 1888). For 1899, *Voenno-konskaia perepis' 1905 goda*, p. 83. For 1912, *Statisticheskii ezhegodnik Rossii 1912 g.*

Sizes of Harvests (and seed requirements):
For 1883–1887, Tsentral'nyi statisticheskii komitet, *Statistika Rossiiskoi Imperii. T. IV. Srednyi urozhai*, pp. 32–33, 40–41. Volume to weight conversions made as per averages for 1888–1897 data (the earliest available), located in *Svod urozhainykh svedenii za gody 1883–1915*, Moscow 1928, pp. 175–178. For 1895–1899, *Resultats generaux de la recolte de 1897*, (and the same title for 1898, 1899, and 1900).
For 1911–1914, *Statisticheskii ezhegodnik Rossii 1911 g.*, St. Petersburg 1912 (and the same title for 1912–14). Seed requirements adjusted as per RGAE, f. 478, op. 2, d. 237, pp. 13–18.

Industrial Use of Crops:
In the absence of data for 1883–1887 I estimated the number of distilleries and their probable inputs of rye and potatoes, based on trends in the sources for the last twenty years before the First World War.
For 1895–1899, from Meien, *Rossiia v dorozhnom otnoshenii*, pp. 587–620.
For 1911–1914, from RGAE, f. 478, op. 2, d. 237, pp. 13–18; Volchanskii, "O vinokurennoi promyshlennosti, pp. 401–406; *Sbornik statistiko-ekonomicheskikh svedenii po sel'skomu khoziaistvu Rossii i inostrannykh gosudarstv. God piatyi*, pp. 176–177.

Net Exports or Imports of Agricultural Products:
In the absence of data for 1883–1887, I have used the data for 1880–1884, appearing in Chelintsev, *Russkoe sel'skoe khoziaistvo pered revoliutsii*, pp. 224–225.
For 1895–1899, from Meien, *Rossiia v dorozhnom otnoshenii*, pp. 587–620.
For 1911–1914, from A. Brianskii, "Sel'sko-khoziaistvennye raiony Tambovskoi gubernii," pp. 36–66; RGAE, f. 478, op. 2, d. 237, pp. 13–18; RGAE, f. 478, op. 2, d. 236, p. 4.

The question naturally arises as to how the figures in this table compare to estimates of nutrition required for subsistence. The best estimates of the day fell around 16–17 *puds* per capita (Wheatcroft, "The Reliability of Russian Pre-War Grain Output Statistics," pp. 167–168). Lower and higher norms could be found: a government publication used 15 *puds* as the subsistence norm, while one scholar put the figure at 20 *puds* of grain and potatoes (respectively, *Stoimost' proizvodstva glavneishikh khlebov*, p. 75; and Arkhangel'skii, *Ocherki po zemel'nomu stroiu Rossii*, Kazan 1920, p. 213). Part of the disagreement stemmed from regional variation in natural resources. Unlike peasants in the northern half of Russia, peasants in Tambov and areas south of it had relatively little meadow and pastureland. They were compelled to feed some of the grain they grew to their animals.* By any interpretation, grain and potato consumption was quite low in Tambov after the 1880s. Geographic comparison reinforces this conclusion. Grain consumption alone for the period 1906–1910 in Moscow province was 19.0 *puds* per capita, Vladimir 19.4, Kaluga 17.1, Kostroma 20.0,

*See Part III for analysis of this.

Nizhegorod 21.1, Smolensk 19.7, Tver 17.3, Iaroslavl 15.5 (Bauer, *Vladimirskii krai*, pp. 81–82). If potatoes were included in these calculations they might all exceed the pre-war level in Tambov.

II. Vegetable, Meat, and Dairy Consumption

Although direct data are lacking, indirect indications point to decline. The area of garden plots increased by just 11% 1881–1917, while the peasant population rose by 64% (*Sbornik ocherkov*, p. 45). Potatoes or hemp, not vegetables, took over most of the space there (see, e.g., Sakharov, *Sel'sko-khoziaistvennye raiony*, p. 80; Egarmin, "Zhelatel'naia reforma na krest'ianskom ogorode," p. 21; *SSS*, Temnikov, p. 86; *ibid.*, Elatma, p. 32). Since potatoes grown in the garden plots were registered as field crops after 1893 (see ** in table), the lion's share of production from the garden plots is already included in the table.

Meat consumption must have dwindled, as peasant pig and sheep holdings per capita declined dramatically 1880/84–1898–1912. Pigs per 100 capita of the peasant population: 23.2–16.1–10.8; sheep: 137.5–94.6–84.1 (*Materialy po podvornomu obsledovaniiu zhivotnovodstva*, vol. 2, prilozhenie, pp. 15–16; *Podvornoe obsledovanie zhivotnovodstva*, prilozhenie 1). The sheep in Tambov were possibly the smallest in all of Russia (Pridorogin, "Zakliuchenie professora Moskovskogo sel'sko-khoziaistvennogo instituta M. I. Pridorogina po kachestvennomu obsledovaniiu zhivotnovodstva v Tambovskoi gubernii v 1913 g.," p. 835). Comparable statistics for poultry do not exist. Meanwhile, dairy consumption held fairly steady. The number of cattle per 100 capita was 28.0—25.8—26.9 (*Materialy po podvornomu obsledovaniiu zhivotnovodstva*, vol. 2, prilozhenie, pp. 15–16; *Podvornoe obsledovanie zhivotnovodstva*, prilozhenie 1).

III. Crude Mortality Rate

1867–1885: 35 per 1,000

1888–1897: 37.5 (36.9, if the cholera or famine year 1892 is excluded)

1899–1912: 32

Sources: SSS, *Kratkii svod*, pp. 52–53; V. P. Semenov-Tian-Shanskii, *Rossiia*, vol. 2, p. 160; Robbins, *Famine in Russia*, appendix (for 1892 mortality rate); *Ezhegodnik Rossii 1904 g.*, (and subsequent annuals, for the period 1899–1912).

All of the mortality figures are slightly understated, since infants expiring in the few days between birth and registration with their parish were not counted (Molleson, *Kratkii ocherk zabolevaemosti*, pp. 250–251).

IV. Condition of Army Recruits

The percentage of recruits deemed physically unfit for service (because of short stature, small circumference of the chest, illness, or disability) increased from 12.3% for 1874–1883 to 15.5% for 1894–1901 [*Kom tsentra*, vol. 1, pp. 28–29]. Meanwhile, it appears that the army lowered its standards of judging fitness in this period. They were accepting recruits of smaller stature and with smaller chests, even after raising the age of induction by three months in 1893 (On the lowered standards, see e.g., Pukalov, "Zapiska V. P. Pukalova o meropriiatiiakh," pp. 118–120; Kovalevskii, "Doklad N. N. Kovalevskogo," pp. 66–67; Zhbankov, "Fizicheskoe razvitie prizyvaemykh," pp. 195–196; and Boris Mironov, "The Peasant Commune after the Reforms of the 1860s," p. 28. On the adjusted age of induction, Zhbankov, *op. cit.*, p. 195).

BIBLIOGRAPHY OF ALL BOOKS, JOURNALS, AND ARCHIVES CITED

Abbreviations

ES	=	*Entsiklopedicheskii slovar'*
GARF	=	Gosudarstvennyi Arkhiv Rossiiskoi Federatsii
GATO	=	Gosudarstvennyi Arkhiv Tambovskoi Oblasti
k otsenke	=	*Statisticheskie dannye k otsenke zemel'*
Kom tsentra	=	*Materialy Vysochaishe uchrezhdennoi 16 noiabria 1901 g. komissii*
KSE	=	*Krest'ianskaia sel'sko-khoziaistvennaia entsiklopedia*
PATO	=	Partiinyi Arkhiv Tambovskoi Oblasti
PERSKh	=	*Polnaia Entsiklopediia Russkogo Sel'skogo Khoziaistva i soprikasaiushikhsia s nim nauk*
RB	=	*Russkoe Bogatstvo*
RGAE	=	Rossiiskii Gosudarstvennyi Arkhiv Ekonomiki
RTsKhIDNI	=	Rossiiskii Tsentr Khraneniia i Issledovaniia Dokumentov Noveishei Istorii
SKhL	=	*Sel'sko-khoziaistvennyi listok*
SKhVIuV	=	*Sel'sko-khoziaistvennyi Vestnik Iugo-Vostoka*
SKhZh	=	*Sel'sko-khoziaistvennaia Zhizn'*
SSS	=	*Sbornik statisticheskikh svedenii po Tambovskoi gubernii*
TGV	=	*Tambovskie gubernskie vedemosti*
TMK	=	*Trudy mestnykh komitetov o nuzhdakh sel'sko-khoziaistvennoi promyshlennosti.*
TVEO	=	*Trudy Vol'nogo Ekonomicheskogo Obshchestva*
VSKh	=	*Vestnik Sel'skogo Khoziaistva*
ZG	=	*Zemledel'cheskaia Gazeta*
ZhMGI	=	*Zhurnal Ministerstva Gosudarstvennykh Imushchestv*
ZhTGZS	=	*Zhurnaly Tambovskogo Gubernskogo Zemskogo Sobraniia*

Archives

Gosudarstvennyi Arkhiv Rossiiskoi Federatsii
Gosudarstvennyi Arkhiv Tambovskoi Oblasti
Hoover Institution Archive
Partiinyi Arkhiv Tambovskoi Oblasti
Rossiiskii Gosudarstvennyi Arkhiv Ekonomiki
Rossiiskii Tsentr Khraneniia i Issledovaniia Dokumentov Noveishei Istorii

Periodicals and Newspapers

Agronom
Agronomicheskii zhurnal
Annals of American Academic Political and Social Science
Anthropological Linguistics
Biblioteka dlia chteniia
Biulleten' Tambovskogo gubernskogo statisticheskogo biuro
Critical Review
Economic Development and Cultural Change
Environmental History
Etnograficheskii sbornik (Imperial Russian Geographical Society)
Etnograficheskoe obozrenie
Explorations in Economic History
Ezhegodnik agrarnoi istorii vostochnoi evropy
Ezhegodnik Ministerstva Finansov
Human Ecology
Istoricheskie zapiski
Istoricheskii Vestnik
Iuridicheskii Vestnik
Izvestiia Kostromskogo Gubernskogo Zemstva
Journal of European Economic History
Journal of International Development
Journal of Leisure Research
Journal of Modern History
Journal of Social History
Kaluzhskie gubernskie vedemosti
Khar'kovskii sbornik
Khutor
Khutorianin
Kratkii sel'sko-khoziaistvennyi obzor Tambovskoi gubernii za ... goda
New York Times Book Review
Novaia derevnia
Otechestvennye zapiski
Planovoe khoziaistvo
Politics and Society
Puti sel'skogo khoziaistva
Progress in Geography
Russian Review
Russkaia Mysl'
Russkie Vedemosti
Russkii Vestnik
Russkoe Bogatstvo
Sam sebe agronom
Samarskii zemledelets
Saratovskie gubernskie vedomosti
Science
Sel'skoe Blagoustroistvo
Sel'skoe Khoziaistvo i Lesovodstvo

Sel'sko-khoziaistvennaia Zhizn', Tambov 1912–1916.
Sel'sko-khoziaistvennyi listok, Balashov 1907–1918.
Sel'sko-khoziaistvennyi Vestnik, St. Petersburg.
Sel'sko-khoziaistvennyi Vestnik Iugo-Vostoka
Sel'sko-khoziaistvennyi vestnik Novgorodskogo Gubernskogo Zemstva
Severnyi Vestnik
Shatskoe Khoziaistvo
Slavic Review
Slavonic and East European Review
Sotsiologicheskie isledovaniia
Sovetskaia etnografiia
Sovremennye zapiski
Sovremennyi mir
Staroe i Novoe (Tallinn)
Statisticheskii ezhegodnik po Moskovskoi gubernii za ... god
Tambovskie gubernskie vedemosti
Tekushchaia sel'sko-khoziaistvennaia statistika Kurskogo gubernskogo zemstva
Trudy Komstromskogo nauchnogo obshchestva po izucheniiu mestnogo kraia
Trudy Vol'nogo Ekonomicheskogo Obshchestva
Vestnik Evropy
Vestnik Finansov, Promyshlennosti i Torgovli
Vestnik Novouzenskogo Zemstva
Vestnik opytnogo dela Tsentral'noi Chernozemnoi Oblasti
Vestnik Orlovskogo obshchestva sel'skogo khoziaistva
Vestnik Pskovskogo gubernskogo zemstva
Vestnik Russkogo Sel'skogo Khoziaistva
Vestnik Sel'skogo Khoziaistva
Vestnik Usmanskogo uezdnogo zemstva
Volzhskii Vestnik
Voronezhskii istoriko-arkheologicheskii vestnik
Voprosy istorii
Voprosy kolonizatsii
World Development
Zapiski Belorusskogo Gosudarstvennogo Instituta Sel'skogo Khoziaistva
Zapiski Imperatorskogo Russkogo geograficheskogo obshchestva po otdeleniiu etnografii
Zapiski Lebedianskogo Obshchestva Sel'skogo Khoziaistva
Zemledel'cheskaia gazeta
Zemledel'cheskii Zhurnal
Zemleustroistvo i zemlepol'zovanie
Zemskii Agronom
Zemskoe Delo
Zemstvo
Zhivaia starina
Zhurnal Ministerstva Gosudarstvennykh Imushchestv
Zhurnal Sel'skogo Khoziaistva
Zhurnal Sel'skogo Khoziaistva i Ovtsevodstva
Zhurnal zemlevladel'tsev
Zhurnaly Kozlovskogo Uezdnogo Zemskogo Sobraniia
Zhurnaly Tambovskogo Gubernskogo Zemskogo Sobraniia
Zhurnaly zasedanii Kurskogo Gubernskogo Zemskogo Sobraniia
... god v sel'sko-khoziaistvennom otnoshenii

Interviews

I found ten men who had run their own farms in various parts of Tambov before mass collectivization began in 1929. The best information was provided by Fedor Lokhin, village Pokrovskoe, Lipetsk *uezd*, and Fedor Abramenkov, village Novo-Tomnikovo, Shatsk *uezd*.

Books and Articles

A. S., "Sel'sko-khoziaistvennye kursy v Lysykh gorakh," *SKhZh*, 1914, nos. 8–9.

A. S., "Sev i seialki," *ES*, vol. 63.

Adams, John, "Peasant Rationality: Individuals, Groups, Cultures," *World Development*, vol. 14, 1986, no. 2.

Afrosimov, A. M., "Opyt otsenki rabot v dvorianskikh pomest'iakh po uezdam," *Zemledel'cheskii Zhurnal*, 1834, no. 20.

Agronomicheskii otchet (za 1911–1912 g.) i doklady, Elets 1912. Elets uezd zemstvo publication.

Aksakov, I. S., *Pis'ma iz provintsii*, Moscow 1991.

Ali, M., and D. Byerlee, "Economic Efficiency of Small Farmers in a Changing World: A Survey of Recent Evidence," *Journal of International Development*, vol. 3, 1991, no. 1.

Alekseev, G., "Ocherki novoi agrarnoi politiki," *Sovremennyi Mir*, September 1911.

Allen, Robert C., "Enclosure, Farming Methods, and the Growth of Productivity in the South Midlands," in George Grantham and Carol S. Leonard, eds., *Agrarian Organization in the Century of Industrialization: Europe, Russia, and North America*, vol. 1.

Amanor, Kojo Sebastian, *The New Frontier. Farmers' Response to Land Degredation: A West African Study*, London 1994.

Andersen, Elaine Slosberg, *Speaking with Style: The Sociolinguistic Skills of Children*, New York 1990.

Anfimov, A.M., *Ekonomicheskoe polozhenie i klassovaia bor'ba krest'ian Evropeiskoi Rossii, 1881–1904 gg.*, Moscow 1984.

——, *Krest'ianskoe khoziaistvo Evropeiskoi Rossii 1881–1904 gg.*, Moscow 1980.

Anikin, S. "Chego prosit derevnia," *Vestnik Evropy*, February 1909.

——, *Plodnaia osen'*, Saransk 1989.

Animelle, N., "Byt Belorusskikh krest'ian," *Etnograficheskii sbornik*, vyp. 2, St. Petersburg 1854.

Anonymous, "Doklad (No. 17-i) o formakh krest'ianskogo zemlepol'zovaniia i pooshchreniia k dobrovol'nomu razseleniiu krest'ian v predelakh ikh nadelov," in *TMK* Orel.

Anonymous, "Doklad po voprosu ob umen'shenii kolichestva prazdnichnykh dnei vo vremia letnykh sel'sko-khoziaistvennykh rabot putem perenosa prazdnovaniia na drugoe vremia," jn *TMK* Riazan.

Anonymous, "K voprosu ob opakhivaniia," *Etnograficheskoe obozrenie*, 1910, nos. 3–4.

Anonymous, "Lozhnyi styd," *Vestnik Usmanskogo uezdnogo zemstva*, 1914, no. 1.

Anonymous, "Molochnoe stado v gorode Saratove," *SKhVIuV*, 1911, no. 12.

Anonymous, "O sostoianii sel'skogo khoziaistva v iuzhnoi Rossii v 1851 g.," *ZhMGI*, 1852, no. 7.

Anonymous, "O vliianii krest'ianskoi reformy na khlebnuiu proizvoditel'nost' v Voronezhskoi gubernii," *TVEO*, 1867, vol. 4, vyp. 5.

Anonymous, "O vrede past'by skota po ozimiam," *Shatskoe Khoziaistvo*, 1915, nos. 22–23.

Anonymous, "Opytnye zamechaniia o molot'be i preimushchestvenno o sberezhenii pri nei zernovogo khleba," *Kaluzhskie gubernskie vedemosti*, 1840, no. 10.

Anonymous, "Po voprosu ob uluchshenii dela organizatsii tekushchei statistiki," *ZhTGZS ocherednoi sessii 1910 goda*, Tambov 1911.

Anonymous, "Pol'za i vred prinosimie boronoi", reprinted from the Khar'kov journal *Khliborob* in *Sel'sko-khoziaistvennyi listok*, 1912, no. 4.

Anonymous, "Pravil'naia obrabotka propashnykh rastenii," *Shatskoe Khoziaistvo*, 1915, no. 12.

Anonymous, "Predstoiashchii posev ozimykh khlebov v sviazi s tekushchimi sobytiami"—anonymous report from *Zemledel'cheskaia Gazeta*, reprinted in *Shatskoe Khoziaistvo*, 1915, no.13.

Anonymous, "Prodolzhenie opytnykh zamechaniia o molot'be zernovogo khleba," *Kaluzhskie gubernskie vedemosti*, 1840, no. 11.

Anonymous, "Zapiska o vozdelyvanii i sbyte khlebov v Lebedianskom uezde," in *Zapiski Lebedianskogo Obshchestva Sel'skogo Khoziaistva. Za 1858 god.*, Moscow 1859, ch. 1.

Antsiferov, A. N., *The Cooperative Movement in Russia During the War*, New Haven 1929.

Antsiferov, A. N., D. Bilimovich, M. O. Batshev, and D. Ivantsov, *Russian Agriculture During the War*, New Haven 1929.

Apsit, Ia. G., "Kak nado rabotat'," *Khutorianin*, 1915, no. 38.

Arkhangel'skii, A., "Selo Davshino, Iaroslavskoi gubernii, Poshekhonskogo uezda," *Etnograficheskii sbornik*, vyp. II, St. Petersburg 1854.

——, "Znachenie plugopolol'nykh rastenii v khoziaistve i obshchie pravila razvedeniia ikh v poliakh," in *Volzhskii Vestnik*, vyp. 1, 1861, otdel II.

Arkhangel'skii, P., *Ocherki po zemel'nomu stroiu Rossii*, Kazan 1920.

Arnol'd, M. F., "Posevnye semena krest'ianskikh khoziaistv Bezhetskogo uezda," in *Trudy 1-ogo Vserossiiskogo sel'sko-khoziaistvennogo s"ezda*, vyp. 5.

Arnol'd, V. F., *Obshchie cherty agronomicheskoi tekhniki i sel'sko-khoziaistvennoi ekonomiki krest'ianskikh khoziaistv Khersonskogo uezda*, Kherson 1902.

Artsybashev, D. D., "Semidesiatiletie russkogo sel'sko-khoziaistvennaia mashinostroeniia," in GUZiZ, Departament Zemledeliia. *1912. Ezhegodnik.*, St. Petersburg 1913.

Ashin, K. S., *Obshchestvenno-agronomicheskie etiudy: sbornik statei po voprosam organizatsii mel'kogo khoziaistva*, Khar'kov 1911.

Astrov, P. I., "Ob uchastii sverkhestestvennoi sili v narodnom sudoproizvodstve krest'ian Elatomskogo uezda Tambovskoi gubernii," in M. N. Kharuzin ed., *Sbornik svedenii dlia izucheniia byta krest'ianskogo naseleniia Rossii (obychnoe pravo, obriady, verovanii i pr.)*. Vyp. 1, Moscow 1889.

Astyrev, A., *V volostnykh pisariakh*, St. Petersburg 1886.

Astyrev, N., "Krest'ianskoe khoziaistvo v Voronezhskom uezde," *Iuridicheskii Vestnik*, 1886, no. 1.

Atkinson, Dorothy, *The End of the Russian Land Commune, 1905–1930*, Stanford 1983.

Aukhagen, O., *Kritika russkoi zemel'noi reformy*, St. Petersburg 1914.

Ault, Warren O., *Open-Field Husbandry and the Village Community: A Study of Agrarian By-Laws in Medieval England*. Transactions of the American Philosophical Society, new series, vol. 55 pt. 7, Philadelphia 1965.

Avrekh, A. L., ed., *Tambovskoe krest'ianstvo: ot kapitalizma k sotsializmu (vtoroi polovina XIX–nachalo XX v.v.)*, Vyp. 1–2, Tambov 1996, 1998.

Avrekh, A. L., V. L. D'iachkov, and V. V. Kanyshev, "Sotsial'nye i fiziologicheskie aspekty kogortnogo analiza demograficheskogo povedeniia krest'ian v kontse XIX–nachale XX v.v.," in Avrekh, ed., Vyp. 2.

B. M., "O khlebnoi statistike," *SKhVIuV*, 1912, no. 17.

——, "Ob uchete urozhaia khlebov," *SKhVIuV*, 1911, no. 13.

B. V., "Pis'ma s dorogi," *Agronom*, 1924, nos. 2–3.

B. V., "Rol' kormovykh rastenii v krest'ianskom khoziaistve", *SKhZh*, 1912/13, no. 9.

Baitsur, I. M., "O znachenii kooperativnykh uchrezhdenii i s.-kh. obshchestv dlia s.-kh. uluchshenii i o vzaimootnoshenii etikh uchrezhdenii," in *Zhurnaly ...* (August–September 1911).

Balov, A., "Rozhdenie i vospitanie detei v Poshekhonskom uezde," *Etnograficheskoe obozrenie*, 1890, no. 3.

Bal'shakov, N., "Kooperativnoe proizvodstvo sel'sko-khoziaistvennykh mashin i orudii," *VSKh*, 1916, no. 8.

Baraboshkin, N. S., *Issledovanie i kharakteristika semennogo materiala krest'ianskikh khoziaistv Khar'kovskoi gubernii*, Khar'kov 1913.

Baranovich, M., *Materialy dlia geografii i statistiki Rossii, sobrannye ofitserami General'nogo Shtaba. T. 19, Riazanskaia guberniia*, St. Petersburg 1860.

Bartlett, Roger, ed. *Land Commune and Peasant Community in Russia: communal forms in Imperial and early Soviet society*, London 1990.

Barykov, F. L., et al, eds., *Sbornik materialov dlia izucheniia sel'skoi pozemel'noi obshchiny*, St. Petersburg 1880.

Bater, James, and R. A. French, eds., *Studies in Russian Historical Geography*, 2 vols., London, 1983.

Bauer, A. A., *Ukhod za parom i rzhanym polem*, n.p. (Moscow or Vladimir) 1921.

Bazhaev, V. "Kooperatsiia sel'skokhoziaistvennaia v Rossii," in *PERSKh*, vol. 12.

Becker, Gary S., *The Economic Approach to Human Behavior*, Chicago 1976.

——, "The Economic Way of Looking at Behavior: The Nobel Lecture," *Hoover Institution Essays in Public Policy*, 1996.

Beketov, B. A., *Voronezhskaia guberniia v sel'skokhoziaistvennom otnoshenii. Otchet po komandirovke v 1893 g. ot Imperatorskogo Moskovskogo Obshchestva Sel'skogo Khoziaistva*, Moscow 1894.

Bekhteev, A., "Ukladka kopen," *ZG*, 1889, no. 21.

Beliaev, K., "Iz sel'skokhoziaistvennoi praktiki," *ZG*, 1884, no. 25.

Beliaev, T. K., "Shkola i agronomicheskaia pomoshch' naseleniiu," in *Zhurnaly soveshchaniia zemskikh agronomov Tambovskoi gubernii* (August–September 1911).

Belokonskii, I. P., *Derevenskie vpechatleniia (iz zapisok zemskogo statistika)*, St. Petersburg 1900.

Bel'skii, S., *Novaia zemledel'cheskaia Rossiia. Ocherki zemleustroistva*, 2nd ed., St. Petersburg n. d.

Ber, V., "Ob uborke khlebnykh rastenii," *TVEO*, 1865, vol. 3, vyp. 2.

Berezov, F., "Nazrela-li dlia iugo-vostoka potrebnost' v zootekhnicheskom opytnom uchrezhdenii?," *SKhVIuV*, 1911, no. 20.

Berezovskii, A. E., "Zapiska A. E. Berezovskogo o vozmozhnosti uluchsheniia sel'skokhoziaistvennogo proizvodstva v Rossii," in *TMK Simbirsk*.

Bers, A. A., "Rol' ritma v zhizni narodov," *Etnograficheskoe obozrenie*, 1902, no. 3.

Bideleux, Robert, "Agricultural Advance Under the Russian Village Commune System," in Bartlett ed., *Land Commune and Peasant Community in Russia*.

——, *Communism and Development*, London–New York 1985.

Bilibin, V., "Doklad Upravy o deiatel'nosti uezdnogo i uchastkogo agronomov," in *Otchet ob agronomicheskoi deiatel'nosti*.

Bilimovich, A. D., "The Land Settlement in Russia and the War," in A. N. Antsyferov, *Russian Agriculture During the War*.

Biriukovich, V. V., compiler, *Sel'sko-khoziaistvennaia tekhnika. Svod trudov mestnykh komitetov po 49 guberniiam Evropeiskoi Rossii.*, St. Petersburg 1903.

Blank, A., "Po povodu predstoiashchei v 1914 godu v Tambove oblastnoi konskoi vystavki," *SKhZh*, 1912/13, no. 25.

Bliokh, I. S., *Sravnenie material'nogo byta i nravstvennogo sostoianiia naseleniia v cherte osedlosti evreev i vne ego*, Tom V, St. Petersburg 1891.

Bloch, Marc, *French Rural History. An essay on its basic characteristics*, translated by Janet Sondheimer, Berkeley 1966.

Blount, Ben G., "Parental Speech and Language Acquisition: some Lao and Samoan examples," *Anthropological Linguistics*, vol. 14, 1972.

Blum, Jerome, *The End of the Old Order in Europe*, Princeton 1978.

——, "The Internal Structure and Polity of the European Village Community from the Fifteenth to the Nineteenth Century," *Journal of Modern History*, 1971, no. 4.

——, "Michael Confino's *Systemes agraires et progres agricole*," *Journal of Modern History*, 1971, no. 3.

Bobovich, I. M., "Puti agrotekhnicheskogo progressa v Severo-Zapade Rossii v poreformennyi period," in *Severo-zapad v agrarnoi istorii Rossii*, Kaliningrad 1986.

Bobynin, N. N., "Agronomicheskaia pomoshch' naseleniiu Tambovskoi gubernii," *SKhZh*, 1915 and 1916 (throughout).

——, "Zemstvo i kooperatsiia," *SKhZh*, 1914, nos. 4–5.

Bogdanov, I. M., *Gramotnost' i obrazovanie v dorevoliutsionnoi Rossii i SSSR*, Moscow 1964.

Bogdanov, N., "Zapiski khoziaina," *SKhZh*, 1912/13, no. 24.

Bondarenko, V. N., "Ocherki Kirsanovskogo uezda," *Etnograficheskoe obozrenie*, 1890, no. 3.

Borisov, B., "Leto 1871 goda v Ekaterinoslavskoi, Khar'kovskoi i Kurskoi guberniiakh. Sel'sko-khoziaistvennyi eskiz puteshestvuiushchego agronoma," *TVEO*, 1871, vol. 3, vyp. 3.

Borisov, N. K., "Klever, korneplody i kartoshka pri mnogopol'i," *KSE*, vol. 6.

Borodavkin, L. M., and K. V. Kamenskii, *Krest'ianskaia rozh' Bronnitskogo uezda Moskovskoi gubernii*, St. Petersburg 1913.

Box, Louk, "The Experimenting Farmer: A Missing Link in Agricultural Change?" in J. Hinderink ed., *Successful Rural Development in Third World Countries*, Amsterdam 1988.

Braslavskii, P, *Sel'sko-khoziaistvennye besedy o vozdelyvanii maslichnogo podsol'nechnika v krest'ianskikh khoziaistvakh*, Pavlovsk 1908.

Braudel, Fernand, *The Identity of France. Volume Two: People and Production*, translated by Sian Reynolds, New York, HarperCollins, 1991.

Brianskii, A., "Sel'sko-khoziaistvennye raiony Tambovskoi gubernii," in *Biulleten' Tambovskogo gubernskogo statisticheskogo biuro*, 1924, no. 4.

Brooks, Jeffrey, *When Russia Learned to Read. Literacy and Popular Literature, 1861–1917*, Princeton 1985.

Bruk, B. L., *Kak naladit' krest'ianinu svoe khoziaistvo na chernozeme*, Moscow 1925.

——, *Obshchinnoe travoseianie na chernozeme*, Voronezh 1924.

——, *Organizatsiia obshchinnogo sevooborota*, Voronezh 1922.

Brunst, V. ed., *Trudy oblastnogo s"ezda predstavitelei zemstv i sel'skikh khoziaev Iuga Rossii.*, 3 vols., Ekaterinoslav 1910.

Brutskus, B., *Agrarnyi vopros i agrarnaia politika*, Petrograd 1922.

Brzheskii, N., *Ocherki po agrarnomu bytu krest'ian*, St. Petersburg 1908.

Bubrin, P., "Posevnoi material," in *PERSKh*, vol. 7.

Bunin, I. A., *Sobranie sochinenii v vos'mi tomakh*, Moscow 1993–.

——, *Light Breathing and Other Stories*, translated by Olga Shartse, Moscow 1988.

Bunin, N., "Khoziaistvennye zapiski i vedemosti g. Bunina," *Zemledel'cheskii Zhurnal*, 1832, no. 5.

——, "Vedemost' o zemledel'cheskikh rabotakh, proizvedennykh v imeniiakh pomesh-chikov Bunina i Pavlova, Tambovskoi gubernii Usmanskogo uezda," *Zemledel'cheskii Zhurnal*, 1832, no. 7.

Burds, Jeffrey, *Peasant Dreams and Market Politics. Labor Migration and the Russian Village, 1861–1905*, Pittsburgh 1999.

——, "The Social Control of Peasant Labor in Russia: The Response of Village Communities to Labor Migration in the Central Industrial Region, 1861–1905", in Kingston-Mann and Mixter, eds.

Burnaby, Fred, *A Ride to Khiva: Travels and Adventures in Central Asia*, 3rd ed., London–Paris–New York 1876.

Buromskii, I. D., "Protsessy sozrevaniia pshenitsy, rzhi, iachmenia, ovsa i maisa," *Puti sel'skogo khoziaistva*, 1926, no. 6–7.

Bushinskii, K. S., "Vozrazhenie K. S. Bushinskogo na dokladnuiu zapisku Mirovogo Posrednika V. A. Iozefi o khutorskom khoziaistve," in *TMK Podol'sk*.

Bushnell, John, "Peasants in Uniform: The Tsarist Army as a Peasant Society," in Eklof and Frank, *The World of the Russian Peasant*.

Bystrov, V. P., "O povtornykh kursov dlia agronomov," *Agronom*, 1924, no. 1.

Calina, Josephine, *Scenes of Russian Life*, London 1918.

Campbell, Bruce M. S., and Mark Overton, eds., *Land Labor, and Livestock: historical studies in European agricultural productivity*, Manchester 1991.

Chaev, Iu., "Poslushnitsa. (Iz sovremennoi deistvitel'nosti.)" *Istoricheskii Vestnik*, 1914, no. 8.

Chaianov, A. V., *Organizatsiia krest'ianskogo khoziaistva*, in his *Izbrannye trudy*, Moscow 1993.

Chebalak, N. M., *Sbornik statei po sel'skomu khoziaistvu dlia krest'ian*, Voronezh 1915.

Chekhov, A. P., *Sobranie sochinenii v dvenadtsati tomakh*, Moscow 1960–64.

Chelintsev, A. N., *Opyt izuchenii krest'ianskogo sel'skogo khoziaistva na primere Tambovskoi gubernii*, Khar'kov 1919.

——, *Russkoe sel'skoe khoziaistvo pered revoliutsii*, Moscow 1928.

Chelman, V. N., "Odna iz blizhaishchikh zadach kooperativnykh uchrezhdenii," *SKhZh*, 1912/13, no. 24.

Cheredeev, V. M., "Odno iz sredstv obezpecheniia urozhaev v nashem uezde," *Sel'sko-khoziaistvennyi Listok*, 1912, no. 1.

Chermenskii, P. N., *Ot krepostnogo prava k Oktiabriu v Tambovskoi gubernii*, Tambov 1928.

Chernenkov, N. N., *K kharakteristike krest'ianskogo khoziaistva*, Moscow 1918.

Cherniaev, V. V., "Sel'sko-khoziaistvennye mashiny i orudiia na Khar'kovskikh skladakh i mekhanicheskikh zavedeniiakh," in *Khar'kovskii kalendar' za 1887 god*, Khar'kov 1886.

——, "Sostiazanie pakharei i plugov v g. Tambov," *ZG*, 1871, no. 24.

Chernyshev, I. V., *Krest'iane ob obshchine nakanune 9 noiabria 1906 godu. K voprosu ob obshchine*, St. Petersburg 1911.

——, *Obshchina posle 9 noiabria 1906 g., po ankete Vol'nogo Ekonomicheskogo Obshchestva*, 2 vols., Petrograd 1917.

——, *Sel'skoe khoziaistvo dovoennoi Rossii i SSSR*, Moscow-Leningrad 1926.

Chernyshev, K. P., "Doklad K. P. Chernysheva po voprosu o semeinykh razdelakh," in *TMK*, Tambov.

Chikhachev, D. N., "Dokladnaia zapiska Predsedatelia Mogilevskogo Uezdnogo Komiteta D. N. Chikhacheva o perekhode krest'ian k khutorskomu khoziaistvu i unichtozhenii chrezpolosnogo pol'zovaniia zemleiu," in *TMK*, Podol'sk.

Chirikov, E. N., "Dobryi barin," in Lebedev, *Derevenskie letopisi*.

Chizhikov, N., "Nuzhny li pokazatel'nye uchastki," *Agronom*, 1926, no. 4.

Christensen, J. J., "Diseases of Wheat," in the entry "Wheat," *Encyclopedia Americana*, Danbury (Conn.) 1999, vol. 28.

Christian, David, *Living Water. Vodka and Russian Society on the Eve of Emancipation*, Oxford 1990.

Chuikov, N. A., *Kurskaia guberniia v sel'skokhoziaistvennom otnoshenii. Otchet po komandirovke v 1893 g. ot Imperatorskogo Moskovskogo Obshchestva Sel'skogo Khoziaistva*, Moscow 1894.

Chuprov, A. I., *Melkoe zemledelie i ego osnovnye nuzhdy*, 2nd ed., Berlin 1921.

——, "Obshchinnoe zemlevladenie," in *Nuzhdy derevni, po rabotam komitetov o nuzhdakh sel'sko-khoziaistvennoi promyshlennosti* St. Petersburg 1904, vol. 2.

——, *Rechi i stati*, 2 vols., St. Petersburg 1909.

Comrie, Bernard, and Gerald Stone, *The Russian Language in the Twentieth Century*, Oxford 1996.

Confino, Michael, *Domaines et Seigneurs en Russie vers la fin du XVIII siècle; étude de structures agraires et mentalites economiques*, Paris 1963.

——, *Systèmes Agraires et Progrès Agricole: l'assolement triennale en Russie aux XVIII–XIX siècles; étude d'economie et de sociologie rurales*, Paris 1969.

Conte, C., "Colonial Science and Ecological Change. Tanzania's Mlalo Basin, 1888–1946," *Environmental History*, 1999, no. 2.

Danilov, V. P., *Rural Russia Under the New Regime*, Bloomington (Indiana) 1988.

Daragan, D., *Mysli sel'skogo khoziaina po raznym zemskim voprosam*, St. Petersburg 1884.

Dashkevich, L., "Likvidatsiia Bankovskikh zemel' i zemleustroistvo v Kirsanovskom uezde," *Vestnik Evropy*, October 1909.

Deilidovich, V., "Ocherk sel'skogo khoziaistva v Kaluzhskoi gubernii," in *Pamiatnaia knizhka Kaluzhskoi gubernii na 1861 god*, Kaluga 1861.

Demidov, A., *Zhizn' Ivana. Povest'*, Moscow 1923.

Dmitriev, S. *Opyt prakticheskikh zamechanii Kinishemskogo zemledel'tsa o sel'skom khoziaistve Kostromskoi gubernii*, 2nd ed., Moscow 1855.

Dmitrieva, T. G., "Problema natsional'nogo kharaktera v proze I. A. Bunina," in *I. A. Bunin i russkaia literatura XX veka.*

Dnevnik Totemskogo krest'ianina A. A. Zamaraeva. 1906–1922 gg., Moscow 1995.

Dobroliubov, N. A., *Selected Philosophical Essays*, Moscow 1948.

Dobrosel'skii, P. P., "Byt' ili ne byt' obshchine. Zapiska P. P. Dobrosel'skogo," *TMK*, Khar'kov.

Doklad Bogorodskoi uezdnoi zemskoi upravy po veterinarnoi chasti, (Bogorodskoe uezdnoe zemskoe sobranie, ocherednoi sessii 1913 goda) Moscow 1914.

"Doklad komissii po punktu Ch: pooshchrenie k dobrovol'nomu razseleniiu krest'ian v predelakh ikh nadela," in *TMK*, Khar'kov.

"Doklad Lipetskoi agronomicheskoi organizatsii," in *Trudy 7-ogo soveshchaniia zemskikh agronomov Tambovskoi gubernii.*

"Doklad o formakh krest'ianskogo zemlepol'zovaniia i pooshchreniia k dobrovol'nomu razseleniiu krest'ian v predelakh ikh nadelov," in *TMK*, Orel.

Doklad sel'sko-khoziaistvennoi komissii Tambovskoi gubernskoi zemskoi upravy, Tambov 1910.

"Doklad Upravy o deiatel'nosti agronomicheskoi organizatsii v 1912 godu i smetnykh predolozheniiakh na 1913 god na sel'sko-khoziaistvennye meropriiatiia," in *Morshanskoe Uezdnoe Zemskoe Sobranie ocherednoi sessii 1912 goda*, Morshansk 1912.

"Doklad Upravy ob agronomicheskoi pomoshchi vsemu naseleniiu Kozlovskogo uezda," in *Zhurnaly Kozlovskogo Uezdnogo Zemskogo Sobraniia chrezvychainogo zasedaniia 8 iiunia i ocherednoi sessii 29 i 30 sentiabria i 1–3 oktiabria 1912 g.*, Kozlov 1913.

Doklady i rezoliutsii 1-ogo Tambovskogo okruzhnogo soveshchaniia po povysheniiu urozhainosti, Tambov 1929.

Doklady ob agronomicheskoi organizatsii, Tambov 1911 (Tambov uezd zemstvo publication).

Doklady Tambovskoi gubernskoi zemskoi upravy Tambovskomu zemskomu sobraniiu ocherednoi sessii 1912 goda, po agronomicheskomu otdelu, Tambov 1912.

Drozdov, V. P., *Okolo zemli. Ocherki po zemleustroistvu.*, St. Petersburg 1910.

Dubrovskii, S. M., *Stolypinskaia agrarnaia reforma. Iz istorii sel'skogo khoziaistva i krest'ianstva Rossii v nachale XX veka*, Moscow 1963.

Egarmin, E., "Zhelatel'naia reforma na krest'ianskom ogorode," *Vestnik Usmanskogo uezdnogo zemstva*, 1914, no. 2.

Eklof, Ben, "Peasant Sloth Reconsidered," *Journal of Social History*, 1981, vol. 14, no. 3.

——, "Peasants and Schools," in Eklof and Frank, *The World of the Russian Peasant.*

Eklof, Ben, and Stephen Frank, eds., *The World of the Russian Peasant*, Boston 1990.

Ekonom, "O vrede, proizvodimom na domashnykh zhivotnykh ot nesvoevremennogo krovopuskaniia i neumestnogo upotrebleniia slabitel'nykh sredstv," *TGV*, 1851, no. 12.

Elenev, F. P., "1868 god v Smolenskoi gubernii," *Russkii Vestnik*, June 1892.

Ellis, Frank, *Peasant Economics. Farm Households and Agrarian Development*, 2nd edition, Cambridge UK 1993.

Elwert, Georg, "Social Transformation as an Endogenous Process Dealing with Strangers: A Comparison of Three African Rural Communities," paper presented to the Program in Agrarian Studies, Yale University, November 1997.

Emel'ianov, I. N., "K voprosu o kharaktere agrarnogo kapitalizma v pomeshchich'em khoziaistve Orlovskoi gubernii v period imperializma." *Ezhegodnik po agrarnoi istorii vostochnoi evropy 1970 g.*, Riga 1977.

Encyclopaedia Britannica, 11th ed., New York, 1910–1911.

Engel, Barbara, "The Woman's Side: Male Outmigration and the Family Economy in Kostroma," in Eklof and Frank, *The World of the Russian Peasant.*

Engel'gardt, A. N., *Iz derevni: 12 pisem, 1872–1887*, 6th ed., Moscow 1960.

Engel'gardt, A. N., *Ocherk krest'ianskogo khoziaistva v Kazanskoi i drugikh Sredne-Volzhskikh guberniiakh*, Kazan 1892.

Entsiklopedicheskii slovar', (Brokgauz-Efron), 86 vols., St. Petersburg 1890–1907.

Eremeeva, Iu. S., "Agronomicheskaia pomoshch' naseleniiu," *TVEO*, 1909, no. 3.

——, "Ob usloviiakh agronomicheskoi raboty v derevne," in *Trudy pervogo Vserossiiskogo sel'sko-khoziaistvennogo s"ezda v Kieve 1–10 sentiabria 1913 g.*, Kiev 1914, vyp. 2.

——, "Ustroistvo krest'ianskogo khoziaistva," *Zemleustroistvo i zemlepol'zovanie*, 1908, no.10.

Ermolenko, G., "O semenakh i podgotovke ikh k posevu," *Shatskoe Khoziaistvo*, 1915, no. 16.

——, "Sornye travy," *Shatskoe Khoziaistvo*, 1915, no. 12.

Ermolov, A. S., *Organizatsiia polevogo khoziaistva. Sistemy zemledeliia i sevooboroty*. 5th ed., St. Petersburg 1914.

——, *Narodnaia sel'sko-khoziaistvennaia mudrost' v poslovitsakh, pogovorkakh i primetakh*. 4 vols., St. Petersburg 1905.

——, *Narodnye primety na urozhai*, St. Petersburg n. d. (1908?).

Ermolov, D., "Iz Bobrovskogo uezda (Voronezhskoi gubernii)," *Zemledel'cheskaia Gazeta*, 1876, no. 1.

Eropkin, A., "Ob upadke zemledeliia i ego nuzhdakh," *Russkaia mysl'*, 1902, no. 5.

Erpulev, I. N., "K voprosu ob uluchsheniiu krest'ianskogo zemlepol'zovaniia v chernozemnom polose", *VSKh*, 1909, no. 2.

Ertel', A. I., "Samarskaia derevnia (fotografiia)," *Etnograficheskoe obozrenie*, 1910, nos. 3–4.

——, *Sobranie sochinenii A. I. Ertelia v semi tomakh*, Moscow 1909.

——, *Volkhonskaia baryshnia. Povesti.*, Moscow 1984.

Esikov, S. A., "Trekhpol'naia sistema i zemskaia agronomicheskaia pomoshch'," in Avrekh, ed., *Tambovskoe krest'ianstvo*, Vyp. 1.

Evans, George Ewart, *Ask the Fellows Who Cut the Hay*, London 1975.

——, *The Crooked Scythe*, London 1993.

Ezhegodnik Cherdynskogo uezdnogo zemstva i kalendar na 1914 god, Cherdyn 1913.

Ezhegodnik Rossii ... goda (title changed in 1911 to *Statisticheskii ezhegodnik Rossii ... goda*), St. Petersburg 1905–1914.

Fabrichno-zavodskoi promyshlennosti Evropeiskoi Rossii v 1910–1912 gg., Petrograd 1914–15.

Fabrikant, A. O., "Po povodu zasukha i agronomov," *Agronom*, 1924, no. 1.

Farnsworth, Beatrice, "The Litigious Daughter-in-Law: Family Relations in Rural Russia in the Second Half of the Nineteenth Century," in Farnsworth and Viola, *Russian Peasant Women*.

Farnsworth, Beatrice, and Lynne Viola, eds., *Russian Peasant Women*, Oxford 1992.

Federov, V. A., "Kul'tura i byt srednevolzhskoi derevni po materialam Etnograficheskogo biuro V. N. Tenisheva," in Iu. V. Smykov, ed., *Krest'ianskoe khoziaistvo i kul'tura derevni srednego povolzh'ia*, Ioshkar-Ola 1990.

Fenin, Aleksandr I., *Coal and Politics in Late Imperial Russia. Memoirs of a Russian Mining Engineer*, DeKalb, Ill. 1990.

Fenoaltea, Stefano, "Transaction Costs, Whig History, and the Common Fields," *Politics and Society*, vol. 16, nos. 2–3.

Fenomenov, Ia. A., *Sovremennaia derevnia*, 2 vols., Leningrad 1925.

Fet, A. A., "Iz derevni," *Russkii vestnik*, April 1864.

——, "Zametki o vol'no-naemnon trude," *Russkii vestnik*, May 1862.

Filipchenko, A. E., "V zashchitu serpa," *ZG*, 1889, no. 17.

——, "Variatsii vo rzhi nyneshnogo urozhaia," *ZG*, 1890, no. 28.

Finnegan, Ruth, "Literacy," in *The Encyclopaedia of Social and Cultural Anthropology*, London 1996.

Firsov, B. M., and I. G. Kiseleva, *Byt velikorusskikh krest'ian-zemlepashtsev*, St. Petersburg 1993.

Fomin, G. I., *Kulachnye boi v Voronezhskoi gubernii*, Voronezh 1926.

Fon-Gagen, S. A., "Iz Usmanskogo uezda, Tambovskoi gubernii," *Vestnik Russkogo Sel'skogo Khoziaistva*, 1893, no. 24.

Fortunatov, A., "Mertvyi inventar' v russkom krest'ianskom zemledelii," *Vestnik Russkogo Sel'skogo Khoziaistva*, 1889, no. 7.

——, "Sel'skokhoziaistvennaia ekonomika," in *ES*, vol. 57.

Foster, George M., "Peasant Society and the Image of the Limited Good," *American Anthropologist*, 1967.

Frank, Stephen P., "'Simple Folk, Savage Customs?' Youth, Sociability, and the Dynamics of Culture in Rural Russia, 1856–1914," *Journal of Social History*, 1992, no. 4.

Frankovskii, V. G., "Odin iz vidov agronomicheskoi pomoshchi naseleniiu. Volostnye sel'sko-khoziaistvennye sovety Valuiskogo uezda (Voronezhskoi gubernii)", in Brunst, *Trudy oblastnogo s"ezda predstavitelei zemstv i sel'skikh khoziaev Iuga Rossii*, vol. 2.

Friedman, Jeffrey, and Adam McCabe, "Preferences or Happiness? Tibor Scitovsky's Psychology of Human Needs," *Critical Review*, vol. 10, no. 4 (Fall 1996).

Frierson, Cathy A., "'I Must Always Answer to Law...' Rules and Responses in the Reformed Volost' Court," *Slavonic and East European Review*, vol. 75, 1997, no. 2.

——, *Peasant Icons: Representations of Rural People in Late Nineteenth Century Russia*, Oxford 1993.

——, "*Razdel*: the Peasant Family Divided," in Farnsworth and Viola, *Russian Peasant Women*.

——, "The Volost' Court Debate, 1870–1912," *Slavonic and East European Review*, vol. 64, 1986, no. 4.

Friesen, Leonard G., "Bukkers, Plows, and Lobogreikas: Peasant Acquisition of Agricultural Implements in Russia before 1900." *Russian Review* 53, no. 3 (1994): 399–418.

Fursova, S. V., "Rasprostranenie gramotnosti i obrazovaniia sredi krest'ianskogo naseleniia Tambovskoi gubernii v poreformennyi period," in Avrekh, ed., *Tambovskoe krest'ianstvo*, Vyp. 2.

Ganeizer, E., "V Tambovskoi Manchzhurii (iz putevykh zametok)," *Sovremennye zapiski*, 1906, no. 1.

Garin-Mikhailovskii, N. G., *Sobranie sochinenii v piati tomakh*, Moscow 1957–58.

Garshin, A., *O semenakh dlia poseva i sornykh travakh*, Chernigov 1909.

Gil'tenbrandt, A., "Sel'sko-khoziaistvennye zametki po puti ot g. Starogo Oskola, cherez Tim, Shchigry i Maloarkhangel'sk, do g. Orla," *TVEO*, 1869, vol. 1, vyp. 4.

Glukhikh, F. S., "Iz nevedomogo mira," in *Krasen chelovek uchen'em*.

Golosa krest'ian: Sel'skaia Rossiia XX veka v krest'ianskikh memuarakh, Moscow 1996.

Goppe, A. A., "Razvedenie repchatogo luka na poliakh," *SKhVIuV*, 1911, no. 11.

Gorelkin, F. M., "Selo Verkhne–Spasskoe, Tambovskogo uezda," *SKhZh*, 1914, no. 3.

Gorev, M., *Agronom priekhal*, Leningrad 1925.

Goriachkin, V., "Sokha," in PERSKh, vol. 9, St. Petersburg 1905.

Goriushkin, L. M., G. I. Bochanova, and G. A. Nozdrin, *Opyt narodnoi agronomii v Sibiri*, Novosibirsk 1993.

Gorizontov, A., "Khoziaistvenno–statisticheskoe opisanie Penzenskogo uezda," *TVEO*, 1859, vol. 1, nos. 1, 3.

Gorskii, A. V., "Kooperativnye tsentry," in *Trudy 7-ogo agronomicheskogo soveshchaniia Tambovskogo gubernskogo zemstva*.

Gosudarstvennyi Sovet. Sessiia 5-aia, *Stenograficheskii otchet*, St. Petersburg 1910.

Grabovskii, A. N., *Kak pereiti na shirokie polosy*, Moscow 1929.

Gregory, Paul R., *Before Command: an economic history of Russia from emancipation to the first five-year plan*, Princeton 1994.

Gregory, Paul R., and Robert C. Stuart, *Soviet Economic Structure and Performance*, 4th edition, New York 1990.

Grekov, V., "Ob organizatsii artel'nykh tomatnykh zavodov," *SKhVIuV*, 1912, no. 19.

Grigg, David, "Ester Boserup's Theory of Agrarian Change," *Progress in Geography*, 1979, no. 1.

——, *Population Growth and Agrarian Change. An Historical Perspective.* Cambridge 1980.

——, *The Transformation of Agriculture in the West*, Oxford 1992.

Gromyko, M. M. and T. A. Listova, eds. *Russkie: Semeinyi i obshchestvennyi byt*, Moscow, 1989.

Gromyko, M. M., *Trudovye traditsii krest'ian Sibiri*, Moscow 1977.

Gruzinov, I., "Byt krest'ian Tambovskoi gubernii," *Zhurnal zemlevladel'tsev*, 1858, no. 5.

Gudvilovich, V., "Stoimost' vypasa skota na parovykh poliakh v Tambovskom uezde," *SKhZh*, 1912/13, no. 8.

Guliaev, V. R., *Perspektivy mnogopolia v chernozemno-rzhanykh raionakh povolzh'ia*, Petrovsk 1925.

Guy Michael, Louis, "My Russian Experience, 1910–1917" unpublished manuscript in the Hoover Institution Archive.

Haxthausen, August von, *Studies on the Interior of Russia*, edited by S. Frederick Starr, transl. by Eleanore L. M. Schmidt, Chicago 1972.

Heilbroner, Robert, *The Worldly Philosophers*, 3rd edition, New York 1967.

Hindus, Maurice, *Broken Earth*, New York 1926

——, *The Russian Peasant and the Revolution*, New York 1920.

Hoch, Steven L., *Serfdom and Social Control in Russia. Petrovskoe, a village in Tambov.* Chicago 1986.

——, "Tall Tales: Anthropometric Measures of Well-Being in Imperial Russia and the Soviet Union, 1821–1960," *Slavic Review*, Spring 1999.

Hoffmann, Richard C. "Medieval Origins of the Common Fields," in *European Peasants and Their Markets. Essays in Agrarian History*, William N. Parker and Eric L. Jones, eds., Princeton 1975.

Hutchinson, John F., *Politics and Public Health in Revolutionary Russia, 1890–1918*, Baltimore 1990.

I. A. Bunin i russkaia literatura XX veka: po materialam mezhdunarodnoi nauchnoi konferentsii, posviashchennoi 125-letiiu so dnia rozhdeniia I. A. Bunina, 23–24 oktiabria 1995 g., Moscow 1995.

Iakimenko, N. A., "O sotsial'nom sostave krest'ian-pereselentsev v Rossii 80-kh godov XIX–nachala XX veka," *Otechestvennaia istoriia*, 1993, no. 1.

Iakovlev, Ia. A., *Nashe derevnia. Novoe v staroe i staroe v novoe.* Moscow 1924.

Iakovlev, G., "Poslovitsy, pogovorki, krylatye slova, primety i pover'ia, sobrannye v slobode Sagunakh Ostrogozhskogo uezda," *Zhivaia starina*, 1906, vyp. 4, otdel II.

Iakovlevich, Ia., "Novoe i staroe v Russkom sel'skom khoziaistve," *Russkaia Mysl'*, 1913, no. 7.

Iakushkin, P. I., *Sochineniia*, St. Petersburg 1884.

Ianovskii, A., "Vygon," *ES*, vol. 14.

Iarilov, Ars., "Iz sel'sko-khoziaistvennoi zhizni i literatury," *VSKh*, 1916, no. 1.

Ionson, Doctor, "O sel'skom khoziaistve v Rossii. Putevye zametki o raznykh guberni-iakh." *TVEO*, 1861, vol. 1, vyp. 4.

Iozefi, V. A., "Osoboe mnenie Mirovogo Posrednika V. A. Iozefi po voprosu o vvedenii khutornogo khoziaistva u krest'ian Mogilevskogo uezda, Podol'skoi gubernii," in *TMK*, Podol'sk.

Iudin, A., "Glavneishie pravila khraneniia i ukhoda za sel'sko-khoziaistvennymi mashi-nami i orudiiami," *SKhL*, 1912, no. 2.

——, "Kak khraniatsia mashiny i orudiia v krest'ianskom khoziaistve," *SKhVIuV*, 1912, no. 13.

——, "Kak vybrat' vremia uborki khlebov", *SKhL*, 1913, no. 7.

——, "Ob ukhode za sel'sko-khoziaistvennymi zhivotnymi," *SKhL*, 1913, no. 9.

——, "Ochistka i sortirovanie semian," *SKhL*, 1913, no. 3.

Iurevich, P., "Agronomicheskie puteshchestviia po Rossii," *ZhMGI*, 1852, no. 7.

Iur'evskii, B., *Vozrozhdenie derevni*, Petrograd 1914.

Iurin, N. T., *Khutora i otruba v Tambovskoi gubernii. Rezul'taty obsledovaniia 1912 goda.*, Tambov 1913.

Iurlov, V., "Neskol'ko slov o zhnitve i uborke khleba naimom v Samarskoi gubernii," in *Volzhskii Vestnik*, vyp. 1, Simbirsk n. d. (1861?).

Ivanitskii, N. A., *Materialy po etnografii Vologodskoi gubernii*, in *Sbornik svedenii dlia izucheniia byta krest'ianskogo naseleniia Rossii*. Vyp. 2, Moscow 1890.

Ivaniukov, I., "Krest'ianskoe khoziaistvo Tambovskoi gubernii," *Russkaia Mysl'*, 1887, no. 1.

Ivanov, A. I., "Verovaniia krest'ian Orlovskoi gubernii," *Etnograficheskoe obozrenie*, 1900, no. 4.

Ivanov, V. V., "Sovremennaia derevnia v Khar'kovskoi gubernii," *Khar'kovskii sbornik*, vyp. 7, Khar'kov 1893.

——, ed., *Zhizn' i tvorchestvo krest'ian Khar'kovskoi gubernii. Ocherki po etnografiiu kraia*, Khar'kov 1898, vol. 1.

Ivanova, P. V., *Zhizn' i pover'ia krest'ian Kupianskogo uezda, Khar'kovskoi gubernii*, Khar'kov 1907.

Ivlev, S., "Malenkaia proba," *SKhZh*, 1914, no. 6.

Jasny, Naum, *Competition among Grains*, Stanford 1940.

Johnson, Allen W., "Individuality and Experimentation in Traditional Agriculture," *Human Ecology*, vol. 1, no. 2, 1972.

Johnson, Robert E., "Family Life-Cycles and Economic Stratification: A Case Study in Rural Russia," *Journal of Social History*, vol. 30, no. 3 (Spring 1997).

Kabanov, B., "Zabytaia mysl'," *Russkie Vedemosti*, 1910, no. 38.

Kabanov, V. V., *Kooperatsiia, revoliutsiia, sotsializm*, Moscow 1996.

——, *Krest'ianskaia obshchina i kooperatsiia Rossii XX veka*, Moscow 1997.

——, "Puti i bezdorozh'ia agrarnogo razvitiia Rossii v XX veke," *Voprosy istorii*, 1993, no. 2.

Kahan, Arcadius, *Russian Economic History. The Nineteenth Century*, Chicago 1989.

Kalashnikov, G. A. and A. M., "Selo Nikol'skoe (Starobel'skii uezd)," in V. V. Ivanov, ed., *Zhizn' i tvorchestvo krest'ian Khar'kovskoi gubernii*.

Kallinikov, I., "O sobiranii skazok v Orlovskoi gubernii," *Zhivaia starina*, 1913, vol. 22.

——, "Skazochniki i ikh skazki," *Zhivaia starina*, 1915, vol. 24.

Karamzin, P., "Ob uborke zernovykh khlebov i poteriakh ot nee proiskhodiashchikh", in A. Sovetov and V. Dokuchaev, eds., *Materialy po izucheniiu Russkikh pochv*, vyp. 1, St. Petersburg 1885.

Karev, N. A., "Iz Bolkhovskogo uezda, Orlovskoi gubernii," *Vestnik Russkogo Sel'skogo Khoziaistva*, 1893, no. 24.

Karonin, S., "Kuda i kak oni pereselilis'," in Lebedev, *Krest'ianskie sud'by*.

——,"Uchenyi," in Lebedev, *Krest'ianskie sud'by*.

Karyshev, N., "Zemledelie (ekon.)," in *ES*, vol. 23.

Kassa melkogo kredita Tambovskogo uezdnogo zemstva, *Doklady o deiatel'nosti kassy za period vremeni s 25 oktiabria 1915 goda po 15 oktiabria 1916 goda i o meropriiatiiakh kooperatsii*, Tambov 1916.

Kaufman, A. A., *Agrarnyi vopros v Rossii*, Moscow 1918.

Kazantsev, N., "Domashnee ptitsevodstvo v chernozemnykh uezdakh Orlovskoi gubernii," *Sel'skoe Khoziaistvo i Lesovodstvo*, 1865, ch. LXXXVIII.

Kazimirov, N., "Zemskaia statistika," *VSKh*, 1914, no. 9.

Keller, V. B., and I. A. Romanenko, *Pervyi itogi agrarnoi reformy*, Voronezh 1922.

Kerans, David, "The Workhorse in Late Imperial Russia. An Exploration." Forthcoming.

——, "Agricultural Evolution and the Peasantry in Russia. Tambov Province, 1880–1915," Ph. D. dissertation, University of Pennsylvania 1994.

Kerridge, Eric, *The Common Fields of England*, Manchester 1992.

Kharchenko, P., "Obrabotka para—kak ona obychno vedetsia i kak ona dolzhna vestis'," *ZG*, 1890, no. 46.

Kharizomenov, S., "Lentochnaia obrabotka polia pri razbrosnom i riadovom posevakh," in *SKhVIuV*, 1911, no. 15.

Khar'kovskii kalendar na 1887 god, Khar'kov 1886.

Khar'kovskii sbornik, vyp. 1, Khar'kov 1887.

Khatunskii, S., *Okolo volosti*, Moscow 1910.

Khizniakov, V., "Zemstvo i kooperatsiia," *VSKh*, 1914, no. 9.

Khurtin, K. P., "Moi opyty s podsolnukhom," *Sam sebe agronom*, 1926, no. 17.

Khvostov, N. A., "Doklad N. A. Khvostova o polozhenii sel'skogo khoziaistva v Eletskom uezde," *TMK*, Orel.

Kingston-Mann, Esther, "Peasant Communes and Economic Innovation: A Preliminary Inquiry," in Kingston-Mann and Mixter, *Peasant Economy*.

Kingston-Mann, Esther, and Timothy Mixter, ed., *Peasant Economy, Culture and Politics of European Russia, 1800–1921*, Princeton 1991.

Kiselev, A. P., "Tochnoe opredelenie prazdnikov v kotorye vospreshchaetsia rabotat'," in *TMK*, Podol'sk.

Kishkin, M. S., "Dannye i predpolozheniia po voprosu ob uluchshenii byta krest'ian v Kirsanovskom uezde, Tambovskoi gubernii," *Sel'skoe Blagoustroistvo*, 1859, no. 2.

——, "O zemledelii, skotovodstve i sel'skikh promyslakh v Kirsanovskom uezde," *Zapiski Lebedianskogo Obshchestva Sel'skogo Khoziaistva. Za 1859 god.*, Moscow 1860, ch. 2.

Klements, A., "Zametka o konnoi molot'be v privolzhskom krae," in *Volzhskii vestnik. Vyp. 1.*, Simbirsk n.d. (1861?).

Klepikov, S. A., *Pitanie russkogo krest'ianina*, Moscow 1920.

Klopov, S. A., "Posevnoe zerno rzhi i ovsa v Belorussii," *Zapiski Belorusskogo Gosudarstvennogo Instituta Sel'skogo Khoziaistva*, vyp. 3, Minsk 1924.

Kliuev, S., *Chto nado znat' o pochve i ee obrabotke*, Leningrad 1925.

Kliuss, G. A., "Luga," *ES*, vol. 35.

——, "Molot'ba", *ES*, vol. 38.

Knipovich, V. M., *Sel'sko-khoziaistvennoe raionirovanie*, Moscow 1925.

Kochetkov, V., "Sel'sko-khoziaistvennye besedy i chteniia, kak sredstvo obshchest-venno-agronomcheskogo vozdeistviia," *Zemskii agronom*, 1913, no. 3.

Koefoed (also spelled Kofod), C. A., *My Share in the Stolypin Agrarian Reforms*, Odense 1985.

Kofod, A., *Russkoe zemleustroistvo*, St. Petersburg 1914.

Kolchin, A., "Verovanie krest'ian Tul'skoi gubernii," *Etnograficheskoe obozrenie*, 1899, no. 3.

Kondratiev, N., and N. P. Oganovskii, *Perspektivy razvitiia sel'skogo khoziaistva SSSR*, Moscow 1924.

Konevodstvo v Kazanskoi gubernii, Kazan 1904.

Kononov, M. A., "Zapiska M. A. Kononova po voprosam o nuzhdakh sel'skokhoz-iaistvennoi promyshlennosti, predstavlennaia Kozlovskomu Uezdnomu Pred-voditel'iu Dvorianstva," in *TMK*, Tambov.

Konovalov, I., "Budni sovremennoi derevni," *Sovremennyi mir*, 1911, no. 6.

——, "Derevenskie kartinki. (Zametki)." *Russkoe Bogatstvo*, 1911, no. 1.

——, "Na khutorakh. (Zametki derevenskogo nabliudatelia)," *Russkoe Bogatstvo*, 1910, nos. 1–2.

——, "V derevne," *Sovremennyi mir*, 1909, no. 2, otdel II.

Kordatov, A. V., "Chernukhinskaia volost', Nizhegorodskaia uezda," in *Sbornik statis-ticheskikh i spravochnykh svedenii po Nizhegorodskoi gubernii*, Nizhnii-Novgorod 1880.

Korinfskii, A. A., *Trudovoi god russkogo krest'ianina*, 10 vols., Moscow 1904.

——, *V mire skazanii. Ocherki narodnykh vzgliadov i poverii.*, St. Petersburg 1905.

Korolenko, V. G., *V Golodnyi god*, St. Petersburg 1894.

Korolev, F., "Zernosushil'nia," in *ES*, vol. 24.

Korostovetz, V., *Seed and Harvest*, translated from German by Dorothy Lumby, London 1931.

Koshelev, A., "Ob urochnykh rabotakh," in *Zhurnal Sel'skogo Khoziaistva*, 1852, no. 2.

Kositsyn, G., "Doklad instruktora-sadovoda o meropriiatiiakh po sadovodstvu i ogorodnichestvu v Morshanskom uezde," in *Morshanskoe Uezdnoe Zemskoe Sobranie ocherednoi sessii 1912 goda*, Morshansk 1912.

Kosogorov, A., "Russkoe narodnoe vospitanie," *Zhivaia starina*, 1906, vyp. 4, otdel V.

Kostikov, N., "Pis'mo kursista o Gusevykh zemskikh nedel'nykh sel'sko-khoziaistven-nykh kursakh", *SKhL*, 1912, no.1.

Kostritsyn, M., "Iz nabliudenii nad mestnogo skotovodstva," *SKhVIuV*, 1911, no. 5.

Kostromskaia derevnia v pervoe vremia voiny, Kostroma 1916 (*Trudy Kostromskogo nauchnogo obshchestva po izucheniiu mestnogo kraia. Vyp. 5*).

Kostrov, N. I., *Opyt issledovaniia krest'ianskogo khoziaistva v agronomicheskom otnoshenii*, Khar'kov 1913.

——, and N. Nikitin and A. Emme, *Ocherki organizatsii krest'ianskogo khoziaistva, po materialam biudzhetnykh issledovanii nachala XX veka*, Moscow 1926.

——, and A. Ia. Tarasov, *Ocherki po tekhnike sel'skogo khoziaistva*, Moscow 1927.

Kotov, A. A., *Opyt issledovaniia tekhniki krest'ianskogo khoziaistva*, Minsk 1925.

Kotsonis, Yanni, *Making Peasants Backward*, London 1999.

Kovalevskii, N. N., "Doklad N. N. Kovalevskogo Khar'kovskomu Gubernskomu Komitetu o nuzhdakh sel'sko-khoziaistvennoi promyshlennosti," in *TMK*, Khar'kov.

Koval'kovskii, A. K., *Zemstvo i zemskaia agronomicheskaia rabota*, Kostroma 1915.

——, *Znachenie sortirovki i ochistki posevnogo materiala i bor'ba s sornymi rasteniiami*, n. p. 1912.

Kozhevnikov, N., "Bych'i sluchnye punkty gorodov v riadu mer massovogo uluch-sheniia skotovodstva," *SKhVIuV*, 1911, no. 13.

Kozlov, Kh. P., "Khoziaistvennyi otchet," *Zapiski Lebedianskogo Obshchestva Sel'skogo Khoziaistva. Za 1858 god.*, Moscow 1859, chast' 1.

Kozlov, V. Kh., "Zapiska po voprosam Ch, Sh, ShCh," in *TMK*, Tambov.

Krasen chelovek uchen'em. Materialy o vospitanii i obrazovanii detei v seleniiakh Sibiri (konets XIX–nachalo XX vv.), Novosibirsk 1995.

Krasil'nikov, I. P., "Kakim zernom nado seiat'," *Sel'sko-khoziaistvennyi vestnik Novgorodskogo Gubernskogo Zemstva*, 1916, no. 1.

Krasil'nikov, M., "Chto znaet Ufimskaia derevnia ob agronomakh," *Zemskii agronom*, 1913, no. 3.

Krasnoperov, I., "Sel'sko-khoziaistvennaia kooperatsiia v evropeiskikh i vneevropeiskikh stranakh," *Sel'sko-khoziaistvennyi vestnik*, 1914, no. 5.

Krasnozhenova, M. V., "Rebenok v krest'ianskom bytu," in *Krasen chelovek uchen'em*.

Krasovskii, V. E., "Undorovskaia obshchina. Simbirskaia guberniia," in Barykov, *Sbornik materialov*.

Kratkii obzor sostoianiia narodnogo obrazovaniia v Tambovskoi gubernii v 1914–15 uchebnom godu, Tambov 1917.

Kratkii ocherk ob otkhozhikh promyslakh Tambovskoi gubernii v 1899 g., Tambov 1901.

Kravchenko, F., "Piatnadtsat' let izucheniia klimata Tambovskoi gubernii," in *Piatnadtsat' let Tambovskoi opytnoi stantsii (1912–1927 gg.)*, Voronezh 1928.

Krest'ianskaia sel'sko-khoziaistvennaia entsiklopediia, 7 vols., Moscow 1925–28.

Krest'ianskoe dvizhenie v Rossii iiun' 1907 g.–iiul' 1914 g. Sbornik dokumentov, Moscow-Leningrad 1966.

Krest'ianskoe dvizhenie v Rossii v 1796–1825 gg. Sbornik dokumentov, Moscow 1961.

Krest'ianskoe dvizhenie 1905–07 gg. v Tambovskoi gubernii, Tambov 1957.

Kriukov, F., "Mel'kom (Vpechatleniia proezzhego)," *RB*, 1914, nos. 8–9.

Krokhalev, F. S., *O sistemakh zemledeliia. Istoricheskii ocherk*, Moscow 1960.

Kurbatov, Ignatii E., "O derevenskikh detiakh," *Saratovskie gubernskie vedomosti*, 1894, no. 6.

Kushchenko, G. A., "K dinamike krest'ianskogo khoziaistva (krest'ianskoe khoziaistvo Surazhskogo uezda Chernigovskogo gubernii po dannym dvukh perepisei–1882 i 1911 g.)," in *Statisticheskii vestnik. Kniga 1-aia, 1915–16*, Moscow 1916.

Kushner, P. I., ed., *Russkie. Istoriko-etnograficheskii atlas.* Moscow 1967.

Kuskov, P., "O sel'sko-khoziaistvennykh obshchestvakh malogo raiona v Saratovskoi gubernii," *SKhVIuV*, 1911, no. 17.

Kuprianov, F. M., "O vliianii tipa pluga na kharakter obrabotke pochvy v krest'ianskom khoziaistve", in *Trudy 8-ogo soveshchaniia zemskikh agronomov Tambovskoi gubernii*, Tambov 1914.

Kuprin, Alexander, "The Song and the Dance," in his *A Slav Soul and Other Stories*, translated by Stephen Graham, London 1916.

Kuznetsov, S. V., *Traditsii russkogo zemledel'tsa: praktika i religiozno-nravstvennye vozzreniia*, Moscow 1995.

Kuznitskii, S., "Agronomiia i krest'ianskoe khoziaistvo," *Agronom*, 1924, nos. 2–3.

Kviatkovskii, A., "Zernosushilki", in *Sel'sko-khoziaistvennaia zhizn'*, 1912/13, no. 1.

L. B., "Iz tekushchei zemskoi agronomicheskoi deiatel'nosti," *VSKh*, 1916, no. 8.

Lachinov, General-Maior, "Otchet chlena-korrespondenta Imperatorskogo Vol'nogo Ekonomicheskogo Obshchestva, General-Maior Lachinova, s 1841 goda po 1856 god, to est', za 15 let," *TVEO*, 1857, vol. 3, vyp. 1.

Lavrent'ev, S., "Ob uborke khleba i v chastnosti ob uborke ego v syruiu pogodu," *Zemledel'cheskaia gazeta*, 1886 no. 43.

Lebedev, Iu. V., comp., *Derevenskie letopisi*, Moscow 1990.

——, comp., *Krest'ianskie sud'by. Raskazy russkikh pisatelei vtoroi poloviny XIX veka*, Moscow 1986.

——, comp., *Pis'ma iz derevni. Ocherki o krest'ianstve v Rossii vtoroi poloviny XIX veka*, Moscow 1987.

Levashev, I., "Sovremennoe sostoianie krest'ianskogo konevodstva v Tambovskoi gubernii," *Sel'skoe Khoziaistvo i Lesovodstvo*, 1896, no. 11.

Levitov, A. I., *Stepnye ocherki*, Moscow 1874.

Lewin, Moshe, "The *Obshchina* and the Village", in Roger Bartlett, ed., *Land commune and peasant community in Russia: communal forms in Imperial and early Soviet society*, London 1990.

Lindeman, K., "Chrezzernitsa," *Vestnik Russkogo Sel'skogo Khoziaistva*, 1889, no. 5.

Lintvarev, G. M., "Doklad G. M. Lintvareva o nuzhdakh sel'sko-khoziaistvennoi promyshlennosti," in *TMK*, Khar'kov.

Lipetskii zemlevladelets, "Iz Lipetskogo uezda, Tambovskoi gubernii," *Zemstvo*, 1881, no. 39.

Listova, T. A., "Traditsii trudovogo vospitaniia v derevne," in *Russkie. Istoriko-etnograficheskie ocherki*, Moscow 1997.

Lockheed, M. E., D. T. Jamison, and L. J. Lau, "Farmers, Education, and Farm Efficiency: A Survey," *Economic Development and Cultural Change*, 1980.

Loury, Glenn C., "Incentive Effects of Affirmative Action," *Annals of American Academic Political and Social Science*, 523, September 1992.

Luchebul', M., "Ozhivaiushchee delo," *Agronom*, 1924, nos. 2–3.

Luginin, S., "Volostnye sudy," *Russkii Vestnik*, March 1864.

Lukin, A. S., "K voprosu vvedeniia sevooborotov v zemel'nykh obshchestvakh," *Agronom*, 1927, no. 4.

L'vov, G. E., *Vospominaniia*, Moscow 1998.

Lyons, Amelia, *Among the Gentry*, Nottingham 1998.

Macey, David A. J., *Government and Peasant in Russia, 1861–1906: the prehistory of the Stolypin reforms*, Dekalb, Ill. 1987.

Maksimov, A., "Narodnye sredstva bor'by s epidemiiami," in *Russkie Vedemosti*, April 5th, 1911.

Mal'nev, I., "Rezul'taty vol'nonaemnogo truda v Borisoglebskom uezde v 1864 godu," *TVEO*, 1865, vol. 3, vyp. 1.

Manzhin, V., "Kormlenie loshadei v neurozhainye gody'," *Novaia derevnia*, 1921, no. 1.

Maress, L. N., "Proizvodstvo i potreblenie khleba v krest'ianskom khoziaistve," in A. I. Chuprov and A. S. Posnikov, eds., *Vliianie urozhaev i khlebnykh tsen na nekotorye storony russkogo narodnogo khoziaistva*, vol. 1, St. Petersburg 1897.

Masal'skii, V. I., *Iavleniia progressa v sovremennom krest'ianskom khoziaistve*, n.p. n.d. (1908).

Mashkin, A., "Byt krest'ian Kurskoi gubernii Oboianskogo uezda," *Etnograficheskii sbornik*. Vyp. 5., St. Petersburg 1862.

Maslov, P., "Nuzhna li krest'ianskoi zhenshchine gramota," *Vestnik Novouzenskogo Zemstva*, 1912, no. 3.

——, "O semenakh i podgotovke semian k posevu," *Vestnik Novouzenskogo Zemstva*, 1912, nos. 3, 5.

Maslov, S., *Mirskoi chelovek. Iz zhizni sovremennoi krest'ianskoi intelligentsii.*, Moscow 1916.

Maslov, S. L., *Plugi i drugie uluchshennye orudiia v krest'ianskom khoziaistve Kazanskoi gubernii*, Kazan 1905.

Maslov, Sem., "Nashe sel'skoe khoziaistvo i voina," *VSKh*, 1916, no. 2.

Materialy dlia otsenki zemel' Saratovskoi gubernii.

Vyp. 3. Sevooboroty i sistemy polevodstva. Chast' I, krest'ianskoe khoziaistvo. Saratov 1906.

Vyp. 4. Raspredelenie polevykh kul'tur. Chast' I, Krest'ianskoe khoziaistvo. Saratov 1904.

Vyp. 5. Tekhnika polevodstva. Chast' I. Krestianskoe khoziaistvo. Saratov 1904.

Materialy dlia otsenki zemel' Tul'skoi gubernii. Opyt issledovaniia vzaimootnosheniia elementov krest'ianskogo khoziaistva. T. 1, vyp. 2. Novosil'skii uezd, Tula 1914.

Materialy po podvornomu obsledovaniiu zhivotnovodstva Tambovskoi gubernii v 1912 g., 2 vols., Tambov 1914. Tambov provincial zemstvo publication.

Materialy po podvornomu obsledovaniiu zhivotnovodstva Tambovskoi gubernii v 1912 godu. Kozlovskii uezd, Tambov 1913.

Materialy po raionnomu kachestvennomu obsledovaniiu zhivotnovodstva Tambovskoi gubernii v 1912 godu, 2 vols., Tambov 1915. Tambov provincial zemstvo publication.

Materialy Vysochaishe uchrezhdennoi 16 noiabria 1901 g. komissii po izsledovaniiu voprosa o dvizhenii s 1861 g. po 1900 g. blagosostoianiia sel'skogo naseleniia sredne-zemledel'cheskikh gubernii, sravnitel'no s drugimi mestnostiami Evropeiskoi Rossii. 3 vols., St. Petersburg 1903.

Matossian, Mary, "Climate, Crops, and Natural Increase in Rural Russia, 1861–1913," *Slavic Review*, vol. 45, no. 3 (Summer 1986).

Matseevich, K. A., "K voprosu o zemskoi agronomicheskoi organizatsii v Saratovskoi gubernii," in *Zhurnaly Ekonomicheskogo Soveta Saratovskogo Gubernskogo Zemstva*, Saratov 1903.

——, "K voprosu ob ocherednykh zadachakh obshchestvennoi agronomii," in *Trudy pervogo Vserossiiskogo sel'sko-khoziaistvennogo s"ezda v Kieve.*

Matsuzato, Kimitaka, "The Fate of Agronomists in Russia: Their Quantitative Dynamics From 1911 to 1916," *Russian Review*, 1996, no. 2.

Matveev, S., "V volostnykh starshinakh," *Russkoe Bogatstvo*, 1912, no. 2.

McCloskey, Donald. "The Persistence of English Common Fields." in William N. Parker and Eric L. Jones, eds., *European Peasants and Their Markets. Essays in Agrarian History.*, Princeton 1975.

Medvedev, B., "Kursy sel'sko-khoziaistvennogo mashinostroeniia v Saratove," *SKhVIuV*, 1912, no. 19.

Meien, V. F., *Rossiia v dorozhnom otnoshenii*, vol. 2, St. Petersburg 1902.

Meisi (Macey), D., "Zemel'naia reforma i politicheskie peremeny: fenomen Stolypina," *Voprosy istorii*, 1993, no. 4.

Meister, G. K., ed., *Svodka rezul'tatov issledovanii 1924 g. sortovogo sostava iarovoi pshenitsy, prosa i podsolnechnika v Saratovskoi gubernii*, Saratov 1927.

Merinov, P., "K voprosu ob uluchshenii senokosov," *SKhZh*, 1912/13, no. 18.

Mertvyi, A. P., *Sel'skokhoziaistvennye vospominaniia (1879–1893 gg.)*, St. Petersburg n. d.

Meshcherskii, A. P., "Pervaia stupen'. (Pis'mo iz derevni)." *Russkii Vestnik*, 1895, no. 7.

Mestnyi agronomicheskii personal sostoiavshii na pravitel'stvennoi i obshchestvennoi sluzhbe 1 ianvaria... g. Spravochnik., St. Petersburg 1912, Petrograd 1914.

Mezentsov, V. I., "Doklad V. I. Mezentsova po punktu M," *TMK*, Khar'kov.

Miasoedov, G., "Nastavlenie o tom, kak osmatrivat' pri pokupke loshad' i vvodit' ee v khoziaistvo," *Zhurnal Ministerstvo Gosudarstvennykh Imushchestv*, 1846, Smes'.

Michael, Louis Guy, "My Russian Experience, 1910–1917," unpublished manuscript, Hoover Institution Archive.

Mikhel'son, V., "O sredstvakh k uluchsheniiu skotovodstva v zapadnykh guberniiakh srednei polosy Rossii," *Zhurnal Ministerstva Gosudarstvennykh Imushchestv,* St. Petersburg 1846, otdel II.

Miklashevskii, V., "Soznatel'nyi vybor krest'ianskogo pluga," *Vestnik Orlovskogo Obshchestva Sel'skogo Khoziaistva,* 1914, no. 11.

Miliukov, Paul, *Russia and its Crisis,* Chicago 1906.

Miller, A., "Novouzenskoe zemstvo i obshchestvennaia agronomiia," *Zemskii agronom,* 1913, no. 3.

Miller, Alice, *For Your Own Good: Hidden Cruelty in Child-Rearing and the Roots of Violence,* translated by Hildegard and Hunter Hannun, New York 1983.

Milov, L. V., *Velikorusskii pakhar' i osobennosti rossiiskogo istoricheskogo protsessa,* Moscow 1998.

Milovskii, V., "O poseve khlebov," in *Sel'sko-khoziaistvennyi listok,* 1914, no. 4.

Minin, A. N., "Agronomiia i zemleustroistvo v ikh otnoshenii k derevenskoi bednote," in *Trudy pervogo Vserossiiskogo sel'sko-khoziaistvennogo s"ezda v Kieve.*

——, "Odno iz reshenii konflikta: agronomiia—kooperatsiia," *VSKh,* 1916, no. 1.

——, "Sel'skoe khoziaistvo", in *Voronezhskii krai.*

——, "Zemlepol'zovanie i zemleustroistvo," in *Voronezhskii krai.*

Minkh, A. N., "Kolenskaia volost'," in *Saratovskii sbornik. Materialy dlia izucheniia Saratovskoi gubernii. T. 1.,* Saratov 1881, otdel 1.

Mironov, B. N., *Khlebnye tseny v Rossii za dva stoletiia (XVIII–XIX vv.),* Moscow 1985.

——, "The Peasant Commune after the Reforms of the 1860s," in Eklof and Frank, *The World of the Russian Peasant.*

——, "Semia: Nuzhno li ogliadyvat'sia v proshloe?," in A. G. Vishnevskii, ed., *V chelovecheskom izmerenii,* Moscow 1989.

——, *Sotsial'naia istoriia Rossii (XVIII–nachalo XX v.),* 2 vols., St. Petersburg 1999.

Mitchell, B. R., *European Historical Statistics, 1750–1970,* New York 1978.

Molleson, I. I., *Kratkii ocherk zabolevaemosti i smertnosti naseleniia Tambovskoi gubernii v trekhletie 1898, 1899 i 1900 g.g.,* Tambov 1904.

Monin, S., "S miakotnykh zemel' Voronezhskogo uezda. Rezul'taty poseva rzhi shampanskoi, ivanovskoi, i prosto-mestnoi," *ZG,* 1886, no. 47.

Moon, David, *The Russian Peasantry, 1600–1930. The World the Peasants Made,* London 1999.

Morachevskii, V. V., ed., *Agronomicheskaia pomoshch' v Rossii,* Petrograd 1914.

——, ed., *Spravochnik po sel'sko-khoziaistvennoi periodicheskoi pechati na 1915 g.,* Petrograd 1915.

Morozov, P., "Otchet po selu Pantsyrevke, izbrannomu Penszenskim obshchestvom sel'skogo khoziaistva mestom dlia opytov raznogo roda, za 1851 god," *ZhMGI,* 1852, no. 8.

Morozov, S. D., "Demograficheskoe povedenie sel'skogo naseleniia evropeiskoi Rossii (konets XIX–nacalo XX v.)," *Sotsiologicheskie issledovaniia,* 1999, no. 8.

Morshanskoe uezdnoe zemstvo, *Otchety uchastkovykh agronomov za 1911 god,* Morshansk 1912.

Moshkov, V. A., "Gagauzy Benderskogo uezda," in *Etnograficheskoe obozrenie,* 1902, no. 4.

Mosolov, P., "Pis'ma zemleustroitel'ia," *Shatskoe Khoziaistvo,* 1914, nos. 4, 5.

M-ov, S., "Melkii kredit i zemstvo," *VSKh,* 1914, no. 9.

Mozzhukhin, I. V., *Zemleustroistvo v Bogoroditskom uezde Tul'skoi gubernii,* Moscow 1917.

Muizhel, V. V., *Khutor No. 16 i drugie rasskazy,* Petrograd 1916.

Murav'ev, A., "Shkol'noe obrazovanie," *Izvestiia Kostromskogo gubernskogo zemstva*, 1915, no. 6.

N. B., "Bol'noi vopros", *SKhZh*, 1914, no. 13.

N. M., "Besedy o krest'ianskom khoziaistve", *SKhZh*, 1914, nos. 10–11.

———, "Ob"edinenie kooperativov," *SKhZh*, 1912/13, nos. 17, 18.

Naidich, D. V., "Orudiia i sposoby molotby i veianiia," in P. I. Kushner ed., *Russkie. Istoriko-etnograficheskii atlas.*, Moscow 1967.

———, "Pakhotnye i razrykhliaiushchie orudiia," in P. I. Kushner ed., *Russkie. Istoriko-etnograficheskii atlas.*, Moscow 1967.

Nair, Kusum, *The Lonely Furrow: Farming in the United States, Japan and India*, Ann Arbor (Michigan) 1969.

Narodnyi komissariat zemledeliia RSFSR, *Stenograficheskii otchet II-ogo Vserossiiskogo agronomicheskogo s"ezda 27 ianvaria–5 fevralia 1929 g.*, Moscow 1929.

Nebol'sin, P. I., *Okolo muzhichkov*, St. Petersburg 1862.

Nefedov, N. F., "Ivan voin," in Lebedev, *Krest'ianskie sud'by*.

Neruchev, M., "Istochniki sel'skokhoziaistvennogo znaniia v narode," *Severnyi Vestnik*, 1886, no. 12.

Nemirovich-Danchenko, V. I., *With a Diploma*, translated by W. J. Stanton Pyper, London 1915.

Neustupov, A. D., "Verovaniia krest'ian Shapshenskoi volosti, Kadnikovskogo uezda," *Etnograficheskoe obozrenie*, 1902, no. 4.

Neverov, A. S., *Sobranie sochinenii v chetyrekh tomakh*, Kuibyshev 1957.

Nikolaev, I. V., "O iaichnoi torgovli i predpolozheniiakh k ee razvitiiu," in *Zhurnal soveshchaniia zemskikh agronomov pri Tambovskoi gubernskoi zemskoi uprave, 5–8 marta 1911 g.*

Nikonov, F., "Byt i khoziaistvo malorossov v Voronezhskoi gubernii," *TVEO*, 1864, vol. 3, vyp. 3,5.

———, "Byt i nravy poselian-velikorussov Pavlovskogo uezda, Voronezhskoi gubernii," *TVEO*, 1861, vol. 4, vyp. 1.

Noarov, V. "Krest'ianskie biudzhety Tambovskoi gubernii v 1923–1924 gody," *Biulleten' Tambovskogo gubernskogo statisticheskogo biuro*, 1926, no. 8.

Nol'dshtein, R. G., "Chto dokazyvaet 'Opyt ekonomicheskoi otsenki' A. N. Minina," *Agronom* 1924, nos. 2–3.

Novikov, A. I., *Zapiski zemskogo nachal'nika*, St. Petersburg 1899.

Novikov, Iu. F., "O nekotorykh zakonomernostiakh razvitiia tekhniki obrabotki pochvy v Rossii", in *Materialy po istorii sel'skogo khoziaistva i krest'ianstva SSSR, sb. 5*, Moscow 1962.

Novyi entsiklopedicheskii slovar' (Brokgauz—Efron), St. Petersburg 1910–1914.

Obelkevich, James, *Religion and Rural Society: South Lindsey 1825–1875*, Oxford 1976.

Obolenskii, V., "Ocherki khutorskoi Rossii. Staroe i novoe v zhizni derevni Nikolaevsk-ogo uezda Samarskoi gubernii," *Russkaia Mysl'*, 1913 no. 2, otdel II.

Ocherk ekonomicheskoi zhizni krest'ianskogo naseleniia Starobel'skogo uezda i prichin ego zadolzhennosti 1849–1893 gg. Khar'kov 1893.

Odinokov, M. F., "Kindiakovskaia ekonomiia E. M. Persi-French," in GUZiZ, Departament Zemledeliia. *1912. Ezhegodnik.*, St. Petersburg 1913.

Oganovskii, N. P., *Agrarnaia evoliutsiia Rossii posle 1905 g.*, Petrograd 1918.

———, ed., *Sel'skoe khoziaistvo Rossii v XX veke*, Petrograd 1923.

———, "Sovremennyi agrarnyi vopros i kooperativy," in *Biblioteka "Kooperativnoi Zhizni": Pervyi sbornik statei*, Moscow 1914.

———, "Tambovskaia guberniia," *Entsiklopedicheskii slovar'* (Granat).

Oganovskii, N. P., "Zemleustroistvo," in *Novyi Entsiklopedicheskii Slovar'*, vol. 18.

Ogloblin, N. N., "Razval. (Iz provintsial'nykh nastroenii)." *Istoricheskii Vestnik*, 1913, no. 4.

Oldenburg, S.S., *The Last Tsar: Nicholas II, his Reign, and his Russia*, Transl. Leonid I. Mihalap and Patrick J. Rollins. Lake Breeze, Fla. 1975.

——, *Tsarstvovanie Nikolaia II-ogo*, Moscow 1992.

Oleinik, I., "K voprosu o programmakh i itogakh obshchestvenno-agronomicheskoi raboty," *VSKh*, 1916, no. 21.

Olishev, Aleksei, "Opisanie godovoi krest'ianskoi raboty v Vologodskom uezde, s primechaniiami," *TVEO*, 1766, ch. 2.

Olson, David R., *The World on Paper: The Conceptual and Cognitive Implications of Writing and Reading*, Cambridge 1994.

Ong, Walter J., *Orality and Literacy*, London 1982.

Opyt sel'skokhoziaistvennogo obzora Saratovskoi gubernii za 1886 g., Saratov 1886.

Orlova, V. D., "Religioznyi faktor demograficheskogo povedeniia krest'ian Tambovskoi gubernii v XIX—nachale XX v.," in L. V. Milov ed., *Osobennosti Rossiiskogo zemledeliia i problemy rasseleniia IX—XX vv.*, Moscow 1998.

Orlovskaia guberniia v sel'sko-khoziaistvennom otnoshenii 1890 g., Orel 1890.

Ortiz, Sutti, "Reflections on the Concept of 'Peasant Culture' and 'Peasant Cognitive Systems'," in Shanin, ed., *Peasants and Peasant Societies*.

O'Rurk, L., "O skotovodstve v sele Khokhlovke, Kurskoi gubernii," *TVEO*, 1872, vol. 1, vyp. 1.

Osennye sel'sko-khoziaistvennye raboty v edinoi trudovoi shkoly, Moscow 1919.

Osipov, N. O., "Kak ia khodil v narod," in *Istoricheskii Vestnik*, February 1899.

Otchet o deiatel'nosti agronomicheskogo personala za 1912 sel'sko-khoziaistvennyi god, Tambov 1912. Tambov uezd zemstvo publication.

Otchet o deiatel'nosti pravitel'stvennoi agronomicheskoi organizatsii v Orlovskoi gubernii za 1912 god, Orel 1912.

Otchet ob agronomicheskoi deiatel'nosti, Tambov 1910. Tambov uezd zemstvo publication.

Otchet Tambovskoi gubernskoi zemskoi upravy Tambovskomu gubernskomu zemskomu sobraniiu ocherednoi sessii 1912 goda. Otnositel'no agronomicheskoi deiatel'nosti uezdnykh zemstv Tambovskoi gubernii za 1912 god, Tambov 1913.

Otchety uchastkovykh agronomov i instruktorov Morshanskogo zemstva za 1913 god, Morshansk 1915.

Otchety uchastkovykh agronomv za 1914 god, Borisoglebsk 1915. Borisoglebsk uezd zemstvo publication.

Ovchinnikov, M., "O lentochnom poseve prosa," *SKhZh*, 1912/13, no. 6.

Overton, Mark and Bruce M. S. Campbell, "Productivity Change in European Agricultural Development," in Campbell and Overton, *Land Labor, and Livestock*.

P. "Pervyi vserossiiskii Sel'sko-Khoziaistvennyi s"ezd v g. Kieve," in *SKhVIuV*, 1913, no. 19.

P. D., *Russkii sotsializm i obshchinnoe zemlevladenie*, Moscow 1893.

P. L., "O molot'be khlebov katkami," *SKhZh*, 1914, no.12.

Paduchev, P., "Iz Kozlova, Tambovskoi gubernii", *Vestnik Russkogo Sel'skogo Khoziaistva*, 1889, no. 21.

Pallot, Judith, "Agrarian Modernization on Peasant Farms in the Era of Capitalism," in Bater and French, eds., *Studies in Russian Historical Geography*, London 1983, vol. 2.

Pallot, Judith, "The Development of Russian Peasant Landholding, 1861–1917," in Bater and French, eds., *Studies in Russian Historical Geography*, vol. 1.

———, "Khutora and Otruba in Stolypin's Program of Farm Individualization," *Slavic Review*, no. 43, Summer 1984.

———, *Land Reform in Russia, 1906–1917. Peasant Responses to Stolypin's Project of Rural Transformation*. Oxford 1999.

———, "The Stolypin Land Reform," in Pallot and Shaw, *Landscape and Settlement*.

———, and Dennis J. B. Shaw. *Landscape and Settlement in Romanov Russia, 1613–1917*. Oxford 1990.

Pares, Bernard, *My Russian Memoirs*, London 1931.

———, *Russia Between Reform and Revolution*, ed. by Francis B. Randall, New York 1962.

Pasvoldsky, Leo, and Harold G. Moulton, *Russian Debts and Russian Reconstruction. A Study of the Relation of Russia's Foreign Debt to Her Economic Recovery.*, New York–London 1924.

Pavlov, N. A., *Zapiski zemlevladel'tsa*, Petrograd 1915.

Pavlovsky, George, *Agricultural Russia on the Eve of the Revolution*, New Haven 1930.

Pelevin, A. N., "Pol'za sortirovaniia semian," *Izvestiia Kostromskogo gubernskogo zemstva*, 1915, no. 3.

———, "Sortirovanie semian i ego pol'za," *Izvestiia Kostromskogo Gubernskogo Zemstva*, 1915, no. 6.

Pel'tsikh, L. A., *Propashnoi klin. Gibel' trekhpolki*. Kirsanov 1926.

———, *Trekhpolka ili mnogopol'e?* Tambov n. d. (1927?).

Peremeny v zemledel'cheskoi tekhnike krest'ian Nizhegorodskoi gubernii, Nizhnyi Novgorod 1893.

Perkins, J. A., "The Agricultural Revolution in Germany, 1850–1914," *Journal of European Economic History*, 1981, no. 1.

Pershin, P. N., *Uchastkovoe zemlepol'zovanie v Rossii. Khutora i otruba, ikh rasprostranenie za desiatiletie 1907–1916 gg. i sud'by vo vremia revoliutsii (1917–1920 gg.)*, Moscow 1922.

———, *Zemel'noe ustroistvo dorevoliutsionnoi derevni. T. 1, Tsentral'no-promyshlennyi, Tsentral'no-chernozemnyi i Severo-zapadnyi*, Moscow 1928.

———, *Zemleustroistvo i agronomiia*, Moscow 1923.

Persidskii, I., "Razdelenie truda v krest'ianskom khoziaistve Riazanskoi gubernii," in *Ekonomicheskii obzor Riazanskoi gubernii. 1911 god. No. 1*, Riazan 1911.

Pervaia vseobshchaia perepis' naseleniia Rossiiskoi Imperii, 1897 g. vol. 42 Tambovskaia guberniia. St. Petersburg 1904.

Pestrzhetskii, I. L., "O nedugakh khoziaistva i stroia zhizni sel'skikh obyvatelei," *TVEO*, 1894, no. 6.

Petrov, A., "Zametki i nabliudeniia sel'skogo khoziaina," *Vestnik Russkogo Sel'skogo Khoziaistva*, 1890, no. 3.

Pisemskii, A. F., *Sobranie sochinenii v deviati tomakh*, vol. 2, Moscow 1959.

Podgorskii, B., "Na pashne," *Staroe i Novoe*, 1931, no. 1.

Pod"iachev, S. P., *Zhizn' muzhitskaia*, Berlin 1923.

———, *Moia zhizn'*, Moscow-Leningrad 1930.

Podvornoe i khutorskoe khoziaistvo v Samarskoi gubernii, Samara 1909

Podvornoe obsledovanie zhivotnovodstva Tambovskoi gubernii v 1912 godu, Tambov 1914. Tambov provincial zemstvo publication.

Pogozhev, A. V., *Uchet chislennosti i sostava rabochikh v Rossii. Materialy po statistike truda*. St. Petersburg 1906.

Pokrovskii, I. S., "Doklad I. S. Pokrovskogo o nekotorykh meropriiatiiakh, napravlennykh k podniatiiu sel'skokhoziaistvennoi promyshlennosti v Simbirskom uezde," in *TMK*, Simbirsk.

Pokshishevskii, V. V., *Tsentral'no-Chernozemnaia Oblast'*, Moscow-Leningrad 1929.

Polevoe khoziaistvo Penzenskoi gubernii, Penza 1928.

Polnaia entsiklopediia Russkogo sel'skogo khoziaistva i soprikasaiushikhsia s nim nauk. 12 vols., St. Petersburg 1900–1912.

Pomp, Marc, and Kees Burger, "Innovation and Imitation: Adoption of Cocoa by Indonesian Smallholders," *World Development* 1995, vol. 23, no. 3.

Ponomarev, N. V., "Uluchsheniia v krest'ianskom sel'skom khoziaistve," in *TVEO*, 1894, no. 6.

Popkin, Samuel, *The Rational Peasant*, Berkeley 1979.

Posashev, F., "Ob obrabotke zemli sokhoi i plugom," *ZG*, 1886 no. 5.

——, "Razvedenie probshteiskoi i shampanskoi rzhi," *ZG*, 1886, no. 33.

——, "Sel'skoe khoziaistvo v Eletskom i Dankovskom uezdakh," *TVEO*, 1874, vol. 2, vyp. 1.

Posnikov, A., *Obshchinnoe zemlevladenie* vyp. 2, 2nd ed., Odessa 1876.

Postan, M. M., ed., *The Cambridge Economic History of Europe*, vol. 1, 2nd ed., Cambridge 1966.

Postnikov, V. E., *Iuzhno-russkoe krest'ianskoe khoziaistvo*, Moscow 1891.

Potekhin, A. A., "Krest'ianskie deti," in Lebedev, *Krest'ianskie sud'by*.

Pouezdnye itogi Vserossiiskoi sel'sko-khoziaistvennoi i pozemel'noi perepisi 1917 goda, Moscow 1923.

Pravikovskii, V. S., "O pokupke novykh sortov semian," *Sel'sko-khoziaistvennyi vestnik*, 1914, no. 1.

Preobrazhenskii, V., *Opisanie Tverskoi gubernii v sel'sko-khoziaistvennom otnoshenii*, St. Petersburg 1854.

Pridorogin, M. I., "Zakliuchenie professora Moskovskogo sel'sko-khoziaistvennogo instituta M. I. Pridorogina po kachestvennomu obsledovaniiu zhivotnovodstva v Tambovskoi gubernii v 1913 g.," *ZhTGZS ocherednoi sessii 1913 goda*, Tambov 1914.

——, "Zhivotnovodstvo v Tambovskoi gubernii," *SKhZ*, 1914, no. 1.

Prishvin, M. M., *Dnevniki. 1914–1917.* Vol. 1, Moscow 1991.

——, *Sobranie sochinenii*, vol. 1, Moscow 1982.

Proekt obshchikh osnovanii otsenki zemel' i lesov Tambovskoi gubernii po zakonu 8-ogo iiunia 1893 goda. vol. 1 Zemlia pakhotnaia., Tambov 1906.

Proekty osnovnykh pravil i polozhenii reguliruiushchikh sel'sko-khoziaistvennuiu deiatel'nost' Borisoglebskogo uezdnogo zemstva Tambovskoi gubernii, Borisoglebsk 1913. Borisoglebsk uezd zemstvo publication.

Prokopovich, S. N., *Opyt ischisleniia narodnykh dokhodov po 50 guberniiam Evropeiskoi Rossii 1900–1913 g.*, Moscow 1918.

Prokudin-Gorskii, S. M.; Photographs for the Tsar: the pioneering color photography of Sergei Mikhailovich Prokudin-Gorskii commissioned by Tsar Nicholas II / edited with an introd. by Robert H. Allshouse. New York, Dial Press, 1980.

Protas'ev, E., "O poroke, svoistvennom krest'ianam i prepiatstvuiushchem uluchsheniiu ikh byta," *Zhurnal zemlevladel'tsev*, 1859, no. 9, section VI.

Pukalov, V. P., "Zapiska V. P. Pukalova o meropriiatiiakh, mogushchikh ostanovit' upadok sel'sko-khoziaistvennoi promyshlennosti v tsentral'nykh i vostochnykh guberniiakh," in *TMK*, Simbirsk.

Pupishskii, S., "K voprosu o rekonstruktsii sel'skogo khoziaistva cherez sel'skokhoziaistvennuiu kooperatsiiu," *Planovoe khoziaistvo*, 1928, no. 9.

Putintsev, A., "Iz etnograficheskikh vpechatlenii i nabliudenii (Korotoiakskii uezd Voronezhskoi gub.)," *Voronezhskii istoriko-arkheologicheskii vestnik*, 1921, no. 2.

Rall, A. F., "Doklad A. F. Rallia po voprosu o mery borby s sel'sko-khoziaistvennym krizisom," in *TMK*, Tambov.

Ransel, David, "Introduction," in Semyonova Tian-Shanskaia, *Village Life in Late Tsarist Russia*.

Rashin, A. G., *Naselenie Rossii za 100 let*, Moscow 1956.

Rasprostranennost' trakhomy v Kazanskoi gubernii, Kazan 1914.

Razmery posevnoi ploshchadi i urozhai khlebov i trav v Samarskoi gubernii v 1899 godu, Samara 1900.

Reshetnikov, F. M., "Tetushka Oparina," in Iu. V. Lebedev, *Krest'ianskie sud'by*.

Resultats generaux de la recolte de 1897 (and 1898, 1899, and 1900), St. Petersburg 1898 (1899, 1900, 1901).

Reynolds, Rothay, *My Russian Year*, London 1913.

Rezanova, E. I., "Derevnia Salomykova, Oboianskogo uezda, Kurskoi gubernii," in *Kurskii sbornik. Vyp. III. Materialy po etnografii Kurskoi gubernii*, Kursk 1902, chast' II.

Richards, Paul, *Indigenous Agricultural Revolution*, London 1985.

Ridley, "How Far From the Tree? Reconstructing our evolutionary history using modern genetic data," *New York Times Book Review*, August 20th, 2000.

Rittikh, A. A., *Zavisimost' krest'ian ot obshchiny i mira*, St. Petersburg 1903.

Rklitskii, M. V., *Iz proshlogo i nastoiashchego chernozemnoi derevni. Ekonomicheskie ocherki, stat'i i zametki.*, Poltava 1914.

Robbins jr., Richard G., *Famine in Russia, 1891–1892. The Imperial Government Responds to a Crisis.* New York 1975.

Robinson, Geroid T., *Rural Russia under the Old Regime*, New York 1932.

Rodionov, D., "Vol'nonaemnyi trud v sele Varko-Veshnaima, Simbirskoi gubernii, Karsunskogo uezda," *TVEO*, 1865 vol. 3, vyp. 3.

Rogger, Hans, *Russia in the Age of Modernization, 1881–1917* London and New York, 1983.

Rogoza, I. D., "Zaniatye pary v lesostepi," *KSE*, vol. 4.

Rolofs, E. A., *Mnogopol'e na chernozeme*, Tambov 1925.

Romanov, N., *Gruntovye dorogi Tambovskoi gubernii i ikh sovremennoe znachenie*, Tambov 1897.

——, *Selo Kamenka i Kamenskaia volost', Tambovskogo uezda*, Tambov 1886.

——, "Tambovskaia guberniia," in *ES*, vol. 64.

Romer, F. E., "Schastlivchik," *Vestnik Evropy*, 1884, nos. 9, 10.

Root, Hilton, *Peasants and King in Burgundy. Agrarian Foundations of French Absolutism*, Berkeley 1987.

Rossiia 1913 god. Statistiko-dokumental'nyi sbornik, St. Petersburg 1995.

Roth, H. L., *Agriculture and Peasantry of Eastern Russia*, London 1878.

Rudnev, Ia., "O sistemakh zemledeliia v zaorenburgskom krae. Pis'ma iz-za Orenburga." *TVEO*, 1869, vol. 1, vyp. 4.

Rusov, A. A., *Opisanie Chernigovskoi gubernii*, Chernigov 1898–1899.

Rybnikov, N., *Krest'ianskii rebenok*, Moscow 1930.

Ryndziunskii, P. G., "Gorodskie i vnegorodskie tsentry ekonomicheskoi zhizni sredne-zemledel'cheskoi polosy Evropeiskoi Rossii v kontse XIX v." in L. V. Cherepnin, ed., *Iz istorii ekonomicheskoi i obshchestvennoi zhizni Rossii*, Moscow 1976.

Ryshkov, A., "O molot'be," *TVEO*, 1857, vol. 4, vyp. 1.

S. D., "Po povodu konkursa odnokonnykh plugov, ustraivaemogo Shchigrovskim obshchestvom sel'skogo khoziaistva," *ZG*, 1884, no. 21.

Sabo, V. S., "Otchet o deiatel'nosti uchastkovykh agronomov za 1913–14 g.," *Shatskoe khoziaistvo*, 1914, nos. 15–16.

Saburova, L. M., "Sel'sko-khoziaistvennye postroiki dlia obrabotki i khraneniia zerna," in Kushner, *Russkie*.

Sadovnikov, Doctor, "Kratkii ocherk razvitiia zemskoi uchastkovoi meditsiny v Tambovskoi gubernii," in *SKhZh*, 1914, nos. 4–5.

Safonov, A., "Tema izbitaia, no eshche ne izzhitaia," *Agronom*, 1926, no. 5.

Sakharov, N. A., *Sel'sko-khoziaistvennye raiony Tambovskoi gubernii*, Tambov 1928.

Saltykov-Shchedrin, M. E., *Melochi zhizni*, Moscow 1955.

Samarin, Iu. F., *Sochineniia*, Vol. 2, Moscow 1878.

Savchenko, K., "Kakoi nam nuzhen uchastkovyi agronom?," *Agronom*, 1924, nos. 2–3.

Sazhin, Iu. E., "Boronovanie ozimykh posevov vesnoiu," *SKhZ*, 1912/13, no. 6.

Sazonov, G. P., *Voprosy khlebnoi promyshlennosti i torgovli, razrabotannye zemskimi uchrezhdeniiami*, St. Petersburg 1891.

Sboev, V. A., *O byte krest'ian v Kazanskoi gubernii*, Kazan 1856.

Sbornik ocherkov po voprosam ekonomiki i statistiki Tambovskoi gubernii. vyp.1, Tambov 1922.

Sbornik statisticheskikh svedenii po Oboianskomu uezdu (Kurskoi gubernii), Moscow 1883.

Sbornik statisticheskikh svedenii po Samarskoi gubernii.

Vol. 2, Stavropol'skii uezd, Samara 1884.

Vol. 5, Bugul'minskii uezd, Samara 1887.

Vol. 6, Nikolaevskii uezd, Samara 1885.

Sbornik statisticheskikh svedenii po Tambovskoi gubernii, 24 vols., Tambov 1880–1896.

Vol. 1, Borisoglebskii uezd, Tambov 1880.

Vol. 2, Kozlovskii uezd, Tambov 1881.

Vol. 3, Morshanskii uezd, Tambov 1882.

Vol. 4, Temnikovskii uezd, Tambov 1883.

Vol. 5, Spasskii uezd, Tambov 1883.

Vol. 6, Shatskii uezd, Tambov 1884.

Vol. 7, Elatomskii uezd, Tambov 1884.

Vol. 8, Lipetskii uezd, Tambov 1885.

Vol. 9, Usmanskii uezd, Tambov 1885.

Vol. 10, Kirsanovskii uezd, Tambov 1886.

Vol. 11, Lebedianskii, uezd, Tambov 1886.

Vol. 12, Tambovskii uezd, Tambov 1886.

Vol. 14, Kratkii svod dannykh o krest'ianskom naselenii, zemlevladenii i khoziaistve po vsei gubernii, Tambov 1890.

Vol. 16, Chastnoe zemlevladenie Kirsanovskogo uezda, Tambov 1891.

Sbornik statistichesko-ekonomicheskikh svedenii po sel'skomu khoziaistvu Rossii i inostranykh gosudarstv. God piatyi., St. Petersburg 1912 (and *God desiatyi*, Petrograd 1917).

Sbornik svedenii po Evropeiskoi Rossii za 1882 god, St. Petersburg 1884.

Scitovsky, Tibor, "My Own Criticism of *The Joyless Economy*," *Critical Review*, vol. 10, no. 4 (Fall 1996).

Scott, James C., *The Moral Economy of the Peasant*, New Haven 1976.

——, *Seeing Like a State*, New Haven 1998.

Scribner, Sylvia, and Michael Cole, "Cognitive Consequences of Formal and Informal Education," *Science*, November 9th, 1983.

Selivanov, N., *Obshchinniki*, Samara 1918.

Selivanov, V. V., "God russkogo zemledel'tsa. (Zaraiskii uezd, Riazanskoi gubernii)." in Lebedev, *Pis'ma iz derevni*.

Sel'skokhoziaistvennye statisticheskie svedeniia po materialam, poluchennym ot khoziaev.

Vyp. 1. *O kolichestve semian ... pri poseve ... , o tom, chto nazyvaetsia srednim i khoroshim urozhaem ..., o vremeni zhatve ....*, St.Petersburg 1884.

Vyp. 7. *Vozdelyvanie kartofelia v Evropeiskoi Rossii*, St. Petersburg 1897.

Vyp. 8. *Gustota poseva polevykh rastenii v Rossii*, St. Petersburg, 1898.

Vyp. 11. *Primenenie i rasprostranenie v Rossii sel'skokhoziaistvennykh mashin i orudii*, St. Petersburg 1903.

Vyp. 12. *Sostoianie travoseianiia v Rossii*, St. Petersburg 1905.

Sel'sko-khoziaistvennye mashiny i orudiia v Evropeiskoi i Aziatskoi Rossii v 1910 godu, St.Petersburg 1913.

Sel'sko-khoziaistvennyi obzor Nizhegorodskoi gubernii za 1894, Nizhnyi-Novgorod 1895.

Sel'sko-khoziaistvennyi obzor Samarskoi gubernii za 1898–1899 god. Vyp. 1, Samara 1899.

Sel'sko-khoziaistvennyi obzor Vologodskoi gubernii. 1905–1906 sel'sko-khoziaistvennyi god. Vyp. 2, Vologda 1907.

Sel'sko-khoziaistvennyi promysel v Rossii, St. Petersburg 1914.

Semenov, D. P., "Promysly i zaniatiia naseleniia", in V. P. Semenov-Tian-Shanskii, ed., *Rossiia, vol. 2*.

Semenov, M. S., "Vo khmeliu. (Iz zhizni sovremennoi derevni)." *Istoricheskii Vestnik*, 1913, no. 8.

Semenov, S. T., *Dvadtsat' piat' let v derevne*, Petrograd 1915.

Semenov-Tian-Shanskii, V. P., ed. *Rossiia. Polnoe geograficheskoe opisanie nashego otechestva, vol. 2 Sredno-russkaia chernozemnaia oblast'*. St. Petersburg 1902.

——, ed. *Rossiia. Polnoe geograficheskoe opisanie nashego otechestva. Vol. 9 Verkhnee Podneprov'e i Belorussiia*. St. Petersburg 1905.

Semenova Tian-Shanskaia, Ol'ga, (spelled Semyonova) *Village Life in Late Tsarist Russia*, Bloomington 1988.

Semushkin, V., "Kartofel, kak korm dlia skota", *SKhZh*, 1914, no. 3.

Sen, Amartya K., "Rational Fools: A Critique of the Behavioural Foundations of Economic Theory," in Frank Hahn and Martin Hollis, eds., *Philosophy and Economic Theory*, Oxford 1979.

——, "Rationality, Joy and Freedom," *Critical Review*, vol. 10, no. 4 (Fall 1996).

Serezhnikov, Vl., "Sel'sko-khoziaistvennyi krizis v Astrakhanskoi gubernii i ocherednye zadachi agronomii," *SKhVIuV*, 1912, no. 3.

Sev, F., "Sortirovka semian. Iz agronomicheskoi praktiki Nikolaevskogo uezda." *Samarskii zemledelets*, 1910/11, no. 3.

Shachtman, Tom, *The Inarticulate Society: Eloquence and Culture in America*, New York 1995.

Shanin, Teodor, *The Awkward Class. Political Sociology of Peasantry in a Developing Society: Russia 1910–1925*, Oxford 1972.

Shanin, Teodor, ed., *Peasants and Peasant Societies*, 1st ed., N.Y. 1971.

Sharkov, V. V., "Obrabotka krest'ianskoi pashni," *Sel'sko-khoziaistvennyi Vestnik*, 1914, no. 2.

Shaternikov, M. E., *Otchego v krest'ianskom khoziaistve semena plokhi i kak ikh uluchshit'*, Moscow 1912.

Shidlovskii, K. I., compiler, *Kratkii obzor glavneishikh ostrozaraznykh zabolevanii v 16-ti guberniiakh zemskoi Rossii za 1899–1902 gg.*, 4 vols., Moscow 1901–1904.

Shil'der-Shul'dner, E. A., *Krest'ianskie nadely i prichiny ikh maloi proizvoditel'nosti*, St. Petersburg 1907.

Shishkov, V. Ia., *Sobranie sochinenii v vos'mi tomakh*, Moscow 1960–1962.

Shlippenbakh, N., "Sredstvo protiv vymochki ozimei i o sodeistvii luchshemu urozhaiiu iarovykh khlebov," *Zemledel'cheskii Zhurnal*, 1832, no. 5.

Shorygin, D. M., "Chto govoriat korrespondenty tekushchei statistiki Moskovskogo uezda o deiatel'nosti agronomov," *VSKh*, 1916, no. 4.

———, "O polozhenii zemskikh sel'sko-khoziaistvennykh skladov i o merakh k uluchsheniiu postanovki dela v nikh," in *Zhurnaly soveshchaniia zemskikh agronomov* (March 1912).

Shostak, Vasilii, "Zamechaniia o sel'skom khoziaistve v Khersonskoi gubernii," *ZhMGI*, 1846 otdel IV.

Shustikov, A. A., *Plody dosuga*, Iaroslavl 1900.

Shuvaev, K. M., *Vymiranie i vozrozhdenie derevni. Selo Novo-Zhivotinnoe i derevnia Mokhovatka Voronezhskogo okruga Tsentral'no-Chernozemnoi oblasti.*, Moscow–Leningrad 1929.

Sigov, V. K., "Narodnyi kharakter i sud'ba Rossii v tvorchestve I. A. Bunina," in *I. A. Bunin i russkaia literatura XX veka.*

Simmel, Georg, *The Sociology of Georg Simmel*, London 1971.

Simonova, M. S., "Ekonomicheskie itogi Stolypinskoi agrarnoi politiki v tsentral'nochernozemnykh guberniiakh," *Istoricheskie zapiski*, vol. 63, 1958.

Skosyreva, A. N., "Khod sozrevaniia ozimoi rzhi na raznovremennogo podniatikh parakh—presnykh i udobrennykh," in *Vestnik opytnogo dela Ts. Ch. O. 1929*, Voronezh 1930.

Skrebitskii, A., comp., *Krest'ianskoe delo v tsarstvovanii Imperatora Aleksandra II. Materialy dlia istorii osvobozhdeniia krest'ian. Tom III. Gubernskie komitety, ikh deputaty, i redaktsionnye komissii v krest'ianskom dele.* Bonn 1865–66.

Slicher Van Bath, B. H., *The Agrarian History of Western Europe, A.D. 500–1850*, London 1963.

Slomka, Jan, *From Serfdom to Self-Government*, London 1942.

Smith, R.E.F., *Peasant Farming in Muscovy*, Cambridge 1977.

Smith, R.E.F., and David Christian, *Bread and Salt. A Social and Economic History of Food and Drink in Russia.* Cambridge 1984.

Snabzhenie krest'ianskogo naseleniia sel'sko-khoziaistvennymi mashinami i orudiiami, po materialam obsledovaniia NKRKI RSFSR, Moscow 1925.

Snezhkov, V., "Sel'skokhoziaistvennyi soiuz uezdnykh i gubernskikh zemstv," in *Zhurnaly Tambovskogo Gubernskogo Sobraniia chrezvychainnoi sessii 1911 goda.*

Sobichevskii, V., "Botva," *ES*, vol. 8.

———, "Vspashka," *ES*, vol.13.

Soimonov, M., "Kozlovskaia gorka," *ZG*, 1878, no. 6.

Sokolov, Iu. M, and E. V. Gofman, eds., *Tambovskii fol'klor*, Tambov 1941.

Sokolovskii, N., "Istoriia odnogo khoziaistva i Krest'ianskii Bank. Iz derevenskikh vpechatlenii," *Vestnik Evropy*, 1892, no. 1.

Sokolovskii, N. M., "V odnom iz zalokhust'ev. Ocherki i nabliudeniia." *Russkoe Bogatstvo*, 1895, no. 3.

Sokovnin, P., "Zemskaia khronika. Zemskaia agronomiia v Morshanskom uezde", in *ZG*, 1895, no. 46.

Solov'ev, I., "O krest'ianskikh pastbishchakh," *SKhVIuV*, 1913, no. 13.

———, "Sravnitel'naia urozhainost' i dokhodnost' na pokazatel'nykh i sosednykh poliakh v Atkarskom uezde za 1912 g.," *SKhVIuV*, 1913, no. 4.

———, "Urozhai glavneishikh khlebov na pokazatel'nykh poliakh Gubernskoi Zemleustroitel'noi Komissii v Atkarskom uezde v 1911 g.," *SKhVIuV*, 1911, no. 21.

Solov'ev, I. P., *Obzor agronomicheskoi pomoshchi v raionakh zemleustroistva Tambovskoi gubernii za 1914 god*, Tambov 1915.

Solov'ev, Ia. A., *Sel'sko-khoziaistvennaia statistika Smolenskoi gubernii*, Moscow 1855.

Solov'ev, K. N., *Rodnoe Selo. (Byt, nravy, obychai i pover'ia)*., n. p., 1907.

Solov'ev, M., "O polozhenii uchastkovogo agronoma v Tambovskoi gubernii," in *Zhurnaly soveshchaniia zemskikh agronomov* (August–September 1911).

Sontsov, I. I., "O nailuchshem vremeni kos'by i zhatvy khlebov," *Vestnik Russkogo Sel'skogo Khoziaistva*, 1893, no. 51.

"Soobrazheniia o nuzhdakh sel'sko-khoziaistvennoi promyshlennosti v Vilenskoi gubernii, sostavlennye sovetom Vilenskogo sel'sko-khoziaistvennogo obshchestva," in *TMK*, Vilna.

Sovetov, A., and V. Dokuchaev, eds., *Materialy po izucheniiu Russkikh pochv*, 2 vols., St. Petersburg 1885.

Sovetov, A. V., "Kratkii ocherk agronomicheskogo puteshestviia po nekotorym guberniiam tsentral'noi chernozemnoi polosy Rossii v techenie leta 1874 goda," *TVEO*, 1876, vol. 3, vyp. 4.

——, *O chernozemnoi polose Rossii. Iz putevykh zametok*, n.p., n.d.

——, "Sevooborot," in *ES*, vol. 63.

——, "Zhatva", *ES*, vol. 22.

Spiski naselennykh mest Tambovskoi gubernii. Vyp.4. Kozlovskii uezd, Tambov 1927.

Spisok lits sluzhashchikh po vedomstvu MVD, St. Petersburg 1907 (internal publication of Ministerstvo Vnutrennykh Del, held at Hoover Institution library).

Srednyi urozhai v Evropeiskoi Rossii za piatiletie 1883–1887 gg., St. Petersburg 1888.

Stakhovich, A. A., "Ob obshchei finansovoi politiki i ee vlianii na sel'sko-khoziaistvennuiu promyshlennost', in *TMK*, Orel.

Stakhovich, M., *Istoriia, etnografiia i statistika Eletskogo uezda*, Moscow 1858.

Statisticheskie dannye k otsenke zemel' Tambovskoi gubernii, po zakonu 8-ogo iiunia 1893 goda. 12 vols., Tambov 1898–1907.

vyp. 1, Lipetskii uezd, Tambov 1898.

vyp. 2, Shatskii uezd, Tambov 1899.

vyp. 3, Kozlovskii uezd, Tambov 1900.

vyp. 4, Lebedianskii uezd, Tambov 1901.

vyp. 5, Usmanskii uezd, Tambov 1901.

vyp. 6, Temnikovskii uezd, Tambov 1903.

vyp. 7, Borisoglebskii uezd, Tambov 1903.

vyp. 8, Elatomskii uezd, Tambov 1900.

vyp. 9, Kirsanovskii uezd, Tambov 1904.

vyp. 10, Tambovskii uezd, Tambov 1904.

vyp. 11, Spasskii uezd, Tambov 1903.

vyp. 12, Morshanskii uezd, Tambov 1907.

Statisticheskie svedeniia po zemel'nomu voprosu v Evropeiskoi Rossii, St. Petersburg 1906.

Statisticheskie tablitsy Rossiiskoi imperii. Vyp. 2. Nalichnoe naseleniia imperii za 1858 god. St. Petersburg 1863.

Statisticheskii ezhegodnik po Simbirskoi gubernii za 1911 god, Simbirsk 1913.

Statisticheskii ezhegodnik Rossii 1911 g., St. Petersburg 1912 (and the same title for 1912–14).

Statisticheskii ezhegodnik 1907 g., Khar'kov 1908.

Statisticheskii ezhegodnik 1908 g., Khar'kov 1909.

Statisticheskii spravochnik po Khar'kovskoi gubernii, Khar'kov 1911.

Statistika Rossiiskoi Imperii. T. IV. Srednyi urozhai v Evropeiskoi Rossii za piatiletie 1883–1887 gg., St. Petersburg 1888.

Statistika zemlevladeniia 1905 g., vyp.20, Tambovskaia guberniia, St. Petersburg 1906.

Stebelsky, I., "Agriculture and Soil Erosion in the European Forest-Steppe," in Bater and French, eds., *Studies in Russian Historical Geography*, vol. 1.

Steensberg, Axel, *Ancient Harvesting Implements*, Copenhagen 1943.

Stenograficheskii otchet 2-ogo Vserossiiskogo agronomicheskogo s"ezda. 27 ianvaria–5 fevralia 1929 g., Moscow 1929.

Stenograficheskii otchet 3-go Vserossiiskogo soveshchaniia zemorganov, 28 fevralia–7 marta 1926 g., Moscow 1926.

Stepanov, V., "Razvedenie zemlianiki i klubniki na priusadebnykh zemliakh," *SKhZ*, 1914, nos. 10–11.

Stepniak (S. M. Kravchinskii), *The Russian Peasantry. Their Agrarian Condition, Social Life, and Religion*, New York 1888.

Stoimost' proizvodstva glavneishikh khlebov. Vyp. 2. Statisticheskie svedeniia po materialam, poluchennym ot khoziaev, Petrograd 1916.

Stoliarov, I., *Zapiski russkogo krest'ianina*, Paris 1986.

Strakhov I., *Sel'sko-khoziaistvennaia arkhitektura*, Moscow 1900.

Strekalov, N., "Udobnyi perekhod iz trekhklinnogo polevodstva v plodosmennoe mnogopol'e," *ZG*, 1851, nos. 21–22.

Studenskii, G. A., *Intenzivnost' i psevdo-intenzivnost' v krest'ianskom sel'skom khoziaistve*, Samara 1927.

——, *Problemy organizatsii krest'ianskogo sel'skogo khoziaistva*, Samara 1927.

Sukhanov, N., *K voprosu o sel'sko-khoziaistvennoi evoliutsii Rossii*, Moscow 1923.

Sumtsov, N. F., *O tom, kakie sel'skie pover'ia i obychai v osobennosti vrednye*, Khar'kov 1901.

——, *Ocherki narodnogo byta (iz etnograficheskoi ekskursii 1901 g. po Akhtyrskomu uezdu Khar'kovskoi gubernii)*, Khar'kov 1902.

Sushchestvuiushchii poriadok vzimaniia okladnykh sborov s krest'ian za 1887–1893 gg. Vyp. 1., St. Petersburg 1894.

Svod statisticheskikh svedenii po sel'skomu khoziaistvu Rossii k kontsu XIX veka. 3 vols., St. Petersburg 1903–1906.

Svod urozhainykh svedenii za gody 1883–1915, Moscow 1928.

Tambovskii gubernskii komitet ob uluchshenii byta pomeshchich'ikh krest'ian, *Proekt polozheniia ob uluchshenii byta pomeshchich'ikh krest'ian v Tambovskoi gubernii*, n.p., n.d.

Tarachkov, A., *Putevye zametki po Orlovskoi i sosednim s neiu guberniiam*, Orel 1861.

Tarnovskii, G., "O pol'ze sveklosakharnykh zavodov v Rossii v vidakh uluchsheniia khlebopashestva," *Zhurnal sel'skogo khoziaistva i ovtsevodstva*, 1850, no. 1.

Teitel', A., *Agronomicheskaia pomoshch' naseleniiu na putiakh svoego razvitiia. Istoriko-metodologicheskii ocherk*, Moscow 1929.

——, "K voprosu o podgotovke deiatelei po obshchestvennoi agronomii," *Zemskii agronom*, 1913, no. 2.

Terpigorev, S. N., *Sobranie sochinenii S. N. Terpigoreva*, Vol. 1, St. Petersburg 1899.

Thomas, Keith, *Religion and the Decline of Magic*, New York 1971.

Titov, K. M., "Uchastkovyi agronom i rassloenie derevni," *Agronom*, 1927, no. 2.

Tiumenev, A., *Ot revoliutsii k revoliutsii*, Leningrad 1925.

Tkachenko, A. A., "Prostranstvennaia identifikatsiia sel'skikh zhitelei," in Z. V. Rubtsova, ed., *Derevnia tsentral'noi Rossii. Istoriia i sovremennost'*, Moscow 1993.

Toren, M. D., "Sposoby uborki khlebov", in P. I. Kushner, ed., *Russkie. Istoriko-et-nograficheskii atlas*, Moscow 1967.

Tolstoi, L. N., *Sobranie sochinenii v dvadtsati tomakh*, Moscow 1960–65.

Tret'iakov, S. F., "K voprosu ob izmeneniiakh pochvy pod vliianiem priemov ee kul'tury", in *Trudy 1-ogo Vserossiiskogo Sel'sko-khoziaistvennogo S"ezda*, vyp. 5, Kiev 1914.

Trifonov, A. A., *Ot trekhpol'ia k mnogopol'iu*, Orel 1924.

——, *Pochemu neobkhodimo podnimat' par rano?*, Moscow 1925.

——, *Pochemu neobkhodimo podnimat' par rano?*, Moscow 1929.

——, *Zaniatoi par v severo-chernozemnom khoziaistve*, Moscow 1924.

Troitskii, D. F., "Iz nabliudenii nad kul'turoi ozimykh khlebov," *SKhVIuV*, 1911, no. 3.

——, "O kul'ture maslichnogo podsolnechnika," *SKhVIuV*, 1911 no. 9.

Troitskii, P., "Selo Lipitsy i ego okrestnosti, Tul'skoi gubernii, Kashirskogo uezda," *Etnograficheskii sbornik. Vyp. 2*, St. Petersburg 1854.

Trostianskii, Ch. K., "Khoziaistvenno-statisticheskoe opisanie severo-vostochnoi chasti Morshanskogo uezda," in *Zapiski Lebedianskogo Obshchestva Sel'skogo Khoziaistva*, 1858, chast' 1, Moscow 1859.

Trotsky, Leon, *The Russian Revolution*, edited by F. W. Dupee, translated by Max Eastman, New York, 1959.

Trube, R. A., "Doklad R. A. Trube k voprosu ob uluchshenii formy krest'ianskogo polevogo khoziaistva chernozemnykh gubernii," in *TMK*, Khar'kov.

Trubetskoi, E., "Novaia zemskaia Rossiia. Iz nabliudenii zemskogo deiatelia," an article originally published in *Russkaia mysl'*, 1913, no. 12, reprinted in *Zemstvo*, 1994, no. 3.

Trudy mestnykh komitetov o nuzhdakh sel'sko-khoziaistvennoi promyshlennosti. 79 vols., St. Petersburg 1903–1906:

vol. 4, Vilenskaia guberniia, St. Petersburg 1903.

vol. 25, Orlovskaia guberniia, St. Petersburg 1903.

vol. 31, Podol'skaia guberniia, St. Petersburg 1904.

vol. 34, Riazanskaia guberniia, St. Petersburg 1903.

vol. 39, Simbirskaia guberniia, St. Petersburg 1903.

vol. 41, Tambovskaia guberniia, St. Petersburg 1903.

vol. 45, Khar'kovskaia guberniia, St. Petersburg 1903.

Trudy podsektsii statistiki X-ogo s"ezda russkikh estestvoispytatelei., Chernigov, 1900.

Trudy pervogo Vserossiiskogo sel'sko-khoziaistvennogo s"ezda v Kieve 1–10 sentiabria 1913 g., 2 vols., Kiev 1914.

Trudy podsektsii statistiki XI-ogo s"ezda russkikh estestvoispytatelei., St.Petersburg, 1902.

Trudy 7-ogo soveshchaniia zemskikh agronomov Tambovskoi gubernii pri Tambovskoi gubernskoi zemskoi uprave, Tambov 1914.

Trudy 8-ogo soveshchaniia zemskikh agronomov Tambovskoi gubernii pri Tambovskoi gubernskoi zemskoi uprave 17–19 oktiabria 1913 g., Tambov 1914.

Trudy tsentral'nogo statisticheskogo upravleniia. t. 5, vyp. 2, Pouezdnye itogi Vserossiiskoi sel'sko-khoziaistvennoi i pozemel'noi perepisi 1917 goda, Petrograd 1922.

Trunov, A. N., "Poniatiia krest'ian Orlovskoi gubernii o prirode fizicheskoi i dukhovnoi," in *Zapiski Imperatorskogo Russkogo geograficheskogo obshchestva po otdeleniiu etnografii. vol. 2*, St. Petersburg 1869.

Ts., "Iz sel'skoi zhizni," *Vestnik Usmanskogo uezdnogo zemstva*, 1914, no. 1.

Tsentral'no-Chernozemnaia Oblast'. Statisticheskii spravochnik, Voronezh 1929.

Tseny na rabochie ruki v sel'skom khoziaistve Chernigovskoi gubernii, Chernigov 1912.

Tul'tseva, L. A., "Obshchina i agrarnaia obriadnost' Riazanskikh krest'ian na rubezhe XIX–XX vv.," in Gromyko and Listova, eds., *Russkie*.

Tumanova, A. S., "Sel'skokhoziaistvennye obshchestva Tambovskoi gubernii na rubezhe XIX–XX stoletii," in Avrekh, ed., *Tambovskoe krest'ianstvo*, Vyp. 2.

Turgenev, I. S., *Polnoe sobranie sochinenii i pisem v dvadtsati vos'mi tomakh*, Moscow–Leningrad 1963.

Urozhai khlebov, trav i proch. v Tambovskoi gubernii za piatnadtsatiletie 1896–1910 gg., Tambov 1917.

Urusov, S., "Issledovanie sovremennogo sostoianiia ptitsevodstva v srednem raione Evropeiskoi Rossii," *Sel'skoe Khoziaistvo i Lesovodstvo*, 1896, no. 11.

Ushakov, D. N., "Materialy po narodnym verovaniiam velikorussov," *Etnograficheskoe obozrenie*, 1896, nos. 2–3.

Uspenskii, D. I., "Tolki naroda (neurozhai—kholera—voina)," *Etnograficheskoe obozrenie*, 1893, no. 2.

Uspenskii, G. I., "Iz putevykh zametok," *Otechestvennye zapiski*, 1883, no. 5.

——, "Krest'ianin i krest'ianskii trud," in Lebedev, *Pis'ma iz derevni*.

——, *Polnoe sobranie sochinenii*, Moscow 1949.

Uspenskii, N. V., *Povesti, rasskazy i ocherki*, Moscow 1957.

——, "Propazha," in Lebedev, *Krest'ianskie sud'by*.

Ustinov, A., "Ob uborke za zimu sel'sko-khoziaistvennykh orudii i mashin," *Shatskoe Khoziaistvo*, 1914, no. 20.

Uvarov, A., "Kniga i opyt," *Shatskoe Khoziaistvo*, 1914, nos. 4.

V., "Literaturnaia letopis'," *Biblioteka dlia chteniia*, 1856, no. 2.

V. I., "Deiatel'nost' zemstv v oblasti narodnogo obrazovaniia", SKhZh, 1914, no. 4–5.

Vagin, A., "O nekotorykh priemakh povyshenii urozhaev ozimoi rzhi, iachmenia i ovsa v Petergofskom uezde," *Sel'sko-khoziaistvennyi Vestnik*, 1914, no. 6.

Vainshtein, A. L., *Narodnoe bogatstvo i narodnokhoziaistvennoe nakoplenie predrevoliutsionnoi Rossii*, Moscow 1960.

——, *Oblozhenie i platezhi krest'ianstva v dovoennoe i revoliutsionnoe vremia*, Moscow 1924.

Vakar, B. A., *Rezul'taty obsledovaniia tekhniki krest'ianskogo sel'skogo khoziaistva v raione Tambovskoi opytnoi stantsii*, Tambov 1927.

Van Beusekom, M. M., "From Underpopulation to Overpopulation. French Perceptions of Population, Environment, and Agricultural Development in French Sudan (Mali), 1900–1960," *Environmental History*, 1999, no. 2.

Varzar, ed., *Statisticheskie svedeniia o fabrikakh i zavodakh po proizvodstvam, ne oblozhennym aktsizom, za 1900 g.*, St. Petersburg 1903.

——, *Statisticheskie svedeniia po obrabatyvaiushchei fabrichno-zavodskoi promyshlennosti Rossiiskoi Imperii za 1908 g*, St. Petersburg 1912.

Vasil'chikov, A. I., *Sel'skii byt i sel'skoe khoziaistvo v Rossii*, Moscow 1881.

Vasil'ev, N. M., *Kak obrabatyvat' parami i ukhazhivat' za ikh*, Borisoglebsk 1912.

Vasil'ev, V., "Kursy po sel'skomu khoziaistvu i ogorodnichestvu v Krestetskom uezde," *Zemskii agronom*, 1913, no. 7.

Veber, K., "O kovke loshadei. Iz zametok o proshlogodnei Gamburgskoi vystavke skota." ZG, 1884, no. 29.

Veber, K. K., *Zemledel'cheskie mashiny i orudiia*. 2 vols., St. Petersburg 1896–97.

——, *Ocherk sel'skogo khoziaistva Tambovskoi gubernii*, Tambov 1922.

Verbov, S. F., *Na vrachebnom postu v zemstve. Iz vospominanii*, Paris 1961.

Vermenichev, I., A. Gaister, and G. Raevich, *710 khoziaistv Samarskoi derevni*, Moscow 1928.

Vikhliaev, P. A., *Vliianie travoseianiia na otdel'nye storony krest'ianskogo khoziaistva*. Vyp. 8., Moscow 1914.

Viter, G., "O kreditnykh tovarishchestvakh Shatskogo uezda," *Shatskoe Khoziaistvo*, 1915, no. 9.

Vnukov, R. Ia., *Protivorechiia staroi krest'ianskoi semi*, Orel 1929.

Vodovozova, E., "Zakholustnyi derevenskii ugolok posle padeniia krepostnogo prava," *Russkoe Bogatstvo*, 1911, no. 2.

Voenno-konskaia perepis' 1888 (and 1899–1901, 1905 and 1912) *goda*, St. Petersburg, 1891 (1902, 1907, 1914).

Volchanskii, F., "O vinokurennoi promyshlennosti Tambovskoi gubernii," *SKhZh*, 1912/13, no. 11.

Volin, Lazar, *A Century of Russian Agriculture, from Alexander II to Khrushchev*. Cambridge, Mass. 1970.

Vol'nov, Ivan, *Povest' o dniakh moei zhizni*, 3rd edition, Moscow-Leningrad 1927.

Volosatov, F., "Selo Tugolukovka, Borisoglebskogo uezda," *SKhZh*, 1914, no.7.

Vonzblein, M., "Agronomiia obshchestvennaia," in *PERSKh*, vol. 12, St. Petersburg 1912.

Vorob'ev, S., "Sel'sko-khoziaistvennye kursy v selenii Lipiagakh," *SKhZ*, 1914, nos. 10–11.

Vorob'ev, S. O., *Rol' faktorov urozhaia v razlichnykh estestvenno-istoricheskikh zonakh Ukrainy*, Odessa 1926.

Voronezhskii krai, Voronezh 1928.

Voronov, I., *Materialy po narodnomu obrazovaniiu v Voronezhskoi gubernii*, Voronezh 1899.

Voronov, I. K., ed., *Naselenie i khoziaistvo Voronezhskoi gubernii*, Voronezh 1925.

Voronov, I. K., *Effektivnost' uslovii i sposobov obrabotki krest'ianskoi pashni*, Voronezh 1928.

Vorontsov, V., *Krest'ianskaia obshchina*, Moscow, 1892.

——, *Progressivnye techeniia v krest'ianskom khoziaistve*, Moscow 1892.

Vsevolozhskii, E., "Ocherki krest'ianskogo byta Samarskogo uezda," *Etnograficheskoe obozrenie*, 1895, no. 1.

Vvedenskii, I., "Zemledeliia i kooperatsiia," *Voprosy kolonizatsii*, 1913, no. 12.

Weber, Eugen, *My France: politics, culture, myth*, Cambridge (Massachusetts) 1991.

——, *Peasants Into Frenchmen: the modernization of rural France, 1870–1914*, Stanford 1976.

Wheatcroft, Stephen G., "Crises and the Condition of the Peasantry in Late Imperial Russia." in Esther Kingston-Mann and Timothy Mixter, eds., *Peasant Economy, Culture, and Politics of European Russia, 1800–1921*, Princeton 1991, pp. 128–172.

——, "The Reliability of Russian Pre-War Grain Output Statistics," *Soviet Studies*, 1974, no. 2.

Wilbur, Elvira, *Peasant Economy, Landlords and Revolution in Voronezh*, (Ph.D. Dissertation, History) University of Michigan 1977.

Williams, Harold W., *Russia of the Russians*, London 1915.

Winter, Nevin O., *The Russian Empire of Today and Yesterday*, London 1914.

Worobec, Christine, *Peasant Russia. Family and Community in the Post-Emancipation Period*, Princeton 1991.

Wrong, Dennis H., "Cultural Relativism as Ideology," *Critical Review*, 1997, no. 2.

Yaney, George, *The Urge to Mobilize: Agrarian Reform in Russia, 1861–1930*, Urbana (Illinois) 1982.

Z-n, A., "O prichinakh izmel'chaniia i boleznennosti naroda," *Zhurnal zemlevladel'tsev*, 1858, no. 5.

Zalenskii, R., "K metodike ucheta urozhaia zerna po obmolotu vsei delianki v polevom opyte," *VSKh*, 1915, no. 31.

Zasodimskii, P. V., "Ot sokhi k ruzh'iu," in Lebedev, *Krest'ianskie sud'by*.

Zelenin, D., *Russkaia sokha, ee istoriia i vidy. Ocherk iz istorii russkoi zemledel'cheskoi kul'tury*, in *Pamiatnaia knizhka Viatskoi gubernii i kalendar' na 1908 god*, Viatka 1908.

Zemets, "Gubernskoe agronomicheskoe soveshchanie v g. Orle," *Zemskoe Delo*, 1913, no. 22.

Zernova, A. V., "Materialy po sel'sko-khoziaistvennoi magii v Dmitrovskom krae," *Sovetskaia etnografiia*, 1932, no. 3.

Zhbankov, D., "Fizicheskoe razvitie prizyvaemykh k otbivaniiu voinskoi povinnosti" in *Meditsinskaia beseda*, 1904, nos. 7–8.

Zhikharev, N., "Ocherk razvitiia strakhovaniia voobshche i zemskogo strakhovaniia v chastnosti," *SKhZh*, 1914, nos. 4–5.

Zhurnaly soveshchaniia zemskikh agronomov Tambovskoi gubernii pri Tambovskoi gubernskoi zemskoi uprave

5–9 marta 1911 g., s dokladami, Tambov 1911.

30–31 avgusta i 1–2 sentiabria 1911 goda, Tambov 1911.

5–8 marta 1912 g., Tambov 1912.

Zhurnaly i doklady 5-ogo agronomicheskogo soveshchaniia zemskikh pri Tambovskoi gubernskoi zemskoi uprave 3–6 sentiabria 1912 g., Tambov 1912.

Zhurnaly zasedanii sel'sko-khoziaistvennoi komissii pri Lipetskoi uezdnoi zemskoi uprave za 1910, 1911 i 1912 gg., Lipetsk 1912.

Zhurnaly zasedanii sel'sko-khoziaistvennoi komissii Tambovskogo uezdnogo zemstva, 1909–1910 gg., Tambov 1911.

Zimin, M. M., *Koverninskii krai (nabliudeniia i zapisi)*, Kostroma 1920 (*Trudy Komstromskogo nauchnogo obshchestva po izucheniiu mestnogo kraia. Vyp. XVII*)

Zinov'ev, P., "Borokskaia obshchina," in F. L. Barykov et al, eds., *Sbornik materialov dlia izucheniia sel'skoi pozemel'noi obshchiny*, St. Petersburg 1880.

Zlatovratskii, N. N., *Derevenskie budni*, in Lebedev, *Pis'ma iz derevni*.

Zolotarev, D., "Etnograficheskie nabliudeniia v derevne RSFSR (1919–1925 gg.)," in *Materialy po etnografii, t. III, vyp. 1*, Leningrad 1926.

Zubrilin, A. A., *Chem obrabatyvat' zemliu i ubirat' urozhai*, Moscow 1924.

——, "Nedostatki trekhpol'ia," *KSE*, vol. 6.

Zverev, V. V., "N. F. Daniel'son, V. A. Vorontsov: Kapitalizm i poreformennoe razvitie russkoi derevni," *Otechestvennaia istoriia*, 1998, no. 1.

Zvonkov, A. P., "Ocherk verovanii krest'ian Elatomskogo uezda Tambovskoi gubernii," *Etnograficheskoe obozrenie*, 1889, no. 2.

Zyrianov, P. N., *Krest'ianskaia obshchina Evropeiskoi Rossii, 1907–1914 gg.*, Moscow 1992.

A MINIATURE GLOSSARY

Terms Concerning Land

Arable land—Land tilled and sown with crops. In almost all communes, this land was split up into furlongs (each one often called a *delezh*, among other names) on the basis of soil quality and distance from the village. In turn, these chunks were divided into strips among the commune's households, in accordance with their family composition (**the "open fields"**). In virtually all communes, this land was periodically subject to repartition, as families' compositions fluctuated (**"communal tenure," "repartitional tenure," "the repartitional commune"**).

Delezh (furlong)—*see* entry "Arable land."

Komassatsiia—A land organization process, designed to widen the arable strips throughout the commune's fields. Two measures are involved: re-evaluating the arable land so as to minimize the number of furlongs (*see* entry "Arable land"), and arranging for households to swap strips so as to connect them as much as possible (*okruglenie*—*see* entry below—essentially).

Okruglenie—A technique whereby individual households would arrange to position some or all of their strips of arable land alongside each other, thus minimizing the number of separate strips.

Farm Organization Terms

The Three-Field System, The Three Arable Fields—Peasants throughout central Russia farmed almost exclusively in the three-field system. The arable land was divided into the following thirds:

> **Winter Field, or Rye Field**—Land sown with rye in August, reaped in the following July. Rye was the primary consumption crop. Peasants did not raise wheat in Tambov.

> **Spring Field**—Land usually sown with oats, in April, or millet, in May. Oats was a fodder crop, millet a consumption crop. Both crops were reaped in August, ordinarily, oats ripening first.

> **Fallow Field**—Land left unsown from the spring crop harvest in August until the rye sowing in the following August. Tillage in preparation for the August sowing began already in the spring.

This arrangement formed the three-field system. On any given strip of land the rye sowing followed fallow, a spring-sown crop followed the rye, and fallow followed the spring-sown crop [Glossary Table 1]:

Glossary Table 1. The Three-Field System

Year / Field	#1	#2	#3
1	Fallow	Winter grain	Spring crop
2	Winter grain	Spring crop	Fallow
3	Spring crop	Fallow	Winter grain

Some Tillage Terms

Ziab—Tillage in the fall of land to be sown in the following spring ("Fall tillage").

Dvoenie—A second tillage of the fallow field, about a month after the raising of fallow.

Lomka—This is a harrowing performed after the sowing of millet or oats, just as sprouts are appearing. The main idea is to kill weeds.

Supplemental Categories of Land

Meadow—Grasslands, usually left as such because they were unsuitable for grain growing. The grass would be scythed down in June, ordinarily, and stored as hay for winter feed. Additionally, peasant communes allowed their herds to graze on the meadows. The herds would visit the meadows for a short time at the beginning of spring, and come back after haymaking.

Pasture—Lands unable to qualify as meadows, for paucity of grass growth. Here animals were grazed on whatever might grow during part of the summer.

Private plots, "home garden plots"—Small plots, in Tambov usually 1–2 acres in size, where families usually raised vegetables. While these lands were generally subject to repartition, their proximity to the family's dwelling made it awkward to transfer them in whole or in part to new holders. Thus most communes were less strict about redistributing garden plot land than they were about arable land.

A Miscellany of Other Terms

Dvor—peasant household.

Peasant commune—normally organized on the basis of a single village, the commune was the peasantry's organ of self-administration. The communal assembly (*skhod*—see separate entry) elected one or more "Elders" to handle business not deemed to require the assembly's direct involvement.

Skhod—the communal assembly, where heads of households convened to attend to certain categories of village business.* The *skhod* oversaw all matters concerning the redistribution of land between member households, the disposition of land with respect to systems of farming and the grazing of herds, and the purchase or rental of non-village lands (or, rarely, of agricultural equipment) by the community. The *skhod's* involvement in agricultural matters did not as a rule extend any further than this.

Otkhod—Peasant migrant labor, of whatever kind.

Promysly—Local, non-agricultural work supplementing farm income. Crafts, quarry work, carpentry, hauling, etc.

Province (*Guberniia*)—(For practical purposes, the province was the largest administrative unit in Russia. There were 50 provinces in the European portion of the Russian Empire.

Uezd—Sub-division of the province. There were 10–15 *uezd*s in most provinces, 12 in Tambov.

Volost'—Sub-division of the *uezd*. There were c. 400 *volost*s in Tambov (the number occasionally fluctuated).

*Rules governing participation and voting privileges in the *skhod* were not uniform in peasant practice. Some villages granted these rights to all men aged 21 and over. Others recognized younger men, down almost to ten-year-olds. Near the end of the Imperial period the central government finally decided to draw the line at age 17. "Vozrast' izbiratelei sel'skikh skhodov," in *Vestnik Usmanskogo Uezdnogo Zemstva*, 1913, no. 5, p. 26.

SOME RUSSIAN WEIGHTS
AND MEASURES

Arshin	= 28 inches or 71 centimeters
Desiatina	= 2.7 acres, 1.09 hectares
Kopna	= 4 crosses (52 sheaves, usually)
Krestets (cross)	= 13 sheaves, usually
Pud	= 36 pounds, 16.4 kilograms
Sazhen	= 7 feet, 2.13 meters
Vedro	= 3.5 gallons or 12.3 liters
Vershok	= 1.75 inches, 4.1 centimeters
Versta	= 0.66 miles or 1.07 kilometers
Zolotnik	= 0.15 ounces or 4.26 grams

NOTE ON DATES

Until 1918 the Russian calendar trailed the Western by 13 days. Unless otherwise noted, all dates in this book are given in the old style.

INDEX